O6F

HISTORY OF NEW TESTAMENT TIMES

WITH AN INTRODUCTION TO THE APOCRYPHA

HISTORY OF NEW TESTAMENT TIMES

With an Introduction to the

APOCRYPHA

~~~~~~

by

ROBERT H. PFEIFFER

Harvard University and Boston University

~~~~~~

HARPER & BROTHERS PUBLISHERS
New York

To my Uncle
G. A. PFEIFFER
who has lived up to his motto
GIVING GOOD VALUE
GETTING GOOD VALUE

CONTENTS

~~~~~~

FOREWORD   xi

PART I: JUDAISM FROM 200 B.C. TO A.D. 200
(A) PALESTINIAN JUDAISM

I. POLITICAL HISTORY   5
1. Hellenistic Domination (332-175 B.C.)   8
2. The Maccabean Rebellion (175-142)   9
3. The Rule of the Hasmoneans (142-63)   19
4. The Rule of the Romans (63 B.C.-A.D. 66)   24
5. The War Against the Romans (66-73)   41

II. RELIGIOUS HISTORY   46

III. LITERARY HISTORY   60

(B) HELLENISTIC JUDAISM

IV. HELLENISM   93
1. Historical Sketch   94
2. General Characteristics   97
3. Hellenistic Literature   101
4. Hellenistic Science   110
5. Hellenistic Scholarship   114
6. Hellenistic Philosophy   116
7. Hellenistic Religion   127

V. THE JEWS IN THE LANDS OF THEIR DISPERSION   166
1. The Jews in Mesopotamia   168
2. The Jews at Elephantine   169
3. The Alexandrian Jews   172
4. Small Jewish Settlements   179
5. Hellenistic Judaism   181

VI. ALEXANDRIAN-JEWISH LITERATURE   197
1. Historical Writings   200

2. Epic and Dramatic Poetry 210
3. Philosophy 212
4. Jewish Propaganda Works Attributed to Gentiles 224

PART II: THE BOOKS OF THE APOCRYPHA

I. I ESDRAS (THE GREEK EZRA) 233
  1. Relation to Chronicles-Nehemiah 236
    A. I Esdras and the Hebrew-Aramaic Text 237
    B. I Esdras and the "LXX" 246
  2. The Story of the Three Youths 250

II. THE BOOK OF TOBIT 258
  1. Literary Problems 264
  2. Religious and Ethical Teaching 278

III. THE BOOK OF JUDITH 285
  1. Historicity and Date 291
  2. Literary Characteristics 297
  3. Religious Teaching 301

IV. THE REST OF THE CHAPTERS OF THE BOOK OF ESTHER ... 304

V. THE WISDOM OF SOLOMON 313
  1. Critical Problems 319
    A. Original Language 319
    B. Authorship 321
    C. Date and Place of Composition 326
    D. Greek Philosophy in the Book of Wisdom 328
  2. Literary Characteristics 329
  3. Religious Teaching 334

VI. ECCLESIASTICUS BY SIRACH 352
  1. The Author, Jesus ben Sira 364
  2. The Teaching of the Book 372
    A. Religion 373
    B. The Law 381
    C. Wisdom 385
    D. Morals 392
  3. The Style of Ecclesiasticus 398

VII. THE BOOK OF BARUCH   409

   1. Unity of the Book   411
   2. Authorship and Date   413
     A. Baruch 1:1-3:8   413
     B. Baruch 3:9-4:4   417
     C. Baruch 4:5-5:9   421
   3. Religious Teaching   423

VIII. THE EPISTLE OF JEREMY   426

IX. ADDITIONS TO THE BOOK OF DANIEL   433

   1. The Greek Texts   438
   2. The Song of the Three Holy Children   444
   3. The History of Susanna   448
   4. Bel and the Dragon   455

X. THE PRAYER OF MANASSES   457

XI. I MACCABEES   461

   1. Comparison between I and II Maccabees   472
   2. Literary Features of I Maccabees   483
     A. The Hebrew Text   483
     B. Speeches, Prayers, and Documents   486
     C. The Author   491
     D. The Greek Text   497

XII. II MACCABEES   499

   1. Jason of Cyrene   506
   2. The Epitomist   519

APPENDICES

  I. ABBREVIATIONS   525

  II. SELECTED BIBLIOGRAPHY   531

  III. INDEX OF AUTHORS   543

  IV. INDEX OF SUBJECTS   555

CONTENTS

VII. The Book of Baruch 400
    1. Unity of the Book 411
    2. Authorship and Date 415
        A. Baruch 1:1-3:8 416
        B. Baruch 3:9-5:9 417
        C. Baruch 4:5-5:9 421
    3. Religious Teaching 429

VIII. The Epistle of Jeremy 426

IX. Additions to the Book of Daniel 433
    1. The Greek Texts 455
    2. The Song of the Three Holy Children 441
    3. The History of Susanna 445
    4. Bel and the Dragon 465

X. The Prayer of Manasses 487

XI. I Maccabees 491
    1. Comparison between I and II Maccabees 472
    2. Literary Features of I Maccabees 484
        A. The Hebrew Text 485
        B. Speeches, Prayers, and Documents 486
        C. The Author 491
        D. The Greek Text 492

XII. II Maccabees 496
    1. Jason of Cyrene 500
    2. The Epitomist 519

APPENDICES

I. Chronological 527
II. Selected Bibliography 531
III. Index of Authors 543
IV. Index of Subjects 550

FOREWORD

"If you steal from one author, it's plagiarism;
if you steal from many, it's research."
Wilson Mizner

After eight years, later than anticipated, I present here the sequel and completion of my *Introduction to the Old Testament*. The unexpectedly warm reception and generous appraisal of that book had encouraged me to write an *Introduction to the Apocrypha* in the same style and for the same public; but after completing it, I could not resist the temptation to preface it with a history of the period in which the Apocrypha were written.

The incredibly favorable reviews and astonishing wide circulation of the first volume produced in me a sense of duty—a most distressing feeling—urging the completion of the work. In addition to what seemed to me a royal command to undertake this considerable labor, I may adduce two other reasons as my excuse for inflicting on long-suffering readers another bulky tome.

First of all, like other writers of manuals, I was convinced (O blissful illusion!) that my book was needed, for no other book in existence presented the same information quite as well! Otherwise no university instructor who does not expect academic promotion or other advantages from his book, would ever submit to the labor and mental agony involved in its preparation—unless he was utterly insane. When I began to teach a course on "The Intertestamental Period" at the Boston University School of Theology twenty-five years ago, I could find no textbook for my students except the five-volume antiquated English translation of Emil Schürer's great *Geschichte des Jüdischen Volkes*, out of print in English and German; I had luckily purchased a copy of the last German edition, and thus prepared a lecture course!

The second reason is merely the momentum derived from the fun of teaching that course through the years. If the students had not shown interest in the subject and given me every encouragement, I might merely have written an introduction to the Apocrypha. Here instead are two books in one: a summary of the history, religion, and literature of Judaism from 200 B.C. to A.D. 200 (much briefer than Schürer's); and an introduction to the Apocrypha (much more detailed than Schürer's or any other known to me). Although New Testament problems and publications have

xi

remained outside the scope of the book, it may possibly help students understand the world in which Christianity arose, and thus supplement my friend Morton Scott Enslin's excellent *Christian Beginnings* (Harper, 1938).

This book is "research" only as defined by Mizner above; the victims of my "scholarly" depredations have been duly mentioned, and are here thanked for invaluable help; notably so in the field of Hellenism. As I strayed into it with the best of motives, I hoped Cervantes was right when he said that heaven always favors good intentions (*Siempre favorece el cielo los buenos deseos*), although fully aware of their alleged use in paving hell.

It is now my pleasant duty to express my appreciation to Miss Julie Eidesheim for her expert editorial work on the manuscripts of both my books; to my former students Ralph Lazzaro (instructor in the Harvard Divinity School) and Dr. Morton Smith, for reading the whole manuscript of this volume critically; another former student, Mr. Herbert Yarrish, read some chapters of it. My learned Harvard colleague and good friend, Professor Robert P. Blake, generously read the book in proof. My wife not only bore patiently the tedious clatter of my typewriter and my morose mood during the preparation of the book, but, besides encouraging me at all times, took upon herself the correction of the proofs and the preparation of the indices. In partial payment of the costs of publication, the Lucius N. Littauer Foundation, the Harvard Semitic Museum, and Mr. G. A. Pfeiffer have generously contributed funds. To them all, and particularly to Mr. Pfeiffer to whom the book is dedicated in appreciation of constant help and counsel, I express here my deep and lasting gratitude.

January, 1949   R. H. P.

PART I

JUDAISM FROM 200 B.C. TO A.D. 200

A. PALESTINIAN JUDAISM

POLITICAL HISTORY

The independence of the Judeans came to an end in 586 B.C., when Nebuchadnezzar destroyed Jerusalem and deprived the Davidic dynasty of its throne. Except for the brief Maccabean interlude (141-63 B.C.), the Jews never again (until 1948) had a government of their own which was not subject to alien authority. Nevertheless, alone of all ancient nations, the Jews did not lose their nationality when they were deprived of land and state.

A small country on the main line of communication between the valley of the Nile and the lands of the Euphrates and the Tigris rivers, Palestine was destined to be the battleground of the great empires surrounding her: Egyptians, Hittites, Syrians, Assyrians, Babylonians fought for the possession of this buffer state, until it passed under the rule of the great empires of the Persians (538-332), of the Greeks (332-141), of the Romans (63 B.C.-A.D. 395), of the Byzantines (395-636, except for the period 614-628 when Palestine was ruled by Chosroes II, the last great Sassanian king of Persia), of the Caliphs (636-1099). Following the ephemeral kingdom of the Crusaders (1099-1187), after various vicissitudes, Palestine was governed by the Ottoman Turks (1516-1917, except for the Egyptian rule in the years 1833-1840) and the British (since 1917; as a mandate of the League of Nations, from April 25, 1920, to May 15, 1948). It was only when no great empire had the urge and the capacity to conquer Palestine that the country enjoyed a breathing spell under its own native rulers: this actually happened only before 1500 B.C., then while the Israelites and Judeans were in power (*ca.* 1150-586 B.C.), and finally under the Hasmoneans (141-63 B.C.).

The significance of the Jews in history (aside from their contributions to culture) is primarily due to their unparalleled success in preserving a strong national feeling, based on literature and religion, after the loss of political independence. We may even say that after 586 B.C. the history of the Jews is primarily a process of trial and error aiming at national survival; at last about A.D. 200 all other means for the preservation of the nation were discarded in favor of Rabbinic Judaism. Military uprisings, apocalyptic dreams of a future triumph over the Gentiles, avoidance of mixed marriages, punctilious performance of the Temple rites, and other remedies eventually proved less effective than the study and observance of the Law, as promoted in school and synagogue. The Jews survived primarily as "the people of the Book"; their history after A.D. 70 is primarily the history of their literature. Their self-preservation as a people depended on the preservation of their national religion, the practice of which included the observance of ancient customs which originally did not always have a direct connection with the worship: thus dietary laws, sabbath, and circumcision were ancient practices the original significance of which had been forgotten for centuries; but by remaining faithful to such customs inherited from their ancestors the Jews incidentally separated themselves from the Gentiles and in turn were regarded with scorn or hostility by the other subjects of the Hellenistic and Roman rulers.

Of external facts in the life of the Palestinian Jews from 586 to the events preceding the Maccabean rebellion (175 B.C.) almost no information has survived, except what may be gleaned from Haggai, Zechariah 1-8, Nehemiah's Memoirs, and possibly—but not certainly—the Book of Ezra. From Haggai and Zechariah we learn that the Temple was rebuilt in 520-516; and also that some Jews, stirred by the widespread insurrections raging when Darius (521-485) ascended the Persian throne, believed that the Lord was shaking the kingdoms in order to give to the Jews independence and dominion. So certain did this hope seem to a group of Jews, including apparently Haggai and Zechariah, that they proceeded to crown Zerubbabel, a descendant of David, as the Messianic king. But Darius conquered all his enemies and the Persian authorities in Jerusalem "liquidated" the unfortunate Zerubbabel at once, even though they granted to the Jews complete freedom in religious and cultural matters.

This liberalism of the Persian rulers, nay, their special manifestations of favor toward the Jews,[1] are conspicuous in Nehemiah's work (444 B.C.), when he revived the pitiful congregation in Jerusalem through restoration of its fortifications (apparently dismantled by a hostile neighboring people) and through social and spiritual reorganization.

Modern historians and Jewish tradition begin a new epoch in the time of Nehemiah. But while Jewish tradition extols Ezra as the restorer of the Law that Moses had received from God, modern historians (at least since the critical researches of A. Kuenen, W. H. Kosters, and C. C. Torrey) are apt to express doubts about Ezra's contribution and to place more emphasis on Nehemiah's activity. In any case, the Persian government

[1] See B. Meissner, *Die Achämenidenkönige und das Judentum* (Sitzungber. d. Preuss. Akad., Phil.-hist. Kl., 1938, pp. 6-26). A tragic illustration of Persian concern for the Jews may be detected at Elephantine in Upper Egypt, where a Jewish colony thrived during the Persian rule of Egypt but appears to have been exterminated when Egypt became independent in 404 B.C.

(538-332 B.C.), by protecting Judea from external aggression and internal tumults and by allowing the Jews full autonomy in their religious and cultural development, was ideally suited to further the transition from kingdom to nation, from state to holy congregation. The publication of the final edition of the Law of Moses (the Pentateuch) about 400 B.C. proved far more significant for the future than the rebuilding of the Temple (520-516), for eventually the Law brought into being the synagogue—the most vital and original institution of Judaism. The *Pax Persiana* not only furthered the growth and diffusion of early Judaism, (as later the *Pax Romana* was to become a condition for the expansion of Christianity), but, as E. Meyer has observed, tended to transform local deities into cosmic gods, national cults into personal and universal religions—a tendency which the Jews, in spite of their concern with the preservation of nationality and religion, could not evade; on the contrary, with Jeremiah and the Second Isaiah (Is. 40-55) Judaism was disclosing at least in germ the characteristics of a personal and universal religion even before Cyrus conquered Babylonia in 538.

Owing to historical circumstances, two apparently contradictory tendencies appear in Judaism during the Persian period. On the one hand, the Second Isaiah proclaimed that Jehovah was the only God in existence, hence his worship should eventually become the sole religion of mankind. On the other hand, however, the apocalypses proclaimed the future subjection of all nations to the Jews and the Law served to separate the Jews from the Gentiles. This contradiction appears in all religions which claim sole and absolute validity: of necessity they are utterly intolerant of other cults, but at the same time zealous in missionary work leading to the conversion of all men to the true religion. Such attitudes, unless clothed with great tact and circumspection, inevitably provoke animosity on the part of outsiders: the hostility of the Alexandrians and others against the Jews in the Hellenistic and Roman periods is in a sense the reaction to Jewish enthusiasm and conviction.

In these remarks on the Palestinian Jews during the Persian period, the familiar traditional topics of the "Exile," the "Return," and the "Restoration" have been deliberately omitted, as also the work of Ezra. These notions we owe to the Chronicler, writing about the middle of the third century. They reflect his dogmas rather than his historical information, and they have prevailed so long simply because no historical sources have been available aside from Haggai, Zechariah, and Nehemiah. These writings, however, sufficiently prove that the actual course of events was far different from the idealized picture conceived by the Chronicler's vivid imagination. All that can be said is that an insignificant minority of the Judeans was exiled by Nebuchadnezzar, that even if Cyrus allowed the Babylonian Jews to return, extremely few were sufficiently heroic to leave a prosperous country in which they were acquiring wealth to go to the far-from-fruitful ruined homeland around Jerusalem. Thus Judea remained destitute until after Nehemiah had come to reorganize and encourage the dejected congregation depicted in the Book of Malachi.

1. Hellenistic Domination (332-175 B.C.)

With lightning speed Alexander of Macedon conquered the Persian Empire of Darius III. His decisive victories were at the Granicus River near Troy (334), at Issus (333), and at Gaugamela near Arbela (331); Tyre was captured after a siege of seven months and Gaza fell after two months in 332; in the same year Jerusalem surrendered to the Greeks without a struggle.[2] So Alexander "advanced to the ends of the earth, and took spoils from many peoples; and the earth was quiet before him" (I Macc. 1:3; cf. Dan. 8:5-7). But the storm broke at the death of the young conqueror in 323. "And when he [the he-goat] was strong, the great horn [Alexander] was broken; and in its place there came up four *others* [cf. LXX] [Cassander, Lysimachus, Seleucus I, and Ptolemy I] toward the four winds of heaven" (Dan. 8:8; cf. 11:3 f.).

Alexander's empire was not divided into four parts immediately after his death, as one might assume from Daniel's vision. Ptolemy I Lagos (305-285 [d. 283] B.C.) made himself king of Egypt and founded a dynasty which remained in power there until the Roman conquest in 30 B.C. Lysimachus was the master of Thrace, Antipater (soon followed by his son Cassander) ruled Macedon and Greece. Seleucus at first lost Babylonia, his portion of the empire, but he recovered it in 312. The lust for conquest of Antigonus, the ruler of Phrygia, brought about a coalition of the other Diadochi (or "successors" of Alexander) against him and, after a period of hostilities in which the fortunes of war fluctuated, Antigonus finally met his end at the decisive battle of Ipsus (Phrygia) in 301. Then was the empire divided between Lysimachus, Cassander, Seleucus, and Ptolemy.

During this time (323-301) Palestine, like other buffer states located between contending kingdoms, passed in rapid succession from the possession of Ptolemy (who took it from Laomedon in 320) to that of Antigonus (315), and so forth. Ptolemy defeated Demetrius, son of Antigonus, at Gaza (312), but lost Palestine again a year later: the victory, however, allowed Seleucus to reconquer Babylonia and thus found the Seleucid kingdom. The year 312-311 fixes the Seleucid Era,

[2] The dramatic story of Alexander's meeting with the high priest Jaddua (Josephus, *Antiquities* 11:8, 4 f. [§§325-329]) is not a legend, but fiction pure and simple.

according to which events are dated in I Maccabees (1:10; 7:1; 10:1; etc.) and in later histories.

But after the battle of Ipsus, Ptolemy occupied Palestine and Phoenicia, which remained under the rule of the Ptolemies of Egypt for over a century—until Antiochus III the Great (223-187) conquered these lands for the Seleucids of Syria (Dan. 11:13-16) through his victories at Gaza (200) and Panium or Banias (198), where Caesarea Philippi was to be built.

Jewish history under the Ptolemies is utterly obscure. The author of Dan. 11:6-12 (our best historical source, as explained by Porphyry and Jerome) knows of no events in this century other than matrimonial difficulties and mutual hostilities between Ptolemies and Seleucids. The Jews were apparently granted considerable autonomy and were allowed to develop their culture undisturbed, as long as they paid the taxes and remained submissive.

The Jews, however, were chafing under foreign domination, despite their apparent obedience to their Ptolemaic rulers: we are told that they welcomed Antiochus III in 198, giving him all possible aid. They imagined to have gained something through the change, but this illusion was short-lived. Disastrously defeated by Lucius Cornelius Scipio at Magnesia in 190 B.C. (Dan. 11:18), Antiochus was forced to pay Rome an enormous indemnity, and died (187) while plundering a temple in Elymais (Dan. 11:19). His son Seleucus IV (187-175) sent forth an exactor (Dan. 11:20), Heliodorus, to raise funds due to Rome (cf. II Macc. 3), but Seleucus IV was eventually assassinated by him (Dan. 11:20); his brother Antiochus IV Epiphanes (175-164) succeeded him. The new king, by adding to the fiscal burdens (weighing heavily on the Jews since the battle of Magnesia) forcible Hellenization and proscription of Judaism, precipitated the Maccabean revolt (Dan. 11:21-45).

2. *The Maccabean Rebellion* (175-142)

In a keen analysis of the historical sources, Elias Bickermann (*Der Gott der Makkabäer*, pp. 17-35. Berlin, 1937) has discovered four conflicting explanations of the Maccabean rebellion, dictated by bias or circulated as propaganda.

1. Pagan Theories. a. The Seleucid theory justified the oppressive measures of Antiochus Epiphanes through a previous rebellion of the Jews, who had sided with the Ptolemies against Antiochus during his Egyptian campaign of 168. This version transfers the plundering of the Temple in 169 to 168, when Jerusalem was attacked and Judaism proscribed. Thus the sacrilegious robbing of a temple was justified in the eyes of the Greeks and Romans. This version was presented presumably in lost parts of Polybius, in allusions by Tacitus, and in sections of II Maccabees and Josephus.

b. The Anti-Semitic theory is an interpretation of the preceding one and is found in Diodorus 34:1 and Tacitus, *Histories* V, 8; it is attacked by Josephus (*Against Apion* 11:7 [§§90-97]). According to this version, Antiochus led a crusade against Jewish barbarism as the champion of Hellenic culture.

2. *Jewish Theories. a.* In opposition to the official Seleucid explanation, Daniel, II Macc. 1:7, and in a measure II Maccabees in general, regard Antiochus as insignificant (being merely, in Isaiah's words, "the rod of God's anger") and attribute the misfortunes of the Jews to a divine judgment against them: not Antiochus, but the Lord punishes the Jews (cf. II Macc. 5:17 f.).

b. In contrast to the anti-Semitic theory, I Maccabees (which was written to glorify the Maccabees) regards the persecution of the Jews as an outburst of abominable pagan fury abetted by apostate Jews: "And there came out of them a wicked root, Antiochus Epiphanes . . . there went out of Israel wicked men . . ." (I Macc. 1:10 f.). The world is rent asunder into God's people and the heathen; the gulf between them is impassable. Israel, the innocent victim of pagan attack, is certain that God will destroy its foes (I Macc. 4:8-11).

These four theories, as Bickermann shows (*op. cit.*, pp. 36-49), have been variously advanced by theologians and historians through the centuries, down to our own time. On the basis of our sources, we may attempt to summarize the course of events impartially (if possible) as follows:

While in 180 Seleucus IV had failed to obtain large sums from the Jews through Heliodorus' ill-fated attempt to plunder the private funds deposited in the Temple (assuming a kernel of truth in II Macc. 3),[3] Antiochus IV Epiphanes[4] found it more profitable to sell the office of high priest to the highest bidder. Soon after his accession, Antiochus deposed the high priest Onias and appointed in his place his brother Joshua (who took the Greek name of Jason). Onias had faced the opposition of the Tobiads, strong supporters of the Seleucids and of the Hellenization of the Jews. Onias offended his friends, the opponents of the Tobiads, by going to Antioch for help, thus making it easy for Jason, the most ardent of the Hellenizers, to supplant him. Jason collaborated with Antiochus not only in raising funds but also in furthering Greek

---

[3] See E. Bickermann, "Héliodore au temple de Jerusalem" (*Annuaire de l'Institut de Philologie et d'Histoire orientales et slaves* VII [1939-44] 5-40).

[4] "[*Theós*] *epiphanês*" means "[the god] who manifests [or reveals] himself." Polybius (XXVI, 10; quoted by Athenaeus X, p. 439) reports the sarcastic pun "*epimanês*" (madman).

customs among the Jews, in accordance with the king's policy to introduce a uniform Greek culture throughout his realm (I Macc. 1:41-43).
For Jason not only paid to Antiochus 440 talents of silver for the office
of high priest, but he also promised 150 more if he were allowed to build
a gymnasium and an ephebeum (II Macc. 4:8 f.).[5]

Having been granted these requests, Jason proceeded to build a
gymnasium under the citadel and induced young noblemen to wear the
petasus (the broad-brimmed Greek hat); young priests forsook the altar
to compete in discus throwing (II Macc. 4:10-15; cf. I Macc. 1:13 f.).
Some young Jews even submitted to surgery to disguise their circumcision while exercising nude in the palaestra (I Macc. 1:15). Thus East
and West met in Jerusalem, but could not be combined. For such Greek
innovations as athletic exercise, sport, bathing for hygienic purposes,
nudity in the presence of others, wearing hats with a rim were profoundly repellent in the Semitic world, particularly to the Jews, whose
customs, hallowed by the observance of centuries and traced back to
divine revelation, seemed irreconcilable with such Greek practices.[6] The
conservative Jews, horrified by what they considered a repudiation of the
divine covenant and a union with the heathen (I Macc. 1:15; cf. II Macc.
4:11), banded themselves together under the name of Hasîdîm (Pious;
Asidaîoi in Greek), regarding the Hellenizers as wicked apostates; in all
probability out of this movement eventually arose the Pharisees.

After three years in office (175-172 or 174-171), Jason was deposed
and fled into Transjordania: a certain Menelaus (Menahem) outbid
him in Antioch by three hundred talents of silver (II Macc. 4:23-26).
He is said (loc. cit.) to have been the brother of Simon, a high Temple
official (II Macc. 3:4),[7] and was obviously the leader of the Tobiads,
although not necessarily related to them by blood. Menelaus found it
difficult to raise the enormous sum he had promised, even though he had
few scruples about appropriating Temple vessels and selling others to

[5] It is generally assumed that the last words of II Macc. 4:9 mean that Jason also
petitioned for the Jews of Jerusalem the title of "Antiochenes," or citizen of Antioch,
the capital of the kingdom. Another explanation is that Jerusalem should be named
"Antioch." E. Bickermann (Gott der Makkabäer, pp. 59-65), however, argues that
these interpretations are not correct: the text means "to register the Antiochenes in
Jerusalem," i.e., to organize them into a políteuma or dêmos (a corporation with
certain civic rights), not merely a club or an association.

[6] When Jason sent a gift of three hundred drachmas to Tyre on the occasion of
the quinquennial games in honor of Heracles, the envoys refused to have the money
used for the sacrifices and had it assigned to outfitting the navy (II Macc. 4:18-20).

[7] Simon (and consequently Menelaus) was a Benjamite according to the Greek
text of II Macc. 3:4, but a member of the Bilgah (Neh. 12:5) priestly family
according to the Latin text. On the other hand, "Benjamin" may be a corruption of
"Miniamin," an order of priests (cf. G. F. Moore, Judaism, Vol. 1, pp. 52-58). F. M.
Abel ("Simon de la tribu de Bilga" in Miscellanea Giovanni Mercati, Vol. 1, pp. 52-58
[Studi e Testi, Vol. 121]. Città del Vaticano, Biblioteca Apostolica Vaticana, 1946)
defends the reading "Bilgah."

Phoenician merchants (II Macc. 4:30-32). But there is reason to doubt that, according to II Macc. 4:33-38, he induced Andronicus to assassinate the former high priest Onias III, who in the illusory security of Apollo's temple at Daphne was thundering against the spoliation of the Temple. In spite of all opposition and of his financial difficulties, Menelaus was becoming more and more a *persona grata* to Epiphanes (even if not all of II Macc. 4:39-50 is historical). In the late summer or fall of 169, Menelaus even allowed Antiochus, returning from his first Egyptian campaign, to plunder the Temple of all treasures, even stripping gold plating from the façade (I Macc. 1:20-24; Dan. 11:25-28; cf. II Macc. 5:15 f., where the sacrilege is dated erroneously one year later). The value of the booty is said to have been 1,800 talents of silver (II Macc. 5:21).

A year later (168) Antiochus was achieving military success in his second campaign against Egypt when the Roman legate, Popilius Laenas, handed him an ultimatum from the Roman Senate and forced him to withdraw his troops at once (Polybius XXIX, 11; cf. Dan. 11:29 f.). The bad temper of Antiochus was not improved by reports that Jerusalem was seething with tumults (II Macc. 5:11). What actually happened is not entirely clear, but the account in II Macc. 5:5-8, which is our sole source of information, is probably based on fact. The Jews were divided into two parties: the great majority, opposed to Hellenization and to Antiochus, was pro-Egyptian at heart; the Tobiads and their supporters, under the leadership of Menelaus, were loyal to Antiochus and consequently anti-Egyptian. Under these circumstances it was not difficult for Jason, when Jerusalem was stirred by the false rumor that Antiochus was dead, to seize the city with a force of only one thousand men. He presented himself, we may surmise, as the leader of the Oniads and forced the Tobiads to seek refuge in the citadel. But Jason soon threw off the mask and revealed himself as animated by self-seeking ambition rather than by a constructive national program: he soon began to slaughter without mercy the very citizens who were opposed to Menelaus (presumably because they detested Jason's ardor for Hellenism). Finally, driven out friendless, he wandered about for a time and died among the Spartans. Whether Antiochus was right or wrong in regarding these disorders as open rebellion against his rule, it is generally admitted that the commotion arose from party politics more than from the conflict between Judaism and Hellenism.

The king sent Apollonius the "mysarch" (Mysian commander) to Jerusalem with an army of 22,000 men (II Macc. 5:24).[8] After slaying

[8] The name "Apollonius" is not given in I Macc. 1:29, where through an error "collector of tribute" is given instead of "mysarch" (J. Wellhausen, *Nachricht. d. Gesellsch. d. Wissensch. zu Göttingen* 1905, p. 161).

treacherously many of its inhabitants (5:25 f.; I Macc. 1-30), he demolished the city walls and many houses (I Macc. 1:31), and south of the Temple, on the eastern hill,[9] he built the *Acra* (1:33) which was not only, according to the meaning of the word, a fortified citadel or acropolis occupied by a body of troops, but a miniature city ("polis") inhabited by pagan Syrians (I Macc. 3:45; 14:36) and pro-Syrian Jews—a group called "a sinful nation, wicked men" (1:34; cf. 6:21-24). These "sons of the Acra" (4:2) remained a thorn in the flesh of the pious Jews (1:36), a humiliating symbol of alien domination, for almost thirty years (until 142-141).

Soon after (or in 167, a year later, according to E. Bickermann), Epiphanes, realizing that ultimately the Jewish opposition to him was rooted in religion, decided to proscribe Judaism. As the Samaritan temple was dedicated to Zeus Xenios, so the Temple in Jerusalem became a sanctuary of the Olympian Zeus (II Macc. 6:1 f). "The abomination of desolation" (Dan. 9:27; 11:31; 12:11; I Macc. 1:54) is a sarcastic distortion of the Semitic name ("the Baal of Heaven") of the Olympian Zeus and indicates a small Greek altar in his honor erected over the large altar of sacrifices. Swine were offered thereon in December, 168. The high priest Menelaus and his subordinate clergy ceased to officiate in the Temple: the Jewish cultus had come to an end.

At the same time all religious observances ordained in the Law of Moses were forbidden in Palestine (but not elsewhere in the Seleucid kingdom) under penalty of death, notably circumcision, Sabbath rest, celebration of the festivals. The mere possession of a scroll of the Law was a capital offense, for the edict ordered the destruction of every copy of the Pentateuch. Conversely, the worship of heathen gods became compulsory, and altars for this purpose were erected all over the land.[10]

The reaction of the Jews to these detestable measures and to the resulting religious persecution—perhaps the first in history—was threefold. Some, either through inclination or through fear, forsook the religion of their fathers and complied with the royal edict (I Macc. 1:43, 52). The Hasidim, or Pious (*Asidaîoi* in I Macc. 7:13; II Macc. 14:6), on the contrary, offered passive resistance to the new law and, either secretly in the towns or openly in the wilderness, continued to obey the Mosaic statutes, preferring to die rather than violate even the least of the dietary commandments (I Macc. 1:62 f.). Their motto is well expressed in the Book of Daniel (3:17 f.), which a Hasid composed to

[9] On the location of the Acra see E. Schürer, *Geschichte*, Vol. 1, p. 198, n. 37; also the map Plate XVII, C in *The Westminster Historical Atlas of the Bible* edited by G. E. Wright and F. V. Filson (Philadelphia, 1945).

[10] For all these measures see especially I Macc. 1:41-64 and II Macc. 6:1-11; and also Dan. 7:25; 8:11 f.; 9:27; 11:31-33; 12:11; Josephus, *Antiquities* 12:5, 4 (§§251-254).

encourage loyalty to the Lord at any cost during the persecution: whether their God would deliver them from the king's hand or not, they would not serve his gods. Some of the Hasidim died valiantly as martyrs for their faith (I Macc. 1:60 f.; 2:29-38; Dan. 11:32b-33, 35) and thus became the heroes of the earliest Golden Legend (in II Macc. 6:10-7:42; cf. IV Macc.). Finally, a third group, chiefly rural, under the leadership of Judas Maccabeus decided to defy openly the royal edict and to fight for their faith.[11]

In the mountain village of Modin (now el-Medije), between Jerusalem and the sea, lived "Mattathias, the son of John, the son of Simeon, a priest of the sons of Joarib, from Jerusalem . . . And he had five sons": John, Simon, Judas Maccabeus, Eleazar, and Jonathan (I Macc. 2:1-5). When a royal officer came to Modin to enforce the decree ordaining pagan sacrifices for the Jews, Mattathias in his zeal killed a Jew who was ready to perform the ceremony as also the officer, and fled forthwith to the mountains with his sons leaving all his property (2:15-28). Thus began the Maccabean rebellion which, after the death of Mattathias in 167-166 (2:69 f.), was led by his son Judas Maccabeus.

After the king's troops had massacred about a thousand Hasidim on the Sabbath (2:29-38), Mattathias and the Hasidim decided to fight for their lives on the Sabbath; they went through the country attacking apostate Jews and pagans, pulling down altars, circumcising infants, and generally upholding the observance of the Law of Moses (2:39-48).

The Syrian authorities underestimated the valor of Judas, who "was like a lion in his deeds, like a lion's whelp roaring for his prey" (3:4), and the difficulties of the mountainous terrain, ideally suited to the guerrilla warfare in which Judas excelled. So the Maccabees were successful in defeating the Syrians under Apollonius, whose sword Judas carried henceforth (3:10-12), and in driving back Seron at the pass of Bethhoron (3:13-24). While in 166-165 Antiochus Epiphanes was engaged in a campaign against the Parthians (3:31, 37), Lysias as his regent in Syria (3:32-36) sent Ptolemy, Nicanor, and Gorgias, at the head of a considerable army, against Judas (3:38-41). After religious and military preparations for a battle which seemed hopeless, Judas met the enemy at Emmaus (3:42-60). While Gorgias was marching against the Jewish

[11] In principle there was an irreconcilable difference between the Hasidim, relying on divine help, and the Maccabees, relying on military and diplomatic measures. Consequently the Hasidim at first mistrusted Judas and his "little help" (Dan. 11:34a), observing that he welcomed to his ranks men whose valor excelled their faith and morals. But eventually, during the emergency, the Hasidim gave their support to Judas (I Macc. 2:42-44; cf. 7:12 f.; II Macc. 14:6) and even consented to fight in self-defense on the Sabbath (I Macc. 2:40 f.): thus, as the Book of Enoch (90:6-9) says symbolically, horns grew on the little lambs. But after 164 the Hasidim and the Maccabees disagreed more and more.

position with a strong body of troops, Judas suddenly attacked the enemy camp at Emmaus; Gorgias, upon his return, seeing the camp in flames and Judas ready for battle, fled into Philistia (4:1-25).

A year later, in the fall of 165, Lysias intervened in person. He circled Judea and camped at Beth-zur (Bethsura), south of Jerusalem (I Macc. 4:26-29). Divergent conclusions in regard to the ensuing events have been reached by historians, unable to reconcile the conflicting reports of I and II Maccabees. The following account seems the most probable to the present writer. Whether Lysias and Judas fought an inconclusive battle (nay, whether a decisive victory was won by Judas, according to I Macc. 4:34 f.) or not, Lysias entered negotiations with Judas and, possibly through the friendly intervention of a passing Roman embassy, a peace treaty abrogating the proscription of Judaism was signed with the approval of Antiochus Epiphanes (II Macc. 11). So Judas and his men went up to Jerusalem and cleansed the Temple, where for three years sacrifices had been offered to the Olympian Zeus: the worship of Jehovah was inaugurated anew, according to I Macc. 4:52, on the 25th of Chislev (December) of 165—on the very day in which it had been profaned three years before (4:54). The day was celebrated annually ever since as the Hanukkah (Rededication) Feast (4:59; II Macc. 1:9; 10:1-8; Ps. 30, superscription; John 10:22). Josephus (*Antiquities* 12:7, 7 [§325]) says that it is called "Lights" (*phôta*); the illumination of the houses during eight days is indeed characteristic of its celebration.[12]

The achievement of religious liberty should have marked the end of the hostilities begun for this purpose, particularly since Antiochus Epiphanes died in 164. It appears, in reality, that the Hasidim became again pacifists. But the Maccabees, as J. Wellhausen says, "did not turn immediately from wolves into lambs." They soon had occasion to wage war again because of pogroms in regions where the Jews were a small minority;because the Acra continued to dominate Jerusalem, and because Judea was still subject to the Seleucids. The Book of Daniel reflects only the struggle for religious freedom before 164, the Book of Judith both that and the war for political independence ended in 141, and finally the Book of Esther the campaigns for vengeance against the enemies of the Jews following 141.

After fortifying the Temple hill in Jerusalem and Beth-zur at the southern border of Judea (I Macc. 4:60 f.), Judas fought successfully

[12] H. Ewald (*Geschichte des Volkes Israel*, 3rd ed., Vol. 4, p. 407), followed by J. Wellhausen (*Israel. und Jüd. Gesch.*, 7th ed., p. 245, n. 1), regards Dedication (and the German Christmas) as a winter solstice feast. See also R. Kittel, *Die hellenistische Mysterienreligion und das Alte Testament*, pp. 17-24 (BWAT N.F. 7), Stuttgart, 1924. W. W. Hyde, *Paganism to Christianity in the Roman Empire*, pp. 249-256. University of Pennsylvania Press, 1946.

against neighboring peoples, the Idumeans, the "Children of Baean" (unknown), and the Ammonites (5:1-8). The Gentiles in Gilead (Transjordania) and Galilee countered by persecuting the Jews in their midst, until Simon attacked them in Galilee and Judas in Gilead. The Jews in both regions were brought to Judea for safety (5:9-54). At the same time, however, Joseph and Azarias, who had been left in command in Jerusalem, were defeated by Gorgias when they attempted to attack Jamnia (5:55-64). During a second campaign against the Edomites, Judas took Hebron and, in Philistia, destroyed the temples of Ashdod (Azotus; 5:65-68).

When young Antiochus V Eupator became king under the tutelage of Lysias at the death of Antiochus Epiphanes in 164-163 (6:1-17; cf. the legends in II Macc. 1:13-16 and ch. 9), Judas rashly decided to besiege the Acra in Jerusalem (6:18-27). But Lysias and the young king defeated Judas at Beth-Zacharias (south of Bethlehem), captured Bethzur, lifted the siege of the Acra, forced Judas to accept terms of peace, and razed the fortifications around the Temple (6:28-63). The freedom of religion was confirmed again, and Menelaus was removed from the high priesthood and executed.

In 162-161 Demetrius I Soter, the son of Seleucus IV and therefore the cousin of Antiochus V, escaped from Rome, and became king after ordering the assassination of Lysias and Antiochus V (7:1-4). Alcimus (in Hebrew Jakim, abbreviated from Eliakim) led a delegation of Hellenizing Jews to Demetrius, was appointed high priest, and was installed by Bacchides with the approval of the scribes and the Hasidim—for Alcimus was of the seed of Aaron. Although Judas and his band had been forced to leave Jerusalem, Alcimus foolishly killed sixty Hasidim who had formerly supported the Maccabees; consequently he lost all support in Jerusalem and had to appeal to Demetrius for help (7:5-25). The king sent Nicanor at the head of the army, but he was defeated by Judas and was slain at the battle of Adasa, near Beth-horon, on the 13th of Adar (7:26-50; cf. II Macc. 14-15)—an event celebrated annually (7:49) on the day before Purim (II Macc. 15:36; Esth. 9:20-32). For a time Judas was again at the head of his nation and he may have attempted to strengthen his position through negotiations with Rome (even though the dossier in I Macc. 8 can hardly be authentic). But when Demetrius sent a powerful army under the command of Bacchides, Judas could not prevail and fell fighting valiantly at Elasa in 161 (9:1-22).

The Hellenizing party led by Alcimus was again in control (9:23-27), but the Maccabees chose Judas's brother Jonathan as their military leader (9:28-31). For the moment, however, they could merely live as freebooters in the wilderness of Tekoa (9:32-34), as David had in his outlaw days: whenever robbed, they raided in revenge (9:35-42). Bacchides was unable to cope with Jewish guerrilla bands (9:43-49), but he forti-

fied a number of garrison towns in Judea and took hostages (9:50-53).
Alcimus tore down the wall in the Temple courts separating Jews and
Gentiles, but died soon after; and Bacchides returned to Antioch
(9:54-57). At the request of the Hellenizers, Bacchides returned two
years later (in 158), but could accomplish nothing against Jonathan; so
he made peace with him and never came back (9:58-72). Thus during
the following five years (158-153) Jonathan was left undisturbed in
Michmash and consolidated his power (9:73). Except for a few aristocrats, the Jewish nation was generally opposed to Hellenization and
accepted more and more the leadership of the Hasmoneans who succeeded
Judas. At the same time the Seleucids, through their dynastic quarrels,
not only became less and less able to lend support to unpopular Hellenizing high priests, but were forced to make concessions to the Hasmoneans
in order to obtain their help.

An Ephesian youth of low birth, Balas, pretended to be the son of
Antiochus Epiphanes. Aided by the enemies of Demetrius I (Attalus II
king of Pergamum, Ptolemy VI Philometor of Egypt, Ariarathes V of
Cappadocia), officially recognized by the Roman Senate, and supported
by the Syrians opposed to Demetrius, Balas took the name of Alexander
and in 153 began his fight for the Syrian throne. In this emergency
Demetrius granted Jonathan the power to raise troops and free the
hostages, withdrew the Syrian garrisons in Judea except those at Beth-zur
and in the Acra, and allowed Jonathan to fortify Jerusalem (10:1-14).
But Balas Alexander offered far greater concessions to Jonathan for his
help: he appointed him high priest and sent him a purple robe and a
golden crown. So Jonathan, clad in the sacred vestments, officiated at
the Feast of Tabernacles in 153 (10:15-21) and wisely rejected all the
other alluring promises of Demetrius I (10:22-47), who died fighting in
150 (10:48-50). In the same year Jonathan was greatly honored: when
Balas married Cleopatra, the daughter of Ptolemy VI, he was appointed
strategos and *meridarches* (military and civil governor) of Judea
(10:51-66).

Jonathan remained loyal to his benefactor even after a legitimate
claimant to the throne, Demetrius II Nicator (son of Demetrius I),
appeared in 147. When Apollonius, the governor of Coele-Syria, passed
over to Demetrius and challenged Jonathan, the latter was victorious at
Joppa and Ashdod (where the temple of Dagon was destroyed), and
received from Balas the city of Ekron as his reward (10:67-89). But
when Ptolemy VI turned against his son-in-law Balas and took away from
him his daughter Cleopatra, giving her to Demetrius II in marriage, Jonathan's help could not save Balas, and he was assassinated in 145
(11:1-19).

Jonathan, however, felt strong enough to besiege the Acra and to
demand of Demetrius, as the price of lifting the siege, three districts of

Samaria and complete freedom from taxation, except for a payment of 300 talents (11:20-37). Such concessions, soon to be increased, indicate how low had sunk the power of the Seleucids—and how cleverly Jonathan took advantage of their plight.

A former general of Balas, Tryphon, brought Antiochus VI (son of Balas) from Arabia, to rule in place of Demetrius II (11:38-40). When a rebellion broke out in Antioch against Demetrius, he was saved from death by three thousand Jewish soldiers sent to his help by Jonathan (11:41-51).

In 144, when Demetrius failed to keep his promises to Jonathan (11:52 f.) and was sorely pressed by Tryphon (11:54-56), Jonathan gave his support to Antiochus VI and Tryphon (11:57-59) and proceeded to subject Philistia to them (11:60-62). He defeated an army of Demetrius at Hazor in Galilee (11:63 f., 67-74a) while his brother Simon forced the capitulation of Beth-zur (11:65 f.).[13] When the forces of Demetrius rallied at Hamath on the Orontes, Jonathan scattered them again (12:24-30). On his way back he punished the Zabadean Arabs in the Lebanon (12:31) and passed through Damascus (12:32). Simon had taken Ashkelon and occupied Joppa (12:33 f.). Then Jonathan set about fortifying Jerusalem and other towns of Judea (12:35-38).

Jonathan and Tryphon did not trust each other, for each sought only his own advantage in their alliance against Demetrius. When Tryphon came to Scythopolis (Beth-shean) in 143, Jonathan met him with a strong army; but overcome by flattery and false promises, Jonathan came to Ptolemais and was cast into a dungeon (12:39-53).

Simon, who was *stratego̅s* (military governor) of the coastal districts from the Ladder of Tyre to the Egyptian border (11:59), hurried to Jerusalem and was elected leader in place of his brother Jonathan (13:1-11). Simon sent money and hostages to Tryphon for the liberation of Jonathan, even though he had reason to mistrust Tryphon (13:12-19). Actually Tryphon, far from keeping his word, tried to invade Judea, had Jonathan killed in Bascama (13:20), and—after assassinating Antiochus VI—made himself king (13:31 f.). Simon, while continuing the fortifications begun by Jonathan, obtained concessions from Demetrius II, and conquered Gazara, the ancient Gezer,[14] making his son John Hyrcanus

[13] According to I Macc. 11:74b-12:23, Jonathan interrupted this campaign to go to Jerusalem and send friendly embassies to Rome and Sparta. The dossier in ch. 12 is no less suspect to some scholars than the one in ch. 8. On Beth-zur see: O. R. Sellers and W. F. Albright in BASOR No. 43 (October 1931), pp. 12-13; O. R. Sellers, *The Citadel of Beth-zur.* Philadelphia, 1933.

[14] The excavations on the site have disclosed a curious sidelight of Simon's occupation of Gezer. One of the Gentiles in the city, obviously forced by Simon to work at the construction of a government palace, inscribed an imprecation on a stone that he placed into the wall. The inscription, written carelessly in Greek, reads as follows: "(Says) Pampras, 'May fire (?) follow up Simon's palace.'" See: R. A. Stewart Macalister, *The Excavations of Gezer,* Vol. I, pp. 211 f. London, 1912.

governor thereof (13:53; cf. 16:1, 19, 21). Finally, by forcing the capitulation of the Acra in Jerusalem on the 23rd of Iyyar (May), 142 (an annual celebration for two or three centuries), Simon made the Jews independent from the Seleucids (13:33-52): thus "was the yoke of the heathen taken away from Israel" (13:41).

3. The Rule of the Hasmoneans (142-63)

The chief merits of Simon (according to 14:4 f., and the ode in his honor in 14:6-15) were the securing of Joppa as a Jewish harbor and the conquest of Gazara, Beth-zur, and the Acra: thus he made Israel prosperous, pious, and strong. In September, 141, a grateful nation conferred upon Simon and his descendants the legitimate and permanent authority as ruling high priests (14:25-49):[15] thus the rule of the Hasmonean dynasty received national recognition. As the first independent ruler of his family, Simon was probably the first to establish an era according to which documents were dated (13:42)—possibly the era of Jerusalem as an independent city rather than of Simon's first year of rule—indeed the first to be recognized by the Roman Senate as a friendly independent ruler (14:16-19, 24; 15:15-24).[16]

When in 138 Demetrius II, after long wars with the Parthian king Mithridates I, was taken prisoner, his brother Antiochus VII Sidetes wrote from Rhodes confirming the authority of Simon (15:1-9) and besieged Tryphon in Dor, Phoenicia (15:10-14, 37). Certain of his final victory over Tryphon, Sidetes, however, refused Simon's help and ordered him to return the conquered cities of Joppa and Gazara, as also the Acra in Jerusalem, or pay for them an indemnity of 1,000 talents of silver (15:25-31). Simon offered only 100 talents (15:32-36). So Cendebeus was sent against the Jews, but Judas and John, the sons of Simon, defeated him, and the attack was not renewed in Simon's lifetime (15:38-16:10). Like his brothers, Simon died a violent death: his son-in-law Ptolemy, governor of Jericho, assassinated him together with his two sons Mattathias and Judas in 135 (16:11-17). But John Hyrcanus, who was in Gazara, was warned in time and became high priest in the place of his father (16:18).

John Hyrcanus (135-104)[17] began his rule inauspiciously, but succeeded in ending it with the Jewish state at the height of its power. He failed

---

[15] Psalm 110, which in Hebrew has the acrostic "Simeon" and contains the divine oracle, "Thou art a priest forever after the order of Melchizedek" (the Hasmoneans were *not* sons of Aaron), may have been composed for this occasion.

[16] O. R. Sellers and W. F. Albright (BASOR No. 43, p. 13) have concluded from the excavations at Beth-zur that Simon did not coin money, despite I Macc. 15:6. H. Willrich (ZAW N.F. 10 [1933] 78 f.) agrees with this conclusion.

[17] Our principal sources of information for Hyrcanus (since his history, named in I Macc. 16:23 f., has not survived) are Josephus, *Antiquities* 13:8-10 and *War* 1:2.

to punish Ptolemy because the latter was holding his mother as a hostage. Worse still, in the year 130 (or, less probably, 134) Antiochus VII Sidetes, who had been defied by Simon, attacked Hyrcanus in person, devastated Judea, besieged Hyrcanus in Jerusalem, and forced his capitulation and the payment of a considerable indemnity. Soon afterward Hyrcanus was forced to accompany Sidetes in his campaign against the Parthians. But the king's death in 129, when he threw himself from a cliff to escape captivity, was fortunate for the Jews. Then ended, however, the rule of the Seleucids east of the Euphrates.

The unpopular weakling Demetrius II, who had been freed by the Parthians, now ruled in place of his able brother, Antiochus VII. Stupidly Demetrius began to war against Ptolemy VII Physcon, and the latter, according to accepted tactics, set up against him a fraudulent pretender who, like Balas, called himself Alexander, but in Syria was known as Zabinas (meaning "bought and paid for"). Demetrius was defeated and was assassinated on the point of landing at Tyre (125). His son Antiochus VIII Grypus (125-113, 111-96), however, succeeded in ridding himself of Zabinas (122), but was driven away in 113 by his cousin Antiochus IX Cyzicenus, son of Sidetes (113-111, 111-95). Even when Grypus occupied most of Syria in 111, Cyzicenus remained the master of Coele-Syria until his death in 95.

Such dynastic dissensions were most advantageous to Hyrcanus, who became again an independent ruler at the death of Antiochus VII Sidetes (129) and, as Josephus (*Antiquities* 13:10, 1) says, contributed nothing to later Seleucid kings either as a subject or as a friend. Like his predecessors, he negotiated with the deceitful pretender (Zabinas) rather than with the real Seleucids. In any case, Hyrcanus knew how to take advantage of the plight of that dynasty to enlarge the borders of his limited province. The Hasmoneans had progressed from the attainment of religious freedom to the elimination of the high priestly aristocracy, to political independence, and, after some attempts by Jonathan and Simon with limited results, to conquest under Hyrcanus.

With the manifest intention of restoring to the Jews the kingdom of David in its whole extent, John Hyrcanus fought successfully in the east, north, and south. After conquering Medaba and Samaga in Transjordania, he captured Shechem and the Samaritan temple on Gerizim, subjugating the Samaritan sect. The Idumeans were subjected and forced to adopt Judaism. The attack on Samaria, which was a Greek city, caused him more trouble, but after a siege of one year he razed it to the ground (fulfilling the prophecy in Mic. 1:6), in spite of the opposition of Antiochus IX Cyzicenus (whose intervention seems to have been frustrated by the Romans). At the same time he gained possession of Scythopolis (Beth-shean).

whose passion was besieging cities,[21] broke out in a violent rebellion when Janneus returned to his capital without his army. It is not certain that the Pharisees, usually pacifists, were now the instigators of violence: in any case the rebels hired Demetrius III Eucerus (son of Grypus) and defeated Janneus in a decisive battle (88). A patriotic reaction, at the sight of the Jewish king wandering as a fugitive in the mountains, turned the tables after Demetrius departed: six thousand Jews went over to Janneus and he was able to regain his throne and wreak bloody vengeance on his enemies.

Hostility from without began anew after the crushing of internal opposition. In 86 Antiochus XII Dionysus (son of Grypus) wished to cross Judea in order to attack the Nabatean king Aretas in his own country. Janneus, instead of helping him defeat their common foe, built a wall fortified with wooden towers and a moat from Joppa inland, to divert the Syrians. Antiochus XII broke through anyhow, but was defeated and slain in battle by Aretas, who thus became master of the country as far as Damascus. He invaded Judea and defeated Janneus at Adida, forcing him to sue for peace. Undeterred by this, Janneus fought with success in Transjordania (83-80), where he captured Pella, Gerasa, Seleucia, Gamala, etc. During the last three years of his life (79-76) he was afflicted by an ailment due to his intemperance and seemed to seek relief in war. When he died while besieging Ragaba in Perea, he had almost restored to the Jews the kingdom of Solomon.

Alexandra (76-67), the widow of two kings, succeeded her husband Janneus on the throne;[22] and her eldest son, Hyrcanus II, became high priest (without civil authority). Her abler and more energetic second son, Aristobulus II, she kept in check. Although we do not know whether the stories of the opposition of the Pharisees against John Hyrcanus I and especially against Janneus are historical, and whether Janneus on his deathbed actually advised Alexandra to give some authority to the Pharisees (Josephus, *Antiquities* 13:15, 5), it is certain that under Alexandra (who was the sister of a famous Pharisee, Simon ben Shetach) for the first time the Pharisees were admitted to the Senate (Sanhedrin) and played an important role in the government. Nicholas of Damascus (quoted by Josephus, *War* 1:5, 2), who was not overly fond of the Pharisees, said with some exaggeration that "the advantages of royalty were theirs, the cost and the troubles were Alexandra's. . . . While she governed other people, the Pharisees governed her." Her reign was peaceful and prosperous—the calm before the storm. By strengthening

---

[21] His coins exhibit his dual function with two types of inscriptions: "Jehonathan the King" (in Hebrew) and "Of King Alexander" (in Greek); other coins have the earlier type of inscription: "Jehonathan (or Jonathan) the high priest and the *cheber* [senate or congregation] of the Jews" (in Hebrew).

[22] On Alexandra see Josephus, *Antiquities* 14:1-4; *War* 1:6-7.

Hyrcanus was followed at his death by his son Aristobulus (10
According to Josephus, the new ruler imprisoned his brothers (
exception of Antigonus) and his mother.[19] The lady he let starve
in prison; his brother Antigonus, whom he dearly loved, he sle
through a diabolical plot, he came into his presence fully arme
said to have died brokenhearted over this unjust execution.
standing these family tragedies (if they be historical), he is sai
been an able ruler. He was the first of his line to adopt the re
although his coins are inscribed in Hebrew, "Judah the high p
the *chebar* (= senate or congregation) of the Jews." Aristobuli
father) must have secured a foothold in Galilee and begun t
it, for he forcibly circumcised the Itureans in the Lebanon.

At his death, Salome Alexandra, his widow, freed the brotl
prison and married the oldest, Janneus (Hebrew, Jonathan) .
(103-76), who was then twenty-four years of age (thirteen year
than she was).[20] Psalm 2, having the Hebrew acrostic "For J:
and his wife," was probably sung at the wedding and c
ceremonies; if so, it correctly anticipated the main aim of Ja
break the heathen with a rod of iron and dash them in pie
potter's vessel (Ps. 2:9) in order to restore David's kingdom
extent.

He began his campaigns with an attack against Ptolemai:
Akko) on the coast. The inhabitants appealed for help to
Lathyrus, who was in control of Cyprus after his mother, Clec
had driven him out of Egypt. Defeated by Lathyrus in 100, Ja
saved from complete disaster by the forces of Cleopatra, altl
queen was at first inclined to retain control of Palestine.
discouraged, Janneus began operations east of the Jordan,
conquered Gadara and Amathus; continued them in Philistia,
took Raphia and Anthedon; and destroyed Gaza after a year's s
About a year later Janneus returned to Transjordania, but he
contact with the powerful kingdom of the Nabateans in E
capital was Petra). The Nabatean king, Obadas, objected
interference in the lands of Moab and Ammon, which he regai
own sphere of influence; he completely destroyed the army o
in a ravine (94).

The bitter resentment in Jerusalem against the bellicose h

[18] Chief sources of information on Aristobulus: Josephus, *Antiquities*
1:3.

[19] J. Wellhausen surmises, not without reason, that they were his step
stepmother.

[20] Our chief sources for Janneus are Josephus, *Antiquities* 13:12-15; W

the army and fortifying strategic points she escaped attack. When Tigranes, king of Armenia, was besieging Ptolemais and threatened to put an end to the independence of the Jews (69), she wisely refrained from war and sent him gifts. He was soon compelled to return to Armenia, which the Roman Lucullus was laying waste. Her only military expedition, led by her son Aristobulus II to Damascus, failed completely. When she died at the age of seventy-three, the power of the Hasmoneans and the independence of the Jews were about to expire.

Even before the death of his mother, Aristobulus II (67-63)[23] had taken measures to rule after her. He had the support of the veterans of Janneus, who had felt slighted during the reign of Alexandra. Hyrcanus II, the high priest and legitimate successor, was weak and indolent by nature. When his forces were defeated at Jericho, he surrendered to Aristobulus all his rights to the high priesthood and to the royal crown; thus three months after his mother's death Hyrcanus II was allowed to retire peacefully to private life.

The change was far from agreeable to Antipater, who was presumably, like his father Antipater, military governor of Idumea; he was the father of Herod the Great. He saw that opportunities for attaining authority and power were far greater under a weakling like Hyrcanus than under an ambitious ruler like Aristobulus. He persuaded Hyrcanus that his life was in danger and brought him to Petra, where Aretas, king of the Nabateans, agreed to place Hyrcanus on the throne in exchange for twelve frontier towns conquered by Janneus. So Aristobulus, defeated by Aretas and forsaken by many of his troops, fortified himself in the Temple at Jerusalem, supported chiefly by the priests (65). The war between the brothers was inviting Roman intervention.

Following Lucullus, who in 69 had checked the conquests of Mithridates king of Pontus, and Tigranes, king of Armenia, Pompey had been sent to the Near East and had broken the power of Mithridates and confined Tigranes to Armenia (66). Pompey's legate Scaurus heard in Damascus of the war between Aristobulus and Hyrcanus, and went to Judea, where both sides presented their pleas and promised four-hundred talents. Scaurus ordered Aretas to lift the siege and, pending the decision of Pompey, left Aristobulus in power. The latter pursued the Nabateans and inflicted considerable losses on them.

Pompey came to Damascus in the spring of 63. There he listened not only to the pleas of Aristobulus and Hyrcanus, but also to those of the Jewish people, who wished neither and preferred the abolition of the monarchy in favor of the earlier priestly government. Pompey promised to settle the matter after his campaign against the Nabateans. But

[23] Our best sources of information on Aristobulus II are: Josephus, *Antiquities* 14:1-4; *War* 1:6-7.

Aristobulus aroused suspicion: he promised to deliver Jerusalem, but Pompey's general Gabinius found the city's gates locked against him. So the Jewish king was placed under arrest. The followers of Hyrcanus opened the gates to the Romans, but their opponents fortified themselves on the Temple hill. Pompey, after a siege of three months, made a breach in the northern fortifications, and a horrible butchery ensued. Pompey entered the Holy of Holies, but he ordered the continuation of the services and did not plunder the Temple. The Jewish community thus passed under Roman rule and lost all non-Jewish cities conquered by the Hasmoneans: the Mediterranean coastal harbors, the Transjordanian towns (Pella, Gadara, Hippus, etc.), and Samaria, Scythopolis, as also other districts. The reduced Jewish state was placed under Hyrcanus II, as high priest without the royal title. In 61 Aristobulus was forced to march in Pompey's triumph at Rome. Numerous Jews had been brought there as slaves and, after their manumission, became the nucleus of the flourishing Jewish community in Rome.

4. The Rule of the Romans (63 B.C.-A.D. 66)

Antipater was the power behind the throne, while Hyrcanus II was the high priest and ethnarch of the Jews (63-40 B.C.).[24] Antipater, as well as his son Herod later, carried out punctiliously the Roman policies. At the same time, if we may judge from Ps. of Sol. 8, the Pharisees seemed pleased with the passing of bellicose high priests and did not object to Roman rule.

After a few years of peace, the storm broke again in 57, when Alexander, the son of Aristobulus II, having previously escaped from Pompey on the way to Rome, took possession of the strongholds of Alexandrium, Hyrcania, and Machaerus. The new proconsul of Syria, Gabinius, sent Mark Antony against him and personally forced his surrender at Alexandrium. Then Gabinius deprived Hyrcanus of civil power and divided the Jewish territory into five districts (Jerusalem, Gazara, Amathus, Jericho, and Sepphoris). The following year (56) Aristobulus (with his son Antigonus) attempted to seize the Jewish state, but was easily recaptured at Machaerus. In 55 another rebellion of Alexander's was put down by Gabinius on his way back from Egypt. In 54 the successor of Gabinius as proconsul of Syria, M. Licinius Crassus, plundered the treasures in the Temple at Jerusalem (valued at about 10,000 talents of silver), but he soon fell at Carrhae (53) in battle against the Parthians. While C. Cassius Longinus was governor of Syria (53-51), Pitholaus (a veteran of the

[24] Our best sources for the rule of Hyrcanus II are: Josephus, *Antiquities* 14:5-13; *War* 1:8-13.

rebellion of Aristobulus) attempted a revolt in Galilee; the only result was the sale of a multitude of Jews into slavery.

The Roman civil war that began in 49 with Caesar's crossing of the Rubicon determined the policy of the Jewish leaders, decided primarily by Antipater. Caesar freed Aristobulus in Rome, that he might fight against Pompey, but Aristobulus was poisoned at once, while his son Alexander was beheaded in Antioch on Pompey's orders. But after Pompey's defeat at Pharsalus (48) and his assassination in Egypt the same year (cf. Ps. of Sol. 2), Hyrcanus II and Antipater passed over to Caesar's side and in 47 came to his help while he was fighting in Egypt. Their reward came the same year when Caesar, turning a deaf ear to the pleas of Antigonus (the last surviving son of Aristobulus), appointed Hyrcanus again as hereditary high priest and ethnarch of the Jews and made Antipater a Roman citizen free from taxation, and governor of Judea. The harbor of Joppa and other districts were added to Jewish territory. The Jews in the Dispersion were also favored; so that Caesar's death, on the ides of March of 44, was mourned by Jews everywhere more than by any other non-Roman nation.

Antipater, who had gained Caesar's favor for the Jews, was not thanked by them, for they knew that he was concerned chiefly about himself and his sons, Phasael and Herod, whom he appointed prefects of Judea and Galilee, respectively. Herod (the later king of the Jews), though only twenty-five years of age, proved himself a man of energy and initiative: he executed a bandit chief (or perhaps a political rebel) named Hezekiah, together with many of his followers. This abuse of authority provoked an immediate reaction in Jerusalem: legally only the Sanhedrin could impose the death penalty. But when Herod appeared before that supreme court, he came clad in purple, with a bodyguard, and Hyrcanus (upon the instructions of Sextus Caesar) adjourned the meeting when it seemed that Herod would be condemned. Herod came back with an army, but refrained from violence upon his father's and brother's entreaties: he thought it sufficient for his future to have made a show of strength before the nation, and returned to Galilee. Sextus Caesar appointed him military governor of Coele-Syria at this time (47-46).

Sextus Caesar was assassinated in 46, and C. Bassus, who belonged to the party of Pompey, made himself master of Syria; the war between Caesar's and Pompey's followers continued unabated. Antipater was an adherent of Caesar. After Caesar's assassination in 44, Mark Antony took up his cause against the assassins, M. Brutus and C. Cassius. Cassius came to Syria and received the support of both contending parties there; he raised an enormous sum for the war (Antipater paid 700 talents). But Antipater was poisoned by the butler of Hyrcanus, bribed by Malichus who wished to become master of Judea. Herod promptly avenged his father's death.

The departure of Crassus in 42 left Syria, which had been forced to supply great sums, in a state of anarchy. Antigonus thought the time ripe for another attempt to conquer Palestine, but Herod frustrated his efforts. When Brutus and Cassius were defeated at Philippi by M. Antony and Octavian in the late fall of 42, Roman Asia passed under the dominion of Antony. With great alacrity Herod—a protégé of Cassius—offered his services and allegiance to Antony who, in spite of Jewish appeals against him, eventually appointed Phasael and Herod as tetrarchs of the Jewish state, with the approval of Hyrcanus who had been ruler in name only (fall of 41).

In 40, while Antony was enjoying the hospitality of Cleopatra or was occupied with the problems of Italy, the Parthians under Pacorus (son of King Orodes) and Barzaphranes invaded Syria. The Jews welcomed them as deliverers from the Romans and gave their support to Antigonus, who had made an agreement with the Parthians. When Hyrcanus and Phasael went to Barzaphranes to negotiate, they were thrown into a dungeon: Phasael killed himself, and Hyrcanus was taken to Babylonia after Antigonus had bitten off his ears to make him unfit for the high priesthood. Herod succeeded in placing his family in the fortress of Masada and went to Rome to seek help from Antony.

Thus Antigonus became king and high priest of the Jews for three years (40-37),[25] the last of the Hasmonean line to sit on the throne. Personally he could evoke little enthusiasm,[26] but so deep was the hatred for Herod and the Romans that he had the backing of Jews of all classes. Through the good offices of Mark Antony and Octavian (Augustus), who recognized Herod's ability and loyalty to Rome, Herod was appointed king of the Jews by the Roman Senate, and left Rome a week after his arrival (late in 40). In 39 Ventidius had driven the Parthians out of Syria, but upon payment of tribute had left Antigonus unmolested. Herod, through the help of Silo, the lieutenant of Ventidius, conquered Joppa and delivered his family, still besieged in Masada. But the Roman troops went into winter quarters, and in 38 could not help Herod, owing to a new Parthian invasion; Herod was busy pacifying Galilee at the time. After the victory of Ventidius over the Parthians (June, 38), Herod went to see Antony at Samosata. During his absence his brother Joseph had been defeated and killed by Antigonus, and the Galileans had

[25] On the rule of Antigonus see: Josephus, Antiquities 14:14-16; War 1:14, 1-18, 3. The inscription on his coins reads: "Of king Antigonus" (in Greek) and "Mattathias the high priest" (in Hebrew).

[26] To gain the throne Antigonus had not only pledged to the Parthians 1,000 talents, but also 500 Jewish women.

rebelled. Nevertheless, Herod succeeded, before winter, in conquering all of Palestine except Jerusalem. Finally in 37, after a laborious siege, Jerusalem was taken with the help of Sosius. At the request of Herod, Antigonus was executed by order of Antony—the first captured king the Romans had ever put to death.

Thus, after three years, Herod could ascend his throne; and ruled from 37 to 4 B.C.[27] Herod proved himself a ruler of ability and energy, although he did not succeed in gaining the respect and affection of the Jews—who, alluding to his Idumean origin, sarcastically called him "half-Jew." From the Roman point of view Herod earned the title of "Great," for he carried out in his corner of the Roman world the great plans of Augustus. His position was that of a *rex socius*, or allied king, enjoying full autonomy and freedom from tribute, but entirely subservient to Rome in matters of foreign relations and particularly war, when he was expected to furnish military contingents.

Early in his reign Herod was faced by the opposition of the aristocracy in Jerusalem, of the surviving Hasmoneans (especially the ladies), of Cleopatra, and of the Jewish nation in general. In 37 he frightened the aristocrats by executing forty-five of the richest and noblest among the supporters of Antigonus, and confiscating their patrimony—thus providing some of the funds needed to preserve Antony's favor. In the spring of that year, after a five-year engagement, Herod married Mariamne, the granddaughter of Hyrcanus II and Aristobulus II. His mother-in-law Alexandra (mother of Mariamne and daughter of Hyrcanus) gave him serious trouble. Herod, who had appointed an obscure Jew from Babylon, Ananel, to the high priesthood (since Hyrcanus after his return from Parthian captivity was not available, having lost his ears), was forced by Alexandra to make her 17-year-old son Aristobulus (III) high priest (early in 35). Herod discovered that Alexandra was planning to flee with Aristobulus to Cleopatra (who had supported her claims) and had prepared caskets in which to get out of Jerusalem; he arranged to have Aristobulus "playfully" drowned by his companions in a swimming pool at Jericho (late in 35). Through Cleopatra, Alexandra induced Antony to summon Herod to explain this murder, but at Laodicea Herod was completely justified by Antony, partly through his arguments and partly

[27] The biography of Herod given by Josephus (*Antiquities*, books 15-17) is derived for the most part from the lost history of Nicholas of Damascus, Herod's secretary and friend. It is therefore an excellent contemporary source, even though showing Herod in the best light. A much briefer account of Herod is given by Josephus in *War* 1:18-33. It is believed that in *Antiquities*, Book 15, Josephus used, in addition to Nicholas, a source unfriendly to Herod, but in *War I* Nicholas is his only source. See H. St. John Thackeray, *Josephus: the Man and the Historian*, pp. 65-67. New York, Jewish Institute of Religion, 1929.

through cash payments (34). Antony told Cleopatra that it was not proper to investigate too closely the official acts of a king, lest he cease to be really a king (Josephus, *Antiquities* 15:3, 8 [§76]). During his absence Herod had left his wife Mariamne in charge of his uncle Joseph (the husband of his sister Salome), with instructions that she should be killed if he did not return alive—so great was his jealous love for her. Upon his return, Salome accused Joseph of illicit intercourse with Mariamne; when Herod discovered that his wife knew of his secret instructions, he had Joseph executed (34).

As for Cleopatra, she obtained from Antony the coastlands south of the Eleutheros (except for Tyre and Sidon), and the region of Jericho, rich in palm trees: Herod was thus obliged to pay tribute to the Egyptian queen from the latter district, which was part of his kingdom (34).

Finally, in regard to the fourth hostile group—the people—Herod used a variety of remedies. Knowing of the great influence of the Pharisees on the Jews, he cultivated the friendship of two famous rabbis, Pollio (Abtalion) and his pupil Sameas (Shemaiah), who during the siege of Jerusalem had advised the people to receive Herod.[28] The Pharisees had no objection to foreign rule, provided the Jews could freely practice their religion and the Pharisees could inculcate the meticulous observance of the Law of Moses—both written and unwritten. Herod showed his favor to the people and tried to gain their loyalty by remitting taxes in years of scarcity and by distributing imported grain in times of famine. On the other hand, Herod instituted drastic repressive measures against his opponents and organized an elaborate secret police.

Herod's position, however, was not threatened by these four enemies, but by the war between Octavian and Antony. When Antony had given to Cleopatra certain Nabatean districts in 34, she made Herod responsible for the collection of the tribute from the recalcitrant Malichus, thus arousing open hostility between the two strongest rulers on Egypt's Asiatic border. When Herod was preparing an expedition against Malichus, who had refused to pay the tribute, the Roman civil war broke out. Herod wished to bring help to Antony, but (fortunately for him!) Cleopatra forced him to march against Malichus instead and, when Herod had prevailed, she even helped Malichus continue the fight— to "destroy one of those kings by means of the other" (Josephus). When in the spring of 31 an earthquake killed, according to Josephus (*War* 1:19, 3), 30,000 subjects of Herod (10,000 according to *Antiquities* 15:5, 2), the Nabateans refused to negotiate and were thoroughly beaten by Herod, but with a desperate effort. Antony's downfall at Actium (September of 31) seemed fatal to his friend Herod, but after executing the aged Hyrcanus II, who willy-nilly might become a rival, Herod

[28] The famous last "pair" of teachers of the Law, Hillel and Shammai, flourished during the reign of Herod.

appeared before Octavian (Augustus) at Rhodes and was confirmed as king of the Jews (spring of 30). In the fall of 30, after Antony and Cleopatra had committed suicide following Octavian's invasion of Egypt, Herod saw Octavian in Egypt and received from him, besides Jericho, additional territories: Hippus, Gadara, Samaria, Gaza, Anthedon, Joppa, and Strato's Tower (later called Caesarea on the Sea). At the end of 29 Herod ordered the trial and execution of his favorite wife Mariamne, accused of infidelity by his mother Kypros and his sister Salome. A passionate nature driven to extremes, Herod after Mariamne's death longed desperately for her, seeking comfort in orgies and hunts until he fell seriously ill. Alexandra his mother-in-law plotted to gain the kingdom if he died, and was executed in 28. The elimination of the relatives of Hyrcanus II was completed when his sister Salome reported that her second husband, the Idumean Kostobar, was sheltering some distant relatives of the Hasmoneans, the sons of *Babas* (corrected to *Sabba* by Niese), and Herod had them all executed.

The importance of Herod in the history of the world consists in his successful realization of the plans of Augustus, principally in two spheres. First of all, he brought some order into the wild regions east of the Jordan (lying between the two Arab kingdoms of the Nabateans and the Itureans), inhabited by Bedouins who recognized no alien government. These raiders in Trachonitis hindered the communications with Damascus. In 23 Augustus gave Herod not only Trachonitis, but also Batanea and Auranitis, and three years later even the Iturean tetrarchy of Zenodorus.[29] Herod proved himself worthy of Roman confidence, in spite of the difficulties of the task, which was continued by his son Philip. This work made possible the organization of the Roman province of Arabia, which became the gateway between East and West.

In the second place, Herod furthered the cultural plans of Augustus, who wished to encourage the development of a uniform Graeco-Roman civilization in the whole empire. Herod was a great admirer of Hellenism and profoundly devoted to Augustus his overlord. So he supported the emperor cult and built temples to the divine Augustus in non-Jewish cities. Samaria, destroyed by Hyrcanus I and rebuilt by Gabinius, Herod beautified after renaming it Sebaste (the present name is still *Sebastiyye*) in honor of Augustus (Greek, *Sebastós*): there the ruins of the Herodian temple to Augustus are still impressive. For the quadrennial (or quinquennial) games in honor of Augustus he built hippodromes, amphitheaters, stadia, and theaters. In Jerusalem he built a theater, and in its vicinity an amphitheater; later (in about 24) he built the fortified royal palace, one tower of which (the so-called David's tower) is still extant, and the Tower Antonia north of the Temple.

More important was the rebuilding of Strato's Tower, begun in 22 and

[29] Josephus, *Antiquities* 15:10, 1 and 3; *War* 1:20, 4.

dedicated as Caesarea (on the Sea) in 10-9 B.C. The artificial harbor was made safe for ships by means of a long wide breakwater made of heavy stones brought from a considerable distance (*Antiquities* 15:9, 6). Two of the enormous pillars of the local temple to Augustus now stand in the Piazzetta near the Piazza S. Marco in Venice.[30]

Within his kingdom Herod built lavishly. New cities or restored towns were named in honor of his relatives: Antipatris (formerly Kapharsaba), Kypros (a stronghold near Jericho), Phasaelis; or of himself (two fortresses were called Herodeion); or of the family of Augustus (Agrippeion, formerly Anthedon). The old Hasmonean fortresses destroyed by Gabinius were rebuilt on a larger scale: Alexandreion, Hyrcania, Machaerus, and Masada; new ones rose at Gaba in Galilee and Esbon in Perea.

Far beyond his borders Herod left tokens of his building activity: at Rhodes, Nikopolis (near Actium), Antioch, Ashkelon, Tyre, Sidon, Beyrouth, Tripolis, Ptolemais, Damascus, and even at Athens and elsewhere, he contributed to the construction of temples and palaces.

But by far the most famous of his edifices is the rebuilt Temple in Jerusalem. The reconstruction began in 20 B.C. and was still continuing forty-six years later, in the time of Jesus (John 2:20); it was not actually finished until after A.D. 62—a few years before its destruction in A.D. 70. Its magnificence became proverbial, even though in reality (as in the case of the Temple of Solomon) the royal palace surpassed the Temple in size and luxury (Josephus, *War* 1:21, 1).[31] The rebuilding, done mostly by priests and Levites, did not interfere in the least with the sacred services.

The cultural aims of Augustus were likewise furthered in the literary realm. Herod surrounded himself with men having a good Greek training in rhetoric and philosophy. Chief among them was Nicholas of Damascus, whose universal history in 144 volumes was utilized by Josephus, who derived from it most of the biography of Herod (cf. note 27, above). Nicholas was sent by Herod on diplomatic missions. Other well-educated courtiers are mentioned by Josephus.

As in the case of David, the last years (13-4 B.C.) of Herod's reign were embittered by family troubles and court intrigues. Herod had ten wives, although not all at one time (according to Mishna *Sanhedrin* II, 4, a king may have eighteen wives). The members of Herod's family and his descendants may be listed concisely as follows:[32]

[30] This is stated by E. Renan (*Histoire du peuple d'Israël*, Vol. 5, p. 273. Paris, 1894), but I have been unable to discover his sources of information. The pillars unquestionably were brought from the Near East and were set up in 1180.

[31] The Temple of Herod is described in Josephus, *Antiquities* 15:11; *War* 5:5; Philo, *De Monarchia* II, 2 (II, 223 M.); Mishna *Middoth*.

[32] Josephus is our source of information as follows: for the parents, brothers, and sisters of Herod, see *Antiquities* 14:7, 3; *War* 1:8, 9; for the wives and children of Herod, see *Ant.* 17:1, 2-3; *War* 1:28, 4; in particular, for the descendants of Mariamne, see *Ant.* 18:5, 4; 19:9, 1; *War* 2:11, 6.

I. Children of Antipater (d. 43 B.C.) and Kypros I[33]

1. Phasael (d. 40 B.C.). His s. Phasael was h. of Salampsio (da. of Mariamne I) and f. of Kypros III (w. of Agrippa I).
2. Herod the Great (see II, below).
3. Joseph (d. 38 B.C.).
4. Pheroras (d. 5 B.C.).
5. Salome I (d. ca. A.D: 10), her husbands were: a. Joseph (d. 34 B.C.), her uncle, b. of her f. Antipater; b. Kostobar (d. 25 B.C.), f. of Berenice I (w. of Aristobulus, s. of Mariamne I); c. Alexas.

II. Wives (and descendants) of Herod (d. 4 B.C.)

1. Doris (da. of Antigonus s. of Aristobulus II), m. of Antipater (d. 4 B.C.).
2. Mariamne I (granddaughter of Hyrcanus II and Aristobulus II) m. of: a. Alexander (d. 7 B.C.; h. of Glaphyra, da. of Archelaus, king of Cappadocia); b. Aristobulus (d. 7 B.C.); c. Salampsio (w. of Phasael); m. of Kypros III. d. Kypros II. Aristobulus was the h. of Berenice I (da. of Salome) and f. of Herod of Chalcis (h. of Berenice II), of Agrippa I (d. A.D. 44; h. of Kypros III), and of Herodias (w. of: a. Herod s. of Mariamne II; b. Antipas). Agrippa I was the f. of: a. Agrippa II (d. A.D. 100); b. Berenice II (w. of: a. Herod of Chalcis; b. Polemon of Cilicia); c. Drusilla (w. of: a. Azizus; b. Felix).
3. Mariamne II, m. of Herod (h. of Herodias, and f. of Salome II who asked for the head of John the Baptist and later married her uncle Philip).
4. Malthace, m. of Archelaus (third h. of Glaphyra, widow of Alexander [2. a. above] and Juba, king of Lybia) and of Antipas (second h. of Herodias).
5. Cleopatra, m. of Philip (d. A.D. 34; h. of his niece Salome II).

Since Herod's family (including his brother and sister) lived in the immense royal palace at the western edge of Jerusalem, together with many courtiers and attendants, and since the ladies moved about the palace at will, jealousies and gossip were rampant. Herod was strongly attached to his kin and yet suspicious of any encroachment on his supreme authority; he wished to hear all the gossip, but was unable to check on its validity.

Within the family, the proud bearing of Mariamne and her sons, who despised those in whose veins did not course the noble Hasmonean blood, aroused the hostility of the rest, particularly of Salome—although

[33] Abbreviations: b. (brother); d. (date of death); da. (daughter); f. (father); h. (husband); m. (mother); s. (son).

one of the sons of Mariamne, Aristobulus, had married Salome's daughter Berenice. Accusations against these two sons, Alexander and Aristobulus, began in 14 B.C., three or four years after they had returned from Rome, where they had received their higher education. To counterbalance their arrogance Herod recalled from exile his oldest son, Antipater (14 B.C.) and even named him heir apparent. A year later Antipater went to Rome with Agrippa to be introduced to Augustus. From there he continued to sow suspicion against Alexander and Aristobulus in Herod's mind, until the king of the Jews appeared before Augustus, who set his mind at ease (12). But Antipater returned to Judea and there, while pretending to defend his half brothers, he was secretly inciting others to slander them. Herod was again suspicious of them and markedly cold toward them; but he did not fully trust the other side, except Antipater. When Alexander was arrested, his father-in-law Archelaus, king of Cappadocia, succeeded in restoring friendly relations between father and son—but not for long. Finally Herod accused the sons of Mariamne (Alexander and Aristobulus) before Augustus and received permission to deal with them as he wished, although he was advised to have a tribunal of friends and Roman officials meet at Beyrouth to judge the two young men. Almost unanimously a court so constituted condemned them to death, and they were executed at Samaria (*ca.* 7 B.C.). Antipater began to plot with his uncle Pheroras, tetrarch of Perea, but was accused by Salome. Antipater went to Rome, still the heir apparent by Herod's testament (6), but his plots came to light after the death of Pheroras (5). Without arousing his suspicions, Herod summoned him back: unable to clear himself, he was kept in prison. Herod made a second testament, naming Antipas as his successor (5). Seriously ill, Herod, having received permission from Augustus, executed Antipater five days before his own death.[34] Herod had previously made a new will in which he designated Archelaus as king of Judea, Antipas as tetrarch of Galilee and Perea, and Philip as tetrarch of Trachonitis, Batanea, and Gaulinitis. So Herod died at Jericho in 4 B.C., not long after the birth of Jesus of Nazareth (6 or 5 B.C.).

A verdict on Herod, as on most of the great political personalities in human history, [35] depends on one's point of view and personal preferences. For the Romans Herod was a trustworthy and able vassal king, a liberal patron of the arts, and a strong champion of law and order; for the Jews, conversely, he was a self-seeking tyrant, a hypocritical "half-

[34] Augustus (according to Macrobius, *Saturnalia* 2:4, 11) coined the Greek pun, "It is better to be Herod's pig (*hŷn*) than his son (*hyión*)."

[35] Thus, for instance, A. Manzoni began his ode on Napoleon (*Cinque Maggio*), composed upon receiving the report of his death, with the words "Fu vera gloria? Ai posteri l'ardua sentenza" (Was it true glory? To posterity [belongs] the difficult verdict). But posterity is almost as prejudiced as the contemporaries!

Jew" wholly pagan at heart, a bloodthirsty oppressor and robber of the people.

Although Herod had the right to decide the succession, he stipulated that Augustus should approve his testament. After crushing a rebellion at the cost of many lives, Archelaus went to Rome, followed by Antipas, Salome their aunt, and finally Philip. All, except the last, were animated by mutual jealousy. At the same time an embassy from Jerusalem recited Herod's crimes and begged for self-government under Roman supervision.

While Augustus deliberated, riots broke out again in Judea.[36] P. Quintilius Varus, the governor of Syria, had left a legion in Jerusalem after Archelaus had departed and the procurator Sabinus had been sent by Augustus to take charge. Sabinus, however, misused his authority and illicitly entered Herod's palace to examine his estate. Attacked by the Jews, particularly by the pilgrims who had come to celebrate Pentecost, Sabinus plundered the Temple after setting fire to one of its porches, and was besieged in Herod's palace. The flames of rebellion spread to Idumea, Jericho, Galilee, and Perea. In various places adventurers put themselves at the head of masses which apparently expected the Messianic age imminently. The prompt intervention of Varus at the head of two legions stopped all riots and brought death or slavery to thousands of Jews (4 B.C.).

Finally Augustus approved Herod's testament, except that he made Archelaus ethnarch until he proved himself worthy of the royal title. Thus the realm of Herod was divided into three parts, each of which now experienced vicissitudes of its own.

Archelaus (4 B.C.-A.D. 6)[37] was the least liked of Herod's sons; his rule was recklessly despotic. His marriage with Glaphyra (the widow of his half brother Alexander), being illegal according to the Mosaic Law because she had three children by Alexander, shocked the faithful, as also his arbitrary removal of high priests. His extensive building operations did not make him popular. Finally, after a delegation of noblemen from Jerusalem and Samaria had complained of his misgovernment to Augustus, he was exiled in A.D. 6 to Vienna (south of Lyons) in Gaul. Thus Judea became a Roman province (A.D. 6-41).

Herod Antipas (4 B.C.-A.D. 39)[38] was the tetrarch of Galilee and Perea (territories separated by Samaria and the Dekapolis). Like his father he was clever (Jesus called him a fox, Luke 13:32) and vainglorious,

[36] For the disturbances following Herod's death, see Josephus, *Antiquities* 17:9-11; *War* 2:1-6.

[37] On Archelaus, see Josephus, *Antiquities* 17:13; 18:1-4; *War* 2:7-10; Philo, *Embassy to Gaius.*

[38] See, on Antipas, Josephus, *Antiquities* 18:2, 1 and 3; 18:4, 5; 18:5, 1-3; 18:7, 1-2; *War* 2:9, 1 and 6; Matt. 14:1-11; Mark 6:14-28; Luke 3:19 f.; 9:7-9; 13:31 f.; 23:7-12.

although more easygoing and indolent. He rebuilt Sepphoris (burned to the ground by Varus) and fortified it for the defense of Galilee. Bethramphtha (renamed Livias in honor of the empress, and later called Julias) was likewise strengthened for the protection of Perea. To secure himself from Nabatean attacks, he married the daughter of their king Aretas. His most ambitious and important building operation was Tiberias, named in honor of Tiberius (14-37). In spite of its magnificence, pious Jews refused to settle there on account of the ancient cemetery on which it was built, and it was occupied by a very mixed population.

His marriage to Herodias (the former wife of his brother Herod), in whose veins flowed the Hasmonean blood of her grandmother Mariamne I, seems to have been a union based on real affection, but brought much trouble to Antipas. The Nabatean king, Aretas, father of his (repudiated) first wife, engaged in guerrilla warfare against him, and in 36 inflicted a serious defeat on his troops. Vitellius was ordered to punish Aretas, but upon hearing of the death of Tiberius (March of 37) he was glad to leave in the lurch his enemy Antipas (who seems to have acted as a spy in the Near East for Tiberius). The people saw in Antipas's defeat a divine punishment for the previous execution of John the Baptist, who was beheaded for having denounced his marriage with Herodias.[39] Antipas did not enjoy the favor of Gaius Caligula (37-41) as formerly that of Tiberius. When the new emperor gave to Herodias' brother Agrippa I the tetrarchy of Philip, with the royal title (37), the sister's jealousy knew no bounds. Only a few years before, the young wastrel, pursued by creditors, had gladly accepted from Antipas the position of market overseer (agoranómos, cf. Josephus, Antiquities 18:6, 2 [§149]) at Tiberias; now he surpassed her husband in rank and authority! She gave no rest to Antipas until he reluctantly consented to go and request the royal title from Caligula. But as the two appeared before the emperor, a letter from Agrippa accusing Antipas of plotting with the ruler's enemies was delivered to Caligula. Since Antipas could not deny that he had collected a large supply of weapons, he was exiled to Lugdunum (Lyons on the Rhone, or in the Pyrenees); Herodias chose to go with him. His tetrarchy was added to Agrippa's domains.

Philip (4 B.C.-A.D. 34)[40] is called "the tetrarch of the region of Iturea and Trachonitis" (Luke 3:1); Josephus omits Iturea, but adds Batanea, Auranitis, Gaulanitis, and Panias. In these northeastern parts of Herod's kingdom the Jews were in the minority and, to some extent, were recent colonists. Philip is praised for the justice and benevolence of his rule,

---

[39] So according to the well-known Gospel story (cf. the preceding note). Josephus (Antiquities 18:5, 2), however, attributes the execution to the king's fear of a rebellion, resulting from John's great influence on the masses.

[40] See on Philip, Josephus, Antiquities 18:2, 1; 18:4, 6; 18:6, 10; War 2:9, 1 and 6.

which gained him the affection of his subjects. He married his niece Salome, the daughter of Herodias. He built his capital, Caesarea Philippi (Matt. 16:13; Mark 8:27), near one of the sources of the Jordan, not far from the site of Panias, the ancient sanctuary of Pan.[41] Bethsaida, where the Jordan enters Gennesareth, he rebuilt and called Julias in honor of the daughter of Augustus. His coins, bearing the head of Augustus or of Tiberius, are the first ones struck by a Jewish ruler which have a human image on them. At his death in 34 his tetrarchy was incorporated into the Roman province of Syria, but a few years later (in 37) it was given by Caligula to Agrippa I as his kingdom, to which were added eventually the tetrarchy of Antipas (in 39) and (under Claudius) the ethnarchy of Archelaus (in 41) so that finally Agrippa until his death in 44 ruled over the kingdom of his grandfather Herod except for Iturea.

From A.D. 6 to 41 the ethnarchy of Archelaus (i.e., Judea, Samaria, and Idumea) was governed by Roman procurators.[42] The new prefect of Syria, P. Sulpicius Quirinius ("Cyrenius") came to Judea in A.D. 6 to enroll the inhabitants as provincials, and thus took a census for purposes of taxation.[43] This humiliating evidence of Roman rule provoked a violent reaction on the part of the patriots but did not disturb the pious. The Jewish authorities in Jerusalem succeeded in calming the spirits, at least for the moment, but in Galilee—which, being ruled by Antipas, was not included in the census—Judas the Galilean (usually regarded on insufficient evidence as the son of Hezekiah whom Herod had executed in 47-46 B.C. [Josephus, *Antiquities* 14:9, 2]) called the people to arms against the Romans and the Herods, but he was soon killed (Acts 5:37).[44] It is by no means certain (although not impossible) that this Judas, together with a Pharisee named Sadduk, founded the party of the *Zealots:* Josephus (*Antiquities* 18:1, 6) calls Judas's movement "the fourth sect of Jewish philosophy" but reserves the term "Zealot" (cf.

[41] See G. A. Smith, *The Historical Geography of the Holy Land*, pp. 447-451, 473-476.

[42] The procurators for this period are the following: Coponius (6-9), Marcus Ambibulus (9-12), Annius Rufus (12-15), Valerius Gratus (15-26), Pontius Pilate (26-36), Marcellus (36-37), Marullus (37-41).

[43] Josephus, *Antiquities* 17:13, 5; 18:1, 1; *War* 7:8, 1. The reference to the "first census made when Quirinius was governor of Syria" in Luke 2:2 has caused much discussion (see E. Schürer, *Geschichte*, Vol. 1, pp. 508-543; cf. E. Klostermann, *Lukas*, in *Handbuch zum Neuen Testament*, Vol. 2, pp. 392-395. Tübingen, 1919). It seems probable that in Luke 2:1-5 the reference is to the historical census of Quirinius in A.D. 6, but that an error was made in dating it more than ten years too early (when Herod the Great was still alive) and in assuming that it embraced the whole Roman world; in any case Joseph and Mary would not have been required to go from Nazareth to Bethlehem to be enrolled in the census. According to M. S. Enslin (*Christian Origins*, pp. 409 f. [cf. p. 155, n. 1]. New York, 1938) the census of Luke 2 is imaginary, and probably "the account is his [Luke's] own creation."

[44] See J. Spencer Kennard, Jr., "Judas of Galilee and his Clan" (JQR N.S. 36 [1946] 281-286).

Luke 6:15; Acts 1:13; the Aramaic form "Cananean" occurs in Matt. 10:4; Mark 3:18) for the rebels of 66. In any case, we may say that as the Pharisees are the heirs of the Hasidim so the Zealots are the heirs of the Maccabees: intolerant of foreign rule, they did not expect, like Daniel and the Pharisees, the Kingdom of God miraculously from heaven, but endeavored to achieve it by fighting the Romans.

Judea (as also all of Palestine after the death of Agrippa I in 44) was an imperial province under a procurator of equestrian rank: he was not subject to the legate of Syria, but directly responsible to the Roman emperor. The procurator resided ordinarily in Caesarea on the Sea, in the praetorium of Herod (Acts 23:35), and came to Jerusalem ordinarily only on the occasion of the annual festivals, to keep order, residing in Herod's palace. The taxes, for which the Sanhedrin was responsible, together with the tolls and customs collected by the publicans, flowed into the *fiscus* (imperial treasury) not the *aerarium* (senatorial treasury): "render unto Caesar" (Matt. 22:21 and parallels) had therefore a literal meaning in Judea. Augustus changed the procurators often; Tiberius left them for many years—out of consideration for the subjects, so that they be not repeatedly fleeced by newly arrived avid procurators (Josephus, *Antiquities* 18:6, 5).

Josephus has almost no information about the first four procurators (*Antiquities* 18:2, 2). The best known is the fifth, Pontius Pilate (26-36), who crucified Jesus (*ca.* 30) to please the mobs. In a letter to Caligula, Agrippa I judged him to be "of nature inflexible, and, owing to stubbornness, harsh" (Philo, *Embassy to Gaius* 38 [II, 590 M.]). In contrast with the customary Roman respect for Jewish religious feelings, Pilate smuggled military insignia bearing the emperor's image into Jerusalem by night, but had them removed when the Jews showed themselves ready to die rather than tolerate this violation of the Ten Commandments. Later they even forced him to remove from Herod's palace in Jerusalem some golden shields inscribed with the emperor's name.[45] On another occasion Pilate was forced to attack and disperse a crowd that protested against the use of Temple moneys to pay the costs of an aqueduct for Jerusalem.[46] Other instances of Pilate's ruthless massacres are recorded (Mark 15:7; Luke 13:1; 23:19). Finally he brought about his own downfall through his harshness: he fell upon large crowds of credulous Samaritans gathered to witness the discovery of the sacred objects allegedly hidden by Moses on Mount Gerizim (A.D. 35). Vitellius, the legate of Syria, sent Pilate to Rome to justify himself of his unwarranted executions (36) and appointed Marcellus in his place (Josephus, *Antiquities* 18:4, 1-2). On this and on later occasions Vitellius showed con-

---

[45] Josephus, *Antiquities* 18:3, 1; *War* 2:9, 2-3; Philo, *Embassy to Gaius* §38 (II, 589 f. M.).

[46] Josephus, *Antiquities* 18:3, 2; *War* 2:9, 4.

sideration for the feelings of the Jews: thus, for instance, he released to the Temple authorities the garments of the high priest, which had been kept in the Tower Antonia.

Herod Agrippa I[47] now took the center of the Jewish stage for a few years (37-44). An inveterate spendthrift in serious financial trouble in his youth, Agrippa was beloved of the patriotic Jews as the heir of the Hasmoneans (through his grandmother Mariamne I), and the favorite of the Pharisees for his observance of the divine ordinances, and allegedly also for his hostility against the early Christians (Acts 12). After many adventures and difficulties, some of which he overcame through the help of his devoted wife and cousin Kypros, his luck changed when Caligula followed Tiberius on the throne (37). The first act of the new emperor was to free Agrippa from prison, giving him the tetrarchy of Philip with the title of king. A year and a half later (38) Agrippa left Rome and went to his kingdom by way of Alexandria. There, innocently or through his grand airs, he became the object of the sarcastic mockeries of the pagan mobs. With insane anti-Semitic hatred, which the Roman governor, A. Avillius Flaccus, did nothing to check, the enemies of the Jews demanded that statues of Caligula be set up in all synagogues and that the Jews be deprived of civic rights. Then a horrible pogrom broke out. Flaccus was exiled and executed; his successor, C. Vitrasius Pollio, restored order. The Jews sent an embassy to Caligula in 40, under the leadership of the famous philosopher Philo; but their enemies sent a rival embassy led by Apion (cf. Josephus, *Against Apion*), a demagogic orator and anti-Semitic writer. After many humiliations the Jews returned, having accomplished nothing. The civic rights and religious freedom of the Jews were, however, restored by Claudius (41-54) at the beginning of his reign,[48] and the chief anti-Semitic rabble-rousers were eventually executed.

But the Alexandrian outrages had produced serious repercussions in Palestine. When the Jews in Jamnia destroyed an altar in honor of Caligula, the emperor decided that a statue of himself should be erected in the Temple. The legate of Syria, Publius Petronius (who later wrote the *Satiricon*) was ordered to execute this insane commission (winter of 39-40). The reluctant legate did his best to delay matters. He ordered the statue in Sidon and went to Ptolemais. Innumerable Jews came to him there, lamenting and weeping. He wrote to Caligula asking for more time. In November he was still in Tiberias, where thousands of wailing Jews during forty days implored him not to desecrate the Temple. Finally Petronius wrote Caligula recommending that his plan be aban-

[47] See on Agrippa I, Josephus, *Antiquities* 18:6; 19:5-9; *War* 2:9, 11; Acts 12 (where he is called Herod). For the anti-Semitic outbreaks in Alexandria after Agrippa's visit there, see Philo, *Against Flaccus* and *Embassy to Gaius*.

[48] Cf. H. A. Wolfson, "Philo on Jewish Citizenship in Alexandria" (JBL 63 [1944] 165-168).

doned. But before receiving this letter Caligula, upon the entreaties of Agrippa I, had rescinded the order and sent instructions to Petronius not to change anything in the Temple, but to allow altars for the emperor's worship to be erected outside of Jerusalem. When Caligula received the letter of Petronius (January of 41), he ordered him to kill himself; but since the news of Caligula's death (January 24, 41) reached Petronius before this letter, he disregarded the order.

When Agrippa I arrived in Palestine after the tumults in Alexandria (38), his first public acts were pious deeds: he presented to the Temple the golden chain that Caligula had given him in exchange for the iron chain of his imprisonment, and made other donations. In Palestine Agrippa was a strict Jew. The Pharisees, Josephus, and the Talmud sang his praises; the Jews were devoted to him. But he foolishly dabbled in foreign affairs, as when he started building a mighty wall north of Jerusalem and when he called a conference of Roman vassal princes at Tiberias. In both instances the Roman authorities intervened at once, and he lost their confidence. When he died suddenly (in 44) at the age of about fifty-four,[49] Claudius reorganized the kingdom of Agrippa into a Roman province (44-66).

The procurators[50] failed to reconcile the Jews to Roman rule; even the wisest and best intentioned among them unwittingly offended the religious scruples of the Jews, while the worst of them contributed to precipitate the disastrous war of 66-70.

Fadus claimed again the custody of the high priestly vestments, which had been in Roman care from 6 to 36. Granting a petition of the Jews, however, Claudius entrusted Herod of Chalcis and, after his death in 49, Agrippa II with the vestments, and with the appointment of the high priests. A prophet named Theudas attracted a crowd when he promised to cross the Jordan on dry land, but Fadus promptly executed him.[51]

Under Tiberius Alexander (a nephew of the philosopher Philo), who had forsworn Judaism, a serious famine caused great suffering in Judea (Josephus; and Acts 11:28-30). Alexander crucified two rebel leaders, James and Simon, the sons of Judas the Galilean.

Tumults continued under Cumanus (48-52). During the Passover celebration, a Roman soldier offended the Jews by an indecent gesture; some

---

[49] The two independent accounts of his death (Acts 12:19-23; Josephus, *Antiquities* 19:8, 2) differ in the details, but agree in some of the basic facts.

[50] These are the procurators from 44 to 66: Cuspius Fadus (44-*ca.* 46), Tiberius Alexander (*ca.* 46-48), Ventidius Cumanus (48-52), Antonius Felix (52-60), Porcius Festus (60-62), Albinus (62-64), Gessius Florus (64-66). For the history of this period, see Josephus, *Antiquities* 20:1 and 5-11; *War* 2:11-14.

[51] Josephus, *Antiquities* 20:5, 1. In Gamaliel's speech (Acts 5:36), allegedly pronounced before the death of Theudas, the movement of Theudas is wrongly dated *before* that of Judas the Galilean in A.D. 6.

persons were killed in the ensuing riots. On a plundering expedition, a
Roman soldier tore up a scroll of the Law: a multitude of Jews came to
Caesarea and gave Cumanus no rest until the offender had been exe-
cuted. Some Galilean Jews were murdered in a Samaritan village and,
since Cumanus took no measures, Eleazar and Alexander, at the head of
a strong band, laid waste villages and massacred defenseless people in
Samaria. Quadratus, the legate of Syria, executed the culprits and sent
the leading Jews and Samaritans together with Cumanus to Rome.
Claudius, upon the plea of Agrippa II, freed the Jews and executed the
Samaritans; Cumanus, however, was exiled.

The time of Felix (51-60) marks the beginning of that constant tension
and open hostility between Jews and Romans which inevitably led to
war. Even though he was a freedman, he married in succession three
royal princesses; Suetonius, however, exaggerates when he calls him
"husband of three queens." One of them was Drusilla, daughter of
Agrippa I and sister of Agrippa II, whom he persuaded to divorce Azizus,
king of Emesa. His drastic measures against the Zealots who advocated
war against Rome not only increased their popularity with the masses,
but resulted in the rise of the *Sicarii*, or Assassins,[52] the most fanatical
and homicidal among the Zealots. The high priest Jonathan (like many
others) fell by their daggers, being considered (to use modern language)
a "collaborationist." It is said that Felix hired Sicarii for this murder.
Religious fanaticism was flaming by the side of patriotic ardor, and was
similarly repressed by Felix. A Jewish prophet from Egypt gathered a
multitude in the wilderness, promising to lead them to the Mount of
Olives to see the walls of Jerusalem fall to the ground at his word. But
this credulous mob was attacked by Felix, and the Egyptian disappeared
in flight (Josephus, *Antiquities* 20:8, 5; *War* 2:13, 2; Acts 21:38). Such
measures tended to unite both types of fanatics (patriotic and religious),
as well as the mass of the people, into a single party pledged to fight
Rome through terrorism, plunder, and assassination until final victory was
achieved.

While the Apostle Paul was a prisoner of Felix in Caesarea (Acts
23-24) about 58-60, riots broke out in that city between Jews and Gentiles
after the Jews had tried to curtail the civic rights of the Gentiles, because
the city had been founded by Herod.

Festus (60-62) was an able and honest administrator, but the situation
was beyond cure. Nero (54-68) decided the quarrel at Caesarea in favor
of the "Hellenes," the masters of the city according to his verdict. The
resulting bitterness of the Jews was one of the causes of the war in 66-70.
Festus, after several hearings, sent Paul to Rome at his own request
(Acts 24:27-27:2). In spite of the efforts of Festus to pacify the country,

[52] Josephus, *Antiquities* 20:8, 5 and 10; *War* 2:13, 3; Acts 21:38.

the Sicarii and the religious fanatics were as active as ever. Military forces had to be used against an "impostor" who promised salvation and deliverance from woes to those who followed him into the wilderness.

After Festus died in office, anarchy prevailed in Jerusalem until the arrival of his successor, Albinus (62-64). The high priest Ananus (son of the Annas mentioned in the Gospels) had several of his enemies stoned—including (according to the report in Josephus, *Antiquities* 20:9, 1, which may be a Christian interpolation) James "the brother of Jesus called the Christ." Agrippa II deposed Ananus after three months, appointing Jesus the son of Damneus. When the latter was deposed in favor of Jesus the son of Gamaliel, street battles were fought between the followers of the two rival high priests. The avarice, nepotism, and cruelty of the high priests of this period[53] are denounced in the Talmud (*Pesaḥim* 57a, where four families are mentioned: those of Boethus, Annas [or Ananus], Cantherus, and Ishmael son of Phabi): "They are high priests, and their sons are treasurers, and their sons-in-law are superintendents (of the Temple), and their servants beat the people with sticks."

Far from attempting, like Festus, to restore law and order, Albinus deliberately stirred the trouble to his own gain: he arrested indiscriminately the followers of the former high priest Ananias, who was favorable to the Romans, and their enemies the Sicarii, but he released all who paid the required bribe. When Albinus was recalled, he executed convicted criminals, but freed all the other prisoners and thus (according to Josephus) filled the land with robbers.

Gessius Florus (64-66), if we believe Josephus, was so wicked and violent that by comparison Albinus seemed to be a public benefactor: at least Albinus sinned in secret, but Florus ostentatiously exhibited his crimes publicly. He did not limit himself to robbing individuals, but plundered entire towns; and, upon payment of bribes, he allowed robbers full freedom of action. The situation became so intolerable for the Jewish nation that (as Josephus says) it preferred to be destroyed at one stroke rather than bit by bit; and so from 66 to 70 it fought heroically in a war that was doomed to end in tragic defeat. Four years before the war (in 62) a farmer named Jesus the son of Ananus appeared in Jerusalem during the celebration of the Feast of Tabernacles and cried aloud continuously, "A voice from the east, a voice from the west, a voice from the four winds, a voice against Jerusalem and the holy house, a voice against the bridegrooms and the brides, a voice against this whole people!" (Josephus, *War* 6:5, 3). No prophecy was ever fulfilled more tragically.

[53] A list of the high priests from 37 B.C. to the last one elected by the people in A.D. 67, with dates and references to ancient sources, is given in E. Schürer, *Geschichte*, Vol. 2, pp. 269-273.

5. *The War Against the Romans* (66-73)

The spark that started the conflagration, as frequently happens, was an event which did not seem particularly significant at the time. In Caesarea the Gentiles had humiliated the Jews by achieving, through Nero's decision, superior civic rights; to this detriment, derision was soon added. The "Hellenes" hindered the access to a synagogue in Caesarea by building shops in front of it and once, during the Sabbath services, sacrificed a bird near the entrance of the synagogue. The Jews obtained no satisfaction from Florus, in spite of their bribes (Josephus, *War* 2:14, 4-5). Jerusalem restrained its fury, but when Florus took 17 talents from the Temple treasury, baskets were passed around sarcastically to raise a collection for that indigent Florus! The procurator took bloody vengeance for the insult. When the Syrian legate Cestius Gallus sent to Jerusalem the tribune Neapolitanus, the city was bitter but calm. Agrippa II made an impression when he showed how futile rebellion against Rome would be, but when he was forced to admit that obedience to the emperor meant obedience to Florus he lost his hold on the people (*War* 2:14:6 ff.). The war party, led by Eleazar, the son of the former high priest Ananias Nedebai (an aristocrat carried away by the movement), gained the upper hand: by stopping the sacrifices in behalf of Nero in 66, Eleazar openly rebelled against Rome. Meanwhile Masada fell into the hands of the rebels, and its Roman garrison there was massacred to the last man (*War* 2:17, 2).

The authorities and the leaders of the Jews (the Sadducees, the Pharisees, and the Herodians) joined in an effort to save the people from war and ruin. Their appeals for help brought insufficient forces from Agrippa, but none from Florus. Defeated by the rebels, the Jewish higher classes withdrew into Herod's palace, while the insurgents captured the tower Antonia, and were reinforced by Menahem, the son of Judas the Galilean, with his band of Zealots well provided with weapons from Masada. The Jewish leaders and soldiers were allowed free exit from Herod's palace; but the Roman troops, after some resistance in the three strong towers of the palace, capitulated and were butchered on the spot. The aristocracy thus lost all authority, but strife broke out between Jerusalem's rebels, led by Eleazar, and the provincials, led by Menahem (who had slain the high priest Ananias, the father of Eleazar); soon the latter were driven out or killed, and Menahem was slain (Josephus, *War* 2:17, 3-10).

Riots like these spread to other cities: where the Jews were in the majority, as at Machaerus and Jericho, they dispersed or slew the Roman garrisons; where the Gentiles prevailed, as at Caesarea, Ashkelon, Scythopolis, Damascus, and Alexandria, horrible pogroms broke out; only in the domains of Agrippa and a few other districts were the Jews safe (*War* 2:18, 1-8).

In October of 66, Cestius Gallus, the legate of Syria, began the siege of Jerusalem. Apparently convinced that he lacked the necessary forces, he turned back and when the Jews surrounded him at the pass of Beth-horon he abandoned his war material and fled in panic (*War* 2:18, 9-2:19, 9).

This victory united all the Jews for war against Rome: the influential men—the former authorities—now regained the helm and organized the nation for war. Joseph son of Gorion and the high priest Ananus were put in charge of Jerusalem's defense; Jesus son of Sapphias and Eleazar son of Ananias were sent to Idumea. Joseph son of Matthias (the later historian Flavius Josephus) became the governor of Galilee (*War* 2:20), where John of Giscala son of Levi stirred up the people against him (*War* 2:21).

Nero chose his most experienced military commander, Vespasian, to crush the rebellion in Judea. In the spring of 67 Vespasian was at Ptolemais, in command of three legions (the 15th had been brought by his son Titus from Alexandria) and of auxiliary troops, reaching a grand total of 60,000 men (*War* 3:1-4). During the good season of 67 Vespasian conquered Galilee (*War* 3:6-4:2), but John of Giscala (i.e., *gûsh ḥalab* [mass of milk], a village in Galilee) and his band of Zealots succeeded in escaping to Jerusalem (*War* 4:2, 2-5). Their arrival plunged the city into a bloody civil war during the winter of 67-68. Through Idumean help, John became the master of Jerusalem, and the former leaders and aristocrats were executed or assassinated (*War* 4:3-5; 4:6, 1).[54] Vespasian decided to let the Jews destroy themselves through civil war within the walls of Jerusalem, and in March of 68 began operations in Perea, which was conquered by his lieutenant Placidus, and later he subjected western Judea and Idumea, thus gaining the mastery of the whole territory around Jerusalem, which could now be besieged (*War* 4:6, 2-8, 1; 4:9, 1). But upon receiving the report of Nero's death (June, 68) Vespasian interrupted the operations for a year. In June of 69, how-ever, he was forced to fight in Judea and became master of all Palestine except Jerusalem, Herodium, Masada, and Machaerus (*War* 4:9, 2-9). During these operations, the chief of a band of Zealots, Simon Bar-Giora ("son of the proselyte"), who had become master of Idumea during Vespasian's inactivity, found it expedient to enter Jerusalem. In the spring of 69 he was welcomed there by the enemies of John of Giscala, who had been terrorizing the population. As a result the city now had two mutually hostile tyrants instead of one (*War* 4:9, 10-12).

[54] The Christian community in Jerusalem left the city at this time, or shortly before (Eusebius, *Hist. Eccl.* 3:5, 2-3; Epiphanius, *Haeres.* 29, 7; *de mensuris* 15).

When the legions on the Rhine proclaimed Vitellius as emperor, following the ephemeral rule of Galba and Otho, the legions in Egypt and the Near East acclaimed Vespasian as the emperor in July of 69. So, after placing his son Titus in command, Vespasian went to Alexandria, where he heard that Vitellius had been murdered (December, 69), and arrived in Rome early in the summer of the following year (*War* 4:10-11).

In Jerusalem a third leader had sprung up in the meantime: Eleazar the son of Simon. In the battles among the three, considerable amounts of provisions were consumed by fire (*War* 5:1, 1-5). Titus, at the head of four legions (in addition to the 5th, 10th, and 15th, also the 12th) and auxiliary troops (5:1, 6), arrived at Jerusalem in April of 70; at the time of the Passover celebration John of Giscala overcame Eleazar in the Temple court, and henceforth only two masters remained within the city (5:2; 5:3, 1).

The topography of Jerusalem and the siege operations are described by Josephus (*War* 5:4-5 and 5:6-13; 6:1-3) with considerable detail; it is clear from his account that famine contributed to the fall of the city no less than military operations. Finally the gates were burned on the 9th of Ab (*ca.* August) of 70, and the following day the battle raged within the Temple courts. The sacred buildings were accidentally set on fire—contrary to the orders of Titus, if we believe Josephus—and the ensuing butchery of helpless Jews was horrible (*War* 6:4-6). John of Giscala and his band escaped to Herod's palace, where after a weak resistance they were captured together with Simon and his men. After a siege of five months, all of Jerusalem, plundered and burning, was occupied by Titus on the 8th of Elul (*ca.* September): only the three towers of Herod's palace were left standing in the leveled city (*War* 6:7-9; 7:1-2).

Titus celebrated his triumph in Rome in 71. As we can still see sculptured on his triumphal arch, the golden seven-armed candlestick and the table of showbread from the Temple were carried in the triumphal procession; later they were deposited in Vespasian's temple to Peace (*War* 7:5, 3-7). But the war in Palestine was not yet ended. Lucilius Bassus, the successor of Vettulenus Cerealis as governor of Judea, conquered Herodium without great difficulty but Machaerus only after a long siege (*War* 7:6, 1-4). Finally Masada—the strongest position of all—fell to the successor of Bassus, Flavius Silva, in April of 73 after the defenders, on the exhortation of Eleazar, killed their families and then themselves (*War* 7:8-9). Some of the Jewish rebels fled to Alexandria, where the resulting agitation in 73 caused the closing of the Jewish temple founded by Onias at Leontopolis about 163 B.C. (*War* 7:10); others caused riots at Cyrene (7:11).

In the midst of the bewilderment, misery, and chaos that followed the destruction of the Temple and the ruin of Judea, Jonathan ben Zakkai, after escaping from Jerusalem before its destruction, obtained permission to reopen at Jamnia his school for the study of the Law. There he established a rabbinical council of scholars (*Bêth Dîn*, High Court) which was purely Pharisean in. membership but continued some of the functions of the defunct Sanhedrin (which had, conversely, been mainly Sadducean in character). Thus the Pharisees preserved the Jewish national religion to the present day by identifying it substantially with the observance of the written and the oral law.

The loss of the Temple in 70, which ended all public and private sacrifices for the expiation of sins, at first seemed to some Jews a calamity without remedy. It is related, however, that Johanan ben Zakkai told a grieving disciple of his that deeds of mercy were an atonement as good as the Temple sacrifices, as Hos. 6:6 makes clear. Soon the study of the ritual laws became a substitute for the cult, and repentance followed by good works took the place of sacrifices offered in expiation of sin. For two or three centuries the synagogue had been a far more significant institution than the Temple for the majority of the Jews, and thus the transition from a religion of cult to one of observances had been anticipated and came to pass without a serious crisis.

Agrippa II, who ruled before and after the war, may claim our attention at this point. He was seventeen years of age at the death of his father Agrippa I in 44, and remained in Rome until after 50, when he succeeded his uncle Herod as king of Chalcis in the Lebanon. At the same time he appointed the high priests and had charge of their vestments (until 66). In 53 he exchanged Chalcis for the tetrarchies of Philip and Lysanias. Nero added to his dominions parts of Galilee and Perea (Tiberias, Tarichea, and Julias). According to gossip (Josephus, *Antiquities* 20:7, 3; Juvenal, *Satires* VI, 156-160), Agrippa had incestuous relations with his sister Berenice, the widow of Herod of Chalcis. The Apostle Paul made his defense before Agrippa and Berenice (Acts 25:23-26:32). From a high tower which Agrippa built by his palace in Jerusalem he enjoyed watching the priests in the Temple, until they shut off his view with a wall. He was more Roman than Jew, and helped Titus in the war against the Jews. After the war he was rewarded with additional territory in the north. But at his death in 100 his kingdom was incorporated by Trajan into the province of Syria, and the rule of the Herods came to its end.

Twice again, after the war against Vespasian and Titus, did the Jews fight disastrously against Rome. Under Trajan (98-117) rebellions broke out in Egypt and Cyrene (115-116) and brought death to thousands of Jews. Rebellions were likewise crushed with great loss of life in Cyprus and in Mesopotamia.

Far more serious was the war in Palestine in the days of Hadrian (117-138).[55] Two reasons for the rebellion are recorded: Hadrian's law forbidding circumcision (rescinded for the Jews, but not for other nations by Antoninus Pius), according to Spartianus; Hadrian's order in 130 to rebuild Jerusalem as Aelia Capitolina and erect a temple to Jupiter Capitolinus (Zeus) on the site of Jehovah's Temple, according to Dio Cassius. To the Jews who hoped to rebuild their Temple, this prospect was doubly shocking: first, because the erection of the temple to Jupiter would make it impossible to rebuild the Temple; and secondly, because the holy place would be profaned by an "abomination of desolation" as defiling as that of Epiphanes.

The leader of the rebellion (132-135) was "Simon, Prince of Israel" (according to the legend on the coins), called usually Bar Kozibah (presumably meaning "native of Kozibah"). Rabbi Akiba saluted him as "the Star out of Jacob" (Num. 24:17), and his name was accordingly punned as Bar Cocheba (son of the star, star-man), and so he is called in Christian writings. That the ruins of Jerusalem were occupied by the Jews at the beginning of the revolt is indicated by coins of the first year bearing the name of the city, and others bearing the inscription "of Jerusalem's liberation." After three years and a half, the last refuge of Bar Cocheba, Bether (really Beththter, presumably the modern Bittir, a few miles southwest of Jerusalem) was taken and the war was ended. Jerusalem, called now *Colonia Aelia Capitolina* (or *Aelia*), became a Roman colony. The temple to Jupiter was erected on the holy site. No Jew could enter Aelia under penalty of death. Even in the fourth century the Jews were allowed to enter the city only once a year, on the anniversary of its destruction by Nebuchadnezzar (9th of Ab), to weep on the site of the Temple.

The revolt of Bar Cocheba marks the last flaming outburst of militant Messianic hope.[56] Normative Judaism relinquished the utopian dreams of apocalyptic writings to the Christians, and retrenched itself increasingly within the citadel of the written and the oral law, thus separating itself more and more from the Gentiles. The final break between the Christian Church and the synagogue took place at this time when the Nazarenes—a Jewish-Christian group worshiping in the synagogues but teaching that Jesus was the Messiah—were forced to become a sect, equally repudiated by the Rabbis and by the Bishops. Henceforth the teachers of the Law—scribes and Pharisees, Tannaim, Amoraim, Geonim, rabbis—became the leaders of Israel.

[55] See for the literature on the subject J. Juster, *Les Juifs dans l'empire romain*, Vol. 2, pp. 190-194. Paris, 1914.
[56] On later apocalyptic literature, see M. Buttenwieser, *Outline of Neo-Hebraic Apocalyptic Literature*. Cincinnati, 1901.

CHAPTER II

RELIGIOUS HISTORY

"Moses received the Torah [the written and unwritten Law] from Sinai and delivered it to Joshua, and Joshua to the Elders, and the Elders to the Prophets, and the Prophets delivered it to the men of the Great Synagogue." This famous utterance at the beginning of the *Sayings of the Fathers* (*Pirqê Abôth*, a treatise of the Mishna dating from about A.D. 200) stresses the basic Jewish conviction that the true religion was revealed to Moses and was transmitted intact to later generations by an unbroken chain of reliable witnesses. The revelation to Moses embodied in the Pentateuch—perfect and definitive—was neither supplemented (except for the reading of Esther at Purim) nor changed by the inspired prophets who followed him. At last the Scriptures were completed in the time of Ezra and the "Men of the Great Synagogue," after whom divine inspiration ceased forever. These convictions of the Jews in the period we are considering (200 B.C.-A.D. 100) must be kept in mind in order to understand their religion and literature; modern notions about historical development and evolution of religion, had they not been entirely alien to their thought, would have been regarded as perniciously heretical.

The Jews were thus aware of a new era beginning after Ezra and Nehemiah and the last inspired prophets. Modern historians agree in regarding that time, when the Pentateuch was codified (about 400 B.C.), as the beginning of a new religious epoch. The only difference is that the Jews believed that the whole Hebrew Bible was canonical at the time and that nothing was added later, while modern critics limit the Scriptures in 400 to the Pentateuch. In either case, after 400 B.C. divine revelation was believed to be embodied in a book (the Pentateuch) on which the pious meditated day and night (Ps. 1:2). This sacred book of the Law, the delight and joy of the Jews, united the nation, which was scattered in many lands and no longer independent (except in 142-63 B.C.), into a divine commonwealth, the holy congregation, whose ruler was Jehovah, the only God. Jehovah is the "refuge and strength" (Ps. 46) of the congregation; for the individual, even though he walk through the valley of death, he is a shepherd (Ps. 23), a "father in fidelity and righteousness" (Jub. 1:25).

In its various manifestations, Judaism in the period under present consideration may be understood on the basis of these premises. The religion of Israel had been purely national in scope, but since the sixth century it had been developing in two directions, without, however, discarding the notion that Jehovah, now the sole God in existence, was still as in earlier times the God of the Jews in a peculiar sense. But more and more, as the implications of monotheism were apprehended, Judaism overflowed the national limitations to become a universal faith for all peoples and a personal religion for every individual. The principal factors in this development are negatively the end of the monarchy in 586 and positively the resulting transformation of the nation into the holy congregation. But the same tendencies may be noted, during the Persian period, among other nations.[1] Without political independence, nationality could have only a religious and cultural meaning.

The *universalistic* and *individualistic* tendencies were grafted on the ancient *national religion* of Israel in the sixth century, if not earlier. After 500 B.C., Judaism is characterized by the interplay of all three tendencies.

The ancient religious nationalism of Deborah and the J document, created by Moses at the crossing of the Red Sea—Jehovah is the God of Israel, Israel is the people of Jehovah—was moralized in the Deuteronomic Code (621 B.C.) under the influence of the reforming prophets. This relationship between the national deity and the people now is no longer inevitable, but morally conditioned: Jehovah made Israel his own peculiar nation through a formal covenant, requiring on Israel's part the observance of the Law.

During the following centuries the religious nationalism of Israel developed in three directions: devotion to the present, past, and future commonwealth of the Jews.

The longing for political independence did not become militant and successful until after 164 B.C. A Jewish kingdom in the present became the ideal of many Jews at that time. The historical summary in the preceding chapter has shown how, after Judas Maccabeus had achieved religious liberty in 164, war was continued for political independence, attained in 142 and preserved until 63 B.C. While some of the Hasmonean rulers and many of their followers pursued purely mundane aims with mundane means (an attitude illustrated in the canonical Book of Esther and later by the Zealots), others regarded the Hasmonean kingdom as the result of divine intervention. Thus the author of I Maccabees (5:62)

---

[1] E. Meyer, *Geschichte des Altertums*, Vol. III, pp. 167-174. Stuttgart, 1901. The time about the sixth century, as has often been noted, saw a remarkable spiritual awakening in widely separated areas. It is enough to mention Jeremiah, Zoroaster, Buddha, Confucius, Thales.

does not hesitate to regard the Hasmoneans as "the seed of those by whose hand deliverance was given unto Israel" (by God), exactly as in the case of the Judges of old. This point of view is also illustrated in the Book of Judith and in some Psalms. Psalm 2 actually speaks of Alexander Janneus in terms of a Messiah in the flesh, and Ps. 110 emphatically states that the Lord had made Simon high priest (and ruler) according to the order of the (legendary) priest-king Melchizedek of Gen. 14. In general, however, the Hasidim (Pious), like their successors, the Pharisees, looked askance at this realized commonwealth and preferred the theocratic rule of God as revealed to Moses, or God's future miraculous kingdom on earth. The Hasmonean rulers were far from realizing the ideal of the ruler of the golden age to come, so nobly described in Is. 9:6 f. (Hebr. 9:5 f.); 11:1-5.

According to the Priestly Code in the Pentateuch (fifth century), through the covenant with Abraham and the Law revealed to Moses, the universal God established the Jewish theocracy in the dim past.[2] Its divine ruler had placed at its head Aaron and, after him, his first-born descendants—the high priests. The Temple worship was the most important function of the holy commonwealth. The Temple is God's dwelling on earth (Tob. 1:4; Syr. Bar. 7:1), prepared since the creation of the world (Ass. of Mos. 1:17 f.). God will punish the Jews if they allow it to be profaned (Jth. 8:21), but when God decided that Nebuchadnezzar should destroy it, first he had the angels hide the sacred vessels underground and breach the walls, then after God had forsaken the Temple the enemies were invited to enter (Syr. Bar. 6-8; cf. II Macc. 2:4-8).

The Temple services were considered by many as essential to the preservation of the right relation between Israel and Jehovah; their interruption by Epiphanes (168-165) was regarded in Daniel and I-II Maccabees as a supreme disaster. Sirach becomes lyrical when he remembers the high priest Simon officiating in the Temple (Ecclus. 50), although he is primarily interested in wisdom and Torah. The zeal in the payment of the Temple tithes (Tob. 1:4-8; cf. Jth. 11:13), the enthusiasm animating the hymns on Jerusalem and its Temple (Tob. 13), and the paramount role assigned to the Temple in the future restoration (Tob. 14:4-7) indicate the reverence of many Jews for their sanctuary. In Jubilees and in the Testaments of the Twelve Patriarchs, Levi (the ancestor of the priests) is the most honored of the patriarchs; both books disclose an intense interest in the sacrificial worship.[3] And yet from the

[2] Paul, in Rom. 9:4, alludes to the holy commonwealth in the past, as well as to the future Kingdom of God promised in the prophetic oracles.

[3] Jub. 6:3 f.; 7:2-6; etc. Test. Levi 9. For references in the Apocrypha to the Temple and its service, see R. Marcus, *Law in the Apocrypha*, pp. 93-112. New York, 1927.

sources that have survived we gain the impression that between 200 B.C. and A.D. 70 the Temple worship played a minor and decreasing role in the religion of the Jews (the Psalter, composed in the course of several centuries, is particularly significant in this regard). Consequently, the shock of the Jews when the Temple was destroyed in A.D. 70 was far less acute than could have been expected.

As the Temple rituals tended to become a survival from ancient days and were gradually losing their significance, the Law became central in Judaism (after 400 B.C.) and there was a shift from ritual to observance, from sacrifices to good deeds. While the study and fulfillment of the Torah tended to stress the personal type of religion, it also strengthened the sense of solidarity among the Jews and gave to "the congregation of the righteous" (Ps. 1:5) an extraordinary cohesion, a sense of isolation in the midst of heathenism, and the power to withstand the utmost buffets of the world.

Specifically, during the period under consideration the Law built up the divine commonwealth (believed to have originated in the time of Moses) in three ways. First of all by ordaining the observance of certain ritual practices not connected with the Temple, and which characterized the Jews in the eyes of the Greeks and Romans. Chief among them are circumcision (I Macc. 1:14, 48; 2:46; Jub. 15:25-34; Ass. of Mos. 8:3), the Sabbath (I Macc. 2:34, 41; Jub. 2:25-33; 50:6-13), and the horror of idolatry (Bel; Epist. of Jer.; Jub. 11:4, 16; 12:3-8; 20:8; Enoch 46:7) and of swine's meat (I Macc. 1:47; 2:23).[4] In general, the other legal prescriptions regulating the conduct of individuals—notably those intended to preserve the purity of the race (prohibition against mixed marriages) and separation from the heathen—contributed to strengthen the national self-consciousness of the Jews.

The conviction that God has revealed in the Pentateuch and in other parts of Scripture his mind and will, the assurance that national (and individual) hopes would not be realized until the people lived in accordance with God's Law, made it imperative to teach to all Jews the divine revelation. The need for general education created two distinct institutions, the synagogue and the school; their importance in strengthening and perpetuating the spiritual commonwealth of the Jews cannot be overestimated. Nothing is known of the beginnings of these two institutions, but they were flourishing at the beginning of the period we are

---

[4] References to passages in Graeco-Roman authors alluding to Sabbath and circumcision will be found in Schürer, *Geschichte*, Vol. 3, pp. 153, 552 f. and in Th. Reinach, *Textes d'auteurs grecs et romains relatifs au Judaïsme*, Paris, 1895. It is manifestly impossible to give more than a few selected references to the Jewish apocryphal writings in this summary. Full references for every topic will be found in the detailed index at the end of R. H. Charles, *Pseudepigrapha*.

concerned with (200 B.C.).[5] The synagogue, even if ultimately derived from the addresses of Ezekiel to the Babylonian Exiles, was (after 400) the place where the Pentateuch was read and studied by local congregations; later, readings from the Prophets and other books, as well as prayers, were added. The oldest preserved synagogue prayers are the Eighteen [*Shemoneh Esreh*] Benedictions. At least as early as the first century of our era, as we know from Philo and the New Testament, an expository sermon abounding in scriptural quotation and allusion helped to familiarize the laity with the Bible. The Bible was also taught in the schools, together with wisdom. Ecclesiasticus consists mainly of the classroom lectures of Ben Sira: wisdom, for him, was both the Jewish religion and its revealed charter, the Pentateuch. After A.D. 70 the Jewish academies were organized, in which scholars discussed with great subtlety and erudition the juristic interpretation of the Law and codified the unwritten law in the Mishna (the extant codification, by Judah ha-Nasi, dates from about A.D. 200). The subsequent learned discussions on points of law were added to the Mishna and produced the Jerusalem and Babylonian Talmuds, finally edited about A.D. 500.

Thus Judaism strove to realize the ancient pattern of its invisible commonwealth revealed to Moses. At the same time another commonwealth, to be realized by God in the future, kindled the hopes of the Jews after their loss of political independence: the Kingdom of God in the Messianic Age. This miraculous glorification of the Jews in the future assumed several forms. In texts of the Old Testament later than Jeremiah (23:5; cf. 33:14-33) in 586, the restoration of David's dynasty and kingdom is repeatedly predicted. In the Palestinian literature later than 200 B.C., the figure of the Messiah[6] is lacking from the apocalyptic visions in Daniel, Jubilees, Enoch 1-36 and 91-108, Assumption of Moses, Slavic Enoch; conversely, the Messiah plays an important role in Enoch 37-71, Test. of Judah 24, Test. of Levi 18, Ps. of Sol. 17 and 18, II (IV) Ezra 7:28 f., 11:36-12:3, 31-34, Syr. Bar. 29:3; 30:1; 36-40; 53; 72-74, Apocalypse of Abraham 31.

In accordance with earlier promises, contained in the Old Testament, the Messiah will deliver Israel from its foes and restore the kingdom of David (Ps. of Sol. 17; cf. Ecclus. 45:25; 47:11, 22; 48:15; I Macc. 2:57). However, the tendency was more and more to regard the Kingdom of God as universal (or as celestial) and the Messiah's rule as merely a passing phase in the transformation of the world at the end of time.

[5] Strangely no reference is made to synagogues in the literature of Palestinian Jews before the Christian Era, unless they are called "the meeting places of God" in Ps. 74:8. Some scholars have discovered allusions to the synagogues in Enoch 46:8; 63:6. The earliest reference to a school is in Ecclus. 51:23 (Hebr.), "lodge *in my house of instruction* [*beth midrashi*]," dating from *ca.* 180 B.C.

[6] "Messiah" is the transcription of the Aramaic *Meshiach* (anointed), translated into Greek as *Christós* (Christ).

Thus we have reached the universalistic tendency of Judaism, which is manifest in apocalypses as also elsewhere. The future salvation of all mankind (through the mediation of Israel) was first proclaimed enthusiastically by the poet whom we call the Second Isaiah, for want of a better name, in Is. 40-55, about 540 B.C. He recognized that if there is only one God there can be only one religion.[7] In a future day "Jehovah shall be King over all the earth" (Zech. 14:9). The Gentiles will partake of the joys of the coming golden age, provided they become converted to the religion of Jehovah; and this conversion is confidently expected (Tob. 13:11; 14:6 f.; Ps. of Sol. 17:34 [31]; Enoch 10:21; 48:4 f.; 90:30-36) and occasionally attributed to the Messiah (Enoch 48:5; Test. of Judah 24). In fact at times the sinful and apostate Jews are definitely classed with the heathen (Syr. Bar. 41-42). Such a point of view comes to light even more clearly in the teaching about individual retribution after death, to which we now turn.

The glorious utopian future, as has been briefly noted, was variously conceived with or without a Messianic king, for the exclusive benefit of the Jews or for all men believing in the one true God. But the strong individualistic trend in Judaism (which begins, like universalism, in the sixth century) inevitably colored the visions of future national or universal bliss. This appears already in Dan. 7 (cf. Enoch 90:20-42): after the destruction of the heathen governments (represented by beasts), worldwide dominion is given in perpetuity to the holy people of the Most High (represented as "one like a son of man," i.e., a figure resembling a human being). Here the writer is still concerned with nations and rulers, not with individuals. But in a later chapter (Dan. 12:1-4), after the death of Antiochus Epiphanes, Michael will arise to defend the Jews; the distress at that time will be unprecedented, but finally the faithful Jews, whose names are inscribed in the book, will be delivered, and the martyrs who laid down their lives for their faith will be raised from the ground to everlasting life; conversely, the deceased apostate Jews and the Hellenizers, who had saved their lives by obeying the decrees of Antiochus Epiphanes instead of God's Law, will be raised from their graves to eternal contempt (cf. II Maccabees). Here the best and the worst individual Jews receive their reward or punishment after death; this individual retribution (confined to Jews) has no connection with the universal judgment of nations in Dan. 7. Going a step further, Enoch 90:20-42 (written not long after Daniel) describes a final judgment of individual angels and Jews, and their final rewards and punishments. In Enoch 21-27 the judgment is not the aftermath of the persecutions of Antiochus Epiphanes and the deliverance of the Jews from the heathen,

[7] Many of the Psalms, at a later period, express the same conviction, particularly the Psalms which exalt Jehovah as the lord of all creation.

but comes at the end of time. In Enoch 45-57 Daniel's "son of man" is identified with the Messiah ("My Anointed" in 48:10; 52:4) who sits in judgment over the living and the dead raised from the underworld and ushers in the golden age on earth. Another picture of the final fate of the righteous and the wicked after death is given in Enoch 91-105.

In the Parables of Enoch (chs. 45-57) the old hope of national restoration under a Davidic king and the following golden age, which has been called earlier in this chapter the commonwealth of the future, is combined in a confused manner with the purely individualistic final judgment and personal retribution following the resurrection. The national and the individual future glorification had been kept separate in the Book of Daniel. In the later apocalypses, written about twenty years after the destruction of Jerusalem in A.D. 70 (II [IV] Ezra 7:26-44; 12:34; Syr. Bar. 40:4; see also Rev. 19:11-21:8, which is substantially a Jewish apocalypse of the same date), the Messianic period belongs to "the present age" (ha- 'olam ha-zeh) and lasts 400 years (II [IV] Ezra 7:28) or 1,000 years (the "millennium," Rev. 20:3). Then come the Last Things, the eschatological determination of the eternal fate of each individual in the "future age" (ha-'olam ha-ba'; see Enoch 71:15, the New Testament, etc.): the new heaven and the new earth, the general resurrection, the last judgment, through which each individual is assigned for all eternity to the bliss of Paradise (Eden) or to the fiery torments of Gehenna.

The individualistic trend does not merely add eschatology to national apocalyptic hopes, but is apparent in every aspect of Judaism after 400 B.C. Sin, retribution, and repentance were collective notions, national in scope, as late as the Deuteronomic Code of 621 B.C., but they were individualized by Ezekiel. As amply shown in the Psalter, religion tended to become personal piety, either an almost mystical relation of the individual to his God, or a passionate eagerness to do God's will as revealed in his Law. Prayer, rather than sacrifice, becomes the true worship. The Wisdom literature and the schools were concerned with the individual rather than with the nation. Fiction writing deals with personal matters (Tobit) as well as with national affairs (Judith).

Although the individual tended to become the center of gravity in Jewish worship and practice, the nation remained, despite the succession of foreign rulers and the wide dispersion outside of Palestine, an inspiration and an ideal, a commonwealth of the spirit or a revived Jewish state in Palestine. In spite of the fact that soon after the rise of Christianity the missionary zeal gave way to the effort of the Jews to entrench themselves within the citadel of the Law, the universality of Judaism, being implicit in its monotheism, could never be obliterated. Thus in the centuries around the beginning of our era even in Palestine—leaving out of consideration here the Jews in the Dispersion—manifold tendencies and conflicting aspirations are manifest, far more indeed than the four philosophical schools described for Greek and Roman readers by Josephus (*Antiquities* 18:1, 2-6; cf. 13:5, 9; 13:10, 5-6; *War* 2:8, 2-14): Pharisees, Sadducees, Essenes, and Zealots.[8] The New Testament lists scribes, Pharisees, Sadducees, Herodians, Zealots, Galileans, Sicarii, Samaritans, and the Disciples of John the Baptist; but such a list is far from comprehensive. For Judaism in the period under consideration was so alive, so progressive, so agitated by controversies, that under its spacious roof the most contrasting views could be held—until a greater uniformity was reached after A.D. 200.

The *scribes* are first mentioned by the Chronicler as one of the professional guilds of Judaism, together with the priests, the Temple singers, and the various Levitical guilds. Ezra is considered by the Chronicler as the founder of the guild of the scribes (Ezra 7:10 f.), probably with no more justification than David's alleged organization of Temple music. Jesus the son of Sira (about 180 B.C.) is the first scribe whose name is known, although the profession had its beginnings between the canonization of the Pentateuch in 400 and the time of the Chronicler, about 250 B.C. Sirach has given us a good description of the work of the scribes, as students of the Law and of life in general, and as teachers of the young (Ecclus. 38:24-39:11). To the scribes, in their threefold capacity of judges, teachers, and jurists, is addressed the motto of the Men of the Great Synagogue: "Be deliberate in giving judgment, and raise up many disciples, and make a barrier about the Law" (*Sayings of the Fathers* [*Abôth*] 1:1).

The *Hasidim* (Pious; also called Assideans from the Greek transcription *asidaîoi*) are the earliest group of Jewish laymen bearing a distinctive name. When Antiochus Epiphanes proscribed Judaism (168 B.C.), the Hasidim (in accordance with Dan. 3:17 f., which expresses their attitude exactly) preferred to die rather than to violate the Law and the tradition of the elders (or oral law) by defending themselves on the Sabbath (I Macc. 2:29-38; cf. 1:62 f.).[9] They were intensely zealous in their

---

[8] At about A.D. 375, Epiphanius (*Panarion* I, 1) lists seven sects (Sadducees, Scribes, Pharisees, Hemerobaptists, Osseans, Nazarenes, and Herodians), and adds four Samaritan sects (Essenes, Sabouaei, Gortheni, and Dositheans), but his information is notoriously unreliable. The Osseans are probably the Essenes. Two other Jewish sects are mentioned elsewhere: Ebionites and Sampsaeans (cf. J. Hastings, *Encyclopaedia of Religion and Ethics*, Vol. 5, pp. 139-145 and 267 f.).

[9] These passages manifestly refer to the Hasidim, although they are not specifically named; their name occurs only in I Macc. 7:13 and II Macc. 14:6; also in I Macc. 2:42 in *codex A* (*codices Aleph* and *B* read "Jews"). The author of the Book of Daniel was presumably a leader of the Hasidim. The martyrdom of the Assideans (*ḥasîdhēkhā*, "thy saints") is probably alluded to in Ps. 79:2, a prayer for help during the persecution by Antiochus.

observance of the Law, and eventually they were willing to fight in the ranks of Judas Maccabeus for religious freedom; but after the end of the religious persecution in 164 they refused to keep on fighting for political independence.

The *Pharisees* were presumably the successors of the Hasidim, although we lack all information about their origin. Their name means "separated," but has been variously interpreted.[10] They are first mentioned, somewhat irrelevantly, in the time of Jonathan (161-143) by Josephus (*Antiquities* 13:5, 9), but actually appear in the flesh as antagonists of John Hyrcanus (135-104) in *Antiquities* 13:10, 5-6; in the Talmud (*Kiddushin* 66a) the story is placed in the time of Janneus (104-76). Quoting Nicholas of Damascus, who was no friend of the Pharisees, Josephus has given us a brief description of the Pharisees as seen by outsiders: "a body of Jews who profess to be more religious than the others, and to explain the laws more accurately" (*War* 1:5, 2). If we disregard the polemic against hypocritical members of the movement, such is the impression we gain from the first three Gospels and from Acts.

In explaining the doctrines of the Pharisees to his Greek and Roman readers, Josephus (possibly quoting Nicholas of Damascus) misleadingly used Greek philosophical terminology (he even compares the Pharisees to the Stoics, in *Life* 2, end) when he said that the Sadducees believed in free will, the Essenes were absolute determinists, and the Pharisees took a middle path, teaching that divine foreknowledge does not prevent the exercise of human free will and that fate and free will are concomitants in human life (*Antiquities* 13:5, 9; 15:10, 4; 18:1, 3; *War* 2:8, 14; *Life* 2, end). The teaching of the Pharisees on the matter of man's free will and God's providence is probably expressed in more accurate terms in Ecclus. 15:11-20; 36:10-15 and especially in Ps. of Sol. 9:7; 5:6, for the Ps. of Sol. were written by Pharisees. As Rabbi Akiba said, "All is foreseen [by God], but free will is given [to man]" (*Sayings of the Fathers* [*Abôth*] 3:19). Similarly Josephus, in describing the difference between Pharisees and Sadducees with respect to the future life, uses terms appropriate to the Platonic doctrine of the immortality of the soul rather than to the Pharisaic resurrection of the body: "All souls are imperishable, but only the soul of the good passes into another body, while the souls of the bad are punished with everlasting punishment" (*War* 2:8, 14); ". . . souls have an immortal vigor, and under the earth there are rewards and punishments . . . [virtuous souls possess] the capability of returning to life" (*Antiquities* 18:1, 3). In Palestinian language, the Pharisaic doctrine of the resurrection is expounded in Ps. of Sol. 3:11-16; 13:9-11.

[10] See G. F. Moore, *Judaism*, Vol. 1, pp. 60-62. Cambridge, U.S.A., 1927.

The most important characteristic of the Pharisees is their punctilious observance of the Law, both written and unwritten (Josephus, *War* 2:8, 14; *Antiquities* 17:2, 4; *Life* 38). The oral law (later codified in the Mishna and the Talmud) or "tradition of the ancients" (Mark 7:3; Matt. 15:2; etc.) consisted of numerous ordinances which interpreted or supplemented the Pentateuch, and consequently embraced a far more extensive and detailed body of legislation. The observance of both types of law on the part of the Pharisees is illustrated in the New Testament in regard to wearing conspicuous tassels (cf. Num. 15:37) and phylacteries (Matt. 23:5), missionary zeal (23:15), gradation in the force of oaths (23:16-22), tithing of wild herbs (23:23; Luke 11:42), straining drinking water for fear of swallowing an impure gnat (Matt. 23:24), ritual washing of cups and dishes (23:25; Mark 7:4; Luke 11:39), ritual ablutions before meals (Matt. 15:2; Mark 7:1-5; Luke 11:38), fasting (Matt. 9:14), long prayers (Mark 12:40; Luke 20:47), abstention even from the appearance of work on the Sabbath (Matt. 12:1 f.; Luke 14:1-6), large donations to the Temple at the cost of the welfare of one's parents (Matt. 15:3-6; Mark 7:8-13), and the like.

The Pharisees were progressive not only in their constant reinterpretation of the Law to adapt it to new conditions, but in all religious fields. They advocated the enlargement of the canon of Scriptures, adding the Prophets (200 B.C.) and the Writings (A.D. 90) to the Torah; they developed exegetical methods by which a scriptural basis could be given to any new law or doctrine; they did not object to new rites in the Temple worship, and new festivals (Hanukkah [Dedication] and Purim); they favored the baptism of the proselytes and the hallowing of the Paschal meal; they were responsible, to a considerable degree, for speculations about wisdom, angels, and demons, as for the flowering of the Messianic hopes and the belief in the resurrection of the body. Certain members of the movement may well have deserved the criticism in the Gospels and in the Talmud, but let us not forget that "Judaism is the monument of the Pharisees" (G. F. Moore, *Judaism*, II, 193).

The Pharisees are often contrasted with two other groups, the uneducated masses and the Sadducees. A man of the common people is called in rabbinical literature *'am hā-'āreṣ* (literally, "people of the land"),[11] the plural of which (*'ammē hā-'āreṣ*) means "the masses." The educated classes were naturally more refined and more pious (since Judaism involved a study of the Scriptures and traditional law) than the "common man," ignorant of the observances and doctrines of his religion; and they treated him with contempt (cf. John 7:49). Jesus and the disciples were

[11] See G. F. Moore, in F. J. Foakes Jackson and K. Lake, *The Beginnings of Christianity* (Part I, The Acts of the Apostles). Vol. I (Prolegomena), pp. 439-445. London, 1920.

regarded by the scribes and Pharisees as belonging to the 'ammē hā-'āreṣ because they did not observe the rules of washings before meals, the refinements in the observance of the Sabbath, and other prescriptions of the oral law.

The *Sadducees*[12] are regularly described as the opponents of the Pharisees. Their name probably means "Zadokites" (descendants or partisans of Zadok, Solomon's priest [I Kings 2:35]). In general, the Pharisees belonged to the middle class, the Sadducees to the wealthy priestly aristocracy. The Pharisees claimed the authority of piety and learning, the Sadducees that of blood and position; the Pharisees were progressive, the Sadducees conservative; the Pharisees strove to raise the religious standards of the masses, the Sadducees were chiefly concerned with Temple administration and ritual, and kept themselves aloof from the masses.

In contrast with the Pharisees, the Sadducees recognized the Pentateuch alone (without other parts of Scripture and without the oral law) as binding, interpreting it more literally and (in criminal law) less leniently than the Pharisees; consequently they denied the resurrection, the judgment, and eternal life, as also (Acts 23:8) the existence of angels and spirits. With the loss of the Temple in A.D. 70 the Sadducees became a small sect without influence on the people.

The third "philosophical sect" of Josephus is that of the *Essenes*—in reality a monastic order, an ascetic and esoteric brotherhood.[13] About four thousand of them lived in Palestine, in various villages (not merely west of the Dead Sea, where their settlement known to Pliny was located). They practiced community of goods, avoided the company of women (although Josephus says one group allowed marriage), and lived under an overseer in the strictest discipline. Novices received an ax (to bury their excrements), an apron (to wear when bathing), and a white garment (their favorite wearing apparel). After one year the novices were admitted to the ablutions, and after two more years on trial they became members of the order. Josephus speaks of four classes, meaning probably children, first-year novices, second- and third-year novices, and members. Slavery, anointing with oil, and oaths were unknown among them; ritual ablutions were *de rigueur* after any kind of pollution (*War* 2:8, 9-10); the Sabbath was observed so rigorously that ordinary bodily

[12] On the Sadducees see: Josephus, *Antiquities* 13:5, 9; 13:10, 6; 18:1, 4; 20:9, 1; *War* 2:8, 14; Mark 12:18-27; Matt. 3:7; 16:1-12; Luke 20:27-40; Acts 4:1; 5:17; 23:6-9. It is worthy of notice that after A.D. 70 heretical movements in Judaism usually advocated a return to the Scriptures interpreted strictly and literally, after the manner of the Sadducean interpretation of the Pentateuch.

[13] Our information on the Essenes is based on the following sources: Josephus, *Antiquities* 13:5, 9; 15:10, 4-5; 18:1, 5; *War* 2:8, 2-13; Philo, *Quod omnis probus liber* §§12-13 (II, 457-459, M.); Philo, in Eusebius, *Praeparatio Evangelica* 8:11 (II, 632-634 M.); Pliny, *Natural History* 5:17.

needs were disregarded (*ibid.*); they considered their own sacrifices as more valuable than those in the Temple, to which they sent only votive gifts. Their common meals, following ablutions, were prepared by priests (to ensure their ritual purity?) and were their chief form of worship. Before dawn they prayed turning toward the east, as if supplicating the sun to rise (*War* 2:8, 5). Josephus compares their teaching to that of the Pythagoreans; he says that they believed that bodies are corruptible but souls immortal, and that the good souls came to lands across the sea similar to the Elysian Fields while the bad went to a murky and cold den for their punishment.[14]

The accidental discovery (in 1896) of the Hebrew documents of the *Covenanters of Damascus* (called, incorrectly, the *Zadokite Work*) shows how limited and fragmentary is our knowledge of sectarian movements in Judaism around the beginning of our era.[15] Scholars are much at variance in their dating of the schism that occurred twenty years after the end of the 390 years of wrath following the destruction of Jerusalem in 586 (1:5 f.): at that time the "Covenanters" went from Judea to Damascus (6:1; 8:6, 15; 9:28, 37) under the leadership of a teacher called "The Star" (9:8) whose coming was predicted in Num. 24:17 and, according to 9:5, in Am. 5:26 f.; 9:11. If, like R. H. Charles, we regard the figure "390" as exact and if we assume on the part of the author a chronological accuracy unparalleled in ancient Jewish literature for the period from 586 B.C. to 175 B.C., we may date the schism and the journey to Damascus soon after 176 B.C. These assumptions have been seriously questioned. The documents themselves were manifestly written some time after the schism; the dates suggested for them are *ca.* 170 (E. Meyer), in the Maccabean period (W. E. Barnes), after the time of Janneus (104-76), when the schism took place (L. Ginzberg), about 80 B.C. (W. H. Ward), about 63 B.C. (A. Bertholet), in the years 18-8 B.C.

[14] The *Therapeutae* described in the *De vita contemplativa* attributed to Philo (II, 471-486, M.) were ascetics of both sexes living all over Egypt in individual houses or cells, meeting only on the Sabbath and on the fiftieth day (following upon the seventh Sabbath), the *Pannychis* ["all night"] festival. They devoted themselves chiefly to meditation and contemplation, after renouncing the pleasures of the world. Eusebius (*Ecclesiastical History* 2:17; cf. 2:16, 2) identifies the Therapeutae with Christian monks. Scholars are divided on the question whether Philo is really the author of this tract.

[15] The *editio princeps* of these documents, discovered in the ruins of a *genizah* (cellar repository for worn-out manuscripts) of old Cairo (Fostat), is that of S. Schechter, *Documents of Jewish Sectaries*, Vol. 1: *Fragments of a Zadokite Work* (Cambridge, England, 1910). English translation in R. H. Charles, *Pseudepigrapha*, pp. 785-834. See also: G. F. Moore, *Judaism*, Vol. I, pp. 200-204; Louis Ginzberg, *Eine unbekannte jüdische Sekte*. New York, 1922. For other publications, see J. Juster, *Les Juifs dans l'empire romain*, Vol. 1, pp. 26-31; L. Rost, *Die Damaskusschrift* (H. Lietzmann, *Kleine Texte*). Berlin, 1933; R. Marcus, in *Proceedings of the American Academy for Jewish Research* 16 (1947) 142. See also, H. H. Rowley, *The Relevance of Apocalyptic*, pp. 71-74. London and Redhill, 1944.

(R. H. Charles), near the end of the second century of our era (M. J. Lagrange), and even in the seventh-eighth (A. Büchler) or eleventh (A. Marmorstein) centuries of our era. It seems fairly certain to the present writer that these documents were composed before the fall of Jerusalem in A.D. 70 and well after 200 B.C., when the eight volumes of the Prophets (Joshua-XII [Minor] Prophets) were canonized (cf. 9:7).[16] Apparently the author of this work was familiar with the Book of Jubilees and the Testaments of the XII Patriarchs (the title of the former is mentioned in 20:1, but L. Ginzberg regards the verse as a gloss) and, in view of the remarkable development of the oral law (Halakah), a date before 100 B.C. is hardly conceivable. We may therefore tentatively assign the work to the period 100 B.C.-A.D. 70.

Aside from the obscure account of the origin and migration of the sect, written in allegorical and apocalyptic language, abounding in Biblical reminiscences (1-9), the work is particularly interesting for its testimony to the early development of the oral law, as expounded in the constitution and the laws of the sect (10-20). The oral law is basically identical with that of the rabbis of the first two centuries of our era, and the teaching of the sect resembles that of the Pharisees—not in the least that of the Sadducees. The oral law, obviously limited here to a selection for laymen from the complete *corpus* (called *Sefer ha-Hāgō*, Book of the Hago; see 11:2; 15:5; 17:5) deals chiefly with lost property, court procedure, ritual bathing, Sabbath observance, defilement of the sanctuary, relations with Gentiles, dietary prescriptions, uncleanness and purifications, the duties of inspectors, oaths, vows, etc. The law is interpreted more strictly than in normative Judaism: marriage with a niece (7:9-11) and bigamy (7:2-7) are classed with incest and fornication, respectively, on the basis of Biblical analogies and interpretation but contrary to the views of the rabbis; the Sabbath laws (13:1-27) and the dietary laws are far stricter than in orthodox Jewish practice: thus, for instance, contrary to Luke 14:5, it is forbidden to rescue an animal which has fallen into a pit on the Sabbath (13:23).

The Covenanters resembled the Pharisees not only in their observance of a body of traditional law, already organized and recorded in writing, but also in a number of doctrines, such as the coming of the Messiah (2:10; 8:2; 9:10, 29; 15:4; 18:8), angels and spirits,[17] "eternal life" (5:6),

---

[16] The Law is quoted as Scripture ten times, the Prophets eleven times, and the Hagiographa once (14:1 refers to Prov. 15:8); see R. H. Charles, *Pseudepigrapha*, p. 789.

[17] Two names for Satan are used: Belial (6:9 f.; 7:19; 9:12; 14:5) and Mastema (20:2). In the Jewish literature of our period Belial (or Beliar) occurs in Jubilees, Testaments of the XII Patriarchs, Martyrdom of Isaiah, and Sibyllines 3:63; Mastema occurs only in Jubilees, unless (as suggested by A. Condamin and C. C. Torrey) *Betomasthem* [variously spelled] in Judith 4:6 is to be interpreted as Beth-Mastem (House of the Devil), a pseudonym of Samaria.

the reconciliation of divine foreknowledge (2:6, 10) with the freedom of the human will (3:1 f.,[18] 7; 4:2, 10).

"The fourth sect of Jewish philosophy," described briefly by Josephus in *Antiquities* 18:1, 6, is often identified, without warrant in the sources, with the party of the Zealots. Similarly its founder, Judas the Gaulonite (Judas the Galilean in Acts 5:37), who led a rebellion when Quirinius was preparing to take the census (A.D. 6), is gratuitously assumed to be the same as Judas, the son of the "bandit" Hezekiah executed by Herod about 47 B.C., a rebel leader whose uprising ten years earlier, immediately after Herod's death (4 B.C.), was crushed by Varus. The Zealots, according to Josephus, are the followers of John of Giscala and appear first in A.D. 66; they are distinct from the Sicarii, or Assassins, in the time of Felix (A.D. 52-60). The fourth philosophy agreed with the Pharisees in religious matters, but they recognized God alone as their Ruler and Lord, and consequently could not recognize foreign rulers. In all probability, like the Maccabees before them, these various patriotic parties and their leaders advocated a war to the finish against foreign domination; none of them, however, regarded its leader as the Messiah (as Bar Cocheba was regarded later).[19]

These Palestinian sects, parties, schools, and movements flourishing during the centuries about the beginning of our era attest, by their contrasting aspirations and tenets, the vitality of Judaism and its manifold variety. We gain the same impression by a perusal of its literature, to which we may now turn our attention.[20]

[18] Note here the reference to man's evil impulse (*yeṣer*), on which see G. F. Moore, *Judaism*, Vol. I, pp. 479-493.

[19] See on these movements, F. J. Foakes Jackson and Kirsopp Lake, *The Beginnings of Christianity*, Pt. I, Vol. 1, pp. 421-425. London, 1920.

[20] After this chapter was set in proof, the discovery of another "Sectarian Document" apparently similar to that of the Covenanters of Damascus (see above, note 15) was made public. Full discussion must await the publication of the complete text; see provisionally: J. C. Trever and Millar Burrows in *The Biblical Archaeologist* (XI:3; September, 1948); Trever in BASOR No. 111 (October, 1948); and H. L. Ginsberg in BASOR No. 112 (December, 1948). See, however, the article of S. Zeitlin in JQR N. S. 39 (1949) 235-247.

CHAPTER III

LITERARY HISTORY

~~~~~~

During the three centuries from 200 B.C. to A.D. 100, Palestinian Jews wrote their books either in Hebrew or in Aramaic, while those living in the lands of the Dispersion, and chiefly at Alexandria, wrote in Greek; this Hellenistic-Jewish literature will be considered in a later chapter.

The Palestinian writings (and a few Hellenistic ones in the Apocrypha) are classified somewhat artificially as canonical, apocryphal, pseudepigraphic, and rabbinical (i.e., sources of rabbinical books actually written later). From a purely Jewish point of view (eliminating Christian preconceptions), a more correct classification[1] would be, canonical, normative, and "extraneous," or "outside," books (the Apocrypha [with the possible exception of Sirach] and Pseudepigrapha).

In an investigation concerned with literary history, doctrinal distinctions are irrelevant. The dogma that certain writings are divinely inspired and therefore canonical is based on faith, and its validity is the subject of theological debate, not of historical research. The latter traces the development of such doctrines without deciding whether they are true or false.

Leaving aside, therefore, the canonical status of these writings in Judaism or Christianity, and the official attitude of the rabbis in their regard, we may classify them in tabular form, according to their date, original language, subject, and style, as follows:

I. PALESTINIAN WRITINGS

A. Written in Hebrew

1. 200-100 B.C.
   a. Lyric poetry. Maccabean and Hasmonean psalms in the Psalter. Other psalms: Ecclus. 39:12-35; 42:15-43:33; 51:1-12 (and the liturgy after 51:12, in the Hebrew); Tob. 13 (possibly written in Aramaic); Jth. 16; Bar. 4:5-5:9.
   b. Wisdom poetry. Ecclesiasticus; Ecclesiastes; Bar. 3:9-4:4.
   c. History. I Maccabees.

[1] Cf. G. F. Moore, *Judaism*, Vol. 1, pp. 125-134.

d. Fiction. Dan. 1:1-2:4a; Judith; Esther.

e. Legends and exhortations. Testaments of the XII Patriarchs; Bar. 1:1-14; 1:15-3:8.

f. Apocalypse. Dan. 8-12.

2. 100-1 B.C.

    a. Lyric poetry. Psalms of Solomon; Prayer of Manasses.

    b. History. The lost life of John Hyrcanus (?).

3. A.D. 1-100.

    a. Wisdom. Sayings of the Fathers (*Pirkē Abōth*), in part; published *ca.* A.D. 200.

    b. History and law. Documents of the Covenanters of Damascus.

    c. Legends. The Lives of the Prophets.

B. Written in Aramaic

1. 200-1 B.C.

    a. Fiction. Dan. 2:4b-6:28; Tobit; Susanna; Bel and the Dragon; Greek Esther (?). The Story of the Three Youths (I [III] Esd. 3:1-4:63) is probably earlier than 200.

    b. Legends. Jubilees; II Macc. 1:1-2:18; the Testament of Job.

    c. Wisdom. Tob. 4:3-21; 12:6-10.

    d. Apocalypse. Dan. 7; Enoch (for the most part).

    e. Polemic. Epistle of Jeremy.

2. A.D. 1-100.

    a. Legends (all containing Christian additions). Martyrdom of Isaiah; Paralipomena of Jeremiah; Life of Adam and Eve (or, in Greek, Apocalypse of Moses).

    b. Apocalypse. Assumption of Moses; Syriac Baruch; II (IV) Esdras; Apocalypse of Abraham (partly Christian).

    c. History. History of the Jewish War of A.D. 66-70, written by Josephus in Aramaic (now lost, except for its rewriting in Greek).

II. JEWISH-HELLENISTIC WRITINGS

1. 200-75 B.C.

    a. Legendary history. Demetrius (shortly before 200)?; Eupolemus; Artapanus; Aristeas; Cleodemus or Malchus; Jason of Cyrene (condensed in II Macc.).

    b. Epic and drama. Philo the epic writer; Theodotus; Ezekiel.

    c. Philosophy. Wisdom of Solomon; Aristobulus.

    d. Propaganda purporting to be written by Gentiles. The Letter of Aristeas (Pseudo-Aristeas); Sibylline Oracle III:97-808; Pseudo-Phocylides; Pseudo-Hecateus.

2. 75-1 B.C.

Legendary history. II Maccabees (beginning with 2:18); III Maccabees.
3. A.D. 1-100.
  a. History. Josephus (*Antiquities of the Jews*; *War of the Jews*); Philo of Alexandria (*Against Flaccus*; *Embassy to Caligula*); Justus of Tiberias (lost history of the Jewish War of 66-70).
  b. Autobiography. Josephus (*Life of Flavius Josephus*).
  c. Philosophy. IV Maccabees; Philo of Alexandria.
  d. Apologetics. Josephus (*Against Apion*); and, to some extent, what has been listed above under 1.*a, c, d*; 3.*a, c.*
  e. Apocalypse. Slavic Enoch (partly Christian); Greek Baruch (partly Christian; possibly later than A.D. 100).

If the preceding conspectus of Palestinian literature is reasonably correct, at least in its main lines, it is clear that the literature *in Hebrew* was either canonical (Psalms, Ecclesiastes, Esther, Daniel) or a conscious imitation thereof. The influence of the Psalter on noncanonical Psalms, of Proverbs on Ecclesiasticus and Bar. 3:9-4:4, of Kings on I Maccabees, of the Song of Deborah (Judg. 5) on Judith, of Gen. 49 and Deut. 33 on the Testaments of the XII Patriarchs, needs no comment. Only Daniel, the first real apocalypse, represents a new trend in literature. *The Sayings of the Fathers,* in spite of echoes of Scripture and resemblance to Proverbs, are in a measure a new type of wisdom book.

Conversely, the *Aramaic* literature was less bound by the Scriptures, more free, unpretentious, and fantastic; as the use of the vernacular shows, it was far more popular. Parts of Daniel alone attained canonical status. For the rest we have popular tales for entertainment and instruction, Biblical legends, apocalypses, and mockery of pagan religions. Josephus wrote his Aramaic history of the Jewish War for "the upper barbarians" (*War*, Preface §1), presumably the Babylonian Jews, but apparently did not attain there as much popularity as he hoped for.

During the second century before our era the persecutions of Antiochus Epiphanes (168-165), the Maccabean rebellion, the achievement of independence under Simon in 142, and the successful wars of conquest in the reign of John Hyrcanus (135-104) were epoch-making events which exercised a decisive influence on the literature written in Hebrew (except on the books of wisdom and legends), but curiously (aside from Daniel) very little on the Aramaic writings.

The dramatic events from the accession of Antiochus Epiphanes to the death of Simon (175-135) were related soberly and objectively, though with considerable pride in the Hasmonean dynasty, in I Maccabees (*ca.* 100 B.C.). The whole gamut from utter despair during the persecution to triumphant exultation after the victories is sounded in the Psalter. In the tragic days of persecution the congregation wept bitterly and cried unto

God *de profundis* in Pss. 44, 74, 79, 83, and others. The achievements of Judas Maccabeus in battle are apparently extolled in Pss. 118, 149. Simon's achievement of independence and the nation's bestowal of the hereditary high priesthood upon him are celebrated in Ps. 110 (which has the acrostic "Simeon" in the Hebrew). The coronation and marriage of Alexander Janneus in the year 104 are commemorated in Ps. 2 (the Hebrew acrostic of which reads, "For A. Janneus and his wife").

A later situation is reflected by the eighteen psalms of the Pharisees known as the *Psalms of Solomon*, composed in Hebrew but extant only in a Greek translation and in a Syriac version made from the Greek text. The author of the 17th of these psalms denounces (in contrast to Pss. 2, 110) the Hasmonean monarchy as illegal, and regards Pompey as the divine agent for its overthrow (as also in Ps. of Sol. 8). After Pompey had taken Jerusalem (63 B.C.) and led away Jewish captives (Pss. of Sol. 2, 8, 17), he was murdered in Egypt (48 B.C.) and his corpse was left unburied (Ps. of Sol. 2). In all probability the other psalms in this collection are likewise to be dated about the middle of the first century B.C. In form there is little to distinguish them from the Psalms of David; some are even supplied with the technical musical notations ("For the Chief Musician," 8:1; "Selah," 17:31 [29]; 18:10 [9]). A sharp distinction between the pious and the sinners (usually interpreted as Pharisees and Sadducees, respectively) dominates most of these psalms. Ps. of Sol. 4 is the portrait of a hypocrite belonging to the upper classes, possibly inspired by a contemporary rascal. Typically Pharisaic teaching about the resurrection (3:16 [12]; 13:9 [11]; 14:6 [9f]), free will (9:4), and the Messianic hope (17; 18) are presented as if they were familiar to the Jews of the time, without the fervor and passion of Daniel, penned a century earlier.

The Book of Daniel was written in the very midst of the persecution of 168-165 B.C., while the "abomination of desolation" stood in the Temple: it was an appeal to the faithful to remain steadfast even unto death, a promise that their God would soon destroy miraculously the heathen empires and give world dominion to the Hasidim—including those slain for their faith, who would be brought back to life. While the psalms of this tragic period were pathetic laments, Daniel unveiled the vision of God's final triumph over the enemies of his Law. Daniel's concern was purely religious; the campaigns of Judas Maccabeus, in contrast with I Maccabees, were deemed insignificant in the sight of God (Dan. 11:34). A few years later Judith expressed an entirely different mood: while the religious fervor of the Hasidim in time of persecution was not yet forgotten, Judith's purpose was to secure the independence of the Jews from the heathen tyrant through a bold *coup de main*. The point of view in Esther seems to be even later: as in the time of John Hyrcanus, the Jews did not fight for their religion nor for political independence any more, but for vengeance against their heathen enemies, who, like the Idumeans under Hyrcanus, adopted Judaism out of fear of the Jews (Esth. 8:17).

The Wisdom Literature (Ecclesiasticus, Ecclesiastes, Bar. 3:9-4:4) did not reflect these stirring events, either because it was written before the accession of Antiochus Epiphanes (Ecclesiasticus, dated about 180), or because it was concerned with individual rather than with national affairs, and thus often had a timeless character.

As early as the third millennium in Egypt, wisdom was the *summum bonum* through which man attains happiness and success. When the Israelites adopted this Egyptian (and later international) notion, they tended more and more to regard wisdom as a peculiar possession of Israel: first they identified it with their own religion and ethics (Proverbs), then with the Law of Moses or the Pentateuch (Sirach and Baruch). After Sirach, no Jewish wisdom book (except Ecclesiastes—if it is later, as seems likely)[2] fails to regard the Law of Moses as Israel's wisdom and as the divine norm of human conduct. The identification of Wisdom and Torah is stressed also in Hellenistic-Jewish writings, but particularly in *Sayings of the Fathers* (*Abōth*) and other rabbinical books.[3] Ecclesiastes is the only dissenting voice: possibly through some vague acquaintance with popular Greek philosophy, he became a skeptic and questioned the value of wisdom and righteousness, for God does not reward and punish human conduct either in this life or in the next. The attribution of Ecclesiastes to Solomon and the pious annotations added to it made possible the canonization of the book, confirmed after some discussion, in A.D. 90.

The Testaments of the XII Patriarchs (probably written in 140-110 B.C.) teach morality not by precept, as the preceding wisdom books, but primarily by example (to which precept is added). Each of the sons of Jacob, when he knew that his death was near, gave to his descendants his parting advice, drawn from his own experience: he dwelt on his own sin or sins, described the resulting misfortunes, and recommended the opposite virtue or virtues. Only Joseph and Issachar could illustrate the value of virtue from their own lives. All, except Gad, add to wise counsel some apocalyptic predictions.

[2] Eccl. 12:13 is of course an editorial addition to the book.
[3] See, J Fichtner, *Die Altorientalische Weisheit in ihrer israelitisch-jüdischen Ausprägung* (Beih. ZAW 62), pp. 79-97. Giessen, 1933. G. F. Moore, *Judaism*, Vol. 1, pp. 263-269.

The noble moral teaching is in the best tradition of orthodox Judaism. It is derived from the letter of the Scriptures by the subtle allegorical and analogical interpretation of scribes and rabbis. Man's moral nature is explained as follows: God created man in his own image (Naphtali 2:5), but gave him a choice of opposite alternatives: "Two ways has God given to the sons of men, and two inclinations" (Asher 1:3)—the good inclination (yeṣer ha-ṭōb, alluded to here for the first time) and the bad (yeṣer hā-raʿ). Consequently, sin is universal; sins against which the patriarchs warn urgently are: fornication, envy, anger, hatred, covetousness, intemperance, deceit, falsehood, and gossip. Inducement to sin comes not only from the evil impulse but also from coquettish women, who caused the fall of the angels (Reuben 5; cf. Gen. 6:1-4), and from the evil spirits whose prince is Beliar. The seven spirits of deceit (Reuben 2:1 f.; 3:3-6)—the counterpart of the seven archangels—are (as in Zoroastrianism) personifications of sins and should not be conceived as actual persons. Beliar, the counterpart of God, however, is a real person: he will eventually be bound (Levi 18:12) and cast into the fire for ever (Judah 25:3) by the Messiah descended from Levi. The Messianic era, on this earth, following the general resurrection, the last judgment, and the punishment of Beliar to which reference has just been made, will consist of an eternal residence of the saved in Eden and the New Jerusalem (Dan. 5:10-13). The author is manifestly a Pharisee and identifies virtue with the observance of the Law (Judah 26:1; Issachar 5:1; etc.). Without disregarding the external observances of a ritual character,[4] the author stresses the more spiritual side of religion and morality. He values particularly patience, prayer, and humility in connection with fasting (Joseph 10:1 f.; cf. Naphtali 8:8; Joseph 4:8; Benjamin 1:4), repentance after sin (Reuben 1:9; 2:1; Simeon 2:13; Judah 15:4; Joseph 6:6; Benjamin 5:4), trust in God (Joseph 1:5 f. [cf. Matt. 25:35 f.]; 2:4), fear of the Lord (Levi 13:1, Zebulon 10:5; etc.), and love for God and man. The earliest combination of Deut. 6:5 and Lev. 19:18 (cf. Matt. 22:37-39; Luke 10:27) is in Issachar 5:2; 7:6; Dan. 5:3; cf. Benjamin 3:4. The author's sense of the inwardness of morality appears in his contempt for good actions performed for an evil purpose and for the illusion that evil actions may be canceled by good ones (Asher 2; cf. Ecclus. 34:20 [Gr. 31:24]); in his condemnation of sins of thought (Issachar 7:2; Joseph 9:2; Benjamin 8:2 [cf. Matt. 5:28]); in his notion of a moral conscience (Reuben 4:3; Judah 20:5; Gad 5:3); and in his emphasis on the motives of actions (Naphtali 2:9; Gad 5:3)—although he goes too far when he implies that the end justifies the means (Asher 4). Many resemblances between the moral teaching of this book and

---

[4] Reuben 1:10; Simeon 3:4; Levi 9:4, 7, 11-14; Issachar 3-6; Joseph 3:4; 4:8; 10:1. On good works, see Reuben 4:1; Levi 13:5; Naphtali 8:5 (cf. Matt. 6:20).

that of Jesus have been noticed. Particularly striking is the exhortation not only to forgive those who offend against us—seeking full reconciliation, and in any case banishing resentment (Gad 6; cf. Matt. 18:15, 35; Luke 17:3)—but to do good unto them and pray for them (Joseph 18:2; cf. Benjamin 5:4; Luke 6:28). Brotherly love, compassion (as God has compassion, Zebulon 5:3; 8:1-3) almsgiving, humility are virtues particularly stressed (also single-mindedness, patience, and temperance)—as illustrated in the description of the good man in Benjamin 4-6. While the Testaments present many close parallels with the Book of Jubilees, they differ radically from it in advocating a friendly attitude toward the Gentiles, whose final salvation is clearly expected.[5]

The little book entitled *The Lives of the Prophets* is another Jewish collection of legends, originally written in Hebrew during the first century of our era. It is preserved in a Greek text extant in various recensions and in a Syriac version from the Greek as also in Latin and Ethiopic texts based on the Greek. All extant versions are edited by Christians, one of the best known being included among the Greek works of Epiphanius, Bishop of Salamis in Cyprus (*ca.* 315-403); another text is attributed to Dorotheus of Tyre. Conceivably, either Epiphanius or Dorotheus could have prepared the Greek translation from the original Hebrew text.[6]

The book contains the legendary lives of the four Major (Isaiah, Jeremiah, Ezekiel, and Daniel) and Twelve Minor Prophets; and of

[5] The Hebrew original of the Testaments is lost, but we have a complete Greek translation (in two redactions), and an Armenian translation from the Greek, which is useful for the elimination of late glosses (which it still lacks) occurring in the Greek. These glosses are partly Jewish and partly Christian: attempts to identify the Christian additions have been made by R. H. Charles (*The Greek Versions of the Testaments of the Twelve Patriarchs, edited from nine manuscripts together with the variants of the Armenian and Slavonic Versions and some Hebrew Fragments.* Oxford, 1908; also in his English version in his *Apocrypha and Pseudepigrapha,* Vol. 2, pp. 296-360; cf. *The Testaments of the Twelve Patriarchs,* translated . . . and edited. . . . London, 1908); F. Schnapp (in Kautzsch, *Apokryphen und Pseudepigraphen,* Vol. 2, pp. 458-460); and W. Bousset (ZNW 1 [1900] 141-175, 187-209, 344-346).

[6] The most important critical editions of the Greek text are the following: I. H. Hall, in JBL 6 (1886) 29-39. E. Nestle, *Marginalien und Materialen.* Tübingen, 1893. Th. Schermann, *Prophetarum Vitae Fabulosae,* etc. Leipzig, Teubner, 1907. C. C. Torrey, *The Lives of the Prophets.* JBL, Monograph Series 1. Philadelphia, 1946. The Syriac text was published by E. Nestle in the second edition of his *Syrische Grammatik.* Berlin, 1888; English translation, 1889 (an incomplete text appeared in the first edition, 1881). I. H. Hall published an English translation of a Syriac text of the *Lives* in JBL 7 (1887) 28-40. For a study of this work, together with an English translation of the Greek critical text, see Torrey's monograph mentioned above; cf. his treatment in *The Apocryphal Literature,* pp. 135-140, and the much longer investigation by Th. Schermann (*Propheten- und Apostellegenden nebst Jüngerkatalogen.* Texte und Untersuchungen, Vol. 31, pp. 1-133. Leipzig, 1907).

Nathan, Ahijah, Joed (Neh. 11:7; identified with Jedo or Iddo in II Chron. 9:29, etc., and with the unnamed prophet of I Kings 13:23-32), Azariah (II Chron. 15:1-15), Zechariah the son of Jehoiada (II Chron. 24:20-22; cf. Matt. 23:35; Luke 11:51), Elijah, and Elisha. The Biblical data on these prophets are alluded to briefly, while legendary embellishments are given more fully. Some of these additions may be summarized here: Before Isaiah was sawn asunder (cf. Martyrdom of Isaiah; Hebr. 11:37) he received water miraculously from a spring which was henceforth called Siloah (sent; cf. John 9:7). Jeremiah, according to a Christian story (the only one included in the original work), told to the author by an Egyptian who had heard it from "the children of Antigonus and Ptolemy, aged men," announced the end of Egyptian idolatry "when a virgin bearing a child of divine appearance [Jesus] would arrive in Egypt." Jeremiah had hidden the ark of the covenant (cf. II Macc. 2:5) until the Lord would come and "all nations would worship a piece of wood [the cross]." Jeremiah destroyed the poisonous snakes of Egypt ('ephōth, "vipers," in Hebrew) by means of the argólai (ḥargōl, Hebr. locust; but in the LXX of Lev. 11:22, snake killer) presumably ichneumones. Ezekiel saved many Jewish exiles in Babylonia by drying up the Chebar canal (Ez. 1:1, etc.) so that they could cross over, and causing its waters to return and drown the Chaldeans; and from that canal he supplied starving exiles with fish which came willingly to be caught. Daniel prayed for Nebuchadnezzar, who had been turned into a beast half bull and half lion. Amos was killed by the son of Amaziah, the priest of Bethel. The mother of Jonah was the widow of Zarephath (I Kings 17:8-24). Habakkuk brought food to Daniel in the den of lions (cf. Bel and the Dragon). When Elisha was born, the golden calf's bellow could be heard in Jerusalem.

The literature *in Aramaic* is generally freer, more popular, less immediately concerned with urging the Jews to observe the written and unwritten law, more under the influence of pagan literature, than the Hebrew writings mentioned above. This is particularly obvious in the fiction written before the beginning of our era. In most cases a Gentile theme (or themes) has been utilized to produce a Jewish book. The Story of the Three Youths (I [III] Esdras 2-4) is apparently of Persian origin; the story of Tobit exhibits some well-known folkloristic motifs and is influenced by the earlier tale of Ahikar, which is certainly not of Jewish origin. Even for the stories of Daniel (Dan. 2-6) and Susanna pagan influence cannot be doubted. Of course Greek Esther and Bel and the Dragon are thoroughly Jewish and strongly antiheathen—like the sarcastic lampoon of idol worship in the Epistle of Jeremy. These Aramaic tales exhibit remarkable imagination in the portrayal of the characters, in the description of their vicissitudes, and in carrying out the plot to a happy ending through divine or human agencies.

The same imagination of these story-tellers was at work on the Hebrew Scriptures (the Law and the Prophets, before the Christian Era) and began to produce the haggadic legends which have been collected and made accessible through the vast learning and literary art of Louis Ginzberg in *The Legends of the Jews* (7 vols., Philadelphia, 1913-1938). Perhaps the earliest as well as the classical example of the imaginative elaboration of Biblical stories is I-II Chronicles (middle of the third century B.C.). After 200, the earliest examples are the Book of Jubilees and the slightly later Testaments of the XII Patriarchs (written in Hebrew).

Jubilees is so called from the chronological scheme for dating the stories related in Gen. 1-Ex. 12. Events are dated according to years, weeks of years, and jubilees, beginning with the creation of the world, thus: "And Leah his [Jacob's] wife died in the fourth year of the second week of the forty-fifth jubilee" (36:21); i.e., $4+7+2156$ [$=44 \times 49$] $=$ year 2167 of the era of creation. Often the day of the month is added for greater exactness. The author also proposed a reform of the calendar. The Jews adjusted twelve lunar months (354 days, 8 hours, 48 minutes) to the solar year (365 days, 5 hours, 48 minutes) by adding a thirteenth month whenever necessary, obtaining about 384 days for this intercalary year. The author proposed instead a solar year of 52 weeks (364 days, more than one day too short) divided into four seasons of 13 weeks each, each season consisting of three months, the first presumably of 31 days and the other two of 30 (6:23-38; cf. 4:17; 5:27; 12:16), or four intercalary days (at the beginning of each season) in addition to twelve months of 30 days (as in Enoch 75:1, which was known to the author, according to Jub. 4:17 f.; in 5:27 months have 30 days). The erroneous calendar of the Israelites, in the author's opinion, has prevented them from keeping each annual festival at the proper time, "on the day of its fixed time" (49:14 f.), as specified long before the time of Moses "on the heavenly tablets" (6:35). Like Enoch 72-82, Jubilees wishes the Jews to have a calendar entirely different from that of the Gentiles (i.e., the Greeks).

In form Jubilees is a revelation made on Sinai to Moses by "the angel of the presence" (2:1, etc.), who constantly refers for information to "heavenly tablets" (3:10, 31; 4:5, 32; and so forth to the end) which the author ostensibly wished to be considered no less inspired than the Scriptures. In this way he could trace back to the beginnings of human history, long before Moses, some of the traditional observances of Judaism which the Pentateuch and the rabbis regarded as first revealed to Moses. Thus the Feast of Weeks (Pentecost), for instance, was celebrated in heaven from the creation to Noah (6:18); and on earth by Noah (6:17) and Abraham (6:19). The ritual of the festivals is described in minute detail (e.g., Tabernacles, 16:21-31; 32:27-29; Passover, 49), and otherwise unknown features are occasionally recorded (as in 16:31). In a number of instances the oral law that the book presents as valid differs from the later practice attested by Philo, Josephus, and the Talmud:[7] the remnant of the first-fruits of the fourth year is to be eaten by the servants of the Temple (7:36) and not by the worshiper himself (Philo and Josephus); olive-tree wood is allowed among other kinds of wood for the sacrifices (21:12-15), but the Mishna (*Tamid* II, 3) forbids the use of olive trees and grapevines; the tithe of cattle is given to the priests (32:15; so Tob. 1:6, *cod. Aleph*, and Philo), and must not be consumed by the worshiper; and so on.

Jubilees is important not only as a record of early Halakah or formulation of traditional oral law, but also for its Haggadah or religious and moral instruction of a non-legal character; here the Haggadah consists chiefly of Biblical legends and apocalyptic hopes. The book follows the narratives of Gen. 1-Ex. 12, but freely omits incidents which seem worthy of oblivion and adds legendary elaborations to others, exactly as Chronicles forgets David's affair with Bathsheba and invents the repentance of Manasses. Like the Chronicler (I Chron. 21:1; cf. II Sam. 24:1), the author attributes to Satan, called Mastema ("the Enemy" in Aramaic), certain actions attributed to God but deemed unworthy of him, such as the suggestion of the sacrifice of Isaac (17:16; 18:9, 12) and the attack on Moses (48:2-4); see also 48:9-12, 15-19; 49:2.[8] Among other haggadic embellishments we may note that Abraham at the age of fourteen successfully stopped the ravens seventy times from eating the seed (11:18-21) and a year later invented a seeder attached to a plow for deep sowing, thus ensuring protection from the ravens' depredations (11:23 f.).[9] Apocalyptic promises are not greatly stressed: Abraham predicted that a period of great sinfulness (when human life would become limited to less than seventy-five years) will be followed after the judgment by a golden age when men will again approach the age of one thousand years of peace and happiness; the bones of the righteous dead will remain in their graves, but their spirits will have much joy (23:11-31).

The author was a Pharisee, deeply devoted to the Law, even though he held some original views on its interpretation. He was strongly opposed

---

[7] See E. Schürer, *Geschichte*, Vol. 3, pp. 377 f.; L. Finkelstein, "The Book of Jubilees and the Rabbinic Halaka" (HTR 16 [1923] 39-61).

[8] Beliar (the name for the devil in the Testaments of the XII Patriarchs) is a mere abstraction in Jub. 1:20; 15:33. Satan (10:11) will eventually be eliminated from this earth (23:29; 40:9; 46:2; 50:5).

[9] Such a plow with seeder is portrayed on a Babylonian seal of the Kassite Period published by A. T. Clay; see J. A. Montgomery in JBL 33 (1914) 157 f.

to any compromise with the heathen (i.e., Hellenism), over whom God appointed spirits who led them astray while He was the ruler of Israel (15:31 f.); and he regarded intermarriage and community of meals with the heathen as apostasy (22:16-20; 30:7-17). Two characteristic Jewish rites, circumcision (15:33 f.) and Sabbath observance (2:25-31; 50:6-13), are sacrosanct and must be strictly kept at all costs. Even the higher ranks of angels have always observed them (2:18; 15:27).

The original Aramaic text seems to have been lost soon after its translation into Greek, which survived only in some patristic and Byzantine quotations. The book is preserved completely only in an Ethiopic version made from the Greek; more than one-fourth of a Latin translation from the Greek has been published. Jubilees was probably written in the second half of the second century B.C., although other dates from the fifth century B.C. to A.D. 60 have been suggested by various scholars.[10]

The Testament of Job is likewise a pre-Christian legendary biography written in Aramaic, though now extant only in a Greek version; it was probably written early in the last century before our era, and translated soon after.[11] The book seems to be the source of the words addressed by Job's wife to her suffering husband in the Greek Bible (Job 2:9, LXX): "How long will you be steadfast, saying 'Lo, I shall wait yet a short time expecting the hope of my salvation?' Behold, your memorial has vanished from the earth: (your) sons and daughters, the pangs and labors of my womb, for whom I labored in vain with agonies. As for you, you sit in the rottenness of worms, remaining all night outdoors. And I, a wanderer and a slave, go about from place to place and from house to house, waiting for the sun to set at last, that I might find relief from my pains and sorrows, which now oppress me. But say a certain word [i.e., blaspheme or curse God] to the Lord and die!" In view of the fact that the Greek text of Job was known to Aristeas, an Alexandrian Jewish historian whose account of Job was excerpted by Alexander Polyhistor (*ca.* 50 B.C.) and preserved by Eusebius (*Praeparatio evangelica* IX, 25; text and translation in C. Müller, *Fragmenta historicorum graecorum*, Vol. 3, p. 220), the Testament of Job cannot be later than 75 B.C., being earlier than the LXX of Job. The notes at the end of the Greek Job contain the misinformation about the ancestry of Job given by Aristeas: Job is identified with

[10] See H. H. Rowley, *The Relevance of Apocalyptic*, pp. 81-85. London and Redhill, 1944; cf. HTR 36 (1943) 19-24.

[11] Cardinal Angelo Mai published the Greek text for the first time in *Scriptorum Veterum Nova Collectio*, Vol. 7, pp. 180-191 (Rome, 1833). The text was reprinted and translated by K. Kohler in *Semitic Studies in Memory of Alexander Kohut*, pp. 264-338 (Berlin, 1897); cf. his valuable article in *Jewish Encyclopedia*, Vol. 7, pp. 200-202. A slightly different text, with a long introduction, was printed by M. R. James, *Apocrypha Anecdota*, 2nd Ser., pp. lxxii-cii, 104-137. Cambridge, 1897. See also, C. C. Torrey, *The Apocryphal Literature*, pp. 140-145.

Jobab, king of Edom, and his mother is erroneously called Bosorra or
Bassara (i.e., the city of Bozrah) through a misunderstanding of Gen.
36:33 ("And Jobab the son of Zerah *of Bozrah* reigned in his stead").
The same identification of Job with Jobab occurs in the Testament of
Job, as also in a fragment of a Targum (i.e., Aramaic version or paraphrase) of Job (cf. E. Schürer, *Geschichte*, Vol. 3, p. 406; L. Ginzberg,
Legends of the Jews, Vol. 5, p. 384). The view that the Testament of
Job was written in Greek by a Christian is defended by Schürer (*op. cit.*,
p. 407) on the basis of some stylistic parallels with the New Testament,
but this evidence (carefully collected by M. R. James, *op. cit.* in note 11,
above) is by no means conclusive: the prohibition of Jewish-Gentile
marriages (Test. of Job 45) is hardly conceivable in a Christian book,
and the linguistic parallels are for the most part Aramaic idioms reproduced in Greek, for which parallels occur in Jewish literature.

The contents of the Testament of Job may be summarized as follows:
Shortly before his death, Job assembled the children from his second
wife, Dinah (daughter of Jacob, cf. Gen. 34), and (after the manner of
Gen. 49 and Deut. 33; cf. the Testament of the XII Patriarchs) in his
farewell address reviewed his past life and gave them his final recom-
mendations. Like his ancestor Abraham, Job forsook idolatry and worshiped the one true God, but by destroying the idols he engaged in a
lifelong battle against Satan. Job had set aside a portion of his enormous
wealth for the benefit of the needy, but Satan obtained permission from
God to reduce Job to wretched poverty, yet could not undermine his
faith. When he was smitten with leprosy, Job sat for seven (48 in the
James edition) years on a dunghill, while his wife Sitidos (from the
Greek *Ausítidos*, of the land of *Ausítis* [Job 1:1, LXX]; Hebr. Uz) became
a water carrier to support him. Finally Satan induced her to invite Job
to curse God and die (cf. above, Job 2:9, LXX). Job rebuked her and
challenged Satan to battle, but he said, weeping, "I yield to you, who
are the great wrestler." Job's three royal friends came to see him and
were horrified by his condition. Sitidos appealed to them to bury the
bodies of her children, but Job declared that they had been taken up
to heaven; they were seen eastward, near the divine throne. Sitidos died
comforted by this vision. Elihu, inspired by Satan, denounced Job. God
forgave Job's three friends, but not Elihu, "the evil one, the son of darkness, the lover of the Serpent," who was cast into the underworld. Job
celebrated his restoration to health with a feast of thanksgiving, became
rich again, married Dinah, and had seven sons and three daughters from
her. Through divine girdles the daughters became able to sing heavenly
hymns. While they glorified God, Job's soul was taken to heaven in a
chariot. The multitude of the poor who had been helped by Job, together
with his family, sang the funeral dirge as his body was taken to the grave.

The religious teaching of the book is characteristic of the Hasidim (Assideans), or strict Jews, living some years after the publication of Daniel in 164 B.C.: emphasis is placed on the resurrection and eternal life, and on such precepts as these: "Forsake not the Lord! Be charitable to the poor and do not disregard the feeble! Take not unto yourselves wives from strangers!"

During the first century of the Christian Era the legends about Biblical characters remained popular, but near the close of the century the rabbinical authorities finally fixed the canon of Scriptures and discarded as futile, if not as unsafe, the popular books of legend and apocalypse. Presumably they were classed at the time with the "outside books" (which included Christian and sectarian writings), the readers of which, according to Rabbi Akiba (d. ca. 132), have no part in the World to Come (Jer. Sanhedrin x, 1, 28a; cf. Bab. Sanhedrin 100b). Later it was said that whoever brings into his house more than the twenty-four books (of the Hebrew Scriptures) brings confusion (Midrash Qoheleth 12, 12). After A.D. 100, in any case, this literature was completely ignored by the rabbis; the Aramaic texts have totally disappeared, and the surviving remnants, in various translations, have been preserved by Christians, for the most part outside the main current of Greek and Latin Christianity.

The Jewish collections of sacred legends must now be reconstructed from extant Christian editions, which are translations, sometimes at several removes from the Aramaic originals written in the first century. Consequently no unanimity of opinion prevails among scholars with regard to these originals.

There are numerous Christian lives of Adam and Eve in a variety of languages. The supposed Jewish book on the subject has been reconstructed chiefly from the Latin Vita Adae et Evae and a Greek book closely parallel to it, published by C. von Tischendorf in Apocalypses apocryphae (Leipzig, 1866) under the erroneous title of "Apocalypse of Moses," and also by A. M. Ceriani (Monumenta sacra et profana, V:1. Milan, 1868).[12] The story begins (chs. 1-17 of the Latin, not in the Greek) with Adam and Eve's repentance after their expulsion from Eden: Adam did penance by standing on a stone in the Jordan with the water up to his neck for forty days, but Eve, deceived by the devil, did not complete her thirty-seven days in the Tigris. Eve gave birth to Cain, who at once ran and brought a blade of grass to his mother (18-21). After the birth of Abel the parents, assailed by premonitions of murder,

---

[12] See the critical introduction and English translation of L. S. A. Wells, in R. H. Charles, Apocrypha and Pseudepigrapha, Vol. 2, pp. 123-154; cf. M. R. James, The Lost Apocrypha of the Old Testament, pp. 1-8. In German: E. Kautzsch, Apokryphen und Pseudepigraphen, Vol. 2, pp. 506-528 (by C. Fuchs).

kept them separated, but Cain slew Abel; then Seth was born (22-24). In a vision related to Seth (25-29, not in Greek), Adam, after eating of the fruit of knowledge, beheld the vicissitudes of the Jews until postexilic times and the Last Judgment. When Adam fell ill, Eve and Seth tried in vain to obtain a drop of the oil of life from the tree of mercy in Eden; on the way Seth was bitten by a beast (30-44). In the Greek (Apoc. of Mos. 15-34), Eve gave a full account of the fall and told the vision of a heavenly chariot at the time of Adam's death. The rest of the book (45-51) deals with the death of Adam and God's mercy for him, at the intercession of the angels, and with the death and burial of Eve.

The book is not particularly important, but it discloses a vivid and poetic imagination, as for instance when we read that when Eve ate of the forbidden fruit all the trees, except the fig tree, lost their leaves; but when God entered Eden on his cherubim chariot, all the trees blossomed forth (Apoc. of Mos. 20:4; 22:3). It is generally inferred from the little apocalypse in ch. 29 that the temple of Herod was still standing (29:6 f.), so that the book was written in Aramaic between 20 B.C. and A.D. 70. A date in the first half of the first century is probable from other indications as well.

The so-called *Martyrdom of Isaiah* is a legendary work comprising with two other tracts a composite Christian book on Isaiah, called the Ascension of Isaiah. This book consists of the Martyrdom (1:1-2a, 6b-13a; 2:1-3:12; 5:1b-14; the rest in these chapters is Christian); the Vision of Isaiah (3:13-4:18, Christian). The work as a whole is extant only in Ethiopic.[13] The extant Ethiopic text was translated from the Greek; it is only for the parts of chs. 1-5 listed above that we may postulate a Jewish original written in Aramaic, but C. C. Torrey regards this assumption as extremely questionable. In brief, chs. 1-5 (omitting 3:13-4:18) tell how Isaiah prophesied to Hezekiah that his son Manasses would serve Beliar instead of Jehovah, and so it actually happened. Isaiah and his followers fled to the wilderness, but a certain Balkira (in Greek and Latin texts *Bechira*, meaning "the chosen one" in Aramaic) accused Isaiah and the prophet was "sawn asunder" (Hebrews 11:37) with a

[13] The Ethiopic text was first published with Latin and English translations by R. Laurence (*Ascensio Isaiae vatis*. Oxford, 1819), and in a critical edition, together with the remnants of the Latin text by A. Dillmann (*Ascensio Isaiae*. Leipzig, 1877). The Vision (chs. 6-11) was known long before, having been printed at Venice in 1522 (reprinted by Gieseler at Göttingen in 1832) according to the text of the Old Latin version. A papyrus sheet of the fifth or sixth century gives 2:4-4:4 in Greek (Grenfell and Hunt, *The Amherst Papyri*, Pt. I, pp. 1-22. London, 1900). All this material, and also the Slavic version of chs. 6-11, was collected by R. H. Charles in his book, *The Ascension of Isaiah translated from the Ethiopic Version* (London, 1900); see also E. Tisserant, *Ascension d'Isaïe* (Paris, 1909) and E. Hennecke (ed.), *Neutestamentliche Apokryphen*, 2nd ed., pp. 303-314 (Tübingen, 1924).

wood (not a "wooden") saw. The interpolated Vision of Isaiah (3:13-4:18) reports that Balkira had been inspired by the devil (Beliar), who was indignant with Isaiah because he had prophesied the coming redemption through Jesus Christ, as also the history of Christianity to the Neronian persecution and the Last Judgment. The Ascension (chs. 6-11) reports that Isaiah was translated in a vision to the firmament, the six lower heavens, and finally to the highest heaven, where he saw the righteous dead and God himself. God announced the coming of Jesus, and Isaiah returned to the firmament. There (ch. 11) he witnessed the future birth, life, crucifixion, and resurrection of Jesus Christ; after which Isaiah took possession again of his earthly body.

As preserved in Greek, Ethiopic, Armenian, and Slavic, the so-called *Paralipomena*[14] *of Jeremiah the Prophet* are manifestly Christian (cf. ch. 9), but a Jewish legendary work may have been utilized. The content is briefly as follows: God, shortly before the fall of Jerusalem in 586, ordered Jeremiah to bury the Temple vessels and go to Babylonia, leaving Baruch in Jerusalem (1-4). Abimelech the Ethiopian, sent by Jeremiah to gather figs in the orchard of Agrippa (*sic!*), went to sleep there and did not awake until sixty-six years later; an old man then informed him of the intervening events (5). Baruch met Abimelech and, according to God's command, wrote to Jeremiah to drive away the foreigners from the midst of the Jews before the nation would return to Jerusalem; the letter and some figs, still fresh after sixty-six years, were delivered to Jeremiah by an eagle (6), which convinced Jeremiah by resurrecting a corpse. When Jeremiah led the Jews back, the men who would not divorce their Babylonian wives were excluded both from Jerusalem and from Babylon, and thus founded the city of Samaria (7-8). Jeremiah fainted while offering sacrifice; regaining consciousness after three days, he praised God for the redemption through Jesus Christ (9). While the last chapter (9) is manifestly Christian, the zeal for the dissolution of mixed marriages is typically Jewish and contrary to the Christian point of view (I Cor. 7:12 f.; I Pet. 3:1). We may regard chs. 1-8 as basically Jewish.

Great imagination is also disclosed in a third type of Aramaic literature, apocalypse, which flourished from 165 B.C. to A.D. 90, after which it was ignored by normative Judaism, although Daniel—the earliest and best specimen—had been included in the Scriptures. Apocalyptic writings purport to be divine revelations made to a noted Biblical character of long ago (from Adam to Ezra, after whom prophecy was said to have

[14] *Paralipomena* (in the title given in Greek manuscripts) means "omitted (or remaining) acts."

ceased). They are usually in the form of visions interpreted by an angel, or in the form of conducted tours through the heavens and other inaccessible parts of the world. The actual date of such books can be determined fairly exactly when they contain a history of the past up to the author's own time, in the form of a prediction of future events. When the author began to predict events which were still in the future, he inevitably became vague or mistaken, and thus unwittingly disclosed his own date.

The *Book of Enoch* (Ethiopic Enoch or I Enoch) is a library rather than a book, probably written in the course of a century (163-63 B.C.). The main divisions of the book are: I. 1-36; II. 37-71; III. 72-82; IV. 83-90; V. 91-105; VI. 106-107; 108. Their contents may be summarized as follows:

I. Introduction (1-5); angels and universe (6-36). A. The angels revealed to Enoch God's appearance in judgment, to punish the sinners and reward the elect (1-5). B. The fall of the angels (cf. Gen. 6:1-4): the fallen angels procreated the giants and taught men the wicked arts of civilization (6-8), but their punishment was imminent and would be followed by the golden age (9-11). Enoch interceded for the fallen angels, but was ordered to proclaim their doom (12-16). Enoch's first journey through the extreme parts of the earth brought him to the place where the fallen angels would be punished (17-20). Enoch's second journey led him from the prison of the angels to the underworld, to the tree of life, to the holy mountain in the middle of the earth (Zion), to the eastern end of the earth, and to the northern, western, and southern ends (21-36).

II. The Parables (or Similitudes) of Enoch (37-71). A. The first parable (38-44): the judgment of the wicked (38); the dwellings of the righteous (39); the millions of angels and the four archangels, Michael, Raphael, Gabriel, Phanuel (40); the "secrets of the heavens" or the mysteries of meteorology and astronomy (41-44). B. The second parable (45-57): the lot of apostates (45); the coming of the Messiah, "the Son of Man" (the elect one), and his wisdom (46-49), the triumph of the righteous (50), the resurrection and the judgment (51), the destruction of the seven metal mountains (52), the valley of judgment and the destruction of mankind through the Flood (53-54), the punishment of the fallen angels and of the heathen kingdoms (55-57). C. The third parable (58-71): the bliss of the saved (58), the secrets of lightning and thunder (59), Leviathan and Behemoth (60), the Messiah's judgment of the elect (61) and his triumph over the rulers of the earth (62-63), the punishment of the fallen angels (64), the prediction of the Flood and of Noah's escape (65:1-67:3), the punishment of fallen angels and earthly rulers (67:4-69:25), conclusion (69:26-29). Enoch taken to heaven and his description of what he saw (70-71).

III. The astronomical book entitled "The Book on the courses of the heavenly luminaries" (72-82): the sun (72), the moon (73), the lunar and solar years (74-75), the twelve winds (76), the four quarters, the seven mountains, the seven rivers, and the seven islands (77), the sun and the moon (78), general summary (79:1-80:1), nature's degeneration as a result of human sin (80-2-8), the heavenly tablets (81:1-4), Enoch's return to his home (81:5-10); the calendar (82).

IV. Two visions (83-90). A. The vision of the Flood (83-84). B. The vision of the history of Israel under the allegory of oxen, sheep, shepherds, and wild beasts (85-90): Adam and Eve (85), the fall of the angels (86) and their punishment by the seven archangels (87-88), Noah and the Flood (89:1-10), from the death of Noah to the Exodus (89:10-27), Moses and Joshua (89:28-40), the Judges and the Kings, to the building of the Temple (89:41-50), decadence to the destruction of the Temple (89:51-67); the four subsequent periods (according to the scheme $12+23+23+12=70$): 1. the Exile (89:68-71); 2. from Cyrus to Alexander (89:72-77); 3. from Alexander to Antiochus Epiphanes and the Maccabean revolt (90:1-12); 4. the Hasmonean rule and the heathen onslaught on the Jews (90:13-19), the final judgment of the wicked (90:20-27), the Messianic age (90:28-42).

V. Miscellaneous. A. Introductory exhortations (92:1-5 and 91:1-11, 18 f.). B. The Apocalypse of Weeks (93:1-10 and 91:12-17, in this order; 93:11-14 seems to be intrusive). Human history is divided into ten weeks, seven actual and three apocalyptic, as follows: 1. Enoch; 2. Noah; 3. Abraham; 4. Moses; 5. building of the Temple; 6. Elijah; 7. an apostate generation (93:3-10); 8. the attack on the wicked; 9. revelation of the judgment; 10. the judgment and the Messianic age (91-12-17). C. Exhortations to the righteous and denunciations against the sinners, whose opposite fates will be determined at the Last Judgment (94-105). D. Appendices: the birth of Noah (106-107); the torments of the sinners and the bliss of the righteous (108).

The dates of the several sections cannot always be determined with accuracy but for general orientation may be set down approximately as follows (all dates are B.C.):[15]

I. A Introduction (1-5): 150-100.

I. B. Angels and Universe (6-36): 100.

II. Parables or Similitudes (37-71): 100-80.

III. Astronomical Book (72-82): 150-100.

---

[15] The latest discussions on the dating of the parts of Enoch are in H. H. Rowley, *The Relevance of Apocalyptic*, pp. 75-80; and C. C. Torrey, *The Apocryphal Literature*, pp. 111-114 (New Haven, 1945). Both reject the theory of R. H. Charles, according to whom chs. 6-39 and 93:1-10; 91:12-17 are pre-Maccabean (so also O. Eissfeldt, *Einleitung in das Alte Testament*, p. 674, for the Apocalypse of Weeks in 93;91) and therefore earlier than Daniel. Torrey dates the whole book about the year 95.

IV. A. First Dream Vision (83-84): 163-130.

IV. B. Second Dream Vision or Apocalypse of the Seventy Shepherds (85-90): 163-130.

V. A. Introduction (92:1-5; 91:1-11, 18 f.): 100-80.

V. B. Apocalypse of Weeks (93:1-10; 91:12-17): 163.

V. C. Final Judgment (94-105): 100-80.

V. D. Appendices (106-108): 100-80.

In its entirety the Book of Enoch is extant only in Ethiopic, a version made from the Greek version of which only a part has survived,[16] made from a Semitic text which, according to Charles, was partly Hebrew (1-5, 37-104) and partly Aramaic (6-36), while C. C. Torrey has convincingly argued that the whole was written in Aramaic (JAOS 62 [1942] 52-60; *The Apocryphal Literature*, p. 114).[17]

The various parts of Enoch dealing with apocalyptic and eschatological matters are far from uniform in their notions of the future. The earliest parts are probably the Apocalypse of Weeks (in 93 and 91) and the Apocalypse of the Seventy Shepherds or of Symbolic Animals, as it is called in German (85-90, together with 83-84). Both sections, like Daniel written shortly before (164), present the panorama of history down to the time of the writer and beyond, culminating in the Last Judgment. But in contrast with Dan. 12:2, neither document clearly proclaims the resurrection from the dead (which R. H. Charles and others erroneously infer from 90:33). It should be perhaps stated that in Daniel, as in these two sections, the glorious future promised to the Jews is terrestrial, not celestial, in spite of the fact that the fallen angels, the seventy shepherds, and the apostate Jews are cast into the fiery abyss (90:20-27): for this abyss is in the midst of the earth (90:26). The New Jerusalem is likewise on this earth (90:28-36), and the Messiah—the white bull with great horns—is a terrestrial ruler (90:37 f.). The Final Judgment is likewise depicted in chs. 1-5, not as a courtroom scene (such as Dan. 7) but as an appearance of the Lord in glory, without any thought of the resurrection: the outlook there is likewise purely terrestrial. There is no reason for assuming that Daniel's new doctrine of the resurrection was immediately adopted by the majority of the Jews— quite the contrary: Ecclesiastes takes pains to deny it.

[16] Chapters 1:1-32:6, in an eighth century Greek manuscript, were discovered in a Christian tomb at Akhmim in upper Egypt (1886-1887) and published by M. Bouriant (1892) and others. Besides some fragments preserved by Syncellus and in manuscripts, chs. 97-107 (ch. 105 is missing) were published from Egyptian papyri by Campbell Bonner, *The Last Chapters of Enoch in Greek.* London, 1937.

[17] F. Perles (OLZ 16 [1913] 481 ff.) argued for a Hebrew original. F. Zimmermann (JBL 60 [1941] 159-172) has maintained that chs. 1-5, 37:1-90:12, 98-104 were written in Hebrew, and the rest in Aramaic.

As in 1-5, so in 6-36 there is no mention of a Messiah. The judgment in 6-36 is not in the immediate future (as in Daniel and in Enoch 85-90) and it is not a vindication of the Jews through their triumph over the Gentiles. It is still far in the future, for a special abode is provided for the souls of the dead in the interim (22:2 f.) and righteous and wicked are separated therein (22:8-13); and after the resurrection (20:8), the wicked Jews will be condemned to eternal torment, while the righteous Jews will enjoy a happy life on earth—after partaking of the fruit of the tree of life. This tree was transplanted from Eden to a high mountain of God (where it was inaccessible) and thence to the Temple for the benefit of the righteous and elect (25:4-6); whether they will also partake of the tree of knowledge (32:3-6) is not stated, but is not to be excluded.

Of the so-called Similitudes or Parables of Enoch (37-71), the first (38-44) gives a general description of the eternal abodes of the wicked and the righteous, after the judgment, while the second (45-57) is important for its development of the theme of the "Son of Man" (cf. Dan. 7:9-14). But while in Daniel the one like a son of man was a symbol of the congregation of the pious Jews, here this figure is definitely an individual, the supernatural Messiah,[18] as sometimes in the New Testament, where the expression may also mean "a human being" or "I" (Jesus). Elsewhere "the Son of Man" occurs in the sense of a superhuman Messiah only in II (IV) Esd. 13:3, 5, 12, 25, 51, cf. 32; and Sibylline Oracles 5:414. In the presence of the Messiah the powerful men of this earth who have not acted justly will be consumed as straw in the flames (48:8-10), while others who witness this will repent (50). Then the (Jewish) dead will rise out of their graves and the righteous will inherit the earth (51). In a deep valley, Enoch saw the angels of punishment preparing instruments of torture and enormous chains for the punishment of the unrighteous rulers and the fallen angels, respectively (53; 54:1-6; 55:3 f.; 56:1-4). The heathen hordes ("Parthians and Medes") will invade Palestine but destroy one another (56:5-8), and the Jews will return from this dispersion (57). Similar is the picture of the Messianic age in the third parable (see chs. 58, 61-64; 67-69).

Such a picture of the judgment and of the final fate of the righteous and the wicked (but without the coming of the Messiah) is painted in chs. 91-105 (omitting the Apocalypse of Weeks in 93; 91, and ch. 105)

[18] On the Son of Man, see Enoch 46:2-4; 48:2 (in the second parable) and Enoch 62:5, 7, 9, 14; 63:11; 69:26 f., 29; 70:1; 71:14, 17 (in the third parable). Other terms for the Messiah are: [God's] Anointed (52:4); the Elect One (39:6; 40:5; 45:3 f.; 49:2, 4; 51:3, 5, 13; 52:6, 9; 55:4; 61:5, 8, 10; 62:1); the Righteous One (38:2; 53:6).

but in a hortatory rather than descriptive style. The skeptical teaching of Ecclesiastes, according to which there is no difference in the fate of the righteous and the wicked either before or after their death (102:6-11), is here disproved by a series of woes against the wicked and assurances to the righteous that even if they die before receiving a reward for their piety they shall be raised from the dead (91:10; 92:3-5) and their spirits will enjoy all joy and prosperity on this earth forever (103:1-4). There is no resurrection for the wicked: after the judgment their spirits will be eternally tormented in the underworld by means of darkness, chains, and fire (103:7 f.), or be actually annihilated there (99:11).

Just as Enoch is explicitly quoted in the Epistle of Jude (vv. 14 f.; cf. Enoch 1:9), so, according to Origen (*De principiis* 3:2, 1), Jude v. 9 refers to the dispute between Michael and the devil for the body of Moses, described in the *Assumption of Moses*. What appears to be the first part of such a work (lacking this dispute) was published by A. M. Ceriani in 1861 in an old Latin version, based on a Greek translation made from the Aramaic original. If such was the case, the first part of this book (Ceriani's text) was apocalyptic, and the second (now lost except for a few quotations) was legendary. It is not certain, as R. H. Charles believes, that the two parts were originally two separate books— the Testament and the Assumption of Moses, respectively.

The contents of the book, as published by Ceriani, is as follows. In Transjordania, after the exodus from Egypt, Moses gave to Joshua the following revelation of the future (1:1-9): Since his life was approaching its end, Moses delivered to Joshua the esoteric books, to be hidden until God's visitation at the end of time (1:10-18). Israel will occupy the land of promise, and twenty kings will rule over Judah (2). But Nebuch-adnezzar will destroy Jerusalem and the Temple, and the captives whom he will exile will remember that all this had been predicted by Moses (3). Through the intercession of Daniel the Lord will again have mercy on them and through Cyrus send the exiles back to Jerusalem, but some of them will lament because they cannot offer sacrifices in the rebuilt Temple—presumably because it stood under the authority of pagan kings and was served by worldly priests (4). Under such Hellenizing high priests ("slaves sons of slaves") as Jason and Menelaus the Jews will be divided on the issue of Hellenism (5).[19] Antiochus IV Epiphanes will then persecute the Jews and force idolatry upon them (8). But "a

---

[19] Chs. 8-9 should be read between chs. 5 and 6, as C. C. Torrey convincingly suggests: a leaf of the Latin text was accidentally misplaced. R. H. Charles regards the transposition as deliberate. C. Lattey (*Catholic Biblical Quarterly* 4 [1942] 11-21), followed by H. H. Rowley (*The Relevance of Apocalyptic*, p. 87), prefers to transfer only ch. 8 after 5.

man of the tribe of Levi named *Taxo*" (i.e., Mattathias),[20] will persuade his seven sons to defy the despot's edict and to choose death rather than transgression of the Law (9). But the Hasmonean rulers will illegally become high priests, only to be wiped out eventually by Herod the Great, who will reign harshly during thirty-four years; his sons (Archelaus, Antipas, and Philip) will rule shorter periods (which is not true of Antipas and Philip). Varus (4 B.C.) will take many captives (6). Then will come the end of time (i.e., the time of the author). It is a time of wickedness, gluttony, iniquity, rapacity (7). But God will manifest himself, Satan will be destroyed, the earth will shake, the sun will be dark, water will disappear, and God will destroy the heathen and Israel will triumph (10). Joshua was greatly perturbed at these words of Moses (11), but Moses reassured him that his own strength was sufficient and that Israel would never be rooted out (12).

The date of this book is clear from ch. 6. The author wrote after the death of Herod the Great and the war of Varus (4 B.C.), but before the end of the rule of Antipas (A.D. 39) and Philip (A.D. 34): we may say after the deposition of Archelaus in A.D. 6 and before A.D. 30, while Jesus was alive.

In this book (ch. 10) the Kingdom of God is no longer terrestrial; there is neither Messiah nor resurrection. The picture presented here seems to be a development of that in Enoch 91-104 (omitting the Apocalypse of Weeks). Without human assistance, the Lord, when he appears in glory, will annihilate Satan; Michael will avenge Israel of its enemies (10:2); God will himself punish the Gentiles, and Israel will, in addition to heavenly bliss, have the unceasing pleasant spectacle of the torments of its enemies in Gehenna (10:10)—a form of eternal amusement which may not appeal to everyone.

The latest Aramaic apocalypses written in Palestine, still extant, date from the tragic aftermath of the war against the Romans in A.D. 66-70. The national ruin not only gave to these writings an extremely pessimistic tone, but naturally stressed the eternal fate of the individual in the invisible world, rather than the Messianic triumph and dominion of the Jews in the visible world. The two books that now engage our attention are II [IV] Esdras and the Apocalypse of Baruch (both written in Aramaic about A.D. 90). The Revelation of St. John is a Christian writing

---

[20] On the identity of "Taxo" see H. H. Rowley, *The Relevance of Apocalyptic*, pp. 128-132. The most plausible suggestion is that of C. C. Torrey (JBL 62 [1943] 1-7; 64 [1945] 395-397; cf. Rowley, in JBL 64 [1945] 141-143), who sees in this cipher a *gematria* of the Aramaic form of "The Hasmonean" (i.e., Mattathias, the father of Judas Maccabeus and his successors). S. Zeitlin ("The Assumption of Moses and the revolt of Bar Kokba" in JQR N.S. 38 [1947] 1-45) identifies *Taxo* with Greek *tóxon* (bow, Hebr. *kesheth*), cf. Zech. 6:12, and refers it to Rabbi Joshua, who opposed the revolt of the Jews against Hadrian (A.D. 132-135).

from about the same time, but it incorporates with slight revisions Jewish apocalyptic writings (notably in Rev. 19:11-21:8 and 21:9-22:20) which seem to be earlier than the destruction of Jerusalem by Titus in 70 and depict at the end of time a golden age on this earth, with the New Jerusalem as the center of the theocracy in which death, sorrow, and wailing will disappear forever.

II (IV) *Esdras*, or the Apocalypse of Ezra, is extant in an old Latin version (in which chs. 1-2 and 15-16 have been added by a Christian hand), printed at the end of the editions of the Vulgate Bible; and in some Oriental versions (Syriac, Ethiopic, Arabic, Armenian, Georgian; also a Coptic fragment) lacking these Christian chapters at the beginning and at the end. The original Aramaic text of the book was lost soon after it was translated into Greek. The Greek version also is lost, but all extant ancient texts were translated from it. Disregarding the four Christian chapters, the book consists of six visions of Shealtiel (*Salatiel*), the father (Ezra 3:2; 5:2; Neh. 12:1) or uncle (I Chron. 3:17) of Zerubbabel; and of Ezra's report on the restoration of the sacred books (ch. 14). A redactor identified Shealtiel with Ezra (3:1; cf. the references to Ezra in 6:10; 7:2, 25; 8:2), although the latter lived a century after him. Shealtiel allegedly saw these visions thirty years after the destruction of Jerusalem in 586 B.C. (i.e., in 556). The first three visions (3:1-9:25) deal with the problem of theodicy, or the reconciliation of God's justice, goodness, wisdom, and power with the evils besetting human life. The last three visions bring comfort to those troubled by that insoluble problem through the assurance that the present age is at its end and a golden age without evil and sorrows is at hand. We may summarize briefly these six parts and ch. 14 as follows:

I. Sin and Israel's misery contradict divine justice (3:1-5:20). In Babylonia in 556 B.C., Shealtiel was troubled by Jerusalem's desolation and Babylon's prosperity (3:1-3) and addressed his complaint to God. God's interventions from the creation to the revelation of the Law to Moses did not remove the evil impulse that Adam passed on to all men (3:4-22). Sin continued in Jerusalem after the building of Solomon's Temple and the city was delivered by God into the hands of his enemies: why did he destroy his people and preserve his enemies (3:23-36)? The angel Uriel answered that the human mind could not comprehend the ways of God (4:1-11). To the complaint that it would have been better for man not to have been created than to sin and suffer without understanding why, the angel replied that it was foolish to attempt to defy the laws of nature and understand what was beyond one's experience (4:12-21). To the objection that the question was not beyond daily experience, since it sought the reason for Israel's ruin at the hand of triumphing heathen, the angel replied that the seed of evil must produce evil fruit; but the age of evil was near its end (4:22-32). "When?" When the treasuries where the souls of the righteous dead were housed became full to the bursting point (4:33-43). In any case the evil time that was past was much longer than the remaining period (4:44-50). The age to come will be preceded by dreadful cosmic signs and great panic (4:51-5:13). The prophet awoke from his trance greatly shaken and fasted for seven days (5:14-20).

II. Renewed complaints about Israel's affliction (5:21-6:34). After those seven days, the seer addressed God again in prayer. Why did he deliver unto the heathen the nation of his choice (5:21-30)? Again the angel demonstrated man's inability to understand God's judgment and his love (5:31-40). The seer inferred that the last generation of men, who would witness the coming of the new age, would be the most fortunate and wondered why all generations could not have lived at that time. The reply is that the generations must follow one another (5:41-49); Mother Earth has become old and the last generations are inferior to the early ones (5:50-55). God alone created the world, and he will bring about its end by himself alone (5:56-6:6). The age to come will follow the present one without any perceptible interval (6:7-10) and will be preceded by the signs of the end (6:11-24; cf. 4:51-5:13)[21] which usher in a time of conversion and salvation (6:25-29). The seer should be of good cheer (6:30-34).

III. The few righteous will be saved in the age to come, but the multitude of the wicked will perish (6:35-9:25). After seven days of fasting (6:35-37) the seer reminded God that he had created the world in six days (6:38-54, cf. Gen. 1) for the benefit of Israel: why then did not the Jews possess the earth (6:55-59)? The angel replied: after Adam's transgression the ways of this earth became narrow and painful for the Jews, who needed to traverse them to reach the future world, which belonged to them alone, leaving this corruptible world to the heathen (7:1-16). Is the bliss of the future age only for the righteous Jews or for all the Jews (7:17 f.)? Reply: for righteous Israel; the Jews have sinned, but the heathen have blasphemed God and his Law as no Jew has done (7:19-25). At the end of this age the Messiah ("My Son") will rule for four-hundred years and die with his generation: then will the primeval silence prevail seven days (7:26-30). The general resurrection, and the final judgment (lasting seven years), will inaugurate the age to come, when Gehenna and Paradise will be revealed (7:31-44).[22] Again it was

---

[21] Worthy of notice are here the sealing of this world and the opening of the book of judgment (6:20), and the blowing of the trumpet (6:23).

[22] The verses numbered here 7:36-105 (as in the Revised Version) are missing from the standard editions of the Vulgate and from the Authorized Version. Consequently 7:36-70 in the Vulgate and the A.V. are here numbered 7:106-140.

stated (cf. 7:17-25) that, though all men were sinful, the Jews alone deserved salvation; a handful will thus be saved, while the heathen, having rejected the Law, must perish (7:45-61). The seer lamented for the human race, but the angel assured him that it deserved its lot (7:62-74). After death, the souls of the wicked did not occupy dwellings, like those of the righteous (cf. 4:35, 41), but wandered about, suffering seven types of torture (7:75-87), while the souls of the righteous were gathered in their chambers and were happy for seven reasons (7:88-101). No intercession of the righteous for the wicked availed anything on the day of judgment (7:102-115). The seer objected that Adam was the cause of human sinfulness, but was assured that each man must wage his own contest in his lifetime and was responsible for his eternal perdition (7:116-131); therefore, despite God's mercy, many were created but few saved (7:132-8:3). Why should God fashion and sustain human beings with such care, only to destroy them—notably in the case of his own people (8:4-19a)? The seer prayed for God's mercy toward Israel (8:19b-36), and God replied that he rejoiced in the righteous and forgot the sinners (8:37-40): the seer should do likewise, for his lot is with the saved (8:41-62). The signs of the end were described a third time (8:63-9:13; cf. 4:51-5:13; 6:11-24), and the small number of the saved was explained a last time (9:14-22). The seer should fast and pray seven more days (9:23-25).

IV. The vision of the Mourning Woman (i.e., Zion) and the New Jerusalem (9:26-10:60). After seven days (9:26-28), the seer lamented that Israel, the receptacle of the Law, must perish, while the Law was eternal (9:29-37). He suddenly saw at his right a mourning woman (9:38). She told him that after thirty years of marriage she gave birth to a son, but he fell dead upon entering his bridal chamber on the wedding night: having fled, she would now fast until she died (9:39-10:4). The seer rebuked her for not weeping over the ruin of Zion (10:5-24). Then her countenance lit up and after a loud cry she disappeared, and a city stood in her place (10:25-28). The angel Uriel explained the vision: the weeping woman, Zion, was barren thirty years, meaning the three-thousand years from the creation to the building of Solomon's Temple; the death of her son was a symbol of the destruction of Jerusalem in 586 B.C.; and the city which appeared, the New Jerusalem, was shown to him for his encouragement (10:29-60).

V. The vision of the Eagle (11-12). In a dream the seer beheld an eagle rising from the sea: it had twelve wings and three heads; from the wings eight "antiwings" (wings with contrary feathers) grew, but they became small. The heads, of which the central was the largest, were at rest. The eagle dominated the whole earth. A voice from within the eagle ordered the wings to rule in succession before the three heads, and so they did, the second ruling more than twice as long as the other eleven. Then two little wings ruled, and nothing was left except the three heads and six small wings: two little wings separated themselves and remained under the head on the right; two others ruled briefly in succession, and the last two were eaten by the heads. The middle head ruled over the earth and disappeared; the two other heads ruled until the one on the right devoured the one on the left (11:1-35). Then a lion shouted at the eagle that it was the fourth beast to which God had given universal dominion, but that now it must disappear to free the earth of its violence (11:36-46). So the remaining body of the eagle was burned (12:1-3a). The angel then gave the interpretation of this vision: the eagle was the fourth of the world kingdoms in Daniel (Dan. 7:7 f., 23), i.e., the Roman Empire[23] (not the Seleucid kingdom, as in Daniel), and the wings and heads were Roman emperors (a total of 23: 12 wings, 8 "antiwings," and three heads). The most probable interpretation is that Julius Caesar is the first wing and Augustus the second (whose rule was reckoned at fifty-six years from his first consulate in 43 B.C.); that the three heads are Vespasian, Titus, and Domitian and that the book was written during the rule of the last (A.D. 81-96). But it appears that the text as we have it has been so supplemented and altered after Domitian that it is no longer comprehensible (12:3b-30). The lion is the Messiah under whose rule the Jews will rejoice until the day of judgment (12:31-34). The seer is to write these things in an esoteric book and teach them to the wise only (12:35-51).

VI. The Man (Son of Man) coming from the sea (13). The seer saw in another dream a storm at sea and a figure of a man (i.e., the Messiah) emerging from the depths of the sea and flying "with" the clouds of heaven (cf. Dan. 7:13). A multitude gathered to fight him, but, flying upon a mountain, he annihilated it through fire proceeding from his mouth; then he gathered a peaceful multitude (13:1-13). The interpretation is that the man from the sea is the one through whom God will redeem his creation after destroying the hostile powers, gathering his subjects (i.e., the ten tribes of Israel), and defending the remnants of the Jews in Palestine (13:14-58).

VII. Ezra's restoration of the sacred books (14). Ezra received a revelation from the Lord: he should instruct his people, and prepare to be taken up from this world to be with the Messiah, for of twelve periods of the world nine and a half have passed (14:1-17); he is ordered to withdraw with five scribes from his people for forty days (14:18-26) and after a final admonition to the people (14:27-36) he dictated ninety-four books to the five scribes, twenty-four (the Hebrew Bible or Old Testa-

[23] The same interpretation of Dan. 7:23 is given in the Babylonian Talmud (*Aboda Zara* 1b).

ment) he was to publish, but seventy (esoteric and apocalyptic) books were intended only for the wise among the people (14:37-48). Then he was taken to heaven (14:49 f.).

This apocalyptic work of the latter part of the first century of our era is one of the most notable and brilliant of the lot. The problem of theodicy in its individual aspect had previously disturbed the author of the Book of Job: if God is almighty and just, why do so many upright persons go through life tormented by sickness and poverty, while they see godless and wicked people prospering and enjoying good health and happiness? The author of Job had concluded that the problem had no rational solution but, except for a few moments, he refused to let his imagination provide an irrational explanation based on belief in the unreal. The author of II (IV) Esdras differed from the author of Job in two respects: he debated the problem of theodicy not only from its individualistic aspects (both Jewish and Gentile), but also from the national point of view, according to which Israel was God's chosen people and suffered beyond its deserts, as shown by the contrast between Jerusalem and Babylon; in the second place, the brilliant author fully realized, like Job, that rational solutions are impossible, and deliberately sought comfort in the world of make-believe. In the years following A.D. 70 it could seem that God had abandoned his people into the hands of heathen plunderers; the situation seemed hopeless unless God miraculously intervened in behalf of his people, and somehow rewarded the righteous Jews who strove to do his will.

The author's doubts were aroused by the following facts: Babylon (i.e., Rome) had triumphed over Zion (3:1-3), Israel had been delivered by God into the hand of the heathen (4:23; 5:23-29; 6:57 f.) instead of being punished by God himself (5:30); Israel's sinfulness (3:25 f., 34; 8:16 f.) was incomparably less serious than that of the heathen (3:31-36), but God had spared his enemies and had destroyed his own people (3:30); if Israel was unworthy of God's mercy, would his Law perish together with Israel, would his holy name be blasphemed by the heathen (4:23-25)? If Israel was God's only chosen people (5:23-27; 6:58), for whom the world was created (6:55; 7:11), why could not Israel possess the earth (6:59)? If it was answered that Adam's fall had brought sin (3:21 f.; 4:30), sorrow, and pain into the world (7:11 f.), and Israel's woes were those common to all mankind (3:7-10), why did God (God alone, 3:4 f.) create Adam with the evil impulse, when he sowed in him "a grain of evil seed" (4:30)? And why did God not restrain its evil influence on Adam's descendants (3:8, 20-22)?

Human conditions in general (as in Job) and Israel's in particular (assuming that it was God's chosen nation) were so tragic and unexplainable that the author sought refuge first in the rational conclusion

that God's ways were incomprehensible to man (4:2-11, 21; 5:36-40)—
but why, then, was man endowed with intelligence (4:22)?—and secondly
in an irrational mirage of a future golden age: the present age was near-
ing its end (4:26-50), the age to come was at hand and would follow
it without interruption (6:7-10), bringing perfect bliss (6:25-28). First
would come the rule of the Messiah for 400 years at the end of this age
(7:26-30), then the resurrection and the judgment (7:31-44). The contrasting fate of the souls of the wicked and the righteous after death
(7:75-101), in their intermediate state before the judgment, anticipated
in a way their eternal bliss in Paradise and their eternal perdition in
Gehenna (7:36-38). Such eschatological outlooks failed, however, to
comfort the seer (i.e., the author), who, though assured of his own
salvation, could not overcome his preference never to have been born
(5:35). He even wished that mankind had never been created, when
he realized that the great mass of mankind—and even the majority in
Israel—would perish without having a part in the bliss of the future
world. None of the explanations given by the angel (7:49-61; 8:1, 3;
etc.) really solved the difficulties in the author's mind.

II (IV) Esdras is a work of a truly great writer and thinker, an
utterly sincere and candid spirit, who strove honestly and earnestly to
solve ultimate problems but finally admitted sadly his failure to explain
the tragic lot of his nation—and of all human beings.[24]

The Apocalypse of Baruch, or *Syriac Baruch* (II Baruch), was written
about the same time as II (IV) Esdras (*ca.* A.D. 90) and presents such
similarities of thought and expression with that book that it is generally
recognized that one of them was influenced by the other, although there
is no agreement as to which one came first. Since it can hardly be disputed that the author of II (IV) Esdras was by far the more original,
more brilliant, and more profound of the two, the present writer (like
O. Eissfeldt and others) is inclined to regard the author of Baruch as
the imitator of a greater thinker. Although both books were soon forgotten by the Jews, Baruch enjoyed far less popularity than Esdras
among the Christians, as shown by the fact that it has survived only in

[24] On the various attempts to analyze II (IV) Esdras into its sources and to deter-
mine the contributions of redactors, see in particular: R. Kabisch, *Das vierte Buch
Esra auf seine Quellen untersucht* (Göttingen, 1889). G. H. Box, *The Ezra Apocalypse*
(London, 1912) and in R. H. Charles, *Pseudepigrapha,* pp. 549-553. W. O. E.
Oesterley, *II Esdras* (Westminster Commentaries. London, 1933). C. C. Torrey, *The
Apocryphal Literature,* pp. 116-123. New Haven, 1945; "A Twice-buried Apocalypse"
(*Munera Studiosa,* edited by M. H. Shepherd, Jr. and S. E. Johnson, pp. 23-39.
The Episcopal Theological School, Cambridge, Massachusetts, 1946). The latest
commentary on this apocalypse is that of W. O. E. Oesterley in the Westminster
series (London, 1933).

a Syriac version (extant complete in a single manuscript) from the Greek text of which a papyrus from Oxyrhynchus preserves parts of chs. 12-14 (printed and translated in R. H. Charles, *Pseudepigrapha*, pp. 487-490). Like Esdras, the Apocalypse of Baruch was originally written in Aramaic and is divided into seven parts, which may be summarized as follows:

I. The fall of Jerusalem in 586 B.C. (1:1-12:4). In the twenty-fifth year of Jeconiah (or Jehoiachin, who ruled three months in 598-597, when he was eighteen years old)—a fantastic date by which the author apparently meant 586 (unless he meant the twenty-fifth year of Jeconiah's life, or 592); contrast the date in II (IV) Esd. 3:1—God revealed to Baruch, Jeremiah's secretary, the coming destruction of Jerusalem (1-4). Baruch complained and was comforted by God (5). On the following day, as the Chaldeans surrounded the city, Baruch saw the earth, obedient to an angelic command, swallow the sacred objects of the Temple (6). The same angel ordered four others, stationed with torches at the four corners of the city, to destroy Jerusalem (7). After they did so, the Chaldeans entered the city and took Zedekiah to Babylon (8). After Baruch's first fast, God sent Jeremiah to Babylonia but Baruch to Zion, where he lamented over its ruin (9:1-12:4).

II. Misgivings of Baruch and divine answers (12:5-20:6). After a second fast lasting seven days, the divine judgment upon the heathen was revealed to Baruch (12:5-13:12). Baruch, however, was troubled by the fact that the righteous Jews failed to save Zion through their merits, and that God's ways were incomprehensible (14). God replied that on account of his sins man failed to understand God; this world was made for the righteous Jews, to give them trouble, and the world to come for their glorification (15). The briefness of this life did not prevent man from acquiring eternal glory if his years were devoted (like those of Moses) to obedience to God's commands (16 f.). If only few followed his example, God is not to be blamed, for he placed life and death before man (18 f.). The fall of Jerusalem hastened the coming of the final judgment (20).

III. The signs of the end and the age to come (21-34). After a third fast of seven days, Baruch prayed (21:1-10) for enlightenment on some disturbing puzzles. Why was human life so miserable (21:11-18)? When would the righteous be rewarded in the age to come (21:19-26)? God replied that until the destiny of the world be accomplished, Baruch should not be troubled by what he failed to understand (22:1-23:2). The total number of mortals who must be born was fixed, and would soon be complete (23:3-7); then would come the judgment (24), preceded by great tribulations (25). These troubles (26) would comprise twelve periods of woes (27 f.)[25] and extend over the whole earth with the exception of Palestine, where the Messiah would be revealed (29:1-3), as also Behemoth and Leviathan—the meat for the Messianic banquet (29:4; cf. II [IV] Esd. 6:49-52; Enoch 60:6-9)—and where the soil would yield miraculous crops, supplemented by the manna from heaven (29:5-8). Then the Messiah would return to heavenly glory or (according to B. Violet, *op. cit.*, p. 246) to rule gloriously on this earth, and the righteous would be raised to happiness, but the wicked consigned to torments (30:2-5). Baruch exhorted the Jews to prepare themselves by observing the Law (31:1-32:1). The Temple would be destroyed again, but would rise again more glorious than ever for all time to come (32:2-4). Let them not be downhearted for the present calamity, for future tribulations would be even more severe (32:5 f.). As Baruch departed, the people complained of being forsaken by him (32:7-33:3), but he promised to return (34).

IV. The vision of the cedar (35-46). After weeping on the ruins of Zion (35), Baruch saw this vision in his sleep. A vine sprang up in front of a forest surrounded by high rocky mountains. A spring came forth from under the vine and near the forest became a stream which uprooted most of the forest and overthrew the mountains surrounding it, leaving only one cedar still standing. After the vine rebuked the cedar, it was consumed by fire while the vine was thriving in the midst of unfading flowers (36 f.; cf. Ez. 17:1-10). In answer to prayer (38), the interpretation was given to Baruch: the forest was the fourth world empire, i.e., the Roman (following the Chaldean, cf. 39:3, the Persian, and the Hellenistic; in Dan. 7 the fourth was the Seleucid kingdom), and the cedar was its last king, executed by "My Messiah" represented by the vine, while the spring represented his dominion (39 f.). Baruch inquired about the fate of apostate Jews and Gentile proselytes (41), and received the desired information (42). He was warned to prepare for further revelations (43) to be made after he had announced to his intimates and to the elders his impending death, assuring them of the glories of the age to come (44-46).

V. The tribulations at the end of this age, the resurrection, and the final lot of the righteous and of the godless (47-52). After another week of fasting (47) and another prayer (48:1-24), the Lord revealed that in the final days of this age the wise would be few and silent; disgrace and strife, oppression and violence, godlessness and weeping would prevail (48:25-41). So Baruch lamented the ruin wrought by Adam and Eve

[25] The reckoning of the time of the end in 28:2 ("two parts a week of seven weeks") is cryptic, and conjectural interpretations vary (cf. E. Kautzsch, *Apocryphen und Pseudepigraphen*, Vol. 2, p. 422, n. *e*). B. Violet (*Die Apocalypsen des Esra und Baruch*, p. 243. Leipzig, 1924) understands two weeks of seven weeks of years each (98 years in all) from the Augustan principate (corresponding to *ca.* A.D. 100).

(48:42-47), and since all men would receive their due, he preferred to think of the final bliss of the righteous (48:48-50). In answer to his plea (49), God described the future resurrection (50) and the final fate of the saved and the damned (51 f.).

VI. Vision of the twelve outpourings of dark and bright rain (53-76). From a cloud rising from the sea, which Baruch saw in a dream, there poured alternatively six black and six bright rainfalls followed by another darker and more devastating than the rest, mingled with fire; finally a clear flash destroyed the cloud and healed the earth, ruling over it and over twelve new rivers ascending from the sea (53). In answer to Baruch's prayer (54), the angel Ramiel was sent to interpret the vision (55), as follows: the black and bright waters represented twelve periods of history from Adam to the Messiah.

<table>
<tr><td colspan="2">Dark Waters</td><td colspan="2">Bright Waters</td></tr>
<tr><td>1.</td><td>Adam's sin (56).</td><td>2.</td><td>Abraham (57).</td></tr>
<tr><td>3.</td><td>Sinful Egyptians (58).</td><td>4.</td><td>Moses, Aaron, Joshua (59).</td></tr>
<tr><td>5.</td><td>Amorite soothsayers (60).</td><td>6.</td><td>David and Solomon (61).</td></tr>
<tr><td>7.</td><td>Jeroboam I, Jezebel (62).</td><td>8.</td><td>Hezekiah (63).</td></tr>
<tr><td>9.</td><td>Manasses (64 f.).</td><td>10.</td><td>Josiah (66).</td></tr>
<tr><td>11.</td><td>The Temple destroyed (67).</td><td>12.</td><td>The Temple rebuilt (68).</td></tr>
</table>

The final dark waters were the tribulations at the end of this age (69-71). The flash of lightning was "My Messiah." He would subjugate all nations which did not know Israel, but destroy those which ruled over the Jews, thus inaugurating the golden age (72-74). Baruch sang a song of thanksgiving (75); he was ordered to instruct the people, and to be ready on top of a mountain forty days later to contemplate the earth in all its details and to be taken alive from among men (76).

VII. Final admonitions of Baruch (77-87). Baruch encouraged the Jews to obey the Law in spite of their present calamity; he wrote a letter to the Babylonian Exiles, sending it by three men; and one to the nine and a half northern tribes, sending it by means of an eagle (77). The text of the latter is given in chs. 78-86. Baruch bound this letter to the neck of the eagle and sent it (87).

The date and the unity of the Apocalypse of Baruch are still discussed by scholars (cf. H. H. Rowley, *The Relevance of Apocalyptic*, pp. 133-135. London, 1944). To the present author the attempts at dissecting it into a number of various works of different date (such as the analysis of R. H. Charles, in *The Apocalypse of Baruch*. London, 1896) are not convincing. Discrepancies in the book are not serious and may be due to the use of divergent sources. The date is close to that of II (IV) Esdras, or about A.D. 90 (32:3 refers to the destruction of the Temple in A.D. 70). The close parallels between the Baruch and the Esdras apocalypse[26] prove that one book was influenced by the other—unless both were written by the same author (which is incredible). Critical opinion is divided on the problem;[27] Esdras is probably the earlier work, chiefly because of its far greater originality and brilliance. Baruch is a veritable thesaurus of Jewish Haggadah known also from rabbinical works of a later date; for numerous typical instances see L. Ginzberg in *The Jewish Encyclopedia* (Vol. 2, pp. 552 f.).

The destruction of Jerusalem by Titus in A.D. 70, and the dreadful suffering of the Jews that followed, produced in the author of Syriac Baruch, as shortly before in the more profound and distinguished writer to whom we owe II (IV) Esdras, a mood of despair, bewilderment, and pessimism (see, e.g., 85:10). The triumph of pagan Rome over holy Zion was inexplicable, and God's reasons and intentions in the matter seemed utterly mysterious. As in an earlier dark period of Jewish history, during the persecutions of Antiochus Epiphanes in 168-165 B.C. (see Daniel), thinkers troubled by these problems could find comfort for the holy congregation of Israel only in utopian dreams. They announced the intervention of Jehovah to destroy the godless ruling empire and to save his people at a not too distant date, either by giving his people the dominion of the whole world (Daniel) or by ushering in the age to come in which the enemies of the Jews would be eliminated from this earth while the pious, living or dead, would enjoy eternal bliss in a land of fantastic fertility (cf. 73-74). With inconsistencies typical of similar eschatological writings, the glorification of the nation under the leadership of the Messiah—involving the reconstruction of Jerusalem (44:7; 71:1), the gathering of the Ten Tribes (78:7; 84:10), and the destruction of the heathen (82:2-9; 85:9)—is loosely connected with the final judgment, the resurrection, and the eternal reward or punishment for each person, the righteous going to Paradise (51:3, 7-14) and the wicked to Gehenna (44:15; 51:1-6). The author was a Pharisee who occasionally, in lamenting the miserable present and in envisioning a glorious future, attained true poetic inspiration and impassioned feeling.

[26] Cf. R. H. Charles, *The Apocalypse of Baruch.* The passages blaming Adam for human misery (II [IV] Esd. 3:7, 21 f.; 4:30; 7:118; Syr. Bar. 17:3; 23:4; 48:42; 54:15, 19) are printed in parallel columns in E. Schürer, *Geschichte*, Vol. 3, p. 310.
[27] Cf. R. H. Charles, *Pseudepigrapha*, p. 477.

B. HELLENISTIC JUDAISM

CHAPTER IV

HELLENISM[1]

~~~~~~~~~~~~~~~~~~~~~~~~~~~~~~~~~~~~

The centuries going from the rule of Alexander the Great (336-323 B.C.) to that of Octavian Augustus (27 B.C.-A.D. 14) are commonly called the Hellenistic period. The culture of this period, since Droysen gave vogue to the term, is incorrectly called "Hellenism"[2] (properly, classical Greek

[1] The brilliant book of Paul Wendland, *Die hellenistisch–römische Kultur in ihren Beziehungen zu Judentum und Christentum* (Handbuch zum Neuen Testament, Vol. I, Part II). Tübingen, 1907; 2nd and 3rd ed., 1912, is still standard and should have been long since translated into English. The following works are the best histories of Hellenism: J. G. Droysen, *Geschichte des Hellenismus*, 2 vols., Gotha, 1836, 1843; 2nd ed., 3 vols. Gotha, 1877. B. Niese, *Geschichte der griechischen und makedonischen Staten seit der Schlacht bei Chaeronea* (Handbücher der alten Geschichte), 3 vols. Gotha, 1893-1903. E. R. Bevan, *The House of Seleucus.* London, 1902; *A History of Egypt under the Ptolemaic Dynasty.* London, 1927. A. Bouché-Leclercq, *Histoire des Lagides*, 2 vols. Paris, 1903 and 1907; *Histoire des Seleucides, Paris,* 1913. W. S. Ferguson, *Hellenistic Athens.* London, 1911; *Greek Imperialism.* London and New York, 1913. F. Baumgarten, F. Poland, R. Wagner, *Die hellenistisch–römische Kultur.* Leipzig and Berlin, 1913. W. Schubart, *Aegypten von Alexander dem grossen bis auf Mohammed.* Berlin, 1922. U. von Wilamowitz-Moellendorff, *Staat und Gesellschaft der Griechen,* 2nd ed. Leipzig and Berlin, 1923. J. B. Bury (and others), *The Hellenistic Age.* Cambridge, 1923. W. Otto, *Kulturgeschichte des Altertums.* Munich, 1925. K. J. Beloch, *Griechische Geschichte,* Vol. 4, in two parts. Berlin and Leipzig, 1925 and 1927. E. Meyer, *Blüte und Niedergang des Hellenismus in Asien.* Berlin, 1925. P. Jouget, *L'impérialisme macédonien et l'hellénisation de l'Orient.* Paris, 1926 (English translation: *Macedonian Imperialism.* London, 1928). J. Kaerst, *Geschichte des Hellenismus,* 2nd ed. Vol. 1, Leipzig, 1917; Vol. 2, 1926. *Cambridge Ancient History,* Vols. VI and following. Cambridge, 1927 ff. W. W. Tarn, *Hellenistic Civilization,* 2nd ed. London, 1930. M. I. Rostovtzeff, *The Social and Economic History of the Hellenistic World,* 3 vols. Oxford and New York, 1941. M. Cary and T. J. Haarhoff, *Life and Thought in the Greek and Roman World.* New York, 1942. C. A. Robinson, *Alexander the Great.* New York, 1947. W. W. Tarn, *Alexander the Great,* 2 vols. Cambridge University Press, 1948. H. I. Bell, *Egypt from Alexander the Great to the Arab Conquest.* Oxford and New York, 1948. On Ptolemaic and Roman-Egypt see also the list in Ida A. Pratt, *Ancient Egypt (1925-1941),* pp. 132-137. The New York Public Library, 1942.

[2] The word "Hellenism" occurs in ancient literature (*hellenismós*), meaning the correct use of the Greek language and, in II Macc. 4:13, the adoption of Greek manners (being a synonym of *allophylismós*, the adoption of foreign customs). Similarly, the verb *hellenízein* and the noun *hellenistēs*, which originally referred to the use of the Greek language, came to mean the adoption of Greek culture; on "Hellenist" in Acts 6:1; 9:29, etc., *see* Jackson and Lake, *Beginnings of Christianity,* vol. 5, pp. 59-74. For the connotations of "Hellenism," in ancient and modern times, see R. Laqueur, *Hellenismus.* Giessen, 1925.

culture), thus avoiding the correct—but dreadful—word "Hellenisticism." In view of the fact that art, science, literature, and philosophy in the early centuries of the Roman Empire were essentially Hellenistic (even Rome's greatest creation, jurisprudence, did not escape Greek influence), we may be allowed in this chapter to call the culture from 300 B.C. to A.D. 200 "Hellenism."

1. Historical Sketch

Philip II, king of Macedon (356-336 B.C.), defeated the Greek states at Chaeronea (338) and settled the perennial "Balkan Problem" by forcing them, with the exception of Sparta, to form a Hellenic League. A year later he received from it the mandate to attack Persia. Philip sent Parmenio to Asia Minor with an army in 336, but was assassinated in the same year. His son Alexander the Great was then twenty years of age: faced by a general revolt, he destroyed Thebes and restored order (335). In 334 he crossed over to Asia with an army of 32,000 infantry and 5,000 cavalry, supported by 160 ships. Through the victories at the river Granicus (334) and at Issus (333), through the conquest of Tyre and Gaza (332), through the expedition into Egypt (332-331), and through the victory at Gaugamela near Arbela (331), Alexander became the master of the Persian Empire. Alexander's great plan was to unite the peoples of Greece and Asia into one nation having a common culture. He symbolized this fusion through marriages of Macedonians with Persians. In Bactria he married Roxana; upon his return from India he married Statira, the daughter of the last Persian king, Darius III, and Parysatis, the youngest daughter of Artaxerxes III Ochus. He induced eighty of his highest officers to marry Persian ladies; 10,000 of his men married native women and during this feast of "fraternization" (in the spring of 324) Alexander paid all the debts of his men, at a cost of almost 10,000 talents (about fifteen million dollars).

When Alexander died in 323, his empire fell apart. After the battle of Ipsus (301), Ptolemy I added Coele-Syria to Egypt, Seleucus I received Syria in addition to Mesopotamia, Asia Minor was divided between Lysimachus and Pleistarchus, and Cassander retained control of Macedon.

The conquests of Alexander and the rule of his successors are less significant politically than culturally in the history of Egypt and Western Asia. The transition from the Persian to the Macedonian rule did not affect the life of populations long used to foreign rule; some of the Persian satraps were even left in office by Alexander until he found it expedient to substitute Macedonian ones. But the Macedonians (notably their upper classes, who had been Hellenized) and the Greeks felt themselves charged with the diffusion of Greek civilization,[3] which even their military success per se confirmed as superior. Alexander, who had been a pupil of Aristotle (384-322), attached to his general staff Greek scholars and scientists, mostly trained by Aristotle: geographers, called Bematists or surveyors (Baeton, Diogenes, Amyntas), whose observations were utilized by Dicaearchus; botanists, notably Theophrastus, whose geography and physiology of plants laid the foundations of scientific botany; historians, both professional (Callisthenes) and amateur (Nearchus described his sea voyage from India; Androsthenes reported his exploration of the Persian Gulf; Ptolemy and Aristobulus reported military campaigns); ethnographers, zoologists, mineralogists, hydrographers, and others. Unfortunately this mass of important scientific material, with the exception of the botanical works of Theophrastus, has been lost, although much of it was preserved indirectly and partially in the works of later Hellenistic and Roman scientists.

It is primarily in the scientific field that the Greeks surpassed all other ancient nations. Egypt, Babylonia, and, at a much later date, China had in very early times reached a relatively high level of civilization, but, owing perhaps to the brilliance of the initial achievement, they soon became fixed and crystallized, never fulfilling their early promises: the Egyptian art of 2800 B.C. is superior to that of 280 B.C. Their achievements are primarily in the field of plastic arts, practical devices, and measures contributing to human comfort. But in the intellectual field there is little to be said: no great literature (aside from Israel and India) was produced in ancient Egypt and Asia; their science remained practical; philosophy (i.e., the feeling that there is a problem of the universe) is unknown outside of India; mathematics as a science of abstract intangibles was inaugurated by the Greeks.

It was thus inevitable that the civilization of Greece should make a great impression on all peoples reached by the armies of Alexander. The Greeks had of course long been aware of their superior culture,[4] and called those who did not speak Greek "barbarians" (literally "babblers, stammerers"): they regarded it as their mission to spread their civilization and regarded language as a primary factor in culture—both entirely new notions. Nevertheless, they found much to admire in Egypt and in the Near East, particularly the great works of art and the mysterious

[3] In modern times this education of the "natives" is quaintly called "the white man's burden," although it usually proves to be quite lucrative. The Bantu in equatorial and Southern Africa say, "At first we had the land and the white man had the Bible. Now we have the Bible and the white man has the land."

[4] As early as 380 B.C., Isocrates could say that as a result of the spread of Athenian culture, "the name 'Hellene' now no longer means racial origin, but indicates spiritual character, mentality; and those called 'Hellenes' are not so much blood relations as those who partake of our education" (*Panegyric* 50).

wisdom of the East (notably in India), which has always fascinated the West (especially when it was idealized and misunderstood). Strangely, however, no Greek scholar ever learned to read hieroglyphs and cunei-forms.

On the other hand, it was inevitable that the peoples of Egypt and Western Asia—notably the upper classes—should be impressed by Greek culture, especially when civilian Greeks, following the armies, settled in their midst. Accordingly, many of the Orientals hastened to talk broken Greek, wear Greek attire (Greek hats, worn by the noblest young Jews in Jerusalem, scandalized the orthodox; see II Macc. 4:12), take part in Greek sports, erect gymnasia, baths, and theaters, being fascinated by Greek customs and fashions and eager for Greek luxuries. These imitators of the Greeks became known as "Hellenists," from the verb *hellenízein*, which Plato used in the sense of "to speak good Greek," but which came to mean "to imitate the ways of the Greeks" (cf. above, note 2). Thus Hellenism spread from Cyrene to the Indus and the Caspian, most con-spicuously in the kingdom of the Seleucids; and in the West it conquered Rome. The chief agent for the Hellenization of these far-reaching countries was the Greek city. The flourishing Greek centers of commerce and culture founded by Alexander and his successors became the standard-bearers of the new civilization.[5] According to Plutarch (*De Alexandri Magni fortuna* I, 5), Alexander founded more than seventy cities—a figure which may not be far from the mark. The most important and famous among them is of course Alexandria in Egypt; Samaria was destroyed by Perdiccas and rebuilt as a Greek city. The greatest of all builders of cities are, however, Seleucus I Nicator (305-280) and Antiochus I Soter (280-261), whose new towns are scattered through Syria (Antioch), Mesopotamia (Edessa; Dura-Europos; Seleucia, the greatest city of the time, which soon eclipsed ancient Babylon), Cilicia, Caria, Lydia, Phrygia, Media, and Iran. These centers of Greek life proved to be at the same time the strength and the weakness of Hel-lenism in Asia. The greatest among them—capitals of kingdoms such as Alexandria, Pergamum, Antioch, Seleucia—attracted the best minds, not only for government service but also for the development of the arts and sciences, and thus became centers of learning to which pupils flocked and from which they eventually spread Greek culture elsewhere. But, as a result of these conditions, Hellenism prevailed only in the cities and chiefly among the upper classes of the native populations. The country-side, where rural folk retained their old languages and customs, was scarcely affected by Hellenism.

[5] On the cities founded by Alexander and his successors see K. J. Beloch, *Griechische Geschichte*, 2nd ed., Vol. 4, Pt. I, pp. 251-262. Some of these new Hellenistic cities are mentioned in the New Testament.

An observer in 200 B.C. would never have doubted the permanence of Hellenism in Western Asia; but a century later the signs of its decay were obvious: it was on the defensive against the Oriental reaction. The rejection of Hellenism in Judea through the victories of Judas Maccabeus was the dramatic forerunner of a general trend which eventually wiped out all traces of Greek culture in Western Asia and Egypt—aside from some archaeological ruins. Like the Philistines before and the Crusaders later, the Macedonians were eventually absorbed in Western Asia, following a striking initial success. Livy (38, 17) already observed this assimilation with the natives when he wrote: "The Macedonians who have colonies at Alexandria in Egypt, at Selencia and Babylon, and at other places scattered over the world, have degenerated into Syrians, Parthians, and Egyptians."

While the Romanization of the West was thorough and bequeathed to modern times the languages derived from vulgar Latin (the Romance languages still spoken in Portugal, Spain, France, Italy, Rumania, and parts of Switzerland) and the solid unity of the Roman Church before the Reformation, the Hellenization of the Near East was only superficial: the Greek language, spoken chiefly in the cities, did not survive the triumph of the old languages (Aramaic or Syriac, Persian, the languages of Asia Minor, Coptic) and later of Arabic; and the Greek Church could not prevent the rise of national churches using Coptic, Ethiopic, Syriac, Armenian, and Georgian in their liturgies—not to speak of the growth of Zoroastrianism and the irresistible spread of Islam. The decline of the Seleucid dynasty, which began with Antiochus IV Epiphanes (175-163), the rise of the Parthian Empire (founded by Mithridates I [171-138]), and the Roman conquests (following the victory over Antiochus III the Great at Magnesia in 190 B.C.) mark the beginning of Hellenism's decadence: when the Romans burned Seleucia to the ground in A.D. 164, they extinguished the torch of Greek culture east of the Euphrates. After the rise of Christianity, only the study of Greek philosophy, especially the works of Plato and (notably in the Syriac Church and in Islam) Aristotle, as also some elements of Hellenistic art, survived the end of Hellenism in the Near East.

2. General Characteristics

It remains now to characterize the Hellenistic culture, the vicissitudes of which have been briefly sketched. The far-reaching changes in the civilization of Greece resulting from the policies of Philip and the conquests of Alexander may be roughly compared to those brought about in Germany by Bismarck, when in 1870, after the victory over France, he founded the German Empire. The culture that was the product of the abiding creations of the genius of Kant, Goethe, Beethoven, and others, came to an end with the final convulsion marked by the works of Nietzsche and Wagner. After 1870 the mental energy of Germany was directed mainly to research in the realm of the physical and natural sciences, as also in philology—if not to industrial production and preparation for war.

The Greek classical culture, reaching its apex at Athens in the age of Pericles, has no rivals. The originality, depth of thought, and perfection of the works of Phidias, Plato, Sophocles, and others are unsurpassed to the present day. It would seem that such genius could best flourish within the confines of a city-state (like Weimar, Florence, Venice), being greatly diluted in an empire. Yet it is only such dilution that makes the highest cultures accessible to the masses: thus they become factors in mankind's progress, which is accordingly nil in the realm of the spirit. Just as the gospel of Jesus had to be transplanted by Paul into the great centers of the Roman world before it became one of the pillars of modern civilization, so the spread of Greek culture through the conquests of Alexander made of Hellenism the other pillar of our civilization. Both the gospel and Hellenism passed through Rome before reaching us, losing thereby the sublime purity and beauty of their beginnings but, by being popularized (or, as they would now say in Europe, "Americanized") almost beyond recognition and made to serve practical purposes in daily life, they gained universal acceptance and produced our modern civilization.

The immediate effect of the end of the *pólis*, the independent Greek city-state, and the rise of great kingdoms and empires through the conquests of Alexander was paradoxically to give to human life both a cosmopolitan and an individualistic aspect.

Even though, as has been noted, Hellenism did not take root in the Near East as deeply as Romanism in the West, the conquests of Alexander did contribute to the education of the "barbarians," to the spread of the Greek language (in the form called *koiné* [*diálektos*], or common [speech]), and thus, to some extent, to the obliteration of the distinction between Greek and "barbarians," inasmuch as they attained the same cultural level (cf. Aristotle's remark in 348, reported by Josephus, *Against Apion* I:22, §§176-182). Besides this creation of a common culture and language over a wide area, Alexander's empire tended to break down more and more the separate nationalities of Western Asia, which had begun to be amalgamated by the Persian Empire. Although the process was by no means completed, and eventually the Jews and the Persians, in strong nationalistic reactions, affirmed their cultural and political separateness, the trend to break down the barriers of nationality, social rank, religion, and culture is unmistakable. The creation of a world

empire per se pointed in the direction of a new conception which in
theory had been partially developed before Alexander, the *oikouménē*
(the inhabited earth), the unity of the human race (*genus humanum,*
Cicero, *De finibus* III, 67), humanity or "One World" (Wendell Willkie),
in which there is "neither Greek nor Jew . . . barbarian, Scythian, bond,
nor free" (Col. 3:11), in which, as Cicero said (*De finibus* III, 63)
referring to Chrysippus, a man on account of the mere fact that he is a
man will not appear to be an alien in the presence of another man. In
this period the Stoics had some vague notion of "the parliament of man,
the federation of the world" (Tennyson), for they conceived a uniform
law applied to all men and according to which, as if according to a
common light, all are ruled (Plutarch, *De Alexandri Magni fortuna* I, 8).
So, at least in principle, the nationalism of the *pólis* and of the small
kingdom tended to be absorbed in the universalism of the world empire.[6]
How the barrier between Greeks and "barbarians" tended to be obliterated
may be seen in the following contrast: Aristotle (fragment 658, edit.
Rose) advised Alexander to practice "hegemony" (leadership) with the
Greeks but "despotism" with the barbarians, caring for the first as for
friends and relatives, but utilizing the latter like plants or animals. A
century later, however, Eratosthenes (in Strabo I, pp. 66-67; cf. Cicero,
De republica I, 58), rejecting this division into masters and servants,
taught that one should judge and distinguish men according to virtue
and wickedness alone—a classification unrelated to the distinction of
races.

This notion of mankind as a whole and the establishment of a world
empire naturally implied, for Alexander, a common culture for *all men*—
a culture basically Hellenic but enriched with Oriental contributions. As
in the case of paint, the vaster the surface over which a culture is
spread, the thinner the veneer will be. Leveling is always downward, to
the standards of the masses. A general, average, Hellenistic culture was
thus developed; national differences tended to disappear; Greek dialects
were losing their identities in the *koinē*—the common international
speech chiefly based on Attic, in which the Septuagint and the New
Testament were written; local juristic practices and principles tended
to be merged into laws for all nations; education, morals, commerce and
industry, and even religion were losing some of their parochial characteristics and coalesced into average forms; and the noblest creation of
the age, Stoic philosophy, taught that the world was one and the individual (whatever his race and rank)—was supreme—thus giving

[6] "If what philosophers say of the kinship of God and men be true, what remains
for men to do but as Socrates did: never, when asked one's country to answer, 'I am
an Athenian or a Corinthian,' but 'I am a citizen of the world'" (Epictetus, *Discourses* I: 9, 1).

philosophical expression to the new cosmopolitan and individualistic spirit. As U. von Wilamowitz-Moellendorff aptly said, "The Stoa sets out solely from the single person and culminates in the wise man for whom individualization is essential. This is diametrically the opposite of the old Hellenic principle which sets out from the community: the ideal conception of Plato is a community, that of Zeno is an individual."

The rise of individualism runs parallel to that of internationalism. Diogenes calls himself *kosmopolítēs* (world citizen): the whole world becomes the fatherland of the sage,[7] who would have approved John Wesley's dictum: "The world is my parish." On the contrary, in the Greek *pólis* of earlier days patriotism was purely local and the interests of the city-state were supreme. The citizen devoted the best of his thought and energy to the conduct of public affairs, his life unfolded within his commonwealth's limits, outside of which he was an alien merely tolerated and without a voice in the administration of the state. As a public servant responsible for the welfare of his city, which depended to a great extent on the decisions reached by the assembly, the citizen left his private affairs largely in the hands of the women and the slaves of his family (like the fortunate husband in Prov. 31:10-31). With the decadence of the *pólis* even before the time of Alexander—due in part to its inability to administer a vast territory, to the rise of political parties more concerned with selfish interests than with the public welfare, and to the bitter strife between Greek cities—and with its final absorption within the kingdom of Philip, the empire of Alexander, and at last within the Roman Empire, participation in the government was precluded to all but a few citizens. The result was a greater concern with private affairs, a greater interest in the home—which gave to womanhood a new importance and dignity—a desire for a successful professional or business career far from the native town, in one of the metropolitan centers of culture or at court, if not in the Hellenistic cities of Asia, which was then the America of the Greeks. The social instinct now found expression in labor unions or craftsmen's guilds, religious and charitable associations, clubs. Individualism and realism are characteristic of Hellenistic art; it excelled in portraits which are true to life.

A good index of this trend from public to private affairs is the Athenian comedy. Aristophanes (d. *ca.* 380 B.C.) satirized on the stage public figures and political movements which displeased his conservative attitude. A century later Menander (342-291 B.C.) was instead the precursor of Molière in presenting wittily or commiseratingly human foibles and domestic troubles, and in depicting standard types of persons such as the misanthrope, the libertine, the miser, the coquette. Menander's contemporary, the botanist Theophrastus (d. *ca.* 287), in his *Characters*

---

[7] Cf. Beloch, *Griechische Geschichte*, Vol. 4, Pt. I, p. 404.

sketched such types as the flatterer, the grumbler, etc.; cf. C. N. Green-ough and J. M. French, A *Bibliography of the Theophrastan Character in English*. Harvard University Press, 1947.

The great political upheavals of the times brought to the fore great personalities of leaders, men of iron will, definite purpose, prompt decision, utter ruthlessness, dazzling daring. Such men were the first two Ptolemies, Seleucus I, Antiochus III, Cassander, Antigonus Cyclops, Demetrius Poliorcetes, Herod the Great, and others. By their side, or alone, are the women who, through intrigue, crime, flirtation, and keen-ness of mind, gain immense political influence or power: Berenice, Cleopatra the Great, some Seleucid queens, Herodias, and others. While the masses worship the emperor and call him *sōtḗr* (savior), men of letters are devoting themselves to a new genre, biography (the books on Alexander; Nicholas of Damascus, whose biography of Herod was abundantly excerpted by Josephus; Plutarch). In its manifold variety and emotional complexity, in the contrasts between pomp and simplicity, sentimentalism and selfishness, puritanism and licentiousness, romanticism and realism, education and propaganda, science and superstition, Hellen-istic life is strangely modern, we almost could say "American"—even though the world was then empty of machines and full of slaves.[8]

This new cosmopolitan and individualistic mentality permeated liter-ature, science, philosophy, and religion; thus it radically modified them and laid the foundation of Roman culture, from which our own has eventually descended.[9]

3. Hellenistic Literature[10]

The decline of the classical literature of the age of Pericles had begun before Alexander. A new spirit which was to prevail in Hellenism, is

[8] Cf. U. von Wilamowitz-Moellendorff, in *Die Griechische und Lateinische Literatur und Sprache* (Kultur der Gegenwart, Part I, Division VIII), pp. 92 f. Berlin and Leipzig, 1905. P. Wendland, *Hellenistisch-römische Kultur*, pp. 19-24. W. W. Tarn, *Hellenistic Civilization*, pp. 3 f.

[9] Cosmopolitan and individualistic tendencies prevail likewise in public administra-tion, social and economic matters, painting and sculpture—subjects which lie outside the scope of the present summary; see for them the works cited at the beginning of this chapter.

[10] In addition to the general works cited at the beginning of this chapter, see the brilliant summary of U. von Wilamowitz-Moellendorff in *Die Griechische und Lateinische Literatur und Sprache* (Kultur der Gegenwart I, viii), pp. 81-197 (for Latin literature see F. Leo, *ibid.*, pp. 316-373). For details, see: F. Susemihl, *Geschichte der griechischen Litteratur in der Alexandrinerzeit*, 2 vols. Leipzig, 1891, 1892. W. von Christ, *Geschichte der Griechischen Literatur*, Vol. 2, 6th ed. by W. Schmid and O. Stählin (I. von Müller's Handbuch der klassischen Altertümswis-senschaft VII, ii, 1). München, 1920. See also M. Rostovtzeff, *Social and Economic History of the Hellenistic World*, Vol. 3, p. 1593, n. 30. Oxford, 1941.

apparent in Euripides (d. *ca.* 407), in contrast with Aeschylus (d. 456) and Sophocles (d. 406 at the age of ninety); and in Aristotle (d. 322), in contrast with Plato (d. 347). Euripides begins to bring drama down to earth, to the level of everyday problems and emotions. In his accurate character drawing, psychological analysis of passion, sense for dramatic conflict in human life, concern with stage effects and audience reaction, Euripides is a precursor not only of the Hellenistic theater, but of the modern one as well—notably in making of love the chief topic in some of his plays. Aristotle, on the other hand, inaugurated a new era by forsaking the brilliant metaphysical and abstract speculations of Plato for research in the humanities and the natural sciences. Aristotle's own classroom lecture notes (*hypomnémata*) were jotted down with little attention to literary form and were later worked over by him and by his pupils into books for publication, which, being intended chiefly as manuals for information, lacked rhetorical art. And yet, as in the case of some modern functional constructions (like suspension bridges), such writings stressing content rather than form have an artistic appeal of their own. In fact such learned works are probably the best products of Hellenistic literature, in which the finest writings are seldom within the realm of belles-lettres.

The rationalism of Aristotle, which had been foreshadowed by the Sophists, and the realism of Euripides eventually had a corrosive effect on Athenian classical poetry, as on Platonic mysticism. The latter, in various admixtures with Orphism and Oriental religions, sank to the level of the credulous masses until it was rescued for philosophy by Posidonius. Poetry had been nourished since Homer by religion and mythology: now traditional religion is in flux, and myths have become fairy tales for children (unless they be interpreted allegorically as vehicles of the deepest truths). This agnostic attitude, together with the humanization of mythical beings in Euripides, robbed ancient myths of their romantic halo and thus dried up the types of poetry nourished by mythical lore: epics, tragedies, and hymns were no longer inspired by faith, their breath of life, and thus became artificial, mere empty shells, skillfully adorned whitened sepulchers. The Alexandrian poetry that had a spark of life found its inspiration outside of mythology in the actual world of men and nature.

The Cretan Rhianus (*ca.* 260 B.C.), author of a *Heraclaeid* and of local sagas in verse (notably on the second Messenian war), Antagoras of Rhodes (about 300-260), and particular Apollonius of Rhodes (*ca.* 270 B.C.), author of the *Argonautica*, wrote epics in Homeric style, but modernized in the manner of novels by means of love interest, adventures, and details drawn from life. But Callimachus had probably such long epics in mind when he said that "a big book is a big evil." Vergil of

Mantua (70-19 B.C.), the great author of the *Aeneid*, is the only successor of Homer worthy of lasting remembrance.

In the third century the seven authors known as the *Pleiad* (a name revived by Pierre de Ronsard [d. 1585] in *La Pléiade*), strove to revive classical tragedy but failed dismally, although they found imitators among Alexandrian Jews. A monologue-drama, written by Lycophron, the *Alexandra* (dealing with Cassandra), and a few fragments are all that survives from the Pleiad.

Other poetic genres showed more vitality—in spite of the fact that their verses proceeded from the pens of erudite scholars and were intended for the intelligentsia. The elegy, which later flourished in Roman literature, was revived in the Hellenistic period by Philetas of Cos (d. *ca.* 280), Hermesianax (*ca.* 290), Euphorion (*ca.* 230), and others. Asclepiades of Samos (*ca.* 290), composed songs and erotic epigrams: his topics ranged from "wine, women, and song" to the sadness of man's lot. In his day, his imitators were Hedylus of Athens and Poseidippus of Alexandria. Leonidas of Tarentum (*ca.* 280) composed more elaborate epigrams, which influenced Phoenician and Syrian poets of the period 130-60 B.C.: Meleager and Philodemus of Gadara in Transjordania (whose erotic epigrams have been compared to the Song of Songs), and Antipatros of Sidon.[11]

The two masters of Hellenistic poetry are Theocritus of Syracuse (*ca.* 280-260) and Callimachus of Cyrene (*ca.* 280-245), the first more inspired as a poet, the second more celebrated (Quintilian calls him *elegiae princeps*) and a far greater scholar. Theocritus, the greatest of bucolic poets, composed graceful—if sophisticated—idyls (imitated, but not surpassed, by Vergil in his *Eclogues*), in which the descriptions of nature's charms and of rustic festivals make us forget that the shepherds of Theocritus are really cultivated gentlemen wearing a rustic disguise. Callimachus composed hymns, epigrams, and notably elegies and idyls (like his *Hekálē*); his chief work (*Aitía*) is a collection of ancient local

---

[11] The Greek Anthology (*Anthologia Palatina*), preserved in a single manuscript of the Palatine Library in Heidelberg (11th cent.), is the fullest collection of Greek epigrams and other brief poems. It is based on the collection of Constantine Kephalas, made at the end of the 9th century. Its 15 books contain about 4,500 brief poems. The standard text is that of H. Stadmüller in the Teubner edition (Leipzig, 1894 ff.); with English translation by W. R. Paton, in the Loeb Classical Library (*The Greek Anthology*). Another source of our knowledge of Hellenistic literature is the mass of classical papyri discovered in the sands of Egypt; see for general orientation, C. H. Roberts, "The Greek Papyri" in *The Legacy of Egypt* (ed. by S. R. K. Glanville), pp. 249-282. Oxford, 1942; K. Preisendanz, *Papyrusfunde und Papyrusforschung*. Leipzig, 1933. Lists of literary texts have been prepared by C. H. Oldfather (*The Greek Literary Texts from Graeco-Roman Egypt*. Madison, Wis., 1923), and H. J. M. Milne (*Catalogue of the Literary Papyri in the British Museum*. London, 1927). Latest edition of texts: D. L. Page, *Greek Literary Papyri*, Vol. 1, Loeb Classical Library, 1942.

legends relating the origin of customs and the founding of Greek cities. Ovid (d. *ca.* A.D. 17), his greatest successor, recognized that his poetic technique surpassed his inspiration (*ingenio non valet, arte valet*).

Hellenistic poetry displays not only great erudition, as in Callimachus, but also scientific knowledge. The best known astronomical poem is the *Phainómena* of Aratus of Soli in Cilicia (d. *ca.* 245). Paul probably quoted the verse "in him we live, and move, and have our being" (Acts 17:28) from its initial invocation to Zeus. The poem describes the constellations and has an appendix on the signs of the weather (cf. Matt. 16:2 f.), leaving open the question whether the stars make the weather or merely point it out in advance. Aratus, however, committed some errors due to misunderstanding. Nicander of Colophon was similarly criticized by Cicero with respect to the lack of agricultural knowledge in his *Georgics* (imitated by Vergil, according to Quintilian). Two other of his technical poems (*Theriaca* and *Alexipharmaca*) deal with antidotes against poisoning through animals and through foods, respectively; they are based on the treatises of Apollodorus and, in spite of their influence on far better Latin poets, they are quite pedantic.

Folk literature flourished by the side of this sophisticated, erudite, and rhetorical poetry: little of it, except the new comedy (Menander, 341-291 B.C.), was spontaneous and natural. On a lower level than the Attic new comedy, the comic burlesques of tragedy (*phlýakes*), presented by grotesquely costumed actors, sent southern Italian and Sicilian audiences into peals of laughter. Through the medium of the Campanian *Atellanae* —ribald farces transplanted to Rome after 210 B.C.—they have survived, in a fashion, to the present day in the Italian Punch-and-Judy shows; the Neapolitan *Pulcinella* is a remote and refined descendant of a rude Syracusan clown. The spoken mime (as distinguished from the sung mime of the Ionians in the East) likewise originated in the West and is a burlesque of the Attic comedy, depicting in caricature scenes from daily life—notably low life. The plot was usually merely sketched and the actors improvised freely. Theocritus[12] and Herodas (*ca.* 240) composed such genre sketches in verse.

Apart from scientific, scholarly, and philosophical works, the prose literature of the Hellenistic period comprises primarily history and fiction, which are not always sharply separated, for historical works (since Herodotus) included legends and fanciful tales, while novels were sometimes built around historical characters. Jewish literature of this period, both Palestinian and Alexandrian, displays the same disregard of a sharp demarcation between fact and fancy. Honestly historical are the books

[12] The three mimes of Theocritus are: *The Sorceresses* (Idyl II), *The Loves of Cynisca* (Idyl XIV), and *The Syracusan Women at the Festival of Adonis* (Idyl XV).

of Ptolemy I on Alexander and the naval report of Nearchus on the voyage down the Indus and to the Persian Gulf; Aristobulus of Cassandreia is more fanciful: all three are preserved in part by Arrian of Nicomedia (second century of our era), our main extant source on Alexander. Less reliable histories of Alexander are those of Clitarchus (about 300 B.C.), whose imaginative account became the most popular and was still enjoyed by Cicero; it is probably the main source of Diodorus Siculus (book 17), of Callisthenes (*ca.* 330 B.C.), and of Hegesis (*ca.* 250), together with the rather trivial and fictitious stories of Onesicritus (a pilot of Nearchus), Chares (a chamberlain), and Ephippus. Historians of the time generally assumed that their task was not merely the exact description of past events, but rather the education and enjoyment of the reader. The purpose of the Epitomist, to whom we owe II Maccabees, as of other historians, was to write so "that they that read may have delight, and that they that are desirous to commit to memory might have ease, and that all into whose hands it comes might have profit" (II Macc. 2:25). Consequently, they stressed drama more than truth, eloquence and moralizing more than facts, propaganda more than objectivity, and rhetorical elegance more than unadorned historicity. The same epitomator, in his defense of rhetorical style, compared himself not to the builder of a house but to its interior decorator (2:29). Such writing for effect (illustrated in its extreme form by this epitomator) dictated the selection of the materials: stories with a moral, tragic events, examples of steadfastness in misfortune, miraculous deliverances, deeply moving pathetic scenes, as when the butler of Darius wept seeing Alexander use his master's table as a footstool (Diodorus 17:66, 4), characterizations, moral verdicts on important persons, detailed descriptions of battles or of scenery were much liked. Although rhetorical devices are not wholly avoided by Polybius (*ca.* 200-120 B.C.), the forty books of his *Histories* (of which books 1-5 and long fragments of others are extant), dealing with Roman expansion from 266 to the destruction of Carthage in 146,[13] are not merely the sole important remnant of Hellenistic historiography but its masterpiece: among Greek historians Polybius is second only to Thucydides.

Apart from the life of Alexander and the history of Roman conquests, Hellenistic historians disclosed a keen interest in the history of Oriental nations:[14] the Jews (I Maccabees in Greek, Jason of Cyrene and II

---

[13] The *Histories* of Polybius were continued by Posidonius of Apamea (or of Rhodes, 135-51 B.C.) who was far better as a Stoic philosopher than as a historian.

[14] The fragmentary surviving texts of these historians are edited with a Latin translation in C. and T. Müller, *Fragmenta historicorum graecorum*, Vols. 1-4. Paris, Didot, 1885. The following work is similar in scope: F. Jacoby, *Die Fragmente der Griechischen Historiker*. 7 vols., Berlin, 1923-1930 (not yet complete). On the individual authors see also C. Wachsmuth, *Einleitung in das Studium der Alten Ge-*

Maccabees, Flavius Josephus), the Egyptians (Hecataeus of Abdera, *ca.* 290 B.C.; Manetho, *ca.* 270 B.C.; Plutarch's *On Isis and Osiris, ca.* A.D. 100), the Babylonians and Assyrians (Berossus, *ca.* 280; the famous chronological canon of reigns by Claudius Ptolemy, second century of our era; Abydenus, early in our era), the Phoenicians (Menander, second century B.C.; Dios; Philostratus; in the first century of our era Philo Byblius, translated the Phoenician mythology of Sanchuniathon); the Indians (Megasthenes).

Out of such national histories were the universal histories compiled. The most important for us is the *Historical Library* (*Bibliothéké historiké*) of Diodorus Siculus (*ca.* 25 B.C.). Only books 1-5 (mythic beginnings) and 11-20 (480-302 B.C.), of the forty books of Diodorus, have survived more or less intact, but abundant fragments of the rest (notably those from the last ten books, preserved by Photius) are known. His method is annalistic. The first part describes the mythical history of non-Hellenic nations (1-3) and of the Greeks (4-6); the second deals with the history from the fall of Troy to the death of Alexander the Great (7-17); and the third part comes down to Caesar's Gallic war in 60 B.C. (18-40). The work is merely a vast collection of extracts strung on a thin thread of original narrative, but it is invaluable for us, having preserved fragments of earlier historians which otherwise would be lost; thus it bridges the gap between Xenophon and Polybius.

Much larger is the work in 144 volumes entitled *Histories*, written by Nicholas of Damascus, the confidential secretary of Herod the Great (37-4 B.C.), in ten years (*ca.* 15-6 B.C.). Fragments of the first seven books (coming down to Cyrus) are preserved. Nicholas is the main source of Josephus for the biography of Herod in books 15-17 of the *Antiquities,* and his sole source in *War* 1, 18-33. Nicholas had written a detailed biography of Herod (Josephus, *Antiquities* 16:7, 1), but we do not know whether it was the final part of his *Histories* or a separate work.[15]

The third universal history was written in Latin, though based on Greek sources, by the Gaul Pompeius Trogus in the latter part of the reign of Augustus (31 B.C.-A.D. 14) and was entitled *Philippic Histories.* We have only an echo of it in the miserable epitome prepared by Junianus Justinus in the second or third century—a wretched opus which enjoyed great popularity among the Church Fathers. The *Prologi* (or table of contents) give us a better idea of the scope of the original work.

---

schichte. Leipzig, 1895. The fragments of minor Hellenistic-Jewish historians are published, in addition to Müller's *Fragmenta,* in W. N. Stearns, *Fragments from Graeco-Jewish Writers.* Chicago, 1908. References to Jewish history in Greek and Roman authors are collected in Th. Reinach, *Textes d'auteurs Grecs et Romains relatifs au Judaïsme.* Paris, 1895.

[15] Cf. H. St. John Thackeray, *Josephus: The Man and the Historian,* pp. 40 f., 65-67. New York, 1926.

The title is taken from the *Philippica* of Theopompus (a Macedonian history). Books 1-6 deal with the Near East to the Persian Wars; books 7-12 with Macedonian history (7-9 to the death of Philip, 10-12 to the death of Alexander); books 12-40 come down to Augustus; two appendixes close the work: books 41-42 deal with the Parthians, and books 42-44 with the founding of Rome, and with the Gauls and Iberians. One of the main sources of Trogus seems to have been the book *On Kings* by his earlier contemporary Timagenes.

The best known world chronicles (*Chronographíai*) are those of Eratosthenes of Cyrene (*ca.* 230-200 B.C.), Apollodorus of Athens (*ca.* 150-100 B.C.), and Sosibius Lakon (second century B.C.?), Castor of Rhodes (*ca.* 50 B.C.), Dionysius of Halicarnassus (d. *ca.* 7 B.C.), Thallus (middle of the first century of our era?),[16] and others down to the Christian chronographers Sextus Julius Africanus (*ca.* 225) and Eusebius of Caesarea (d. *ca.* 340), whose world chronicles were utilized by their Byzantine successors.[17]

Biographies and autobiographies are characteristic of the Hellenistic age. The earliest autobiography (or "confessions") known is the "apology" of Hattushil III, king of the Hittites (*ca.* 1281-1260 B.C.), if we disregard the self-laudatory grave inscriptions of the Egyptian monarchs of the Middle Kingdom in the first half of the second millennium B.C. Nehemiah's memoirs, contained in his book, are something unique in the fifth century B.C. In the Hellenistic period Pyrrhus, Ptolemy VII Euergetes II, and Aratos of Sykion (271-213), wrote their autobiographies. In the Roman period such memoirs were written in Greek (Nicholas of Damascus, Flavius Josephus) and in Latin (Scaurus and Sulla; cf. the *Commentarii* of Julius Caesar). Collections of biographies begin with Clearchus of Soli (*ca.* 300), Antigonus of Carystus (d. *ca.* 220 B.C.), who wrote on the Athenian philosophers of the third century B.C., and with Satyrus of Alexandria (*ca.* 220), a biographer of statesmen, poets, and philosophers. Out of the mass of uncritical and semifictional biographies written in Alexandria, Plutarch of Chaeronea (d. *ca.* A.D. 120) drew the material for his famous *Parallel Lives*, and Diogenes Laërtius (third century of our era) for his *Lives of Philosophers*. Both works are indispensable historical sources in spite of their fusion of fact and fancy.

There is accordingly no hard and fast demarcation between these historical and biographical writings and fiction—particularly historical fiction, such as the *Cryopaedia*, (education of Cyrus) by Xenophon. And

---

[16] Horace A. Rigg, Jr. ("Thallus: The Samaritan?" [HTR 34 (1941) 111-119]), has shown that there is no valid evidence proving that Thallus was a Samaritan.

[17] See the standard work of H. Gelzer, *Sextus Julius Africanus und die byzant. Chronographie.* Vol. 1 (on the chronography of Africanus), Leipzig, 1880; Vol. 2 (on his followers), Leipzig, 1885.

who can tell whether one of the numerous *Lives* of Alexander is romanticized history or historical fiction? As a matter of fact Alexander became the hero of one of the most widespread sagas ever written: the folk tale, like the hero, conquered the world! The innumerable forms of the Alexander sagas in Latin, Greek, French, English, German, Spanish, Danish, Swedish, Icelandic, Flemish, and Czech literatures down to Boccaccio's *Decameron*, ultimately go back to the story written by "Pseudo-Callisthenes" (or "Aesop") at Alexandria in the second century B.C., and preserved in three recensions in Greek and its Byzantine re-writings.[18] Pseudo-Callisthenes ultimately inspired the varied and inter-polated versions in Latin (Julius Valerius, end of the third century A.D.; *Historia de Proeliis*, tenth century), Armenian (seventh century), Pah-lavi (Persian, *ca.* sixth century), Syriac (translated from the Pahlavi, seventh century), Arabic (translated from the Syriac, *ca.* 750-850), Sahidic-Coptic (eighth century; see O. von Lemm, *Der Alexanderroman der Kopten*. St. Petersburg, 1903), Ethiopic (fully Christianized, so that Alexander becomes a saint; sixteenth century), Georgian (early seven-teenth century), etc.[19]

Hellenistic fiction, in accordance with a trend begun in Aramaic liter-ature during the preceding Persian period, became a sea into which poured motifs and plots out of the various Oriental and Western cultures, from the Atlantic to India. Eventually, when this ephemeral fusion came to an end and the individual nations developed their own literatures in a variety of tongues, the great Hellenistic reservoir remained the source of the separate streams pouring out of it and flowing again through the old nationalistic beds.[20] This mutual fertilization between East and West during the Hellenistic period may be illustrated with the story and the

[18] The standard edition of the Greek text is: W. Kroll, *Historia Alexandri Magni* (Pseudo-Callisthenes). Vol. 1: Recensio vetusta. Berlin, 1926. A German critically reconstructed text is given by A. Ausfeld, *Der griechische Alexanderroman*, edited by W. Kroll. Leipzig, 1907.

[19] For European medieval Alexander romances see P. Meyer, *Alexandre le grand dans la littérature française au moyen age.* 2 vols., Paris, 1886. F. P. Magoun, Jr., *The Gests of King Alexander of Macedon.* Cambridge, Mass., 1929 (cf. Magoun in *Byzantion* 16 [1942-43] 315 ff.). The basic investigation of the Oriental versions is that of Th. Nöldeke: "Beiträge zur Geschichte des Alexanderroman" (*Denkschriften der kaiserl. Akademie der Wissenschaften*, Phil.-Hist. Klasse, Vol. 38. Vienna, 1890). E. A. W. Budge has edited and translated the Syriac (Cambridge, 1889) and the Ethiopic (2 vols., 1896) versions. I am indebted to my colleague and friend F. P. Magoun for most of these references. W. W. Tarn, *Alexander the Great*, 2 vols. Cam-bridge University Press, 1948, appeared too late to be used here.

[20] See: K. Kerényi, *Die griechisch-orientalische Romanliteratur in religionsgeschit-licher Beleuchtung* (1927). C. H. Becker, *Das Erbe der Antike im Orient und Okzident* (1931). Miss R. Söder, *Die apokryphen Apostelgeschichten und die roman-hafte Literatur der Antike* (1932). G. E. von Grunebaum, "Greek Form Elements in the Arabian Nights" (JAOS 62 [1942] 277-292; cf. 64 [1944] 62 f., n. 7).

wisdom of Ahikar.[21] The earliest version known is an Aramaic text circulating in the Persian Empire late in the fifth century B.C. It has been suggested that it was ultimately a Babylonian tale written about 550 B.C., translated either directly into Aramaic or into Persian, from which the Aramaic was translated. Whatever be its ultimate origin, we have more or less free renderings into Syriac (from which the Armenian and the Arabic were translated), and into Byzantine Greek, from which the Slavonic text (the basis of the Rumanian version) was rendered. How the plot of the Ahikar tale came to be utilized in the *Life of Aesop* written by Maximus Planudes (d. *ca.* 1310) remains a curious puzzle, but it indicates how fluid and mobile the material of popular fiction could become. Earlier echoes of Ahikar's proverbial wisdom and of his vicissitudes have been noticed in Jewish writings (Psalms, Proverbs, Tobit, Sirach, Jubilees, Testaments of the XII Patriarchs), in the New Testament, and in the Koran (cf. R. H. Charles, *Pseudepigrapha*, pp. 716-719).

In a sense the novel (as distinguished from the short story, which is much earlier) is a creation of the Hellenistic period.[22] Two separate strains combined to create the full-length novel: love and adventure. Love poetry was ancient in Greek literature and flourished in new forms after Alexander; love became the prevailing topic in the New Comedy (although sentimental outpourings are not frequent in it); now romantic love tales relate the joys and sorrows, longings and disappointments of fictitious lovers of present times or of long ago (such as Hero and Leander, Jason and Medea, Pyramus and Thisbe, and others; see in particular Ovid's *Heroides*). The tale of adventures in distant fabulous countries also appears early in Greek literature, beginning with Homer's *Odyssey*; the Gilgamesh Epic furnishes an ancient Babylonian example of such descriptions of marvels and wonders witnessed in imaginary lands. The Sicilian Euhemerus (*ca.* 275)[23] in his *Sacred History*—a philosophical *roman à thèse*—relates that on the (imaginary) island of Panchaea in the Indian Ocean he found an inscription describing the activities of Greek gods (Uranus, Cronus, Zeus) when they were still rulers or conquerors, before they were worshiped as gods by their grateful subjects. This attempt to rationalize mythology, tracing religion to ancestor worship or the cult of the dead, was not new, but gained wide popularity through Euhemerus; it suggested to the author of Wis-

[21] For bibliographical references see the chapter on Tobit.
[22] The standard work is Erwin Rohde, *Der griechische Roman und seine Vorläufer*, 3rd ed. Leipzig, 1914. See also B. Lovagnini, *Le origini del romanzo greco* (1921). The basic work on literary style and literary genres is Eduard Norden, *Die antike Kunstprosa vom VI. Jahrhundert v. Chr. bis in die Zeit der Renaissance.* 2 vols. Leipzig and Berlin, 1898 (reprinted with supplements, 1900).
[23] Cf. T. S. Brown, "Euhemeros and the Historians" (HTR 39 [1946] 259-274).

dom of Solomon (14:15-17) one of the ways in which idolatry began. Journeys to fantastic places are also the subject of the novel on the Hyperboreans by Hecataeus of Abdera (*ca.* 290) and of those of Amometus dealing with the Himalayas, the upper Nile, and Arabia. The most incredibly absurd tales, comparable to those of Baron Munchausen,[24] are those of Antiphanes of Berge, who knows of a country so cold that a man's words froze in the autumn and were not heard until they thawed in the spring (see also Lucian's *True Story*). *Gulliver's Travels*, the journeys to the heavenly spheres in Enoch, or to the moon in Jules Verne's *De la terre à la lune* (1865), some tales from the *Arabian Nights* (like that of *Sindbad the Sailor*), explorations of the abode of the dead like Dante's *Divine Comedy* (see A. Dieterich, *Nekya: Beiträge zur Erklärung der neuentdeckten Petrus-Apokalypse*. Leipzig, 1893; 2nd ed., 1913) have all parallels and antecedents in Hellenistic fiction. According to E. Rohde (*Der Griechischer Roman*, 3rd ed., p. 295), Antonius Diogenes (probably first century of our era), in his novel *Wonders beyond Thule*, was one of the first to combine in his book erotic and fantastic elements and Photius seems to have regarded him as the first among the writers of Greek novels.

4. Hellenistic Science

Such imaginary voyages to the lands "of make-believe" were inspired by the actual explorations by land and sea which, as we have seen, began with the far-reaching conquests of Alexander the Great. Besides the exact measurements of road distances traversed by Alexander, which the Bematists preserved for later geographers, other voyages of exploration supplied important information.[25] Nearchus at the orders of Alexander sailed down the Indus and to the mouth of the Euphrates, thus making known to the Greeks the Indian Ocean. Androsthenes of Thasos explored the eastern coast of Arabia before Alexander's death. The coasts of the Red Sea were explored to a great extent by Philo, a naval officer of the first two Ptolemies. Under Ptolemy II (285-246), Dalios sailed up the Nile south of Meroe (Ethiopia). Two generals of Seleucus I (321-280), Patrocles and Demodamas of Miletus, explored the Caspian Sea (incompletely) and Scythia beyond the Yaxartes, respectively. Agathocles, ruler

[24] The fantastic tales about Baron Karl F. H. von Münchhausen (1720-1797) were written by R. E. Raspe, anonymous author of *Baron Munchausen's Narrative of his Marvelous Travels and Campaigns in Russia*, 1785.

[25] On the geographical knowledge of the Hellenistic period, see in particular, H. Berger, *Geschichte der wissenschaftlichen Erdkunde der Griechen*. Four parts, Leipzig, 1887-1893; 2nd ed., 1903. The best account of Hellenistic and Roman science is: George Sarton, *Introduction to the History of Science*. Vol. 1: From Homer to Omar Khayyam, pp. 124-343. Carnegie Institution of Washington, 1927.

of Syracuse (316-289), campaigned in the region of Carthage. Pytheas of
Messalia (Marseilles) in the time of Alexander navigated along the
coasts of Western Spain, Gaul, and reached the northern end of Scotland
and the mouth of the Elbe. He saw the bright summer nights in the
North and heard of Thule, where the sun never set in midsummer; he
explained correctly the ebb and flow of the tides, connecting them with
the phases of the moon. Megasthenes was sent by Seleucus I as ambassador to the court of Chandragupta (*Sandrokottos* in Greek) and remained in Palibothra or Pataliputra (now Patna) from 302 to 298; his
observations on India (*Indica*) are unfortunately lost except for some
fragments.

Such firsthand observations of lands and seas hitherto unknown to the
Greeks not only contributed to create that cosmopolitan feeling and the
global notion of the *oikouménē* (whole inhabited earth), but also furnished scientific geographers with needed information. Dicaearchus, a
pupil of Aristotle (d. 322 B.C.), proceeded to measure the size of the
earth, the spheric shape of which had been discovered before him, and
reached results which occasionally were almost correct; on his map he
divided the *oikouménē* into a northern and a southern half, separated by
the Mediterranean Sea and the Himalayas, and proved that mountains
and valleys were insignificant irregularities on the surface of an earth
which was much larger than had been previously surmised.

These and other geographic researches, such as the book on harbors
and coastlines by Timosthenes of Rhodes under Ptolemy II, and the
books of Cleon of Syracuse, Nymphodorus, Lycus of Rhegium, and
Timaeus, enabled Eratosthenes of Cyrene, the head of the Alexandrian
library under Ptolemy III (246-221), to calculate anew the size and
circumference of the earth (24,662 miles; in reality, 24,857; see A.
Diller in *Isis* 40 [1949] 6-9), and to surmise that one should reach
India by sailing westward from Spain—the error of Columbus. Discovery of a New World was predicted by Seneca [d. A.D. 65], *Medea*
376-380. Eratosthenes guessed that there was another *oikouménē* in
the southern half of the globe, and prepared the first map of the known
world, which for Mediterranean countries was less inaccurate than we
might expect. His map was superior to the later one prepared for Agrippa
(63-12), the son-in-law and adviser of Augustus, and his scientific method
was far better than that of Strabo (*ca.* 63 B.C.-A.D. 24), whose famous
extant *Geography*, although based on earlier works like that of Artemidorus of Ephesus, deservedly became a "best seller" and a classic.

The conquests of Alexander furthered astronomical studies in two
respects: by the new calculations of the size of the terrestrial globe,
already noted, and by providing information about the Babylonian

observations of the heavenly bodies.[26] The theory of Eudoxus of Cnidus (early fourth century), improved by Callippus (fourth century), did not explain the movements of the planets; and the relative sizes of earth, sun, and moon were being constantly revised. Eudoxus had reckoned that the diameter of the sun was nine times that of the moon, and that the sun was therefore nine times as far from the earth as the moon, but Pheidias of Syracuse at the beginning of the third century figured the ratio twelve to one, the great Aristarchus of Samos (in the time of Ptolemy II, 285-246) adopted the ratio of eighteen or twenty to one, and Archimedes of Syracuse, son of Pheidias (d. 212 B.C.), that of thirty to one. Aristarchus, recognizing thus that the sun must be much greater than the earth (between six to eight times larger in diameter and about three-hundred times in volume) logically concluded that the earth rotated on its axis and moved around the sun—the epoch-making discovery for which N. Copernicus (d. 1543) is famous. Aristarchus even taught that the fixed stars were so far from the earth that the earth's orbit around the sun with respect to the universe was merely like the center of a circle. But the times were not ripe for these brilliant conjectures: Archimedes refused to accept them, and Cleanthes, who succeeded Zeno as the head of the Stoics, accused Aristarchus of ungodliness. Even astronomers like Conon of Samos, active in Alexandria under Ptolemy III (246-221 B.C.), and his pupil Dositheus of Pelusium, rejected the new theories. On the other hand, however, it was no longer possible to accept the system of Eudoxus (according to which sun, moon, and planets moved round the earth in concentric spheres), so Apollonius of Perga (third century) developed the theory of the epicycles according to which the planets moved in an orbit the center of which rotated around the earth: thus, after some improvements by Hipparchus of Nicea (ca. 130 B.C.) originated the Ptolemaic system of astronomy, so named after Claudius Ptolemaeus (second century of our era), which prevailed until Copernicus and J. Kepler (d. 1630) proved it to be false. Only Seleucus of Babylon (middle of the second century B.C.) adopted the theory that earth and planets moved around the sun, but the immediately following scientific decline consigned the theory to oblivion until modern times.

Mathematical studies[27] made possible this progress in astronomy. Euclid (ca. 300 B.C.) wrote in Alexandria those famous *Elements*

[26] On Hellenistic astronomy, see T. Heath, *Aristarchus of Samos* (1913) and the article of Hultsch, "Astronomie," in Pauly-Wissowa's *Realenzyklopädie*. On Babylonian influence see H. Gressmann, *Die hellenistische Gestirnreligion*, pp. 4-7. (Beih. zum Alten Orient 5. Leipzig, 1925).

[27] Geminus, a pupil of Posidonius, wrote a comprehensive history of ancient mathematics.

(*stoicheia*) which remained the standard textbook of geometry almost to the twentieth century. Archimedes of Syracuse, who is said to have shouted, "*Eureka!*" (I have discovered [it]) in his bath when he determined that a body immersed in a fluid loses in weight an amount equal to that of the fluid displaced, fixed more exactly the ratio of diameter to circumference of a circle, found that a hemisphere has two-thirds the volume of a cylinder of the same circumference and height, and founded the theory of the spiral. The work of Archimedes and of Conon of Samos on conic sections was surpassed by the outstanding work (*perì kónōn*) of Apollonius of Perga (third century), which marked the ultimate achievement of antiquity on the subject. Apollonius likewise arrived at a more accurate ratio of the diameter to the circumference than Archimedes had obtained and he was possibly the discoverer of trigonometry, unless this honor belongs to Hipparchus (*ca.* 130 B.C.) The latter is usually regarded as the discoverer of the precession of the equinoxes (although some historians attribute it to the Babylonian Kidinnu [Greek, Kidenas] of Sippar, third century); he calculated the sun's mass as 1,880 times that of the earth, and its distance 1,245 earth diameters from it; Posidonius (*ca.* 80 B.C.) said 6,545. In reality the sun's volume is 1,300,000 times that of the earth; and while the diameter of the earth is less than 8,000 miles, its average distance from the sun is 92,900,000 miles: in both cases Hipparchus figured about one-tenth of the ratios discovered by modern astronomers.

Archimedes invented mechanical devices such as endless screws, and Ctesibius of Alexandria soon after him invented catapults and other machines operated through air pressure, as also a water clock. On these foundations Philo of Byzantium composed his standard treatise on mechanics.

In the field of natural sciences, the outstanding work was done by Theophrastus (d. *ca.* 287), a pupil of Aristotle. His *History of Plants*, presenting the information on exotic plants which the campaigns of Alexander had made known to the Greeks, and his *Theoretical Botany*, dealing with plant physiology, laid the foundation of the science. His pupil Strato of Lampsacus, and the latter's pupil Lycon (*ca.* 270-226), who headed the Peripatetic school in succession after Theophrastus, carried on zoological researches, but with these men biological sciences, which had hardly advanced beyond the work of Aristotle, ceased to be cultivated except for practical or medical purposes.

Hippocrates (d. *ca.* 377) was called the "Father of Medicine" and the "Hippocratic Oath," still administered to physicians, is ascribed to him. In the early third century Alexandria became the medical center: through dissections and, if we believe A. Cornelius Celsus (early first century

A.D.), the author of a great scientific encyclopedia of which only the eight books on medicine are extant (*Proemium*, I, 4; cf. Tertullian, *De anima* 10, cf. 25), even vivisections on criminals, anatomy and physiology made notable progress. Herophilus of Chalcedon (*ca.* 300), a pupil of Praxagoras of Cos, discovered the nerves and their functions, recognized that the arteries contained blood (not air) and that their pulsations originated in the heart: thus he almost determined the circulation of the blood, the discovery of which made William Harvey (1578-1657) famous. Erasistratus of Iulis in Ceos, his younger contemporary, distinguished more accurately motor and sensory nerves, performed serious operations, studied the digestive process, but went back to the theory that arteries carried air except in certain diseases when blood entered them. These two outstanding physicians continued the traditions of the Hippocratic school of Cos and the school of Cnidus, respectively. A third school, the empiric, was founded by Philinus of Cos, a pupil of Herophilus: stressing medical experience rather than theory, it regarded anatomy and physiology as secondary in practical therapy. This school became important about 200 B.C. with Serapion of Alexandria; with Heraclides of Tarentum it contributed to the knowledge of drugs. Asclepiades of Bithynia (first century B.C.) even dispensed with drugs: he prescribed diets, bathing, massage, and exercise. Moreover, by the side of medicine, miraculous cures were reported at the sanctuaries of Serapis and Asclepios—ancient pagan parallels to Lourdes and St. Anne de Beaupré.

5. Hellenistic Scholarship

The achievements of Hellenistic scholars are no less epoch-making than those of the scientists whose work has just been sketched. The vast amount of writing in the fields of history and biography has been mentioned in speaking of Hellenistic literature. Here a word should be added about works on the history of arts, sciences, and literature. The Peripatetic school deserves the credit of initiating such studies, following the example of its founder. Aristotle (d. 322) had collected material for a history of Attic drama; he laid the foundations of science as well as of learning in the following ages, and Dante rightly called him "il maestro di color che sanno" (*Inferno* IV, 133) or the teacher of the learned ("the professors' professor," as a modern journalist would say). Duris of Samos (*ca.* 300), a pupil of Aristotle's pupil Theophrastus, wrote the first history of painting and sculpture, and was followed by other historians of art: Xenocrates of Athens (*ca.* 280-260), Antigonus of Carystus (*ca.* 230), Adeus of Mytilene and Callixenus of Rhodes (late third century). Pupils of Aristotle wrote histories of science: Meno a history of medicine, Eudemus of Rhodes a history of mathematics and astronomy, Theophrastus a systematic history of natural sciences. A colleague of Aristotle, Aristoxenus of Tarentum (*ca.* 330), not only wrote a brilliant work on the theory of music and rhythm which is still extant,[28] but through his biography of Pythagoras inaugurated the history of philosophy, continued by the art historian Antigonus of Carystus for the period after Aristotle; but the lives of philosophers by Diogenes Laërtius (third century A.D.) are our chief source of information (together with the works of Cicero). Aristoxenus also wrote biographies of the great dramatists. But the real founder of literary history was presumably Chamaeleon of Heraclea Pontica (*ca.* 280), a pupil of Theophrastus, the author of a history of Greek poetry from Homer to Aristophanes (d. *ca.* 380 B.C.). He was probably inspired by his learned countryman, Heraclides (d. after 330), a pupil of Plato and a rival of Aristotle, who wrote extensively on scientific subjects as also on the history of music and literature. In his *Life of Greece* Dicaearchus presented a history of culture; he also wrote a book on the poet Alcaeus (*ca.* 600). The last work of the Peripatetic school in the field of literary history was the comprehensive treatise, after the manner of Chamaeleon, prepared by Hieronymus of Rhodes (*ca.* 250).

The preparation of critically edited texts of the Greek classics and of commentaries on them had begun before Alexander, but reached such a degree of accuracy and thoroughness in the Hellenistic period that, as in the case of mathematics and physical sciences, it became the standard in medieval and modern times. The first critical edition of the Homeric poems was prepared by Antimachus of Colophon about 400 B.C.; after Aristotle himself had apparently edited a Homeric text for his pupil Alexander, such critical studies were pursued in his school by Dichaearchus and Chamaeleon, and particularly by Praxiphanes of Mytilene, a pupil of Theophrastus. He proved that the exordium of Hesiod's *Work and Days* was spurious, while his pupil, the poet Aratus of Soli (author of the *Phaenomena*) edited the *Odyssey*.

Another school was founded by the poet Philetas of Cos (*ca.* 300), the compiler of a dictionary which was widely used. His pupil Zenodotus of Ephesus became the librarian of the Museum in Alexandria and prepared the standard critical edition of the Homeric epics, omitting many spurious verses. Aristarchus of Samothrace (*ca.* 220-150), likewise Museum librarian at Alexandria, edited the text of the *Iliad* and *Odyssey* prepared by Zenodotus (revised by another librarian, Aristophanes of Byzantium [*ca.* 257-180]), dividing each poem into twenty-four books, and thus substantially gave us our current printed text of Homer.

[28] Cf. W. R. Arnold, in *Old Testament and Semitic Studies in Memory of William R. Harper*, Vol. 1, pp. 167-204. Chicago, 1908.

Zenodotus also initiated the immense work of cataloguing the Library of the Museum. He was assisted by two able scholars, Alexander of Pleuron and Lycophron of Rhegium, who classified the tragedies and comedies, respectively. The work of cataloguing the library was finally completed by the great poet Callimachus, who probably succeeded Zenodotus as librarian: his monumental catalogue (*Pinakes,* Tablets) in 120 papyrus scrolls was a literary history giving biographies and bibliographies of the authors represented in the library. A number of pupils of Callimachus became eminent scholars, but his successor as librarian was the great scientist Eratosthenes (see above), who wrote a great work on Attic comedy.

Thus during the two centuries from 300 to 100 B.C. Alexandrian scholars, through critical texts, philological and historical commentaries, and learned research, not only made the Greek classics available and comprehensible, but laid the foundation of critical and exegetical methods, soon adopted in Alexandria by Jews like Philo, and Christians like Origen, in their study of the Bible, and eventually blossoming in the research technique of modern times.

Dictionaries and grammars also grew out of the Alexandrian literary researches. The Stoic philosopher Chrysippus (d. *ca.* 204 B.C.) raised an important philological problem: does analogy or anomaly contribute most to linguistic development? Dictionaries were prepared at Alexandria: lists of words considered classical (prepared to determine the authenticity of classical passages), lists of words belonging to certain dialects, vocabularies for individual authors, and other types of dictionaries were used in Hellenistic centers of learning. The first systematic Greek grammar was prepared by Dionysius Thrax in Rhodes (*ca.* 100 B.C.) and still survives. Although it is an elementary textbook and makes no contributions to philology, it became an ancient "best seller." It is not only the ancestor of all grammars of the Greek language down to our times, but it is the parent of Latin, Syriac, and Armenian grammatical studies. The Indians are of course the earliest and greatest grammarians in the world (Panini's Sanskrit grammar, the earliest extant, dates from *ca.* 350 B.C.), but their work has not influenced Western philologists until recent times. Before then, for better or for worse, all European grammars were more or less indebted to Dionysius Thrax.

6. Hellenistic Philosophy[29]

Alexandria with its Museum and Library was the center of scholarly and, to a lesser degree, scientific research; but Athens remained the

[29] The chief general sources are, Diogenes Laërtius, *Lives of the Philosophers* (*de clarorum philosophorum vitis,* libri decem), dating from the third century of our era, and the philosophical works of Cicero (d. 43 B.C.) and Plutarch (d. *ca.* A.D.

home of the schools of philosophy and kept the flame of pagan thought alive until Justinian (527-565) in 529 closed the school of Athens.

The Hellenistic schools, of which the most influential was the Stoa, soon departed from the metaphysics of Plato (d. 347) and Aristotle (d. 322), and going back to Socrates (d. 399) stressed the problems of human life, notably the conduct and happiness of the individual. The empire of Alexander and the monarchies into which it divided at his death in 323 created a cosmopolitan and individualistic attitude toward life which philosophy could not ignore.

Soon after 323 we find in Athens several schools. Aristotle's Peripatetic school headed by Theophrastus was incorporated by the state and bought the garden near the Lyceum where Aristotle had taught; Epicurus of Samos (d. 270) came from Lampsacus and opened his school in 306; Zeno of Citium on Cyprus (d. 262) had come to study with Crates of Thebes (a Cynic) in 312, and in 301 he began to teach in the "Painted Porch" (*poikílē stoá*) adorned with frescoes of Polygnotus, near the market (his pupils were accordingly called "Stoics"); the fourth school was Plato's Academy. The Cynics, led by Crates (d. *ca.* 300), a disciple of Diogenes of Sinope (d. 323), professed poverty (like Diogenes, who lived in a tub), and owned no meeting place. The first four were endowed by Marcus Aurelius (d. A.D. 180). Besides these five schools, active in Athens shortly before 300 B.C., the Skeptic school was founded by Pyrrho of Elis (d. *ca.* 275 B.C.) in his homeland. Rhodes and Rome eventually became, for a time, centers of Stoic teaching. Cyrene and Megara gave their names to the two remaining schools.

In the field of philosophy the famous schools founded by Plato and Aristotle soon lost ground and importance. The Old Academy under the leadership of Speusippus (347-339) and Xenocrates of Chalcedon (339-314) developed Plato's thought as he had conceived it in his last years, but modified it in some points. Their successors (Polemo of Athens [314-270], whose best pupil was Crantor; and Crates of Athens [270-264]) stressed ethics and religion: thus the philosophical system of Plato disintegrated and decayed. The Middle Academy, headed by Arcesilaus of

120). The standard work, even though antiquated in occasional details, is still Eduard Zeller, *Die Philosophie der Griechen in ihrer geschichtlichen Entwickelung*, 3 vols., Tübingen, 1844-52; 5th ed., 5 vols., 1892-1909; in English: E. Zeller, *Stoics, Epicureans, and Sceptics*, 1880; *History of Greek Philosophy*. London, 1881. For later bibliographies, see F. Überweg, *Grundriss der Geschichte der Philosophie*, Vol. 1; 12th ed. by Prächter, Berlin, 1926; and also individual articles in Pauly-Wissowa, *Realenzyklopädie*. Good general summaries of Hellenistic philosophy will be found in *Allgemeine Geschichte der Philosophie*, pp. 200-287 (by H. von Arnim). Kultur der Gegenwart I, 5. Berlin and Leipzig, 1909. W. Windelband, *Geschichte der antiken Philosophie*, 3rd ed. by A. Bonhoffer (I. von Müller's Handbuch der klassischen Altertums-Wissenschaft V; I, 1). München, 1912.

Pitane (d. 241), followed by Lakydes of Cyrene (d. 216), completed this dissolution first by a return to Socrates's critique of superficial opinions, then by a frank adoption of the skepsis of Pyrrho. The New Academy, founded by Carneades of Cyrene (d. 129) and continued by Clitomachus, included also Philo of Larissa and Antiochus of Ashkelon, the teachers of Cicero. Carneades, the greatest skeptic of antiquity, attacked Stoicism and as a member of a philosophical embassy in Rome in 155 displayed his virtuosity there by lecturing brilliantly for and against justice. The New Academy joined to its theoretical skepticism a practical theory of probabilities, and eventually, like other schools, reached its end in eclecticism.

Aristotle's Peripatetic school (the Lyceum) followed an entirely different course, as has been noticed above in dealing with science and scholarship. Under its first head, the botanist Theophrastus (d. 287), the school carried on the scientific work of the master: Aristoxenus of Tarentum wrote on musical theory; Eudemus of Rhodes wrote a history of mathematics and astronomy; Dicaearchus wrote a history of Greek culture, the *Constitution of Sparta*, and prepared a map. The successor of Theophrastus, Strato of Lampsacus (d. 269), was the last important Hellenistic physicist; like Aristoxenus and Dicaearchus, he strove to overcome Plato's dualism (the world of ideas and the world of material objects) which Aristotle had not solved, for he still contrasted God and world, spirit and nature, form and matter: he asserted the immanence of reason (against Aristotle's transcendence) in the soul. After him the Peripatetic school ceased to deal with philosophical problems, except for Critolaus of Phaselis (*ca.* 155). Lycon of Troas, who headed it from 269 to 225, devoted himself to pedagogy. His successor Ariston of Ceos wrote books on morals, while, as we have seen, other members of the school, in Alexandria and Athens, turned more and more to humanistic scholarship: we may mention again Clearchus of Soli, Duris, Chamaeleon, Hieronymus of Rhodes. The final and, for the future, most important contribution of the Peripatetic school was the collection, edition, and explanation of the works of Aristotle. Tyrannion (*ca.* 90 B.C.) prepared a critical edition of the works of the master, and Andronicus of Rhodes (*ca.* 70 B.C.), the eleventh head of the Peripatetic school, arranged and interpreted them. This work was continued by the latest members of the Peripatetic school, of whom Alexander of Aphrodisias (*ca.* A.D. 200) was probably the greatest. The complaint of Seneca (d. A.D. 65) was justified for both the Academy and the Peripatetic school in his time: *quae philosophia fuit, facta philologia est* (*Epistle* 108, 23; "what was once philosophy has become philology"); cf. Epictetus, *Manual,* No. 49.

The endeavor to overcome the dualism of Plato, which Aristotle had narrowed (but not suppressed) by bringing together in existing objects

Plato's ideas and matter as inseparable form and matter, remained the chief metaphysical problem of Hellenistic philosophy. In Aristotle the dualism appeared chiefly in the contrast between God—pure act, pure form, pure thought, unmoved mover—and the world. Even in the Peripatetic school, as we have seen, Strato rejected Aristotle's dualism in the cosmos, by finding there nature alone without God, and in the soul, by denying the transcendence of reason and asserting the soul's unity. Epicureans and Stoics likewise in different ways reached the *one* beyond the *two.*

Epicurus of Samos (342-270) was much impressed as a young man by the atomism of Democritus of Abdera (early fourth century B.C.) and the *ataraxía* (impassiveness) of Pyrrho, whose skepticism, however, he rejected. Epicurus recognized only two disciplines in philosophy: physics and ethics. His notions of the physical world are chiefly derived from Democritus: nothing exists except atoms moving in empty space. The atoms are of different sizes, have weight and form, and are indestructible. They move downward in space at different speeds and, due to collisions between atoms, they are capable of deviating slightly from the vertical direction, making possible the formation of bodies having spontaneous motion—and even the freedom of the human will, which is the foundation of ethics. Since everything is the result of a combination of atoms, the souls are dissipated at death; and popular religions are immoral and false superstitions. The gods exist, but live serenely outside of our world, in interstellar spaces, unconcerned with terrestrial affairs and needing no worship, although being perfect they are worthy of it. In his ethical teaching Epicurus followed the Cyrenaic school, founded by Aristippus (d. *ca.* 360), according to which pleasure (*hēdonē*) is the aim of life and virtue is the capacity to enjoy pleasure. But Epicurus did not stress, like Aristippus, the pleasures of the senses, such as the delights of love and the enjoyment of banquets, but rather the lack of pain attained through insight. Insight leads us to virtue, which ensures serenity of mind in the midst of misfortune, or *ataraxía* (impassiveness). The great poem of T. Lucretius Carus (d. 55 B.C.) *On Nature (De rerum natura)*, one of the masterpieces of world literature, is the fullest exposition of the teaching of Epicurus now extant. It seems likely that Ecclesiastes, and Wisd. of Sol. 2:1-9, contain more or less distorted echoes of the hedonism of Epicurus.

After Aristippus, the first hedonist, new tendencies appear in the Cyrenaic school. Hegesias (*ca.* 300 B.C.) realized that pleasure, which was the aim of man for Aristippus, was unattainable, for life brought more sorrows than joys; he became therefore so pessimistic that he was called *ho peisithánatos* (the persuader to die), for he taught that deliverance from pain came only in death. Theodorus, his contemporary, was less gloomy: he believed that through insight and righteousness one might attain a constant happy mood enabling one to enjoy life. His attack on popular religion, which gained him the nickname of "the atheist" (*átheos*), made an impression on his pupil Euhemerus of Messene (Sicily) who, in his philosophical novel *Sacred History* depicted Zeus and other gods as ancient divinized kings.

The school of the Cynics was founded by Antisthenes of Athens (d. *ca.* 370), a pupil of Gorgias and of Socrates, and gained popularity through Diogenes of Sinope (d. 323), called "the insane Socrates," and his pupil Crates of Thebes (d. *ca.* 300) who, with his wife Hipparchia, gave away his property and lived on alms. The Cynics had no interest in scientific research but stressed the right life. Virtue, according to Antisthenes, was attained not through learning and reflection but through practice (*áskēsis*). Virtue, the *summum bonum* which alone brings happiness, is the capacity to reduce our wants to a minimum: thus, after becoming emancipated from externals, we attain inner freedom and joy. Spiritual and physical *pónos* (toil and trouble), poverty, humiliations, false accusations, are consequently more desirable than pleasure. The political ideal of the Cynics was a world state: one flock and one shepherd. In religion they stressed monotheism against the popular myths and cults. One of the last and most brilliant members of the school was Menippus of Gadara (Transjordania) in the third century B.C., the author of biting satires partly in verse and partly in prose—a literary genre which reached its perfection in the satires of Horace (d. 8 B.C.) which were composed entirely in hexameters. After Menippus the Cynics became itinerant evangelists to the lowest classes.

The Megarian school was founded by Euclides of Megara (d. 374 B.C.). He gave a concrete content to the Eleatic abstract Being—the sole reality according to Parmenides of Elea (*ca.* 470 B.C.), for *éstin eînai* (being is)—by identifying it with the Good, under the influence of his teacher Socrates. This sole existing reality is called by various names (God, Reason, Insight, one of the virtues) but it is eternally invariable; likewise there is but a single virtue, namely, knowledge. A later head of the Megarians, Stilpo of Megara (d. *ca.* 300) combined this teaching with the ethics of the Cynics, and thus had a deep influence on his pupil Zeno, the founder of the Stoic school. Stilpon argued that if the sole existing Being is the Good, the Good must have all the attributes of what really exists; virtue must be the state in which the mind is separated from all pain and all change, and the *summum bonum* must be complete apathy and autarchy of the soul, its indifference to external goods, as the Cynics taught. However, for the Cynics what is perceived through the senses was the only reality, while for the Megarians it did not exist at all.

A similar moral ideal was presented by the Skeptical school founded by Pyrrho of Elis (d. 275 or 270 B.C.). Our information on this school in pre-Christian times is limited to echoes of the teaching of Timon of Phlius (d. *ca.* 230), Pyrrho's pupil; the school was revived after him by Aenesidemus of Knossos (first century B.C.) and came to its end with Sextus Empiricus (*ca.* A.D. 200), some of whose works are preserved. Like Epicureanism, Pyrrhonism had its roots in the atomism of Democritus: Pyrrho was a pupil of the latter's follower Anaxarchus, with whom he reached India in Alexander's expedition. Doubts about the possibility of human knowledge had of course been raised by the Sophists in the fifth century. Pyrrho argued that either sense-perception or reason may at times deceive us, and no truth may confidently be expected from such deceivers, particularly since we possess no reliable criterion for determining what is true. Sense and reason can inform us merely about phenomena, never about the ultimate reality: our knowledge is always relative, never absolute. Consequently, Timon could sum up his teaching in three questions: What is the nature of things? How should we behave in relation to them? What do we gain if we behave correctly?[30] The three following words concisely give the philosopher's attitude to these three problems, in the same order: *akatalepsía* (incomprehensibility), *epoché* (suspension of judgment), and *ataraxía* (impassiveness). Since things are unknowable, they are indifferent (*adiáphora*). The Skeptics suspended judgment not merely in physical and metaphysical matters, but also in value verdicts, refusing to commit themselves as to whether something was beautiful or ugly, good or bad, just or unjust. For such value judgments would produce attraction or repulsion, desire or avoidance, and thus disturb the serenity of the soul, the supreme happiness and peace of *ataraxía,* which is substantially the same as the Epicurean serenity, the Cynic inner freedom, the Megarian autarchy of the soul, and the Stoic apathy. All these schools strive toward the self-sufficiency of the individual and his indifference to external occurrences.

The Stoic school was the most successful and the most characteristic school of the Hellenistic and Roman periods: it offered the most acceptable solutions to the metaphysical problem (how to overcome the dualism of Plato and Aristotle) and to the practical problem about the attainment of the peace of mind that most schools of philosophy made the goal of their ethical teaching.

Zeno of Citium in Cyprus (d. 262), the founder of the Stoa, had among his teachers the Cynic Crates, the Academist Polemon, and the Megarians Stilpon and Diodorus Cronus. His greatest pupil, who followed him as the head of the Stoa, was Cleanthes of Assus (d. 232), called "the donkey" by his comrades on account of his clumsiness. He

[30] Aristocles, quoted by Eusebius, *Praeparatio evangelica* XIV:18, 2.

allowed some gifted Stoics, like Ariston of Chius, Herillus of Chalcedon, and Dionysius of Heracleia (Pontus) to found other schools or to follow other masters. Chrysippus of Soli in Cilicia (d. 206) was the successor of Cleanthes: an indefatigable scholar, his writings filled 705 scrolls (100 of our printed volumes) and fixed in all details the standard teaching of the Stoa for his successors (Zeno of Tarsus, Diogenes of Seleucia, Antipatrus of Tarsus, and Archedemus).[31] "If Chrysippos were not, the Stoa would not exist" (Diogenes Laërtius 7, 180). A second phase of Stoicism, characterized by a more eclectic acceptance of Platonic and Aristotelian teachings, began with Panaetius of Rhodes through whose friend Scipio Africanus the Younger (185-129) Stoicism was taught in Rome. In 129 Panaetius became the head of the Stoic school in Athens, and Cicero (106-43) in his *De officiis* not only preserved the basic teaching of Panaetius' book *On Duties*, but passed it on to Ambrose of Milan (d. A.D. 397) and thus to Christianity. Posidonius of Apamea in Syria (d. 51 B.C.), the greatest pupil of Panaetius and the teacher of Cicero, was the last original Hellenistic thinker.[32] Finally, in the Roman Empire, the leading Stoics were Lucius Annaeus Seneca of Cordoba (d. A.D. 65), the tutor of Nero; C. Musonius Rufus of Volsinii (first century of our era); Epictetus of Hierapolis in Phrygia (d. *ca.* A.D. 130), whose teaching has been preserved by his pupil Flavius Arrian (d. *ca.* A.D. 150) in two books, the *Diatribaí* (Discourses) and the famous *Encheirídion* (Manual), a brief extract thereof; and Emperor Marcus Aurelius Antoninus (161-180), whose *Meditations* (Greek title: *Eis heautón* [For Himself]), the justly classical swan song of Stoicism, well express the aspirations of a noble mind.

The Stoics defined the *sophía* (wisdom), which is the goal of philosophy, as "the knowledge [or science] of divine and human things and of their causes";[33] and they subdivided it into logic, physics, and ethics,

Logic is the science of language and thought, of words (grammar) and what they mean (concepts, judgments, conclusions): it is the study of *lógos*, which means both word and reason (cf. John 1:1), either a

[31] The surviving fragments of the early Stoics have been edited in the standard work of Hans von Arnim (J. ab Arnim), *Stoicorum veterum fragmenta*, 3 vols. Leipzig, Teubner, 1903-1905; Vol. 4 by M. Adler, 1924. The main secondary sources on Stoicism are the fragmentary seventh book of Diogenes Laërtius, Plutarch, Cicero, and Seneca. Aside from the general works previously listed, the following are still basic on the Stoa: L. Stein, *Die Psychologie der Stoa*, Vols. 1-2, Berlin, 1886-1888. A. Bonhoffer, *Epiktet und die Stoa*. Stuttgart, 1890. A. Schmekel, *Die Philosophie der mittleren Stoa*. Berlin, 1892. A. Dyroff, *Die Ethik der alten Stoa*. Berlin, 1897.

[32] The basic work on Panaetius and Posidonius is still Schmekel's *Die Philosophie der Mittleren Stoa*, mentioned in the preceding footnote.

[33] References to this definition by Plutarch, Cicero, and Seneca are quoted by C. L. W. Grimm, *Kurzgefasstes Exegetisches Handbuch zu den Apokryphen*, Vol. 4, p. 305. Leipzig, 1857. This definition is quoted in IV Macc. 1:16 and Philo, *De congressu eruditionis gratia* 14 [M I, 531].

thought in the mind or an expression on the lips. The Stoic teaching on grammar, on dialectics (discrimination between truth and falsehood), and on epistemology (according to which knowledge is based on sensations tested and directly apprehended, in contrast with imagination and general concepts) need not be considered in detail here, but the notion of *lógos* is basic for us, since it influenced Hellenistic Judaism and Christianity. This *lógos* is a faculty which dumb animals lack: men share it with the gods. It is the capacity to pass from a mass of individual sensations to general concepts and conclusions. The human *lógos* is essentially identical with the cosmic reason molding matter into natural objects; consequently, even though not infallible like the divine *lógos*, human reason can reproduce the thoughts of cosmic reason and thus understand reality.

The *lógos* has brought us to the second branch of philosophy, physics (and metaphysics). Plato in the *Timaeus* portrays the eternal immaterial God creating the world and implanting in it a universal rational soul (which was made before matter) to rule over it intelligently, administering the immutable laws of nature. Aristotle (*Metaphysics*), instead, did not regard the immaterial God as the creator of the world: both God and the world existed from eternity and God was merely the cause of motion and of its laws. The Stoics went a step further in eliminating the dualism between God and the world. God for them is material and existed from eternity in the primeval fire, out of which he created the world. In this world of ours God functions as the mind or soul of the world, the cosmic *lógos*, and reaches out to all parts of the universe through his innumerable seminal *lógoi* (*lógoi spermatikoí*) or powers (*dynámeis*). Thus reality is one, an organism in which body and soul are inseparable, for God is immanent in the world. The immaterial realities of Plato and Aristotle become spirit (*pneûma*), which is material and, in various degrees of refinement (from that of God himself to that in a stone), permeates all matter, which the Stoics, in contrast to the atomists, regarded as infinitely divisible. In this pantheistic conception, the immanent God is the ultimate cause of all motion (without being Aristotle's motionless *movens non motus*) and of all phenomena: this single chain of cause and effect, this necessary relationship of all phenomena ultimately originating in God is called *heimarménē* (fate). Such a notion had obvious repercussions on human conduct.

We thus come to the third field of philosophy, ethics. The divine primeval fire is not only the determining cause of all that exists (fate), but at the same time the cosmic all-knowing reason and purposeful mind, the benevolent *prónoia* (providence); cf. Wisd. of Sol. 14:3; 17:2; IV Macc. 9:24; 13:18; etc. The same God causes all events and uses them for the attainment of the noblest goals, but in him there is no conflict between fate and providence. In the seminal *lógoi*, likewise, determinism and purpose are one, and Chrysippus could say that whatever happens through fate happens also according to providence. Cleanthes, on the contrary, denied this, saying that what happened through providence also happened through fate, but not vice versa. Thus Cleanthes was able to explain the presence of evil in the world as the effect of fate without the influence of providence. Conversely, Chrysippus, stressing the unity of the cosmos, could not admit that any evil ever came into the world without the consent of providence. He refused to admit that man's serenity could be disturbed by physical pain or other external evil, which as a matter of fact was no actual evil. As for moral evil, he proved that it was in harmony with divine providence by showing that moral good could not exist without moral evil, and was implicit in human freedom of the will. Man, the goal of all creation, could be an image of God only if he were free to live according to reason, thus collaborating with God, or to decline to do so. If man refuses to fulfill this purpose he sinks to the level of animals: from the cosmic point of view this is no more a real evil than the fact that there are plants and animals besides men. Man has a higher freedom than beasts when he deliberately chooses to follow the dictates of reason, rather than the compulsions of nature. This goal is fully achieved only by the sage, who becomes as free as God, for whom necessity and freedom are one and the same notion. The soul of man grows out of the soul of animal as the *lógos* or reason develops within the highest part of the soul, the *hēge-monikón* (the governing faculty). Only the souls that have attained wisdom and virtue live on as ghosts—but not forever. The cosmos, as Heraclitus had taught, emerges from fire as a new universal order (*diakósmēsis*) and later returns to the primitive simplicity of the fiery divine substance (*ekpýrōsis*, conflagration), eventually being born anew (*palingenesía*) and repeating the process through eternity.[34] As everything else, the souls of the wise are merged with the divine substance in the process of *ekpýrōsis*, but in the palingenesis the souls are reborn, without any memory of their previous existence, however. Such are the theoretical foundations of the practical philosophy of the Stoics. In accordance with their times, they regarded happiness as the goal of human life. For Zeno such happiness was logical agreement of our thoughts, and harmony of our feelings, volitions, and actions with our thoughts; Cleanthes changed this harmonious life into the famous "life in harmony with nature"—whatever that may mean. Chrysippus clarified the formula by stating that it meant both life in harmony with human nature and cosmic nature; for they are basically the same, "nature"

[34] For echoes of this doctrine in Judaism and Christianity, see E. Schürer, *Geschichte des jüdischen Volkes*, Vol. 2, pp. 636-638. The word *palingenesía* in its cosmic sense occurs in Matt. 19:28.

(*phýsis*) being taken in a comprehensive sense, including soul and reason. In other words, for Chrysippus harmony with nature meant harmony with the *lógos* which determines both universal law and moral law: human reason, when fully developed, agrees with divine reason. Thus the human ideal is the full realization of the possibilities of human nature: the attainment of this goal is called virtue. Therefore, life in harmony with nature means virtuous life and alone brings happiness: virtue is its own reward. But virtue must always be a goal, never the means to another end, otherwise it ceases to be virtue and the supreme good. In practice, everything must be subordinated to the attainment of this goal. Things and actions either contribute to life according to the will of God, or hinder it, or finally, doing neither, they are irrelevant. Consequently, what most men regard as good (like wealth, honors, position, health) or as bad (as poverty, disgrace, ruin, pain) are intrinsically indifferent matters: their moral value depends entirely from the use we make of them. They affect only our animal nature, but as reasonable beings we are independent of externals: the wise can say with Dante, (*Inferno* 2:93), "fiamma d'esto incendio non m'assale" (the flame of this conflagration does not attack me). Such things as are indifferent (*adiáphora*) from the point of view of the supreme goal of life are, however, significant to our animal nature and are therefore to be preferred or to be rejected (*proēgména* or *apoproēgména*)—not actually good or bad—by the sage. The same applies to human actions: they are good, bad, or indifferent inasmuch as their influence on right living is positive, negative, or nil. Indifferent actions may be absolutely so or may affect our physical existence: the latter constitute a common zone of conduct between wise and fool, at least in regard to the action per se, without reference to the motive. There are thus the *katórthōma* (virtuous action), the *hamártēma* (sinful action), and the *kathēkon* (proper, correct, legal action). An action in the third category is virtuous when performed by the wise (all of whose actions are necessarily virtuous) and sinful when performed by a fool (all he does is sinful).

This absolute contrast between good and evil, theoretically without gradations in virtue and vice, divided mankind, at least in principle, into two classes: the wise and the fools, no less sharply distinguished than the saved and the damned of St. Augustine (d. 430), Calvin (d. 1564), or, for that matter, a good old-fashioned revival meeting.[35] There is no

---

[35] Logically of course there is only truth and falsehood, right and wrong, with no middle ground. There is "the way of life and the way of death" (Jer. 21:8), wisdom and folly (Eccl. 1:17; 2:12; 7:25), the narrow gate and way leading to destruction (Matt. 7:13 f.); see in general, for Jewish literature, H. L. Strack and P. Billerbeck, *Kommentar zum Neuen Testament*, Vol. 1, pp. 460-463. Prodicus of Ceos (d. *ca.* 400 B.C.) gave the earliest and best exposition of the doctrine of the two ways in his apologue of the choice of Heracles, summarized by Xenophon (d. *ca.* 355 B.C.) in *Memorabilia* II, 1:21-34.

gray between black and white: even a fool may make slow progress in wisdom, but he becomes a sage instantly; in other words, a man is one or the other. In practice even Zeno, however, admitted a sort of middle class, the *prokópton* (the one advancing morally and intellectually) and common sense showed that men were either incurably bad (rare), average (the great mass), progressing, (many), or wise (very few).

The sage, or wise man (*sophós*), exemplifies the Stoic ethical ideal. Epictetus (*Discourses* IV, 3:9-12) expresses it thus: "I am free, I am a friend of God ready to render him willing obedience. Of all else, I may set store by nothing—neither by my own body, nor possessions, nor office, nor good report, nor, in a word, anything else." The sage must be selfless, passionless, pitiless, serene. He has achieved *autárkeia* (independence, self-sufficiency) and *apátheia* (impassibility, freedom from emotions). Having the first, he cannot be affected by the course of events in the world around him; his happiness is entirely an inner state, without connection with happenings independent from his will. By attaining the second he has rooted out from himself the passionate emotions rebellious against the *lógos*; he has substituted desire for greediness, caution for fear, joy for pleasure; he has banished compassion, which is mourning for another's misfortune, since mourning is excluded entirely; he has reached the stage in which "pious reason (*logismós*) is the absolute ruler (*autodéspotos*; also *autokrátōr*) over the passions" (IV Macc. 1:1, the theme of the book; cf. 1:7, 9, 13 f., 19, 30; 2:6 f., 10, 24; 6:31; 7:16; 13:1; 16:1; 18:2). Freedom from greediness leads to temperance (*sophrosýnē*); freedom from fear becomes courage (*andreía*); both of these virtues presuppose the insight and knowledge (*phrónēsis*, prudence) of right, wrong, and indifferent; and in turn are presupposed by justice (*dikaiosýnē*), which is the knowledge of what belongs to God and every person, and acting accordingly.[36] While the first three virtues stress individualism, justice is practiced in human society. Later Stoics, beginning presumably with Panaetius, added benevolence to justice (Cicero, *De officiis* I, 7:20); compassion and mercy were stressed by Seneca, Epictetus, Marcus Aurelius. Seneca (*De clementia*) discussed in detail the problem of how strict justice can be reconciled with clemency: the unfortunate should be helped, without grieving with them; punishment should not be omitted, but should be determined after due consideration of human frailty and of extenuating

[36] These four Stoic cardinal virtues were first determined by Plato in connection with the four parts of the soul. The Stoics modified their meaning slightly; from them they were adopted by the Alexandrian Jews (Wisd. of Sol. 8:7; IV Macc. 1:2-4, 6; cf. 5:23-24, where they are harmonized with the Law of Moses and piety takes the place of prudence; for Philo, see H. A. Wolfson, *Philo*, Vol. 2, p. 218, n. 134; cf. C. Siegfried, *Philo von Alexandria*, p. 272. Jena, 1875). The ethics of the Stoics in general had a considerable influence on the teaching of Philo; see E. Bréhier, *Les idées philosophiques et religieuses de Philon d'Alexandrie*, 2nd ed., pp. 252-259. Paris, 1925; but cf. Wolfson, *op. cit.*, Vol. 1, pp. 111-112.

circumstances. Elsewhere Seneca condemns Roman gladiatorial fights and warlike spirit. The social trend begins with the second basic instinct (race preservation; the first is self-preservation), which produces devotion to the family. From this we pass to ever-wider circles of fellow human beings until we reach all of mankind. The *lógos* proves that all men are brothers, being children of the same heavenly Father: "they are by nature your kinsmen, your brothers, the offspring of God" (Epictetus, *Discourses* I, 13:3). All beings endowed with reason (*lógos*), i.e., all gods and men (but not animals), are a single society, a single state in which reason is law; they have duties toward the other members of the world state, piety being their duty toward the gods. All men were indeed members of this organism "whether Jews or Greeks, whether bond or free" (I Cor. 12:13; cf. 12:12-26).

If the mental faculty is common to us, then the *lógos* by which we are reasonable beings is common. If this is so, also the *lógos* which commands us what to do and what not to do is common. If this is so, then there is likewise a law in common. If this is so, we are fellow-citizens, and if so we are members of the same community. If this is so the world is, so to say, a single state.

Marcus Aurelius IV, 4

In this world state, individual states are like houses (or households) within a city (*ibid.* III, 11). This great idea of the world state, according to Epictetus (*Discourses* I, 9), goes back to Socrates, who, when asked to what country he belonged, replied, "I am a citizen of the world [*kósmios*, meaning obviously *kosmopolítēs*]." According to the Stoics, in the words of St. Paul, "there is neither Greek nor Jew, circumcision nor uncircumcision, Barbarian, Scythian, bond nor free" (Col. 3:11) for those who "put off the old man with his deeds; and have put on the new man, which is renewed in knowledge after the image of him that created him" (Col. 3:9 f.). Such a cosmopolitan view did not, however, prevent the Stoics from participating ably and actively in the administration of their own particular countries, and this is one of the reasons for the popularity of this school in Rome, where Emperor Marcus Aurelius (VI, 44) could say, "As [Marcus Aurelius] Antoninus my state and fatherland is Rome, but as a man it is the world." Whether the world state was suggested to Zeno by Alexander's empire or not, this great conception furnished a philosophical basis for the Roman Empire and for Paul's notion of a universal Christian Church in which social, national, and racial differences are no longer significant.

7. Hellenistic Religion

In the Greek world after Alexander five types of religion attracted adherents: the city cults in honor of the Olympian gods, the personal striving for salvation in the mystery religions, the beliefs in chance and fate, the teaching of philosophical schools like the Stoa, and the Oriental religions (including Judaism and Christianity).

The traditional worship of the Olympians[37] was declining long before Christianity brought it to an end.[38] Nothing had contributed more to delineate the individual character of the Olympians, to create a common Greek religion by the side of the local cults, to humanize (and consequently to moralize) the gods than the Homeric poems (tenth to eighth centuries B.C.)—the basis of Greek education and mentality (on which the best study is W. Jaeger's *Paideia*).[39] Homer, however, had no influence on the celebration of the local rituals and festivals, and on personal religion.

Before Alexander several trends were at work to undermine the worship of the Olympians. The austere bourgeois morality and the common sense of farmers characteristic of Hesiod (eighth century) contrast sharply with the Homeric world of noble heroes and proud knights, in which the common man appears only once in Thersites (who is thrashed into silence when he speaks his mind in the assembly) aside from faithful old family retainers. In the sixth century a new spirit appears in Greek

[37] The standard works on the Olympian gods are the following. L. F. A. Maury, *Histoire des religions de la Grèce antique.* 3 vols. Paris, 1857-1859. O. Gruppe, *Griechische Mythologie und Religionsgeschichte.* 2 vols. Handbuch der Klassischen Altertumswissenschaft, edited by I. von Müller, V, 2. München, 1897-1906. L. R. Farnell, *The Cults of the Greek States.* 5 vols. Oxford, 1896-1909. A. B. Cook, *Zeus.* 3 vols. Cambridge, 1914 ff. O. Kern, *Die Religion der Griechen.* 3 vols. Berlin, 1926-1938. M. P. Nilsson, *Geschichte der griechischen Religion.* Vol. 1 [to Alexander]. Handbuch der Altertumswissenschaft V, ii, 1. München, 1941. Summaries: L. R. Farnell, *Outlines of Greek Religion* (reprinted from the article "Greek Religion" in J. Hastings, *Encyclopaedia of Religion and Ethics*). London, 1920. M. P. Nilsson, *History of Greek Religion* (expanded translation of Chant. de la Saussaye, *Lehrbuch der Religionsgeschichte,* 4th ed. by A. Bertholet and E. Lehmann. Vol. 2, pp. 280-417. Tübingen, 1925). Oxford, 1925. G. Murray, *Five Stages of Greek Religion.* London, 1925. A. Gercke and E. Norden, editors, *Einleitung in die Altertumswissenschaft* II, 4: S. Wide and M. P. Nilsson, *Griechische und Römische Religion.* 4th ed. Leipzig and Berlin, 1931. See also the general histories of religion and the encyclopaedias.

[38] On the decline and end of paganism after the birth of Christianity see especially: V. Schultze, *Geschichte des Untergangs des griechich-römischen Heidentums.* 2 vols. Jena, 1887, 1892. G. Boissier, *La fin du paganisme.* Paris, 1891. J. Toutain, *Les cultes païens dans l'empire romain.* Bibliothèque de l'Ecole des Hautes Etudes, Sciences Religieuses, Vols. 20 and 25. Paris, 1905, 1911. A. Dieterich, *Der Untergang der antiken Religion* (in: *Kleine Schriften,* pp. 449-539. Leipzig, 1911). G. Wissowa, *Religion und Kultus der Römer,* 2nd ed. München, 1912. A. Harnack, *Die Mission und Aubreitung des Christentums,* 2 vols., 3rd ed. Leipzig, 1915 (English translation of the 2nd ed. London, 1908). J. Geffcken, *Der Ausgang des griechich-römischen Heidentums.* Heidelberg, 1929. Books on pagan criticism of Greek religion, and particularly of polytheism and image worship, will be found listed in Part II, Chapter V (The Wisdom of Solomon), note 22.

[39] W. Jaeger, *Paideia.* Translated by G. Highet. Vol. 1. Oxford, Blackwell, 1939. Vol. 2. Oxford University Press, 1943. Vol. 3, Oxford University Press, 1944.

religion, about the same time when new heights were reached in China (Lao-tse and Confucius), India (Buddha and the Upanishads), Iran (Zoroaster), and Israel (Jeremiah, Deuteronomy, and the Second Isaiah). The cults of Demeter, a country goddess of farmers worshiped in the Eleusinian mysteries, and of Dionysus, whose orgiastic rites originated among Thracian barbarians, as also the later Orphic religion, likewise coming from Thrace, offered to the average man the hope of a blessed immortality, unknown to Homer. Greek philosophy was born in the same century, and investigated the origin of the universe: one of the early philosophers, Xenophanes of Colophon (sixth century) ridiculed the human tendency to represent the gods as men and recognized but a single god, the thinking universe; another, Heraclitus of Ephesus, not long after him, attacked rituals and idolatry and saw in primeval fire the first principle and mind of the world. Even more corrosive for religion was the agnosticism and skepticism of the Sophists in the fifth century. Strange as it may seem, the superb poetry of Pindar (d. 443) and Aeschylus (d. 456), which was superficially in agreement with Homer, through its profound moral and monotheistic piety actually taught a new religion, akin to that of philosophers like Socrates and Plato. Sophocles (d. 406) was more conservative than Aeschylus; but Euripides (d. 406)—bitterly attacked by the reactionary Aristophanes (d. *ca.* 380), particularly in *The Frogs* (as Socrates in *The Clouds*)— openly censured the conduct of the Homeric gods and even, following Protagoras of Abdera (fifth century), seemed at times to doubt their existence.

So the Hellenistic period witnessed the twilight of the Olympian gods, at least in the minds of the cultivated Greeks. New factors, in addition to the mystical and rationalistic attacks just mentioned, contributed to the decay of traditional beliefs. The old religion was intimately connected with the *pólis*, or city-state, which was absorbed into kingdoms and empires after Philip of Macedon (382-336), the father of Alexander, conquered Greece through his victory at Chaeronea (338). So shaken were the old convictions that when Hellenistic rulers were worshiped as gods hardly anyone protested in the name of religion. Seleucus I Nicator (d. 280) was revered as "Zeus victorious," Antiochus I Soter [savior] (d. 261), his son, became "Apollo savior," Antiochus IV Epiphanes [(god) manifest] (d. 164) called himself "god" and was represented as the Olympian Zeus on his coins (cf. Dan. 11:36). Demetrius I Poliorcetes (d. 283) was celebrated as the only god (the son of Poseidon and Aphrodite), received the Parthenon in Athens as his residence, and saw his mistress Lamia receive divine honors as Aphrodite Lamia in Athens and Thebes.[40] This apotheosis of rulers received a sort of philosophical vindication

[40] K. J. Beloch, *Griechische Geschichte*, 2nd ed., Vol. 4, Pt. I, p. 434. Berlin, 1925.

through Euhemerus, who, in his fictional *Sacred History*, presented Zeus and other gods as human kings, divinized after their death; thus he contributed to the dethronement of the Olympians. Moreover, the allegorical interpretation of Homer, introduced by Theagenes of Rhegium before Plato (cf. J. Tate, in *Classical Review* 41 [1927] 214 f.; *Classical Quarterly* 23 [1929] 142-154), stripped the ancient myths of even the semblance of fact: Aristotle dismissed popular beliefs as nothing but fables. Finally, the influence of Egypt and the Near East proved decisive: as early as Herodotus Oriental deities were identified with Greek ones (Melkart of Tyre was called Heracles, Amon was called Zeus, etc.); they were adopted by the Greeks, but no Greek god received more than passing formal worship in Asia and Africa.[41] Antiochus IV Epiphanes alone in 168 attempted to force his subjects to worship the Olympian Zeus exclusively, but failed dismally.

While the Homeric deities were losing their hold on the faith of the Greeks, their public worship was flourishing: festivals were celebrated as splendidly as ever, temples continued to receive votive gifts, divine oracles were still requested by the authorities, notably from Apollo at Delphi. We even hear of deities appearing visibly to their devotees, as Artemis Leucophryene at Magnesia in 221 B.C.—an event celebrated annually as a national festival sanctioned by the Delphic oracle.[42] This is not the sole instance of a religion stressing pomp and circumstance in the public worship when it has ceased to be a living faith, a genuine inner force.

As has been noted, personal religious feeling and the quest for immortality found little satisfaction in the national cult of the Olympians; in Egypt, likewise, the masses sought immortality through Osiris when the official worship of Amon-Re failed to promise it to them. In the Hellenistic period, the earlier Eleusinian mysteries in honor of Demeter, the enthusiastic and orgiastic cult of Dionysus (from which came the Attic drama), and the Orphic mysteries continued to flourish;[43] at the same time a number of Oriental cults attracted Greek adherents—particularly among the women.

[41] On Hellenistic cults in Syria, see O. Eissfeldt, *Tempel und Kulte syrischer Städte in hellenistisch-römischer Zeit* (AO 40). Leipzig, 1941.

[42] Such divine apparitions explain how Paul and Barnabas could be regarded as Hermes and Zeus by the people and the priesthood of Lystra in Lycaonia (Acts 14:11-13).

[43] On the Greek mystery religions, see in particular: C. A. Lobeck, *Aglaophamus*. Königsberg, 1829. O. Kern, *Orpheus*. Berlin, 1920; *Orphicorum Fragmenta*. Berlin, 1922. V. Macchioro, *Zagreus: studi sul'orfismo*. Bari, 1920. E. Rohde, *Psyche*. 10th ed. Tübingen, 1925. R. Reitzenstein, *Die hellenistischen Mysterienreligionen*. 3rd ed. Leipzig-Berlin, 1927. See also below, note 83.

The mysteries of Demeter at Eleusis, as in those of Dionysus, Adonis,[44] Attis, and Osiris, depict the death and resurrection of a deity (symbolizing the revival of nature in spring). In this case, Persephone (Kore), the daughter of Demeter, is carried to the underworld by Hades (Pluto) and may come back to the world of sunshine not more than eight months every year. Through initiation rites which, being secret, are not known in detail, the *mýstai* (initiates) believed that they secured a happy immortality.[45] On the island of Samothrace the mysteries of the two *Kábeiroi* (Cabiri) gods, said to be of Phrygian origin, were associated with those of Demeter and Dionysus; aside from other future benefits, the initiates enjoyed the right of asylum. Later the mysteries of Hecate flourished on the island of Aegina.

Dionysus was originally a fertility god and in Greece became the god of wine (Bacchus): his female devotees (maenads) danced wildly in the night, bearing torches, and after being overcome by "divine" frenzy tore living animals apart and devoured their bloody flesh, reputedly the body of Zagreus, i.e., Dionysus (see Euripides, *Bacchae*). In their enthusiasm, in the rapture of their ecstasy, the devotees were lifted above themselves to the divine plane, forgot their misery, and for a moment achieved the ineffable experience of mystical union with the deity, which was a foretaste of eternal bliss.

Orpheus was a Thracian singer whose lyre tamed savage men and beasts until the maenads tore him apart. Orphism, named after him, not only taught the death and resurrection of Dionysus, but also furnished that exact information on life after death of which echoes come down to modern times. The body is considered as the tomb of the soul (*sôma-sêma*, body-grave; cf. Plato, *Gorgias* 493a), "man is the dream of a shadow" (Pindar, *Pythian Odes* 8, 95 cf. Sophocles, *Ajax* 126; Wisd. of Sol. 2:5; etc.). After death, the Orphic initiates, who had been purified in this life through special rites, and through strict diet and conduct had remained pure, enjoyed an immortality about which opinions ranged from a state of eternal ebriety (Plato, *Republic* II, 363c) to the pleasures of a delightful countryside (Aristophanes, *Frogs* 154-157). The wicked, conversely, went to a horrible hell first described in Orphic interpolations near the end of book XI (576-600) of the *Odyssey* (Tityus, Tantalus, Sisyphus).[46]

[44] The earliest form of the Adonis myth is found in the mythological poem from Ras Shamra on Aleyan Baal, translated by Cyrus H. Gordon in *The Loves and Wars of Baal and Anat*, Princeton University Press, 1944; see also Julian Obermann, *Ugaritic Mythology*, Yale University Press, 1948.

[45] Homeric *Hymn to Demeter* 480 f.

[46] The basic study of Greek notions about heaven and hell is: A. Dieterich, *Nekyia*. Leipzig, 1893. Second ed., 1913. See also E. Rohde, *Psyche*, and the standard books on Greek religion cited in note 37, above. The great Polygnotus (5th cent.) depicted at Delphi some of the infernal torments: he represented the

And next you'll see great snakes and savage monsters
In tens of thousands. . . . Then weltering seas of filth
And ever-rippling dung: and plunged therein,
Whoso has wronged the stranger here on earth,
Or robbed his boylove of the promised pay,
Or swinged his mother, or profanely smitten
His father's cheek, or sworn an oath foresworn.

. . . But now I've got thee fast.
So close the Styx's inky hearted rock,
The blood-bedabbed peak of Acheron,
Shall hem thee in: the hell-hounds of Cocytus
Prowl round thee; whilst the hundred-headed Asp
Shall rive thy heart-strings: the Tartesian Lamprey
Prey on thy lungs: and those Tithrasian Gorgons
Mangle and tear thy kidneys, mauling them,
Entrails and all, into one bloody mash.

Aristophanes, Frogs 143-150 and 469-477
(Translated by B. B. Rogers)

Hardly anything has survived from the ancient Orphic literature, which must have been fairly abundant—to judge from its echoes in later descriptions of heaven and hell, such as are found, aside from *The Frogs* of Aristophanes, in Plato (*Republic* II, 363, and at the end of the work; *Gorgias* 524 ff.; *Phaedo* 112 f.), in Plutarch (*De sera numinis vindicta* 566 f.), and in Lucian of Samosata in the second century of our era (*Vera historia* 126 f.). Orphic literary remains have been collected by O. Kern (*Orphicorum fragmenta.* Berlin, 1922). The inscriptions on gold leaf found in tombs in southern Italy and in Crete, which contain instructions about the correct behavior in the underworld, are a genuine, though meager, supplement to Orphic literature.[47]

We do not know whether Orphic ideas of future life influenced the descriptions of paradise and hell in Judaism before A.D. 200 (see Testament of the XII Patriarchs, Enoch, Syriac Baruch, IV Esdras, Sibylline Oracles;[48] cf. Luke 16:19-31; 23:43; Rev. 14:10; 19:20; 20:10; 21:1-22:5;

---

visit of Odysseus to Hades adding some scenes not found in *Odyssey* XI. Plato, who was much impressed by Orphism, like Polygnotus described the Danaïdes who are punished in Hades (for killing their husbands) by being forced to carry water in sieves or leaky vessels.

[47] The text of these Orphic texts will be found in: A. Olivieri, *Lamellae aureae Orphicae.* H. Lietzmann's *Kleine Texte*, No. 133. Bonn, 1915; Gilbert Murray, in the appendix to Jane E. Harrison, *Prolegomena to the Study of Greek Religion*, 3rd ed., Cambridge 1922. See especially, I. M. Linforth, *The Arts of Orpheus.* University of California Press, 1941.

[48] For references to heaven and hell in these Jewish writings, see: E. Schürer, *Geschichte*, Vol. 2, pp. 644-646; L. Couard, *Die religiösen und sittlichen Anschauungen der alttestamentlichen Apokryphen und Pseudepigraphen*, pp. 240-244. Gütersloh, 1907; R. H. Charles, *The Apocrypha and Pseudepigrapha*, Vol. 2, Index, under "Heaven" and "Hell." Oxford, 1913.

etc.), but the so-called *Apocalypse of Peter*[49] (a Christian book dated about A.D. 135) is unquestionably indebted to Orphism (see particularly Dieterich's *Nekyia*) and introduced precise notions about heaven and hell into Christianity, where eventually they inspired Dante's master-piece, *The Divine Comedy*. Orphism is important also for having stressed the sense of sin and guilt, and for showing a way which, through puri-fications and right living, led to eternal salvation.[50]

Before leaving these two genuinely Hellenic types of religion (even though some of their elements originated abroad)—the cult of the Olympians and the mysteries—it should be noted that the rapid rise and fall of kingdoms and rulers after the death of Alexander produced a sense of insecurity, a feeling that blind chance (*týchē*) ruled human affairs and destinies (cf. Eccl. 3:10-15; 7:13 f.; 9:1, 11 f.; Wisd. of Sol. 2:1-5). As early as the seventh century the poet Archilochus had said, "Tyche [chance, good and bad luck] and Moira [fate], O Pericles, give all things to a man." Personified and divinized, Tyche was widely wor-shiped in the Hellenistic and Roman periods, as Pliny the Elder (who died A.D. 79 investigating the eruption of Vesuvius) observed:

In the whole world, indeed, in all places and at all times, *Fortuna* [i.e., *Tychē*] alone is invoked and celebrated. She alone is accused, alone she is indicted as guilty, alone she is thought about, alone she is praised, alone she is censured and is reviled: mutable, even deemed by many blind, fickle, capricious, unreliable, variable, and favorable to the unworthy. To her are debited all expenses and credited all payments; and in the entire reckoning of mortals she alone enters both assets and liabilities. And we are so subject to chance that chance itself takes the place of god, whom she proves to be unreliable.

Pliny, Naturalis Historia II: v, 22

Tyche became the patron goddess of a number of Near Eastern Hellenistic cities. Thus Antioch in Syria recognized Tyche as its patron goddess, after Eutychides (according to Pausanias [6:2, 7], second century of our era) had carved her image with surpassing art. Each man had his own fortune or *daímōn* (Latin, *genius*). Besides Tyche, Fate, called *Heimarménē* [*Moîra*] (decreed [destiny]), *Moîra* (goddess of Fate), or *Anánkē* (necessity), was recognized as the deciding factor in

---

[49] See on this book A. Dieterich, *Nekyia*, 2nd ed., 1913; M. R. James in JTS 12 (1910-1911); E. Hennecke, *Neutestamentliche Apokryphen*, 2nd ed., pp. 314-327. Tübingen, 1924. F. Cumont, *After Life in Roman Paganism*. New Haven, 1922. An English translation of the extant fragments will be found in M. R. James, *The Apocryphal New Testament*, pp. 506-521. Oxford, at the Claredon Press, 1924.

[50] In view of a popular misunderstanding, it seems necessary to remark that moral living (as shown in the first quotation from Aristophanes, above; see also *Frogs* 454 ff.) was a requirement for future salvation in the mystery cults, particularly Orphic. In this point there is no basic contrast between Orphism and Christianity.

human events.[51] While some Stoics identified God with Heimarmene, Philo of Alexandria criticized them for making "fate and necessity into gods" (see H. A. Wolfson, *Philo*, Vol. 1, p. 329).

The determinism of the Stoics had its roots in astrology, a subject on which some of them (Diogenes of Seleucia, second century B.C.; Posidonius of Apamea, *ca.* A.D. 100) wrote books.[52] Astrology originated in Babylonia: "Chaldean" means astronomer in Greek (Aristotle, *Fragmenta* No. 35, V. Rose, Leipzig, 1886; cf. Cicero, *De divinatione* I: 1, 2), Latin (Tacitus, *Annals* II, 27; etc.), and Biblical Aramaic (Dan. 1:4; 2:2; etc.); Sextus Empiricus (*ca.* A.D. 200) even calls astrology "*chaldaikḗ*" in his book *Against the "mathematici"* (i.e., astrologers). From the Babylonians, the Greeks derived the notion that the planets were gods (we still call them by divine names: Mercury, Venus, Mars, Jupiter, etc.), that their positions were omens whose interpretation disclosed the future, and that the heavenly bodies influenced human life. Similarly, the identification of the signs of the Zodiac is a Babylonian contribution to Greek (and modern) astrology and astronomy. Some Greeks said the stars and planets through the influences (*apórrhoiai*, ethereal fluids or occult powers) emanating from them actually determined human fate; others said they merely disclosed it.[53] In either case astrology leads to fatalism, which may or may not prove deadly to religious faith and practice. Curiously, the masses in antiquity (as in modern times) have failed to see the sharp contrast between fatalism and divine help; between a predetermined fixed chain of cause and effect and freedom of the will, moral responsibility, rewards and punishments. The more intelligent, however, realized that logically worship is meaningless in a world in which every event is so inexorably determined that the gods are helpless. Such was the attitude of Emperor Tiberius (A.D. 14-37): "He was rather unconcerned about the gods and sacred things, but decidedly devoted to astrology (*mathematica*) and fully convinced that everything is produced by fate" (Suetonius [d. after 125], *Lives of the Caesars: Tiberius* 69). The contradiction between faith and fate was recognized by the Aristotelian Alexander of Aphrodisias (*ca.* A.D. 200) in his book *Perì heimarménēs* (On Fate), an attack on fatalism, and was succinctly

---

[51] See the well-documented book of W. C. Greene, *Moira: Fate, Good, and Evil in Greek Thought*. Harvard University Press, 1944.

[52] On Greek astrology and fatalism, see: A. Bouché-Leclercq, *L'astrologie grecque*. Paris, 1899. R. Reitzenstein, *Poimandres*, pp. 69 ff. Leipzig, 1904. F. Cumont, *The Oriental Religions in Roman Paganism*, translated from the French by G. Showerman. Chicago, 1911; *Astrology and Religion among the Greeks and Romans*. London, 1912. H. Gressmann, *Die hellenistische Gestirnreligion* (Beihefte zum "Alten Orient," No. 5). Leipzig, 1925. F. Boll, *Sternglaube und Sterndeutung*, 3rd ed. by W. Gundel. Leipzig 1926. The sources have been collected by Boll and Cumont in the *Catalogus codicum astrologorum graecorum*. 11 vols. Brussels, 1898-1929.

[53] See E. Pfeiffer, *Studien zum antiken Sternglauben* (*Stoicheia* II). Leipzig, 1916.

stated by the Christian poet Commodianus (third or fourth century) in the question, "If the fates of birth bestow [all], why do you beseech the gods?" Conversely, another Christian, Firmicus Maternus (fourth century) before his conversion to Christianity stressed the omnipotence of fate, but at the same time invoked the gods to help him resist the influence of the stars. The Stoics, however, revered the supreme power of the universe without requesting anything and submitted gladly and unreservedly to the vagaries of destiny no matter how cruel.

The measures of the state (as early as 139 B.C. the astrologers were banished from Rome) and the opposition of the Christian Church, beginning with Clement of Alexandria (d. ca. 220)[54] and culminating with St. Augustine (d. 430) (City of God 1 ff.; Epistle 246, to Lampadius; etc.), failed to suppress astrology, which is still flourishing in our time and still supplies horoscopes as it did two millennia ago. The same is true of magic, a vast and fascinating subject which still awaits a thorough historian for the Hellenistic-Roman period.[55]

In the philosophical schools of the Hellenistic period every conceivable attitude toward current religions seems to be represented, from rationalistic unbelief and scorn for the worship, to "fundamentalistic" acceptance of traditional faith and ritual.

The most acute, far-reaching, and thorough attack on religion in all its aspects, from the point of view of rationalistic skepticism, is that of Carneades of Cyrene (d. 129 B.C.), the founder of the New Academy.[56] He objected to the familiar argument that religion is universal among men (consensus gentium) by pointing to atheists and, in arguing with the Stoics, gleefully quoted their doctrine about the foolishness of the great majority of men. He points out the absurdity of conceiving the gods in human form and with human passions. He undermines the Stoic combination of pantheism with traditional religion by showing that the allegorical interpretation is false and incapable of making the myths appear rational; and by disproving the identification of divine powers with the Olympian gods through the following sorites, which eliminated the distinction between divine and earthly: if Zeus is god, then also his brother Poseidon; and if so, every sea, every river, every little brook would be a god. By such reasoning he questioned the whole Stoic cosmology

[54] Cf. P. Wendland, Die Hellenistisch-Römische Kultur, p. 81.

[55] A brief summary, with bibliography, will be found in F. Cumont, The Oriental Religions in Roman Paganism, ch. 6. See also the articles in the encyclopaedias, particularly Darembourg, Saglio, and Pottier, Dictionnaire des Antiquités; Pauly-Wissowa, Realenzyklopädie; W. H. Roscher, Ausführliches Lexicon der griechischen und römischen Mythologie; J. Hastings, Encyclopaedia of Religion and Ethics.

[56] Cf. P. Wendland, Hellenistisch-Römische Kultur, pp. 62 f. Our chief source is Cicero's book On the Nature of the Gods.

and theology: the doctrine of the divinity and animation of the cosmos, the divine providence, the right plan and purpose of the world (which in the presence of evil is unbelievable), fatalism, astrology, and divination. And yet this intellectual skepticism did not result in a total rejection of religious practices: the doctrine of probability leaves open the door to beliefs and conduct based on them.[57]

Only the Cynics, of all Hellenistic philosophers, took the final step: opposed, like the Sophists, to all conventions, they mocked, often in a vulgar manner, whatever their contemporaries regarded as holy. To attain the soul's complete freedom and true happiness, they strove to become indifferent to all external circumstances and rejected the refinements of civilization, including all good manners and traditional beliefs, from etiquette to worship. And yet they were monotheists, and became popular preachers advocating the simple life in accordance with nature, dedicated to the pursuit of virtue.

The religious point of view of the Epicureans is intermediate between the New Academy and the Cynics. Theoretically Epicurus eliminated religious worship by assigning to the gods a serene existence in the astral spaces of an atomic world, and denying that in their perfect calm and bliss they take the slightest interest in human affairs. But in practice Epicurus advocated a new kind of piety, in contrast with the common one that had its roots in fear (*Primus in orbe deos fecit timor* [Statius (*ca.* A.D. 45-95), *Thebais* III, 661], on the earth terror at first made the gods) and self-interest. The new piety expects nothing from the gods, neither rewards nor punishments; in men who have attained *ataraxía* (impassiveness) it springs from admiration for ideal divine beings and is a joyful contemplation of beauty. Without excluding participation in the ancestral religious rites,[58] the new faith contrasts sharply with it. "Godless is not he who annihilates the gods of the masses, but he who attributes to the gods the notions of the masses" (H. Usener, *Epicurea*, p. 60. Leipzig, 1887). Rites, oracles, divination, myths, and particularly the Stoic doctrines are absurd, for in this atomic world Epicurus can discover no trace of divine presence or activity. Epicurus summarized

---

[57] A similar separation of reason and faith may be noted in Ecclesiastes. Rationally he concluded that God was too far and too indifferent to human beings to enter into communion with them, or to change the fixed course of events for their benefit; and yet he recommended external conformity to traditional rites and mechanical fulfillment of religious obligations (Eccles. 5:1-7 [H. 4:17-5:5]; 7:15-18; 8:2).

[58] Cicero (*De natura deorum* I, 85) reports that he knew Epicureans who worshiped every divine image (*novi ego Epicureos omnia sigilla venerantes*). That Epicurus actually made concessions to popular religious tenets and beliefs may be inferred from the following words of Sextus Empiricus (*Adversus physicos* I, 58): "According to some, Epicurus in his popular exposition allows the existence of God, but in expounding the real nature of things he does not allow it." See also Wendland, *Hellenistisch-römische Kultur*, p. 61.

his attitude in twelve Greek words, found among some fragments of his work *On Nature* discovered at Herculaneum.[59]

> There is nothing to fear in God.
> There is nothing to feel in death.
> What is good is easily procured.
> What is bad is easily endured.

In his great poem, *De rerum natura* (*On Nature*), T. Lucretius Carus (d. 55 B.C.) expounded brilliantly the teaching of his master Epicurus on physics, psychology, ethics, and religion. With a passionate zeal—which paradoxically is intensely religious—he denounces *religio* (which to him means superstition and popular cults) as a great evil for mankind. In considering Agamemnon's sacrifice of his daughter Iphigenia, he exclaims with a shudder,

> *Tantum religio potuit suadere malorum!*[60]
> *De rerum natura* I, 101

True piety has no more to do with traditional religious rites for Lucretius than for Amos and Isaiah:

> *Nec pietas ullast velatum saepe videri*
> *vertier ad lapidem, atque omnis accedere ad aras,*
> *nec procumbere humi prostratum et pandere palmas*
> *ante deum delubra, nec aras sanguine multo*
> *spargere quadrupedum, nec votis nectere vota.*[61]
> *De rerum natura* V, 1198-1202

For the superstitious fear of the gods Lucretius substituted the light of reason, the freedom of the spirit, and a happiness which is not perturbed by the prospect of the dissolution of the personality at death.

While the traditional worship and belief was attacked in the name of reason and morals,[62] various attempts were made to preserve something out of the wreckage as a basis for the religion of cultivated men.[63] While

---

[59] J. C. Orelli, *Fragmenta librorum ii et xi De natura.* Leipzig, 1818. A. Voghano, *Epicuri et Epicureorum scripta in herculanensibus papyris servata.* Berlin, 1928.

[60] "Such crimes was religion able to instigate!"

[61] "Nor is it piety at all to be often seen covered with a veil, turning oneself towards a stone, and to come near all altars; nor to prostrate oneself prone to the ground and stretch out the hands in front of the shrines of the gods; nor to drench altars with abundant blood of four-legged victims; nor to join vows to vows."

[62] The most important books on ancient criticism of Greek religion are listed later in this book, in note 22 of the chapter on the Wisdom of Solomon (Part II, Ch. V).

[63] The reader will immediately think of modern parallel attempts to bring Christianity "up-to-date." The Modernistic Movement in Roman Catholicism, some of whose leaders were A. F. Loisy (d. 1940), G. Tyrrell (d. 1909), E. Bonaiuti (d. 1947), was brought to an end by the encyclical *Pascendi* (1907) of Pope Pius X. Innumerable publications by liberal Protestants have attempted to reconcile Christianity with modern science and philosophy, thus supplying the "intelligentsia" with an acceptable faith: a good recent example is J. S. Bixler's *Religion for Free Minds* (New York, 1939).

Stoicism primarily provided the educated classes with rational faith and morals, using elements of the traditional cults as much as possible, some other apologetic attempts to salvage something from the shipwreck of the old religion may be mentioned first. It is only superficially that these appear to be radical attacks on religion—such they seemed indeed after the beginning of our era—but in reality they are conservative in tendency.

It was manifestly quite difficult for an intelligent and educated Greek or Roman to revere and worship Zeus, Apollo, Aphrodite, Athena, and the other Olympians so superbly depicted by Homer as immortals with human traits. Unless the Homeric gods were to be regarded as characters of fiction, as some thinkers said, they must be something quite different from what Homer says they are. Hellenistic writers suggested that they were in reality men, heavenly bodies, or natural elements which had been deified in dim antiquity.

Hecataeus of Abdera (*ca.* 290) in his book on Egypt (*Egyptiaká*)[64] identified the ancient Egyptian gods with heavenly bodies and elements (eternal gods), or with rulers (divinized mortals). Sun and moon were worshiped as Osiris and Isis; similarly for the elements: the *pneûma* (spirit) of the world is Zeus, fire is Hephaestus, earth is Demeter, water is Oceanus, air is Athena. The gods also appeared in Egypt as holy animals. The earliest kings of Egypt, divinized for their contributions to culture: Helios (so called after the sun), Cronus and Rhea, Zeus and Hera, whose sons were Dionysus (called Osiris) and Demeter (called Isis), Typhon, Apollo. From Egypt these deities passed to Greece; Belos introduced Egyptian wisdom to the Chaldeans, Danaus led a colony to Argos (Peloponnesus), the Athenians came from Sais. Even the Colchians (east of the Black Sea) and the Jews, as shown by the practice of circumcision, came from Egypt. Hecataeus did not originate this sort of speculation in which fact and fancy are thoroughly mixed, for traces of it can already be detected in Herodotus, but he apparently set the pace for others. Euhemerus, not long after, in his fictional *Sacred History* reported his discovery on the island of Panchaea of an inscription on a golden pillar reporting the deeds of three ancient kings, Uranus, Cronus, and Zeus, who eventually became Greek gods. This book was translated into Latin by Ennius (d. 169 B.C.), the famous author of tragedies and of an epic (*Annales,* Annals), and thus "Euhemerism," or the theory that pagan gods were deceased beloved kings, became popular (cf. Wisd. of Sol. 14:15-17); as in the case of "America," the name "Euhemerism" did not commemorate the name of the original discoverer. Some years before Euhemerus, Megasthenes, who in 302

---

[64] Most of the extant text is published in C. Müller's *Fragmenta historicorum Graecorum* II, 384-396. Most of Book I of Diodorus Siculus, *Historical Library,* is based on Hecataeus.

went to India as ambassador of Seleucus I Nicator, in his book on India (*Indica*) celebrated Dionysus and Heracles as men who were divinized for their contributions to civilization (text in C. Müller, *Fragmenta hist. graec.* II, 418-20).

The attempt to make Greek religion rational and sensible not only made of the gods divinized human beings, but also identified them with natural objects and forces (Hecataeus). The divine character of heavenly bodies had been recognized by Pythagoras, Plato, and Aristotle before Chaldean astrology popularized this notion, which in the Wisdom of Solomon was regarded as the noblest form of paganism: "But either fire, or wind [*pneûma*], or swift air, or the stars in their courses, or stormy water, or the luminaries of heaven who rule the cosmos, they regarded as gods" (or: "the luminaries of heaven, they regarded as the gods who rule the cosmos") (Wisd. of Sol. 13:2; cf. Philo, *De decalogo* 12 [M II, 189]). Besides the heavenly bodies, as this passage of Philo shows, the four natural elements also were divinized and identified with the gods of popular religion: "For they call the earth Kore, Demeter, Pluto; the sea Poseidon . . . the air Hera, the fire Hephaestus" [and also, "and the sun Apollo, and the moon Artemis"] (Philo, *ibid.*); cf. the Epistle to Diognetus 8:1 f.[65] The worship of the elements (including the heavenly bodies) eventually proved less important in the spiritualization of personal piety than the belief that the gods were divinized mortals who had greatly benefited mankind during their lifetime. The discovery of God in the greatest of men was one of the most profound and significant phases of Hellenistic-Roman religion.[66] The noblest and most momentous application of this thought was the recognition that the

[65] The doctrine of the four elements (earth, water, fire, air) was apparently first propounded by Empedocles (*ca.* 450) and was systematized by Aristotle, who added a fifth (ether). The elements were regarded as gods by Prodicus of Ceos (5th cent.) and with more philosophical reasoning by Xenocrates (d. 314). Philo mentions the four elements several times (cf. Wolfson, *Philo*, Vol. 1, pp. 154, 260, 310, 400). The Wisdom of Solomon omits the earth in 13:2 and the air in 19:18-20, which deals with God's transmutation of the elements (cf. Philo, *Life of Moses* I, 17). In Greek the elements are occasionally called *archaí* (principles), but the usual word is *stoicheîa*, which occurs in the Apocrypha (Wisd. 7:17; 19:17; IV Macc. 12:13) and the New Testament (II Peter 3:10, 12, which refer to the Stoic doctrine of the cosmic conflagration); cf. the Shepherd of Hermas, Vision III, 13:3. Reference to the pagan worship of the *stoicheîa* (probably both the four elements and the heavenly bodies) is made in Gal. 4:3, 9; Col. 2:8, 20; for the literature on these passages, which is abundant, see W. Bauer, *Griechisch-deutsches Wörterbuch zu den Schriften des Neuen Testaments*, under *stoicheîon* (2nd ed. of E. Preuschen's *Handwörterbuch*). Giessen, 1928; 3rd ed., Berlin, 1937.

[66] The worship of rulers, unless a mere formality, has its roots in this notion. In an attenuated form this practice was continued in the Roman Catholic canonization of the saints (cf. Cicero, *De republica* VI, 13, 16, 26, 29, etc., where benefactors of the fatherland enjoy eternal bliss in heaven after death).

sublime words and deeds of Jesus were manifestations of his divinity. That service to mankind lifts man to the realm of the divine was stated clearly by Pliny (*Natural History* II: V, 18 and 19): "For a mortal to help a mortal—that is god; and this is the path to eternal glory . . . it is an extremely ancient custom, in rendering thanks to well-deserving ones, to include such persons among the deities." And of Jesus we read that "God anointed Jesus of Nazareth with the Holy Ghost and with power: who went about doing good, and healing all that were oppressed of the devil; for God was with him" (Acts 10:38).

The noblest and most influential religion for the intellectuals was provided by Stoicism, which was at the same time a system of metaphysics, a way of life, and a monotheistic faith practicing the popular cults. The first two aspects have been sketched above, speaking of philosophy; the third one may be summarized here.

God is the active principle of the universe producing, out of the passive physical elements, the cosmos with all its phenomena. In a rhythmic process comparable to breathing, God produces the cosmos and then allows it to return to chaos, repeating this cycle through eternity. God is not immaterial, but consists of spirit and ether; mentally he is reason (*lógos*), fate (*heimarménē*), providence (*prónoia*). Immanent in the world like the soul in the body[67] (in contrast with the transcendent deity of Plato and Aristotle), God is present and active in every part of the universe: "For in him we live, and move, and have our being" (Acts 17:28).[68] "For of him, and through him, and to him, are all things" (Rom. 11:36) or, as Marcus Aurelius said, "Of thee [i.e., Nature] are all things, in thee are all things, to thee are all things" (*Meditations* IV, 23): everything originates in God, exists through him, and returns to him.[69] Men, as Epictetus said, are "fragments of God." None of the Stoics has described more eloquently the Stoic notion of the deity than Cleanthes (third century B.C.) in his famous *Hymn* (usually called *Hymn to Zeus*).[70]

[67] Seneca (*Quaestiones Naturales* II, 45), for instance, calls God, "ruler and guardian of the universe, soul and spirit of the world."

[68] The speech of Paul to the Athenian philosophers on the Areopagus, as reported in Acts, contains a good popular exposition of Stoic philosophy in Acts 17:24-28; see, for details, E. Norden, *Agnostos Theos: Untersuchungen zur Formengeschichte religiöser Rede*, pp. 13-30. Leipzig, 1923.

[69] For other New Testament and Stoic parallels, see Norden, *op. cit.*, pp. 240-250.

[70] The Greek text was published by H. von Arnim, *Stoicorum veterum fragmenta* I, 537. The translation of the initial invocation printed here is by J. Adams, *The Vitality of Platonism*, p. 105. Cambridge, 1911. It is also printed in W. J. Oates, *The Stoic and Epicurean Philosophers*, pp. 591 f. New York, 1940; this volume contains the writings of Epicurus, Epictetus, Lucretius, and Marcus Aurelius in English translations.

O God most glorious, called by many a name
Nature's great king, through endless years the same;
Omnipotence, who by thy just decree
Controllest all, hail, Zeus, for unto thee
Behoves thy creatures in all lands to call.
We are thy children, we alone, of all
On earth's broad ways that wander to and fro,
Bearing thine image wheresoe'r we go.

In such a pantheistic system God was for all practical purposes identified with Nature and for man "to live according to Nature" meant to be in harmony with God: such is the ideal of the sage. Its attainment requires daily self-examination, constant self-restraint, unending battle and self-training. Life, as the early Christians likewise knew, was a race to be won, a battle to be fought (II Tim. 4:7 f.; cf. Phil. 3:12-14; I Tim. 6:12; Hebr. 12:1; etc.), after undergoing severe athletic training.

God says to you, "Give me a proof, whether you have observed the rules of athletics, eaten what you should, exercised, obeyed the trainer."

Epictetus, *Discourses* III, 10:8

Through such discipline the sage strove to attain a state of absolute dependence on God and absolute independence from externals, which for Epictetus was freedom resulting from bondage under God.

Friend, lay hold with a desperate grasp, ere it is too late, on freedom, tranquillity, and greatness of soul! Lift your head high, as one escaped from slavery! Dare to look up to God and say, "Deal with me henceforth as thou wilt; thou and I are of one mind. I am thine; I refuse nothing that seems good to thee; lead where thou wilt; . . . ."

Epictetus, *Discourses* II, 16:41

He who realizes that he has God for his maker, and father, and kinsman is free from sorrows and fears (Epictetus, *Discourses* I, 9:4-7). Consequently, for the sage the religion of forms had no meaning in comparison to the religion of the spirit:[71] prayer was not a request for liberation from some evil or for the granting of some good, but merely the endeavor to free the mind from fears and desires (Marcus Aurelius IX, 40), indeed it was the communion of the mind with God; sacrifices, offerings, images, temples, divination, magic are in themselves insignificant; personal

[71] Zeno, the founder of the Stoic School, opposed the erection of temples because what the architect and builders made was not something sacred (according to Plutarch and Diogenes Laërtius). Seneca denied the value of prayer inside or outside of temples: "Hands should not be lifted to heaven nor should the sacristan be requested to allow us to come near the ears of the (divine) image, as if we could be heard better; God is near you, with you, in you" (*Epistle* 41, 1). Expiations and other rites are merely comforts for diseased minds (Seneca, *Naturales Quaestiones* II, 35:1). See also Seneca, *Epistle* 115, 5; Epictetus, *Discourses* I, 16.

immortality was replaced with a sense of divine kinship. True worship, according to Seneca (*Epistle* 95, 47), does not consist in lighting lamps on the sabbaths, since the gods need no light, and men hardly enjoy soot; nor in morning homages or sitting outside the temples; nor in carrying linen and scrapers, and holding Juno's mirror. God needs no servants, for he serves mankind and is at hand everywhere for all; the worship of the gods is first of all to believe in the gods, then to recognize their majesty and goodness; whoever imitates the gods has adequately worshiped them.

And yet, even though in theory the Stoics regarded the whole *cura et cerimonia*[72] of religion (as Cicero called it), the whole apparatus of public worship, as futile and empty forms, in practice they strove to discover a reality behind the shadow, a truth in the myths, a justification for the traditional faith and practice. They not only were aware of the value of religion in human society but found nourishment for their religious aspirations in the current worship. They harmonized their theology with popular polytheism by identifying the gods with individual divine powers emanating from the divine cosmic soul, usually called Zeus (Jupiter). Seneca (quoted by Lactantius, *Institutions* I:5, 26 f.) accordingly distinguishes between the various deities which we worship singly, and the God of gods whose ministers they are. Through allegorical interpretation of the ancient myths and fanciful etymologies the Stoics succeeded in combining the most advanced philosophy and science with the crassest superstitions. Zeus (poetic *Zén*) is connected with *zén* (to live), and its accusative *Día* with *diá* (by means of, through); Hera is *aér* (air). Some gods are heavenly bodies or natural elements; others, like Athena (reason, providence), mental functions. Ares (thoughtlessness) and Aphrodite (debauchery) are assailed by Athena (reason): this illustrates the moralizing interpretation of Homer; in other interpretations of the Homeric myths the gods were explained as forces, elements, or phenomena of nature.

The Stoic teachers did not merely instruct a small circle of disciples, as Plato and Aristotle did, but, following the example of the Cynics (beginning with Diogenes of Sinope, who died in 323 B.C.), they left the classroom and went out to the market place where they addressed the masses. Before the beginning of our era the Stoic preachers could hardly be distinguished from their Cynic colleagues. These mendicant philosophers on the open road, like the early Christian missionaries later, went about the Graeco-Roman world bringing to the lower classes a message of redemption. They taught that external advantages are worthless in comparison with virtue, which is the source of peace of mind and happiness; the goals of men are insignificant in comparison with the

[72] "Concern and rites."

simple life in accordance with nature. Like modern evangelistic appeals
to conversion, these street-corner addresses were intended to kindle the
emotions of uneducated masses: they consisted of anecdotes, observations
of life, puns, easily remembered maxims, contrasts, sarcastic or impassioned attacks on the sinners, calls to repentance. Such popular addresses
in the vigorous (if not vulgar) vernacular gave rise to a body of written
literature; Bion of Borysthenes in Sarmatia (ca. 280) out of this material
created a new literary genre, the diatribe.[73] This written composition is
a well-arranged, dramatic, animated imitation of the "soapbox" addresses.
Of the latter the best example is in Horace, Satires II, 3, a brilliant transcription in hexameters of a Stoic sermon on the insanity of all those who
have not attained Stoic wisdom. Besides being an excellent and almost
unique example of a popular Stoic address, this poem is the greatest
satire ever written. In reality other satires of Horace, as also the later
ones of Persius (d. A.D. 62) and Juvenal (d. ca. A.D. 140) have much in
common with the diatribe: Horace (Epistles II, 2:60) actually names
the diatribes of Bion as his model. Jewish-Hellenistic authors imitated
the diatribe in the Wisdom of Solomon and particularly in IV Maccabees,
a rhetorical discourse on the Stoic theme that "devout reason is supreme
ruler over the passions."

So in Rome, in the last century before our era and especially in the
two following centuries, Stoicism contributed not only a noble philosophy
and religion for the intellectuals, but also moral and religious propaganda
among the masses. Posidonius of Apamea[74] (d. ca. 50 B.C.), the disciple
of Panaetius (d. ca. 110 B.C.) and the teacher of Cicero, was the last great
creative thinker of Greece and exercised a deep influence on later eclectic
philosophers[75] and even on Christianity. Through him Cicero became
acquainted with the book of Panaetius On Duty (Perì toû kathékontos)
and under its influence wrote his own De officiis (On duties) in two
books, which was utilized by Ambrose, Bishop of Milan (d. 397) in his
basic treatise of Christian ethics, De officiis ministrorum (On the duties
of the clergy).[76]

[73] See in particular P. Wendland, Hellenistisch-Römische Kultur, pp. 39-53.
[74] See I. Heinemann, Poseidonios' Metaphysische Schriften, 2 vols. Breslau, 1921-
28.
[75] Posidonius influenced the ideas about God and spirit in Vergil's Aeneid (VI,
724 ff.) and Georgics (IV, 218 ff.), as also his ideas about the afterlife in Aeneid
VI; similarly Ovid's notions about the Golden Age and cosmology; M. Terentius
Varro (d. 27 B.C.) in discussing religion in 16 of the 41 books of his Rerum human-
arum et divinarum antiquitates likewise discloses the influence of Posidonius (see
Augustine, City of God IV, 27; VI, 2 ff.).
[76] It may be noted, incidentally, that certain similarities between Stoicism and
Christianity were noted in antiquity: it was said that Paul met Seneca in Rome and
letters allegedly exchanged between them were forged (C. L. Barlow, Epistulae
Senecae ad Paulum et Pauli ad Senecam [quae vocantur]. American Academy in
Rome, 1938). Jerome even included Seneca among Christian authors. On mutual

After Posidonius, however, the Stoics devoted themselves increasingly to the practical aspects of their doctrine instead of theoretical speculations, more to propaganda among the masses than to academic teaching and writing. In fact, as in the case of most New Testament writings (notably the Epistles of Paul), the literature to a great extent is merely subservient or supplementary to the oral message: Epictetus (like his teacher Musonius) wrote nothing, but Arrian faithfully recorded his *Discourses* (*Diatribai*), only about half of which are extant, and made a selection of them in the *Manual* (*Encheiridion*). Like the Apostles, the Cynics and Stoics became primarily preachers and pastors, their message became more and more ethical and religious. They stressed the need of realizing the nature and value of one's soul, of disregarding all external circumstances to pursue virtue, of being born again (*transfigurari*; Seneca, *Epistles* 53, 8; 94, 48; cf. *Epistle* 6). In detail, the philosophers discussed the duties toward one's country, parents, children; they gave advice concerning marriage relations, clothing, diet, home, old age, friendship, education, and all situations of human life. A more inward and profound religious feeling, a more spiritual kind of prayer (cf. Persius, *Satire* II, in the form of a letter; Juvenal, *Satire* X, a diatribe) were increasingly stressed, together with a sense of the divine calling of the Cynic and Stoic itinerant preacher. To a young pupil eager to devote himself to this spiritual calling Epictetus spoke as follows:

If a man were to undertake so great a task without God, he would be hated by God and his activity would make him a public laughingstock. . . . The philosopher . . . must be free from desires and passions . . . his soul must be pure. . . . Death? Let it come when it will, let it smite the whole or a part. Exile? Can any man cast me outside of the world? . . . Furthermore the true Cynic must know that he is sent as a messenger (*ángelos*) from Zeus to men to teach them concerning good and evil, to show them that they are in error looking for these where they are not to be found and not noticing where they really are. . . .

Epictetus, *Discourses* III, 22

Noble as was the Cynic-Stoic ideal of a life devoted to the practice of virtue under the guidance of reason, the control of the will, and the

relations between Stoicism and early Christianity, see: Bruno Bauer, *Christus und die Caesaren*. Berlin, 1879 [an uncritical attempt to prove that Christianity arose after A.D. 70 as a Jewish transformation of Stoicism]. Th. Zahn, *Der Stoiker Epiktet und sein Verhältniss zum Christentum*. 2nd edit. Erlangen and Leipzig, 1895. K. Kuiper, *Epictetus en de Christelijke Moraal*. Amsterdam, 1906. P. Wendland, *Hellenistisch-römische Kultur*, pp. 50-53; 120-153. G. H. Gilbert, *Greek Thought in the New Testament*. New York, 1906. The view advanced by Zahn and Kuiper that Epictetus was influenced by the New Testament has been convincingly refuted by A. Bonhöffer, *Epiktet und das Neue Testament*. Giessen, 1911.

judgment of conscience,[77] it did not suffice: it could not be attained
without divine aid. "No man is good without God. Can any rise superior
to fortune save with God's help?" (Seneca, *Epistle* 41, 2). Human longing
for God, before the rise of Christianity, found satisfaction in mystical
philosophies and in the mystery religions.

Mysticism had its roots in Orphism, Pythagoras, and Plato, in their
teaching about the conflict of mind and matter in man, and the possible
deliverance of the soul from earthly bondage. Posidonius gathered together the various philosophical and religious strains into a great system
of philosophy based on exact sciences and culminating in mysticism. He
stresses the conflict of body and soul in the moral sphere (cf. Paul's
"works of the flesh" and "works of the spirit" in Gal. 5:16-25). The human
soul is a portion of the fiery cosmic spirit, descending from heaven to
earth to be imprisoned in the body and polluted by its passions. Here
it yearns for communion with God and full knowledge, but they can be
attained only through deliverance from the body and return to God:
"For now we see through a glass, darkly; but then face to face" (I Cor.
13:12).

Another mystical school, combining Pythagorean mysticism with Platonic philosophy (not without Stoic influence), is usually called Neo-
Pythagoreanism because it revered Pythagoras (*ca.* 530 B.C.) as the
perfect sage, in possession of esoteric truth through divine revelation.
Consequently, whatever doctrines were regarded as true were attributed
to the ancient founder and his disciples and, since hardly any genuine
writings had come down from that period, Pythagorean books were
freely forged. Parallels in other religions, likewise dominated by the
principles of authority, divine revelation, and tradition, will at once occur
to the reader. The movement appears in Rome with Nigidius Figulus, a
friend of Cicero; its most famous representative was Apollonius of Tyana
in the time of Nero (54-68), who was regarded as a miracle worker and
the incarnation of the Pythagorean ideal sage. The influence of this
school was widespread and is notably obvious in the writings of Philo of
Alexandria (*ca.* A.D. 40)[78] and of Plutarch of Chaeronea (d. *ca.* 120).

[77] The concept of a moral conscience (*syneídēsis*, meaning both consciousness and
conscience) originated in Hellenism and was current in popularizing philosophy,
whence it passed to the Romans (*conscientia*), to Alexandrian Jews (Wisd. 17:11
[Greek 17:10]), Josephus, and some of the writings of the New Testament (chiefly
Paul's epistles; Acts 23:1; 24:16; Hebrews; I Peter). For the literature on the
subject, see W. Bauer's New Testament Dictionary, under *syneídēsis*.

[78] On the Pythagorean 'numerology' in Philo, see: E. Bréhier, *Les idées philosophiques et religieuses de Philon d'Alexandrie*, 2nd ed., pp. 43 f. Paris, 1925. K.
Staehle, *Die Zahlenmystik bei Philon von Alexandreia* (Tübingen Dissertation). Berlin
and Leipzig, 1931. Other Pythagorean echoes in Philo are discussed in E. R. Goodenough, "A Neo-Pythagorean Source in Philo Judaeus" (*Yale Classical Studies* 3
[1932] 117-164). I. Heinemann, *Philons griechische und jüdische Bildung*, pp. 550-
554. Breslau, 1932.

In turn the writings of Philo were apparently known to Ammonius surnamed Saccas ("sack bearer," because he had been a porter), and to his pupils Plotinus (d. A.D. 270), the founder of Neoplatonism, Longinus (d. 273), and Origen (d. *ca.* 254), the first great Christian theologian.[79] Plotinus, whose writings were edited by his pupil Porphyry (d. *ca.* 304), in six *Enneads* or fifty-four (6×9) treatises, taught that the godhead "cannot be grasped by thought," is ineffable and absolute; it is "the One" (*tò hén*), "the Primal [Being]" (*tò prôton*), which "neither thinks, wills, or desires." It is beyond existence, above all relations with anything else, without qualities: we cannot say what it is, but only what it is not. And yet it is the cause of all that exists, it is the primary power (*prôtē dýnamis*), a pure, unconditioned, creative activity. To the objection that if the One produces the many they were contained in it potentially, Plotinus answers that the One does not possess energy distinct from itself, but it is creative energy; the One is perfect and as such possesses the capacity to produce other beings; its very existence automatically produces, just as the sun radiates light without changing in the least. The world is an emanation from the One; it is its shadow, its image seen in a mirror—in other words, an illusion, an unreal and imperfect copy of the One. "The sensuous life is mere stage-play, all the misery in it is only imagination, all grief a mere deception of the actors." Man's supreme goal is the return of his soul to God, which implies its deliverance from the body, its cleansing (*kátharsis*) from all that separates it from God, and the ecstatic rapture in which the notion of multiplicity disappears and the soul reaches the One, attains the *unio mystica*. Such a supreme achievement is permanent only for purified souls after death; in this life the experience is brief and rare: Plotinus attained it four times in six years, Porphyry only once in his lifetime.

Neoplatonism was a rival of Christianity (Porphyry wrote *Against the Christians* in fifteen books) and yet it influenced Christian mysticism, notably in Augustine, Boethius (d. 524), Pseudo-Dionysius the Areopagite (a body of fifth-century writings attributed to Paul's convert named in Acts 17:34), Scotus Erigena (who translated these writings into Latin and explained the original, about 858), and others. The intellectual basis of European mysticism is Neoplatonic. The last Neoplatonists are Iamblichus of Chalkis in Syria (d. *ca.* 330), a pupil of Porphyry; Proclus (d. 485); and finally his pupil Damascius, who, when Justinian closed the philosophical school at Athens in 529, found refuge at the court of Chosroes I, King of Persia. Thus, after a development of

[79] The influence of Philo on Christian theologians of the Alexandrian School is obvious, but some scholars doubt his influence on pagan philosophers; see, however, H. A. Wolfson, *Philo*, vol. II, pp. 158-160.

a thousand years, Greek philosophy reached its sad end, but it had previously passed on the torch to Christianity.[80]

Besides mystical philosophies, the foreign mystery cults offered satisfaction for the widespread longing for communion with the deity. A few foreign deities and their worship had gained admission into Greece before Alexander: Thracian and Phrygian deities (Cybele, Sabazios, etc.) had followed Dionysus; Adonis (Tammuz) and the Semitic Aphrodite came from Phoenicia; Amon and Isis from Egypt. These deities were revered in Greece for the most part by private cultic associations (*thíasoi*, confraternities; *éranoi*, meals in common; at Rome they are called *collegia*) of foreigners, exactly as in our times immigrants into the United States have formed congregations worshiping according to the traditional practices of their homelands. Eventually, however, native Greeks were allowed to join these associations and occasionally foreign deities were identified with Greek ones: the Phrygian Cybele after being identified with Rhea, the mother of Zeus, became "the Great Mother [*Magna Mater* in Rome] of the gods." Amon became Zeus, Astarte became Aphrodite, Isis became Demeter. Greeks and Romans were hospitable to foreign gods and did not doubt the existence of a multitude of gods unknown to them; they even erected altars to unknown gods (*theoì ágnōstoi*), as Pausanias (second century of our era) reports (I: 1, 4; V: 14, 8); whether the broken inscription on an altar excavated at Pergamum (*theois ag . . .*) should be restored *theoîs agnóstois*, "to unknown gods" (as A. Deissmann, *Paulus*, pp. 178 ff. [Tübingen, 1911], suggests) must remain in doubt.[81]

After the death of Alexander (323 B.C.) the increased contacts between East and West tended to fuse the Greek and Oriental religions—a process

[80] A good summary on the development of philosophy and religion from 100 to 529 with bibliographical references will be found in: J. Geffcken, *Der Ausgang des griechisch-römischen Heidentums.* Heidelberg, 1929. A more concise and popular treatment, stressing Christianity more than paganism, is that of W. W. Hyde, *Paganism to Christianity in the Roman Empire.* University of Pennsylvania Press, 1946.

When completed, the following work will be especially valuable, *Reallexicon für Antike und Christentum, Sachwörterbuch zur Auseinandersetzung des Christentums mit der antiken Welt,* ed. by Th. Klauser in co-operation with F. J. Dölger and H. Lietzmann (both deceased), and particularly with J. H. Waszink and L. Wenger. Fascicules 1-7, columns 1-1120. Leipzig, K. W. Hiersemann, 1941-1944.

[81] Paul's famous reference to "an altar with the inscription, TO THE UNKNOWN GOD" (Acts 17:23) in Athens raises serious difficulties, for such an inscription would have been in the plural, TO UNKNOWN GODS. But Paul's argument for monotheism could not have been introduced by a polytheistic inscription. It therefore seems likely that the author of Acts, or whoever composed the speech in Acts 17, by changing the plural to the singular made the inscription to read as a dedication to the sole true God: such is the conclusion of O. Pfleiderer, P. Wendland, and E. Norden (see E. Norden, *Agnostos Theos,* p. 121, n. 1). The pertinent Greek and Latin material is discussed in detail by E. Norden, *op. cit.,* pp. 56-124.

which scholars call "syncretism." Besides the earlier identification of foreign with Greek gods, cult and theology identified Isis with Demeter; Artemis, Aphrodite, Athena, Nemesis, and Tyche as one; Osiris with Dionysus, Attis, and Adonis; Serapis with Asclepius, Zeus, Pluto, Dionysus; Bendis (a Thracian goddess) with Artemis, Hecate, and Persephone; The Zoroastrian deities Ahura-Mazda (Ormazd), Verathragna, and Anahita, through the spread of Mithraism, became Zeus, Heracles, and Artemis, respectively.[82]

The cults of foreign gods in Greece (and later in Rome) soon tended to assume the form of "mysteries," following the pattern of the earlier Eleusinian and Orphic mysteries. Mysteries are characterized by secret rites, esoteric doctrines, initiation rites; they allegedly purified men from carnal taint, expiated their sins, removed their guilt, brought the initiates into communion and mystical union with the deity, assured them of their triumph over death or deliverance from the cycle of reincarnations, and promised eternal bliss in the future world (G. F. Moore).[83]

[82] P. Wendland, *Die Hellenistisch-römische Kultur*, p. 79.

[83] In addition to the works listed above, note 43, see the following works on the mysteries, particularly in the Roman period, and their relations to Christianity: G. Boissier, *La fin du paganisme*. Paris, 1891; *La religion romaine d'Auguste aux Antonins*, 6th ed. Paris, 1906. J. G. Frazer, *Osiris, Attis, Adonis*. London, 1907. J. Toutain, *Cultes païens dans l'Empire Romain*. 2 vols. Paris, 1907, 1911. T. R. Glover, *The Conflict of Religions in the Early Roman Empire*, 3rd edit. London, 1909. F. Cumont, *The Oriental religions in Roman Paganism*. Chicago, 1911 (*Les religions orientales dans le paganisme romain*, 4th ed. Paris, 1929; German translation, 3rd ed., 1931). A. Jakoby, *Die antiken Mysterienreligionen und das Christentum*, 1910. G. Wissowa, *Religion und Kultus der Römer*, 2nd ed. München, 1912. H. Graillot, *Le culte Cybèle mère des dieux à Rome et dans l'Empire Romain*. Paris, 1912. F. Cumont, *Les mystères de Mithra*, 3rd ed. Bruxelles, 1913. C. Clemen, *Der Einfluss der Mysterienreligionen auf das älteste Christentum*. Giessen, 1913. H. A. A. Kennedy, *St. Paul and the Mystery Religions*. London, 1913. F. Legge, *Forerunners and Rivals of Christianity*. 2 vols. Cambridge, 1915. L. Friedländer, *Darstellungen aus der Sittengeschichte Roms in der Zeit von August bis zum Ausgang der Antonine*, 9th ed. by G. Wissowa. 4. vols. Leipzig, 1919-21. K. Deissner, *Paulus und die Mystik seiner Zeit*, 2nd ed. Leipzig and Erlangen, 1921. J. Leipoldt, *Sterbende und auferstehende Götter*. Leipzig and Erlanger, 1923. N. Turchi, *Fontes historiae mysteriorum aevi hellenistici*. Rome, 1923. R. Petazzoni, *I misteri*. Bologna, 1924. C. Clemen, *Religionsgeschichtliche Erklärung des Neuen Testaments*, 2nd ed. Giessen, 1924. W. R. Halliday, *The Background of Early Christianity*. Liverpool, 1925. G. La Piana, "Foreign Groups in Rome during the First Centuries of the Empire" (HTR 20 [1927] 183-403; see pp. 282-340). H. W. Willoughby, *Pagan Regeneration*. Chicago, 1929. A. Loisy, *Les mystères païens et le mystère chrétien*, 3rd ed. Paris, 1930. A. D. Nock, *Conversion*, Oxford, 1933. G. Kittel, *Die Religionsgeschichte und das Urchristentum*. Gütersloh, 1933. E. R. Goodenough, *By Light Light*. Yale University Press, 1935. W. Schubart, *Die Religiöse Haltung des frühen Hellenismus* (AO XXV, 2). Leipzig, 1937. T. von Scheffer, *Hellenistische Mysterien und Orakel*. Stuttgart, 1940. J. Carcopino, *Aspects mystiques de la Rome païenne*. Paris, 1941. J. Klausner, *From Jesus to Paul*. Translated by W. F. Stinespring. New York, 1943. S. J. Case, "Pagan Antecedents of Christianity" (*Religion in the Making* 3 [1943] 108-130). W. W. Hyde, *Paganism to Christianity in the Roman Empire*. University of Pennsylvania Press, 1946.

Foreign deities were officially worshiped in Rome at an early date. In the sixth century B.C. the old triad Jupiter, Juno, Quirinus became Jupiter, Juno, Minerva—an Etruscan triad which was identified with the Hellenic Zeus, Hera, Athena. From Latin neighbors came Hercules, Castor and Pollux, and Diana. Greek deities were introduced early likewise, generally from southern Italy. Following a famine, and in accordance with an oracle obtained from the Sibylline Books, a temple (*aedes Cereris*) was erected to Demeter, Dionysus, and Kore [Persephone] in 493 B.C., but their names were changed to Ceres, Liber, and Libera. Apollo had been introduced as healer from the plague (*Apollo medicus*), possibly when Tarquinius Superbus (534-510) obtained the Sibylline Books from Cuma; his first real temple was dedicated in 431. Hermes was identified with Mercury, Poseidon with Neptune, in the fifth century. Finally in 217 six divine couples were reverenced in Rome, all Greek deities with Roman (mostly Etruscan) names: Jupiter and Juno, Neptune and Minerva, Mars and Venus, Apollo (alone retaining the Greek name) and Diana, Vulcanus and Vesta, Mercury and Ceres. A temple was dedicated to Aesculapius (the Greek Asclepius of Epidaurus) in 291; the god was soon associated with Hygeia (Greek *Hygíeia*, goddess of health) or Salus. Pluto and Persephone became *Dis* (*pater*) and Proserpina; Hebe became Iuventas.

Near Eastern deities began to arrive at Rome late in the third century. In 204, during the Second Punic War (218-201), the Senate obtained from Attalus, king of Pergamum, the holy stone of Cybele (*Mater Deum Magna*, great mother of the gods) of Pessinus in Phrygia, identified with the Cretan Rhea; and in 191 her temple was erected on the Palatine. Before our era the orgiastic cult of Cybele was restricted to foreigners, except for a few official rites: the springtime festive processions (charmingly described by Lucretius, *On Nature* II, 598-643), the *Ludi Megalenses*, and the washing of the image of the *Magna Mater* in the Almo. These ceremonies, even if performed by Phrygian priests, were restrained and did not offend the Roman *decorum*. In 92 B.C., however, Roman soldiers under Sulla were attracted to the worship of Mâ (a manifestation of Cybele, the great mother) in Comana (Cappadocia), where her great temple (described by Strabo, *Geography* XII, ii:3 [p. 535]) was located, and introduced her ecstatic cult into Rome (where Mâ was identified with Bellona). Caracalla (211-217) gave official recognition to this worship.

Attis was probably introduced into Rome together with Cybele.[84] Like

[84] G. Showerman ("Was Attis at Rome under the Republic?" in *Transactions of the American Philological Association* 21 [1900] 46-59) concludes from the lack of decisive evidence that Attis was introduced in Rome long after Cybele, not before the beginning of our era. Most scholars, however, believe that in Rome Cybele and Attis were worshiped together from the beginning. On Attis see in particular H. Hepding, *Attis, seine Mythen und sein Kult*. Giessen, 1903. The myth of Attis has

Adonis in Syria, Attis in Phrygia was a dying and rising god of vegetation: Cybele is Mother Earth, Attis is the vegetable kingdom. The myth, of which varying recensions are recorded, told in essence that Cybele was enamored of Attis, an effeminate youth, and when he was unfaithful to her she drove him mad, so that he emasculated himself under a pine tree and died; violets grew up where drops of his blood fell on the ground. How Attis was raised from the dead is not recorded in ancient texts, but his resurrection is to be inferred from the rituals of his cult.

The annual festival of the Cybele-Attis mysteries was reorganized and officially sanctioned by Claudius (A.D. 41-54). Attis became more prominent than Cybele because he promised to his devotees the salvation of the soul and life after death. On March 15 (designated as *Canna intrat*, the reed enters) the *Cannophori* (reed-bearers) carried reeds in procession, allegedly commemorating the finding of the infant Attis among the reeds by the river Gallus. On March 22 (called *Arbor intrat*, the tree enters) the *Dendrophori* (tree-bearers) bore a pine tree, adorned with violets and bandaged like a mummy—a symbol of the dead Attis—to the temple of Cybele on the Palatine. On March 24 (called *Dies sanguinis*, day of blood) the mourning for Attis reached its climax.

> The Archigallus or high-priest drew blood from his arms and presented it as an offering. . . . Stirred by the wild barbaric music of clashing cymbals, rumbling drums, droning horns, and screaming flutes, the inferior clergy whirled about in the dance with waggling heads and streaming hair, until rapt into a frenzy of excitement and insensible to pain, they gashed their bodies with potsherds or slashed them with knives in order to bespatter the altar and the sacred tree with their flowing blood.
>
> J. G. Frazer, *Adonis, Attis, Osiris*, Vol. 1, p. 268. 3rd ed.
> The Macmillan Company, 1914.

Presumably, although no evidence is available for Rome, the neophytes aspiring to become *galli* (eunuch priests of Cybele and Attis) unmanned themselves during these wild transports, which resemble those of dancing dervishes. On March 25 (called *Hilaria*, good cheer) the resurrection of Attis was celebrated joyfully: masquerades, banquets, and merrymaking of every kind marked the day in which license prevailed. On March 26 (called *Requietio*, rest) the worshipers were allowed to relax from the strain of the two days of great excitement. Finally on March 27 (called *Lavatio*, washing) the cycle of festivities closed with the washing of the silver image of Cybele, with its face of black stone, in the brook Almo. Aside from these annual public rites celebrating the death and resur-

---

inspired a poetic masterpiece, the 63rd ode of Catullus (d. 54 B.C.) describing in 93 verses the frenzied madness of Attis, his self-emasculation, his escape to Cybele's temple, his lament and longing for his fatherland, and his lasting enslavement in that temple under the watch of a lion.

rection of Attis, his cult comprised secret and probably mystic sacraments by which the novice entered into communion with the god and gained the assurance of eternal life. The only rite about which some information is available is the baptism of blood, called the *taurobolium*. The earliest reference to it is dated in A.D. 134 at Pozzuoli, in honor of the celestial Venus; the last celebration known occurred at Rome in 394. At first the rite was patriotic, being performed for the welfare of the community; later it became, like baptism, a personal purification and regeneration. The later significance is illustrated by the inscription of S. A. Aedesius, who dedicated an altar to Attis and Cybele: *taurobolio criobolioque in aeternum renatus* (born again unto eternity through a taurobolium and a criobolium).[85] In the taurobolium the devotee descended into a pit covered with a platform of planks pierced by many small holes. A bull adorned with garlands of flowers, its forehead shining with gold leaf, was mortally stabbed on the breast by the high priest, so that the devotee below was drenched in the blood of the bull and emerged from the pit convinced that his sins had been washed away and he had passed from death unto life (Prudentius [Christian poet, d. *ca.* 410], *Perì stephánōn* 1006-50).

Egypt's contribution to Graeco-Roman religions was a group of deities closely connected with Osiris, i.e., Isis, her son Harpocrates (Horus the infant, as distinguished from Horus the elder), and Serapis. This triad dominated the religion of Egypt in the Ptolemaic period. Osiris appears already in the Pyramid texts, the oldest religious writings known (*ca.* 2400-2300 B.C.) as the god of the waters, the fields, and the plants; he triumphed over death, becoming the king of the underworld. From his death and resurrection (as in the cults of Tammuz-Adonis and Attis, who were likewise fertility gods) the ancient Egyptians—first the Pharaohs, then the nobles, and finally the commoners—drew their hope of a happy immortality.[86]

The best complete account of the Osiris myth is that of Plutarch (*De Iside et Osiride* 12-20), which, though late, since Plutarch died about A.D. 120, agrees substantially with the fragmentary ancient Egyptian accounts and therefore may be regarded as reliable. We may summarize

[85] *Corpus inscriptionum latinarum*, Vol. 6, No. 510. The "criobolium" is a sacrifice of a ram in honor of Attis corresponding to the sacrifice of a bull in honor of Cybele in the taurobolium.

[86] For Osiris and his cult in ancient Egypt before Alexander, see especially J. H. Breasted, *Development of religion and thought in Ancient Egypt*. New York, 1912. Breasted's *The Dawn of Conscience* (New York, 1933) is mainly a popularization of the earlier, far more valuable, work. See also, A. Erman, *Die Religion der Ägypter*, pp. 40-42, 68-87, etc. Berlin and Leipzig, 1934. A. H. Gardiner, *The Attitude of the Ancient Egyptians to Death and the Dead* (Fraser Lecture, 1935). Cambridge University Press, 1935.

it as follows: The earth-god Geb (identified with Cronus) and the sky-goddess Nut (identified with Rhea) had four children, the gods Osiris and Seth (or Set; Greek, Typhon) and the goddesses Isis and Nephthys; Osiris married Isis, Seth married Nephthys. Osiris became the god of the earth and taught the Egyptians agriculture and gave them laws. But Seth plotted against him: having taken the measure of Osiris' body, he fashioned a richly decorated chest and brought it to a banquet, where he promised to give it to the guest who would fit into it exactly. After the others had tried, Osiris lay down in it and fitted it perfectly. The conspirators slammed the lid down, nailed it fast, poured molten lead on it, and floated it to the sea on the Nile. As Isis wandered among the swamps of the Nile delta, guided by seven scorpions, she came to the house of a woman who, frightened by the scorpions, shut the door in her face. But a scorpion crept in and stung the woman's child to death. Through her spells Isis restored his life and soon after gave birth to Horus in the swamps. (Isis had been impregnated by the corpse of Osiris.) Buto, the goddess of Lower Egypt, hid the infant from the wrath of his uncle Seth. But one day Isis found her son stretched out lifeless in his hiding place after a scorpion had stung him. Upon her entreaties, the sun-god Re sent down Thoth, the god of wisdom, to teach her the spell through which she revived her son.

In the meantime the chest containing Osiris had reached the Mediterranean and the waves of the sea had brought it ashore at Byblus in Phoenicia, where a tree sprung up quickly and enclosed the chest inside its trunk. The king of Byblus admired the tree and made it into a pillar of his house. Isis received word of this and came to Byblus and became the nurse of the queen's child. Having revealed herself as a goddess, Isis obtained the pillar, cut the chest out of it, and gave the trunk of the tree to the king, who placed it in a temple of Isis where the people worshiped it. Isis brought the chest to Egypt and hid it, while she went to the city of Buto to see Horus. But Set-Typhon found the chest while he was hunting in the light of the full moon. In his fury he tore the body into fourteen pieces and scattered them far and wide. In a papyrus boat Isis sought the pieces and buried them where she found them; that is why there are so many graves and shrines of Osiris: the backbone was at Busiris, the head at Abydos (and also at Memphis), and so forth.[87] When Horus had grown to young manhood he decided to avenge the murder of Osiris. The combat with Seth was furious and lasted some days; Horus lost an eye, but Seth's mutilation was even more serious. Finally Thoth separated the fighters and healed their wounds. Seth was

[87] According to Strabo (*Geography* XVII, 1:23 [p. 803]), Isis buried coffins of Osiris in many places, but hid his corpse carefully so that Seth could not find it; cf. Diodorus Siculus I, 21:5-11.

declared defeated and recognized Horus as the new ruler of mankind, while Osiris became the king of the deceased. For Osiris really died and the members of his family, but their souls are alive: that of Osiris is the phoenix bird, that of Isis is the star Sirius, that of Horus is Orion.[88]

The myth of Osiris was represented as a "mystery," a "passion play" in the time of Sesostris I (1980-1935 B.C.) of the XIIth Dynasty (Middle Kingdom) of Egypt near Abydos, which became the center of the Osiris cult. A high official of Sesostris III (1887-1879), Ikhernofret (or Igernefert), inscribed on a stela at Abydos the outline of the sacred drama, in which he played an important role.[89] Eventually this sacred performance of the death and resurrection of Osiris was given in many Egyptian sanctuaries. Herodotus (2:170 f.) saw the grave of Osiris in Sais (northern Egypt) and reports that on a lake in the vicinity "the representation of his sufferings is performed at night, and the Egyptians call it 'mysteries.' " The institution of these mysteries was attributed to Isis herself (Plutarch, De Iside et Osiride 27), and they were believed to be "the remedy which gives immortality" (Diodorus Siculus I, 25).

The religion of Osiris, which before Alexander had become so general in Egypt that Herodotus (2:42) could say that Osiris and Isis were the only gods worshiped by all the Egyptians, was preserved in substance but Hellenized in form (the liturgy was in Greek); Osiris had been identified with Dionysus and Isis with Demeter long before, as Herodotus testifies, and the Osiris religion received the character of the Eleusinian and Dionysiac mysteries. So these cults spread throughout the Hellenistic and Roman worlds. One important change was the substitution of Serapis (or Sarapis) for Osiris. The legend telling of the origin of the Serapis cult in Alexandria, as related by Tacitus and others,[90] is well known and frequently accepted as history. A youth of great comeliness and gigantic stature appeared to Ptolemy I Soter (323-285) in a dream and ordered him to fetch his image from Sinope in Pontus; after great difficulties the

[88] For classical sources for the study of Egyptian religion, in addition to Plutarch, see Th. Hopfner, *Fontes historiae religionis Aegyptiacae*, Parts 1-5 (in C. Clemen, Fontes historiae religionum ex auctoribus Graecis et Latinis). Bonn, 1922-1925. On the spread of Egyptian cults in Europe, see among others G. Heuten, "La diffusion des cultes egyptiens en Occident" (In RHR 104 [1931] 409-416); S. Dow, "The Egyptian Cults in Athens" (HTR 30 [1937] 183-232).

[89] This stela was published with full commentary by H. Schaefer, *Die Mysterien des Osiris in Abydos unter König Sesostris III*, nach dem Denkstein des Oberschatzmeisters I-cher-nofret im Berliner Museum (in K. Seethe's *Untersuchungen zur Geschichte und Altertumskunde Aegyptens* IV, 2). Leipzig, 1904. An English translation is available in J. H. Breasted, *Ancient Records of Egypt*, Vol. 1, pp. 661-670. University of Chicago Press, 1906. See also Breasted, *Development of Religion and Thought in Ancient Egypt*, pp. 287-290; and A. Moret, *Mystères égyptiens*. 3rd ed. Paris, 1922.

[90] Tacitus, *Histories* 4:83 f.; Plutarch, *De Iside et Osiride* 27-29; Athenodorus of Tarsus, in C. Müller, *Fragmenta historicorum graecorum* vol. 3, pp. 487 f.

Alexandrian ambassadors brought back the statue; Tacitus says that according to rumor the statue of its own accord went on board the vessel, which reached Alexandria in the record time of three days. Tacitus adds, however, that according to others the statue was brought by Ptolemy III Euergetes (246-221) from Seleucia ("a city of Syria"), or that Ptolemy I fetched it from Memphis.[91] In any case, if Serapis was really a foreign deity, an Egyptian etymology of the name was at once discovered by the Egyptian priest Manetho and the Greek Timotheus of Eleusis: Serapis is the compound name *Asar-Hapi,* Greek Osiris-Apis (Osarapis, Sarapis); and they, according to Plutarch, determined the character of the god (whose cult is a combination of Osirian and Eleusinian religions).

Greeks and Romans were attracted to the cults of Serapis and Isis, the most 'refined of all Oriental cults then current in the West, as modern Californians are attracted by exotic Hindu philosophies and practices such as Vedanta and yoga, or synchretistic faiths like theosophy. Both Serapis and Isis were deities whose character was vague and thus capable of unlimited development. Serapis, according to Tacitus (*Histories* 4:84), was identified with four deities: Aesculapius, Osiris, Jupiter (Zeus), and Dis pater (Pluto, the ruler of the underworld). At first, like Osiris and Pluto, he was the lord of the depth of the earth and of the dead; then he was invoked in mortal dangers, whether through illness or other menacing circumstances, and assumed the attributes of Aesculapius, the god of healing; the stories of his miraculous deliverances took the place of nonexistent myths about this god. Finally he was equated to Zeus, *ut rerum omnium potentem* (as having power over all things), and became a universal god (*pantheus*), the closest approach to monotheism in Graeco-Roman paganism. In an oracle reported by Macrobius (fourth-fifth century) in his *Saturnalia* (I:20, 17), Serapis speaks as follows of himself:

> The heavenly world is the head, the sea the belly,
> The earth is feet for me, the ears lie in the ether,
> And the eye is the far-shining bright light of the sun.

Isis likewise became a universal deity, after absorbing the goddesses of Egypt and, beginning with Demeter (Herodotus 2:59 and 156), of Greece (Io, Artemis, Hera, Aphrodite, Athena, Nemesis).[92] Apuleius in his famous novel *Metamorphoses* (*Metamorphoseon libri XI,* or (as

[91] Assuming that Serapis came from Memphis, some scholars have explained the origin of the Sinope story. The hill near Memphis on which the Serapeum (temple of Serapis) rose was called *Sen-Hapi* (dwelling of Apis), in Greek *Sinōpion,* which sounded like Sinope in Pontus.

[92] Plutarch (*De Iside* 27), on the authority of Archemachus the Euboean and of Heracleides Ponticus, identifies Isis with Persephone (Persefassa).

Augustine called it) *The Golden Ass* (*De asino aureo*), composed probably between A.D. 151 and 157, supplies the best information available
on Isis and her mysteries, omitting of course their esoteric secrets. In the
story, Lucius fell in love with the chambermaid of a witch. He saw the
witch transform herself into an owl and begged the maid to change him
into a bird. But she used the wrong concoction and turned him into a
donkey. Led away by a band of thieves before he could be restored to
human shape, Lucius with his human soul in a donkey's body underwent
great trials and tribulations until (in book XI) through meditation and
faith in Isis he was saved. When Isis appeared to Lucius in all her
majesty (XI, 5) she described herself as follows:

Begetter of nature, mistress of all the elements, primal offspring of the ages,
supreme deity, queen of the shades of the dead, first of the heavenly beings,
uniform manifestation of gods and goddesses, I who by my nod control the
luminous summits of the sky, the wholesome breezes of the sea, and the
gloomy shades of the underworld: whose unique name, in manifold forms, in
diverse ceremonies, in various titles the whole world adores.

A Greek hymn, preserved in an inscription found in Cius in Bithynia
(A. Boeckh, *Corpus ·Inscriptionum Graecarum*, No. 3724. Berlin, 1828-
1877), after praising Anubis and Osiris, continues as follows.

Zeus is he, the son of Cronos, he is the mighty Amon,
The immortal king, and revered as Serapis.
Thee also, blessed goddess and mother, many-named Isis,
Whom heaven brought forth on the glittering waves of the sea,
And who didst bring up darkness as the light for all men;
Thou who as the oldest bearest the scepter on Olympus,
And as divine mistress rulest the earth and the seas,
Thou who viewest everything—much good hast thou given to men.[93]

The worship of Serapis spread all over Egypt under the patronage of
the Ptolemies: the Greek rhetorician P. Aelius Aristides (second century
of our era) counted forty-two temples of Serapis in Egypt, the chief ones
being at Alexandria,[94] Memphis, and Abydos. The Ptolemies not only
made of Serapis the god of the dynasty and one of the main gods of
Egypt, but they spread his worship abroad, chiefly where they had

[93] Other lists of attributes and titles of Isis will be found in F. Hiller von
Gaertringen, *Inscriptiones Cycladum praeter Tenum* (Inscriptiones Graecae XII: v,
1), No. 14; and in B. P. Grenfell and A. S. Hunt, *The Oxyrhynchus Papyri* Parts
1-18. London, 1898-1941: Part 11, No. 1380 (1915). See also, for other texts, O.
Gruppe, *Griechische Mythologie und Religionsgeschichte*, p. 1563, n. 2.

[94] The site of the Serapeum of Alexandria has been excavated. See, E. Breccia,
Les fouilles dans le Sérapéum d'Alexandrie en 1905-1906 (Service des antiquités
de l'Égypte. Annales. Vol. 8, pp. 62-76). Cairo, 1907. The excavations were begun
by G. Botti (d. 1903), the founder of the important Museum of Greek and Roman
Antiquities in Alexandria.

diplomatic representatives or occupation troops. Pausanias about A.D. 170 mentions temples of Serapis, usually together with those of Isis, at Athens (1:18, 4), Corinth (2:4, 6), Messene (4:32, 6), Sparta (3:14, 5), and other Greek localities (2:34, 10; 3:22, 13; 3:25, 10; 7:21, 13; 9:24, 1). From the island of Delos, on which the Serapeum was probably built during the reign of Ptolemy II Philadelphus (285-286), the worship of Serapis spread farther. His temples are recorded in Cyprus, Antioch, Smyrna, Carthage, Sicily. At Puteoli (Pozzuoli, near Naples, where Paul landed; see Acts 28:13) a Serapeum is recorded in 105 B.C. From Rome, finally, the worship of Serapis reached the provinces on the Rhine and the Danube.

The Isis cult proved itself even more widespread and more popular than the Serapis cult. It was practiced in almost all localities where Serapis was worshiped, and also in all parts of Gaul. The temple of Isis at Pompeii, enlarged when it was rebuilt following its destruction through an earthquake in 63 B.C., had probably been built when the Serapeum of Puteoli in the vicinity was erected, not later than 105. Not far away stood the Isis temples in Herculaneum and Stabiae (Castellamare). Much earlier is the Iseum of Syracuse, dating from the rule of Agathocles (316-289). But the most beautiful and most important temple of Isis stood on the Nile island of Philae (at the southern border of Egypt) and is still magnificent, even though the buildings are almost completely submerged from January to July when the Assouan dam is closed and the Nile water is collected above it in a great lake. The oldest temple of which traces remain was built there about 370 B.C., but Ptolemy II Philadelphus (d. 289) is the real founder of the extant temple, which was restored and amplified down to the time of the Roman emperors of the third century of our era. It was the last vestige of Graeco-Roman and Egyptian paganism: while the patriarch of Alexandria, Theophilus, burned the famous statue of Serapis, ruined the Serapeum, and thus ended the cult of Serapis in Alexandria in 391, during the reign of Theodosius (379-395), it was not until the reign of Justinian (527-565) that the temples of Philae were closed to the Isis cult and some of their rooms used for Christian worship. But inscriptions on the walls of these temples still attest that multitudes of pagan pilgrims came to honor Isis there.

Isis apparently gained a foothold in Rome in the time of Sulla (80 B.C.); but the Roman consuls and the Senate in the period 58-48 B.C. repeatedly destroyed the altars and shrines of Isis, presumably because members of the Isiac associations (mostly foreigners) had a part in the tumults stirred up by Clodius at this time.[95] Nevertheless the cult survived and flourished soon after, attracting chiefly freedmen and women, and not only wives or courtesans of the demimonde (Juvenal [6, 489] calls Isis

[95] Cf. G. La Piana in HTR 20 (1927) 291 f.

a procuress!), but also respected ladies of the aristocracy. Augustus and his prime minister Maecenas repressed the cult; and Tiberius in A.D. 19, when a lady was induced by attendants of the Isis temple to commit immoral acts, threw the image of the goddess into the Tiber, crucified her priests, and deported to Sardinia 4,000 Isiac adherents of military age to fight the brigands there.[96] Thus, like Judaism before and Christianity later, the religion of Isis had its martyrs and confessors!

Beginning with Caligula (A.D. 37-41), however, the Isis cult enjoyed imperial favor and began to flourish and to attract new devotees. Finally, in 394, three years after the destruction of the Serapeum in Alexandria, Rome saw the last procession of Isis and Cybele: Rufinus, the prime minister of Theodosius, was responsible for crushing, as he said, *caput ipsum idolatriae* (the very head of the idolatry).

The earliest description of the public rites in the Isis cult in Rome is that of Tibullus who, falling ill in Corfu (30 B.C.), begged Delia to pray Isis to heal him.

Of what use is now your Isis to me, Delia? Of what help for me are now the bronze instruments (i.e., the sistrum) so often agitated by your hand? Of what use, indeed, your devotion to sacred rites, your pure ablutions, which I remember, and the chaste bed on which you reclined? Now, O goddess [Isis], now aid me (for you can heal, as the numerous paintings in your temples attest).[97] As my Delia will render the songs she has vowed, she will sit, clothed in linen, before the sacred doors and, twice daily [i.e., at matins and vespers], with flowing hair, she will sing your praises, a striking figure in the midst of the crowd of Pharos[98] worshipers.

Tibullus, *Elegies* I:3, 23-32

Here Tibullus describes the daily worship of Isis; for in contrast with Roman temples, which were opened only occasionally, the Egyptian temples were opened daily with appropriate ritual (*matutinas apertiones templi*, Apuleius, *Metamorphoses* XI, 20). Every morning the temple singer awoke Isis by singing a morning hymn in Egyptian (cf. Porphyrius, *De abstinentia* 4, 9); then, as Egyptian priests did from time immemorial,

---

[96] Josephus, *Antiquities* 18:3, 4; Tacitus, *Annals* 2, 5.

[97] Ex-voto paintings depicting deliverances from diseases or dangers can be seen in Roman Catholic churches in Italy and elsewhere. That Isis in particular had many such paintings in her shrines is also attested by Juvenal (12, 8): *pictores qui nescit ab Iside pasci?* (who is unaware of the fact that painters are nourished by Isis?).

[98] Pharos, an island in the bay of Alexandria, was famous for its lighthouse (one of the wonders of the ancient world) over 400 feet high, built by Ptolemy II Philadelphus in 265-247. Isis had a famous shrine on this island; see, for other references, O. Gruppe, *Griechische Mythologie*, p. 1569, n. 1. According to the Letter of Aristeas §301, the Septuagint translation of the Pentateuch was made in a secluded house on this island in the time of Ptolemy II, perhaps while the lighthouse was being built.

the temple was purified by sprinkling Nile water in it and burning incense; and the deity was clothed, adorned with jewels, and fed.

That ritual was chiefly the concern of the clergy; Tibullus describes the participation of the devotees. Moreover, these, aside from the public worship, enjoyed a personal relation with Isis and received private instruction from her. A Roman matron would (according to Juvenal 15, 522-531), presumably as a penance ordained by Isis, on a cold winter dawn break the ice of the Tiber to immerse herself three times and, even though she disliked the water, she would dip her head into the current; then, naked and shivering, she would make the circuit of the Campus Martius (on which the shrine of Isis was built by Caligula or Nero) on her bleeding knees. Indeed, Juvenal proceeds, if Io (i.e., Isis) should order it, she would go to the extreme end of Egypt to bring back Nile water to sprinkle the Isis shrine. At times, however, as Juvenal (15, 535-541) observed, the deity was less exacting: when on the holy days of abstinence a wife had slept with her husband—a sin deserving a severe penalty—the Isiac high priest through tears and mumbled meditations obtained the forgiveness of Osiris, after the silver snake had been seen moving its head: Osiris allows himself to be bribed by a fat goose and a thin round sacrificial cake! And yet Isis punished sin (Juvenal 13, 90-96): an embezzler expected no mercy from Isis, saying, "Let Isis do as she wishes with my body, let her smite my eyes angrily with her sistrum if only, even though blind, I may keep the funds which I deny were entrusted unto me. Consumption, suppurating boils, an amputated leg are not too much to pay for such a sum."

In the third place, besides the daily ritual and the penitential system, the Isiac cult included the great annual festivals. The mystery drama celebrated at Abydos, as we have seen, during the twelfth dynasty was substantially re-enacted annually in Rome, beginning with October 28. Shrieking loudly Isis searched for the body of Osiris, followed by Nephthys and Anubis (cf. Ovid, *Metamorphoses* 9, 693), until at last on October 31 (called *Heureusis*, finding) the people shouted for joy when Osiris was found (Juvenal 8, 29): the merry celebration lasted three days, the last of which was called *Hilaria* as in the cult of Cybele-Attis. Both festivals expressed the gladness over the revival of nature in spring, over the triumph of life over death.

In the fourth place, the cult of Isis included the initiation rites and the esoteric knowledge that was taught only to the initiates after a solemn vow of secrecy. These rites and doctrines resembled those of the Eleusinian mysteries, which is not surprising since Timotheus the Eumolpid, who together with Manetho organized the Serapis worship under Ptolemy I, came from Eleusis. Owing to the secrecy of mystery initiation rites, however, little is known to us except what Apuleius reports in his *Golden*

Ass (book XI), vaguely and mysteriously. Lucius approached the borders
of death and walked to the threshold of Proserpina, having crossed all
the elements, and returned therefrom. He saw the sun at midnight,
shining with a white light, and came into the presence of the gods of
the underworld and of the gods of the upper world, so that he could
worship them close at hand. On the morrow he was shown to the crowds
on a high platform, in front of the image of Isis; he wore a cloak embroidered with the figures of mythical animals, he held a lighted torch
and wore a crown of palm leaves in the shape of sunrays. These last
details, identifying the initiate with the sun, seem to be alien to the Isis
cult and typical of the mysteries of Mithra, to which we must now turn
our attention. It would seem that in the first-degree initiation Isis was
the main figure, but that in the final degree, the third initiation, Osiris
held the center of the stage.

Before coming to Mithra a word may be said about Syrian deities, who
played a relatively unimportant role at Rome. Until a late period only
Tammuz-Adonis attracted the attention of the Romans. Even though we
have no information about his official or public worship at Rome and in
the West (as in Jerusalem, according to Ez. 8:14), the Adonis myth in
its Hellenistic form was frequently used by Roman poets.[99]

Atargatis was the first Syrian deity to be worshiped in Rome, having
been introduced by prisoners taken during the war against Antiochus
III the Great, in 192-188 B.C. Syrian servants and Syrian merchants practiced the cult soon after in Sicily, Rome, and the harbors of Ostia, Naples,
and Puteoli. The name Atargatis is a compound of the names of the
goddess 'Atar (Astarte, Ishtar) and the god 'Ate (opportune time); the
Greeks shortened Atargatis to *Derketō* (English, Derceto); see Strabo
XVI: 4, 27 (p. 785); Pliny, *Natural History* V:23, 81 .The center of her
worship was at Heliopolis, west of the Euphrates on the road from Aleppo
to Harran: the native name was *Mabog* (according to Pliny, *loc. cit.*),
pronounced *Bambyce* by the Greeks (Strabo XV: 2, 27 [c. 748]); the
modern name is Membidj. The worship there is described by Lucian,

[99] On the Adonis myth in its earliest known Syrian form, at Ras Shamra-Ugarit
(Northern Phoenicia) in the 14th century B.C., see Vivian and Isaac Rosensohn
Jacobs, "The Myth of Moth and 'Aleyan Ba'al" (HTR 38 [1945] 77-109); for the
English version of the pertinent mythological poems, see C. H. Gordon, *The Loves
and Wars of Baal and Anath*. Princeton University Press, 1943. For later forms of
the Adonis myth and for the Adonis cult, see W. W. von Baudissin, *Adonis und
Esmun*. Leipzig, 1911. J. G. Frazer, *Adonis, Attis, Osiris*. 3rd ed., London, 1919.
The earliest form of the myth is Sumerian: Inanna (Babylonian, Ishtar) descended
to the underworld to deliver from death the shepherd Dumuzi (Babylonian, Tammuz); see S. N. Kramer, *Sumerian Mythology*, pp. 83-103. American Philosophical
Society, *Memoirs*, Vol. 21. Philadelphia, 1944. The Adonis feast in Alexandria is
described by Theocritus (*Idylls* XV).

De Dea Syra.[100] A temple of Atargatis is mentioned at Carnion in Gilead (II Macc. 12:26; cf. I Macc. 5:43); another, more important one, was at Ashkelon. Atargatis was the consort of Hadad or Rimmon (cf. Zech. 12:11). She was represented as a mermaid at Ashkelon, but as a woman at Heliopolis (Lucian), and was regarded as the goddess of fertility, the protector of the community and its social and religious life, and the inventor of useful appliances. She became, like Cybele, a great nature goddess. In Rome she was called the Syrian goddess (*Dea Syra* or *Deasura*). Fishes (as also doves) were holy to her and forbidden as food to her worshipers, except to her priests and initiates on the festivals. Sacred prostitution is reported at her sanctuary in Heliopolis. Apuleius (*Golden Ass* VIII, 25 f.) regarded Atargatis as "almighty and all-bearing" (*omnipotens et omniparens*; a variant reading for the latter is *omnia parens*, mother of all things) and described her clergy (*op. cit.* VIII, 24 ff.; cf. Lucian, *Lucius* 50 ff.) as a band of wandering charlatans who shrieked and whirled wildly at the sound of flutes, and in their frenzy scourged and cut themselves; then they took a collection and further increased their income by divination and theft.

Besides Tammuz-Adonis of Byblus, other gods from Syria and Phoenicia reached Rome. The Baal of Doliche (northwest of Heliopolis and east of Apamea on the Euphrates) was brought to Rome under Vespasian; he was a war-god represented standing on a bull, holding the battle-ax in his right hand and the lightning bolt in his left, like Teshub, the ancient Hurrian-Hittite weather-god (akin to Adad). He was called Jupiter Dolichenus in Rome, and was closely associated with Jupiter Heliopolitanus worshiped at Heliopolis, the modern Baalbek (about 60 miles north of Damascus), where the ruins of his temple (begun by Antoninus Pius, 138-161, and completed by Caracalla, 211-217) and the better preserved temple of Bacchus are among the most impressive Roman buildings in existence. Like Jupiter Dolichenus and Jupiter Heliopolitanus, Hadad, the consort of Atargatis, the god of Hierapolis and Damascus, was likewise identified with Jupiter Optimus Maximus (Jupiter Capitolinus) and called Jupiter Damascenus; but their cults retained in Rome their foreign character and never became really Roman. The gods of Palmyra were Belsamin (i.e., heavenly Baal, a name also current in Phoenicia and Syria; cf. O. Eissfeldt in ZAW N.F. 16 [1939] 1-31), identified with Zeus, Malak-Bel (meaning messenger of Baal or, less probably, King Baal), Yarkhi-Bol (lunar Bel), Agli-Bol (bull-Baal or chariot-Baal?). The solar Baal of Palmyra was named *Sol dominus imperii romani* (the Sun, lord of the Roman Empire) by Aurelian (270-275), who erected a temple to him in Rome (274). So previously Elagab-

[100] Doubts have been expressed about Lucian's authorship of this work, but Eduard Meyer and others are probably correct in regarding it as authentic.

alus, or Heliogabalus (218-222), a priest of the sun-god Elagabalus
(meaning "god of the mountain"?) at Emesa (Homs) in his youth, had
proclaimed this god, under the name *Sol invictus Elagabalus* (invincible
sun) as the supreme, if not the sole, god of the Roman Empire.

The worship of Mithra proved to be one of the most popular in the
Roman Empire and, according to some scholars, a serious rival of Christianity. "If Christianity had been checked in its growth by some deadly
disease, the world would have become Mithraic" (E. Renan, *Marc
Aurèle et la fin du monde antique*, p. 579. 4th ed. Paris, 1899). (But
such guesses beginning with an "if" are fanciful flights of the imagination
into the realm of make-believe, not sober statements of historical facts.)

Mithra had long been worshiped before his popularity attained its
peak in the third century of our era, declining after Constantine, through
the Edict of Milan (313), declared Christianity a legal religion. The
Mithra cult came to its end (after the vain effort of Julian the Apostate
[361-363] to revive it) with the edicts of Theodosius I (379-395) repress-
ing paganism and closing its temples "throughout the whole world."[101]

Mithra is first known early in the second millennium B.C. as one of
the gods of that group of ancient Indo-Europeans who called themselves
Aryans (i.e., Indo-Iranians) and were the ancestors of the Vedic Indians
and the early Iranians: these Aryans appeared in Western Asia in the
sixteenth century B.C. The earliest written mention of Mithra occurs in
a treatise between Shubbiluliu, king of the Hittites (*ca.* 1390-1350 B.C),
and Mattiwaza (*ca.* 1360), king of Mitanni.[102] Among the many gods
who witness the treaty we find "Mitra, Varuna, Indar, the Nasatya."[103]

[101] The bibliography on Mithra earlier than 1915 is given in Ida A. Pratt, *List of
Works in the New York Public Library relating to Persia*, pp. 88 f. The New York
Public Library, 1915. The basic works are still: F. Cumont, *Textes et monuments
figurés relatifs aux mystères de Mithra*. 2 vols. Bruxelles, 1896 and 1899; cf. Cumont,
Les mystères de Mithra. Paris, 1902; 3rd ed., 1913; English translation by T. J.
McCormack, *The Mysteries of Mythra*. Chicago, 1910. A. Dietrich, *Eine Mithras-
liturgie*. Leipzig, 1903; 2nd ed. by R. Wünsch, Paris and Berlin, 1910; 3rd ed.,
Leipzig, 1922. In addition to the general works on Greek and Roman religions, and
on the mysteries, which have been listed in previous notes, only the discovery of
a Mithraeum at Dura-Europos deserves special mention; see, M. Rostovtzeff, "Das
Mithräum von Dura" (*Römische Mitteilungen* 49 [1934-35] 180-207); *Dura-
Europos and its Art*. Oxford, 1938. Dura-Europos Preliminary Report: *Seventh and
Eighth Seasons*. Yale University Press, 1939.

[102] The text of this treatise in Hittite was found in the excavations at Boghaz-
Keui (ancient Hattushash, the Hittite capital) in Asia Minor by H. Winckler in
1906, and was published by H. H. Figulla and E. F. Weidner in *Keilschrifttexte aus
Boghazköi*, Vol. 1, No. 1. Leipzig, 1916. German translation by E. F. Weidner in
Boghazköi Studien, Vol. 8, 33. Leipzig, 1923. English Translation: D. D. Luckenbill,
in AJSL 37 [1921] 162-171.

[103] Lines 55-56 of the reverse of this tablet read, *ilâni* (*pl*) *mi-it-ra-aš-ši-il ilâni*
(*pl*) *u-ru-wa-na-aš-ši-il ilu in-dar ilâni* (*pl*) *na-ša-ti-ia-an-na*.

It appears from this inscription that in the early part of the fourteenth century B.C., if not earlier, the Aryans had two groups of gods, the gods of nature and the gods of human society. In the first group, Indar (better known as Indra) is the god of storms, shattering the enemy with his thunderbolt, and the two Nasatya (later known as the Asvins) on their war chariot, helping those in mortal danger, are the Indian Dioscuri (Castor and Pollux). Mitra (later Mithra) and Varuna are the gods who embody the basic principles of human civilized society. Mithra means "compact" in Iranian; Mithra is the guardian of the observance of contracts between individuals and covenants between nations. Varuna is invoked in the taking of oaths. The two groups were called by the early Aryans Daevas or Daivas (Indra and the Nasatyas) and Asuras (Mithra and Varuna), respectively. Among the Iranians the Daivas were eventually degraded to the status of demons, and Varuna disappeared, having probably been absorbed by Ahura-Mazda, the supreme god of Zarathustra (Zoroaster), the great religious reformer who probably lived about 650-600 B.C. In the Zend-Avesta, the holy book of Zoroastrianism which grew about the prophetic teaching of Zoroaster (chiefly preserved in the *Gathas*), Mithra is second only to Ahura-Mazda (Lord Wisdom) or Ormazd, and almost his equal: "Ahura-Mazda spoke to Spitama Zarathustra, saying 'Verily, when I created Mithra, the lord of wide pastures, O Spitama, I created him as worthy of sacrifice, as worthy of prayer as myself, Ahura-Mazda'" (Avesta, *Yasht* X, 1). He was then a god of light, "the god of celestial light" (E. Benveniste, *The Persian Religion*, according to the chief Greek texts, p. 54. Paris, 1929). "Who first of the heavenly gods reaches over the Hara [cf. *Yasht* X, 50] before the undying, swift-horsed sun; who, foremost in a golden array, takes hold of the beautiful summits, and from thence looks over the abode of the Aryans with a beneficent eye?" (*Yasht* X, 13). Mithra is the guardian of mankind, present everywhere, the patron of compacts and the avenger of perfidy, but also the victorious hero on the battlefield, like Indra for the early Indians, and the promoter of agricultural prosperity. "We sacrifice to Mithra, the lord of wide pastures, who is truth-speaking, a chief in assemblies, with a thousand ears, well-shapen, with ten thousand eyes, high, with full knowledge, strong, sleepless, and ever-awake" (*Yasht* X, 7, etc.). "He, first and foremost, strikes blows with his club on the horse and his rider"(*Yasht* X, 101). He is called "increase-giving, fatness-giving, cattle-giving, sovereignty-giving, son-giving, cheerfulness-giving, and bliss-giving" (*Yasht* X, 65). Thus Mithra became, so to say, a manifestation in the visible world of the supreme god Ahura-Mazda, who had withdrawn far beyond the sun; Mithra, is halfway between Ahura-Mazda and the god of darkness and ignorance, Angra-Mainyu (Ahriman, "the evil spirit"); "therefore the Persians call Mithra 'tòn mesítēn' [the mediator]" (Plutarch, *De Iside et Osiride* 46). This explains the prominence of Mithra when the Zoro-astrian religion spread to Babylonia, Asia Minor, and, after the victory of Pompey over the Cilician pirates in 67 B.C. (cf. Plutarch, *Pompey* 24) and his conquest of the kingdom of Mithridates, king of Pontus (65 B.C.), to Rome. Before Mithra reached Rome he had become a solar deity. P. Jensen (ZA 2 [1887] 195) has called attention to a cuneiform tablet from the library of Ashurbanipal (668-625 B.C.) in Nineveh in which *Mi-it-ra* (manifestly Mithra) is identified with the Babylonian sun-god Shamash: if this interpretation is correct, this would be the second earliest written mention of Mithra (the next one being Herodotus I, 131, where Mithra is erroneously identified with Ishtar). In any case an inscription of Antiochus I of Commagene (69-38 B.C.) identifies Mithra with the Greek solar gods: *"Apollo-Mithras-Helios-Hermes"* (Cumont, *Textes et monuments*, Vol. 2, pp. 89-91, 187-189). In later inscriptions we find *"Helios Mithras"* in Greek and *"deus Sol invictus Mithras"* in Latin. It was not until Vespasian's consolidation of the eastern frontier of the empire (Commagene and Armenia), and especially after the Parthian war of Trajan in 113-117 and the reign of Hadrian (117-138), that the cult of Mithra became popular in the Roman Empire, and surpassed all other foreign cults in the abundance of widespread shrines and inscriptions until the triumph of Christianity. The spread of the cult was primarily due to the Roman army, stationed from Britain, the Rhine, and the Danube to the edge of Sahara in North Africa. War prisoners and slaves from Asia Minor and Western Asia likewise established far-flung centers of Mithra worship, as also merchants along the great trade routes, notably in the upper Adige (the Brenner route to the Danube) and in Dacia (north of the Danube): see the map in Cumont's *Textes et monuments*. It was in Greece and the lands where Hellenistic culture was prevalent that Mithraism had little success.

A sanctuary of Mithra, or Mithraeum, consisted of a *pronaos*, or pil-lared vestibule, from which a stairway led to the underground cella simulating a cave and therefore called *spēlaion* (Latin, *spelaeum*), grotto (cf., e.g., Justin Martyr, *Dialogue with Tryphon* 78, 6). These crypts were small, few could hold as many as one hundred men (no women were admitted), but usually not more than fifty could find room in them. This indicates that they were used for initiation rites rather than for regular services. When required, several Mithraea were in use (four in Ostia). On the two walls at the sides of the entrance were two stone benches; between them, in the center of the hall, stood two altars, while in a recess on the back wall facing the entrance was the bas-relief of *Mithra tauroctonus* showing the god in Phrygian costume slaying the sacred bull, while a scorpion attacks its genitals, a serpent drinks its blood, and a dog springs toward the wound. According to the myth, Mithra was born from a rock (cf., e.g., Justin Martyr, *op. cit.* 70, 1), subdued in a cave the bull created by Ahura-Mazda; the bull escaped, but was then reluctantly sacrificed by Mithra by order of the sun (whose messenger was the raven). The dying bull brought life to the earth despite the efforts of Ahriman, who sent the scorpion to defeat this purpose. The dog is the friend of Mithra and the serpent probably symbolizes the fertilized earth.

As Jerome reports in his *Epistle* 107, the initiate (*sacratus*) passed through seven degrees corresponding perhaps to the seven planetary spheres through which the soul passed on the way to the abode of the blest: *corax* (raven), *cryphius* (hidden; probably to be read *nimphus*, bridegroom, in accordance with inscriptions found at Dura-Europos), *miles* (soldier), *leo* (lion), *Perses* (Persian), *heliodromus* (courier of the sun), and *pater* (father). On occasion, appropriate garments corresponding to these designations were worn. Until the third degree (*miles*) the neophytes were called "servants"; beginning with the fourth (*leo*) they became "participants," and at their real initiation they took the oath of secrecy. According to Tertullian (*De corona militis* 15), the *miles* in the cave, "appropriately in a military camp of darkness," was offered a garland with a sword inserted into it as if he were acting his martyrdom; after placing it on his head he removed it to his shoulder saying that Mithra was his crown; he was then branded on the forehead with a red-hot iron. Other rites were baptism by immersion, passage through flames, and simulation of death (Porphyry, *De antro nympharum* 15). The *leo* initiate partook sacramentally of bread and wine: Justin Martyr (*First Apology* 66, 4) says that evil demons imitated the eucharist in the mysteries of Mithra.[104] The chief festival of Mithra was on December 25, the *dies natalis invicti solis* (the birthday of the invincible sun):[105] the day was sacred to the sun in other religions, for it marked the rebirth of the sun after December 21, the shortest day of the year when the sun seemed to be on the way to expire. Special services were held on *Sunday*, which in English and German still has a pagan name, the day of the sun-god, but which Italian and French decently Christianized by calling it the Lord's Day ([*dies*] *dominica: domenica, dimanche*).

Christianity, like the mystery religions, spread in the Roman world as a religion of salvation, offering a happy immortality to its faithful. It

[104] Tertullian (*De praescriptionibus haereticorum* 40) says that the devil imitates the divine sacraments in the mysteries of the idols: he baptizes his faithful promising expiation of sins through this bath, marks his soldiers on the forehead, celebrates the oblation of bread, introduces "the image of the resurrection" [i.e., a mock resurrection], and ransoms the crown under the sword (cf. above, *De corona* 15).

[105] On the origin of Christmas, see R. Kittel, *Die hellenistische Mysterienreligion und das Alte Testament*, pp. 17-36. BWAT N.F. 7. Stuttgart, 1924. W. W. Hyde, *Paganism to Christianity in the Roman Empire*, pp. 249-256.

also admitted to its sacraments only the initiates, it also told of a being who died and was raised from the dead to bring salvation to those united mystically with him. The resemblance of Christianity's rites to those of Mithraism was noted, as we have seen, by Justin Martyr (d. *ca.* 165) and Tertullian (d. *ca.* 230), who regarded Mithraism as a devilish imitation of Christianity. But eventually Christianity, which differed from all other cults by refusing in the most absolute manner (like Judaism) any participation in pagan rites, triumphed in the Roman and Greek worlds in spite of the persecutions, which were particularly severe under Decius (249-251) and Diocletian (in 303-304). Christ proved himself mightier than Caesar! The Church, however, through its victory enrolled into its ranks multitudes who could not forget their pagan practices and beliefs. *Graecia capta . . . victorem cepit* (Horace, *Epistles* 2:1, 156; "conquered Greece her conqueror subdued"). So a legacy was passed on by the mystery religions of expiring paganism, and it has been transmitted through the years to the twentieth century. The Oriental aspirations, the Greek spirit, the Roman practice did not wholly die.

CHAPTER V

THE JEWS IN THE LANDS OF THEIR DISPERSION

The settlement of Judeans and Israelites in foreign lands, followed in later centuries by the rise of flourishing colonies of Jews outside of Palestine, is not a unique nor even an exceptional phenomenon[1] until the Middle Ages, when the scattered Jewish communities lacked a common fatherland. Quite aside from great movements of populations known from time immemorial—such as the Aramean migrations after 1200 B.C.—forcible or voluntary settlements abroad of large civilized urban groups are well known at least since Tiglath-pileser III (745-727 B.C.) inaugurated the Assyrian policy of deporting to distant regions a part—often the best—of defeated peoples.

The technical term for the settlement of Israelites and Jews abroad, beginning with the deportation by Tiglath-pileser III in 732 B.C. (II Kings 15:29),[2] is the Greek word *diasporá* (the Dispersion), which occurs in II Macc. 1:27 (in the sense of the dispersed Jews) and in Judith 5:19 (in the sense of the land of the Babylonian Exile).[3] Alexandrian Jews even spoke of the Jewish Dispersion as the sending forth of colonies, in the Greek manner (Agrippa, in Philo, *Embassy to Gaius* 36 [II, 587 M]; cf. *Against Flaccus* 7; *On Contemplative Life* 3).

In the second half of the Hellenistic period and in the early part of the Roman period (*ca.* 200 B.C.-A.D. 200), with which we are here concerned, the Jews were scattered throughout the civilized countries of the Mediterranean world. "Every country will be filled with thee and every sea," the Sibyl sang ominously in 140 B.C. (Sibyl. 3:271). Philo (*Against*

---

[1] The Phoenicians and the Greeks furnish the most familiar ancient parallels. Long before, Assyrian merchants established commercial colonies in Cappadocia (about 1850 B.C.).

[2] See also Tiglath-pileser's fragmentary report in D. D. Luckenbill, *Ancient Records of Assyria and Babylonia*, Vol. I, p. 293, §816 (cf. §779).

[3] See also, elsewhere in the LXX, Deut. 28:25; 30:4; Is. 49:6; Jer. 15:7; 34:17; Ps. 146:2 (Hebr. 147:2); etc. Strangely, *diasporá* never translates the Hebrew *gōlāh*, which means both deportation (Jer. 29:16; 48:7; and elsewhere) and the Exiles in Babylonia (Jer. 28:6; 29:1, 4, 20, 31; and elsewhere. In the LXX, Jer. 28-29 are 35-36, and Jer. 48 is 31). The regular translation of Hebr. *gōlāh* and *gālûth*, as well as of Aramaic *gālûthā* (Ezra 6:16; Dan. 2:25; 5:13; 6:14), is *apoikía* (*apoikesía*), or *aichmalosía*. The word *diasporá* occurs also in Ps. of Sol. 8:34 f. and in the New Testament (John 7:35; James 1:1; cf. I Peter 1:1, which refers to Christians).

Flaccus §7 [II, 524 M]) explained this dispersion not as a punishment, as did the Sibyl, but as the result of the immense number of Jews, which no country could contain, so that "they dwell in the great majority of the most attractive regions in Europe and Asia, both in islands and in continents." Josephus (*War* 2:16, 4 [§398]; 7:3, 3 [§43]) similarly testifies to the presence of Jews throughout the civilized world and quotes an otherwise lost passage of Strabo to the same effect. Particular countries and regions in which there were Jewish settlements are listed in I Macc. 15:16-24 (allegedly countries to which the Roman Senate appealed in behalf of the Jews) and in a letter of Agrippa I to Caligula (quoted by Philo, *Embassy to Gaius* 36 [II, 587 M.]); see also Acts 2:9-11.

So much has been written by scholars on the Diaspora that only brief selected lists of publications can be given here on the Diaspora in general,[4] and on the Jewish settlements in Egypt, notably at Alexandria,[5] and later in Rome,[6] in particular. In the centuries with which we are

[4] "Dispersion" by H. Guthe (in *Encyclopaedia Biblica*, Vol. 1, cols. 1106-1117; 1899). "Diaspora" by Th. Reinach (in *Jewish Encyclopedia*, Vol. 4, pp. 559-574; New York, 1903). E. Schürer, *Geschichte*, Vol. 3, pp. 1-188; Leipzig, 1909. J. Juster, *Les Juifs dans l'empire romain*, Vol. 1, pp. 179-212; Paris, 1914. F. J. Foakes Jackson and Kirsopp Lake, *The Beginnings of Christianity*, Vol. 1, pp. 137-168. London, 1920. Hans Lietzmann, *Geschichte der alten Kirche*, Vol. 1, pp. 64-101; Berlin and Leipzig, 1932. Ch. Guignebert, *Le monde juif vers le temps de Jésus*, pp. 279-306; Paris, 1935 (English edition, *The Jewish World in the Time of Jesus Christ*, pp. 211-237. London, 1939). M. S. Enslin, *Christian Beginnings*, pp. 78-98. New York, 1938. J. Klausner, *From Jesus to Paul* (Translated from the Hebrew by W. F. Stinespring), pp. 7-30. New York, 1943. See also the map of the Diaspora in A. Deissmann, *Paulus.* Tübingen, 1911.

Fairly full lists of Jewish settlements, with references to inscriptions and other sources, will be found in the sections of the Schürer and Juster books cited above.

[5] F. Stähelin, *Der Antisemitismus des Altertums in seiner Entstehung und Entwicklung*, Basel, 1905. A. Bludau, *Juden und Judenverfolgungen im alten Alexandria*, Münster i.W., 1906. U. Wilcken, "Zum alexandrinischer Antisemitismus" (Abhandlungen d. Königl. Sächsisch. Gesell. d. Wiss. 57 [1909] 783-839). B. Motzo, "La condizione giuridica dei Giudei di Alessandria sotto i Lagidi ed i Romani" (*Atti della Regia Accademia delle Scienze di Torino* 48 [1912-13] 577-598). A. Neppi Modona, "La vita pubblica e privata degli Ebrei in Egitto nell'età ellenistica e romana" (*Aegyptus* 2 [1921] 253-275; 3 [1922] 19-43). H. I. Bell, *Jews and Christians in Egypt*, London, 1924; and *Juden und Griechen im Römischen Alexandreia* (Beiheft 9 zum "Alten Orient"), Leipzig, 1926. L. Fuchs, *Die Juden Aegyptens*, Wien, 1924. H. S. Jones, "Claudius and the Jewish Question at Alexandria" (*Journal of Roman Studies* 16 [1926] 17-35). E. R. Goodenough, *The Jurisprudence of the Jewish Courts in Egypt*, New Haven, Conn., 1929. W. W. Tarn, *Hellenistic Civilization*, pp. 190-193. 2nd ed., 1930. A. Tscherikover, *Ha-Yehudim we-ha-Yewanim ba-Tekufah ha-Hellenistit*, Tel-Aviv, 1931; and *The Jews in Egypt in the Hellenistic-Roman Age in the Light of the Papyri*, Jerusalem, 1945 [in Hebrew, with an English summary]. H. A. Wolfson, "Philo on Jewish Citizenship in Alexandria" (JBL 63 [1944] 165-168); *Philo*, Vol. 1, pp. 3-86.

[6] A. Bludau, "Die Juden Roms im ersten christlichen Jahrhundert" (*Katholik* 1 [1903] 113-134; 193-229). M. Radin, *The Jews among the Greeks and Romans.* Philadelphia, 1915. G. La Piana, "Foreign Groups in Rome during the first centuries of the Empire" (HTR 20 [1927] 183-403, especially pp. 341-393).

concerned here the Jewish community at Alexandria is of outstanding significance and will be considered in some detail.

1. The Jews in Mesopotamia

Before the conquests of Alexander the Great the most important foreign settlements of Jews were in Mesopotamia, Egypt, and Persia. The ultimate fate of the Northern Israelites deported in 734 by Tiglath-pileser III (II Kings 15:29),[7] and in 722 by Sargon II (27,290 inhabitants of Samaria, according to the Assyrian records), is a mystery which has fascinated later generations and has thus given rise to fantastic legends about the "lost Ten Tribes,"[8] beginning with Tobit, ch. 1, according to which most of these exiles were apostates but some, like Tobit, remained true to the written and oral Law of Moses (which in reality had never been observed in the Northern Kingdom of Israel). The Testaments of the Twelve Patriarchs assume with no basis of fact that the "Ten Tribes" were still in existence in the days of the author (cf. also Ass. of Mos. 3:5-14), exactly as Josephus, drawing on his imagination, could glibly assert that from the time of Ezra "the Ten Tribes are beyond [= east of] the Euphrates till now, countless myriads and incapable of being numbered" (Antiquities 11:5, 2). According to II [IV] Esdras (13:39-45) the Ten Tribes exiled by Shalmaneser, after crossing the Euphrates miraculously, settled in a distant unknown and uninhabited country called, in the Latin text, Arzareth (i.e., 'eres 'ahereth, "another land" [cf. 13:40], in Deut. 29:25-28 [H. 29:24-27];[9] cf. Schiller-Szinessy in Journal of Philology 3 [1870] 114), and in the Syriac version Arzaph ("end land," located "at the end of the world").

But we must resist the temptation to indulge here in the fascinating speculations of later date about the "Lost Tribes," which have been identified with the Ethiopians, the Scythians, the Nestorians, the Shindai (holy class) of Japan, the Afghans, the Peruvians, the North American

[7] The deportations reported under Shalmaneser V (727-722) in II Kings 17:6; 18-11 (and on the basis of these passages in Tob. 1:2, where Enemessar is an error for Shalmaneser) are questionable on account of the doubtful historicity and genuineness of these texts.

[8] Cf. the summary in The Jewish Encyclopedia, Vol. 12, pp. 249-253. New York, 1906; see also Schürer, Geschichte, Vol. 3, p. 10, n. 19; Encyclopaedia of Religion and Ethics, Vol. 11, pp. 167 f.; H. L. Strack and P. Billerbeck, Kommentar zum Neuen Testament aus Talmud and Midrasch, Vol. 2, pp. 606-608, 682 f.; Vol. 4, pp. 903-906.

[9] About A.D. 100 this passage was used as a proof text concerning the ultimate fate of the Ten Tribes. According to the Mishna (Sanhedrin X, 3 end), Rabbi Akiba quoted Deut. 29:28 (Hebr. 29:27), "And the Lord . . . cast them into another land, as it is this day," to prove that the Ten Tribes would never return, for "as this day goes and never returns, so they go never to return." But Rabbi Eliezer said, "As the day becomes dark and then light again, so to the Ten Tribes, for whom darkness has come, light will shine again."

Indians, and last but not least, the Irish and the English—to mention but a few.

Twenty-one years after the fall of Samaria and the deportation of less than 28,000 of its inhabitants, Sennacherib (705-681) devastated the kingdom of Judah (in 701) and deported many Judeans—though hardly the incredible number of 200,150 given in his official report. These Judeans, exiles, presumably transplanted into Assyria, like the earlier North Israelitic exiles of 722, apparently were gradually absorbed by the native population among which they lived, and thus disappeared from history as a distinct national and religious group.

The real Jewish Diaspora begins in 597. Nebuchadnezzar (according to the reliable figures given by Jeremiah in Jer. 52:28-30) deported the following numbers of men: 3,023 Judeans in 597; 832 inhabitants of Jerusalem in 586; and 745 Judeans in 581. The total of 4,600 men exiled to Babylonia by Nebuchadnezzar, with the addition of the women and children of their families, may represent a total deportation of 18,000 people at most. They were the ancestors of the flourishing Jewish colonies in Babylonia, particularly in the vicinity of Nippur on the Chebar canal. Very few of the "Babylonian Exiles" and of their descendants ever settled again in Judea, the fanciful stories of the Chronicler notwithstanding. In accordance with Jeremiah's advice (Jer. 29:5-7), they built houses, planted orchards, married, had children, and saw them marry, thus furthering the peace and prosperity of the communities in which they lived. Nevertheless, they retained, in contrast with the earlier exiles, their religious and ethnic individuality in the midst of the Babylonians, primarily because they remained faithful to the Book of the Law of Moses (i.e., the Deuteronomic Code) found in 621, listened to the pleas of Ezekiel and the Second Isaiah, and retained close contact with Jerusalem (cf., e.g., Zech. 6:10). In the first century of our era the most important Jewish centers in Babylonia were at Nehardea and Nisibis [not the well-known Nisibis in northern Mesopotamia] on the lower Euphrates, relatively near Seleucia and Ctesiphon on the Tigris (Josephus, *Antiquities* 18:9, 1 and 9; on the history of Nehardea, see, in brief, *Jewish Encyclopedia*, Vol. 9, pp. 208 f.).[10] Asineus and Anileus, Nehardea weavers, in the time of Tiberius, founded an ephemeral Jewish state near Nehardea (Josephus, *Antiquities* 18:9).

2. *The Jews at Elephantine*

In contrast with these Jewish settlements in Mesopotamia, those in Egypt were voluntary rather than the result of forcible deportations. The

[10] For the literature on the Babylonian Diaspora, see Juster, *Les Juifs*, Vol. 1, p. 201, n. 1.

earliest Jewish migration to Egypt of which we have a sure record occurred in 586 when some Judeans forced the prophet Jeremiah to go with them to Tahpanhes in the Nile Delta (Jer. 43). At least half a century later (if not actually before 586),[11] a Jewish military colony manned the fortresses at Elephantine (*Yeb*) and Syene (modern Assouan) at the extreme southern border of Egypt; Cambyses, king of Persia, unquestionably found Jews there when he conquered Egypt in 525.[12]

This Jewish colony, flourishing at Elephantine during the fifth century, is of particular importance as the only settlement of Jews outside of Palestine before 300 B.C. from which original records and detailed genuine information have come down to us.[13] Founded as a military garrison for the defense of the southern border of Egypt, and consisting primarily of Jewish mercenaries divided into regiments (*dgln*) at the service of the Persian king, this settlement, during a century of peace, became more and more a civilian community. These soldiers had wives and children, bought and sold houses and lands, added to their salary through commercial activity, and engaged in litigation before civil judges; even the women owned property and fought civil cases in courts of law.

This early Jewish settlement resembles later ones, even though it differs from them in some important respects. The most striking difference is the failure of these Jews—for they were unquestionably Jews and called themselves so (*yhwdy*)—to observe the Law of Moses. Totally disregarding the Deuteronomic Code of 621 B.C. (if they knew it at all), they built a temple to Jehovah (*Yhw*) on that remote island on the Nile, in violation of the law of Deut. 12, and, worse still, apparently recognized other deities besides the Lord (notably Ashim-Bethel, Anath-Bethel, Anath-Yahu, Cherem-Bethel; or Ashim, Anath, Bethel, Cherem). Whether the five gates of the temple were named after these five deities must remain in doubt. A similar transgression of the Law was denounced

[11] According to the Letter of Aristeas (§13) Psammetichus (I [663-609] or, much more probably, II [593-588, cf. Herodotus 2:30]) sent an army of Jews to fight against the Ethiopians (cf. Schürer, *Geschichte*, Vol. 3, pp. 31 f.). Moreover, Jeremiah (24:8) seems to know of Jews living in Egypt before 586, and in 44:1 he refers to settlements in the Delta (Migdol, Tahpanhes, and Noph [Memphis]), and also in Upper Egypt (Pathros, i.e., Egyptian *p-to-rês(y)*, meaning, "South Land").

[12] *Elephantine Papyri*, No. 1, lines 13-14 (in the editions of E. Sachau and A. Ungnad), dated 408 B.C. Text and English translation in A. Cowley, *Aramaic Papyri of the Fifth Century*, pp. 111-114. Oxford, 1923.

[13] The literature on the Elephantine Papyri is very considerable. In addition to Cowley's *Aramaic Papyri*, the standard work in English (see the preceding footnote), the reader may find lists of works on the subject in Ida A. Pratt, *Ancient Egypt*, pp. 346-350. New York Public Library, 1925; and its supplement (*Ancient Egypt, 1925-1941*, p. 244. New York Public Library, 1942). An important investigation (A. Vincent, *La religion des Judéo-Araméens d'Éléphantine*. Paris, 1937) is listed in the latter work on p. 204.

by Jeremiah (ch. 44) when he inveighed against the Judeans in Egypt who burned incense to other gods, and notably to the Queen of Heaven.

The religion of the Jews at Elephantine was thus similar to the popular religion of the Judeans before 621 and was influenced neither by the prophetic teaching nor by the Law of Moses in Deuteronomy and in the rest of the Pentateuch. In the temple of Jehovah (*Yhw*) there (built before 525 B.C.) regular sacrifices and offerings were presented, "meal offering (*minhah*), incense, and burnt offering (*'lwh*, Hebr. *'ōlāh*)." Despite this express, though possibly unconscious, violation of the Law, these Jews regarded their temple as legitimate. When fanatical Egyptians destroyed it in 411, they petitioned Johanan, the high priest in Jerusalem (who naturally disregarded the request), and later the governor of Judea, Bagoas, for permission to rebuild it. Characteristically, in 419 Hananiah wrote a letter to the Jewish garrison in Elephantine apparently to commend to them, in accordance with the wishes of King Darius, the observance of Passover and Unleavened Bread as prescribed by the Priestly Code (middle of the fifth century) in the story of Ex. 12 (Sachau No. 6; Ungnad No. 6; Cowley No. 21 and p. xxiv; cf. W. R. Arnold, in JBL 31 [1912] 1-33). Manifestly these remote colonists knew nothing about the developments in Judaism from 621 to 419 B.C.

But apart from the fact that the Jewish settlement at Elephantine did not observe the Law of Moses, its vicissitudes resemble those of later groups of Jews living among Gentiles. The Jews of Elephantine did not live in a ghetto, but their language (Aramaic), customs, and religion marked them as a distinct group, living apart from the Egyptians, and having at its head a chief and his council.[14] While in general this community was self-contained and socially self-sufficient, commercial contacts with the Egyptians were inevitable and intermarriage was not unknown. Litigation, even among Jews, was settled by Persian-Egyptian courts according to Persian law (which was basically Babylonian, to judge from the Elephantine papyri).

The latent but persistent hostility between the Jews and the Egyptians at Elephantine and Assouan has innumerable parallels when a compact minority in the midst of a people resists assimilation and clings to its own culture and faith. In addition to the usual causes of friction in such a situation, it seems that at Elephantine the Egyptians strongly resented the devotion of the Jews to the Persian authorities, whom the Egyptians

---

[14] Cf. "Yedoniah and his companions" (Sachau, and Ungnad, No. 6; Cowley No. 21; dated in 419). Priests apparently formed a substantial part of the council, for in another papyrus (Sachau 12, Ungnad 11, Cowley 38), which is undated, the heads of the community are, "Yedoniah, Uriah, and the priests of the God *Yhu*"; cf. "Yedoniah and his companions, the priests who are in Yeb the fortress" (Sachau, and Ungnad, 1; Cowley 30; dated 408 B.C.), etc.

naturally considered alien despots.[15] As long as the Persians were able to control Egypt, the Egyptian hostility to the Jews was confined to thoughts and words. A hitherto unnoticed sign of such unfriendliness may be perhaps detected in the history of Herodotus. The Greek historian visited Elephantine (Herod. 2:29) sometime between 460 and 454 B.C., when the Jewish colony was flourishing there. And yet he says that the Ethiopians (i.e., Nubians) inhabit half of the island and the Egyptians the other half (2:29), without a word about the Jews, although he adds (2:30) that Psammetichus had established garrisons against the Ethiopians on the island, and in his own day the Persians controlled those garrisons, now occupied by Persians. It would seem that the guide who led Herodotus through the Island and gave him the information that is recorded was an Egyptian who deliberately ignored the Jews or called them Persians; even in Palestine, Herodotus never mentions the Jews by name, although he came into direct contact with them.

In 411, when the Persian rule in Upper Egypt was weakening, Waidrang the governor ordered his son Nephayan, the commander of the garrison at Syene, to destroy the Jewish temple at Elephantine. From all indications, that sanctuary of Jehovah was not rebuilt soon after, as E. Schürer (*Geschichte*, Vol. 3, p. 25) surmised. On the contrary, the situation of the Jews in Elephantine, whose petitions for the rebuilding of their temple (see Cowley, *Aramaic Papyri*, pp. 108-126) remained unheeded, deteriorated rapidly, owing to the growing relaxation of Persian authority and the consequent increased boldness and impertinence of the Egyptians. When in 404 the Persian rule in Egypt came to its end, the sudden ominous absence of all Jewish records after that year may indicate that the celebration of Egyptian independence included a massacre of the Elephantine Jews—detested both as Persian mercenaries and as worshipers of alien gods (the priests of Khnum demanded the destruction of the Jewish temple). If this inference be correct, this was the first pogrom in the history of the Jews.

3. The Alexandrian Jews

The dramatic history of the Jewish colony on Elephantine has been related, even though it is considerably earlier than the period studied in this book, because it is the earliest and the typical example of the tragic fate of many Jewish settlements through the centuries: it marks the beginning of anti-Semitism.

Several Jewish settlements in Egypt are known in the Hellenistic

[15] The reciprocally friendly relations between the Achaemenian Persian rulers (538-330 B.C.) and the Jews have been described in some detail by B. Meissner in *Die Achämenidenkönige und das Judentum* (Sitzungsberichte der Preussischen Akademie der Wissenschaften, Phil.-hist. Klasse 1938).

period,[16] but by far the most important is that at Alexandria, where Jews were settled by Alexander the Great when he founded this famous harbor city (331 B.C.)—if we believe the plausible statements of Josephus (*War* 2:18, 7 [§487]; *Against Apion* 2:4 and 6 [§§35 and 72]) and Emperor Claudius (Josephus, *Antiquities* 19:5, 2 [§281]). Under the Ptolemies a special quarter of the city was set aside for the Jews (Josephus, *War* 2: 18, 7; Strabo, quoted in Josephus, *Antiquities* 14: 7, 2): it was located near the royal palace, in the northeastern part of the city (Josephus, *Against Apion* 2:4). At a later period, however, the Jews lived and had their synagogues in every part of the city (Philo, *Against Flaccus* 8 [II, 525 M]; *Embassy to Caius* 20 [II, 565 M]), although of the five quarters of the city two were called "Jewish" on account of the prevalence of Jews there (*Against Flaccus*, loc. cit.).[17]

The question whether the Jews enjoyed full Alexandrian citizenship or not has been much discussed by historians (see the works cited above, in note 5). Although Josephus (*Against Apion* 2:4; *War* 2:18, 7) asserts that when Alexander founded the city he gave the Jews and Macedonians equal rights, which later rulers did not curtail, it is now generally admitted that the Alexandrian Jews constituted a *políteuma* (corporation, community) within the city, enjoying a position higher than the metics (or settlers) but not quite on a par with citizens.[18] They did enjoy almost a complete equality of rights (at least in the case of the Jewish upper classes), and in fact even "isopolity," or the possibility to become full citizens if they wished—provided, of course, they renounced their ancestral religion and worshiped the gods of the *pólis*, or city-state. Isopolity is attested by Josephus not only for Alexandria (Josephus, *Antiquities* 19:5, 2 [§281]; etc.: cf. III Macc. 2:30), but for Antioch (Josephus, *War* 7:3, 3; *Antiquities* 12:3, 1), and even for Cyrene (*isonomía*, equality of legal rights, see Josephus, *Antiquities* 16: 6, 1) where according to Strabo (Josephus, *Antiquities* 14:7, 2) the population was divided into four classes: citizens, peasants, metics, and Jews. Such

[16] *The Letter of Aristeas* (§§12-14, cf. §§15-27 and 35-37), for instance, greatly exaggerates the figures when it reports that Ptolemy I, presumably after the battle of Gaza in 312, transported to Egypt 100,000 Jews of which 30,000 were drafted into the army and settled in various garrisons, while the rest were reduced to slavery. But there is no reason to doubt that this story is based on fact, even though there is no other confirmation, for Josephus (*Against Apion* 2:4 [§§44-47] and *Antiquities* 12:1) draws his information from Pseudo-Aristeas and is therefore not an independent witness.

[17] It is clear from this situation of the Jews that they did not live in an Alexandrian "ghetto," as some historians have asserted (e.g., K. J. Beloch, *Griechische Geschichte*, Vol. 4, Pt. I, p. 265. 2nd ed. Berlin and Leipzig, 1925). On the contrary, the Jews enjoyed in Alexandria considerable civic rights.

[18] The letter of Claudius (41-54 A.D.) to the Alexandrines (H. I. Bell, *Jews and Christians in Egypt*, pp. 14. London, 1924) proves that the Jews were *not* full citizens. Philo indirectly admits this fact (H. A. Wolfson, JBL 63 [1944] 165-168).

isopolity was the subject of a quarrel between Jews and Gentiles at Caesarea shortly before A.D. 60 (Josephus, *Antiquities* 20:9, 7) and thus became one of the causes of the Jewish War of 66-70.

In the earliest reference to the Jewish *políteuma* in Alexandria (Letter of Aristeas §310) we find at its head a council of elders and leaders (archons?), just as the Jewish *políteuma* at Berenice in Cyrenaica was governed by a council of nine *árchontes* (archons, chief magistrates), according to a Greek inscription probably dating from 13 B.C. (*Corpus Inscript. Graec.* 5361; cf. E. Schürer, *Geschichte*, Vol. 3, p. 79 f.). Later, in the time of Augustus (A.D. 11), there was an ethnarch at the head of the Alexandrian *políteuma* (Strabo, quoted by Josephus in *Antiquities* 14:7, 2 [§§115-118],[19] cf. the letter of Claudius in 19:5, 2 [§281]), although Philo (*Against Flaccus* 10 [II, 257 f. M]) reports that at the death of the "genarch" (ethnarch) Augustus appointed a senate (*gerousía*) to administer the Jewish affairs. H. I. Bell (*Juden und Griechen*, p. 13) would harmonize these apparently contradictory statements by assuming that after the authority of the council was assumed by an ethnarch, Augustus appointed a senate over which the ethnarch probably presided. In any case, the ethnarch is no longer mentioned after Augustus, possibly because he acted only as chairman of the *gerousía* (comprising probably 71 members): Philo speaks repeatedly of the *gerousía* and of the *árchontes* at its head (cf. Schürer, *Geschichte*, Vol. 3, p. 78, n. 14), never of an ethnarch. It is thus clear that the Jews in Alexandria before the reign of Caligula (A.D. 37-41) enjoyed a considerable degree of autonomy, although as Jews they did not possess the full Alexandrian citizenship.

In Alexandria, as elsewhere during the Hellenistic and Roman periods, the Jews were not especially well liked by their Gentile neighbors.[20] The main reason for this unpopularity was clearly stated by the Jewish author of the Book of Esther (3:8): they were a nation "scattered abroad and dispersed among the people" in the whole Mediterranean world, "and their laws are diverse from all people; neither keep they the king's laws." For the masses, like children occasionally, dislike and distrust instinctively foreign or different people in their midst. The Jews kept themselves as much apart from the Gentiles as possible and tenaciously clung to their own customs, fearful, after the attempt of Antiochus

---

[19] A. Segrè (*Jewish Social Studies* 6 [1944] 388 f.) believes that Strabo exaggerates the power of the ethnarch when he asserts that the ethnarch governed the Jews, administered justice among them, supervised their contracts and their laws as if he were the chief of an independent state (*polis*). It seems probable, however, that ordinarily Jews were judged by their own magistrates in their own courts.

[20] See I. Heinemann in Pauly-Wissowa, *Realenzyklopädie des klassischen Altertumswissenschaft*, new ed. by W. Kroll and K. Mittelhaus, Supplementary Vol. 5, cols. 3-43.

Epiphanes to Hellenize them forcibly, of losing their national individuality and religious peculiarity.

During the rule of the Ptolemies (323-30 B.C.) this dislike for the Jews on the part of the Greeks in Alexandria expressed itself merely in words, to the best of our knowledge. The extant Alexandrian tracts attacking the Jews, to be named in the next chapter, and the Jewish rejoinders seem to indicate that the controversies remained oral or literary and did not degenerate into physical violence—notwithstanding the alleged persecutions of the Jews alluded to in the Wisdom of Solomon and III Maccabees.

This mutual dislike grew considerably after Octavian's conquest of Egypt, following his victory over Mark Antony at Actium (31 B.C.) and the suicides of Antony and Cleopatra VII in 30 B.C. Although the Jews had enjoyed the special favor of the Ptolemies (the tale of III Maccabees is fictitious), they promptly turned their loyalty to the Romans and received a reward for their alacrity. The Greeks in Alexandria, on the contrary, took no pains to hide their hostility against the conquerors and against their Jewish protégés, who were receiving special favors from the Romans.[21]

During the rule of Octavian Augustus (30 B.C.-A.D. 14) and Tiberius (A.D. 14-37) the Romans succeeded in keeping peace between the two unfriendly Alexandrian groups. They even discriminated in favor of the Greeks in order to gain their favor, as when Germanicus (the nephew of Tiberius, father of Caligula, grandfather of Nero) in A.D. 19 distributed grain in Alexandria to the Greeks, but not to the Jews (Josephus, *Against Apion* 2:5 [§63]).

Serious disturbances occurred, however, in the time of Caligula (37-41). A. Avilius Flaccus had been governor of Egypt under Tiberius (32-37), and Philo (*Against Flaccus* §3 [II, 518 M]) has nothing but praise for his administration in those years. But in his fear of the disfavor of Caligula, he purchased the support of the Greeks in Alexandria by promising to countenance, if not to encourage, their plots against the Jews (Philo, *ibid.* §§3-4). If the Jews were striving for full citizenship, his hostility to them has a rational explanation (cf. H. I. Bell, *Jews and Christians*, p. 16). When Agrippa I was passing through Alexandria in 38, after Caligula had crowned him king of Batanea and Trachonitis, the Jews unwisely received him publicly with pomp and ceremony. The Greeks, who remembered that two or three years earlier Agrippa had come to the city destitute and pursued by his creditors, subjected him

---

[21] Before Caligula's rule, only Sejanus, who was the close adviser of Tiberius from 19 to 31, succeeded in oppressing the Jews (see Schürer, *Geschichte*, Vol. 3, p. 61). The attitude of Tiberius after 31 is insufficiently known (cf. Juster, *Les Juifs*, Vol. 1, p. 224, n. 3).

to cruel mockery by dressing up an imbecile as king and addressing him as *"Marin"* (Aramaic for "our lord"). Later, fearful of Caligula's displeasure, the Greeks hit on the diabolical suggestion to place statues of the emperor, who demanded divine worship for himself, in every synagogue.

Flaccus, aware of his insecure position particularly after allowing a friend of the emperor's to be insulted by the mobs, could only welcome this "red herring" and in an edict branded the Jews as "aliens" unwilling to worship the emperor. Thus encouraged, the mobs drove the Jews into a single one of their quarters, inaugurating thus the indignity of the ghetto, and plundered their vacated homes and shops. A horrible pogrom followed, in which no mercy was shown even to helpless women and children. Then the mobs burned some synagogues and desecrated the rest by placing in them statues of the emperor. Flaccus intervened at last—by having 38 members of the Jewish senate publicly flogged! Finally, Jewish women were forced to eat swine meat in the theater, and were tortured if they refused. When the tumults came to an end, the Jews found themselves in a critical economic situation and may have been prevented from practicing some of their religious rites.

Soon thereafter Flaccus was exiled, and eventually was executed by order of Caligula. Persecutions ceased under the new governor, C. Vitrasius Pollio; but the synagogues remained closed until the death of Caligula. In the winter of 38-39 the Jews sent to Caligula the philosopher Philo at the head of an embassy, while Apion led the embassy of the Greeks. Caligula mocked the Jews and granted them nothing, finally dismissing them with the remark that those who could not recognize his divinity were more to be pitied than censured.[22]

Upon his accession, Claudius (41-54) issued a decree (preserved by Josephus, *Antiquities* 19:5, 2). This text, which is extremely favorable to the Jews, may not have been reproduced verbatim by Josephus. Although it has been regarded by some scholars as a forgery, it is apparently authentic in substance. Claudius confirmed in it the privileges and rights of the Jews, previously abrogated by "the madness of Gaius"; thus the Alexandrian "ghetto" was abolished.[23] In his unquestionably genuine letter to the Alexandrines (A.D. 41), published by Bell (*Jews and Chris-*

[22] All these events are related by Philo in his two works, *Against Flaccus* and *Embassy to Caius*; and in brief by Josephus, *Antiquities* 18:8, 1 (§§257-259); for later events at Alexandria, see Josephus, *op. cit.* 19:5, 2 (§§278-285); *War* 2:18, 7 f. and a number of papyri (cf. Schürer, *Geschichte*, Vol. 1, pp. 67 f.; Juster, *Les Juifs*, Vol. 1, pp. 125-128), in particular a letter of Claudius to the Alexandrines (published and translated by H. I. Bell, *Jews and Christians in Egypt*, pp. 23-29; for the other papyri, see p. 19 f.). For summaries of the Alexandrian tumults, see Juster, *op. cit.*, Vol. 2, pp. 182-186, 201; H. I. Bell, *Juden und Griechen.*

[23] Philo, *Embassy* §§18 ff. [II, 563 f. M].

tians), Claudius refused to commit himself as to whether Jews or Greeks were responsible for the recent riots (or rather the war) soon after his accession, but expresses unyielding indignation against whoever caused this renewed outbreak (or, "whoever will cause another outbreak"). He will not tolerate "this baneful and obstinate mutual hostility." He exhorts the Alexandrines to be "forbearing and kindly" toward the Jews' long residents of the city, not insulting their traditional worship but allowing them "to observe their customs" as in the time of Augustus; he confirmed the free practice of these customs. On the other hand, the Jews must not intrigue for additional prerogatives, nor send two separate Jewish embassies (representing opposed Jewish factions), nor strive "in gymnasiarchic and cosmetic games" (restricted to the ephebi, youths enjoying full citizenship). They should enjoy the prosperity of a city not their own, but refrain from inviting to Alexandria Jews from Syria and other parts of Egypt (as reinforcements against the Alexandrines? cf. Philo, *Embassy* §129), lest he take vengeance on them as men who bring a general plague upon the whole world (cf., for the language, Acts 24:5).

Thus Claudius refers indirectly to the tumults that began in 38, and directly to an outbreak early in his reign, in which the persecuted Jews, emboldened by the death of Caligula, were the aggressors (cf. Josephus, *Antiquities* 19:5, 2 [§278]). His letter is fair and impartial, expressing good intentions toward both sides, but warning troublemakers of drastic measures against them. In reality, two of the chief Greek rabble-rousing demagogues (Isidore and Lampon; cf. Philo, *Against Flaccus* §§4, 15-17) active in stirring the riots in 38, were condemned to death by Claudius.

Later, the patriotic fervor, the religious ferment characterized by Messianic hopes, the passionate hatred of the Romans, and the feverish agitation of the spirits in Palestine, which precipitated with tragic fatality the disastrous war of A.D. 66-70, inevitably had their repercussions among Alexandrian Jews, whose nervous tension tended to magnify minor incidents until they seemed to be national catastrophes.

After the outbreak of the great rebellion at Caesarea in 66, the Alexandrines assembled in the theater to arrange for an embassy to Nero. Some Jews were discovered in the crowd, and a cry went up, "Enemies! Spies!" Three of them were caught and led away (to be burned alive, according to Josephus). The Jews of Alexandria rushed to deliver them, attacked the crowd with stones, and threatened to burn the people in the theater. When the governor, Tiberius Alexander, an apostate Jew and a nephew of Philo, failed to persuade some of the most hotheaded Jews to desist, he sent against them two Roman legions and a force of 2,000 men from Cyrene on their way to Judea. After bitter fighting in the Jewish "Delta" quarter, 50,000 Jews (according to Josephus) lost their lives, and many houses went up in flames. When the governor withdrew the troops, the Alexandrian riffraff continued the plundering (Josephus, *War* 2:18, 7 f.).

These drastic measures, mercilessly bloody as they were, proved effective. After the Jewish war had ended with the fall of Masada (April of 73), some Jewish fanatics (Sicarii, or assassins) fled to Alexandria and, when the parties of law and order among the Alexandrian Jews opposed their insane plans for a rebellion there, they began to murder the Jewish leaders. But in the Jewish senate the Sicarii were accused of causing the ruin of Judea and of plotting now that of the Jewish Diaspora; this verdict prevailed. Six hundred Sicarii were arrested on the spot, while those who fled to Upper Egypt were soon seized but, despite all tortures, refused to recognize Caesar as their lord (Josephus, *War* 7:10, 1). Vespasian, fearing further tumults, ordered the governor, M. Rutilius Lupus, to close the temple of Onias at Leontopolis, which had been dedicated 236 years before (not 343 years, as Josephus says) and, after the destruction of Jerusalem, had been the only Jewish temple in existence—in fact the last one to the present day (Josephus, *War* 7:10, 2-4).

As a result of the destruction of the Temple in Jerusalem in 70, the Temple tax of a third of a shekel (Neh. 10:33 f.), raised later to half a shekel or two drachmae (Ex. 30:11-16), paid to the sanctuary by all male Jews twenty years of age or older (cf. Matt. 17:24-27; Mishna *Sheqalim* entire), was ordered paid by *all* Jews (including women and children) to the temple of Jupiter Capitolinus in Rome (Josephus, *War* 7:6, 6 [§218]; Dio Cassius 66:7, 2; cf. Juster, *Les Juifs*, Vol. 1, pp. 377-385; 2, pp. 282-286; H. I. Bell, *Juden und Griechen*, pp. 34-43).

Under Trajan (98-117), when the Jews rebelled everywhere in 114-115, the Alexandrian Jews defeated the governor, M. Rutilius Rufus, and almost destroyed Alexandria, but they were prevented from joining the Jews of Cyrene, so that peace was gradually restored at Alexandria (see Juster, *Les Juifs*, Vol. II, pp. 185-190; cf. Vol. 1, pp. 126 f.).

Hardly had Hadrian (117-138) finished putting down this rebellion when he caused an even bloodier war, either by forbidding circumcision or by rebuilding Jerusalem as *Aelia Capitolina* and erecting therein a temple to Jupiter Capitolinus. The repercussions of this war of Bar Cocheba (132-135) in Alexandria are not known, but the Jews there were probably so dejected and exhausted that a rebellion on their part was out of the question. The later vicissitudes of the Alexandrian Jews are almost unknown, until Cyril, Bishop of Alexandria, expelled them in 414 after some riots (see Juster, *Les Juifs*, Vol. 2, pp. 175 f.). Although some Jews settled in Alexandria later, the history of Hellenistic Judaism may be regarded as ended at that time, following by a few years the official end of Alexandrian paganism (391). Both rivals had long since contributed noble teachings to Christianity.

4. Small Jewish Settlements

In the third century before our era Jews continued to come to Egypt and settled not only in Alexandria but also in other parts of the country. Greek inscriptions (cf. Schürer, *Geschichte*, Vol. 2, pp. 499 f., n. 4, inscriptions a. and b.) from the time of Ptolemy III Euergetes (246-221 B.C.) bear witness to the existence of synagogues (*proseuchai*) at Schedia and at Leontopolis (the latter having the right of asylum). Under later Ptolemies we hear of a number of other synagogues, where the Jews gathered on the Sabbaths and holydays to listen to the reading and exposition of the Pentateuch. The Law of Moses was read in the original Hebrew with a Greek oral rendering, or eventually in the Greek version called the Septuagint, which had been prepared in Alexandria about 250 B.C. The rest of the Old Testament and the Apocrypha were eventually added to the Torah (or Law) before the beginning of our era, with the possible exception of Ecclesiastes (the extant Greek of which dates from about A.D. 100). About 160 B.C. the high priest Onias escaped from Jerusalem and built at Leontopolis (contrary to the law of Deut. 12) a small replica of the Jerusalem Temple; there sacrifices to Jehovah continued to be offered until A.D. 73. Jews were growing in numbers, prestige, and riches during the second and first centuries before our era, until early in our era (Philo, *Against Flaccus* 6) they were said to number one million (or one-sixth or -seventh of the total population of Egypt). Opinions among scholars vary as to the occupations of the Jews in Egypt: some say the majority were farmers living in villages, others that they were merchants living in cities; in any case both groups were well represented as were tax collectors and public officials (soldiers were not so many as in the early periods).[24]

While in Alexandria the Jews constituted a *políteuma*, an organized semiautonomous community, in Rome they lacked a civic government of their own and, like all new and small Jewish settlements, were still organized into synagogue associations, such as Jews from abroad established in Jerusalem: five such synagogues are named in Acts 6:9, including the synagogue of the Libertines (the descendants of the Jews taken to Rome as slaves by Pompey and eventually freed [Philo, *Embassy to Gaius* §23 [II, 568 M]) built by Theodotus and supplied with a hostel.[25]

[24] From a study of the Greek papyri, V. Tcherikover (*The Jews in Egypt in the Hellenistic-Roman Age*) infers that the Jews were chiefly merchants, artisans, peasants, shepherds, cattle owners, bankers, tax collectors, and government officials. For details, see J. Juster, *Les Juifs dans l'Empire Romain*, Vol. 2, pp. 291-314.

[25] For the literature on the inscription of Theodotus, commemorating the opening of the synagogue and of the accommodations for Jews from abroad, see M. N. Tod, *Journal of Hellenic Studies* 43 [1923] 37; 45 [1925] 198. The present writer published the text and translation of this inscription in the *Methodist Review* (New York) 110 [1921] 971 f.

In Rome and in other localities where the Jews lacked civic organization the synagogue tended to assume community functions quite distinct from strictly religious matters (as in medieval Jewish communities).

Both types of community organization of the Jews in the Dispersion resemble, at least in form, the civic and religious associations of Gentiles living abroad (notably Phoenician and Egyptian).[26] The *políteuma* is manifestly of Gentile origin and apparently goes back to those new settlements established by Alexander, which lacked the organization of a Greek *pólis* and included several nationalities in addition to the Greek (cf. Tarn, *Hellenistic Civilization*, pp. 129 f.). But even the synagogue, notably outside of Palestine, had some resemblance to Gentile cult associations. While the Hebrew term *kenēseth* (assembly), like the Greek term *proseuchē* (originally "prayer," then place of prayer, sanctuary), emphasized the religious purposes for which the synagogue was originally established, the Greek term *synagōgē* (literally, a gathering of people) was used for the meeting of the members of a pagan cultic association on a festal occasion, and then for the association itself (Schürer, *Geschichte*, Vol. 2, p. 505), and among Jews indicated the political as well as the religious functions of the organization. It was inevitable that the early Jewish colonies abroad, which had a strong national and political solidarity, tended to become private associations of worshipers, including foreign proselytes, in which, however, the religious emphasis did not suppress the political functions. In the Jewish inscriptions the terms *políteuma, laós* (people), *éthnos* (nation) give way to *synagōgē* (congregation).

The status of the Jews in the Dispersion gradually thus became unique in the Graeco-Roman world. It is the basic contradiction in Judaism (and a reason for its vitality) that it regarded itself both as a nationality—nay, as a people—and as the worship of the only God in existence, who was also Jehovah, the God of Israel. In Gentile cities the Jews were a colony of settlers who, whether they enjoyed full citizenship or not, participated in the life of the town; but at the same time they constituted a religious congregation observing with utmost rigor Jehovah's revealed Law and strictly refraining from any contact with the religious life of the town. Thus, for instance, at Sardis in Asia Minor about 50 B.C. the Jews were both Roman and Sardian citizens, and yet they had their own assembly (*sýnodos*) and court of law (Josephus, *Antiquities* 14:10, 17 and 24). That the native populations resented this anomaly appears, for instance, from the situation at Ephesus in 14 B.C.: when the Ephesians required that the Jews who enjoyed full citizenship either forsake it or worship the city's deities, M. Agrippa confirmed the privileges of the Jews, whose

[26] See Schürer, *Geschichte*, Vol. 3, pp. 96-105. G. La Piana, in HTR 20 (1927) 183-403.

cause was ably defended by Nicholas of Damascus in the name of Herod the Great (Josephus, *Antiquities* 12:3, 2; 16:2, 3-5). The Romans regularly granted to the Jews, as to all nations, full religious freedom (cf. e.g., Josephus, *War* 6:6, 2); but local conflicts were inevitable as long as the ancient notion prevailed that citizenship could not be severed from the worship of the tutelary deities of the *pólis*.

5. Hellenistic Judaism

In other respects as well the situation of the Jews in the Hellenistic world was somewhat anomalous. Jewish religious life in Palestine was so systematized by scribes, Pharisees, and rabbis that the average Jew was seldom in doubt about what was right and wrong—even though the finer points of juristic interpretation were the object of learned and subtle discussions in the academies. But abroad, in a foreign environment where an alien culture and religion prevailed, the fidelity of the Jews to ancestral faith and practices was severely tested. The author of the Book of Ecclesiastes, well aware of the pervasive Hellenistic culture, began to question the good old Jewish religion in which he had grown up. He was unable to justify rationally its basic tenets and even reached some agnostic, if not skeptical, conclusions. The Wisdom of Solomon seems to depict (2:1-20) the deep impression made on some prosperous Jews in Alexandria by the theoretical and practical teaching of Epicurus: thus led astray, blinded by their wickedness, they failed to understand the secret purposes of God (2:21 f.) and ceased to belong to Jehovah's congregation.

Such spiritual defections from the faith of the fathers seldom led to an actual break from the synagogue, and even more rarely to an actual apostasy from Judaism—as in the case of Tiberius Alexander, nephew of Philo and son of the Jewish *alabarch* (Arabarch) or river-custom inspector in chief (wrongly believed to mean the chief of the Jews in Alexandria), who after adopting paganism became governor of Judea (A.D. 46-48) and later of Egypt.[27] In reality the great majority of the Jews of the Dispersion fulfilled the ordinances of the Law of Moses to the best of their ability, but could not fully escape the influences of the Hellenistic milieu. The most obvious, pervasive, and subtle of such influences was the Greek language, in the Hellenistic stage of its development (called the *koiné*, or common [dialect]). It is true that Aramaic was gradually displacing Hebrew as the vernacular of the Palestinian

---

[27] For instances of various degrees of apostasy, see J. Klausner, *From Jesus to Paul*, pp. 25-30. In Smyrna, during the time of Hadrian (117-138), among the citizens who made gifts to the city a Greek inscription lists "the former Jews" (*hoi potè Ioudaîoi*); see *Corp. Inscr. Graec.*, No. 9897; cf. Schürer, *Geschichte*, Vol. 3, p. 14.

Jews, but after all the two languages were very closely related and in fact had many words in common, while Greek was bound to introduce Western modes of thought alien to Hebrew and Aramaic. The overtones of the Hebrew *Yahweh* (Jehovah) or *Adonai* (Lord), and the Greek *Kýrios* (Lord), to a sensitive ear are totally different, for *kýrios* is a common divine term in the mystery religions. Even without adducing such contrasting works as the Palestinian Ecclesiasticus (with its notion of a miserable future life in the underworld) and the Wisdom of Solomon (with its Platonic doctrine of the immortality of the soul and the rewards or punishments after death), it is sufficient to compare the Hebrew Bible with its translation into Greek (the Septuagint or LXX) to note how subtly different, in spite of a basic agreement, Palestinian and Hellenistic Judaism really are. That the Hebrew Bible could not be reproduced intact into Greek was noted two millennia ago by the translator of Ecclesiasticus into Greek; in apologizing for the imperfections of his own rendering he remarked, in the preface to his translation, that what was originally spoken in Hebrew does not have the same force when translated into another language; and that "the Law, the Prophecies, and the rest of the books" in Greek are quite different from their form in the original language. It was necessary for the translators to attribute to Greek words shades of meaning hitherto unknown in order to render Hebrew ideas alien to the Greeks (e.g., *dikaiosýnē* [righteousness], *nómos* [law], *dóxa* [glory]). Conversely, current meanings of Greek words inevitably gave to expressions in the LXX a sense quite at variance with the original.[28]

The extent of Hellenistic culture in the LXX is a matter of dispute, although its presence cannot be denied, for the LXX contains reminiscences of Greek poetic literature in the Book of Job, mythological terms (Sirens, Titans, *Amaltheias keras* [rendering Keren-happuch in Job 42:14]),[29] and other typically Greek words like "cemetery" (Jer. 2:23), *dídrachmon* (Hebr. shekel), and *obelós* (Hebr. gerah). The Greeks appear twice in place of the Philistines (Is. 9:12; Jer. 26:16, LXX [H. 46:16]) and the wool trade of Miletus is referred to in Ez. 27:18, LXX. Traces of Greek philosophy, mystery cults, and other cultural elements of Hellenism have been discovered by some scholars in the pages of the LXX, but their conclusions have not been generally ac-

---

[28] See in general, C. H. Dodd, *The Bible and the Greeks*, pp. 3-95. London, 1935.
[29] See H. A. Redpath, "Mythological Terms in the LXX" (AJT 9 [1905] 34-45); H. St. John Thackeray, *The Septuagint and Jewish Worship* (Schweich Lectures for 1920), pp. 51-54. London, 1921; J. Ziegler, *Untersuchungen zur Septuaginta des Buches Isaias* (Alttest. Abhandl. XII. 3), p. 191. Münster i.W., 1934; I. L. Seeligmann, *The Septuagint Version of Isaiah* (Ex Oriente Lux, No. 9). Leiden, 1948. The King James Version erroneously introduces *Satyrs* in Is. 13:21; 34:14.

cepted.[30] Moreover, it should never be forgotten that, after the time of Alexander, Hellenistic culture and language were far from unknown even among the Palestinian rabbis.[31] But in conclusion Ralph Marcus (*op. cit.* p. 244) is fundamentally right when he says that "the Greek elements of the LXX are merely superficial and decorative, while the Jewish elements are deep-lying, central, and dominant."

As in the case of the Septuagint, so for the culture of the Alexandrian Jews in general, Hellenism is merely the garb of Judaism. The differences between Palestinian and Hellenistic Judaism are chiefly a matter of emphasis—even when the authors of the Wisdom of Solomon and IV Maccabees, and especially Philo, adopted some of the tenets of Greek philosophy. Jews, unless they renounced the ancestral religion, never adopted the spirit of Hellenism; despite appearances, they merely accepted forms. We should not give too much importance to traces of seeming paganism among Diaspora Jews, as when two Jews at the temple of Pan at Apollonopolis Magna (Edfu in Upper Egypt) in the second century of our era praise "the god"—one of them for deliverance, presumably from shipwreck (Schürer, *Geschichte*, Vol. 3, p. 50). Of course the ambiguous term "god" (*theos*) could mean Jehovah, as *hýpsistos* or *ho theós ho hýpsistos* (the Highest, God the Highest, the LXX's rendering of El 'Eliōn [the highest God, cf. Gen. 14:20], but also a title of Zeus and other gods) did when used on Jewish inscriptions in Greek (cf. C. H. Dodd, *The Bible and the Greeks*, pp. 11-13; W. W. Tarn, *Hellenistic Civilization*, pp. 195 f.). Of course, some strict Jews denounced such latitudinarian practices, like the Christian author who called the Jews at Smyrna and Philadelphia the "Synagogue of Satan" (Rev. 2:9; 3:9), i.e., worshipers of Zeus, assuming that "Satan's seat" at Pergamum (Rev. 2:13) was the famous altar of Zeus there.[32]

And yet, in spite of appearances, the Jews in the Dispersion were true to the Law of Moses and only superficially Hellenists. Rare indeed was the Jew who, like the one who conversed learnedly with Aristotle in Asia Minor in 348 B.C.,[33] "became a Greek not only in his language, but also in his soul." In Rom. 2:17-25, out of his observations extending over a vast area in the Roman world, the Apostle Paul has given us a picture

[30] A good summary of the problem of "Jewish and Greek Elements in the Septuagint," with numerous bibliographical references, has been published by Ralph Marcus in the *Louis Ginzberg Jubilee Volume*, pp. 227-245 (New York, American Academy for Jewish Research, 1945).

[31] See S. Krauss, *Griechische und Lateinische Lehnwörter im Talmud, u.s.w.* 2 vols. Berlin, 1898-1899; S. Lieberman, *Greek in Jewish Palestine*. New York, 1942.

[32] For other examples of Jewish contacts with pagan religions, see J. Klausner, *From Jesus to Paul*, p. 26. For M. Friedländer's defense of this liberalism in the Diaspora and its influence on Christianity, see *ibid.*, p. 28, n. 71.

[33] Josephus, *Against Apion* I: 22 (§§176-182); cf. E. Silberschlag in JBL (1933) 66-77.

of the Jews living "among the Gentiles" (2:24)—a picture which is the counterpart of the description of the best and the worst features of heathenism in the preceding verses (1:18 ff.). The ideal Jew in the Diaspora knew the Law, boasted of his God (Rom. 2:17), endorsed the highest ethical principles (2:18), and tried to convert the heathen to his religion (2:19 f.); and yet, as in all churches, reality was sadly at variance with such ideals (Rom. 2:21-25). Paul's summary of Hellenistic Judaism in Rom. 2:17-20 is confirmed by all available sources and may serve as our outline here.

That the Law was the decisive factor in the life of Jews in the Dispersion there is no doubt whatsoever. Even such philosophically minded Hellenistic Jews as the author of the Letter of Aristeas and Philo, who attempted to rationalize some of those prescriptions of Moses which puzzled the Gentiles by using freely the allegorical interpretation, kept the Law punctiliously themselves and denounced the Jews who violated its literal import (Philo called them "sons of Cain"). The sarcastic remarks of Roman writers such as Horace, Juvenal, and Tacitus indicate clearly that what mostly impressed the Gentiles about the Jews was their observance of the following prescriptions: circumcision, Sabbath rest, and avoidance of swine meat.[34] These rites, together with monotheism, imageless worship, and ethical conduct, were indeed the essential characteristics of the Jewish religion in the Diaspora. The Temple worship (aside from Elephantine and Leontopolis) was strictly avoided outside of Jerusalem, in accordance with Deut. 12. The religion of the Diaspora is in fact foreshadowed by the Priestly Code in describing the patriarchal religion before Moses: special prominence is given to Sabbath, circumcision, and morality (Gen. 17:9-14, 23-27; 17:1) in Abraham's religion; his observance of the Sabbath (established long before, Gen. 2:2 f.) is taken for granted.

It is precisely in the matter of the observance of the Law that we note one of the most significant differences between Palestinian and Hellenistic Judaism. In Judea, where the Jews constituted the bulk of the population, it was essential—nay, inevitable—for them to provide for their ever-changing society an ever-developing body of law (civil as well as religious). They did not, of course, make any changes in the Pentateuch after it was canonized in 400 B.C. (apart from a few insignificant ones), but, by subtle juristic interpretations, definitions, and casuistry, the scribes, Pharisees, and rabbis were able to supply, in the oral law, a fluid body of prescriptions which was always abreast of the times and provided

[34] See, e.g., Horace, *Satires* I, 9:68-72; Persius, *Satires* 5:179-184; Juvenal, *Satires* 6:160; 14:96-106; Tacitus, *Histories* V, 3-5. Cf. Schürer, *Geschichte*, Vol. 3, pp. 150-173; Th. Reinach, *Textes d'auteurs grecs et romains relatifs au Judaisme*, Paris, 1895. Horace (*Satires* I, 4:142 f.) alludes also to Jewish efforts to convert the Gentiles.

specific rules of conduct. Until it was finally codified and published in the Mishna by Rabbi Judah the Patriarch (about A.D. 200), this "tradition of the ancients" was unwritten and growing.

The situation was obviously different in the Diaspora, where the Jews were a minority in the midst of cities having a Hellenistic civilization. Here the best the Jews could do was to remain faithful to ancestral customs and obedient to the Law revealed to Moses; a juristic development such as was incessantly carried on at least until about A.D. 450 in Palestine[35] was unknown in the Diaspora, except in Babylonia (where the Babylonian Talmud was completed about A.D. 500). The knowledge of Hebrew (the language of the Mishna) and Aramaic (the language of the *Gemara*, or post-Mishnaic discussions in the two Talmuds) required by this juristic elaboration was not sufficiently available to Greek-speaking Jews in the Hellenistic-Roman cities. Moreover, it was natural for them to adopt from their Gentile neighbors institutions without parallels in the written and oral law, although not directly in conflict with Judaism. Thus, for instance, Jews formed or joined trade associations and guilds, as shown by the epitaph of a certain P. Aelius Glycon of Hierapolis (east of Ephesus): he bequeathed a sum to the guild of purple-dippers with the stipulation that they adorn his grave with a crown annually on the feast of Unleavened Bread, and likewise to the guild of carpet weavers who were to adorn his grave on the Feast of Pentecost (see Schürer, *Geschichte*, Vol. 3, p. 18). It became customary among Diaspora Jews to confer the current Gentile honors—such as crowns and chief seats at the synagogues (instead of the chief seats at the games)—and record them on inscribed stelae placed in the synagogues and occasionally even in the amphitheater; to dedicate synagogues to the king; to confer on women titles and honorary positions such as "chief of the synagogue," "mother of the synagogue," etc.; to free slaves in the synagogue with the obligation that the freedman would honor the synagogue and attend it regularly, as pagans freed slaves by fictitiously selling them to a temple (see Schürer, *Geschichte*, Vol. 3, pp. 91-96).

Although there is thus no indication of independent jurisprudence among the Hellenistic Jews, we know that they took special pains to observe the Law of Moses individually and collectively, to the best of their ability. The laws of the Gentiles among whom they lived, even when some local institutions and practices were adopted, remained alien and external—even when they could not be disregarded. Whenever possible, the Jews not only fulfilled the religious ordinances of Moses, but had their own courts of law, which decided the cases (as at Smyrna; see Josephus, *Antiquities* 14:10, 17), "according to the law of their fore-

[35] After its codification, the Mishna was subjected to the interpretations and juristic discussions recorded in the Jerusalem Talmud.

fathers." Indeed, they even had a slight acquaintance with the growing unwritten law formulated by Palestinian jurists (see S. Belkin, *Philo and the Oral Law*. Cambridge, Mass., 1940).

The second basic feature of Diaspora Judaism, noted by Paul after the knowledge of the Law, is the boast about God, about monotheism (Rom. 2:17). This "boasting" is indeed a characteristic feature of the Dispersion. In Judea, in the midst of an almost compact Jewish population, monotheism was taken for granted. In the Diaspora, conversely, it became a constant source of pride, and was contrasted with the crass polytheism of the pagan masses. In striving against the dangers of assimilation, in defending Judaism against the attacks of the Gentiles, and in missionary efforts to convert the heathen, the Diaspora Jews inevitably placed the main emphasis on their noble conception of a sole, universal God: the words ascribed to Paul in Athens (Acts 17:22-29) sound like a missionary address of a Diaspora Jew. This stressing of monotheism may be illustrated not only in Josephus (*Against Apion* III, 23 f.), but also in a passage of the geographer Strabo (XVI; 2, 35) which echoes a Jewish source. Moses taught, says Strabo, that the Egyptians, as also the Lybians, were mistaken in representing the deity as animals, and even the Greeks in representing it in human form. "For God is the one single thing which embraces us all, and earth and sea, which we call heaven, world, and nature." Here, as often elsewhere (cf. Acts 17:29), imageless worship is the corollary of the recognition that aside from the just and omnipotent sole Creator of all things there is no god. This "boasting" of their superior knowledge of the true God naturally led the Jews to ridicule the pagan worship of images. Sarcastic descriptions of idolatry are of course familiar in Palestinian literature since the Second Isaiah, the first Jewish monotheist (Is. 40:18-20; 41:6 f.; 44:9-20; cf. Jer. 10:2-5, 9, 14 f.; Ps. 115:4-8 = Ps. 135:15-18; the Epistle of Jeremiah), as also in Hellenistic literature (e.g., Wisd. of Sol. 13:10-19; 15:7-17).[36] But Hellenistic Jews do not confine themselves to scoffing at the representation of pagan gods by means of statues; they go deeper into the matter and attack the very notion of a plurality of gods, the questionable conduct of the gods, their helplessness and subjection to men (Josephus, *Against Apion* II, 34-35); they even attempt to explain rationally the origin of various types of paganism (Wisd. of Sol. 13:1-9; 14:12-21; Josephus, *ibid.* 36). Another difference may be noted: while the Hellenistic polemic was primarily addressed to pagans, the Palestinian was addressed to Jews only, since Hebrew and Aramaic were unknown to the majority of pagans, and expressed the "rabbinic resentment against the heathen world that

[36] Cf. R. H. Pfeiffer in JBL 43 (1924) 229-240; G. F. Moore, *Judaism*, Vol. 1, pp. 362-364; L. Wallach, in HUCA 19 [1946] 389-404.

had crushed Jewish secular . . . independence" (L. Wallach, *op. cit.* p. 401). The Alexandrian Jewish polemic against heathenism influenced not only rabbinic writings, but even more the early Christian apologies.[37]

The third characteristic mentioned by Paul is the knowledge of God's will and the approval of the most excellent things (Rom. 2:18) or, as we now would say, the observance of divinely revealed ethical principles. Here the differences between Palestinian and Hellenistic Jews are somewhat elusive. This identification of the moral ideal with the will of God probably goes back to Amos and became basic in Judaism; in our period no Jew doubted that the Law of Moses embodied the divinely revealed moral ideals. Ben Sira identified wisdom (i.e., the moral ideal) with the Law. While Alexandrian Jews held the same opinion and derived the precepts for right conduct from the Pentateuch (as can be seen abundantly in Pseudo-Aristeas and Philo), in Wisdom (particularly 7:22-8:1) the Pentateuch is more in the background (see, however, 16:6; 18:4, 9), while wisdom, proceeding from God, is man's guide (cf. Prov. 8) and teaches him the four cardinal virtues (Wisd. 8:7). While Stoic philosophy is even more prominent in IV Maccabees, other Hellenistic-Jewish writings such as II and III Maccabees, Sibylline Oracles 3:97-829, and the Letter of Aristeas definitely stress the observance of the Law as the acme of right living (see also IV Macc. 5:19-26; 6:15; 9:2).

All in all, whether influenced by Greek philosophy or not, the moral ideal, as Paul recognized, was a noble one. This needs to be stressed for, under the influence of the attacks of Jesus against the hypocrisy of some Pharisees and Paul's disparagement of "legalism," some Christians tend to cast aspersions on the Jewish ethics of our period. Thus, for instance, W. Bousset (*Die Religion des Judentums*, pp. 154-163; 2nd ed. Berlin, 1906) states that Jewish morality, owing to its connection with the Law, was particularistic (nationalistic and sectarian), disparate (laying equal weight on ritual, civic, and moral duties, whether important or not), casuistic, negative, lacking sincerity (with an emphasis on externalities, leading to hypocrisy), and ecclesiastical (in almsgiving). The error of this, and of similar indictments, is the failure to distingush between the ideal and the reality. That each of the preceding shortcomings may be illustrated in the life and occasionally even in the writings of Jews of the period in question is obvious; that they were inherent in Judaism at its best is a slanderous falsehood.[38] In the noblest

[37] P. Wendland, *Die Hellenistisch-Römische Kultur* (Handbuch zum Neuen Testament I, 2), pp. 150-160. Tübingen, 1907. Cf. Wallach, *op. cit.* pp. 401-403.

[38] " 'In every system, as time goes on, the secondary comes to be regarded as primary and the primary as secondary; the most exalted idea has associated with it disciples who distort and transform it' [Joseph Klausner, *Jesus of Nazareth*. Translated by H. Danby. London and New York, 1925. 2nd ed.]. The fence that Judaism

ethical and religious systems, the moral prescriptions are always far above the practice of even the best; this discrepancy between lofty goals and sordid conduct is by no means confined to Judaism. The contrast between the ideals of Judaism and the wickedness of some Jews, so pointedly and dramatically brought out in Wisd. of Sol. 1-5 and Rom. 2:17-25, is equally true of Christianity. What is more significant than Bousset's ill-disguised polemic is that the ethical system of Christianity and of the modern world in general is ultimately based on the moral ideals of Judaism and of Greek philosophy. While some New Testament parallels to the Apocrypha will be noted in the course of this volume and almost all the pertinent material will be found conveniently in Strack and Billerbeck's great New Testament commentary, a few illustrations from the Testaments of the XII Patriarchs will suffice here to show how close the Sermon on the Mount was at times to earlier Jewish writings.

> Love ye, therefore, one another from the heart; and if a man sin against thee, cast forth the poison of hatred and speak peaceably to him, and in thy soul hold not guile; and if he confesses and repents, forgive him. . . . And if he be shameless, and persist in his wrong-doing, even so forgive him from the heart and leave to God the avenging.
>
> > Testament of Gad 6:3, 7; cf.
> > Matt. 18:15, 21 f., 35
> > (also 5:43-45); Mark 11:25;
> > Luke 6:27 f.; 17:3 f.

> Love the Lord through all your life, and one another with a true heart.
>
> > Testament of Dan 5:3 (similarly Test. of Issachar 5:2; 7:6); cf. Matt. 22:37, 39.

> And if any one seeketh to do evil unto you, do well unto him, and ye shall be redeemed of the Lord from all evil.
>
> > Testament of Joseph 18:2; cf.
> > Luke 6:27 f.; Matt. 5:43-45.

The fourth and last virtue of Diaspora Jews mentioned by Paul is their missionary zeal (Rom. 2:19 f.).[39] A real passion for the conversion of the

---

erected to protect the spirit became to some of its sons more important than the spirit. Yet it never was so to all its sons. Nor was it created to be so to any." (H. R. Rowley, "The Unity of the Old Testament" in *Bulletin of the John Rylands Library*, Vol. 29, No. 2 [February 1946], p. 28).

[39] On Jewish missionary work and on the proselytes, see: A. Bertholet, *Die Stellung der Israeliten und der Juden zu den Fremden* (Berlin, 1896). E. Schürer, *Geschichte*, Vol. 3, pp. 150-188. A. Harnack, *Die Mission und Ausbreitung des Christentums*, pp. 1-12. Leipzig, 1902 (later editions, English translation). I. Lévy, "Le proselytisme juif" (REJ 51 [1906] 1-29). J. Juster, *Les Juifs dans l'empire romain*, Vol. 1, pp. 253-290 (Paris, 1914). G. F. Moore, *Judaism*, Vol. 1, pp. 323-353. F. Gavin, *The Jewish Antecedents of the Christian Sacraments*. London, 1928. F. M. Derwacter, *Preparing the Way for Paul* (New York, 1930). J. Klausner, *From Jesus to Paul*, pp. 31-49 (New York, 1943).

heathen animated some Pharisees in the first century of our era: "For ye compass sea and land to make one proselyte" (Matt. 23:15). But such activity was becoming less pronounced in Palestine, where it seems to have almost come to an end about A.D. 100. In the Dispersion, however, conditions were more favorable for it.

The numerical increase of the Jews during the last three centuries B.C. is due, in part, to the influx of proselytes. In the time of Nehemiah (444 B.C.) the total number of Jews was considerably less than one million (probably little more than half a million), while in the first century of our era the Jews of the Dispersion probably numbered about two millions, while those in Palestine are estimated to have been at least one million (Juster's figure of five millions is incredible).[40]

When Paul said of Israel that it regarded itself as "a light of them which are in darkness" (Rom. 2:19), he appropriately echoed the Second Isaiah, the first explicit advocate of the conversion of the heathen (about 540 B.C.), when he wrote, "I will also give thee for a light to the Gentiles" (Is. 49:6; cf. Enoch 48:4; Luke 2:42; Acts 13:47). These words (according to Justin, *Dialogue with Tryphon* 122 f.) were understood to mean that Israel was the teacher of the nations; or, in the words of the Sibyl, "to all mortals the guide to life" (Sibyllines 3:195). Later writers in the Old Testament reechoed this missionary ideal, and looked forward to the day when all nations would worship Jehovah. But it was first in the Hellenistic period that efforts were made to realize this ideal; the first known step in this direction was probably the translation of the Pentateuch into Greek at Alexandria: the Septuagint, in the original, narrow sense of the word (dating from about 250 B.C.). It is probably at the same time or shortly before that missionary work was begun on a considerable scale in Palestine (II Chron. 30:1-12, 25; the dating in the time of Hezekiah is to be ascribed to the Chronicler's imagination). While the Samaritans "laughed to scorn and mocked" (30:10) the missionaries sent out from Jerusalem—as could have been expected—the Galileans were not wholly unresponsive, and some of their proselytes went to Jerusalem to worship in the Temple (30:11; cf. Ps. 68:28; Tob. 1). The earliest description of such converts is perhaps in Is. 56:6-8—a passage which cannot be dated exactly, but which presumably was written in the early part of the Hellenistic period.[41] The Jewish proselytes were however, still a minority of the Galileans in 164 B.C. (I Macc. 5:14-17, 20-23); the mixed population of northern Galilee and the Itureans were forcibly converted to Judaism by Aristobulus I (104-103 B.C.), according

---

[40] For various opinions on the number of Jews in antiquity, see J. Klausner, *From Jesus to Paul*, pp. 32 f.; and C. C. McCown in JBL 66 (1947) 425-436.

[41] G. F. Moore (*Judaism*, Vol. 1, p. 231) says that its date "probably falls at a relatively advanced time in the Persian period."

to Josephus (*Antiquities* 13:11, 3 [§318]). Similar conversions on the threat of death are recorded for John Hyrcanus (135-104), who imposed circumcision on the Idumeans in southern Judea (Josephus, *Antiquities* 13:9, 1 [§257]), and for Alexander Janneus (103-76), who was apparently no less successful, although he destroyed Pella because the inhabitants refused to adopt Judaism (*op. cit.*, 13:15, 4 [§325]).[42] On the whole, however, conversions to Judaism were obtained by persuasion and took place mostly outside of Palestine and its neighborhood. As Rabbi Eleazar said, "God dispersed the Jews to facilitate proselytism" (Babylonian Talmud, *Pesaḥim* 87b).

The Hellenistic period, after 300 B.C., was especially favorable to the spread of Judaism in the Mediterranean world. The Jews were then establishing colonies in all important civilized communities and thus, outside of Judea, lived in the midst of Gentiles. Even without sending out any missionaries to convert the heathen, the Jews by their mere presence, by their conduct and daily contacts, and primarily through their synagogues, open to all, were attracting many Gentiles to their religion; but at the same time they aroused in some a strong hostility against themselves.

During the Hellenistic and Roman periods, Gentiles ran the whole gamut from highest admiration to most extreme contempt in their attitudes toward the Jews. In a general way it appears that Judaism attracted particularly the lower classes (as did Christianity at the beginning) and women, but was often ridiculed and denounced by people of high education, breeding, and wealth. There are, of course, men of letters, scientists, and philosophers (like Theophrastus, Clearchus of Soli, Strabo, Varro, and others) whose favorable opinions reflect those of the illiterate, humble people; while on the contrary mobs at Alexandria and elsewhere in their insane fury pillaged and slaughtered the Jews. But, on the whole, the references to the Jews in classical literatures (collected by Th. Reinach, *Textes d'auteurs grecs et romains*; cf. Schürer, *Geschichte*, Vol. 3, pp. 150-173; Juster, *Les Juifs*, Vol. 1, pp. 31-34, 45-48, note) are decidedly unfriendly and express disdain rather than hatred.

In a measure Gentile writers merely reciprocated Jewish contempt for heathenism. In the ancient world the Jews alone claimed that theirs was the only true religion and that eventually it would conquer the world. By setting themselves apart from all other nations as the chosen people

---

[42] That such compulsory conversions were only "skin-deep" was well known (the Idumean Herod was called a "half-Jew"). Several varieties of converts for purely worldly motives are enumerated in the Jerusalem Talmud (*Qiddushin* 65b): "love proselytes" (for the sake of marriage), proselytes for a place at the king's table or similar to Solomon's servants (for advancement in the bureaucracy or in high society), "lion proselytes" (out of fear, like the Babylonian colonists in Samaria: II Kings 17:24-28), converts because of a dream understood as a divine order to become Jews, and the proselytes of the days of Mordecai and Esther (Esth. 8:17), compelled by terror of slaughter.

of the only God in existence, and by ridiculing Gentile religions as a foolish worship of wooden and stone idols, as some Jews had done since the days of Second Isaiah (Is. 40-55) and Cyrus the Great, they invited pagan resentment both as a people and as a religious community.

The criticisms against the Jewish nation and religion, which were later repeated by Christians and were used in part by pagans against Christians, are conveniently listed, with references, by Juster (*Les Juifs*, Vol. 1, pp. 45-48) in a long footnote (see also Schürer, *Geschichte*, Vol. 3, pp. 150-173; Th. Reinach, *Textes*, pp. viii-xxii).[43] The Jews, according to pagan slander, are mutually loyal and merciful to the highest degree, but hate all others;[44] they are a useless nation; a nation of slaves; a seditious, cruel, obstinate, daring, cowardly, prolific, sensual, degenerate, dirty, leprous, exclusive, dangerous, and contemptible people. The Jewish religion (*barbara superstitio*, Cicero) is characterized by sad and cold ritual; worship of angels, of a donkey, of heaven and clouds; human sacrifice; contempt for images; circumcision; Sabbath idleness; eating of unleavened bread; abstention from pork and other foods; the Jews are atheists, enemies of the gods, disrespectful toward the emperor, hated by the gods, and sacrilegious.

Despite such abusive attacks, most fully summarized by Tacitus (*Histories* V, 1-13), Judaism had a strong appeal for many Gentiles, first of all because of the universalistic tendencies of Judaism and secondly because of similar trends in Hellenism.

In its essence Judaism was of course not merely a universal monotheistic religion, teaching noble ethics and salvation for all the faithful (whatever their race), but also a revealed religion, demanding strict observance of all its prescriptions, exclusive devotion, and rigorous separation from polluting contacts with heathenism in all its forms. In the Diaspora, however, in opening its gates to the Gentiles, Judaism stressed its points of contact with the noblest Hellenistic teachings rather than its national exclusiveness. No one could seriously object to the basic doctrines of monotheism, moral conduct, God's judgment, and eternal salvation; no one could take offense at the denunciation of polytheism, idolatry, and wickedness.[45]

[43] The latest treatment of the subject is in the essay of R. Marcus which appeared in *Essays on Antisemitism*, edited by K. S. Pinson (Jewish Social Studies Publications, No. 2). New York, 1942. For details, see I. Heinemann, "Antisemitismus" in Pauly-Wissowa, *Realenzyklopädie*, Supplementary Vol. 5, cols. 3-43. Stuttgart, 1931.

[44] *Apud eos fides obstinata, misericordia in promptu; sed adversus omnes hostile odium* (Tacitus, *Histories* V, 5). Juvenal (*Satires* XIV, 103 f.) says even that they will show the right way only to a fellow believer, and will lead only a circumcised man to the spring which is looked for. This separateness of the Jews (Greek, *amixía*), which accomplished the survival of Judaism, is amply attested in Jewish writings (Jub. 22:16-22; Dan. 1:8-16; 30:7-17; Tob. 1:10 f.; etc.).

[45] Paul's indictment of heathenism in Rom. 1:18-32 is more bitter and severe than any extant Jewish attack of this kind (as, for instance, in the Wisdom of Solomon).

And so the Jews met the Gentiles halfway. The latter were attracted to Judaism first as a philosophy and later as one of the Oriental mystery cults offering eternal life. Judaism is called a philosophy by Hellenistic and Roman writers (beginning with Aristotle, according to Clearchus of Soli), as well as by Jewish and Christian apologists (see the references in Juster, *Les Juifs*, Vol. 1, p. 243, n. 2). The synagogue worship, consisting mainly of a scriptural reading and an address, appeared to the Gentiles as a meeting of teachers and pupils of a foreign philosophical school. Nor was the synagogue radically different from some Greek schools in asserting that its textbook was inspired, in singing the praises of the deity, and in observing peculiar prescriptions in regard to food, dress, and purifications. Moreover, Jewish teachings about the character and activity of the sole Creator and about ethical conduct were not only familiar in some Hellenistic philosophies, but were occasionally mentioned without disapproval by ancient writers, such as Hecataeus of Abdera,[46] Strabo (XVI: 2, 35, paraphrased earlier in this chapter), who on the basis of a Jewish source (Schürer) or of Posidonius and a Jewish apology (Th. Reinach) presented Moses as a Stoic pantheist, Varro (116-27 B.C.)[47] and, surprisingly, even the implacable Tacitus.[48]

No less erroneous than the notion that Judaism was a philosophy is the notion that it was a mystery cult; yet under both aspects it drew adherents to itself. Both points of view are suggested in the Wisdom of Solomon—which to some extent is a missionary tract—where Judaism is identified with *sophía* (wisdom) and secures to its true adherents the immortality of the spirit. In contrast with wisdom in Palestinian writings (such as Ecclesiasticus), *sophía* in the Wisdom of Solomon is decidedly tinged with Platonic and Stoic doctrines, and the book's teaching on the immortality of the soul is the opposite of the Pharisaic doctrine of the resurrection of the body which Greek philosophers regarded as absurd (cf. Acts 17:32). IV Maccabees (cf. Philo, *De congressu* 14 [I, 531 M]) defines *sophía* as the Stoics did: "The knowledge of things divine and

---

[46] "[Moses] made no image of the gods at all, since he did not believe that the deity had a human figure" (preserved by Diodorus 40, 3, in Photius; the text is printed in C. Müller, *Fragmenta historicorum graecorum* II, 392; Th. Reinach, *Textes*, p. 16).

[47] In one of his 41 books of *Human and Divine Antiquities*, Varro "says also that the ancient Romans during more than 170 years worshiped the gods without images. 'If this custom had continued, he says, the gods would be honored in a purer fashion.' To support his opinion he adduces, among others, the example of the Jews. He does not hesitate to conclude this passage saying that the first men who raised among nations statues to the gods removed from their countrymen a terror, but added an error" (Augustine, *The City of God* IV:31, 2).

[48] "The Jews conceive merely mentally the one and only deity. They regard as wicked those who fashion with perishable materials, in human figures, this God. He is supreme and eternal, neither imitable nor perishable. They therefore allow no images in their cities, and much less in the temples" (Tacitus, *Histories* V, 5).

human, and of their causes" (1:16; cf. Plutarch, *Placita philosophorum*
I, 1 [this work is erroneously attributed to Plutarch]; Cicero, *de officiis*
I:43, 153; II:2, 5; Seneca, Epistle 89). But IV Maccabees contains also
the Jewish definition of *sophía*: "The culture acquired under the Law,
through which we learn with due reverence the things of God and for
our worldly profit the things of man" (1:17). This book stresses, like
the Book of Wisdom and Philo, the final liberation of the souls from
their prison in the body, in order to receive after death their eternal
reward (IV Macc. 10:15; 13:17; 15:3; 16:13; 17:4 f., 18; 18:23) or their
everlasting punishment (9:9, 32; 10:11, 15; 12:19; 13:15; 18:5, 22).

That one could easily mistake Judaism for an Oriental mystery[49] may
be seen from the characteristics that made these cults popular, as listed
by F. Cumont in ch. 2 of his standard book, *Les religions orientales dans
le paganisme romain* (Paris, 1906; 4th ed., 1929). These cults undertook
to restore to the soul its lost purity, either through ritual washings which
should remove sin (cf. the Jewish baptism for the proselytes) or through
privations and suffering (cf. the fast, afflicting one's soul, and confession
of sins on the Day of Atonement). Their priests became (like the rabbis)
pastors, advising the members of their flock, individually, teaching them
the abstentions and duties required to restore and retain their right
relations with the deity. The holiness attained through such rites and
ascetic practices was the condition of eternal bliss after death—a liberation from the slavery of the spirit to the body; this was the one ray of
hope for the masses, whose wretched state on earth seemed beyond cure.
Nay, the whole world seemed to have become so corrupted that its end
was near (cf. the Jewish apocalypses). These cults thus offered more
beauty in their rites, more truth in their teachings, nobler ideals in their
ethical principles, more comfort in their glance on the invisible world
of eternal bliss, than the traditional religions, which had a national,
public character. The Oriental mysteries raised the spirit, gave to conduct an ideal goal, appealed to the deepest feelings of the individual, and
called him to a new, a spiritual, life.

In this general religious awakening, which marks a new era in the
development of religion, Judaism played an important role in setting
the stage for the triumph of Christianity. It was in harmony with the
general trend toward monotheism and with the general longing for
purification from sinfulness and for eternal bliss; and it could satisfy the
religious aspirations of the nobler spirits better than the mystery cults.
That it failed to attain the missionary success of some of these and did

[49] Such a misconception is attested in Rome in 139 B.C., when the *praetor pere-
grinus* Cn. Cornelius Hispalus forced the Jews to return to Palestine because "they
had tried to corrupt the Roman customs through the worship of Jupiter Sabazius
[error for *Yahweh Ṣebāōth*, the Lord of Hosts]" (Valerius Maximus; cf. Schürer,
Geschichte Vol. 3, p. 58; Th. Reinach, *Textes*, p. 259).

not become the religion of Europe instead of Christianity is due primarily to those obstacles to the conversion of the Gentiles which Paul recognized and removed: circumcision, the ritual and ceremonial prescriptions of the Law of Moses, and particularly the national character of Judaism, which required that its converts become citizens of Israel and renounce (at least in theory) their previous allegiance. For the proselyte was naturalized into the Jewish nation,[50] not initiated into a mystery cult, like that of Mithra, in which nationality played no role; by becoming heir of the scriptural promises which God had made to Israel, he was denationalized and forbidden to participate as formerly in ruler worship, and in civic rites and festivals. As members of a nation, the Jews were granted in Roman law special exemptions and unique religious privileges. Juster (Les Juifs, Vol. 2, pp. 19 f.) rightly stresses the point that both before and after A.D. 70 the Jews were regarded in Roman law as a nation, not as members of a licit religion; the Jewish privileges were conceded only to converts naturalized into the nation; and so the law more and more strove to prevent Gentiles from becoming proselytes or, in other words, members of the Jewish nation (which, of course, cannot be distinguished from the Jewish Church). And, as Paul recognized (Rom. 9:4), the Jewish religious prerogatives ("the adoption, and the glory, and the covenants, and the giving of the Law, and the service of God, and the promises") belong to the nation, to the "Israelites"—but not to the uncircumcized (Eph. 2:11 f.). Thus the ancients were wrong in regarding Judaism merely as a philosophy or as an Oriental cult, but these misconceptions served to make Judaism attractive to many Gentiles.

Some of these converts remained mere adherents, sympathizers, "fellow travelers," who did not take the final step by becoming proselytes. These people on the outside fringe of Judaism have been erroneously called "semiproselytes" or "proselytes of the gate."[51] Their real name in ancient writings is "fearers of God," meaning devout, God-fearing persons, who worship and revere God.[52] From Josephus (War 7:3, 3) and the Book of Acts we get the impression that these Jewish sympathizers (phoboúmenoi or sebómenoi tòn theón, those who fear or revere God),

[50] Philo (de monarchia 7, 51 [II, 219 M]) says the proselytes "have become naturalized in a new and godly commonwealth."

[51] By "proselytes of the gate" (gērê ha-shá'ār) medieval rabbis mean "the strangers who are within Israel's gate" (cf. Ex. 20:10; Deut. 5:15; 14:21; 24:14) or the resident aliens who have not been naturalized; the expression does not occur in the Talmud, which calls the resident alien gēr tôshāb—an expression used in contrast to the gēr ha-ṣedeq or real proselyte observing the "seven commandments of the children of Noah" as also the whole Law of Moses (see Schürer, Geschichte, Vol. 3, pp. 177-180; Strack and Billerbeck, Kommentar, Vol. 2, pp. 715-723).

[52] For the Hebrew and Greek terms, with references, see Schürer, Geschichte, Vol. 3, p. 174, n. 70; G. F. Moore, Judaism, Vol. 1, pp. 325, 338-341; Vol. 3, n. 96; Juster, Les Juifs, Vol. 1, pp. 274 f., n. 6. See also: J. Klausner, From Jesus to Paul, pp. 40-45; H. A. Wolfson, Philo, Vol. 2, pp. 372-374.

sharply distinguished from Jews (a term which includes the proselytes), constituted a conspicuous part of the synagogue congregations (Acts 13:16, 26, 43; 17:4, 17; cf. 10:2, 22; 16:14; 18:7; in 13:43 we find "religious proselytes," a designation which is ambiguous). Josephus tells us that these God-fearing adherents to Judaism sent contributions from the Diaspora to the Temple in Jerusalem (*Antiquities* 14:7, 2 [§110]); that Poppaea, the wife of Nero, was one of them (*op. cit.* 20:8, 11 [§195]); that Izates (d. A.D. 55), the king of Adiabene (the Assyrian provinces east of the Euphrates), together with Queen Helena his mother became an adherent and was eventually circumcised (*op. cit.* 20:2, 3-5 [§§34-53]); see also Schürer, *Geschichte*, Vol. 3, pp. 169-172; Juster, *Les Juifs*, Vol. 1, p. 202, n. 9; G. F. Moore, *Judaism*, Vol. 1, p. 349. Other well-known adherents are the centurion of Capernaum (Luke 7:5), the Ethiopian eunuch (Acts 8:27 f.), and Cornelius, the centurion at Caesarea (Acts 10).

These Gentile adherents of the synagogue were attracted by Jewish monotheism and certain Jewish practices; they rejected idolatry and polytheism, but, objecting to circumcision and Jewish citizenship, they did not take the final steps required of true proselytes. Among Jewish practices which were widely observed by these adherents and even by pagans, Josephus names the Sabbath observance, fasts, lighting the lamps just before the beginning of the Sabbath, and dietary prohibitions (*Against Apion* 2:39; cf. Tertullian, *ad nationes* I, 13). According to Juvenal (*Satires* 14:96-106), it would happen that the son of a Roman who observed the Sabbath and some dietary laws would begin to worship the clouds and the deity of heaven, then he would class pork meat with human flesh, and finally he would be circumcised, would despise Roman laws, and would study, observe, and fear only the Jewish Law, which Moses handed down in a mysterious scroll. Although Josephus (*Against Apion* 2:10 [§123]) says that of the many Greeks who have adopted the Jewish laws some "had not courage enough to persevere and so departed from them again," the number of the faithful God-fearing adherents must have been conspicuous in the Diaspora of the first century of our era. It was primarily among them that Paul found the early believers who constituted the nucleus of the incipient Christian Church, until converted pagans eventually became the great majority in it.

Real proselytes were probably less numerous than these adherents, especially among men. Women, who did not have civic religious duties, were more pious, and were not held back by the requirement of circumcision, constituted the bulk of the proselytes and were presumably the majority even among the adherents. When Hadrian forbade circumcision, Jewish missionary work ceased.

Jewish Law required from the Gentile who wished to become a

proselyte that he be circumcised and baptized, and (before A.D. 70) that he offer a sacrifice.[53] After these three initiatory rites, the neophyte was expected to adopt all Jewish doctrines and laws (". . . every man that is circumcised . . . is a debtor to do the whole Law" [Gal. 5:3]). Thus he became "a naturalized citizen of a new religious commonwealth in which he is on full equality of rights and duties with born Jews" (G. F. Moore, *Judaism*, Vol. 1, p. 328). Human nature being what it is, it could not be expected that the Jews would love the *ger* (proselyte) as one of themselves (cf. Lev. 19:34, which by *ger* meant the resident alien), in accordance to Biblical and post-Biblical exhortation. Although according to Philo and the Talmud the proselyte was "the brother" of the native Jew (cf. H. A. Wolfson, *Philo*, Vol. 2, pp. 352-364), the proselyte became an "Israelite," true, but never a "child of Abraham" (cf. Acts 13:26), and socially he was never quite considered an equal by the majority of native Jews; at times he was the object of criticism, suspicion, and contempt—even down to J. Klausner (*From Jesus to Paul*, pp. 48 f.), who ascribes to these ancient converts "a pagan heart which was covered by only a light wrapping of abstract Judaism." Such an attitude must have contributed to attract not merely Jewish adherents but also Jewish proselytes to Christianity in which "there is no difference between the Jew and the Greek" (Rom. 10:12); for in the Church there can be "neither Greek nor Jew, circumcision nor uncircumcision, Barbarian, Scythian, bond nor free: for Christ is all, and in all" (Col. 3:11).

[53] For the literature on these requirements, see Schürer, *Geschichte*, Vol. 3, pp. 185; Juster, *Les Juifs*, Vol. 1, p. 255, n. 1; Moore, *Judaism*, Vol. 1, p. 331-335. On baptism of proselytes, see in particular H. H. Rowley, "Jewish Proselyte Baptism" (HUCA 15 [1940] 313-334).

CHAPTER VI

ALEXANDRIAN-JEWISH LITERATURE

~~~~~~

In his admirable work on *Philo* (2 vols. Cambridge, Mass.: Harvard University Press, 1947), Harry A. Wolfson states that the Alexandrian Jews, in presenting Judaism to the Graeco-Roman world—which at times regarded their religion as atheism, their laws as inhospitable, and their practices as superstitious—tried to show that "their God . . . is the God of philosophers, that their laws . . . were like the ethics and politics recommended by philosophers, and that their practices . . . could be explained as being based on reason" (*op. cit.*, Vol. 1, p. 19). In other words, substantially the whole Hellenistic-Jewish literature, from the translation of the Pentateuch into Greek (the LXX, about 250 B.C.) to the writings of Philo (d. *ca.* A.D. 50) and Josephus (d. *ca.* A.D. 100), who wrote in Greek although he was a Palestinian, had a double purpose: to defend the Jews and Judaism from the attacks of pagans and to prove the superiority of the Jews and Judaism over other nations and their religions. As appears clearly, for instance, in the Wisdom of Solomon, this literature aimed at keeping the Jews loyal to their ancestral beliefs and practices and at convincing the pagans of the folly of their own polytheism and idolatry. Polemics and apologetics are inseparably blended in all these writings of Alexandrian Jews—omitting, of course, the Greek versions of Palestinian books circulating at Alexandria. Another characteristic of this literature is the mixture of Jewish and Greek thought, which is variously appraised. While H. A. Wolfson asserts that the Hellenization of the Alexandrian Jews was "in language only; not in religious belief or cult" (*Philo* I, 13), Aristotle stated that a Jew whom he met in Asia Minor during his residence there from 348 to 345 B.C. was "Hellenic not only in language but also in soul" (Josephus, *Against Apion* I, 22 [§180]). In any case, while some Jews in Alexandria (as also in Jerusalem about 175-164 B.C.) leaned so far toward Greek culture that they were considered apostates (cf. I. Macc. 1:11-15; Wisd. of Sol. ch. 2; Wolfson, *Philo* I, 78-85; II, 406 f.), the Alexandrian Jewish writings that the Christian Church has preserved for us were all written by stanch defenders of the strict orthodox practices and of the orthodox tenets of normative Judaism, whose Hellenization was more or less superficial and never affected basic convictions.

197

The book *On the Jews* by Alexander Polyhistor (*ca.* 80-40 B.C.)[1] is lost except for quotations by Josephus, Eusebius of Caesarea and Clement of Alexandria; it was an objective, impartial collection of Jewish and pagan excerpts on Jewish history. All other Graeco-Roman works on the Jews—as almost all references to Jews in classical literature—are unfriendly, if not hostile and contemptuous (see Th. Reinach, *Textes d'auteurs grecs et romains relatifs au Judaisme.* Paris, 1895). The following authors wrote books (now lost) against the Jews:[2] Apollonius Molon of Rhodes (*ca.* 100-70 B.C.), Apion Pleistonikes of Alexandria (*ca.* A.D. 50; see Josephus, *Against Apion*), and Herennius Philo of Byblus (A.D. 64-141).

Without composing special books against the Jews, other Hellenistic writers likewise attacked them. In his important history of Egypt (*Aigyptiaká*), Manetho, an Egyptian priest living about 270-250 B.C., reported, as he himself admitted, "from anonymously transmitted tales" (Josephus, *Against Apion* I, 16; cf. I, 26) slanderous fantasies about the early history of the Jews (Josephus, *op. cit.* I, 26-27); Manetho's Hyksos stories in I, 14-16, *pace* Josephus, had no reference to the Jews. Other derogatory fictitious tales about the Jews were told by Mnaseas (*ca.* 200 B.C.) in his travel book (Josephus, *op. cit.* II, 9; cf. I, 23; and *Antiquities* I:3, 6); by Lysimachus (perhaps at the beginning of our era), whose account of the Exodus went beyond Manetho's "in the incredible nature of his forgeries . . . contrived out of his bitter hatred of the Jews" (Josephus, *op. cit.* I, 34-35; cf. II, 2 and 14); by Chaeremon (*ca.* A.D. 50) in his *Egyptian History* (Josephus, *op. cit.* I, 32-33; C. Müller, *Fragmenta histor. graec.* III, 495-499); by the philosopher and historian Posidonius, early in the first century before our era (Josephus, *op. cit.* II, 7); by Tacitus (*Histories* V, 2-5); and by the other authors quoted by Th. Reinach in his *Textes* mentioned above. The vicious and false accusations of these authors against the Jews have been briefly summarized in the preceding chapter.

Comparatively little was written by the Jews to retort the baseless slanders of their adversaries. Indeed we know of only two real "apologies" for Judaism and the Jews:[3] Philo's *Apology for the Jews* (lost, except for the quotation in Eusebius, *Praeparatio evangelica* VIII, 11), and the

---

[1] See E. Schürer, *Geschichte*, Vol. 3, 469-472. The fullest treatment is: J. Freudenthal, *Alexander Polyhistor und die von ihm erhaltenen Reste judäischer und samaritanischer Geschichtswerke.* Breslau, 1875. The surviving parts of the work are also published in C. Müller's *Fragmenta historicorum graecorum*, III, 206-244.

[2] See on them Schürer, *Geschichte*, Vol. 1, 71-73; Vol. 3, 532-544. J. Juster, *Les Juifs*, Vol. 1, pp. 32-34. Schürer (*op. cit.*, 3, 541) denies that Apion wrote a special work against the Jews: while only his book on Egypt is explicitly quoted in connection with the Jews, Eusebius and Jerome (see Schürer, *op. cit.*, p. 543) definitely assert that he wrote a book on the Jews.

[3] Cf. Paul Krüger, *Philo und Josephus als Apologeten des Judentums.* Leipzig, 1906.

work wrongly entitled (since Jerome) *Against Apion,* by Flavius Josephus (Origen and Eusebius cite it under the title, "On the Antiquity of the Jews"). In this work, written about A.D. 95, Josephus argued that the Jews were no less ancient than any other civilized nation (I, 1-23): "I suppose that, by my books of *The Antiquities of the Jews* . . . I have made evident . . . that our Jewish nation is of very great antiquity. . . . Those *Antiquities* contain the history of five thousand years." With great learning (facilitated to a great extent by the convenient collection of texts about the Jews prepared by Alexander Polyhistor) Josephus referred to many non-Jewish historians (Manetho, Herodotus, Dius, Berossus, etc.) and concluded that the Jews were delivered from Egypt almost one thousand years before the siege of Troy (I, 16; in reality the two events are almost contemporary). Josephus was forced to refute, incidentally, slanderous tales about the origin of the Jews told by Manetho, Lysimachus, Chaeremon, and Apion (I, 24—II, 3). Then, after replying to some specific charges made by Apion against the Alexandrian Jews (II, 4-6) and against the Jewish worship and law (II, 7-12)—mostly rather silly charges—Josephus proceeded to a matter that was paramount to Jewish apologists: the accusation that the Jews, being a people of recent origin, had made no contributions to human culture (II, 13). This he refuted by means of a panegyric of the Law of Moses (II, 14-31) and of the law-abiding Jewish nation (II, 32-33; cf. II, 39). Taking the offensive, Josephus pointed out the folly of pagan polytheism (II, 34-36) and the unfriendliness to foreigners, far greater in ancient Greek legislations than in the Mosaic Law (II, 37-38), concluding that this law was the most ancient of all (II, 39), that it influenced Greek philosophers, and was attracting converts to Judaism (II, 40). In closing, he summarized his whole book (II, 41-42).

In the other Hellenistic-Jewish writings the accusations against the Jews were not even mentioned: the authors contented themselves with glorifying the Jews and their religion, and ridiculing paganism: these, in varying guises and different forms, are the dominant themes of this literature. Even the Palestinian books written after 200 B.C. and translated into Greek, becoming part of the Septuagint, have in common this exaltation of the Jews over the pagans. History (I Maccabees) and fiction (Daniel, Bel and the Dragon, Judith, Esther with additions) described the triumphs of Jews over heathen; or presented idealized portraits of exemplary Jewish individuals (Tobit, Susanna). Ecclesiasticus extolled Judaism and deemed Hellenism unworthy of notice. Apocalypses, beginning with Daniel, announced the coming downfall of the heathen empires and the establishment of the Jewish world kingdom. And the Epistle of Jeremy caricatured sarcastically the religion of the Gentiles as an extremely crass and idiotic worship of inanimate idols.

1. Historical Writings

The Alexandrian-Jewish literature pursued its apologetic and polemic purposes with far greater fervor and forthrightness than the Palestinian, as a comparison between the fairly objective I Maccabees (Palestinian) and the fanatic II Maccabees (Alexandrian) will show. Hellenistic-Jewish historical writing was embellished with fiction, to stress the superiority of the Jews over the Gentiles (II Maccabees), or consisted of fiction pure and simple, with the same purpose (III Maccabees, and partly preserved books). Poetry and philosophy were subservient to propaganda, which was not camouflaged successfully (Wisdom of Solomon, Aristeas, Sibylline Oracles, IV Maccabees, etc.). Being utterly convinced that the Law and the other Scriptures were revelations of the sole true God, who had chosen Israel as his people, but living in the midst of people who ridiculed such claims, the Alexandrian Jews could make neither concessions nor compromises: they alone "had a very great light," while over the heathen "was spread a heavy night" (Wisd. of Sol. 17:21 f.).

The only complete historical works are II and III Maccabees and the historical books of Philo and Josephus; only fragments of other writings survive. These fragments have been preserved for us by Eusebius (*Praeparatio evangelica* IX), Clement of Alexandria (*Stromata*), and Josephus; ultimately they seem to go back to the collection of passages on Jewish history made by Alexander Polyhistor; they have been published by C. Müller (*Fragmenta histor. graec.* III, 206-244) and by W. N. Stearns (*Fragments from Graeco-Jewish Writers*. Chicago, 1908); see, in general, Schürer, *Geschichte*, Vol. 3, pp. 468-497.

Demetrius (*ca.* 215 B.C.) was erroneously regarded as a pagan by Josephus; his history of the Jews was entitled *On the Kings in Judea*. Four fragments survive: the life of Jacob, followed by the list of the descendants of Levi down to Aaron and Moses; a demonstration that Zipporah the wife of Moses was a descendant of Abraham and Keturah; the story of Marah (Ex. 15:22-26); a calculation of the number of years elapsed from the deportation of the northern tribes of Israel in 722 B.C. and of Judah in 586 B.C. to the accession of Ptolemy IV Philopator (221-203 B.C.), i.e., 338 years and three months and 573 years and nine months, respectively (which would date 722 B.C. in 794, and 586 B.C. in 559: the interval is actually 136 years instead of 235; perhaps we should read 473 instead of 573); from Sennacherib's deportation in 701 B.C. to Nebuchadnezzar's in 586 Demetrius calculates an interval of 128 years and six months instead of the correct 115. In dealing with Jacob the interest in chronology is likewise apparent; the whole work may have been primarily a determination of Old Testament chronology, to prove the antiquity of Israel.

Pseudo-Hecataeus (*ca.* 200-150 B.C.) is a Greek-writing Jewish historian who assumed the name of the philosopher Hecataeus of Abdera (who was, according to Josephus, *Against Apion* I, 22 [§183], a contemporary of Alexander). He wrote a book entitled *On the Jews* or *On Abraham* (*ibid.* and *Antiquities* 1:7, 2 [§159]), which is quoted in the Letter of Aristeas §31 (cf. Josephus, *Antiquities* 12:2, 4 [§38]) and by Josephus (*Against Apion* I, 22 [§183-204], cf. Eusebius, *Praeparatio Evangelica* IX, 4; and *Against Apion* II, 4 [§43]). The remnants of the book of *Pseudo-Hecataeus* are collected by C. Müller, *Fragmenta historicorum graecorum*, Vol. 2, pp. 392-396. Müller regards, probably unnecessarily, *On the Jews* and *On Abraham* as two separate works of our author; they are probably different titles for the same book (for further details and bibliography, see Schürer, *Geschichte*, Vol. 3, pp. 603-608).

Eupolemus (*ca.* 150 B.C.) has been often identified with the ambassador sent to Rome by Judas Maccabeus (I Macc. 8:17; II Macc. 4:11), but no definite evidence is available on the matter. Like Demetrius, he wrote a book *On the Kings in Judea* and was also interested, although far less intensely, in chronology. He figured that from the Exodus to the fifth year of Demetrius I Soter (162-150 B.C.) and the twelfth of Ptolemy VII [IX] Physcon (170-116 B.C.), i.e., 157 or 158 B.C. (the year 5140 from the creation of the world, according to Eupolemus), 2,580 years had elapsed; by dating the Exodus thus in 2423 B.C. he figured at least one millennium too early (unless his figure 1580 was accidentally increased to 2580 by a coypist). The following fragments of his book have survived: the story of Abraham, probably attributed to him erroneously by Eusebius (Polyhistor apparently quoted it as anonymous); Moses, "the first sage," taught the alphabet to the Jews, then visited the Phoenicians and the Greeks; the history of David and Solomon, including the correspondence of the latter with Suron (i.e., Hiram) of Tyre (based on II Chron. 2:3-16 [Hebr. 2:2-15]; cf. I Kings 5:2-10 [Hebr. 5:16-24]) and with Uaphres, king of Egypt (freely composed on the basis of the preceding); the description of the building of the temple in Jerusalem; and possibly a prophecy of Jeremiah about the coming exile, fulfilled through Nebuchadnezzar's conquest of Jerusalem (Eusebius [*Praep. ev.* IX, 39] does not name the author).

Artapanus (presumably *ca.* 100 B.C.) wrote a book *On the Jews* in which he allowed his fancy to glorify his people by attributing to it all inventions and cultural advances. Abraham taught astrology to Pharaoh Pharethothes. Joseph improved Egyptian agriculture. Jacob and his sons founded the shrines of Athos and Heliopolis. Moses was none other than the Greek Musaeus and the Egyptian Hermes, the real originator of

Egyptian civilization, the first to develop navigation, architecture, strategy, and philosophy; Moses divided Egypt into 36 nomes, taught each nome how to worship God (including the veneration of the ibis and Apis), gave to the priests the knowledge of the hieroglyphic signs, organized the government; Pharaoh Chenephres failed to kill Moses and after the king's death God delivered Israel from Egypt through Moses, by means of miraculous wonders.

Aristeas (presumably *ca.* 100 B.C.) likewise wrote a book *On the Jews.* All we have is a fragment dealing with Job, who (as in the apocryphal end of Job in the LXX) is identified with Jobab son of Zerah of Bozrah (Gen. 36:33), a great-grandson of Esau (Gen. 36:10, 13). The extant corrupt text, however, makes Job a son of Esau and of his wife *Bassara*: the city *Bozrah* was thus taken to be the name of Esau's wife! Our author, as later the author of the Testament of Job, probably drew his misinformation from the apocryphal addition to Job in the Septuagint.

Cleodemus, or *Malchus* (presumably *ca.* 100 B.C.), according to Polyhistor, was a prophet who wrote a history of the Jews in agreement with that of Moses (Josephus, *Antiquities* I, 15). He relates that the three sons of Abraham and Keturah—Apheran (Epher), Asourim (Asshurim), and Japhran (Ephah), cf. Gen. 25:3 f.—gave their names to Africa, the Assyrians, and the city Aphra. They marched with Heracles against Libya and Antaeus; Heracles married Aphra's daughter, who gave birth to Diodorus, the father of Sophonas, or Sophax, from whom the Sophakians received their name.[4]

A fragment quoted by Polyhistor from an *anonymous work* (Eusebius, *Praep. ev.* IX, 18) and a parallel text in a much fuller form (*ibid.*, IX, 17), presumably from the same book although attributed to Eupolemus, relate that Abraham was descended from the giants (Gen. 6:1-4) who built the Tower of Babel after the Flood; Abraham taught the Phoenicians "the circuits of the sun and moon, and all other things" and helped them in war; in Egypt he taught astrology and the other sciences to the priests of Heliopolis; Enoch was, however, the discoverer of astrology (cf. Enoch 72-82; Jub. 4:17-21).

Thallus[5] probably lived during the reign of Tiberius (14-37). There is no compelling reason, as H. A. Rigg, Jr., has shown (HTR 34 [1941] 111-119), to consider Thallus a Samaritan, in accordance with a conjectural emendation in Josephus, *Antiquities* 18:6, 4 (§167): "For there

---

[4] Plutarch (*Lives: Sertorius*, ch. 9) relates that from Heracles and Tinge, the widow of Antaeus, was born Sophax, whose son was Diodorus.

[5] The remnants of his writings are printed in C. Müller, *Fragmenta histor. graec.*, Vol. 3, pp. 517-519; and in F. Jacoby, *Die Fragmente der griechischen Historiker*, Vol. 2-B, p. 256. Berlin, 1929 [Commentary in Vol. 2-D, pp. 835 ff. Berlin, 1930]. See, in general, Schürer, *Geschichte*, Vol. 3, pp. 494 f. R. Laqueur, "Thallos" in Pauly-Wissowa, *Realenzyklopädie*, Reihe II, Band V, cols. 1225 f. Stuttgart, 1934.

was *another* [*allos,* corrected to *Thallos*] Samaritan by birth, a freedman of Caesar [Tiberius]. . . ." According to Eusebius, he composed a universal history "from the capture of Troy to the 167th Olympiad [i.e., 112-109 B.C.]." In reality the work (said to comprise three books) seems to have begun earlier and to have ended later. The fall of Troy was probably dated by Thallus in the year we designate as 1184 B.C., but an extant fragment of his history mentions "Bel, king of the Assyrians," who lived "332 years" before the beginning of the war against Troy (1193 B.C.), or in 1515 B.C. Bel, Cronus the Titan, and Ogygus fought in the ranks of the Titans against Zeus; after their defeat Cronus fled to Tartessos (Tarshish, near Gibraltar), presumably confused with Tartarus (hell), Ogygus to Ogygia (Attica), where he witnessed the great deluge. Other fragments mention Moses, Sardanapalus (i.e., Ashurbanipal, 668-625 B.C.), and Cyrus. The history of Thallus came down at least to A.D. 33, the year in which Julius Africanus dated the crucifixion of Jesus; for Africanus criticizes Thallus for regarding the darkness in that year (Matt. 27:45) as an eclipse (and not as a miracle) (see Müller, *Fragm. hist. graec.,* Vol. 3, p. 519, No. 8; Schürer, *Geschichte,* Vol. 3, p. 495).

The second and third books of the Maccabees belong here, with the other histories embellished with legends and fictitious tales.[6] II Maccabees, for which the reader is referred to Part II, Chap. XI, of this book, deals with actual facts, even though they are often hidden by a thick layer of romance and fiction; III Maccabees (dating from the last century B.C.) purports to be history but is a story invented for the glorification of the Jews, which has nothing to do with the Maccabees and has no basis in reality. Like Judith and Esther, it is the story of an imaginary triumph of the Jews over their enemies; a similar story is told independently by Josephus (*Against Apion* II, 5), who, however, dates the events in the reign of Ptolemy VII (IX) Physcon (170-116 B.C.) instead of the time of Ptolemy IV Philopator (221-203 B.C.). III Maccabees may be summarized as follows.

Ptolemy IV, accompanied by his sister (later his wife) Arsinoë, led his army against Antiochus III the Great (223-187 B.C.) and encamped at Raphia (1:1). There a Jew converted to paganism, Dositheus, saved Ptolemy from a conspiracy (1:2 f.). As Antiochus was on the point of winning the battle of Raphia (217 B.C.), Arsinoë induced the tottering Egyptian troops to fight on to victory (1:4-6). So Ptolemy, having thus conquered Coele-Syria, visited neighboring cities and shrines (1:7). Having received the congratulations of the Jews, Ptolemy visited Jeru-

---

[6] This characteristic type of Hellenistic historical writing is well described by Polybius (XV:34, 1): "I am quite aware of the miraculous occurrences and embellishments which the chroniclers of this event have added to their narrative with a view of producing a striking effect upon their hearers, making more of their comments on the story than of the story itself and the main incidents."

salem and offered sacrifice to the Lord (1:8 f.). He then decided to enter
the Holy of Holies, despite the warnings of the leaders, the prayers of
the priests, and the lamentation of the people (1:10-29). Simon, the
high priest, implored God, the sovereign of all creation who loves Israel
(2:1-11), not to punish his people through heathen profanation of the
Temple (2:12-20). In answer to this prayer God smote the king, who
fell senseless to the ground (2:21 f.) and, having been carried out,
departed uttering bitter threats (2:23 f.). In Egypt Ptolemy circulated
slanders about the Jews (2:25 f.) and decreed that the Jews must participate in the official cult also, in order to practice their own religion;
that they be degraded to the rank of native Egyptians; and be branded
with the picture of an ivy leaf, the emblem of Dionysus (2:27-29).
Only the Jews who willingly joined the Dionysiac mysteries would have
full Alexandrian citizenship (2:30). The great majority of the Jews
remained true to their religion (2:31-33). In his rage, Ptolemy ordered
that all the Egyptian Jews outside of Alexandria be brought to the
capital to be put to death by torture (3:1), while malicious reports were
being circulated about their nation (3:2). Nevertheless, the Jews remained loyal to the king, even though observing the Law of Moses, and
still had many Greek friends (3:3-10). But the king published an edict,
in which he declared that after the successful conclusion of his campaign
in Coele-Syria he was generally well received and had made gifts to
the temples (3:11-16). But at Jerusalem, while apparently welcomed, he
was prevented from entering the Temple to do it honor (3:17-20). Having returned to Egypt, he not only forgave this rudeness, but even
offered the Jews full Alexandrian citizenship and a share in the religious
rites (3:21); they, however, not only refused these privileges, but even
despised the few Jews who had accepted them (3:22 f.). Since it was
clear that the Jews were traitors, he now ordered that they be executed
(3:24 f.). Harboring Jews would be punished with death; informers
against them would be amply rewarded (3:26-28). Places in which Jews
were found in hiding would be destroyed with fire (3:29-30). The publication of this decree produced jubilation among the heathen, but grief
among the Jews (4:1-3). All over Egypt the Jews were chained in the
dark holds of ships (4:4-10) and brought to Schedia to be imprisoned in
the hippodrome outside of Alexandria (4:11). Soon after, the Alexandrian
Jews were likewise placed there (4:12 f.). All of them were to be
registered before their execution (4:14), but after forty days of feverish
work the scribes ceased registering that immense multitude for the
supply of pens and papyrus was (providentially) exhausted (4:15-21).
Ptolemy ordered Hermon, who was in charge of the elephants, to drug
his beasts with incense and wine so that they would slaughter the Jews
(5:1 f.). The king celebrated with banquets, while the Jews in their

fetters (5:3-5) prayed ardently (5:6-8). God caused the king to sleep until late, so that the execution of the Jews was necessarily postponed until the following day (5:9-22). At dawn everything was in readiness (5:23). Heathen multitudes gathered for the spectacle (5:24), while the Jews prayed (5:25). When Hermon invited the king to the execution of the Jews, the king through God's intervention had lost all memory of the matter (5:26-29) and denounced the murderous plan of Hermon (5:30-35). But at another banquet Ptolemy rebuked Hermon for not having destroyed the Jews (5:36-38). The courtiers, astonished at his contradictory orders, assured him that further delay might cause tumults (5:39-41). So the king swore that he would have the Jews crushed by the elephants and would devastate Judea (5:42 f.). The required preparations were made (5:44 f.), and at dawn the king went out to the hippodrome with the elephants and an immense multitude (5:46 f.), while the Jews again beseeched the Almighty (5:48-51). The aged priest Eleazar recalled in prayer God's miraculous deliverances of Israel since the Exodus (6:1-8) and begged God to manifest his power to the heathen by delivering the Jews (6:9-15). As Eleazar finished, the king arrived, the Jews shouted desperately, and two fierce angels came through the opened gates of heaven, filling the army and the king with terror (6:16-20). The elephants began to crush the troops (6:21). The king's anger now turned against his friends (6:22-26); he instantly delivered the Jews (6:27-29) and ordered that they be served rich meals for seven days of rejoicing (6:30-32). The king himself celebrated with a banquet (6:33), while the enemies of the Jews were put to shame (6:34). The Jews ordained an annual celebration of the deliverance and requested permission to return to their homes (6:35-40). Ptolemy wrote his generals a letter (6:41) in which he blamed his friends for what had happened (7:1-5), exculpated the Jews, whose God fought on their side (7:6), ordered them to return, and threatened with divine punishment those who injured the Jews (7:7-9). Before returning to their homes the provincial Jews obtained permission to kill their apostate brethren (7:10-14). Rejoicing in the slaying of over three hundred men (7:15), they departed happily (7:16). At Ptolemais they banqueted again (7:17 f.), made the day an annual festival (7:19), and erected a pillar and a chapel on the site (7:20). Henceforth they were highly respected; they recovered all their property (7:21-23).

The historical and psychological improbabilities of this tale are manifest, and match the rhetorical artificiality, fastidiousness, and preciosity typical of a pretentious but decadent style. The wealth of rare and even new words is unsurpassed in similar writings: more than one hundred words are not found elsewhere in the LXX and fourteen are unknown in all Greek literature. The author's effort to stir the reader's emotions by highly colored dramatic descriptions (1:16-29; 4:3-10; 5:48 f.) has its earlier parallel, if not its model, in II Maccabees (3:15-21), as also his recitals of miraculous manifestations of God (2:21-24; 6:18 f.), and his moralizing reflections (3:21 f.). The religion of the author centers on his faith in divine answer to prayer and in the miraculous intervention of the Almighty in the present, as in the distant past (2:1-13; 6:1-9). Naturally such a faith can dispense with the hope of a future Messianic age or Jewish empire, and of a blessed immortality for the pious: of such notions there is no mention whatsoever in the book, in contrast with II Maccabees. In brief, the purpose of the book is well expressed by Ptolemy when he warns the heathen that any attempt to injure the Jews will be promptly avenged not by human beings but by the most high God from whom escape is impossible (7:9).

This rapid survey of Hellenistic-Jewish historical writing would not be complete without a mention of the historical works of the two out-standing Jewish authors who wrote in Greek: Philo and Josephus.

Philo (d. *ca.* A.D. 50)[7] was primarily a philosopher, but since most of his 38 works are either parts of a running commentary on the Penta-teuch or essays on selected topics in the same, he necessarily deals with Biblical history down to Moses. In his biography of Moses (*De vita Mosis*), he presented him as the wisest of all legislators. His philosophical principles naturally colored this rewriting of Biblical history. In addition to ancient times he also described contemporary events and movements. The book on contemplative life (*De vita contemplativa*)[8] describes the life of the Therapeutae, ascetic hermits devoted to meditation, allegorical study of the Law of Moses, composition of sacred poetry, and contem-plation of God. More important for the political history of the first century of our era is a work which, according to Eusebius (*Ecclesiastical History* II, 5, 1; the sequel [5, 6-6, 3] gives a brief summary of the work), comprised five books: only the third (*Against Flaccus*) and fourth (*Embassy to Caligula* [*legatio ad Gaium*]) survive; perhaps *Against*

---

[7] For a bibliography of publications on Philo, see: H. L. Goodhart and E. R. Goodenough, *The Politics of Philo Judaeus with a General Bibliography*. New Haven, 1938; see also Ralph Marcus, "Recent Literature on Philo (1924-1934)" (*Jewish Studies in Memory of George A. Kohut*, pp. 463-491. New York, 1935). The best works on Philo, for general orientation, are the following. James Drummond, *Philo Judaeus; or the Jewish-Alexandrian Philosophy in its Development and Completion*, 2 vols. London, 1888; E. Schürer, *Geschichte*, Vol. 3, pp. 633-716; Emile Bréhier, *Les idées philosophiques et religieuses de Philon d'Alexandrie*, 2nd ed. Paris, 1925; E. R. Goodenough, *An Introduction to Philo Judaeus*. New Haven, 1940. The most detailed and thorough work on Philo's philosophy is H. A. Wolfson, *Philo*, 2 vols. Cambridge, Mass., 1947.

[8] Philo's *De vita contemplativa* was regarded by Eusebius (*Ecclesiastical History* II, 17; cf. II, 16, 2) as a description of *Christian* monasticism, and the authenticity of this work has been questioned by some scholars; see, e.g., Schürer, *op. cit.*, 3, 687-691; Bréhier, *op. cit.*, pp. 321-24.

Flaccus alludes at the beginning to the second volume (dealing with a plot of Sejanus [d. A.D. 31] against the Jews; cf. Eusebius, *Chronicon*, ed. Schoene, 150-151), while the *Embassy to Caius* at the end possibly refers to the *palinodía* (retraction), i.e., the change for the better of the situation of the Jews after the death of Caligula in A.D. 41, which apparently formed the subject of the fifth book. The general title of the work seems to have been *On Virtues* (*perì aretôn*) and indicated that in the end virtue triumphed over wickedness.[9] The main topic of the book was really the miserable end of the principal persecutors of the Jews, namely, Sejanus, Flaccus, Caligula, and probably also Pilate. The divine vengeance against the enemies of the Jews is stressed in earlier Jewish histories (see, for instance, II Kings 19:36 f.), notably in II Maccabees (3:22-40; 5:6-10; 9:5 f.; 13:4-8; 15:28-35), and in pseudo-histories (Daniel, Judith, Esther, etc.). Notwithstanding this nationalistic bias and religious dogma, these books of Philo are invaluable sources, particularly where they relate events of which Philo was himself an eyewitness.

Josephus, son of Matthias (born in Jerusalem in A.D. 37-38, died after A.D. 100), who assumed Vespasian's family name, Flavius, after he was liberated from captivity in 69, is the most famous of Jewish historians.[10] His life is fairly well known through his autobiography (*The Life of Fl. Josephus*), which deals primarily with his activity as governor of Galilee in 66-67 and was written soon after 100; it supplements his *Antiquities*. Through references to himself in his history of the war of 66-70 (see also *Against Apion* I, 9-10) Josephus has likewise thrown light on his own career.

The first work of Josephus was his history of the war of 66-70 in Aramaic (*War*, Preface), of which we have his translation into Greek,

[9] In contrast with these views which Schürer (*Geschichte*, Vol. 3, pp. 678-682) has defended, L. Massebieau, ("Le classement des oeuvres de Philon," pp. 65-78. *Bibliothèque de l'Ecole Pratique des Hautes Etudes*. Section des sciences religieuses. Paris, 1889) argues that *Against Flaccus* and *Embassy* are separate works.

[10] For details on Josephus the reader is referred to the illuminating lectures of H. St. John Thackeray on *Josephus: The Man and the Historian* (New York, Jewish Institute of Religion Press, 1929). See also G. Hölscher, "Josephus" in Pauly-Wissowa, *Realenzyklopädie der classischen Altertumswissenschaft*, Vol. 9, pp. 1943 ff. Stuttgart, 1916. A general bibliography of publications about Josephus is given in Schürer, *Geschichte*, Vol. 1, pp. 100-106; J. Juster, *Les Juifs*, Vol. 1, pp. 7 f.; R. Marcus in *Proceedings of the American Academy for Jewish Research* 16 (1947) 178-181. The standard edition of the Greek text of Josephus is: B. Niese, *Flavii Josephi Opera*. 7 vols. Berlin, 1887-1895 (the same, *editio minor*, 6 vols. Berlin, 1888-1895). H. St. John Thackeray and R. Marcus have published in seven volumes of the Loeb Classical Library (London and New York; now Cambridge, Mass., 1926-1943) the bulk of the works of Josephus. The old English translation of William Whiston (1667-1752), first published in 1737 and often reprinted, is still the best known. There are now excellent translations in French (Th. Reinach, editor, *Oeuvres complètes de Josèphe*. 6 vols. Paris, 1902-1932) and, at least in part, in Italian (G. Ricciotti, *Flavio Giuseppe tradotto e commentato*. 4 vols. to date. Turin, 1937-1939).

entitled *On the Jewish War* (*Perì toû ioudaikoû polémou; Bellum judai-cum*), in seven books. The contents, in brief, are as follows: Book I: The history from Antiochus IV Epiphanes (175-164 B.C.) to the death of Herod the Great (4 B.C.). Book II: From 4 B.C. to the first year of the war (66-67), inclusive. Book III: The war in Galilee (67). Book IV: Operations following the fall of Galilee up to the beginning of the siege of Jerusalem (68-69). Books V-VI: The siege and fall of Jerusalem (69-70). Book VII: The aftermath of the war (70-73). Having been an eyewitness of many events of this war, Josephus used primarily his own notes as source material (*Against Apion* I, 9). The work was published by order of Titus (*Life* §65) after 75 but before the death of Vespasian in 79.

The Antiquities of the Jews (*Ioudaikē archaiología; Antiquitates judaicae*), in twenty books, deals with the history of the Jews to A.D. 66. The individual books cover the following periods: Book I: From the creation of the world to the death of Isaac. Book II: From Esau and Jacob to the Exodus. Books III-IV: From the Exodus to the death of Moses. Book V: From the death of Moses to the death of Eli. Book VI: From the death of Eli to the death of Saul. Book VII: David. Book VIII: From Solomon to Ahab (853 B.C.). Book IX: From the death of Ahab to the fall of Samaria (722 B.C.). Book X: From Sennacherib's attack (701 B.C.) to the first year of Cyrus (538 B.C.). Book XI: From Cyrus to Alexander's death (323 B.C.). Book XII: From the death of Alexander to the death of Judas Maccabeus (161 B.C.). Book XIII: From the death of Judas to that of Alexandra (67 B.C.). Book XIV: From 67 B.C. to the accession of Herod the Great (37 B.C.). Books XV-XVII: The reigns of Herod the Great (37-4 B.C.) and of Archelaus (4 B.C.-A.D. 6). Book XVIII: From A.D. 6 to the death of Caligula (41). Book XIX: From 41 to the death of Agrippa I (44). Book XX: From 44 to the outbreak of the Jewish war in 66.

Josephus completed his *Antiquities* in 93-94. He had written it for educated Greeks and Romans to prove that the Jews had "formerly been in great esteem" and had not been prevented from keeping their ancestral laws and practicing their religion; and "to take away the causes of that hatred which unreasonable men bear" to the Jews (*Antiquities* 16:6, 8). In the first ten books, dealing with Biblical history and using almost solely the Old Testament as his source, Josephus not only omitted or modified unpleasant incidents but, following Alexandrian Jewish historians (Demetrius, Artapanus, etc.), which he knew through Alexander Polyhistor, as also Philo and the Palestinian Haggadah, he freely added legends and juristic comments to the data furnished by the Pentateuch. In confirmation of his account he eagerly quoted such authorities as Homer, Hesiod, Herodotus, Manetho, Berossus, and others. For the blank period from Nehemiah (432 B.C.) to Antiochus Epiphanes (175) Josephus could give only a few legends or fictitious tales, such as Alexander's visit to Jerusalem (11:8, 4-5), a summary of the Letter of Aristeas (12:2), and rarely an occasional fact gleaned from Greek histories, such as the conquest of Jerusalem by Ptolemy I Lagus (12:1 [§5]; cf. *Against Apion* 1:22 [§§209-211]) reported by Agatharchides of Cnidus.[11] For the period 175-135 Josephus utilized I Maccabees, at times quoting it literally, but often modifying it freely (cf. C. L. W. Grimm's commentary on I Maccabees, pp. xxviii f.) and disregarded I Macc. 14-16; he did not use II Maccabees at all. Down to the year 143 B.C. he also used Polybius (12:9, 1).[12] For the period 135-37 B.C. he cites primarily the lost history of the years 143-27 B.C. by the famous geographer Strabo of Cappadocia, who died about A.D. 20 (the first and last references are 13:10, 4 and 15:1, 2) and the world history of Herod's confidential secretary, Nicholas of Damascus[13] (13:8, 4 to 14:6, 4). Nicholas alone is manifestly Josephus' accurate and detailed source for the life of Herod in books XVI-XVII (in book XV there are traces of a second source, unfavorable to Herod): the history of Herod's last years (14-4 B.C.), told in books 125-144 of Nicholas, is apparently reproduced with hardly any change, in spite of the admission that Nicholas was partial to Herod (16:7, 1). Josephus quotes also book 96 of Nicholas with reference to the Flood (1:3, 6; cf. 3, 9) and book 4 with reference to Abraham (1:7, 2) and David (7:5, 2). The history of Nicholas ended in book 144 with the accession of Archelaus (4 B.C.); consequently, the information available to Josephus from then to A.D. 41 was extremely scanty. The reign of Agrippa I (41-44) is reported in greater detail, presumably because Josephus could obtain information from eyewitnesses and particularly from Agrippa II (d. 100). For the years preceding the outbreak of the war in 66 Josephus could rely on his own memory; but the source from which he derived the exact and full information for the events at Rome in 41, when Caligula died and Claudius succeeded him, is still unknown, as also the source of the dossier of Caesar's and Augustus'

[11] B. Niese (*Geschichte der Griechischen und Makedonischen Staaten*, Vol. 1, p. 230, n. 4. Gotha, 1893) questions the historicity of this event which, in any case, cannot be dated.

[12] On the sources of Josephus for the post-Biblical period, see H. Bloch, *Die Quellen des Fl. Josephus in seiner Archäologia.* Leipzig, 1879; J. Destinon, *Die Quellen des Fl. Josephus in der jüdischen Archäologie Buch XII-XVIII.* Kiel, 1882; F. Schemann, *Die Quellen des Fl. Josephus in der jüdischen Archäologie Buch XVIII-XX* (Doctoral Dissertation, Marburg). Hagen, 1887; G. Hölscher, *Die Quellen der Josephus für die Zeit vom Exil bis zum jüdischen Kriege* (Doctoral Dissertation). Leipzig, 1904.

[13] The remnants of the history of Nicholas of Damascus are published by C. Müller, *Fragm. hist. graec.*, Vol. 3, pp. 343-464; Vol. 4, pp. 661-668. See on Nicholas, Schürer, *Geschichte*, Vol. 1, pp. 50-57.

edicts in favor of the Jews, and other public documents (a complete list, with bibliography, is given by J. Juster, *Les Juifs*, Vol. 1, pp. 132-159). The apologetic tendency of Josephus in the *Antiquities* (cf. 16:6, 1 and 8) unfortunately induces him to select only decrees favorable to the Jews (in 13:9, 2; 14:8, 5; 14:10 and 12; 16:6; 19:5 and 6; 20:1, 2).[14]

The latest Jewish-Hellenistic historian known by name to us is Justus of Tiberias (*ca.* A.D. 110), a rival of Josephus (who refers to him in his *Life*, §§ 9, 12, 17, 35, 37, 54, 65, 70, 74). He wrote a history of the Jewish war of 66-70, in which he criticized Josephus (*Life* §65), and a chronicle of the Jewish kings, which was still known to Photius in the ninth century (see for further details, Schürer, *Geschichte*, Vol. 1, pp. 58-63; H. Luther, *Josephus und Justus von Tiberias* [Doctoral Dissertation]. Halle, 1910).

2. Epic and Dramatic Poetry

Alexander Polyhistor, as has been noticed, is responsible for the survival of a portion of Alexandrian-Jewish historical writings; at the same time the extant fragments of the epic and dramatic Jewish literature in

[14] A word should be said about the references of Josephus to Christian beginnings: for full bibliography see, R. Eisler, *Iēsoûs Basileùs ou Basileúsas*, 2 vols. Heidelberg, 1928-1930 (English abridgment: R. Eisler, *The Messiah Jesus and John the Baptist according to Flavius Josephus' Recently Rediscovered 'Capture of Jerusalem'* etc. English ed. by A. H. Krappe. New York, 1931). *Antiquities* 18:5, 2 reports the execution of John the Baptist in Machaerus (cf. Mark 6:17-29; Matt. 14:3-12; Luke 3:19 f.; 9:7-9). The *Antiquities* passage is cited by Origen (*Against Celsus* I:47) and quoted by Eusebius (*Eccl. Hist.* I:11, 4-6). Scholars seem to be inclined to regard the Josephus passage as authentic, at least in part; see, for discussions and bibliographies, Schürer, *Geschichte*, Vol. 1, 436-441; Martin Dibelius, *Die urchristliche Überlieferung von Johannes dem Taüfer* (FRLANT 15). Göttingen, 1911. J. Juster, *Les Juifs* II, 130 f., n. 3. A second passage (*Antiquities* 18:3, 3; cf. Schürer, *Geschichte*, Vol. 1, 544-549) praises the deeds of Jesus Christ and asserts his resurrection after three days; it was quoted by Eusebius and accepted as genuine until modern times, when it has been generally recognized as a Christian interpolation. A third passage (*Antiquities* 20:9, 1) refers to the trial of "the brother of Jesus, called Christ, whose name was James." Although Eusebius (*Eccl. Hist.* II:23, 21-24) quotes this passage, it is likewise regarded as spurious (cf. Schürer, *Geschichte*, Vol. 1, pp. 548, 581 f.; Juster, *Les Juifs* II, 140 f.); at least the reference to Jesus Christ is of Christian origin, although Josephus might well have reported the execution of James. Finally there are numerous additions about John the Baptist, Jesus, and James in a thirteenth century Slavic version of Josephus' *Jewish War* (II, 7; 9; 11; V, 5; VI, 5). A Berendts (*Die Zeugnisse vom Christentum im slavischem De bello judaico des Josephus*. Texte und Untersuchungen 29. Leipzig, 1906), who first called attention to these additions and translated them into German, believed that they were authentic, for he was convinced that the Slavic version was made on the lost Aramaic text of the *War of the Jews*. It seems certain, however, that the Christian passages were translated from the Greek, having been added in the Greek text of the *War* used for the Slavic version. On this Slavic text in general, see S. Zeitlin, "The Slavonic Josephus" (JQR 20 [1929-30] 1-50, 281); M. M. Creed, "The Slavonic Version of Josephus' History of the Jewish War" (HTR 25 [1932] 277-319); J. S. Kennard, Jr., "Gleanings from the Slavonic Josephus Controversy" (JQR 39 [1948] 161-170); S. Zeitlin, "The Hoax of the 'Slavonic Josephus'" (JQR 39 [1948] 171-180).

Greek were quoted from Polyhistor by Eusebius in the *Praeparatio Evangelica*.[15]

Philo the Elder (*ca.* 100 B.C.), as Josephus (*Against Apion*, I, 23) calls him to distinguish him from Philo the philosopher, composed in rhetorical Homeric hexameters (the meter of the Sibylline Oracles) an epic poem *On Jerusalem*. Eusebius has preserved three small fragments on Abraham, on Joseph, and on the springs and aqueducts of Jerusalem.

Theodotus (*ca.* 100 B.C.) wrote a parallel poem *On Shechem* of which Eusebius has preserved a portion, partly verbatim and partly in summary. The author called Shechem a "holy city" and must therefore have been a Samaritan. After a description of the site of the town, its conquest by the Hebrews is related on the basis of Gen. 34. In the manner of numerous Hellenistic poets, Theodotus composed an epic celebrating the mythical origin and legendary history of his city. He tells us that Shechem received its name from Sikimios the son of Hermes (cf. Shechem the son of Hamor, Gen. 34:2) and he connects the city of the Samaritans with Greek mythology—a procedure known in earlier Jewish-Hellenistic writers.

Ezekiel the dramatist (*ca.* 100 B.C.) is the sole known Jew who wrote tragedies in Greek. Only one of them, *The Exodus*, is partially known through excerpts preserved by Eusebius and Clement of Alexandria. It begins with a long monologue of Moses reviewing his past life, spoken in Midian where he had fled after slaying an Egyptian taskmaster (Ex. 2:11-15). He then met the seven daughters of Reuel (Ex. 2:16) and eventually married Zipporah. In a second fragment Reuel interpreted a dream of Moses as signifying that he would become a ruler and a prophet. A third excerpt describes the divine revelation at the Burning Bush (Ex. 3), and a fourth the divine prescriptions about the departure of Israel from Egypt and the celebration of the Passover (Ex. 11-12). In another, an Egyptian who had escaped from the drowning in the Red Sea related that the Israelites had crossed the sea safely, while the Egyptian troops had perished in the waters. In the final fragment, an Israelite messenger (probably a spy sent ahead of the people) reported to Moses the discovery of an excellent camping site at Elim (Ex. 15:27 and Num. 33:9); there a wonderful bird, almost twice as large as an eagle, the ruler of the other birds, had appeared to him.

Ezekiel manifestly followed the Biblical narrative fairly closely, but felt free to add haggadic embellishments at will. His iambic trimeters lack true poetic inspiration but are adequate in narratives and descriptions. If, as seems probable, this drama was composed for the stage and was

---

[15] For the text, see C. Müller, *Fragm. hist. graec.*, Vol. 3, pp. 213, 219, 229 (Philo); 217-219 (Theodotus). For Ezekiel see: Dübner's edition in the appendix to F. G. Wagner, *Fragmenta Euripidis*. Paris, 1846, pp. vii-x, 1-7; and J. Wieneke, *Ezechielis Judaei poetae alexandrini fabulae quae inscribitur Exagoge fragmenta*. Münster, 1931. See, in general, Schürer, *Geschichte*, Vol. 3, pp. 497-503.

actually performed, it not merely instructed and edified the Jews but gained for them if not friendship, at least a better understanding, on the part of some of the pagan spectators.

3. Philosophy

In appraising a mixed philosophy such as that of the Alexandrian Jews, some scholars regard it as Jewish thought modified by Greek philosophy (Schürer, *Geschichte*, Vol. 3, p. 503), while others, on the contrary, would say that the Jewish thinkers "systematically set about remaking Greek philosophy according to the pattern of a belief and tradition of an entirely different origin." (H. A. Wolfson, *Philo*, Vol. 1, p. 4).[16] It seems probable that both attitudes were current in ancient Alexandria: the Greeks presumably accused the Jews of adopting their own thought and language, and regarded the synagogue as a school of philosophy (G. F. Moore, *Judaism*, Vol. 1, pp. 284 f.), while, conversely, Aristobulus, Philo, and Josephus did not hesitate to assert "the dependence of Greek philosophers upon Moses" (Wolfson, *Philo* Vol. 1, p. 141; cf. Schürer, *Geschichte*, Vol. 3, p. 547)—which meant that Greek philosophy was an imperfect form of Judaism. It is not necessary to enter here into a debate between the two points of view, Jewish and Gentile. What is certain is that Alexandrian Jewish thinkers interpreted Judaism in the light of Greek philosophy and that both Jews and Greeks at times regarded Judaism as a philosophy (for references see Juster, *Les Juifs*, Vol. 1, p. 243, n. 2).

A philosophical conception of Judaism is not yet apparent in the earliest monument of Hellenistic Judaism, the Greek version of the Pentateuch made in Alexandria about 250 B.C. (the "Septuagint" in its original sense, cf. the Letter of Aristeas). The translators were probably Alexandrians who had some familiarity with Greek thought; they strove for an accurate rendering, and if occasionally they appear to echo philosophical teachings, there is no reason for regarding such possible reverberations as deliberate attempts to read Greek philosophy into the Scriptures.[17] When such a conscious identification of the teaching of Moses and of Plato was made later, by Alexandrian Jews, it presupposed an allegorical interpretation of the Scriptures,[18] such as had been adopted in Greece for the philosophical

[16] J. Klausner (*From Jesus to Paul*, pp. 201 f.) combines the two theories when he denounces Hellenistic Judaism as a "compromise."

[17] Cf. J. Freudenthal, "Are there traces of Greek Philosophy in the Septuagint?" (JQR 2 [1890] 205-222). J. Drummond, *Philo Judaeus* I, 156-166.

[18] On the allegorical method used by Greeks and Jews see: C. Siegfried, *Philo von Alexandrien als Ausleger des Alten Testaments*. Jena, 1875. P. Decharme, *Critique des traditions religieuses chez les Grecs*. Paris, 1906. J. Geffcken, "Allegory" in J. Hastings, *Encyclopaedia of Religion and Ethics*, Vol. 1, pp. 327-331. Edinburgh and New York, 1908. E. Bréhier, *Les idées philosophiques et religieuses de Philon d'Aléxandrie*, pp. 35-66. 2nd ed. Paris, 1925. H. A. Wolfson, *Philo*, Vol. 1, pp. 115-138.

interpretation of Homer and Hesiod, beginning with Theagenes of Rhegium (*ca.* 525 B.C. [?]) and others after him. After Philo, this interpretation of the Old Testament passed into Christianity, beginning with Paul (Gal. 4:24 f.; II Cor. 3:13-16; cf. I Cor. 10:1-4) and the Epistle to the Hebrews, continuing with Barnabas, Justin Martyr, and the Alexandrian school (Clement of Alexandria and Origen), and persisting to the present day among those orthodox Protestants who find an allusion to the Trinity in the plurals, "Let us make man in our image . . ." and "Go, let us go down . . ." (Gen. 1:26 and 11:7). Such an allegorical interpretation, in contrast with modern historical and critical methods of interpretation, is the last line of defense of traditional orthodoxy, now as in antiquity.

In Hellenistic Judaism the allegorical method was occasionally employed before Philo. In reality Alexandria—whether Jewish, pagan, or Christian—was the center of allegorical interpretation. In the Wisdom of Solomon, the pillar of salt (Gen. 19:26) is a symbol of incredulity, the pillars of cloud and fire (Ex. 13:21) of wisdom, the brazen serpent (Num. 21:9) of salvation, and the high priestly vestments (Ex. 28:4) of the whole world, the Greek *kósmos* meaning both ornate garment and world (Wisd. of Sol. 10:7, 17; 16:6 f.; 18:24); three of these allegories (omitting Ex. 13) were also used by Philo (*Legum Allegoria* III, 213; II, 79; *De Vita Mosis* II, 117, respectively); Josephus (*Antiquities* 3:7, 7) identified the vestments with earth and heaven. A clever allegory of the Mosaic dietary laws is found in the Letter of Aristeas: the cloven foot and the two separate claws (Deut. 14:6; cf. Lev. 11:3) "teach us that we must discriminate our individual actions with a view to the practice of virtue" (§150; see also §§151 f.); "animals which are cloven-footed and chew the cud [Deut. 14:7; Lev. 11:4] represent to the initiated the symbol of memory" (§153; see also §§154-157; §161). The prohibition of birds of prey as food (cf. Deut. 14:12-19; Lev. 11:13-21) signifies that men "must practice righteousness in their hearts and not tyrannize over any one . . ." (§147); see also §170 on the symbolism of sacrificial victims. Moses did not draw up the Law for the sake of mice and weasels, but for perfecting character (§144; cf. §§163-166); "Does God care for oxen?" asks Paul (I Cor. 9:9), interpreting the law about the threshing ox (Deut. 25:4) allegorically to mean that Christian ministers should receive a fair salary.

Strictly speaking, the allegorical interpretation of Scriptures, by means of which the deepest metaphysical truths were discovered in the most trivial incidents reported in the Bible, was first practiced by Philo, who in this followed Greek models rather than Jewish ones. For the few examples of allegory in the Wisdom of Solomon and the Letter of Aristeas, as also those in rabbinical literature (cf. Wolfson, *Philo,* Vol. 1, pp. 133 f.), are by no means "philosophical allegory of the kind we find in Philo" (*ibid.*). Nevertheless, it was thought long before Philo that the noblest ethical and religious truths had been revealed by God throughout his inspired Scriptures, but often not literally and plainly, but "through a glass, darkly," so that the ignorant failed to discover the deep meaning underlying the literal sense of the scriptural words. Thus the Bible became an inexhaustible mine of truth; every generation of men discovered new verities in it, for, as Paul said, "whatsoever things were written aforetime were written for our learning" (Rom. 15:4; cf. I Cor. 9:10). Consequently, the whole body of teaching in Hellenistic Judaism, even what we know to have been derived from Greek philosophers, was somehow read into the words of Scripture. This basic trend manifests itself in various ways.

In the Wisdom of Solomon (for which see below, Part II, Chap. V) the notion of Wisdom (*sophía*) was manifestly colored by Greek ideas, and yet was allegedly derived from Prov. 8 (cf. Job. 28): Wisd. 9:9, for instance, is a summary of Prov. 8:22-30; and "the worker" in the statement that Wisdom is "the *worker* [*technítes*, artificer, craftsman] of all things" (Wisd. 7:22) translates the Masoretic reading *āmōn* (artificer) in Prov. 8:30 (cf. the LXX *harmózousa*, joiner) instead of *āmūn* (nursling, ward; cf. the Authorized Version). Nevertheless, it would be difficult to discover in the Bible some of the 21 qualities of Wisdom listed in Wisd. 7:22-23, and the descriptions in 7:24-26: "For Wisdom is more mobile than any motion; she pervades and penetrates all things by reason of her pureness. For she is the breath of the power of God, a clear effulgence [or emanation] flowing from the glory of the Almighty. . . ." On the one hand, Wisdom was the universal soul of the Stoics (Wisd. 7:27; 8:1), on the other, the inspirer of prophets (Wisd. 7:27; cf. 7:22) and the helper of Israel's ancient heroes of faith (Wisd. 10). Indeed, throughout the book Jewish and Greek ideas are joined or combined, Biblical proof-texts are tacitly adduced, as in 2:24 ("through envy of the devil came death into the world"), where the serpent of Eden (Gen. 3) is transformed into the devil or one of his agents. See also Wisd. 11:17 (cf. Gen. 1:1 f); 8:7 (cf. Prov. 8:20).

If the Scriptures, rightly interpreted, taught the tenets of Greek philosophy, it was natural to assume that Greek philosophers derived their teachings from Moses. Before Philo, this was asserted in a Jewish-Alexandrian work entitled *An Explanation of the Mosaic Law* (or the like), attributed to Aristobulus. According to Clement of Alexandria and Eusebius, he wrote during the reign of Ptolemy VI Philometor (181-145 B.C.).[19] The first of the three extant fragments of this work (Eusebius, *Praep.*

---

[19] See J. Drummond, *Philo Judaeus*, Vol. 1, pp. 242-252; Schürer, *Geschichte*, Vol. 3, pp. 512-522. The authenticity of this work has been seriously questioned by Elter and others. Schürer defends it, while E. Bréhier, (*Les idées philosophiques et religieuses de Philon d'Aléxandrie*, pp. 47 f.) believes that "the author . . . copied Philo, condensing him, obscuring him, often without understanding him." The text of the extant fragments of this work is printed by W. N. Stearns, *Fragments from Graeco-Jewish Writers*. Chicago, 1908.

Ev. XIII:12, 1-16) dealt with Gen. 1-2: Homer, Hesiod, Pythagoras, Socrates, and Plato were familiar with the Pentateuch in a Greek version made before the Persian conquest of Egypt (525 B.C.), and used it in their works.[20] The words "God said . . . and it was so" (Gen. 1), as Greek philosophers recognized, mean that everything came into being through God's power (*dýnamis*); Orpheus (in spurious Jewish verses) and Aratus attest that God's power permeates everything. The seventh day on which God rested (Gen. 2:1-3) may be called the day in which light was created, inasmuch as the Peripatetics call Wisdom the lamp of life and Solomon declared (Prov. 8:22-30) that Wisdom existed before the world. God's rest means the quiet maintenance of the divine universal order; the significance of the number 7 is explained after the manner of the Pythagoreans. Verses of Homer, Hesiod, and Linus are quoted in this explanation of the Sabbath.

The second fragment (Eusebius, *Praep. ev.* VIII:10), dealing apparently with God's revelation of the Law on Sinai, explains the anthropomorphic expressions referring to God's "hands, arm, face, feet, walking about." We must not be misled thereby and adopt a fairy-tale notion of God's appearance. These words are figurative, as in Greek "hand" means "power." God's descent on Sinai means merely the revelation of his power.

The third fragment (quoted by Eusebius, *Eccles. History* VII:32, 17-18, according to the paraphrase of Anatolius) explains that the Passover is celebrated when the sun stands in the sign of the vernal equinox, while the full moon stands in the sign of the autumnal equinox.

The derivation of Greek philosophy from the Pentateuch, the philosophical interpretation of the Bible (possibly with Gentile readers in mind), the elimination of scriptural anthropomorphisms, the quotation from ancient Greek poets, which characterize this work, will be developed more fully by Philo.

The Fourth Book of Maccabees discloses a deeper knowledge of Greek philosophy than all other Hellenistic-Jewish writings, except Philo's works. It likewise strives to find philosophical ideas in the Old Testament (cf. 1:15-17). Thus, for instance, in 5:23-24 the Law of Moses is said to teach the four cardinal virtues of Plato and the Stoics. This book is in the form of a diatribe or street-corner address on Cynic or Stoic practical philosophy. The author was presumably an Alexandrian Jew living shortly before Philo (about the beginning of our era) and explicitly addresses Jews (18:1). We may summarize it as follows:

1. The introduction (1:1-12). The philosophical (Stoic) theme to be discussed is "whether devout reason [*ho eusebes logismos*] rules supreme over the passions" (1:1; cf. 1:7, 9, 13 f., 19, 30; 2:6 f., 10, 24; 6:31; 7:16;

[20] Philo likewise asserted the dependence of Greek philosophers on Moses; cf. Wolfson, *Philo*, Vol. 1, p. 141.

13:1; 16:1; 18:2). This subject is important both theoretically and practically (1:2-4). The skeptical objection that reason is not the master of
forgetfulness and blameless ignorance, is irrelevant (1:5 f.). The best
example of the supremacy of devout reason is furnished by the martyrdom
of Eleazar, the seven brothers, and their mother (II Macc. 6:18-7:41),
who by their contempt of pain and death fully demonstrated this thesis
(1:7-11). The two parts of the exposition are the theoretical (1:13-3:18)
and the historical (3:19-17:24) (1:12).

2. The philosophical exposition (1:13-3:18). Reason and passions must
now be defined (1:13 f.). Reason is the mind's determination to live
according to wisdom (1:15), which is the knowledge of divine and
human things and of their causes (1:16),[21] i.e., "the culture acquired
under the law" of Moses (1:17). Wisdom is manifested in the four
cardinal virtues: prudence, justice, courage, and temperance (1:18 f.).
The sources of the passions (or emotions) are pleasure and pain (1:20),
and often the passions follow a certain sequence (1:21-27). Reason is
the guide of the virtues and the master of passions: (a) through temperance, which checks our bodily appetites (1:28-35) and controls the
soul's desire to enjoy beauty, which expresses itself in erotic emotion
(2:1-4); (b) through justice, which overcomes the desire to obtain
another's property (2:5-7) and even grants one's own property to another (2:8 f.); (c) through courage, which enables us to place virtue
above family affections and friendship (2:10-12) and to overcome hatred
(2:13 ff.); (d) through prudence, which rules over aggressive passions
and violent anger (2:15-20). God implanted passions in man, but gave
him also a mind which should be directed by the Law (2:21-23). Two
objections may be raised: reason is not the master of forgetfulness and
ignorance (2:24-3:1; cf. 1:5 f.); reason does not extirpate the passions
(3:2-4). As shown by the example of David conquering his thirst (II
Sam. 23:15-17), reason is not the extirpator but the antagonist of passions
(3:5-18).

3. The evidence from history (3:19-17:24). a. Introduction: the events
preceding the Maccabean rebellion (3:19-4:26). When Apollonius
(Heliodorus, in II Macc. 3) attempted to plunder the Temple at Jerusalem for Seleucus IV Philopator (187-175 B.C.; the text reads erroneously
Seleucus Nicanor), angels on horseback prevented this sacrilege (3:19-
4:14). Antiochus IV Epiphanes (175-164 B.C.) appointed Jason as high
priest: Jason introduced Greek institutions in Jerusalem; Antiochus proscribed Judaism and through tortures attempted to force the Jews to
violate the Law of Moses (4:15-26; cf. II Macc. 4:7-17; 5:1-26; 6:1-11).

b. The martyrdom of Eleazar (5-7; cf. II Macc. 6:18-31). Eleazar was

---

[21] Reason and wisdom are here defined in accordance with the teaching of the
Stoics; for references see C. L. W. Grimm's commentary ad loca.

brought before Antiochus (5:1-3), who urged him to partake of swine's meat (5:4-13). Eleazar replied that all transgressions of the Law are equally serious (5:14-21; this view is typically Stoic. cf. Cicero, *Paradoxa Stoicorum* III; cf. Horace, *Satires* I, iii, 115-124), and that Jewish Law is in harmony with Greek philosophy (5:22-26). However he may be tormented, Eleazar will not violate the law (5:27-38). Eleazar was subjected to torture (6:1-11) and, when advised by the courtiers to partake of lawful meat pretending to eat swine's meat (6:12-15; cf. Macc. 6:21 f.), he indignantly refused to save his life through a falsehood contrary to reason, to exemplary conduct, and to bravery (6:16-23; cf. II Macc. 6:23-28). So Eleazar died praying that his suffering might be a ransom for Israel (6:24-30; cf. 17:20-22), and through his martyrdom he proved that devout reason rules over passions (6:31-7:23).

c. The martyrdom of the seven brothers (8-12; cf. II Macc. 7). Seven young brothers and their mother (7:1-4) were exhorted by Antiochus "to share in the Hellenic life" (8:1-11) but were not terrified at the sight of the instruments of torture (8:12-15), although they had many inducements to yield to the king (8:16-28). All seven together (8:29), when the king (8:5-10) invited them to share "in the Hellenic life," replied that the tyrant should put them to death, for so would they win the reward of virtue (cf. 10:15; 13:17; 17:4, 18; 18:23), while he would forever be tormented with fire (9:1-9; on eternal torments cf. 9:32; 10:11, 15; 12:19 [Rahlfs 12:18]; 13:15; 18:5, 22). The first youth, while being tortured (9:10-14), denounced the tyrant (9:15), and in reply to the guards' suggestion to yield (9:16), urged them to increase his torments (9:17 f.); in his last breath he urged his brothers to follow his example (9:19-25). The second youth, likewise, died heroically (9:26-32), as also the third (10:1-11), the fourth (10:12-21), the fifth (11:1-12), the sixth (11:13-26), and the seventh (12:1-20 [Rahlfs 12:1-19]).

d. Reflections on the heroism of the seven brothers (13:1-14:10). Thus their reason won the victory over their passions and their pains (13:1-7); they encouraged one another through the fine example of Shadrach, Meshach, and Abed-nego (Dan. 3:13-23), and that of Isaac (Gen. 22:1-13); through their descent from Abraham; through the eternal punishment of violators of the Law, and conversely their bliss together with their forefathers after the martyrdom; and through loyalty to those on the point of death or already expired, and to brothers (13:8-22). Thus their brotherly love was so strengthened that they could encourage one another to suffer agony (13:23-14:1). So they were praised (14:2-6); the sevenfold companionship of brethren was compared to the seven days of Creation (14:7 f.) and their torments were extolled (14:9 f.).

e. The fortitude and death of the mother (14:11-17:7). Their mother deserved even greater admiration (14:11-20), for in spite of her love she preferred for her sons righteousness rather than escape from death (15:1-7). Witnessing their torments, she urged them to die for their religion (15:8-18). Having the choice of life or death for her sons, she chose the latter, following Abraham's example, and withstood the waves of passion as Noah's ark withstood the waves of the Flood (15:19-32). This mother proves that reason rules over passions (16:1-4). Had she been a coward, she might have wept (16:5-11 [Rahlfs 16:5-10]), but as if she were bringing forth her sons a second time unto eternal life, she entreated them to die for religion's sake (16:12-25 [Rahlfs 16:11-25]). The mother also was now put to death (17:1-7).

f. Concluding praise of the martyrs (17:8-24). A fitting epitaph (17:8-10) should be inscribed on the tombs of these martyrs who received the crown of victory as athletes of righteousness (17:11-24).

4. Peroration (18). Let Israel follow the noble example of these martyrs (18:1 f.), who achieved world renown, eternal bliss, national rebirth, and victory over Antiochus (18:3-5). For the benefit of her sons the mother reviewed her life; she recalled for them the sufferings of Abel, Isaac, and Joseph, the zeal of Phineas, the steadfastness of Daniel and his three friends, and the words of Is. 43:2 (LXX), Ps. 34:19 (LXX, 33:20), Prov. 3:18, Ez. 37:3 (LXX), and Deut. 32:39 (LXX), which their father had taught them while he was alive (18:6-19). The cruel tyrant would be judged by God, but the mother together with her sons would be gathered unto their ancestors (18:20-24).

Although the author was a zealous orthodox Jew trained in "the Law and the Prophets" (18:10; cf. the quotations from the LXX in 18:13-19),[22] he must have attended Greek schools. He has a notable command of the resources of the Greek language, including a vast vocabulary and rhetorical art. His style is far better than that of his historical source, II Maccabees—or the full work of Jason of Cyrene condensed in II Maccabees—and he surpasses in good taste and clearness of diction the ornate and pompous Atticist who wrote III Maccabees.

The argument of the book is presented logically and consistently, even though in reality it begs the question. He proves that devout reason is the absolute master of the passions by regarding reason as the determination to live according to wisdom, which is not merely knowledge but also the observance of the Law of Moses. He then defines the "passions" as moral defects contrary to the four cardinal virtues, but not mental defects such as forgetfulness and ignorance, over which reason has no control. In other words: reason possesses wisdom; wisdom is manifested

---

[22] C. L. W. Grimm in his commentary (cf. the preceding note) believed that the book ended with 18:2 and that 18:3-23 was an addition by a later hand; but, as R. B. Townshend has shown (in R. H. Charles, *Pseudepigrapha*, pp. 655 f.), there is no compelling reason for rejecting 18:3-23.

in the four cardinal virtues that control the passions opposed to them; therefore reason controls these passions. Q.E.D. In harmony with Rabbinic Judaism, he concludes that reason does not extirpate the passions, but enables us to resist them successfully, and also that while there may be small and great sins, any transgression of the Law of Moses, be it in small things or in great, is equally heinous (cf. the Stoic teaching), for it shows contempt for the Law (5:19-20; cf. James 2:10).

The general theme of the book (the supremacy of reason over the passions) as well as many of the special arguments and views presented are clearly Stoic.[23] The famous Stoic paradox "The sage is not merely free but also a king" is echoed in 7:23 and 14:2; the martyrs behave with true Stoic apathy (9:17 f.; 11:25; 15:11, 14); wisdom (1:16) is defined in the Stoic manner. He differs from the Stoics, however, in his more comprehensive conception of the passions and in regarding them as divinely implanted in man (2:21; cf. 1:20) and therefore ineradicable (1:6; 3:2, 5) even though controllable.[24]

As a Jew addressing Jews the author tended to subordinate the Stoic philosophy to the Law of Moses, even though he wished to equate them. On the one hand, he refuted the Greek view that the Law of Moses was a "preposterous philosophy" (5:10), "contrary to reason" (5:22), by asserting that it taught the four Stoic cardinal virtues (5:23 f.). On the other hand, the source of these virtues was wisdom (1:18), which, in its Stoic definition (1:16), was merely "the culture acquired under the Law" (1:17); the Stoic ideal could be realized only by fulfilling the Law (7:17-23). Moreover, it was not natural reason that dominated the passions, but "devout, inspired" reason—and only Judaism could make reason "devout." Thus for the author there was no difference between Zeno and Moses, between Stoic virtues and Mosaic prescriptions, between "moral beauty and goodness" (1:10) and Jewish righteousness. Wisdom and law had already been identified in Judaism long before, but our author failed to go beyond a purely verbal identification of Judaism and Stoicism, and did not produce a real synthesis of the two. Indeed, no Jew believing the Law to be divinely inspired could bring it down to the level of mere human knowledge, as Greek philosophy did.

In two points the author changes the religious teaching of II Macca-

---

[23] H. A. Wolfson (*Philo*, Vol. 2, pp. 271 f.), however, asserts that "guided by Jewish tradition the author comes out in opposition to the Stoics." But C. L. W. Grimm has shown (in his commentary to IV Maccabees, p. 288) how pervasive Stoic teaching is in this book.

[24] In 2:21 f. the author gives us a notion of his idea of a human being. When God created man, He planted at the periphery, near the surface of his being (*periephúteusen*), the passions and inclinations, but He placed the mind (*noûs*) or reason (the ego) on a throne to dominate, under the guidance of the Law, over the senses and passions (cf. 7:20; Rom. 7:25).

bees, from which (or from whose source, Jason of Cyrene) he derived the stories of the Maccabean martyrs (cf. the table of parallels in Charles, *Pseudepigrapha*, p. 665). While II Maccabees repeatedly speaks of the resurrection of the body as the hope of the martyrs and only once (II Macc. 7:36) of "eternal life" (which may be a loose way of speaking of the resurrection),[25] IV Maccabees, like the Wisdom of Solomon, teaches the doctrine of the immortality of the spirit (14:5; 16:13)—"pure and immortal souls" (18:23)—both of the pious (14:6)[26] and of the wicked (13:15); the pious are honored by God and have an abode in heaven (17:5) after achieving "the prize of victory in incorruption in everlasting life" (17:12) or, better, with a slight change in the Greek, "the prize of victory *was* incorruption." They shall stand beside the throne of God and live in blissful eternity (17:18) "unto God" (16:25), having obtained a divine inheritance (18:3). On the contrary, eternal torments are the lot of the wicked (9:9; 10:11, 15, 21; 12:12).[27] In II Maccabees, only the Jews are raised from the dead (II Macc. 7:14).

Another difference between these two books lies in the evaluation of the torments and death of the martyrs. In II Maccabees the martyrs were selected for torment from the midst of a sinful people to be an example of God's punishing justice and to appease his wrath against Israel (II Macc. 7:18, 32 f., 37 f.). But in IV Maccabees the martyrs not only endured pain for God's sake (16:19), and knew that it was unreasonable for the pious to fail to suffer the pains (16:23) that would be compensated through eternal bliss (9:8), but they were offered up as a sacrifice of expiation, a propitiation, a ransom, an atonement, in behalf of the whole nation (6:28; 17:21 f.), after the manner of the suffering servant in Isaiah 53 (in behalf of the Gentiles). This involved, in principle, the moral perfection of these martyrs, exactly as sacrificial victims had to be without blemish. Aware perhaps of this difficulty, the author declared that Eleazar was immaculate (5:37) and holy (7:4); he also let a martyr express the wish that his death *might be* a satisfaction for Israel (6:28), and that his soul be accepted as *a ransom* for them (*antipsychon*).[28] We do not know whether Paul was acquainted with IV Maccabees, but in any case it would seem that the author of IV Macca-

[25] Modern Christians, conversely, generally understand by "resurrection of the flesh" in the Apostles' Creed the immortality of the spirit—a Platonic doctrine which excludes the bodily resurrection.

[26] R. B. Townshend in Charles, *Pseudepigrapha*, p. 679, translates literally, "as if prompted by the immortal soul of religion" (14:6). The meaning, however, seems to be, "so those holy youths, prompted by the immortality of their pious soul . . ."

[27] In this book immortality is not, as in Plato, a quality of the spirit but the result of God's intervention (7:19; 17:17-21; 18:23).

[28] IV Macc. 6:29; cf. 17:22 (Rahlfs 17:21). This word for ransom occurs four times in the epistles of Ignatius of Antioch (Ephesians 21:1; Smyrneans 10:2; Polycarp 2:3; 6:1). Ignatius died a martyr during the reign of Trajan (98-117).

bees, through his notion of expiatory martyrdom, somehow anticipated the main lines of Paul's doctrine of the atonement.[29]

The Alexandrian-Jewish philosophy and the allegorical interpretation of the Scriptures on which it rests reached their culmination and end in the works of Philo of Alexandria (d. about A.D. 50).[30] Soon after Philo's death it was rejected by the Jews, but it furnished to incipient Christianity a philosophical scaffolding for its faith. The works of Philo have been grouped as follows:[31]

1. *Questions and answers* (*Zētēmata kaì lýseis; Quaestiones et solutiones*) on the Pentateuch, of which we have parts of six books dealing with Gen. 1-28 (lacking Gen. 10:10-15:6); and parts of the second and all of the fifth book on Exodus, surviving in Armenian and Latin translations, but lost in the Greek. Here Philo interpreted the books of the Pentateuch both literally and allegorically. For instance, this is the comment on the words "in this generation" (Gen. 7:1):

It is an admirable expression which is meanwhile added, the one which says, "in this generation have I seen thee righteous," that he might not appear to condemn earlier generations, nor cut off the future hope of generations of later times. This is the literal sense. But according to the spiritual meaning, when God will have the mind, the ruler of the soul, which is the head of the family, then he saves likewise the whole family together with him; I mean all parts . . . and the things of the body. As the mind is in the soul, so the soul is in the body. Through good advice all parts of the soul thrive, and its whole house is benefited along with it. When the whole soul is in good condition, then all of its house likewise is found to be benefited with it, namely the body (profits) through sound conduct and continence, after those passionate desires which cause diseases have been destroyed.

Quaest. et solut. II, 11 (surviving in Armenian)

2. *Allegory of the Holy Laws* (*nómōn hierôn allegoría; legum allegoria*) is a purely allegorical commentary on the Pentateuch, consisting of many individual works. We have the parts dealing with Gen. 2-41 either verse by verse (Gen. 2-4) or in longer sections (thus there are two books *de ebrietate* on Gen. 9). Here Philo gives his views on the nature of human

[29] Paul uses *hilastêrion* in the sense of "propitiation" (Rom. 3:25), exactly as in IV Macc. 17:22. In the LXX the word means "mercy seat" (cf. Hebr. 9:5).

[30] For the bibliography on Philo see above, note 7. The reader is referred to the works of Drummond, Goodenough, and Wolfson for a presentation of Philo's teaching, which cannot be adequately described here. The most convenient edition of his works (not yet completed) is: F. H. Colson and G. H. Whitaker, *Philo with an English Translation*, Vols. 1-9. The Loeb Classical Library. Cambridge, Mass., 1929-1941. C. D. Yonge's complete English version (1854-1855) is still useful. The standard edition of the Greek text is that of L. Cohn and P. Wendland, *Philonis Alexandrini opera quae supersunt*. 6 vols. Berlin, 1896-1915; H. Leisegang, *Index Philonis*, 1926-1930.

[31] Cf. the bibliography in H. A. Wolfson, *Philo*, Vol. 1, p. 87, n. 1.

beings, from the points of view of physiology, psychology, epistemology, and ethics. Thus, for instance, commenting on Gen. 2:10 he says, "'River' is generic virtue, goodness. This issues out of Eden, the wisdom of God, and this is the *Logos* [i.e., Word, Reason] of God, for in accordance with that has generic virtue been made. And generic virtue waters the garden, that is, it waters the particular virtues" (*Leg. alleg.* I, 19, 165 [I, 56 M]). The four rivers of Gen. 2:10-14 are the four cardinal virtues of Plato and the Stoics: prudence, temperance, fortitude, and justice. The individual books in the *legum allegoria* series are: *Legum allegoria*, books I (on Gen. 2:1-17), II (on Gen. 2:18-3:1a), III (on Gen. 3:8b-19); On the Cherubim and the Fiery Sword (*de Cherubim et flammeo gladio*, on Gen. 3:24; 4:1); On the Sacrifices of Abel and Cain (*de sacrificiis Abeli et Caini*, on Gen. 4:2-4); That the Worse Usually Waylays the Better (*quod deterius potiori insidiari soleat*, on Gen. 4:8-15); On the Offspring of Cain (*de posteritate Caini*, on Gen. 4:16-25); On the Giants (*de gigantibus*, on Gen. 6:1-4) and That God Is Unchangeable (*quod Deus sit immutabilis*, on Gen. 6:4-12); On Agriculture (*de agricultura*, on Gen. 9:20a and *de plantatione Noe*, on Gen. 9:20b); On Intoxication (*de ebrietate*, of which only the first of two books, dealing with Gen. 9:21, survives); On Temperance (*de sobrietate*, on Gen. 9:24-27); On the Confusion of Languages (*de confusione linguarum*, on Gen. 11:1-9); On the Migration of Abraham (*de migratione Abrahami*, on Gen. 12:1-6); Who Is to Be the Heir of Divine Things (*Quis rerum divinarum haeres sit*, on Gen. 15:2-18); On the Meeting about Education (*de congressu quaerendae eruditionis causa*, on Gen. 16:1-6); On Fugitives (*de profugis*, on Gen. 16:6-14); On the Change of Names (*de mutatione nominum*, on Gen. 17:1-22); (On God [*de deo*, a fragment in Armenian on Gen. 18:2]); On Dreams (*de somniis*; book II, on Gen. 28:12-22 and 31:11-13; book III, on Gen. 37:5-11; 40:5-19; 41:1-36; three other books are lost).

3. Studies on miscellaneous Pentateuchal subjects, seldom utilizing the allegorical method, constituting an introduction to the Law of Moses for a large circle of readers, notably Gentiles.[32] This collection includes the following books:

The Life of the Sage (*bíos sophoú*) Who Has Been Perfected through Education. Book I: *de Abrahamo* (On Abraham), dealing with Enosh, who typifies hope; Enoch, the type of conversion and improvement; Noah, the type of righteousness; Abraham, the type of the virtue acquired through teaching; (Isaac, the type of the natural or inborn virtue, and Jacob, the type of the virtue acquired through practice, are lost).

Book II: *de Josepho* (On Joseph, the type of the statesman); *de*

---

[32] See E. R. Goodenough in HTR 27 (1933) 109-125.

decalogo (On the Ten Commandments); *de specialibus legibus* (an arrangement of all Pentateuchal laws in accordance with the Ten Commandments) I-IV. I (Ex. 20:3-6): *de circumcisione* (On Circumcision), *de monarchia* (On Monotheism) I-II, *de praemiis sacerdotum* (On the Emoluments of the Priesthood), *de sacrificantibus* or *de victimas offerentibus* (On Proper Victims and On those who Offer Sacrifice), *de mercede meretricis* (On the Wages of a Harlot). II (Ex. 20:7-12): *de septenario* (On the Sabbath), *de festo cophini* (on Deut. 26), *de colendis parentibus* (On Honoring the Parents). III (Ex. 20:13-14) and IV (Ex. 20:15-17): *de judice* (On the Judge), *de concupiscentia* (On Covetousness), *de justitia* (On Justice), *de tribus virtutibus* (On Three Virtues recorded with others by Moses: *de fortitudine, de caritate, de poenitentia* [on courage, humanity, and repentance]) (also, *de nobilitate*); *de praemiis et poenis* and *de execrationibus* (On Rewards and Punishments, and On Curses; see Lev. 26 and Deut. 28).

4. Separate historical and philosophical works. On the Life of Moses (*vita Mosis* I-III, or better I-II), addressed to Gentile readers; That Every Good Person Is Free (*quod omnis probus liber*); Against Flaccus (*adversus Flaccum*); The Embassy to Caius Caligula (*de legatione ad Caium*); On Providence (*de providentia*); That Dumb Animals Have an Intelligence of Their Own (*de Alexandro et quod propriam rationem muta animalia habeant*); Assumptions (*hypothetiká*, lost except for the references in Eusebius, *Praep. ev.* VIII, 5-7); On the Jews (or Apology for the Jews, lost except for Eusebius, *Praep. ev.* VIII, 11 [on the Essenes]), possibly identical with the preceding work.

5. Entirely lost works. Three books of *quaestiones et solutiones* on Exodus (cf. above, No. 1); two books of *legum allegoria* (cf. above, No. 2); On Rewards (*perì misthôn* commenting on Gen. 15:1, mentioned at the beginning of *quis rerum divinarum haeres sit*); two books On Testaments (*perì diathēkôn*, mentioned at the beginning of *de mutatione nominum*); three of the five books *de somniis* (cf. above, No. 2); the books on Isaac and Jacob, following *de Abrahamo* (cf. above, No. 3); That Every Bad Person Is a Slave (*perì toû doûlon eînai pánta phaûlon*), the first half and the opposite of *quod omnis probus liber* (No. 4, above), mentioned by Eusebius (*Eccl. Hist.* II:18, 6); three books of a work on the persecution of the Jews at Alexandria, of which only *adversus Flaccum* and *de legatione ad Caium* (No. 4, above) survive; On Numbers (*perì arithmôn*), mentioned in *vita Mosis* III, 11; and possibly a book on the rule of the sage (*perì tês archês toû sophoû*), which Philo says he intended to write (*quod omnis probus liber* §3).

6. Spurious works. *De vita contemplativa* (On the Therapeutae [ascetics] in Egypt), regarded as genuine by some scholars; *de incor-*

ruptibilitate mundi; de mundo; de Sampsone; interpretatio hebraicorum nominum; liber antiquitatum biblicarum; breviarium temporum.

4. Jewish Propaganda Works Attributed to Gentiles

The *Letter of Aristeas*[33] purports to be a letter written by Aristeas, an official of Ptolemy II Philadelphus, king of Egypt (285-245 B.C.), to his brother Philocrates to give him an account of the translation of the Pentateuch into Greek. In reality, all the details of this narrative are fictitious, and the work was written in Greek by an Alexandrian Jew about 100 B.C. The Septuagint (LXX) version of the Pentateuch was indeed prepared about 250 B.C., but hardly by seventy-two elders (six from each tribe of Israel) brought from Jerusalem, and hardly under the auspices of Demetrius of Phalerum, the head of the library at Alexandria, who died *ca.* 283 in exile. We may summarize this epistle (which is in reality only a eulogy of Judaism) as follows:

a. Introduction (§§1-8). Aristeas will give his brother Philocrates an account of his mission to Eleazar (the high priest of the Jews) to further the preparation of a Greek translation of the Jewish law (§§1-8).

b. Preparatory steps (§§9-50). Demetrius of Phalerum, the chief librarian, induced Ptolemy II to add a translation of the Jewish Law to the 200,000 volumes in the Museum (§§9-11). Aristeas thought that the occasion was propitious to request the king to free the Jews enslaved by Ptolemy I (§§12-20), and through a royal decree they were emancipated (§§21-27). Demetrius prepared a memorandum for the king (§§28-32), who wrote a letter to Eleazar the high priest in Jerusalem requesting that seventy-two translators be sent to Egypt (§§33-40). Eleazar replied favorably (§§41-46) and sent 72 elders, who are named in §§47-50.

c. The royal gifts to Eleazar (§§51-82): a sacred table, enormous and richly ornate (§§51-72); golden mixing bowls and polished silver bowls (§§73-78); and golden vials (§§79-82).

d. Description of Jerusalem (§§83-106) and of Palestine (§§107-120): the Temple and its abundant water supply (§§83-91); the work of the priests (§§92-95) and of Eleazar (§§96-99); the citadel or Acra (§§100-104), the city of Jerusalem (§§105-106), and the Palestinian countryside (§§107-120).

e. The seventy-two translators were such noble and able men that Eleazar was greatly concerned about their safe return (§§121-127).

[33] The Greek text has been edited by H. St. John Thackeray in H. B. Swete, *Introduction to the Old Testament in Greek*, pp. 499-574. Cambridge, 1900; and by P. Wendland in the Teubner series of classical texts (Leipzig, 1900). Thackeray has published an English translation (London, 1917), as also H. T. Andrews (in Charles, *Pseudepigrapha*).

f. Eleazar's explanation and defense of the Jewish laws, and particularly of monotheism, purifications, and dietary prescriptions (§§128-171).

g. The royal welcome to the translators (§§172-186).

h. The banquets in the translators' honor during seven successive days and the answer of each translator to a question asked by the king (§§187-300). The questions deal with the art of government, ethics, philosophy, and practical wisdom.

i. The Pentateuch was translated into Greek by the seventy-two translators on the island of Pharos in seventy-two days (§§301-307). The translation was read by Demetrius before the Jewish population (§§308-309), which approved it and recommended that it be preserved without changes (§§310-311). The translation was then read to the king, and its divine origin and sacredness were explained to him (§§312-317). The king dismissed the translators with costly gifts (§§318-322).

This fanciful story of the origin of the Septuagint is merely a pretext for defending Judaism against its heathen denigrators, for extolling its nobility and reasonableness, and for striving to convert Greek-speaking Gentiles to it. The author pleads eloquently for the political independence and emancipation from slavery of the Jews in his own day, who are said to worship the same god as the Greeks (Zeus or Dis) under another name (§§15-16, §19). Eleazar expounded so convincingly the logic of some aspects of Judaism which were occasionally ridiculed (§§128-169) that Aristeas—allegedly a pagan—praised "the holiness and meaning in conformity with nature" of the Jewish Law (§§170-171). He was likewise deeply moved by the Temple rituals (§99). The conversation at the banquets (§§187-294) between Ptolemy II Philadelphus and the seventy-two translators emphasized for the benefit of Gentiles the philosophical insight, ethical nobility, and admirable wisdom of the Jewish translators.

Pseudo-Phocylides, an unknown Jewish-Alexandrian poet living probably in the last century before our era, composed a didactic poem in 230 Greek hexameters and attributed his composition to Phocylides of Miletus (sixth century B.C.), an author of wise sayings, few of which are extant. Our Jewish author moralizes about the problems of daily life, after the manner of Sirach, but deliberately follows the prescriptions of the Pentateuch (even down to such details as Deut. 14:21 and 22:6 f). In order to make the forgery at least apparently plausible, peculiar Jewish prescriptions and polemic against idolatry are entirely omitted. Besides the Pentateuch, the author utilized the Jewish wisdom books (Proverbs, Job, Ecclesiastes, Ecclesiasticus, and Wisdom of Solomon). Although the Church Fathers do not quote this book, it became a textbook in the Byzantine period, and is therefore extant in many manuscripts and printed editions, the first of which appeared in 1495 (for further details and bibliography see Schürer, *Geschichte*, Vol. 3, pp. 617-622; S. Kraus, in *Jewish Encyclopedia*, Vol. 10, pp. 255 f.).

The Sibylline Oracles[34] now surviving are in part the work of Hellenistic Jews. The Sibyl was a prophetess, the pagan counterpart of the Hebrew prophets—as Michelangelo realized when he painted the Sibyls opposite the prophets on the walls of the Sistine Chapel. Vergil's description of how Apollo entered into the Cumaean Sibyl at the moment of inspiration (*Aeneid* 6, 40 ff.) shows that, like the prophets, the Sibyls were thought to be literally and physically filled with the divine spirit at the moment of inspiration. The etymology of "Sibyl" given by Varro, from Aeolic *sios boulla* (Greek *theoû boulê, theoboulê*, counsel of God), is manifestly fanciful, but the real origin of the word, which is *not* a personal name, is unknown. The earliest and foremost of the Sibyls was Herophile the Erythraean (in Ionia, Asia Minor).

According to Plutarch, Heraclitus knew Sibylline oracles in verse which mentioned "many revolutions and upheavals in Greek cities, many appearances of barbarous hordes and murders of rulers." A collection of such oracles was housed in Rome until it was destroyed in the burning of the Capitol in 82 B.C., but a new collection was made under official auspices and kept in secrecy. Many private collections were, however, in circulation; Augustus ordered 2,000 volumes to be destroyed. Most of the oracles were in Greek hexameters (the meter of the *Iliad* and the *Odyssey*).

The extant collection of Sibylline Oracles was preserved, as well as abundantly edited, by Christians, so that it is at times difficult to say whether some verses are Jewish or Christian (pagan material, such as III, 110-154, is scarce). It comprised fifteen books (books IX, X, and XV are lost), of which 4,240 verses are extant. In view of the popularity of the Sibylline Oracles among the pagans, it is not surprising that an Alexandrian Jew living about 140 B.C. should compose some spurious oracles in the same style to teach the truths of the Jewish religion. His example was followed by Jews and Christians in later times. In any case, while the authors of the present collection lived between the second century B. C. and the fifth century of our era, the early oracles were regarded as genuine and ancient by some Jews: Josephus in *Antiquities* I, 4:3 quotes freely Sibylline Oracles III, 97-104, which he presumably read in Alexander Polyhistor's *Chaldaiká*. Christian authors—beginning with Justin Martyr (d. *ca.* 165), and including Clement of Alexandria (d. *ca.* 220), Theophilus of Antioch (d. *ca.* 185), Lactantius (d. *ca.* 325), and

[34] The best edition of the Greek text is that of J. Geffcken, *Die Oracula Sibyllina.* Leipzig, 1902 (cf. his *Komposition und Entstehungszeit der Oracula Sibyllina.* Texte und Untersuchungen 23, 1. Leipzig, 1902). The English translation of H. C. O. Lanchester is published in Charles, *Pseudepigrapha*; another translation of Books III-V was published by H. N. Bate (London, 1918).

Augustine (d. 430)—likewise regarded the oracles as ancient pagan poetry. Celsus (second century), in his book against the Christians, mocked their credulity and accused them of fabricating Sibylline oracles. The oracles generally regarded as Jewish (in books III-V) may be summarized as follows:

1. Book III, about 140 B.C. *a.* Its *Introduction* apparently consisted of two long fragments preserved by Theophilus of Antioch (*ad Autolycum* ii, 36): Lactantius quotes passages from these fragments and from book III as oracles of the Erythraean Sibyl, but passages from other books are attributed to other Sibyls. The two introductory fragments furnish the keynote of the Jewish Sibyl (if not of Alexandrian-Jewish apologetics in general) by stressing the truth of Jewish monotheism, in contrast with the falsehood and folly of pagan idolatry and animal worship.

b. III, 1-92 seems to have originally belonged to book II, which is late. III, 1-45 praises God, the universal Creator, who fashioned "four-lettered Adam" (in Greek, the letters A-D-A-M are the initials for east, west, north, south; cf. also II Enoch 30:13), and denounces the heathen for their idolatry and wickedness. III, 46-62 (obscure) announces the final judgment and the eternal rule of a holy king over the whole world (the Jewish Messiah or Jesus Christ?); then the Latins will suffer and three men (either the first [Pompey, Caesar, and Crassus; 60 B.C.] or second [Antony, Octavius, and Lepidus; 43 B.C.] triumvirate) will bring ruin to Rome. III, 63-92 (probably Christian) describes the initial success and final ruin of Beliar (incarnated in Simon Magus?) "from the stock of Sebaste" (i.e., Samaria); during the world rule of a widow, God will burn up the world.

c. III, 93-96 (Christian?) longs for the rise of the sun that shall never set, which will be obeyed by all.

d. III, 97-294 begins abruptly a history of the world from the building of the Tower of Babel (97-107) to Cyrus (286-294). Following the dispersion of mortals after the destruction of the Tower of Babel (105-109), Cronus, Titan, and Iapetus [Alexander Polyhistor has Prometheus instead of Cronus] ruled peacefully, each having dominion over one-third of the earth (110-116). But after the death of their father Uranus, Cronus and Titan fought against each other (117-121) until the goddesses (122-126) decided that Cronus should first rule supreme (127-128), but that Titan, rather than a future son of Cronus, should succeed him (129-131). When Rhea, the wife of Cronus, gave birth to a boy, the Titans killed him (cf. Rev. 12:4); but when Hera was born, the Titans left, and Zeus, born immediately after, was sent secretly to Phrygia (132-141); similarly Rhea saved Poseidon and Pluto (142-146). The Titans, however, heard of the birth of sons and captured Cronus and Rhea (147-151). War broke out between the Titans and the sons of Cronus (152-156). After Cronus and the Titans died, there arose the kingdoms of Egypt, Persia, Media, Ethiopia, and "Assyrian Babylon"; then those of Macedon, of Egypt again, and of Rome (157-161).

Now the Sibyl began to prophesy (162-164) about the kingdoms of Solomon, the Phoenicians, and other nations of Asia (165-170); of the Greeks and Macedonians (171-174); of Rome (175-190) until Ptolemy VII (192-193), when Israel would be powerful again and be a guide to all mortals (194-195). God's judgment would come upon all kingdoms of the earth, from those of Cronus and Titan down through the centuries (196-210); even Israel would suffer (211-217). There follows a eulogy of Judaism and a history of Israel from Abraham to Cyrus (218-294).

e. III, 295-488 contains prophecies of woes: against Babylon (295-313), Egypt (314-318), the land of Gog and Magog (319-322), Libya (323-333). A comet will presage the cosmic upheavals at the end of this age (334-340) and many cities will fall (341-349), including Rome (350-366). Then will come the Messianic age of peace and prosperity (367-380).

After Alexander (381-387), Antiochus IV Epiphanes and his successors will devastate Asia (387-400).

The fall of Troy will be recorded by blind Homer in the *Iliad* and the *Odyssey*, after obtaining the Sibyl's verses; the accursed Phrygians are (through Aeneas) the ancestors of the Romans (401-432).

The Sibyl proclaims the doom of Lycia (433), Chalcedon (434-435), Cyzicus (436, 442-443), Byzantium (437-438), Krasos in Lycia (439-441), Rhodes (444-448), Persia (449-450), Samos (451-456), Cyprus (57-458), Trallis (459-463), Italy (464-469), Laodicea (470-473), and other cities and nations (474-488).

f. III, 489-808 contains oracles of doom and eschatological predictions. God ordered the Sibyl to proclaim the doom of Phoenicia (489-503), Crete (503-507), Thrace (508-511), Gog and Magog (512-519), and Greece (520-572).

Israel obeys God's law (573-585) and, instead of idols (586-590), worships the true God (591-593) and avoids immorality (594-600), for which God punishes men (601-606a). Men will cast away their idols in the time of Ptolemy VII and Antiochus IV Epiphanes (606b-618), after which "God will give great joy to men" (619-623).

The pagans should worship God (624-631) to avoid the outbreak of his wrath (632-651).

The Messiah (652-655) will enrich the Jews (656-661). God will judge the nations (662-701) and bring peace and prosperity to the Jews (702-731). Greece should cease being arrogant and worship God (732-740). The golden age will come after the judgment (741-761). Therefore men should serve God (762-765), that he might establish his kingdom on earth (766-771) for the benefit of the Jews (672-684). Rejoice, O Virgin of Israel (685-687), for wild animals will become tame (688-695). Cosmic portents will presage the judgment (696-808).

g. III, 809-829 (colophon). The Sibyl came from Babylon, the Greeks say she was born in Erythraea (Ionia), others call her an impostor (809-816a). In reality she is the prophetess of the mighty God, a daughter-in-law and blood relation of Noah (816b-829).

2. Book IV (about A.D. 80, for the destruction of Jerusalem in A.D. 70 [115-116, 125-127] and the eruption of Vesuvius in August of A.D. 79 [130-136] are clearly mentioned). a. Introduction. The Sibyl is the prophetess of the true God (1-23).

b. Happy are the pious Jews (24-34), for they do not imitate the shameless pagans doomed to the fires of hell (35-46).

c. The history of the world (47-139): the Assyrian (47-53), Medic (54-60), and Persian (61-75) empires; the expedition of Xerxes against the Greeks in 491-490 B.C. (76-70), the eruption of Etna (80-82), the Peloponnesian War or the fighting in 446 B.C. (83-85), the conquests of Alexander (86-101), the Macedonian wars of Rome from 214 to 168 B.C. (102-104), the Roman conquest of Corinth and Carthage in 146 B.C. (105-106), the Laodicean earthquake (107-108), the ruin of Lycian Myra (109-113), Rome's Armenian wars in A.D. 43-66 (114), the destruction of Jerusalem in A.D. 70 (115-127), the earthquake at Salamis and Paphos in Cyprus in A.D. 76 (128-129), the destruction of Pompeii through the eruption of Vesuvius in A.D. 79 (130-136), and the return of Nero Redivivus, who was reported to have fled beyond the Euphrates when he died (cf. 119-120), from Parthia (137-139).

d. Woes against various localities (140-161): Antioch (140-42), Cyprus (143-144), Rome (145-148), Caria (149-161).

e. Exhortation to repentance (162-170), to avoid the destruction of the world by fire (171-178).

f. The final judgment (179-192). Following the destruction of the world by fire and the resurrection (179-182), God will judge the world again (183-192).

3. Book V (about A.D. 125). a. The history of Rome (1-51). After the kingdoms of Egypt (1-3), after the conquests of Alexander (4-7), after Aeneas (8-9), and after Romulus and Remus (10-11) shall come Julius Caesar (12-14), Augustus (15-19), Tiberius (20-23), Gaius Caligula (24), Claudius (25-27), Nero (28-34), Galba, Otho, and Vitellius (35), Vespasian (36-37), Titus (38-39), Domitian (40), Nerva (41), Trajan (42-45), and Hadrian (46-50); (Marcus Aurelius (51), was probably added).

b. Woes on several nations (52-227): introduction (52-59), Egypt (60-110), the Near East and Asia Minor (111-136). The calamities wrought by Nero (137-154) will be avenged after a comet, appearing in A.D. 73, presages disaster for Italy (155-161); woe unto Rome (162-178; cf. Rev. 18)! Egypt (179-199), Gaul (200-205), India and Ethiopia (206-213), and Corinth (214-227) are doomed.

c. A poem on violence (*hýbris*), the fountainhead of evils (228-246).

d. A eulogy of the Jews (247-255, 260-285), interrupted by a Christian interpolation on Jesus Christ: Jesus, whose name is the Greek form of Joshua, was nailed on the cross and, like Joshua, stopped the sun (256-259; cf. Luke 23:44).

e. Woes on several nations (286-343): woe on Asia Minor (286-327); a prayer for Judea (328-332); woe on Thrace (333-341) and on Italy (342-343).

f. The end of the world (344-385). God's appearance in power (344-360), cosmic upheavals, the return of Nero redivivus as the Antichrist, the resurrection, and war (361-380) will precede the golden age of the Jews (381-385).

g. A denunciation of Roman immorality (386-402; cf. III, 384-386; Rom. 1:24-31): homosexuality, fornication, incest, and commerce with beasts (386-393) have befouled Rome, whose temple of Vesta will be destroyed because of the burning of the Temple in Jerusalem (394-402) by Titus (403-413).

h. The Messiah (414-433). A blessed man holding God's scepter has come from heaven (414-415) to destroy the heathen and glorify Jerusalem (416-433).

i. Woes on Babylon, Egypt, and other countries (434-511). Babylon will be leveled (434-446). The sea will dry up, Asia Minor will be water, Crete and Cyprus will suffer, Phoenicia will perish (447-457). Octavian will make war to cease (458-463). The Gauls, repulsed at Delphi in 279 B.C., will invade Asia Minor (464-475), and total darkness will afflict all men except the Jews (476-483). Isis and Serapis will be forgotten, and Egypt will worship the true God in the Jewish temple of Onias at Leontopolis in Egypt (484-503; cf. Is. 19:18-21). But Egypt will be destroyed (504-511).

j. The astral battle (512-530). The various stars and constellations, notably those of the Zodiac, fought furiously (512-527) until heaven hurled them to the earth and into the ocean; "they kindled the whole earth: and the sky remained starless" (528-530).

PART II

THE BOOKS OF THE APOCRYPHA

I ESDRAS (THE GREEK EZRA)

~~~~~~

This book is entitled *I Esdras* in the standard Septuagint manuscripts and editions, as also in the Old Latin and Syriac versions; *II Esdras* in Lucian's recension of the Septuagint (where I Esdras is Ezra-Nehemiah); and *III Esdras* in the printed editions of Jerome's Vulgate (Latin) Bible, where it is placed after the New Testament.

This Greek book gives a history of the Jews from the celebration of the Passover in the time of Josiah (621 B.C.) to the reading of the Law in the time of Ezra. It is substantially parallel to Chronicles-Ezra-Nehemiah, but differs in textual recension and occasionally in the order of the stories (Ezra 4:7-24 precedes 2:1); it omits Ezra 4:6, Neh. 1:1-7:5 and 8:13b-13:31, and a few brief clauses, but adds to the canonical books the Story of the Three Youths at the court of Darius (I Esd. 3:1-5:6).[1]

Its contents may be summarized as follows:

1. *The last kings of Judah* (1; II Chron. 35:1-36:21). *a.* Josiah celebrated the Passover with a pomp and ceremony unknown since the time of Samuel and distributed gifts to the clergy (1:1-22 [Gr. 1:1-20]; II Chron. 35:1-19). In spite of Josiah's piety, the divine sentence pronounced against Israel (in I Kings 13:2, 32; cf. II Kings 23:15-18) was confirmed on account of the people's sins (1:23 f. [Gr. 1:21 f.]; not in Chronicles, but see note 1, above). Disregarding an oracle of Jeremiah, Josiah fought against Pharaoh Necho at Megiddo and was fatally wounded (1:25-35 [Gr. 1:23-31]; II Chron. 35:20-27).

b. In the place of Jehoahaz, the choice of the people, Necho made Jehoiakim king of Judah (1:34-35 [Gr. 1:32-36]; II Chron. 36:1-4). But Nebuchadnezzar took Jehoiakim captive to Babylonia (1:39-42 [Gr. 1:37-40]; II Chron. 36:5-8).

c. Jehoiachin [not Joakim] was likewise taken captive to Babylonia (1:43-45 [Gr. 1:41-43]; II Chron. 36:9-10a).

d. Zedekiah also was wicked, and God sent Nebuchadnezzar to destroy

---

[1] The addition in 1:23 f. (Gr. 1:21 f.), explaining why Josiah's piety did not avert Jehovah's punishment of Judah (cf. II Kings 23:24-27 and the addition in the LXX of II Chron. 35:19) is generally considered a gloss, but C. C. Torrey (*The Apocryphal Literature*, pp. 47 f. Yale University Press, 1945) regards it as original.

Jerusalem and to exile the people for seventy years, according to the prophecy of Jer. 25:11 f. (1:46-58 [Gr. 1:44-55]; II Chron. 36:10b-21).

2. *The decree of Cyrus* (2:1-15 [Gr. 2:1-11]; Ezra 1:1-11). This prophecy of Jeremiah was realized in the first year of Cyrus (2:1 f. [Gr. 2:1]; Ezra 1:1), who published a decree allowing the Jews to return and to rebuild their Temple (2:3-7 [Gr. 2:2-4]; Ezra 1:2-4; and, in part, II Chron. 36:22 f.). So the Exiles returned to Jerusalem led by Sheshbazzar, bringing back the Temple vessels (2:8-15 [Gr. 2:5-11]; Ezra 1:5-11).

3. *An adverse official report to Artaxerxes on the rebuilding of Jerusalem and its Temple* (2:16-30 [Gr. 2:12-26]; Ezra 4:7-24). Rathumus (Rehum), Samellius (Shimshai), and other Persian officials west of the Euphrates warned Artaxerxes that the Jews, if they rebuilt Jerusalem and its walls, would revolt (2:16-24 [Gr. 2:12-18]; Ezra 4:7-16; Esdras omits Ezra 4:6). In his reply Artaxerxes forbade the rebuilding of Jerusalem (2:25-29 [Gr. 2:19-24]; Ezra 4:17-22). Thus the work on the Temple was interrupted until the second year of Darius I (2:30 [Gr. 2:25 f.]; Ezra 4:23 f.).

4. *Zerubbabel's* (?) *victory in a debate at the court of Darius I and his reward—permission to rebuild the Temple* (3:1-5:6; retold, with changes, by Josephus in *Antiquities* 11:3). *a.* After a banquet (3:1-3), three guardsmen of Darius I wrote on separate slips what they considered the strongest of all things; and having sealed the slips, they placed them under the king's pillow in the expectation that the wisest of the three would be greatly honored and rewarded by Darius (3:4-9). The three youths wrote respectively: wine, the king, and "women are strongest, but truth triumphs over all things" (3:10-12). In the morning the king, surrounded by his princes and officials, invited each page to expound his view (3:13-17 [Gr. 3:13-16]).

b. The first one argued that wine, through intoxication, made the minds of all men, great and small, a blank (3:18-24 [Gr. 3:17-24]).

c. The second page maintained that men, though powerful, must obey the commands of the king (4:1-12).

d. The third one (Zerubbabel?) proved that women, as mothers and as wives, rule over men and even kings (4:13-32). But truth is supreme, for there is no unrighteousness in it as in wine and in men; it abides and rules forever (4:33-40).

e. Acclaimed as the victor by the audience (4:41) and asked to express his wish by the king (4:42), Zerubbabel merely requested that Darius, in accordance with his vow, rebuild Jerusalem and its Temple, and send back the sacred vessels which Cyrus had vowed to return to the Temple (4:43-46).

f. Darius at once issued orders to facilitate the return of the Jewish

Exiles, to provide the building material needed for Jerusalem, to free all Jews and to exempt their country from tribute, to restore their territory, to contribute to the costs of the restoration of the Temple and of its services; and he sent back the sacred vessels (4:47-57).

g. Zerubbabel praised God (4:58-60) and reported to the Babylonian Jews the king's measures; they celebrated joyfully for seven days (4:61-53). Then the Exiles went to Jerusalem (5:1-3); the most prominent in their midst are named in 5:4-6.

5. *Register of the Exiles who returned with Zerubbabel* (5:7-43 [Gr. 5:7-42]; Ezra 2:1-67; Neh. 7:6-69).

6. *The rebuilding of the Temple* (5:44-7:15 [Gr. 5:43-7:16]; Ezra 2:68-4:5; 4:24-6:22). *a.* Some of the leading returned Jews vowed to rebuild the Temple and made substantial contributions to its cost (5:44-46 [Gr. 5:43-45]; Ezra 2:68-70; Neh. 7:70-73a).

b. In the seventh month (Tishri) an altar was erected on Zion, the Feast of Tabernacles was celebrated, and the regular worship was resumed (5:47-53 [Gr. 5:46-52]; Ezra 3:1-6).

c. After some needed materials were provided (5:54 f. [Gr. 5:53]; Ezra 3:7), the building of the Temple was begun in the second year after the return, in the second month (5:56-65; [Gr. 5:54-62]; Ezra 3:8-13).

d. The enemies of the Jews (in Samaria) were not allowed to cooperate in the rebuilding, but succeeded in stopping the work until the second year of Darius I (5:66-73 [Gr. 5:63-71]; Ezra 4:1-5; 4:24).

e. In the second year of Darius, encouraged by Haggai and Zechariah, Zerubbabel and Joshua resumed the building of the Temple (6:1 f.; Ezra 5:1 f.), but Sisinnes* (Tattenai), the governor of Syria and Phoenicia, reported the matter to Darius (6:3-6; Ezra 5:3-5) in a letter (6:7-22 [Gr. 6:7-21]; Ezra 5:6-17). After a search in Ecbatana, the decree of Cyrus was discovered (6:23-26 [Gr. 6:22-25]; Ezra 6:1-5; cf. I Esdr. 2:3-7), and Darius ordered Sisinnes to allow the rebuilding of the Temple, to provide for the sacrifices at public expense, and to punish violators of this royal decree (6:27-34 [Gr. 6:26-33]; Ezra 6:6-12).

f. In accordance with the decree of Darius, the Temple was completed on the 23rd [the 3rd in Ezra] day of Adar, in the sixth year of Darius (516 B.C.), and solemnly dedicated (7:1-9; Ezra 6:13-18). The Passover was celebrated by the returned Exiles (7:10-15; Ezra 6:19-22).

7. *Ezra's journey to Jerusalem* (8:1-67 [Gr. 8:1-64]; Ezra 7:1-8:36). *a.* Ancestry of Esdras [Ezra] the scribe (8:1-3; Ezra 7:1-6a).

b. High in the favor of Artaxerxes, Ezra led a caravan of Exiles to Jerusalem (8:4-7; Ezra 7:6b-10) in accordance with a royal decree granting him extensive authority in Jerusalem (8:8-24; Ezra 7:11-26). Ezra blessed the Lord (8:25 f.; Ezra 7:27-28a).

c. Ezra gathered the Jews who would go with him from Babylonia to Jerusalem (8:27; Ezra 7:28b) and listed their names (8:28-40; Ezra 8:1-14). At the river Theras (Ezra: Ahava), Ezra noticed the absence of priests and Levites (Ezra: only Levites) from the caravan of returning Exiles, but persuaded a certain number of Levites and Temple servants to join him (8:41-49 [Gr. 8:41-48]; Ezra 8:15-20). After fasting to obtain God's protection, they set forth without any troops (8:50-53 [Gr. 8:49-53]; Ezra 8:21-23). The precious objects were placed in charge of the priests and Levites (8:54-60 [Gr. 8:54-59]; Ezra 8:24-30) and, three days after the arrival in Jerusalem, were deposited safely in the Temple (8:61-64 [Gr. 8:60-62]; Ezra 8:31-34). The returned Exiles offered sacrifice and presented the royal decree to the local authorities (8:65-67; [Gr. 8:63 f.]; Ezra 8:35 f.).

8. *Ezra's concern about mixed marriages* (8:68-9:36 [Gr. 8:65-9:36]; Ezra 9:1-10:44). *a.* Shocked at the toleration of marriages of Jews to Gentile wives (9:68-72 [Gr. 8:65-69]; Ezra 9:1-4), Ezra confessed the national sin to God, who had already shown his mercy to the people (8:73-90 [Gr. 8:70-87]; Ezra 9:5-15).

b. The crowd was stirred by Ezra's prayer, and Jechonias the son of Jeelus [Ezra: Shecaniah the son of Jehiel] urged the people to swear to divorce the foreign wives (8:91-95 [Gr. 8:88-91]; Ezra 10:1-4). So Ezra made the priests and Levites swear (8:96 [Gr. 8:92]; Ezra 10:5).

c. Three days later, in the national assembly, the multitude agreed to divorce foreign wives as Ezra had urged, but asked for the time required to do so (9:1-15; Ezra 10:6-16a). Ezra and others compiled a list of priests and Levites (9:16-25; Ezra 10:16b-24), and of laymen (9:26-36; Ezra 10:25-44), who had foreign wives. I Esdras (9:36) says that they repudiated them, together with their children; but Ezra 10:44 (possibly textually corrupt) seems to say that some of them had children from their wives.

9. *The reading of the Law* (9:37-55; Neh. 7:73-8:13a). On the new moon of the seventh month the congregation was assembled in the Temple (9:37-39; Neh. 7:73-8:1), and at their request Ezra read the Law in their presence (9:40-42; Neh. 8:2-4a), while prominent men stood by him (9:43-47; Neh. 8:4b-6) and the Levites explained it (9:48-53; Neh. 8:7-11). Then the people went away to celebrate and to send presents to the needy (9:54 f.; Neh. 8:12-13a).

1. Relation to Chronicles-Nehemiah

The preceding outline shows that I [III] Esdras is closely parallel to portions of the canonical books of Chronicles, Ezra, and Nehemiah; the only part of the book (aside from 1:23 f. [Gr. 1:21 f.]) that lacks its equivalent in the Hebrew Scriptures is the Story of the Three Youths at the Court of Darius and its sequel (3:1-4:42; 4:43-5:6). This story will be considered separately in a later section of this chapter; here we are concerned solely with the canonical parts of the book, and we shall inquire into their relation first to the Masoretic text, then to its Greek translation commonly called the "Septuagint" (LXX).

A. I Esdras and the Hebrew-Aramaic Text

The Hebrew and Aramaic text of II Chron. 35:1-36:21; Ezra 1-10 (only Ezra 4:6 is omitted in I Esdras); and Neh. 7:73-8:13a appears substantially in a free and idiomatic Greek version in our book, together with the Story of the Three Youths. But differences in the order of the narratives, omissions from the canonical book, and textual variants are obvious. Since the differences are confined to the form and seldom affect the substance, it is unnecessary to examine here the historicity and literary history of the original narratives: these problems are investigated in connection with the canonical books (Chronicles, Ezra, Nehemiah) and have been discussed, for instance, in the present writer's *Introduction to the Old Testament* (pp. 813-838, in particular).

We may assume from the start that Esdras is a translation from a Hebrew-Aramaic original and not, as a few scholars of the last century believed,[2] a revision of our "Septuagint" of Chronicles-Ezra-Nehemiah. This has been demonstrated by E. Nestle (*Marginalien,* pp. 23-29. Tübingen, 1893). A few typical examples, chosen among many, show that I Esdras is the translation of a Hebrew-Aramaic original not always identical with the text from which the LXX was translated. Esd. 1:10 (Gr. 1:11) is a translation of *massoth* (unleavened bread), not of *kemiswath ha-melek* (according to the commandment of the king) in II Chron. 35:2 (Hebrew and LXX). In 1:11 (Gr. 1:12) we read "before the people" (Hebr. *liphnê hā-'ām*) instead of "of the children of the people" (Hebr. *libhnê hā-'ām*) in II Chron. 35:12. Esd. 9:2 reads *wyln* (and he lodged) instead of *wylk* (and he went), as given by Ezra 10:6. In some cases the identical Hebrew (or Aramaic) words were translated differently: *wyhzqm* (II Chron. 35:2) is rendered "arrayed [in their vestments]" in Esd. 1:2, but "and he encouraged them" in the LXX; *'štdwr 'bdyn* appears as "carrying on sieges" in Esd. 2:23 (Gr. 2:17),

[2] C. F. Keil, *Lehrbuch der historisch-kritischen Einleitung in die kanonischen und apokryphischen Schriften des Alten Testamentes,* p. 679. 2nd ed., Frankfurt, 1859; p. 704 in the 3rd ed., 1873. E. C. Bissell, *The Apocrypha of the Old Testament.* New York, 1880. O. Zöckler, *Die Apokryphen des Alten Testaments* (in Strack and Zöckler, *Kurzgefasster Kommentar,* Vol. IX). München, 1891. E. Schürer, "Apokryphen des A. T." (J. Herzog, *Realenzyklopädie für Protest. Theol. und Kirche,* 2nd ed. Leipzig, 1877-1888) and in the first two editions of his *Geschichte des Jüdischen Volkes;* see Vol. 2, p. 713, in the 2nd ed. and the English translation: *A History of the Jewish People,* Vol. 2, Pt. iii, pp. 177 ff. Edinburgh, 1886-1890). E. König, *Einleitung in das Alte Testament,* p. 480. Bonn, 1893.

cf. 2:27 (Gr. 2:21), but as "places of refuge for slaves" in Ezra 4:15, cf. 4:19.

It is true that occasionally the two Greek texts agree rather closely. In some cases they use the same unfamiliar words, for instance, *ekoúphisas*, literally "thou didst alleviate," in the sense of reducing the guilt or punishment for sins (Esd. 8:86 [Gr. 8:84] and Ezra 9:13); and the rare words *lipásmata* (fattening foods; not occurring elsewhere in the LXX, but only in later versions, in Is. 25:6) and *glykásmata* (sweets, sweet drinks; unknown before the LXX, where it occurs elsewhere only in Prov. 16:24 and Ecclus. 11:3) used in I Esd. 9:51 and II Esd. 18:10 (LXX), which translate Neh. 8:10. In one instance both texts (Esd. 1:11 [Gr. 1:12]; I Chron. 35:12) agree in a vocalization at variance with the Masoretic one: they interpret *lbqr* in I Chron. 35:12 as "in the morning" (*labbôqer*, cf. some Hebrew manuscripts; the Syriac has "every morning") in contrast with the Masoretic *labbāqār* ("in regard to the oxen"; so the Vulgate). Both versions misunderstand "in pans" (II Chron. 35:13): I Esd. 1:12 [Gr. 1:13] reads *met' euōdías* ("with fragrance," which, as J. G. Eichhorn recognized in 1795, is presumably an error for *met' euodías*, "with luck"), and II Chron. 35:13 [LXX] *euōdóthē*, "prospered"; but I Esdras is more accurate in translating the verb in the following verse ("and they set them") than the LXX of II Chronicles ("and they ran"). Similarly both versions misunderstand "and he disguised himself" in II Chron. 35:22 (I Esd. 1:28 [Gr. 1:26]; cf. C. C. Torrey, *Ezra Studies*, p. 221, n. 16. Chicago, 1910); and they give to "with force and power" in Ezra 4:23 (inverting the order of the nouns) the meaning of "with horses and power" (LXX) or "with horse and mob" (I Esd. 2:30 [Gr. 2:25]): *hayil* (power) actually means "horses, cavalry" in Arabic and "power, army" in Syriac. In other cases the two versions agree in the terminology when translating our standard Hebrew-Aramaic text (cf. B. Walde, *Die Esdrasbücher der Septuaginta*, pp. 11 f. Bibl. Studien XVIII:4, Freiburg i. B., 1913). Nevertheless, the differences in textual recension, vocabulary, and syntax are so numerous and so characteristic (cf. B. Walde, *op. cit.*, pp. 15-26) that the two Greek texts must be regarded as substantially independent translations, even though the later one may have occasionally made use of the earlier one, unless they both are revisions of an earlier version now lost, as H. Ewald believed (*History of Israel*, Vol. 5, pp. 126-128. London, 1869-83), cf. R. Smend (*Die Listen der Bucher Esras und Nehemias*, p. 16. Leipzig, 1901), and H. St. J. Thackeray (in J. Hastings, *A Dictionary of the Bible*, Vol. 1, p. 759. Edinburgh, 1898).

The mutual relation of the Greek texts will be considered later. Here, having recognized that the Greek Esdras—at least in its canonical parts —is a version from a Semitic original, we must inquire into the relation of this Semitic text to the parallel passages in the Hebrew Bible. The lost original of the Greek Ezra and the parallels in the Masoretic text differ in textual recension, sequence of the stories, and contents, but unquestionably are merely different editions of a text which was still in a state of flux.

1. *Textual differences between the Greek Ezra and the Hebrew Bible.* The reconstruction of the Hebrew-Aramaic prototype of the Greek Ezra presents great difficulties, owing to the translator's blunders and liberties, but, except for some doubtful passages, is not impossible. In general this prototype agrees with the Masoretic text; all instances in which the meaning of the Greek Ezra differs from that of the Masoretic text (whether the variations of the Greek rest on mistranslations or actual variants) are conveniently listed by W. J. Moulton ("Über die Überlieferung und den textkritischen Wert des dritten Esrabuchs" in ZAW 19 [1899] 209-258; 20 [1900] 1-35). In order to determine the instances in which the Semitic prototype of I Esdras really differed from the Masoretic text, the following divergences of the Greek from the Hebrew-Aramaic extant text must be disregarded.

a. Free, idiomatic renderings of the same text. The translator fails to discriminate between the divine names *Lord* and *God*, generally preferring *Lord*, and renders freely divine titles, activities, precepts, and objects (ZAW 19 [1899] 226-230; cf. B. Walde, *Die Esdrasbücher der Septuaginta,* pp. 15-17). He seldom reproduces Semitic idioms verbatim (three instances are given by E. Bayer, *Das Dritte Buch Esdras,* p. 11. [Bibl. Studien XVI, 1]. Freiburg i. B., 1911), preferring Greek forms of speech (examples are given by B. Walde, *op. cit.,* pp. 20 f.). Thus, characteristically, he always renders "beyond the river" (the country west of the Euphrates) with "Coele-Syria and Phoenicia" or "Syria and Phoenicia" (cf. C. C. Torrey, *Ezra Studies,* p. 83), an expression unknown elsewhere in the Septuagint except in II and IV Maccabees. He prefers participial clauses (Walde, *op. cit.,* pp. 18 f.), rendering, for instance, "I did not find there and I sent . . ." with "not having found there I sent" (I Esd. 8:42 f.); or "according to the hand of the Lord his God upon him" (Ezra 7:6) with "having found favor in his sight" (I Esd. 8:4). He does not always reproduce the order of words in the Hebrew-Aramaic (Walde, *op. cit.,* pp. 55 f.) and otherwise translates freely (*ibid.,* pp. 57-62), adding explanatory words (*ibid.,* pp. 62-65), omitting unnecessary clauses (*ibid.,* pp. 69 f.), and paraphrasing as he sees fit (*ibid.,* pp. 65-69).

b. Incorrect translations. The translator (I Esd. 6:8) joins "all" at the end of Ezra 5:7 to what follows and translates ". . . greeting. Let *all* things be known . . ." instead of ". . . *all* peace. Let it be known . . ." Through his tendency to condense, he renders (8:62 [Gr. 8:61]) "And when the third day came, the silver and gold were weighed . . ." instead of "We remained there three days and on the fourth the silver and gold and the vessels were weighed . . ." (Ezra 8:32 f.). Conversely, he says "in two or three days" (9:4) instead of "in three days" (Ezra 10:8). Definitely alien to Hebrew grammar is his rendering "on the new moon of the seventh month" (9:37) instead of "the seventh month" (Neh. 7:73), unless his text read *hōdeš* (without the article) instead of *hā-hōdeš*. For other examples see Walde, *op. cit.*, pp. 70 f.

c. Omissions due to insufficient knowledge of the true meaning of certain words. Some of the Persian and Babylonian words occurring in the Aramaic sections (discussed by C. C. Torrey, *Ezra Studies*, pp. 174-177) were obviously unfamiliar to the translator. In some cases he merely guessed the correct meaning from the context (so for the first three in Torrey's list) but in other instances he left out the obscure words. Thus in 2:19 (Gr. 2:15) he merely gives "tribute" for three Babylonian words (Ezra 4:13, 20; 7:24) indicating three types of taxation (similarly in 2:27 [Gr. 2:22]; 8:22), and leaves the mysterious word *'appethōm* or *'appethōs* (Ezra 4:13; the meanings "revenue," "damage," or "finally" have been suggested) untranslated. The so-called "Septuagint" is equally at a loss in these passages. Another word, occurring in a Hebrew section (Ezra 8:27; cf. I Chron. 29:7), is left untranslated in I Esd. 8:57 (Gr. 8:56): darics (or drachmae); it also puzzled the "LXX," which rendered "gold" in I Chronicles and "to the way *chamanim*" in Ezra (translating the first part of the Hebrew word [*derek*, way] and transliterating the second); Codex A reads "of drachmae *ein*" (with a remnant of the transliteration at the end) and Lucian, combining two readings, "on the way drachmas."

d. Accidental omissions. B. Walde (*Die Ezrabücher*, p. 72) explains the omissions in 1:7, 10, 42 (Gr. 1:44) as due to changes in the order of the words, and those in 1:12, 30, 35, 42, 46, 49 (Gr. 1:13, 32, 37, 44, 48, 51); 5:40, etc. (*ibid.* pp. 72 f.) as resulting from skipping over words located between identical expressions (homoeoteleuton). Other miscellaneous omissions (*ibid.* pp. 73 f.), such as that of the word "all," left untranslated twenty-one times, are probably dictated by the endeavor to produce a smooth and idiomatic translation.

e. Double translations. The translator often gives both possible meanings of a Hebrew or Aramaic word, for instance: "singing hymns to the Lord and praising" (Esd. 5:60 [Gr. 5:57]) for "to praise the Lord" (Ezra 3:10); "and all the people blew trumpets and shouted" (Ezra 3:11). But in some of the instances listed by B. Walde (*op. cit.* pp. 81-88) the prototype used by the translator may have differed slightly from our Masoretic text (so possibly in 2:22-24 [Gr. 2:17 f.]; 5:50 [Gr. 5:49]; 6:25, 28 [Gr. 6:24, 27]).

f. Corruptions of the Greek text. B. Walde (*op. cit.*, pp. 88-92) lists glosses and textual errors which can hardly be attributed to the translator, but are the result of accidents in the later textual transmission.

The preceding textual differences between the Greek Ezra and the Masoretic text may be safely disregarded in a comparison between the text from which Esdras was translated and that of the standard Hebrew Bible. In other instances, however, the matter is not so clear. When the Greek obviously rests on a slightly different and presumably erroneous Semitic text, it is difficult to decide whether the error stood in the proto-type used for the Greek translation or whether the translator read wrongly a badly written word or clause. In listing such errors, B. Walde (*op. cit.*, pp. 74-81) is inclined to adopt the second alternative, without excluding the validity of the first in isolated instances. In reality, however, Walde's list includes cases in which the differences are due to divergent vocalization of the same consonantal text, as in Esd. 2:9 (Gr. 2:6) "horses" (*rekeš*) instead of "goods" (*rekûš*) in Ezra 1:6; or to a confusion of *s* and *sh*(*š*), which were not yet distinguished by the position of a dot as in modern Hebrew: "the chief men with the women" (*hā-sarîm wehā-sarôth*) in 1:32 (Gr. 1:30) instead of "the singing men and women" (*hā-šarîm wehā-šarôth*) in II Chron. 35:25. Other differences, however, must be explained through a prototype at variance with our Hebrew Bible.

In twenty instances the Greek Ezra has actually preserved a better textual recension than the Hebrew Bible (Walde, *op. cit.*, pp. 92-96). A few characteristic examples will illustrate how occasionally the Greek Esdras alone has preserved the original reading and thus enables us to remedy a textual corruption of the Masoretic text. The unintelligible Hebrew text on II Chron. 35:21, "Not against thee, thou ['*attah*], to-day, for unto ['*el*, an error for '*al*, against] the house (*bêth*) of my war," should be revised, in accordance with Esd. 1:27 (Gr. 1:25), to read "I have not been sent ['*ōthêh*, literally, "I come"] by the Lord God against thee, for my war is upon the Euphrates [*perath*, instead of *bêth*; cf. Josephus, *Antiquities* X, 5:1 (§75)]." Presumably the date, "in the second year of Darius' reign" (Esd. 6:1), has accidentally dropped out of Ezra 5:1, unless it was transferred to the preceding verse (4:24); other acci-dental omissions in Ezra 5:8; 6:7, 15; 10:3 may be corrected with the help of Esd. 6:8 f., 27 (Gr. 6:8, 26); 7:5; 8:93 (Gr. 8:90), respectively.

Finally, in the transcription of personal and geographic names the Greek Ezra differs often and radically from the Masoretic text, but only occasionally does it bear witness to better readings; for details see E. Bayer, *Das Dritte Buch Esdras*, pp. 36-72; and B. Walde, *op. cit.*, pp. 96-107).

This cursory textual comparison of the Greek Ezra with the parallel passages in the Hebrew Bible proves beyond cavil that I Esdras was

translated from a text substantially identical with the Masoretic text. The
differences are due either to mistakes made by the translator and errors
resulting from the transmission of the Greek text or to slight recensional
differences in the two forms of the original text. The Greek Ezra "is
simply a piece taken without change out of the middle of a faithful Greek
translation of the Chronicler's History of Israel" (C. C. Torrey, *Ezra
Studies,* p. 18).

2. *Differences in contents and sequence between the Greek Ezra and
Ezra-Nehemiah.* The following table may serve to show these differences
at a glance. References are to the English (*not* the Greek) Bible:

I (III) Esdras	Ezra-Nehemiah (E.-N.)	Josephus, Ant. XI, 1-5
Cyrus (2:1-15)	Cyrus (E. 1:1-11)	Cyrus
Artaxerxes (2:16-30)	(*Cf.* E. 4:7-24)	Cambyses
Darius I (3:1-5:6)	———	Darius I
Darius I [?] (5:7-46)	Cyrus (E. 2; N. 7)	"
Cyrus (5:47-73)	Cyrus (E. 3:1-4:5,24)	"
———	Xerxes (E. 4:6)	———
(*Cf. 2:16-30*)	Artaxerxes (E. 4:7-24)	[see *Cambyses*]
Darius I (6-7)	Darius I (E. 5-6)	Darius I
Artaxerxes (8-9)	Artaxerxes (E. 7-10; N. 7:73-8:13a)	Xerxes

It is apparent from this table that only Josephus observes the actual
chronological sequence of the Persian kings. The canonical Ezra and
even more the Greek Esdras list the kings in a capricious order.[3] In fact,
in Esd. 2:16-5:73 (Gr. 2:12-5:71) the historical order is actually reversed:
Artaxerxes, Darius, Cyrus, instead of Cyrus, Darius, Artaxerxes (not to
speak of the omission of Cambyses and Xerxes). In Ezra 3-5, Xerxes and
Artaxerxes are erroneously inserted between Cyrus and Darius. It seems
apparent from the table that in both books these anachronisms result
from the insertion of narratives in the wrong place: if we remove from
I Esdras the section 2:16-5:73 (Gr. 2:12-5:71), or only 2:16-5:6 (Gr.
2:12-5:6) if 5:7-73 (Gr. 5:7-71) is dated in the time of Cyrus as in Ezra,
and from Ezra the section 4:6-24 (in which 4:24 is harmonistic), the
dynastic sequence is correct in both books.

This situation has puzzled the critics, and they have explained it by
having recourse to one of the three sole possibilities: Ezra is a modification of I Esdras; or I Esdras is derived from Ezra; or both recensions
are descended from a common prototype.

The first hypothesis, according to which I Esdras presents the original

[3] An extremely ingenious explanation of the abnormal order of Persian kings in
Jewish literature has been suggested by C. C. Torrey ("Medes and Persians" in
JAOS 66 [1946] 1-15).

form of the history and is the source of the canonical recension, was presented most forcefully by Sir Henry Howorth, particularly in a series of articles entitled "Some Unconventional Views on the Text of the Bible" (published in PSBA 23 [1901] and 24 [1902]; later articles in this series deal with other matters). He concluded that the order and contents of I Esdras are primary and correct, while the canonical Ezra-Nehemiah is the product of rabbinical rearrangement and curtailment. With the exception of J. Marquart (*Fundamente israelitischer und jüdischer Geschichte.* Göttingen, 1896. P. 42), J. Theis (*Geschichtliche und literarkritische Fragen in Ezra* 1-6, AA II, 5. Münster i. W., 1910, pp. 82 ff.), and P. Riessler,[4] no scholar has apparently shown the slightest inclination to defend this view which, upon close examination, presents insurmountable difficulties.

The second hypothesis, according to which I Esdras is the result of a tendentious revision and rearrangement of the canonical books, is generally held.[5] The most thorough defense of this theory is that of B. Walde (*Die Ezrabücher der Septuaginta*). He concludes that I Esdras is an independent book, preserved almost completely, written in Egypt, composed in Greek (on the basis of the first Greek translation of our canonical books) during the period 150-100 B.C. Walde thus takes issue with E. Bayer (*Das Dritte Buch Esdras*), who also regarded I Esdras as an independent book, but believed that it was composed in Aramaic-Hebrew and later translated into Greek. The latest advocate of the dependence of I Esdras on the canonical books, in their present form, O. Eissfeldt (*Einleitung in das Alte Testament*, p. 632. Tübingen, 1934), does not commit himself with regard to the original language of I Esdras, merely noting that the compiler of the book used Ezra-Nehemiah and that our Greek Esdras represents or presupposes an older and better translation than the so-called LXX of Ezra-Nehemiah.

The third possibility, namely, that I Esdras and the canonical books are derived from a common source (the Chronicler's original book), has been presented with great originality and acumen by C. C. Torrey (AJSL 23 [1907] 116-141; reprinted in his *Ezra Studies*, pp. 11-36). His conclusions may be summarized as follows: The contents and sequence of the Chronicler's history were originally as follows: I and II Chronicles; Ezra 1; I Esd. 4:47-56; 4:62-5:6; Ezra 2:1-8:36; Neh. 7:70-8:18; Ezra

---

[4] After comparing individual passages in I Esd. and in the Hebrew Bible, P. Riessler concludes that "the prototype of I (III) Esd. is earlier and better than the one of the Masoretic Text" (BZ 5 [1907] 157). He considers the canonical book of Ezra as a revision of an earlier form preserved in I Esd. (BZ 2 [1904] 148, n. 1). Ultimately he derives both recensions from a Babylonian prototype (BZ 4 [1906] 113-118). G. Jahn (*Die Bücher Ezra [A und B] und Nehemja.* Leiden, 1909) regards the Hebrew prototype of I Esd. as earlier than the canonical books.

[5] See, for bibliography, B. Walde, *Die Ezrabücher der Septuaginta*, pp. 4-6.

9:1-10:44; Neh. 9:1-10:39 (H. 9:1-10:40); Neh. 1:1-7:69; 11:1-13-31. Soon after 200 B.C. (*Ezra Studies*, p. 339, top of the page) three chapters belonging to the story of Ezra (Neh. 7:70-8:18; 9:1-10:39 [H. 9:1-10:40]) were "accidentally transposed" to the book of Nehemiah, the Story of the Three Youths was interpolated, and Ezra 4:6-24 was transposed before this story. Later Neh. 7:73-10:39 (H. 7:73-10:40) was appended to the story of Ezra, following Ezra 10, while Neh. 7:70-72 was left in Nehemiah's book. At the beginning of the Christian Era two editions of the Chronicler's book were in circulation: both contained the interpolated Story of the Three Youths, but they differed in regard to the position of Neh. 7:73-10:39 (H. 7:73-10:40), which stood in the same place as in the Hebrew Bible in one, but after Ezra 10 in the other. The text in the Hebrew Bible was descended from the first of these recensions, that of I Esdras from the second. At the beginning of the second century of our era, when the canon of the Hebrew Scriptures was fixed for all time, the Story of the Three Youths, being recognized as an interpolation, was removed from the first recension, together with a part of the Chronicler's story (preserved in I Esd. 4:47b-56; 4:62-5:6). The Greek translation of the second recension (i.e., I Esdras), prepared before 150 B.C., was used by Josephus, and has been preserved without radical changes—except for the loss of its beginning and end. Of the condemned second recension, only a fragment (beginning with II Chron. 35:1 and ending with Neh. 8:13) has survived accidentally in our I Esdras, which is not a "book" but the torso of one.[6]

Like C. C. Torrey, G. Hölscher (in E. Kautzsch, *Die Heilige Schrift des Alten Testaments* (4th ed., edited by A. Bertholet, Vol. 2, pp. 495 f. Tübingen, 1923) believes that both the canonical Chronicles-Ezra-Nehemiah and I Esdras were derived from the Chronicler's history.[7] But Hölscher avoids one serious difficulty in Torrey's theory, namely, the excision of a portion of the Chronicler's work (the Story of the Three Youths) from the Hebrew text at the time of the fixation of the canon. The reverence for the text to the last letter exhibited by Akiba and his colleagues at the time militates against such an excision. According to Hölscher, the Chronicler's history, supplemented with the dossier of Aramaic letters, gave for the Persian period only the stories of Zerubbabel

---

[6] In *The Apocryphal Literature* (p. 48. Yale University Press, 1945), C. C. Torrey concludes that I Esdras "does not represent the original form of this portion of the Chronicler's history" but a popular revision thereof which was the sole form of that history circulating in the first century B.C. The canonical text of Ezra-Nehemiah, dating from the second century of our era, is a revision of the earlier text known through I Ezra.

[7] S. Mowinckel (*Statholderen Nehemia; Ezra den Skriftlaerde.* Studier til den jødiske menighets historie og litteratur, I and II. Kristiania, 1916) reaches conclusions similar to Hölscher's.

and Ezra (not Nehemiah's). This text, supplemented with the Story of the Three Youths and some glosses,[8] was rearranged (Ezra 4:6-24 was placed before the Story of the Three Youths) and revised on the basis of the canonical text (cf. I Esd. 9:37 with Neh. 7:72): thus originated the I Esdras recension. The Memoirs of Nehemiah were inserted into the Chronicler's work *after* the compilation of the I Esdras recension, for they were still a separate book in the time of Ben Sira and when II Macc. 2:13 was written. In addition to Nehemiah's Memoirs, the following passages of the canonical Ezra are later supplements: 4:6-24; 5:3-6, 14a, 15; 7:11-26.

The present writer agrees with Torrey, Mowinckel, and Hölscher in regarding the canonical books and I Esdras as different recensions of the Chronicler's history, but without accepting all their individual conclusions about the process of transmission. It is indeed difficult to see how one recension could be derived from the other, but their similarities and differences are readily explained if they have a common source. This prototype presumably contained the material common to both, including the Artaxerxes correspondence (Ezra 4:7-24; I Esd. 2:16-30 [Gr. 2:12-30]) and possibly even Ezra 4:6, although these passages may not have been in the Chronicler's first edition of his work. But the material appearing in only one text could hardly have been in the prototype. Ancient editors were more prone to supplement than to curtail the histories they were revising, unless some material offended their sensibilities. We may accordingly surmise that the common source consisted of I-II Chronicles; Ezra 1-10; Neh. 7:5-8:13 ff., probably without Neh. 13. I Esd. found Neh. 7:5-72 in his prototype (since he reproduces its conclusion, 7:73a), but omitted it as a duplicate of Ezra 2 (reproduced in I Esd. 5:7-47 [Gr. 5:7-46]). That the Memoirs of Nehemiah were still read by Sirach (180 B.C.) as a separate book and not as part of the Chronicler's history was recognized, before Mowinckel and Hölscher, by Th. Nöldeke (ZAW 20 [1900] 89). It is even possible that Josephus read Nehemiah as a separate book in Greek (even though he dates both Ezra and Nehemiah in the time of Xerxes, reserving Artaxerxes for Esther), since he deals with Ezra in *Antiquities* XI, 5:1-5 (§§120-158), and with Nehemiah in 5:6-8 (§§159-183). To the common prototype, the Story of the Three Youths was added in I Esdras, causing the transposition of the Artaxerxes correspondence, with the resulting chronological chaos, and Nehemiah's Memoirs were added in the canonical text. Other differences between the two redactions are due to accidents in transmission and editorial revisions. Incidentally, in the prototype and in I Esdras (which is here the more archaic recension), the separation of Ezra from Chronicles, as a distinct

[8] I Esd. 1:23 f. (Gr. 1:21 f.); 3:12b; "this is Zerubbabel" in 4:13; 4:33-41; 4:43-5:6.

book, had not yet taken place. To go beyond such general conclusions seems precarious, considering our limited evidence.

B. I Esdras and the "LXX"

The conclusions reached in regard to the relation of the Greek Ezra to its Hebrew-Aramaic parallels in the canonical Scriptures, whatever they may be, do not solve the problem of the relation of the two extant Greek texts, I Esdras and the "LXX" of Chron.-Ezra-Neh. This problem must be examined per se.

It may be assumed from the beginning that the two Greek versions were made independently (even though mutual influence is not to be excluded entirely) from two Hebrew-Aramaic texts which were substantially identical. We have noted that the view that I Esdras is merely a revision of the "LXX" has been disproved once for all by E. Nestle, and is now generally regarded as absurd (cf., for details, B. Walde, *Die Ezrabücher der Septuaginta*, pp. 11-26). It could, however, be argued, as H. St. J. Thackeray does (J. Hastings, *Dictionary of the Bible*, Vol. 1, p. 759), that both versions "are to some extent dependent on a lost original," like the two Greek versions of Daniel. This view, which finds support only in a few verbal parallels between the two versions, fails to do justice to the differences in text (illustrated above) and in style. These discrepancies are so far-reaching that they presuppose not revisions of a hypothetical prototype, but its radical rewriting; it seems to be far more plausible to regard the two Greek texts as independent translations.

While I Esdras differs from the Masoretic text in numerous passages, as has been noted, the "LXX" translator reproduces it exactly, except when he failed to understand it (notably in the Aramaic parts) or when his text differed from the extant one (in some instances preserving lost passages; cf. C. C. Torrey, *Ezra Studies*, pp. 87-90). The characteristics of the two versions in the matter of style may be summarized as follows:

The "LXX" translator of the canonical books, in reproducing the Hebrew-Aramaic verbatim, frequently used Semitic expressions and turns of phrase utterly alien to the Greek speech. He made no attempt to write consistently intelligible and idiomatic Greek. One example sufficiently illustrates his procedure: "And they performed the Feast of Tents [Tabernacles] according to the written, and the burnt offerings day in day in number like the judgment a word of the day in its day" (Ezra 3:4, "LXX"). This English gibberish is no more incomprehensible than the Greek from which I have literally translated it! Contrast the free, idiomatic version in I Esd. 5:51 (Gr. 5:50): "And they celebrated the Feast of Tabernacles, as it is commanded in the Law, and sacrifices daily, as it was proper."

In accordance with this concern for the literal rendition of the sacred text our translator regularly reproduces Semitic idioms unchanged, into inelegant Greek: the contrast with I Esdras is particularly obvious in such instances.[9] "The house" is translated literally (*oîkos*) even when it means "the Temple" (*hierón* in I Esdras); the Hebrew idiom "sons of the Exile" (or "of the people, of Judea," etc.) is left unchanged, while I Esdras says "those of the Exile," etc.; his literal "beyond the river" is given idiomatically as "Coele-Syria [or Syria] and Phoenicia" in I Esdras; the idiom meaning "to give instructions" is reproduced woodenly as "to place an opinion" ("to command, decree, write," or the like, in I Esdras); he punctiliously says "day one" meaning the "first day [of the month]" (I Esdras has "the new moon"), "kids from the children of the goats" (II Chron. 35:7; merely "kids" in I Esd. 1:7), and "sons of oxen" (Ezra 6:9; "bulls" in I Esd. 6:29 [Gr. 6:28]).

Another evidence of this translator's concern with the letter of the sacred text is his tendency to transliterate the words which he does not fully understand or which he, out of caution or punctiliousness, wishes to preserve intact. C. C. Torrey presents a list of seventy transliterations in the Greek Chronicles-Ezra-Nehemiah (*Old Testament and Semitic Studies in Memory of William R. Harper*. Vol. 2, pp. 64-71. Chicago, 1908. Reproduced in his *Ezra Studies*, pp. 70-77.)

The literalness of the "LXX" translator appears also in the syntax. He uses "of the king" instead of "royal" in I Esdras (contrast, e.g., II Chron. 35:7 with I Esd. 1:7), and the finite verb instead of the participle found in the more idiomatic version of I Esdras as, for instance, "and he set the priests . . ." (II Chron. 35:2) instead of "having set the priests" (I Esd. 1:2); cf. vv. 5 and 6, etc. The "LXX" retains the infinitive of the Hebrew, while I Esdras uses the participle: for instance, "and in the second year of their coming . . ." (Ezra 3:8), but, "and in the second year after he had come [part.]" (I Esd. 5:56 [Gr. 5:54]). While the "LXX" reproduces mechanically the Hebrew or Aramaic forms, I Esdras uses the participle in the genitive absolute (I Esd. 1:22 [Gr. 1:20]; 2:1; 7:3; 8:1, 4, 68 [Gr. 8:65]; etc.).

In contrast with the slavishness of the "LXX," I Esdras renders the original with great freedom, correctness, and even elegance. Not only are Semitic idioms avoided and participial constructions freely used, as has been noted above, but there is no effort to preserve the order of words in a series. On the contrary, the order is changed frequently and arbitrarily (for a list of examples, see Walde, *op. cit.*, pp. 55 f.), for no sensible reason that we can discover, as in 1:49 (Gr. 1:47), "the leaders of the people and of the priests" ("of the priests and of the people" in II Chron. 36:14). There is no consistency in the order of the parts of speech, for the direct object may precede or follow either the verb or

[9] See B. Walde, *Die Ezrabücher*, pp. 17-22.

the indirect object, the subject may stand before or after the verb: such variations may have been used for stylistic effects. In other ways the translation is very far from literal (cf. Walde, pp. 57-62), and at times it becomes an interpretation rather than a rendition, as in the substitution of "sacrifices" (1:17 [Gr. 1:16]) for "service" (II Chron. 35:16); of "people" (1:36 [Gr. 1:34]) for "land" (II Chron. 36:3); of "give him" (8:19) for "let it be done" (Ezra 7:11); etc. With no concern for literal accuracy, I Esdras omits or adds words and clauses and introduces other changes in the interests of clarity (Walde, pp. 62-74). Even when he misunderstands the original (as in 1:10-12 [Gr. 1:11-13], 38 [Gr. 36]), he produces a plausible narrative, at least in appearance.

It is thus clear, even from this brief list of typical differences, that the two translations are radically unlike in style. The "LXX" discloses servile conformity to the Hebrew and Aramaic original, at the cost of clarity, and thus fails to attain even the pretense of Greek idiomatic expression, not to speak of distinction in diction. On the contrary, I Esdras offers a free version in idiomatic and elegant Greek, perfectly intelligible to readers unacquainted with the original because the translator avoided Hebraisms, made guesses (cf. 2:9 [Gr. 2:8]; 6:4, 9 [Gr. 6:10]) or omissions when he failed to understand the original, and, having command of a rich vocabulary (see W. J. Moulton's list of words in ZAW 19 [1899] 232-234) and familiarity with Greek syntax, was able to express himself lucidly and elegantly. Everything thus indicates that the two translations were made separately, even though the later one may have occasionally utilized the earlier one, and mutual contamination in the course of transmission is not to be excluded.

This raises the problem of the relative dates of the two versions. The search for a solution has been seriously hampered by the intrusion of the meaningless debate about which of the two is the "Septuagint" (LXX) translation. It is idle to call any Greek version of Biblical books other than the Pentateuch (or at most the Pentateuch and the Prophets) the "LXX." The extant texts of the "LXX" are (except for a few early papyrus fragments) a miscellany of separate translations of Biblical books with important differences between the texts used in the various Christian centers. It is generally impossible to determine the original Greek text officially used by the Jews in Alexandria.[10] Consequently, it is critically precarious, if not unsound, to identify either the canonical translation of Chronicles-Ezra-Nehemiah with the "Septuagint" as B. Walde does, or, on the contrary, to regard I Esdras as a fragment of the original "Septuagint" (so Sir H. Howorth, in the *Academy* for 1893 [I, 13], and others).

[10] "Would it not be better," asks C. C. Torrey (*Ezra Studies*, p. 17, n. 4) with good reason, "in the interests of clearness and accuracy, to cease altogether from using the term 'Septuagint' in scientific treatises?"

Leaving the ambiguous and misleading term "Septuagint" out of the discussion, the most plausible conclusions seem to be the following: I Esdras is the extant fragment of a Greek translation of Chronicles-Ezra-Nehemiah made in Alexandria not later than 150 B.C.; the scanty pertinent evidence is adduced by C. C. Torrey, *Ezra Studies*, pp. 82-87. In all probability this translation was the first Greek rendering of the Chronicler's history and was used by Josephus in the first century A.D. Soon, however, it was lost, except for a fragment, called I Esdras, which enjoyed considerable popularity in the early Christian Church, as shown by two recensions of the Old Latin version of it (cf. H. C. York, "The Latin Versions of I Esdras," in AJSL 26 [1910] 253-302), the Syro-Hexaplar version of Paul of Tella, dating from 616-617 (cf. C. C. Torrey, *Ezra Studies*, pp. 1-5), the Ethiopic version (edited by A. Dillmann in 1894), and the references to the Story of the Three Youths in patristic literature (A. A. Pohlmann, "Über das Ansehen des apokryphischen dritten Buchs Esras," in *Tübing. Theologische Quartalschrift* 51 [1859] 257-275; cf. E. Schürer, *Geschichte des Jüdischen Volkes*, 4th ed., Vol. 3, p. 447). Origen included I Esdras in the fifth column of his Hexapla—the column giving the Septuagint. But following the adverse verdict of Jerome (*Preface to Ezra-Nehemiah*), who rejected I Esdras because it was outside of the Hebrew canon of Scriptures, the book lost prestige in the Latin Church: it was omitted from the Complutensian Polyglot and failed to be recognized as canonical at the Council of Trent (cf. H. Pope, in JTS 8 [1907] 218-232), so that in the editions of the Vulgate it is printed as an appendix to the New Testament.

Eventually, this ancient Greek version was discarded in favor of a later one. Exactly so, the old version of Daniel (extant only in the Chigi manuscript and in Paul of Tella's Syro-Hexaplar version), still included in Origen's *Hexapla* as the Septuagint but not cited in his other works, ceased to be read in the churches when Theodotion's recension took its place (Jerome, *Preface to Daniel*), in accordance with Origen's own practice. As a matter of fact Theodotion's edition of Daniel was preferred even before Origen's time (cf. H. B. Swete, *An Introduction to the Old Testament in Greek*, pp. 47 f. Cambridge, 1900; J. A. Montgomery, *Daniel* [in the ICC], pp. 46-50. New York, 1927). It has even been suggested by J. Gwynn (*Diction. of Christ. Biogr.* IV, 977, n.), H. St. J. Thackeray (Hastings' *Dictionary of the Bible* I, 761 b), P. Riessler (*Das Buch Daniel*, pp. 52-56. Stuttgart and Vienna, 1899), and C. C. Torrey (*Ezra Studies*, pp. 84 f.) that I Esdras and the "LXX" of Daniel are the work of the same translator. The canonical "LXX" translation of Chronicles-Ezra-Nehemiah has been attributed to Theodotion (who, according to Jerome, was responsible for the later translation of Daniel) by Sir H. Howorth (*Academy* 43 [1893] 13; PSBA 24 [1902] 167; later, in PSBA 29

[1907] 32 f., he attributed it to Symmachus or Aquila), P. Riessler (BZ 5 [1907] 146), C. C. Torrey (*Old Test. and Sem. Studies in Memory of W. R. Harper*, II, 60-76 [1908] and *Ezra Studies*, pp. 66-82; criticized by B. Walde, *Die Ezrabücher*, pp. 29-53), and J. Theis (*Geschichtliche und literarkritische Fragen in Esra 1-6* [AA II, 5]. Münster i. W., 1910). Unfortunately our information about Theodotion is too meager to allow us to be categorical in attributing questionable portions of the Greek Bible to him. All that can be asserted with some confidence is that I Esdras is a much earlier translation than the canonical "LXX" rendering of Chronicles-Nehemiah. This extant version of the complete work of the Chronicler (whether it be by Theodotion or not) does not seem to be based on the earlier version of which I Esdras alone survives, but appears to be a literal, independent rendering of the Masoretic text, made in the first or second century of the Christian Era. I Esdras was probably saved from oblivion by the Story of the Three Youths, to which we shall now turn our attention.

2. *The Story of the Three Youths*

An important portion of the Greek Ezra (3:1-5:6) has no parallel in the canonical books. It consists of the Story of the Three Youths at the Court of Darius (3:1-4:42), the original end of which seems to have been omitted in favor of the conclusion supplied by the editor (4:43-47) and of the account of the return of the Babylonian Exiles to Jerusalem, under the leadership of Zerubbabel, according to the decree of Darius (4:48-5:6).

This whole section is generally regarded as an interpolated addition to the Chronicler's work; only Henry Howorth (*Transact. of the Ninth Intern. Congress of Orientalists*, II [London, 1893], 79; The *Academy* 43 [1893] 106; PSBA 24 [1902] 335) and J. Marquart (*Fundamente israelitischer und jüdischer Geschichte*, p. 65. Halle, 1896) attribute all of 3:1-5:6 to the Chronicler's pen. C. C. Torrey, however, regards only 4:47b-56 and 4:62-5:6 (*Ezra Studies*, pp. 26-30, 58-61) as an original, slightly edited portion of the Chronicler's work; while H. Ewald (*Geschichte des Volkes Israel*, Vol. 4, p. 96. Göttingen, 1852) and E. Bertheau (*Die Bücher Ezra, Nehemia und Esther* [Kurzgef. Exeg. Handbuch zum A.T. 17], pp. 26 f. Leipzig, 1862) limit the Chronicler's contribution in this section to 5:1-6.

The theory of Torrey is somewhat complicated, but not impossible, assuming that "Darius" has been substituted, in our text, for the Chronicler's "Cyrus." Although it is tempting "to restore a lost half chapter to our canonical Old Testament—a thing which has never been done before, and presumably will never be done again" (C. C. Torrey, *Ezra Studies*, p. 30), we should not overlook the difficulties of this position (cf. the criticisms of E. Bayer, *Das Dritte Buch Esdras*, pp. 127-135; S. A. Cook, in R. H. Charles, *The Apocrypha and Pseudepigrapha*, Vol. 1, pp. 15-19; B. Walde, *Die Esdrasbücher der Septuaginta*, pp. 118-142). The main difficulty in regarding with Torrey I Esd. 4:47-56; 4:62-5:6 as the sequel of Ezra 1 (relating the return of the Exiles under Cyrus) is that in Ezra 1 (and I Esd. 2:1-15 [Gr. 2:1-11]) Sheshbazzar brought back the sacred vessels under Cyrus, while I Esdras tells of Zerubbabel doing the same under Darius. Are Sheshbazzar and Zerubbabel the same person? In I Esdras the two men are quite distinct, and are active under different kings. If, with Torrey, we regard I Esd. 4:47b as the immediate sequel of Ezra 1:11, the words "And *Cyrus* the king wrote for him letters . . ." (4:47b) can only mean that Sheshbazzar (and not Zerubbabel, as in what follows: cf. I Esd. 5:5) was the leader of the Exiles going to Jerusalem.

Although it is far from certain that the Chronicler wrote any part of I Esd. 3:1-5:6, Torrey seems to be right in regarding this section as composite rather than as the work of the author of I Esdras, as claimed by Torrey's Roman Catholic critics.

The original Story of the Three Youths (3:1-4:42, possibly incomplete at the end) is "an important specimen of old Aramaic literature" (Torrey, *Ezra Studies*, p. 30), "a bit of popular wisdom-literature complete in itself, and in its first estate having nothing to do with the history of the Jews" (*ibid.*, p. 37): for the words "this was Zerubbabel" in 4:13 are a notorious gloss. This originally Gentile tale was changed into a Jewish story in two stages: first by identifying the third youth with Zerubbabel through the gloss in 4:13 and by providing a new ending (4:43-47) which refers to Jewish history; and finally by making the story the prelude for the return of the Babylonian Exiles and the rebuilding of the Temple in Jerusalem (4:48-5:6). The Jewish coloring is intensified in these successive stages, as appears even in the designations for God: in the original story we read "the God of truth"[11] (4:40) and the clause "He who makes these things" (4:35); in the first revision, "the King of Heaven" (4:46, repeated in 4:58); and in the third, finally, the unmistakably Jewish expressions "Lord [*despótēs*] of our Fathers" (4:60) and "the God of their Fathers" (4:62).

It may be surmised not only that the story was composed in the Persian (Achaemenian) period (538-331), but that it was Persian in origin. Our Greek text (3:1-4:42) was unquestionably translated from an Aramaic prototype, as has been demonstrated by Torrey (*Ezra Studies*, pp. 23-25; 50-56; cf. E. Bayer, *Das dritte Ezrabuch*, pp. 123-125; B. Walde, *Die Ezrabücher*, pp. 119 f.). The closest parallel to our tale is the Story of

[11] Unless we render with Torrey (*Ezra Studies*, p. 56, note f), "Blessed of God is truth."

Ahikar, extant in fragmentary Aramaic papyri from Elephantine dating
from 450-410 (see A. Cowley, *Aramaic Papyri of the Fifth Century B.C.*,
pp. 204-248. Oxford, 1923). In both works (as in the ancient Egyptian
Story of the Eloquent Peasant) the plot is merely a pretext for the introduction of speeches and wise sayings (cf. the Letter of Aristeas). It seems
probable that, like the author of Tobit, the author of the Story of the
Three Youths was familiar with the Ahikar tale—a possibility which has
apparently never been considered. For in the extant Aramaic fragments
of Ahikar we read, "What is stronger than wine foaming in the press?"
(vi, 79; cf. I Esd. 3:18, 24; 4:14), and the power of the king is likewise
stressed (vii, 100-108; cf. I Esd. 4:1-12). The subject of the third discourse
is not treated in the extant fragments of Ahikar, but there is reference
to truth in x, 158 and to women in xiv, 218 f.

Cowley (*op. cit.*, p. 206 f.) regards the Aramaic text of Ahikar as a
translation from the Persian "or made under Persian influence," but thinks
that the story was "originally composed in Babylonian" about 550 B.C.[12]
It seems more probable, however, to consider the Ahikar story as a
remnant of Persian popular literature, of which other traces survive in
Herodotus, Athenaeus, Plutarch, etc., not to speak of the Avesta (A.
Christensen, *Die Iranier*, p. 297, in the *Handbuch der Altertumswissenschaft* [I. von Müller], edited by W. Otto, III:I; Vol. 3, iii:1. Münich,
1933). If such is the case, it is not to be excluded that the Story of the
Three Youths, in its original form, should likewise be regarded as a survival of this Persian literature.

In reality, quite apart from the setting of the story at the court of
Darius in Susa, the Persian point of view appears here and there. The
exaltation of truth as the mightiest of all things is typically Persian. As
Herodotus (1:136; cf. Strabo, *Geography* 15:3, 18) states, Persian youths
were educated in three fields only: horseback riding, archery, and speaking the truth. Accordingly, Darius I, in his famous Behistun (or Bisutun)
inscription,[13] emphatically declares that, as a worshiper of Ahura-Mazda,
he has given *a true, not untruthful,* account of events (§57) and, conversely, repeatedly declares that it was the Lie (*drauga*) which caused
the rebellious leaders to revolt and lie to the people (§§10, 52, 54, 56,

---

[12] The following scholars also believe that the Ahikar Story was originally written
in Akkadian: A. Schollmeyer (in *Theol. und Glaube* 4 [1912] 660 f.), F. Stummer
(in OLZ 18 [1915] 103-105, and B. Meissner (*Das Märchen des Weisen Achiqar*
[AO 16, 2]. Leipzig, 1917).

[13] The Persian text, with transcription and translation, is given by H. C. Tolman,
A Guide to the Old Persian Inscriptions. American Book Company, 1893 (cf. his
Ancient Persian Lexicon [Vanderbilt University Studies, Oriental Series], Nashville,
1908). For transcription and translation of the Persian, Babylonian, and Elamitic
texts, see F. H. Weissbach, *Die Keilinschriften der Achämeniden* (Vorderas. Bibliothek 3). Leipzig, 1911. For fragments of the Aramaic translation, see A. Cowley,
Aramaic Papyri of the Fifth Century, pp. 248-271.

58, 63); therefore he recommends to future kings to guard earnestly against the lie, punishing severely a liar, if they wish their land to remain secure (§55, cf. §64). The praise of Truth (*alétheia*) in I Esd. 4:34-40 seems to be the echo of a hymn in praise of Asha (Indo-Iranian *Arta*, Avestan *Asha Vahista* [Best Truth], Vedic *Ṛta*), rendered *alétheia* by Plutarch (*de Iside* 47).[14] Asha, or Truth, is the right cosmic order and justice, the Persian deity which, as stated in I Esd. 4, regulates both the course of phenomena in heaven and earth (vv. 34-36) and establishes justice among men (vv. 37-39): therefore to Truth belong "the might, the kingdom, the power, and the majesty for ever and ever" (v. 40; cf. Matt. 6:13).

Seen tentatively in such a light, the Story of the Three Youths acquires an unsuspected significance. It may not be a lost chapter of the Hebrew Scriptures, but it may add a page to the few remnants of Achaemenian Persian literature and perhaps preserve an echo of a hymn to Asha no longer extant in the surviving parts of the Avesta. If my conjecture that the story preserved in I Esdras is Achaemenian in origin does not seem *a priori* impossible, it should be tested by experts on Iranian literature.

How this Persian story became known to the Jews must remain a puzzle, although a lesser one than the familiarity of the remote Jewish colony at Elephantine with the Story of Ahikar, also known to the author of Tobit. More significant is the problem of the influence of Zoroastrianism or of Persian religion in general upon Judaism, a subject on which much has been written without reaching definitive results.[15]

Specifically, here the problem concerns the possible influence of Asha (or Truth's personification in our book) on the personifications of Wisdom and *Lógos* (word, reason) in Jewish writings. There are obvious parallels between the cosmic figures of Truth, and Wisdom as described in Prov. 8 and in the Wisdom of Solomon; and, if the Story of the Three Youths is Achaemenian, dependence could only be assumed on the part of Prov. 8. Although it might be tempting to discover in I Esd. 4 an unsuspected source for the personification of Wisdom, caution is advisable. The author of Prov. 8, in the early Hellenistic period, obviously penned his famous autobiographical account of divine Wisdom, from her childhood at the time of Creation to the writer's time, as a protest against the brilliant heresies of Job 28. He not only personified Wisdom, which

---

[14] See L. H. Mills, "Asha as the Law in the Gathas" (JAOS 20 [1899] 31-53).

[15] For publications earlier than 1915 see, Ida A. Pratt, *List of Works in the New York Public Library relating to Persia*, pp. 107-110. New York, 1915. See also: J. Scheftelowitz, *Die Altpersische Religion und das Judentum*. Giessen, 1920. P. Volz, in *Eucharisterion* I, 323-345 (FRLANT N.F. 19, I). Göttingen, 1923. J. A. Maynard, in JBL 44 (1925) 163-70. W. Bousset, *Die Religion des Judentums im neutestamentlichen Zeitalter*. 3rd ed. by H. Gressmann. Tübingen, 1926. A. von Gall, *Basileia tou Theou*. Heidelberg, 1927.

in Job was merely the blueprint used by the divine Architect in construct-
ing the cosmos out of chaos, but also brought Wisdom out of her inaccessible abode beyond the limits of the world and pictured her standing at
the crossroads to instruct the children of men. Was his personification
inspired by the figure of Truth (Asha) in the Persian-Aramaic Story of
the Three Youths? It is well to recall the wise words of G. F. Moore on
a similar question: "Borrowings in religion . . . , at least in the field of
ideas, are usually in the nature of the appropriation of things in the
possession of another which the borrower recognizes in all good faith as
belonging to him, ideas which, when once they become known to him,
are seen to be necessary implications or complements of his own"
(*Judaism*, Vol. 2, pp. 394 f.). We need not assume that the author of
Prov. 8 actually "borrowed" his personification of Wisdom from our
story. Eager to bring the mysterious cosmic Wisdom of Job 28 into
harmony with the tenets of Judaism, in which no impassable gulf separated God from man, he was bound to realize that Wisdom, to come
into intimate contact with men as their counselor and friend, would have
to be more than an abstraction, more than a plan, and must need be like
a person. If, then, he became acquainted with the eulogy of Truth in
our story, he would be encouraged to proceed with his personification
of Wisdom. As all indicates, he was the first Jew to personify a moral
quality. He could have seized upon the personification of Truth as a
commendable precedent, worthy of imitation; particularly so since Truth
was not only a cosmic power, directing the course of the physical world
as Wisdom in Job (I Esd. 4:34-36), but also the highest standard of
human conduct—justice personified (I Esd. 4:37-40). In contrast with
Job, but in harmony with I Esdras, Prov. 8 minimizes the cosmic functions
of Wisdom (8:22-30), attributing the creation of the world to God (cf.
I Esd. 4:35; Ahura-Mazda, not Asha, was the creator in Zoroastrianism;
cf. *Yasna* 44), but stresses its justice (8:15-20, 31-36).

The personification of Wisdom in Prov. 8 played an important role in
Judaism directly (Ecclus. 24; Wisdom of Solomon) and indirectly (the
Lógos speculations of Philo). Conversely, although our story so impressed
the Jews that it was included in an edition of Chronicles-Ezra-Nehemiah,
I have been able to discover only one colorless example of the personification of Truth in early Jewish writings: "Truth returns to them who practice her" (Ecclus. 27:9). Here Truth has, however, merely the connotation
of moral rectitude, without cosmic functions.[16]

Aside from the possible influence of the story on Prov. 8, a number
of parallels have been pointed out between it and other Jewish writings.

---

[16] It seems clear that if the author of the story in I Esdras had been a Jew influenced by Prov. 8, he would have personified Wisdom (like the author of Wisd. of
Sol.) rather than Truth, which no Jew ever personified vividly.

As is often the case in the study of literary parallels, critics reach at times opposite conclusions in determining which author is the borrower. Thus, for instance, E. Bayer (*Das Dritte Buch Esdras*, pp. 110-117), after pointing out numerous parallels between our story and the Books of Esther and Daniel, concludes that our story was inspired by them. On the contrary, C. C. Torrey (*Ezra Studies*, pp. 47 f.) states positively, "The plainest example of its influence on subsequent writing is found in the book of Esther"; and with less assurance concludes that in regard to the literary relation with Daniel, "there is probably dependence, and the borrower was in that case certainly Daniel."

Manifestly, these conclusions are reached in accordance with a previous determination of the relative dating of these writings. Torrey (*op. cit.*, pp. 39-44) concludes, on the basis of the reference to Apama (or Apame) in I Esd. 4:29, that "The Story of the Youths was written probably while she [Apama, daughter of Artabazus, wife of Ptolemy I Soter, the king of Egypt from 305 to 283] was still living . . . but possibly in the next following generation" (p. 44). Conversely, Bayer (*op. cit.*, p. 116) regards the name Apama, which is not uncommon, as freely chosen; "That the author had in mind a definite personality cannot, anyhow, be demonstrated." Bayer concludes that the story was not composed about 300 B.C., but *after* the Maccabean rebellion (168-165).

The clue discovered by Torrey in the reference to Apama does not seem decisive to the present writer, who, like Bayer, regards the name as fictitious. Moreover, he would rather identify the Darius of the story with the great Darius I, son of Hystaspes (521-485), than with the unlucky Darius III Codomannus (336-330) deposed by Alexander, as Torrey suggests (*op. cit.*, p. 40). For the story is manifestly fiction throughout, including I Esd. 4:29, although (as in the stories of Ahikar, Esther, Daniel, Judith, Tobit, etc.) a famous monarch of the past plays a more or less leading role in the plot. If, as suggested here, the story was originally Persian (composed probably by a Zoroastrian), it would date from the century 450-350 B.C. It presumably circulated in an Aramaic version about 300 B.C. The story (I Esd. 3:1-4:42) was interpolated in the Chronicler's work by an editor, who supplied (at least in part) its Jewish conclusion (4:43-5:6) about 200 B.C. The story was translated into Greek, with the rest of the Chronicler's work, soon after (cf. Torrey, *op. cit.*, p. 339, top of the page). A fragment of this translation, made presumably at Alexandria, survives in our I Esdras. If these conjectures are approximately correct, we may conclude that the Story of the Three Youths in Aramaic had some influence on the authors of Prov. 8, Daniel, and Esther; and in its Greek version it may have been known to the author of the Wisdom of Solomon (cf. the parallels tabulated by L. E. T. André, *Les Apocryphes de l'Ancien Testament*, p. 192. Florence, 1903).

Conceivably the author of the Letter of Aristeas knew our story: I have not noted any very close parallels, but in Arist. §§250-254 the power of women, truth, and the king are discussed. Of course, the first unquestionable quotations from our story are in Josephus.[17] Later, it enjoyed popularity in Christian circles and was not seldom referred to by Church Fathers, beginning with Clement of Alexandria, Origen, and Cyprian.

The popularity of this Gentile tale in Judaism and Christianity is not undeserved. The story is excellent in form and content. It is rightly classed as wisdom literature, but may possibly have been originally a good example of a Zoroastrian popular homily—valuable, if such, as a rare surviving specimen of this type of religious literature.

The author advisedly encloses his teaching within a historical framework—fictitious, but plausible. For the concrete is always more interesting to an audience than the abstract; drama is more gripping than philosophy. With a fine literary sense he builds up to his climax, beginning with the celebration of the power of something purely material and morally inferior—wine, "which seduces the wit of all who drink it" (3:17). He proceeds to a higher level in depicting the absolute power of the king, which may or may not be used for noble purposes. Then, with a touch of humor and pathos, of comedy and tragedy, he shows that the so-called weaker sex is really the strongest. Here he ranges, even more clearly than when speaking of the king, from the noblest (mother love and wifely devotion) to the lowest (selfish whims and silly fancies of coquettes bringing ruin to their lovers): even the king is helpless before a woman's wiles! But mightier than anything else is Truth: *magna est veritas, et praevalet!* (4:41). The eternal ordinances of nature and the moral law in man's heart are supreme! "Two things fill the spirit with ever new and increasing astonishment and awe, the more frequently and continuously reflection is occupied therewith: the starry heaven above me, and the moral law within me" (Immanuel Kant, edition of his works published under the auspices of the Prussian Academy, Vol. 5, p. 161).

Rhetorical art is evident in the three discourses: "It is evident that the form in which they are cast is well studied" (Torrey, *Ezra Studies*, p. 46). Torrey (*op. cit.*, p. 47) presents a good case for the metrical form of the speeches in the Aramaic text from which the Greek was translated, but

---

[17] Josephus (*Antiquities* 11:3, 2 [§34]) had before him the erroneous text of I Esd. 3:3, "Darius . . . slept and *woke up*" (*éxypnos egéneto*; Josephus: *éxypnos gínetai*). Accordingly Josephus, noticing the inconsistency, describes Darius arising from bed in the night and, to pass the time, suggesting to the three guardsmen the subjects which they elaborated in their speeches on the following morning. In the original story, however, the king slept through the night and found the slips with the subjects of the speeches under his pillow. Torrey (*Ezra Studies*, pp. 24, 50) is probably right in regarding "he woke up" as a mistranslation of an Aramaic text reading, "Darius . . . slept. Then *stood on the watch* the three young guardsmen. . . ."

if such was the case the present writer would regard the poetical meter as 4:4, rather than 3:3 as Torrey believes. Whether the Persian original (assuming that the Aramaic text was translated from the Persian) was in poetry must of course remain uncertain.

What gives to the speeches particular charm is not only the fine literary form, but also the unusually acute observations from life of which they are filled. The author discloses a fine psychological sense in describing human experiences. The rewards expected naïvely by the three youths are exactly what three courtiers of a Persian king would hope for (3:5-7). Intoxication at first produces a sense of elation and gladness, through elimination of inhibitions and forgetfulness of one's lacks and limitations (cf. Judg. 9:13; Prov. 31:6 f.), but later come contentiousness, blows, and unconsciousness (3:18-22); the subjects of a despotic ruler are utterly servile to him (4:3-11); men gape with open mouth at a comely woman promenading on the street (4:18 f.); a king will tolerate any impertinence on the part of a woman with whom he is infatuated and even humiliate himself to gain her favor (4:29-31). While some of these vignettes taken from life are universal (e.g., women making men's fine garments, 4:17; men becoming robbers or heroes for the love of women, 4:23 f.; husbands devoted to their wives, 4:25; men ruined by women, 4:26 f.), others seem to be typically Persian (the absolute power of the king, 4:3-12; the people's mastery of land and sea, 4:15; women parading freely without veiling their faces, and thus exhibiting their charms, 4:18 f.).

One of the qualities of style conspicuous in the author's art is the excellent use of irony in the description of the power of wine (3:17-23) and of women (4:18-24), increasing to biting sarcasm in the description of the king's infatuation (4:28-31). Nevertheless, real eloquence is attained in the noble finale in praise of Truth (4:34-40), where the author's impassioned words express his conviction that the universe and human society are both ruled according to eternal Truth—the embodiment of the basic principles of what is forever right: "Great is Truth, and it prevails!"

CHAPTER II

THE BOOK OF TOBIT

The title of the book in the Greek manuscripts is "The Book of the Words of Tobit" (1:1), in the Vulgate, *Liber Tobiae* (Book of Tobias). In contrast with the Greek, the Vulgate does not distinguish the names of Tobit and of his son Tobias, naming both Tobias: "When [Tobit] became a (grown) man, he married Anna of his tribe and of her he begat a son, *giving him his own name*" (1:9, Vulg.). Here, as throughout 1:3-3:15 (Vulg. 1:1-3:15), the Vulgate (as also the Aramaic and Gaster's Hebrew texts) speaks of Tobit in the third person, while the Greek (and other texts) gives the section as an autobiographical account of Tobit in the first person.

The story of Tobit is extant in three principal recensions, each attested in several forms but best preserved in Greek.[1]

I. The Greek text of *Codex Sinaiticus*, or *Aleph* (about A.D. 400),[2] is regarded by a number of scholars as the best now available,[3] and will be considered the basic text here. This recension is also represented, to a great extent, by the *Vetus Latina* (old Latin; sometimes erroneously called *Itala*) version;[4] the *Aramaic* text published by Neubauer (see the

[1] See D. C. Simpson in Charles, *Apocrypha*, pp. 174-180; "The Chief Recensions of the Book of Tobit" (JTS 14 [1913] 516-530). A. Schulte, *Beiträge zur Erklärung und Textkritik des Buches Tobias*, pp. 4-31 (Bibl. Studien 19, 2). Freiburg i. B., 1914. M. Schumpp, *Tobit* (Exegetisches Handbuch zum A. T.), Münster i. W., 1933.

[2] The text of the Sinaiticus has been published by F. H. Reusch (*Libellus Tobit e codice Sinaitico editus et recensitus.* Freiburg i. B., 1870), H. B. Swete (*The Old Testament in Greek*, 2nd ed. Cambridge, 1895-1899), and by A. Rahlfs (*Septuaginta.* Stuttgart, 1935). D. C. Simpson has translated this text into English (with critical apparatus) in Charles, *Apocrypha*, pp. 202-241. The latest edition of the Greek text with critical apparatus is in the Larger Cambridge Septuagint, the work of the late A. E. Brooke (*The Old Testament in Greek*, Vol. 3, Pt. 1: Esther, Judith, Tobit. Cambridge, 1940).

[3] Reusch (*op. cit.*, and TLZ 1878, pp. 333 f.), H. Graetz (MGWJ 1879, pp. 388 ff.), E. Nestle (*Septuagintastudien*, Vol. 3, pp. 5, 22-27; Vol. 4, pp. 9 f. Stuttgart, 1899 and 1903), J. Rendel Harris ("The Double Text of Tobit" in AJT 3 [1899] 541-554; see p. 554), E. Schürer (*Geschichte*, Vol. 3, p. 243), D. C. Simpson (see note 1, above), P. Joüon ("Quelques hébraïsmes du Codex Sinaiticus de Tobie" in Bibl. 4 [1923] 168-174).

[4] Published by P. Sabatier (*Bibliorum sacrorum Latinae versiones antiquae*, Vol. 1, 2nd ed. Paris, 1751), and A. Neubauer (*The Book of Tobit. A Chaldee Text from a unique Ms in the Bodleian Library with other Rabbinical Texts, English Translations, and the Itala.* Oxford, 1878).

preceding note) which was translated from the Greek;[5] the *Münster Hebrew* text,[6] translated from the archetype of Neubauer's Aramaic text; and the Latin *Vulgate*,[7] which influenced the *London Hebrew* version.[8]

II. The Greek text of *Codices Vaticanus* (B) and *Alexandrinus* (A), dating from the fourth and fifth centuries, respectively, is the standard text in the printed editions of the Septuagint.[9] This printed text (chiefly according to the Vaticanus) is translated in the Authorized Version (the Revised Version gives preference to the readings of the Alexandrinus). This recension, found also in some ancient versions from the Greek (i.e., the *Syriac*,[10] the *Hebrew* of Fagius,[11] the *Ethiopic*,[12] the *Coptic* [*Sahidic*],[13] and the current *Armenian*), has been regarded by some scholars as the oldest and best.[14]

[5] Th. Nöldeke, "Die Texte des Buches Tobit" (*Monatsberichte der Berliner Akademie*, 1879, pp. 45-69).

[6] Published in Constantinople in 1516 and by Sebastian Münster in 1542. It has been printed in the *London Polyglot Bible* (Vol. 4), edited by B. Walton (1657), with a Latin translation, and has been edited by Neubauer (*op. cit.*).

[7] In his preface to Tobit, Jerome says that he reluctantly prepared, with the help of an expert in Hebrew and Aramaic, a Latin version of an Aramaic ("Chaldee") text. In reality he apparently merely revised the Old Latin on the basis of the Aramaic. A. Schulte (*Beiträge*, p. 32) regards the Vulgate as the most faithful witness to the lost original.

[8] Extant in a British Museum manuscript (Add. 11639) edited by M. Gaster, *Two unknown Hebrew Versions of the Tobit Legend*, London, 1897 (reprinted from PSBA 18 [1896] 208-222; 259-271; 19 [1897] I-XV, 27-38). Gaster's other Hebrew text is taken from a Midrash on the Pentateuch and is related to Neubauer's Aramaic. The Georgian version follows the recension of the *Codex Sinaiticus*.

[9] The standard text of the LXX is that of the *Sistine Edition* (1586), based chiefly on the Vaticanus. Both the Vaticanus and the Alexandrinus have been published photographically. The Vaticanus for Tobit will be found in the edition of the whole manuscript of C. Vercellone and J. Cozza-Luzi (Rome, 1868-1881), and in the Septuagint editions of H. B. Swete and A. Rahlfs. On the mutual relation of these two manuscripts, see A. Schulte in BZ [1908] 262-265 (cf. *Beiträge* [see note 1, above], p. 17).

[10] The extant Syriac text (first published in the *London Polyglot*, Vol. 4; edited by P. de Lagarde, *Libri Vet. Test. apocryphi syriace*. Leipzig, 1861) in 1:1-7:8 (Gr. 7:9) gives the so-called *Syro-Hexaplar* version made by Paul of Tella in 616-617 from Origen's Greek text in the Hexapla. This text is a close translation of a text belonging to the Vaticanus-Alexandrinus recension. Owing presumably to the loss of the rest in an early manuscript, another version was utilized from 7:9 (Gr. 7:10) to the end of the book; this version was made from a text belonging to Recension III.

[11] A late and periphrastic version, introducing Biblical diction and legalistic prescriptions into the text, first published at Constantinople in 1517, then by P. Fagius in 1542; it appears in the *London Polyglot*, Vol. 4, with a Latin translation.

[12] Edited by A. Dillmann in Vol. 5 (Berlin, 1894) of his *Biblia Vet. Test. aethiopica*.

[13] A. Ciasca (*Sacrorum Bibliorum fragmenta copto-sahidica*, Vol. 1, pp. 219-225. Rome, 1885) has published Tob. 4:16-5:9; 11:14-14:15.

[14] André (*Les Apocryphes*, p. 184) regards the text of the Alexandrinus as the oldest. The following scholars regard the standard text of the Sixtine Edition (chiefly based on the Vaticanus) as the most original: Th. Nöldeke (*Monatsber. d. Berl.*

III. A third recension is attested in the Greek by some minuscule manuscripts (Holmes and Parsons 44, 106, 107) for a portion of the book (6:8-13:8 [Gr. 6:9-13:8]), but they give in the rest a text of Recension II. That this third recension comprised originally the whole book is attested by the Syriac version, which preserves it in 7:9-14:15 (Gr. 7:10 ff.), and by a sixth-century papyrus[15] giving a portion of 2:2-8. This recension, which is later than the two others and often contains readings from both side by side, is first attested in the second epistle of Clement to the Corinthians (16:4, quoting Tob. 12:8).

We may summarize the Book of Tobit as follows:

Superscription of the book (1:1 f.). The Book of the Words of Tobit, of the tribe of Naphtali, who was taken away captive out of Thisbe (upper Galilee) during the reign of Shalmaneser V (727-722 B.C.).

1. *Preliminary information* (1:3-3:17).

A. Tobit's misfortune (1:3-3:6). *a.* An exile in Nineveh, Tobit fulfilled the prescriptions of the Law (1:3). Even before his captivity, while his tribe, Naphtali, sacrified in Dan to Jeroboam's calf (1:4 f.), he observed the Law, taught him by his grandmother Deborah, and went to Jerusalem for the annual festivals, bringing first-fruits and tithes, as well as alms (1:6-8). He married his kinswoman Anna (the name is omitted in the Sinaiticus) and named their son Tobias (1:9). In Nineveh, although he did not eat the food of the Gentiles like other Israelites, he became the purchasing agent of Shalmaneser. He went to Media on this business, leaving at Rages (or Rhagae) (cf. 4:1) on deposit with Gabael ten talents of silver, or more than $20,000 (1:10-14). When Shalmaneser died and his son (*sic!*) Sennacherib (705-681; actually the son of Sargon, 722-705) reigned in his stead, the roads were too unsafe to go to Media (1:15). In Nineveh he had continued his pious works, and buried the corpses of his fellow Israelites (1:16 f.). When Sennacherib sought to kill him for the burial of these victims, he fled (1:18 f.), but all his property was confiscated (1:20). Within forty (or fifty) days, however, Sennacherib was assassinated (cf. II Kings 19:37; Is. 37:38) and Tobit's nephew Ahikar, the cupbearer of Essarhaddon (681-668), arranged for Tobit's return to Nineveh (1:21 f.).

b. Before partaking of a rich dinner at Pentecost, Tobit sent Tobias to invite some destitute pious Israelite to the feast (2:1 f.), but the boy reported that an Israelite lay dead, strangled, on the market place (2:3).

Akad. 1879, pp. 45 ff.), M. Löhr ("Alexandrinus und Sinaiticus zum Buche Tobit" in ZAW 20 [1900] 243-263), E. Schürer (in the 2nd and 3rd ed. of his *Geschichte*), J. Müller (in Beih. ZAW 13, pp. 33-53. Giessen, 1908), J. Goettsberger (*Einleitung*, p. 177. Freiburg, 1928), and others.

[15] Oxyrhynchus 1076, in A. S. Hunt, *The Oxyrhynchus Papyri*, Vol. 8. London, 1911.

Placing the corpse in the house, Tobit washed himself and ate sorrow-fully, remembering Amos 8:10 (2:4-6). Despite the neighbors' mockeries, he buried the corpse after sunset (2:7 f.) and, being in a state of ritual impurity, slept by the wall of the courtyard (2:9). The warm dung of sparrows fell in his eyes and blinded him (2:10). His wife was forced to work for wages as a dressmaker, and one day brought home a small goat which had been given her as a gift: Tobit's suspicion that it had been stolen led to bitter words between them (2:11-14).

c. Deeply grieved, Tobit turned to God in prayer: he recognized that God had justly punished Israel and implored God to release him from a life of distress (caused by reproaches) and allow him to die (3:1-6).

B. Sara's misfortune (3:7-15). On the same day in Ecbatana, Sara, daughter of Raguel, was reproached and, like Tobit, wished to die: one of her maids[16] accused her of murdering in succession the seven men who had married her, but they had been slain by the demon Asmodeus on the wedding night, before they had lain with her (3:7-9). Sara in her grief contemplated hanging herself, but refrained, thinking of her father's disgrace (3:10). So, like Tobit, she prayed God to let her die (3:11-15).

C. God's intervention in behalf of Tobit and Sara (3:16 f.). God heard their prayers and sent Raphael to heal Tobit and to free Sara from Asmodeus, so that she could marry Tobias (3:16 f.).

2. *Tobit sends Tobias to Media* (4:1-5:22 [Gr. 6:1].

A. The reason for the journey (4:1 f.). Having prayed for death, Tobit remembered the money deposited with Gabael in Rhagae (4:1; cf. 1:14) and decided to tell Tobias about it (4:2).

B. Tobit's instructions to his son (4:3-21). a. Tobias shall bury his father, honor his mother, and at her death place her in his grave (4:3 f.). b. He shall observe the Law (4:5) in order to prosper (4:6). In par-ticular he shall be generous in giving alms (4:7-11), marry a wife of his tribe (4:12), love his brethren (4:13), pay his employees promptly (4:14), do to no one what he disliked, be temperate in drinking (4:15), give bread to the hungry (4:16) and place some on the grave of the righteous (4:17), ask counsel of the wise (4:18), and be fervent in prayer (4:19). c. Tobias need not fear poverty, in view of the ten talents of silver deposited with Gabael (4:20 f.).

C. Preparations for the journey (5:1-16 [Gr. 5:17]). a. Tobit gave Tobias a receipt for the money[17] and sent him to seek a companion for the trip (5:1-3). b. Tobias found the angel Raphael, under the guise of an Israelite (5:4-8 [Gr. 5:9]). c. Raphael told Tobit that he was his

---

[16] I. Lévi (REJ 44 [1902] 289 ff.) has conjectured that the original Hebrew text had *'immah* (her mother) rather than *'amah* (a maid). The distress of Sara is easier to understand if her own mother reproached her.

[17] In the Sinaiticus and in some manuscripts of the Old Latin Tobit's autographed statement was divided into two parts: Gabael kept one, Tobit the other.

kinsman Azarias son of Ananias (5:9-13 [Gr. 5:10-14]), and he was hired
to lead Tobias to Media, his wages being a drachma a day and expenses
(5:14-16a [Gr. 5:15-17a]).

D. The departure (5:16b-22 [Gr. 5:17b-6:1]). As Tobias was on the
point of leaving,[18] his mother wept and begged Tobit to suffer the loss
of the money rather than the loss of the son (5:16b-19 [Gr. 5:17b-20]).
But Tobit assured her that the journey would be successful, for God's
angel (cf. 5:16a [Gr. 5:17a]) would accompany Tobias (5:20-22 [Gr.
5:21-6:1]).

3. *The Journey to Media* (6:1-9:6 [Gr. 6:2-9:6]).

A. A fish is caught in the Tigris (6:1-8 [Gr. 6:2-9]). While Tobias
was washing in the Tigris, a fish threatened to devour him (Codices A
and B; Vulgate) or his foot (*Cod.* Sinaiticus) (6:1 f. [Gr. 2 f.]). Upon
instructions of Raphael, Tobias caught the fish and removed its gall,
heart, and liver; they ate part of the fish (and salted the rest [Sinaiticus])
(6:3-5 [Gr. 6:4-6]). On the way the angel explained that the smoke
from the heart and liver exorcized demons, and the ointment from the
gall would cure blindness (6:6-8 [Gr. 6:7-9]).

B. Tobias marries Sara (6:9-8:21 [Gr. 6:10-8:21]). *a.* Raphael told
Tobias that they would lodge at Ecbatana in the home of Raguel, and
that Tobias should marry Raguel's daughter Sara, for she belonged to
him according to the Law of Moses (6:9-12 [Gr. 6:10-13]).[19] Tobias,
who knows of the sudden death of Sara's seven husbands, hesitates,
remembering his duty to bury his parents (6:13 f. [Gr. 6:14 f.]); but
Raphael reminds him of his father's injunction (6:15 [Gr. 6:16]) and
assures him that the demon Asmodeus will flee from the smoke of the
liver and heart of the fish, never to return (6:16 f. [Gr. 6:17 f.]). *b.*
Raguel, his wife Edna, and their daughter Sara welcomed Tobias, and
were deeply moved in hearing that he was their kinsman (7:1-8a [Gr.
7:1-9a]). *c.* Upon the request of Tobias, who refused to eat before being
granted Sara's hand, Raguel performed the marriage on the spot (7:8b-14
[Gr. 7:9b-13]). "Then they began to eat [and to drink (Sinaiticus)]"
(7:15 [Gr. 7:14]). *d.* After Edna had prepared the chamber and comforted her daughter (7:16-18 [Gr. 7:15-17]), Tobias put Asmodeus to

---

[18] Tobias' dog is mentioned in 5:16b [Gr. 5:17b] 11:4 [Gr. 11:3] by Codices A
and B, but in 6:1 [Gr. 6:2] by the Sinaiticus and the Vulgate (in the latter also
in 11:9).

[19] The Pentateuch contains no law (cf. 7:10-12 [Gr. 7:10b-11]) ordaining a
father, under penalty of death, to give his daughter in marriage to a kinsman. The
author manifestly refers to a halakic interpretation of Num. 27:1-11; 36, and
regards the oral law as Mosaic. J. Müller (Beih. ZAW 13, p. 4. Giessen, 1908),
however, interprets 6:12 (Gr. 6:13) according to Recension II (but not according
to the other texts), as follows: Raguel cannot marry Sara to another man according
to the Law of Moses, lest *this other man* [not Raguel] be put to death [like the
seven other previous husbands].

flight through the stench of the burning liver and heart of the fish; Raphael bound the demon tightly, after overtaking him in Egypt (8:1-3). e. In the bridal chamber Tobias and Sara prayed to God, and then slept (8:4-9a). f. Raguel, expecting the worst, had a grave dug for Tobias; but on hearing that he was asleep (8:9b-15) he sang God's praises (8:16 f.), had the grave filled (8:18), and arranged for fourteen days of festivities (8:19-21).

C. Raphael collects the money from Gabael (9). To save time, Raphael went to Rages at the request of Tobias (9:1-4), returning soon with the money and with Gabael, who blessed the newlyweds (9:5 f.).

4. *The return to Nineveh* (10-11).

A. In Nineveh, Tobit and Anna were anxiously waiting for their son's return. Anna mourned for him but, inconsistently, kept watching the road on which he should return (10:1-7a).

B. Tobias would not be entreated to stay with Raguel after the two weeks of festivities were ended (10:7b-10 [Gr. 10:7b-9]); after a moving farewell, he departed with Sara, enriched with half of Raguel's property (10:11-11:1 [Gr. 10:10-13]).

C. In the vicinity of Nineveh, Raphael and Tobias went ahead of the rest of the caravan, bringing the gall of the fish (11:2-4 [Gr. 11:1-3]). Anna saw them in the distance (11:5 f. [Gr. 11:4 f.]). After his mother's embrace, Tobias, according to Raphael's instructions, restored his father's sight by applying the gall of the fish to his eyes (11:7-13 [Gr. 11:6-12]). Tobit embraced his son, blessed God, and went forth to meet Sara: then the wedding was festively celebrated anew (11:14-19 [Gr. 11:12-18]).

5. *Raphael's Departure* (12).

A. Tobit and Tobias agree to give Raphael-Azarias half of the sum brought from Media (12:1-5).

B. Raphael's reply (12:6-15). a. Taking father and son aside, Raphael exhorted them to give thanks to God (12:6 f.) and declared that prayer and alms are preferable to riches (12:8-10). b. He disclosed then that he was one of God's seven angels sent to test Tobit and to heal Sara; he had brought both their prayers and good deeds into the presence of God's glory (12:11-15).

C. Raphael's ascension (12:16-22). Tobit and Tobias were afraid, but Raphael reassured them, urged them to praise God, and told them that he had been present in their midst only as a vision. After ordering them to write down what had taken place, he ascended and they saw him no more (12:16-22).[20] Tobit and Tobias praised God (12:22).

6. *Tobit's psalm of thanksgiving and praise* (13).

[20] On the close parallels between 12:16-22 and the Gospel records of the transfiguration, resurrection, and ascension of Jesus, see D. C. Simpson in Charles, *Apocrypha*, p. 234.

a. The punishment through the Exile (13:1-8). God chastises and shows mercy (13:1-5): when the Exiles, scattered among the Gentiles, turn wholeheartedly to God, he will no longer hide his face from them (13:1-8). *b.* The glorification of Jerusalem (13:9-18). After being punished, Jerusalem should praise God, that the Temple may be built again: then the Exiles and the Gentiles will come joyfully to worship there (13:9-11). Cursed be those who hate Jerusalem, and blessed be those who love her (13:12-14). Jerusalem will be rebuilt of precious stones and gold (13:15-18; cf. Is. 54:11 f.; Rev. 21:18-21).

7. *Epilogue* (14).

A. Tobit was blinded at the age of 62 (Sinaiticus; or 58, Vaticanus; 88, Alexandrinus; 56, Vulgate), and recovered his sight 8 (Vaticanus and Alexandrinus; 2, Vulgate; 7, Syriac) years later, lived to the age of 112 (Sinaiticus) or 102 (Syriac), and was buried in Nineveh (14:1 f.).

B. The last words of Tobit (14:3-11a). *a.* Tobias should go to Media with his family, for Nineveh will be destroyed, in accordance with the prophecy of *Nahum* (so Sinait.; *Jonas,* according to Vat. and Alex.), as also Jerusalem (14:3 f.). But eventually Jerusalem and the Temple will be rebuilt, the Exiles will return (14:5 f.), and all nations shall forsake their idols and worship the true God (14:6 f.). *b.* Tobias shall leave Nineveh as soon as he has buried his parents there, and observe the Law, remembering how Nadab perished through the snare which he had set for Ahikar, who had brought him up (14:8-11a).

C. The end of Tobias (14:11b-15). *a.* After he had honorably buried his parents, Tobias went to Ecbatana and died there at the age of 117 (so Sinait. and Old Latin; Vat. and Syr., 107; Alex., 127; Vulg. [14:16], 99) (14:11b-14). *b.* Before his death Tobias joyfully heard of the destruction of Nineveh, and saw her captives led to Media by Nebuchadnezzar and Assuerus (actually, Nabopolassar and Cyaxares), and he blessed the Lord (14:15).

1. *Literary Problems*

Until comparatively recent times it was assumed that the Book of Tobit related events which had actually happened. The author, of course, tells his story as if it were real history and is not in the least aware of taxing the credulity of his readers—who blindly accepted Old Testament miraculous tales as genuine facts—by introducing among his characters angels like Raphael and demons like Asmodeus. Nevertheless, he seems to have felt some qualms on account of his deception, for at the end of the story he has Raphael declare that his presence among men had not been corporeal but merely a "vision" (12:19).

If such was the case, many of the events narrated are imaginary— mere hallucinations. But thereby the reader is left bewildered: on the one hand, Tobit, Tobias, Sara, and the other human characters are presented as actual persons, living in a definite historical period—from 734 B.C., when Tiglath-pileser III (not Shalmaneser V, according to 1:1 f.; see II Kings 15:29) carried Naphtali into captivity, to 612 B.C., when Nineveh was destroyed by Nabopolassar and Cyaxares (not Nebuchadnezzar and Assuerus, 14:15); some of the characters are even supplied with genealogies (1:1) and other data of vital statistics (14:1 f., 14). On the other hand, everything connected with Raphael-Azarias is illusion.

It is idle to attempt to separate the supernatural from the natural in the tale, for they are too intimately interwoven. To say that what actually happened is that a young man was sent by his blind father to collect a sum of money and married during his journey is to reduce the story to the level of commonplaces hardly worth recording (except in the *personalia* of a provincial newspaper): and we still wonder how the young man collected the money, since his marriage prevented him from reaching his original destination. Moreover, the story as we have it can hardly have been written before 200 B.C., and it is difficult to see how it could be based on a family history written in Ecbatana four hundred years before. Of course no one can prove that such was not the case, but even so the possible historical kernel is insignificant, and the present story, on the author's own admission, is to a great extent unreal.

We may safely assume that the author did not have at his disposal a written account prepared by Tobit and Tobias upon Raphael's order (12:20), and we may proceed to search for actual written sources at his disposal in writing this charming and edifying fairy tale. It is manifest at once that he was well read in the Hebrew Scriptures, which in his day consisted of "the Law and the Prophets"—incidentally a proof that he could not have written before the Prophets were canonized (about 200 B.C.). He knew some of the Writings (canonized in A.D. 90), notably Psalms, Proverbs, and Job; but he apparently did not regard them as canonical and made no explicit reference to them.[21]

The Pentateuch, called "the Law of Moses" (6:12 [Gr. 6:13] and 7:13 [Gr. 7:12], Vat., Alex., Syr.; 1:8, Sinait.) or "the Book of Moses" (6:12 [Gr. 6:13] and 7:13 [Gr. 7:12], Sinait.),[22] was God's supreme revelation for all pious Jews after 400 B.C., and the norm of their life: what it ordains is "an everlasting decree" or a "statute forever" (1:6; cf. Ex. 27:21; Lev. 3:17; Num. 18:23). Tobit's life, as a matter of course, was

---

[21] When the author (in 14:4-7) refers to the return of the Babylonian Exiles to Jerusalem and to the rebuilding of the Temple, he does not quote Ezra, where these events are narrated, but refers to the promises of "the prophets of Israel" (Jer. 25:11; 29:10; Hag. 2:4; the Second Isaiah; Ez. 40-48; etc.).

[22] Already in Chronicles the Pentateuch is called either the Law (II Chron. 23:18; 30:16) or the Book (Book 35:12) of Moses; cf. Ecclus. 24:23.

regulated thereby in ritual matters (1:6-8, 10-12; 2:5, 9; 5:13 [Gr. 5:14])
as also in the practice of honesty (2:13) and of good works (1:16-18; 2:2,
4; etc.). But in Tobit the pious Jew observes not only the written law
codified in the Pentateuch, but also the oral law, or "tradition of the
ancients," which was being formulated by the Scribes and was transmitted orally until it was codified in the Mishna about A.D. 200. Tobit
knows a summary of the Law in negative form (4:15a [not in Sinait.];
Jesus [Matt. 7:12] gives it in a positive form, cf. 14:9). The law on
honoring and loving one's parents (4:3 f.; 14:10) is extended to one's
parents-in-law (10:13 [Gr. 10:12]). The prescription that daughters who
inherit their father's estate because they have no brothers must marry
within their tribe (Num. 27:1-11; 36) seems to be understood, in 6:12
[Gr. 6:13], in the sense that a father who fails to give his daughter (who
will inherit from him) to her next of kin is guilty of a capital offense.
The famous commandment to love one's neighbor as oneself (Lev. 19:19)
is apparently understood as not including in one's charity the unrighteous
Jews (4:17 [not in Sinait.]; cf. Ecclus. 12:1-7; Gal. 6:10; the opposite is
said in Test. of Benj. 4; Aristeas §227; Rom. 12:19-21).

One prescription, if the text of 4:17 (not in Sinait.) (Vulg. 4:18) is
a faithful rendering of what the author actually wrote, even contradicts
Deut. 26:14 (cf. Hos. 9:4; Is. 8:19; Jer. 16:7), where offerings of food
to or for the deceased are regarded as a sin. Such *choaí* (outpourings)
on the graves were an ancient heathen custom, familiar in Egypt from
the earliest times as well as in the Graeco-Roman world (Ovid, *Fasti*
2:566; Lucian, *De luct.* 9). Surprisingly, not only some ancient Israelites
but even Jews after 200 B.C. still placed food on the graves (Ecclus.
7:33), although the practice is regarded as heathen in Ecclus. 30:18
[Gr.]; Epist. of Jer. 32 [Gr. 31]; Wisd. of Sol. 14:15; Sibyl. Or. 8:382-384,
and particularly in Jub. 22:17. In another curious detail the author seems
to disregard the standard Jewish practice: a dog, an unclean animal
according to Deut. 23:18; Ecclus. 13:22 (the modern Moslem likewise
regards dogs as impure), accompanies Tobias on his journey (5:16 [Gr.
5:17] in the Vaticanus and Alexandrinus; 6:1 [Gr. 6:2] in the Sinaiticus
and the Vulgate; 11:4 [Gr. 11:3]; 11:9, Vulgate). While the Aramaic text
(as also the Münster and London Hebrew texts) omits the dog out of
respect for Jewish feelings, Jerome adds a charming touch in 11:9: "Then
the dog who had been along on the journey ran ahead; and, like an
arriving messenger, expressed his joy by wagging his tail."[23]

The author of Tobit was indebted to the Pentateuch not only for the

---

[23] According to M. Rosenmann (*Studien zum Buche Tobit*, Berlin, 1894), the
dog was introduced into the story under the influence of Greek customs and
literature (cf. *Odyssey* 17:290-327). R. Smend (Beih. ZAW 13, p. 153. Giessen,
1908), on the other hand, is inclined to trace the dog back to the Ahikar story.

religious and moral practices illustrated and inculcated in his book, but also for some incidents and scenes in his story. He is also familiar with Isaiah, Jeremiah, and the Minor Prophets.[24] In 2:6 he quotes Amos 8:10 from memory, but fairly accurately, and refers to Nahum's oracle on the fall of Nineveh in 14:4 (in the Vaticanus and Alexandrinus the reference is to Jonah). Like the Jews in general after Ezekiel and the Second Isaiah (cf. the gloss in Amos 3:7), our author read the ancient prophetic oracles not as impassioned appeals to the living generation, denouncing its sins and urging its repentance, but as predictions of God's intervention to change the course of history in a remote future (14:4-7). Since, like his contemporaries, our author read the prophetic books in the light of the glorious predictions of the Second Isaiah (and Jer. 31), it was natural that he would be attracted more by the postexilic additions to the prophetic books than by the ancient authentic oracles (even Amos 8:10, quoted in 2:6, is of questionable authenticity). The following predictions in the prophetic books were familiar and dear to the author: Is. 60:6-10, Mic. 4:2, and Zech. 8:22 (see Tob. 13:11; 14:7); Is. 2:8 and Mic. 5:13 (H. 5:12) (see Tob. 14:6); Is. 66:10 (see Tob. 13:13 f.); Is. 54:11 f. (see Tob. 13:16 f.).

The Jews are not only the heirs of such divine promises, they are "the sons of the prophets" (4:12), for their ancestors Noah, Abraham, Isaac, and Jacob were prophets (4:12; Abraham is called a prophet in Gen. 20:7; the patriarchs in general in Ps. 105:15). The early Christians appropriated for themselves this designation of "sons of the prophets" (Acts 3:25), but in a less literal sense. Incidentally 4:12, assuming without Biblical warrant that Noah married a kinswoman, echoes haggadic legends.[25] Thus, according to Jub. 4:33, Noah's wife was his cousin "Emzara, the daughter of Rakiel [or Bakiel], the daughter of his father's brother."[26]

In addition to the Law and the Prophets, the author of the Book of Tobit was manifestly familiar with Psalms, Proverbs, Job, and other Hagiographa. His story presents some parallels to the much earlier tale of the pious and patient Job (Job 1:1-2:10; 42:10b-17): in both cases a devout and innocent man is afflicted undeservedly through loss of property and illness, is greatly irritated by his wife, whose rebuke only enhances

---

[24] The parallels in legal and narrative matter between Tobit and the Pentateuch are listed by D. C. Simpson in Charles, *Apocrypha*, p. 192, notes 6 and 7, respectively. For his indebtedness to the prophets, see *ibid.*, p. 193, n. 1. He draws information from the Books of Kings in 1:2, 5, 18, 21.

[25] Cf. L. Ginzberg, *Legends of the Jews*, Vol. 5, pp. 145 f. (n. 42), 172 (n. 11), 179 (n. 29). Philadelphia, 1925.

[26] For other parallels between Tobit and Jubilees, see J. T. Marshall in Hastings, *Dictionary of the Bible*, Vol. 4, p. 789.

the hero's faith, and at the end obtains through God the restoration of wealth and health.

Critical opinion is divided on the question whether our author knew Sirach's Ecclesiasticus (written about 180 B.C.): the problem has an obvious bearing on the dating of Tobit. Although the instructions of Tobit to his son in 4:3-21 resemble closely the teaching of Sirach, and numerous parallels in details may be pointed out,[27] the diction is sufficiently different to preclude any certainty about direct borrowing on the part of our author. The evidence adduced by I. Lévi ("La langue originale de Tobit," REJ 44 [1902] 288-291) to prove that the author of Tobit occasionally misunderstood the Hebrew of Sirach is by no means convincing. We must conclude that, if the author knew Ecclesiasticus (which is possible), he failed to quote it verbatim and at most utilized its religious teaching in a general way.

On the contrary, the familiarity of the author of Tobit with the Story of Ahikar[28] is certain, in spite of the tendency of Roman Catholic scholars, who believe that the Book of Tobit is historical and divinely inspired, to regard the explicit references to Ahikar in 1:21 f.; 2:10; 11:18 (Gr. 11:17); 14:10 (in 14:15, Sinait., the name Ahikar is due to an error) as interpolated (cf. A. Schulte, Beiträge, p. 145). A number of Protestant scholars have defended the same view,[29] but have failed to adduce convincing arguments. Neither corruption of the names of Ahikar and his nephew Nadan in the various recensions of Tobit, nor the journey of Ahikar to Elymais (2:10), which is not mentioned in the story, prove that the Ahikar passages are interpolated. Conversely, quite aside from the references to Ahikar, the Book of Tobit presents, both in narrative and in moral teaching, parallels to Ahikar (cf. D. C. Simpson, in Charles, Apocrypha, pp. 191 f.), so that it can hardly be doubted that the author of Tobit knew the story of Ahikar (cf. Schürer, Geschichte, Vol. 3, pp.

---

[27] Cf. Tob. 4:3 with Ecclus. 3:12; Tob. 4:7 with Ecclus. 14:9 f. (cf. Matt. 20:15) and 4:4 f. cf. Matt. 5:7); Tob. 4:10 with Ec. 3:4; 29:12; 40:24 (cf. Prov. 10:2; Dan. 4:27 [H. 4:24]; Mark 10:21); Tob. 4:17 with Ecclus. 12:1-7; Tob. 4:21 with Ecclus. 21:6b.

[28] The earliest (fragmentary) text is furnished by some Aramaic papyri of the late 5th century B.C. discovered at Elephantine (an island on the Nile opposite Assouan), and first published by E. Sachau in 1911; for the text and English translation see: A. Cowley, Aramaic Papyri of the Fifth Century B.C., pp. 204-248. Oxford, 1923. English translation of later recensions (in various languages) are printed in parallel columns in R. H. Charles, Pseudepigrapha, pp. 715-784. See also: F. C. Conybeare, Rendel Harris, and Agnes S. Lewis, The Story of Ahikar. 2nd ed., Cambridge, 1913. For an account of research and a bibliography, see F. Nau, Histoire et sagesse d'Ahikar l'Assyrien. Paris, 1909. See also B. Meissner, Das Märchen vom weisen Achiqar. Leipzig, 1917.

[29] For instance, W. Erbt (Encycl. Biblica, Vol. 4, cols. 5110-5117); J. Müller (Beih. ZAW 13, pp. 13-15); R. Smend (Beih. ZAW 13, p. 63). Th. Reinach (REJ 38 [1899], pp. 11 f.) regards only one reference to Ahikar (14:10 f.) as authentic.

253-255) in *written* form and not, as Margarete Plath (in TSK 74 [1901] 394) believed possible, only from hearsay.[30]

Another probable source of the Book of Tobit, the folk tale of "The Grateful Dead,"[31] was first suggested by Karl Simrock (*Der Gute Gerhard und die dankbaren Toten*, pp. 131 f. Bonn, 1856).[32] But the first Biblical scholar to recognize the significance of folk tales for the study of the origin and meaning of Tobit was E. Renan (*Histoire des origines du Christianisme*, Vol. 6 [*L'Église Chrétienne*], pp. 554-561. Paris, 1879). The earliest and simplest parallel to the tale is told by Cicero (d. 43 B.C.) in *De divinatione* I, 27 (cf. II, 65 f.): after Simonides had buried decently the corpse of an unknown person, he was warned by the deceased not to sail on a certain ship lest he perish through shipwreck; he followed this advice, while all those who sailed died. In spite of certain resemblances, this story may not be directly connected with the cycle of the Grateful Dead, in which after burying a corpse at great personal sacrifice or risk a man (often on a journey) is saved from death or obtains a bride through the good offices of the deceased. In Tobit and numerous other tales of this type two originally distinct motifs are combined: the Grateful Dead and the Dangerous Bride. The latter motif appears in a number of variants: the Poison Maiden,[33] the Ransomed

---

[30] It hardly seems necessary to discuss the views that the Ahikar of Tobit may not be the same person as the hero of the Ahiqar story (L. Ginzberg, in *Jew. Encycl.*, Vol. 1, p. 290; M. Löhr, in E. Kautzsch, *Apokryphen und Pseudepigraphen*, Vol. 1, p. 146); or that the Ahikar story depends from the Book of Tobit (G. Hoffmann, in *Abhandl. für die Kunde des Morgenlandes* 7 [1880] 182 f.; P. Vetter, in *TQ* 86 [1904] 321-364, 512-539; 87 [1905] 321-370, 497-546). For a bibliography on the relation between the Tobit and Ahikar stories, see Schürer, *Geschichte*, Vol. 3, pp. 257 f.

[31] The fullest account in English of this fairy-tale motif is to be found in Gordon Hall Gerould, *The Grateful Dead: the History of a Folk Story* (Publications of the Folk-Lore Society, Vol. 60). London, 1908. For later publications on the subject see: Stith Thompson, *Motif-Index of Folk-Literature*, Vol. 2, pp. 364 f. Bloomington, Ind., 1933. See also H. Gunkel, *Das Märchen im Alten Testament*, pp. 91-93. Tübingen, 1921.

[32] Additional variants of the tale were pointed out by Th. Benfey (*Pantschatantra*, Vol. 1, p. 219. Leipzig, 1859), R. Köhler (*Germania* 3 [Stuttgart 1858] 192-209; reprinted in *Kleinere Schriften*, Vol. 1, pp. 5-20. Weimar, 1898; cf. *ibid.* p. 424), G. Stephens (*Ghost-Thanks or the Grateful Unburied, A Mythic Tale in its Oldest European Form, Sir Amadace*, 1860), M. Hippe (*Archiv f. d. Stud. der neueren Sprachen* 81 [1888] 141-183), G. H. Gerould (*op. cit.*). The latest treatment of the subject known to me is: Sven Liljeblad, *Die Tobiasgeschichte und andere Märchen mit toten Helfern*. Lund, 1927. A list of literary and popular variants of the tale is given there on pp. 44-57; cf. Gerould, *op. cit.*, pp. 7-25.

[33] W. Hertz, "Die Sage vom Giftmädchen" (*Abhandlungen der kön. bayerischen Akad. d. Wissensch.*, philos. philol. Klasse, Vol. 20 [1893], pp. 89-166), reprinted in his *Gesammelten Abhandlungen* (edited by F. von der Leyen [1905], pp. 156-277); cf. Gerould, *op. cit.*, pp. 44-75. A "Poison Maiden" is a woman who, having been nourished with poison, kills the man embracing her.

Woman,[34] the Bride of the Monster (giant, dragon, or the like),[35] and similar subjects. Whether these themes should be regarded as mere variants of the Poison Maiden story (Gerould, *op. cit*, p. 45) or mutually independent motifs (G. Huet "Le conte du 'mort reconnaissant' et le livre de Tobie" in RHR 71 [1915] 18) is not easily determined, but it is unimportant for our present inquiry. What seems certain is that the author of Tobit was familiar with a folk tale combining the motifs of the Grateful Dead and the Dangerous Bride;[36] it is absurd, conversely, to suppose that all similar folk and literary tales are derived from the Book of Tobit.[37]

The two versions of the tale that present the closest parallels with Tobit may be summarized as follows: According to a modern Armenian tale, from Transcaucasia,[38] a man saw a corpse being beaten by the deceased's unpaid creditors and, paying the debt, buried it decently. Later he became poor and considered marriage with a rich maiden, whose five previous husbands had died on their wedding nights. An unknown man offered to become his servant for half of his future wealth and advised him to marry the maiden. On the wedding night the servant cut off the head of a serpent coming out from the bride's mouth and forced a second serpent out of the woman by threatening to cut her in half. Then the servant made himself known as the ghost of the deceased whose corpse had been rescued, and disappeared. In a similar (gypsy) tale heard near Adrianople[39] the ghostly companion, after cutting off

---

[34] Gerould, *op. cit.*, pp. 76-118.

[35] S. Liljeblad, *op. cit.*, pp. 157-247.

[36] This is now generally recognized (cf. *Revue des traditions populaires* 24 [1909] 309 f.). See in particular: Th. Linschmann (*Zeitschr. f. wissensch. Theol.* 25 [1882] 359-362); E. Cosquin (RB 8 [1899] 62-73, 513-520), Margarete Plath (TSK 74 [1901] 402-414); W. Erbt (*Encycl. Bibl.*, Vol. 4, cols. 5126-5128). J. Müller (Beih. ZAW 13 [1908] 2-10); D. C. Simpson (in Charles, *Apocrypha*, p. 188); P. Fiebig (in *Religion in Geschichte und Gegenwart*, 1st ed., Vol. 1, p. 538. Tübingen, 1909); G. Huet (RHR 71 [1915] 9); S. Liljeblad (*Die Tobiasgeschichte u.s.w.*, pp. 157-163); O. Eissfeldt (*Einleitung in das Alte Test.*, p. 640); W. O. E. Oesterley (*Introduction to the Books of the Apocrypha*, pp. 165 f. New York, 1935); etc. Few scholars (like E. Schürer, *Geschichte*, Vol. 3, p. 241) have expressed doubts in the matter, or have denied the connection of Tobit with an ancient fairy tale (H. Preiss, *Zeitschr. f. wissensch. Theol.* 28 [1885] 24-51; J. Sieger, *Katholik* 1904, pp. 367-377; F. Nau, *Histoire et sagesse d'Ahikar l'Assyrien*, p. 21, n. Paris, 1909).

[37] Only J. Sieger (*Katholik* 1904, 376) has feebly suggested it. The two folk tales actually derived from Tobit have unmistakable characteristics: Laura Gonzenbach, *Sizilianische Märchen*, Vol. 2, p. 177 ("Tobia and Tobiola"). Leipzig, 1870. Lydia Schischmanoff, *Légendes religieuses bulgares*, pp. 194-201 (1896).

[38] A. von Haxthausen, *Transkaukasia*, Vol. 1, pp. 333 f. Leipzig, 1856. Th. Benfey, *Pantschatantra*, Vol. 1, p. 219. Leipzig, 1859. R. Köhler, *Germania* 3 (1858) 202 f.; cf. *Orient und Occident*, Vol. 2, p. 328, and Vol. 3, p. 96. G. H. Gerould, *The Grateful Dead*, p. 47.

[39] A. G. Paspati, *Études sur les Tschinghianes ou Bohémiens de l'Empire Ottoman*, pp. 601-605 (1870). F. H. Groome, *Gypsy Folk-Tales*, pp. 1-3 (1899). Gerould, *Grateful Dead*, pp. 47 f.

the head of the dragon emerging from the bride, demands half of the woman. When he takes his sword, she screams and the second dragon is disgorged.

The author of Tobit, intent on writing a deeply religious and highly edifying book, took considerable liberties with the folk tale (as Margarete Plath, TSK 74 [1901] 404-414, has well shown). As a result, it is difficult to determine, for instance, which variant of the Dangerous Bride motif was utilized in the story of Sara: was she the wife of Asmodeus (Bride of the Monster motif), his captive (Ransomed Maiden motif), or the object of his courtship ("the demon loves her" [6:14, Gr. 6:15] in the standard Greek text [Codd. B, A] and the Old Latin)? Or was she a victim of demonic possession (E. Renan; M. Hippe; G. Huet [RHR 71 (1915) 19])? Or, again, was Sara a Poison Maiden (Gerould, *op. cit.*, pp. 45, 73 f.)? The author obviously obscured this crucial point of the tale for his own purposes.

More questionable is the indebtedness of our author to the Egyptian tract extolling Khons of Thebes (suggested by H. Schneider, *Kultur und Denken der Babylonier und Juden,* pp. 638 f. Leipzig, 1910), the *Odyssey* of Homer (C. Fries, "Das Buch Tobit und die Telemachie" in *Zeitschr. f. wissensch. Theol.* 53 [1910-11] 54-87), and pre-Zoroastrian Perso-Medic sources (J. H. Moulton, ET 11, pp. 257-260; *Early Zoroastrianism,* pp. 246-253 [*Hibbert Lectures* for 1912]. London, 1913) in spite of the probable Avestan origin of Asmodeus (*Aeshma Daeva,* the demon of wrath).[40]

We may thus conclude that the sources the author utilized in writing the Book of Tobit were the Law and the Prophets (and undoubtedly Psalms, Proverbs, and Job), the Story of Ahikar, and the Tale of the Grateful Dead. Whatever else he had read or heard has either failed to reach us or cannot be identified positively.

Our second problem is the original language of the book, now extant in three Greek recensions and later versions. Origen did not know of a Hebrew text of Tobit; he tells us that the Jews did not even have it among their apocryphal writings (*Epistle to Africanus,* 13 [Migne, PG 11, 80]). But Jerome (*Preface to Tobit*) found an Aramaic (*chaldaeo sermone conscriptum*) copy of the book; he assures Chromatius (Bishop of Aquileia) and Heliodorus (Bishop of Altino) that he had a Jew render

---

[40] See P. Haupt, "Asmodeus" (in JBL 40 [1921] 174-178). L. Ginzberg, however, denies the Persian etymology of "Asmodeus" (*Jewish Encyclopedia,* Vol. 2, p. 219; cf. *Legends of the Jews,* Vol. 6 [Philadelphia, 1928] p. 299, n. 83): he derives the name from the Hebrew-Aramaic root *sh-m-d* (cf. *Shamdon,* a demon), and interprets it as "the cursed." Moulton (*Early Zoroastr.,* p. 251) refutes this view. The Persian etymology has also been rejected by E. König (*Geschichte der Alttestamentlichen Religion,* p. 552. Gütersloh, 1915) and most recently by J. E. Steinmueller, *A Companion to Scripture Studies,* Vol. 2, p. 130. New York, 1942.

it into Hebrew, and he himself translated the Hebrew into Latin, dictating it to a secretary in a single day (not mentioning that he often utilized the Old Latin version). This Aramaic text of Jerome was hardly a copy of the original text of the book (being presumably a translation from the Greek),[41] but may be the ancestor of the Aramaic text published by Neubauer. Thus, external evidence being irrelevant, the original language of the book can be determined only through an examination of the Greek text.

Origen and Jerome were right in surmising that the current Greek text was a translation from a Hebrew or Aramaic original, although they were unable to find the original text. The view that Greek is the original language of the book seems to be less popular now than formerly.[42] Critical opinion has generally come to regard Tobit as a book written originally in a Semitic language,[43] although still uncertain between Hebrew[44] and Aramaic.[45] In reality, although it can hardly be doubted that the Greek text was translated from a Semitic prototype, it is difficult to determine whether this text was in Hebrew or Aramaic, in view of the uncertainty of the Greek text; on the whole, the evidence seems to favor an Aramaic original.

It seems clear that in its earliest form the Greek text was so literal a rendering that Semitic idioms abounded in it, but that it was repeatedly revised in the interests of a more idiomatic Greek diction. This revision is more pronounced in the Vaticanus than in the Sinaiticus, although the latter has some stylistic improvements still lacking in the Vaticanus. The following instances of "translation Greek" may suffice to illustrate some

[41] A. Schulte (Beiträge, pp. 31-33), who regards Jerome's Vulgate as the most faithful reproduction of the original text, admits that Jerome's Aramaic text was *not* the original text of the book. Th. Nöldeke (Monatsber. der Berlin. Akad. 1879, pp. 45-69) doubts that Jerome's statement is entirely accurate, but he admits that Jerome used an Aramaic text similar to Neubauer's—which is based on a late Greek recension (ibid., pp. 59 f., 67). See also J. Müller (Beiträge, p. 2) and E. Schürer (Geschichte, Vol. 3, p. 244).

[42] A Greek original is postulated by O. F. Fritzsche (Commentary, p. 8), Th. Nöldeke (Monatsber. der Berlin. Akad. 1879, p. 61), E. Schürer (in Herzog, Realencyclopädie, 3rd ed., Vol. 1, p. 643; however, in Geschichte, Vol. 3, p. 230, he presupposes a Semitic original), O. Zöckler (Die Apokryphen in the Kurzgefasster Kommentar, p. 165. München, 1891), M. Löhr (in E. Kautzsch, Apokryphen, p. 136), L. E. T. André (Les Apocryphes, p. 181), H. G. Bévenot (Bibl. Stud. 83 [1926] 55-84). After some discussion, D. C. Simpson (Charles, Apocrypha, p. 182) leaves the question of the original language open. E. J. Goodspeed (The Story of the Apocrypha, p. 13. Chicago, 1939) believes that it probably was composed in Greek by an Egyptian Jew, as a missionary tract.

[43] So E. Schürer (Geschichte, Vol. 3, p. 240) and J. Müller (Beiträge, p. 33).

[44] So H. Graetz (MGWJ 28 [1879] 386 f.), I. Lévi (REJ 44 [1902] 288-291) and P. Vetter (TQ 86 [1904] 526-30).

[45] So J. M. Fuller (in Wace, Apocrypha, Vol. 1, pp. 52-155, 164-171), J. T. Marshall (in Hastings, Dict. of the Bible, Vol. 4, p. 788), and C. C. Torrey (The Apocryphal Literature, pp. 85-87).

typical Semitisms: "*Good* [i.e., better] is little with righteousness *than* much with unrighteousness" (12:8); "I kept *my soul* [i.e., myself] from eating" (1:11); "I am *one* [i.e., the only child] to my father" (3:10); "*One . . . not*" (i.e., none; 3:8); "From the face of the earth" (3:6, Sinait.); "Sons of the righteous" (13:9, 13; meaning righteous individuals); "to stand . . . before [meaning, to serve]" (12:15, Sinait.).[46] Although a Jew could have written this sort of Semitizing Greek, and although occasionally the Greek is so idiomatic that it cannot be rendered literally into Hebrew or Aramaic (e.g., in 4:6; 5:14 [Gr. 5:15]; 7:7; 14:3), our text is in all probability a translation. We lack decisive evidence for determining whether the prototype was Hebrew or Aramaic. Since the characteristics of Hebrew, which are so obvious in the Greek of I Maccabees and Judith, are not in evidence here, I am inclined to regard the original as Aramaic. The author was manifestly familiar with Aramaic fiction, notably the Story of Ahikar, and would be inclined to write his book in the same language.

Our third problem is the date and place of origin. The explicit historical allusions in the book give us no clue for determining its date of composition. As in other short stories written by Jews (Ruth, Jonah, Esther, Judith, etc.), the action takes place long before the time of the author: in the case of Tobit, the events occurred in the period 722-612 B.C. But, as was usually the case, the information about the historical period dealt with is somewhat hazy: the tribe of Naphtali was not deported in the days of Shalmaneser V (1:2) but by his predecessor Tiglath-pileser III (II Kings 15:29); Sennacherib was not the son of Shalmaneser (1:15), but of Sargon;[47] Nineveh was not captured by Nebuchadnezzar and Assuerus (14:15), but by Nabopolassar and Cyaxares (cf. C. C. Torrey, *The Apocryphal Literature*, pp. 87 f.; JAOS 66 [1946] 8).

His geographical notions are likewise dubious.[48] Torrey ("Nineveh in the Book of Tobit" in JBL 41 [1922] 237-245) has convincingly shown that Nineveh in the book is not in its proper location, and has suggested that "Nineveh" is really Seleucia. But the author must really have had in mind Nineveh—even though he had no precise notion of its location— as appears from his reference to the Assyrian kings who resided there and the city's destruction, during the lifetime of Tobias, by "Nebuchadnezzar and Assuerus." If the author really believed that Nineveh had

---

[46] For other examples, see J. Müller, *Beiträge*, pp. 28-33.

[47] The author's error (1:18-21) in assuming that Sennacherib was assassinated when he returned to Nineveh after his siege of Jerusalem in 701 (he actually died in 681) is probably due to II Kings 19:37, which may seem to report events immediately following Sennacherib's return to Nineveh.

[48] The author apparently imagines that Rages (Rhagae) is but a day's camel ride from Ecbatana (9:6), whereas almost two weeks would be required for the journey.

stood on the site of Seleucia, he must have written so long after its destruction that the city's actual location was generally unknown, except perhaps to those living near its site.

Like Daniel, the author refers prophetically to events which would occur long after the death of his characters: Tobit on his deathbed predicted, as a fulfillment of Old Testament prophecies (14:4 f.), the destruction of Nineveh (612) and of Jerusalem (586), the return of the Exiles (538, according to the Book of Ezra), and the rebuilding of the Temple (516), which was not "like the first" (Solomon's), as Haggai (2:3) had heard old people say. From 516 to the Maccabean rebellion the history of the Jews was a blank for the author as for us, except for the activity of Ezra and Nehemiah, which the author disregarded as unimportant. Consequently, Tobit could predict the coming of the "Messianic age" (without a Messiah) after 516 (14:5b-7). This seems to indicate that the author wrote before 168, when the Maccabean rebellion began, and did not know Daniel (written in 164), where the Messianic age is to begin immediately after the rededication of the Temple in 164. Moreover, Tobit knows nothing of the resurrection from the dead, taught by Dan. 12:2.

On the other hand, the author could hardly have written before 200, for, like Sirach (180 B.C.), he knows "the Law and the Prophets," which were edited and canonized about 400 and 200 B.C., respectively. His religious and ethical teaching resembles that of Sirach, and both authors reflect the incipient scribal elaboration of the oral law, or "tradition of the ancients." It is probable that Tobit was written shortly after Ecclesiasticus, but before Daniel, during the decade 180-170 B.C. (although 190-180 B.C. is possible).

Such a second-century date, or a slightly earlier one, is generally proposed by modern scholars.[49] Other dates suggested range from the seventh century B.C. (defended by some Roman Catholic scholars, e.g., C. Gutberlet, *Das Buch Tobias*. Münster i.W., 1877; F. Kaulen, *Einleitung in die Heilige Schrift*. Freiburg, 1876-81, and later editions), to A.D. 116 (F. Hitzig, ZWT 3 [1860] 250-261; F. Rosenthal, *Vier apoc. Bücher aus der Zeit und Schule R. Akibas*. Leipzig, 1885), to the years A.D. 139-141 during the reign of Antoninus Pius (138-161), allegedly portrayed as "Essarhaddon" in Tobit (H. Graetz, *Geschichte der Juden*, Vol. 4, pp. 466 f., second edit.; MGWJ 28 [1879] 513-520; similarly H. Preiss, ZWT

[49] For instance: J. T. Marshall (Hastings, *Dictionary of the Bible*, Vol. 4, p. 788. 1902); L. E. T. André, *Les Apocryphes*, p. 182; E. Schürer, *Geschichte*, Vol. 3, p. 239; D. C. Simpson (Charles, *Apocrypha*, p. 185); J. Goettsberger, *Einleitung in das A.T.*, p. 178 (cf. n. 3); O. Eissfeldt, *Einleitung*, p. 641. 1934; W. O. E. Oesterley, *Introduction to the Books of the Apocrypha*, p. 169. 1935; J. E. Steinmueller, *A Companion to Scripture Studies*, Vol. 2, p. 132. C. C. Torrey, *The Apocryphal Literature*, p. 85.

29 [1885] 50 f.), or even to A.D. 226 (A. Kohut, *Etwas über die Moral und Abfassungszeit des Buches Tobias.* Breslau, 1872). Since the Book of Tobit was known to Pseudo-Clement (II Cor. 16:4 is an echo of Tob. 12:8 f.) in 140 and to Polycarp, Bishop of Smyrna (Phil. 10:2; cf. Tob. 12:9) about 150, such late dates are *ipso facto* excluded; Clement of Alexandria (*Stromata* ii, 23, §139) before 220 actually quoted Tob. 4:16 as Scripture.

We lack definite clues for determining the residence of the author. The book combines the strictest Jewish practices and tenets with Oriental folklore; the action takes place in Nineveh, Ecbatana, and Rhagae, but the Temple in Jerusalem is manifestly at the center of the author's thought. It has therefore been possible to suggest the most varied locations as the home of the author. Following Th. Nöldeke (*Monatsberichten der Berliner Akademie,* 1879, p. 62), several scholars have supposed that Tobit was written in Egypt[50]—a conclusion that is almost certain *if* the book was originally written in Greek as they contend. But if, as seems more probable, the book was written in Hebrew or Aramaic, then it could hardly have been written in Ptolemaic Egypt. The setting of the action in the Diaspora has induced some scholars to look far from Jerusalem for its place of origin, in spite of the fact that Daniel, the Palestinian origin of which can hardly be questioned, describes non-Palestinian locales much more vividly than Tobit, a book in which only Jewish family life (unchanged in Palestine, Assyria, and Media) is depicted in some detail. If the author had lived in Mesopotamia (P. Vetter, TQ 86 [1904] 515-39), he could hardly have assumed that Nineveh was a day's march west of the Tigris (6:1 [Gr. 6:2]), since Herodotus (I, 193; II, 150) still knew, long after the destruction of Nineveh, that it was located on the banks of the Tigris, and the memory of its site has persisted locally through the ages. And it is difficult to believe that if the author had lived in Media (cf. J. H. Moulton, *Early Zoroastrianism,* p. 247) he could have stated that Ecbatana and Rhagae were but a day's march apart (9:6), whereas the journey on camels (9:2) requires almost two weeks. Even less probable are other remote localities, like Persia (A. Kohut). No, the book was written in Palestine, more specifically in Judea (presumably in Jerusalem or its environs), as the religious teaching (similar to Sirach's) indicates (cf. J. Müller, *Beiträge,* p. 24. Beih. ZAW 13. Giessen, 1908). But it echoes some of the feelings of the Jews of the Diaspora.

---

[50] Wm. Robertson Smith ("Tobit" in *Encyclopaedia Britannica,* ninth edit., 1888); M. Löhr (in E. Kautzsch, *Die Apokryphen und Pseudepigraphen,* Vol. 1, p. 136. Tübingen, 1900); André, *Les Apocryphes,* p. 183; D. C. Simpson (in Charles, *Apocrypha,* pp. 185-187); E. J. Goodspeed, *The Story of the Apocrypha,* p. 13.

Our fourth critical problem is that of the integrity of the book, and this is insoluble at present, owing to insufficient evidence. The original text of Tobit, presumably in Aramaic, is hidden from us by the haze of three distinct recensions of the Greek text, not to speak of the other versions. Even if the Codex Sinaiticus comes closest, on the whole, to the lost original, it is precarious to attempt to determine, on the basis of a translation which has not been transmitted intact, what parts of the book are later interpolations.

Beginning with K. D. Ilgen (*Die Geschichte Tobi's*, u.s.w. Jena, 1800), who dated 1:1-3:6 in the seventh century, 3:7-12:22 about 280 B.C., and ch. 13 about 10 B.C., some scholars have attempted to prove that Tobit is the result of a series of additions and revisions. The most radical and elaborate theory of the growth of Tobit (200 B.C.-A.D. 200) is that of W. Erbt (Cheyne's *Encyclopaedia Biblica*, Vol. 4, cols. 5113-5128; 1903). Erbt rejects all allusions to the Ahikar story (as also C. H. Toy, *Jewish Encyclopedia*, Vol. 12, p. 172; 1906; R. Smend, Beih. ZAW 13, p. 63; 1908; J. Müller, *ibid.*, p. 13), the wise sayings in ch. 4 (Toy omits also those in ch. 12), and other parts of the book. Without denying that the book could have reached its final form after a long period of elaboration and growth, we should recognize that none of the arguments advanced and none of the clues discovered can possibly lead us to objectively valid results. In particular, it seems certain (at least to the present writer) that the original author knew the Ahikar story and mentioned its hero; that, following the procedure of Ahikar's tale, he put moral precepts in the mouth of his hero; and that he told his tale substantially as it is preserved, including references to the dog of Tobias. Of course the popularity of the tales of Ahikar and Tobit, attested by variant recensions in several languages, produced inevitably a considerable number of editions differing in matters of detail, although agreeing in basic matters. The text remained in this fluid state for some centuries, and the proverbial sections in chs. 4 and 12 could be expanded or decreased at the pleasure of editors (Codex Sinait. lacks 4: 6b-19), not to speak of other changes. All that can be said of the original work, now beyond recovery, is that it probably did not differ substantially from the story told in Codex Sinaiticus (and may even have contained 4:6b-19).

This incertitude about the precise text of the original work and our dependence on a Greek translation variously transmitted are serious obstacles for a correct appreciation of the literary art of Tobit. Nevertheless, some observations about the structure of the story and its style may be presented here.

In structure, the story of Tobit differs from all other Hebrew and Aramaic short stories. While the Books of Ruth, Jonah, Judith, Dan. 1-6,

Esther, Ahikar, and others relate the adventures of the hero or heroine according to whom they are named in a straightforward manner, in Tobit the troubles of two widely separated households are told—and eventually solved—together. This unusual narrative technique is the result, as has been noted, of the use of two originally distinct folklore motifs: the Grateful Dead and the Dangerous Bride. Their union is effected with considerable skill, although the two tales are not so well fused as in later versions of the combination, so that C. H. Toy (*Jew. Encycl.*, Vol. 12, p. 172) could regard the story of Sara as an addition to that of Tobit.

First the author tells the story of Tobit's piety, good fortune, and misery (1:3-3:6); then the apparently totally irrelevant story of Sara's troubles (3:7-15). The two stories end symmetrically: Tobit and Sara, distressed more by reproach than by calamity, pray for death at the same instant. But God heard their petitions and through Raphael took measures to cure their ills. Thus in the sequel the two stories are joined into one.

After these preliminaries, the main part of the book follows the steps of Tobias as, accompanied by Azarias (Raphael), he journeys to Ecbatana and marries Sara (4-8) and, after Azarias has collected the money from Gabael in Rhagae (ch. 9), returns to Nineveh to restore his father's sight (10-11). The story closes with Raphael's return to heaven (ch. 12), Tobit's psalm of thanksgiving (ch. 13), and the deaths of Tobit and Tobias in their ripe old age (ch. 14).

The story is well constructed, in accordance with a definite plan: no part of the book looks like a later addition. All the characters are indispensable to the plot. They are arranged in pairs (Raphael and Asmodeus; Tobit, Anna, Tobias corresponding to Raguel, Edna, and Sara), with the exception of Sara's maids, Gabael, and of course God behind the scenes. It is only the author's eagerness to inject an intense religious feeling into an originally secular tale that introduces matters which, though valuable per se, contribute nothing to the action. The announcement of divine intervention in behalf of Tobit and Sara (3:16 f.) may relieve the reader's anxiety about their calamities, but decidedly lessens the dramatic suspense. The quotation of the full text of prayers (3:1-6, 11-15; 8:5-8, 15-17), psalms (ch. 13), and aphorisms (4:3-21; 12:6-10; cf. 14:8-11) would be frowned upon in modern short stories, but was entirely in the manner of some ancient didactic tales like the Egyptian Eloquent Peasant, Ahikar, The Three Youths at the Court of Darius (Greek Ezra [I Esdras] 3:1-4:42), Judith, Greek Esther, and others.

Thus, although the book as a whole should be classed as a short novel, it exhibits (in addition to straight narrative prose) other literary genres. The pedantic style of official documents in the title (1:1 f.) and the autobiographical form (1:3-3:6) inspired by Nehemiah serve to give an air of historicity to the book. The psalms, prayers, and aphorisms were of course written by the author in standard meter, although the poetic form is lost to some extent in the Greek translation. Although these poetic sections present abundant parallels with Hebrew poems of an earlier date, they were not quoted from anthologies but composed in Aramaic or Hebrew for their context. The prayers of Tobit and Sara (3:1-6, 11-15) are moving appeals to God *de profundis*, similar in content (request for death) and form: a praise of God introduces the invocation. The prayer of Sara is, however, more personal, as befitting a woman. Tobit's prayer is more standardized: like the liturgical prayers in Ezra 9; Neh. 1 and 9; Dan. 9:4-20; and the prayers of Azariah and Manasses (all influenced by those in I Kings 8 and Jer. 32:17-25), it stresses the national sins, which God punishes, and appeals to his mercy. It may therefore be considered typical, with these others, of Jewish piety after the Exile. The other prayers in the book (8:5-8, 15-17), although not so pessimistic, have the same structure (praise followed by invocation). The psalm of joy in ch. 13 likewise refers to national sin, in the midst of praise for God and expectation of a glorious future.

All in all, Tobit is one of the best extant examples of an ancient Semitic short story. The characters are well traced, the conversations are animated and true to life, the vicissitudes of pious Jewish families in the Dispersion are depicted vividly, and the tale as a whole is dramatically absorbing, psychologically convincing. The combination of fantastic traits (such as the healing powers of the entrails of a fish), with details taken from life (like the dog that accompanies Tobias on his journey), is by no means disturbing in a fairy tale. The style, judging from a translation, is adequate, although lacking the superb brilliance found in the best Old Testament stories. In the silver age of Hebrew-Aramaic literature Tobit may be regarded as a classic. For to these qualities, which atone for the literary defects typical of the time (historical and geographic errors, a naïve assumption that God will intervene to save the pious Jews, and a rather artificial structure of the plot), we must add the nobility of the religious and moral teaching of the book, to which we now turn our attention.

2. Religious and Ethical Teaching

By example and by precept the Book of Tobit inculcates the noble religious and moral principles of Judaism in the first third of the second century B.C. While the events narrated take place among the Jews of the Dispersion, the author has not neglected to stress the worship in the Temple at Jerusalem. Pious Jews went to Jerusalem for the annual festivals, even as the Galileans in the Gospels, in accordance with the "everlasting decree" (1:6; cf. Bar. 4:1; Ecclus. 45:7, Hebrew) of the Law. Tobit, while living in Galilee, went to Jerusalem to celebrate the feasts.[51]

On these journeys to the Temple, Tobit delivered the offerings and tithes required by the Law (1:6-8; cf. 5:13 [Gr. 5:14]). The two principal Greek texts differ, however, in regard to the tithes listed in 1:6-8.

The earlier practice is described in Codex Sinaiticus. Tobit paid to the priests "the first fruits [bikkûrîm], the firstlings [bekōr or bekōrāh], the tithe [ma'asēr] of the cattle [Lev. 27:32], and the first shearings of the sheep [Deut. 18:4]." To the Levites he gave "the tithes of corn, wine, oil, pomegranates, and the rest of the fruits" (cf. Num. 18:21, 24). The "second tithe" on the first, second, fourth, and fifth years of the septennial or sabbatical cycle (according to rabbinical sources) was converted into money which was used at will for feasting in Jerusalem (Deut. 14:22-26). On the third and sixth years this tithe, the "poor tithe," was distributed to needy "orphans, widows, and proselytes" (Deut. 14: 28 f.). No tithe, of course, was paid on the seventh, or sabbatical, year.

The standard Greek text (based on Codices Vaticanus and Alexandrinus), as published by A. Rahlfs, reflects later usage and represents probably, as E. Schürer (Geschichte, Vol. 3, p. 243) believed, a correction made by Jews to the older recension. According to this later text, Tobit presented to the priests for the altar "the first fruits, the tithes of produce, the first shearings." To the Levites he gave the (first) "tithe of all produce." "And the second tithe I sold for money and I spent it for feasting in Jerusalem every year. And the third [tithe] I gave to those to whom it was suitable."

The differences between the two recensions are the following: 1. In the Sinaiticus Tobit gave the second tithe to the poor in the third and sixth years, but consumed it in feasting on the four other years. In the standard text, apparently, he consumed the second tithe in feasting "every year," but at the same time collected a third tithe for the poor. 2. Tobit gave the tithe of the cattle to the priests, according to the Sinaiticus, but the standard text omits this item. 3. In the standard text "the tithes of produce" are given to the priests, and "the third [tithe] of all produce" to the Levites: it would thus seem that the same tithe was paid both to the priests and to the Levites, which is patently absurd.

Although the Sinaiticus furnishes the earlier Jewish regulations about tithes, based on an interpretation of Biblical laws, it is not free from difficulties. In fact, no sources earlier than the Mishna give us a clear

---

[51] Tob. 1:6-8; 5:13 (Gr. 5:14); cf. R. Marcus, Law in the Apocrypha, pp. 86 f. New York, 1927.

picture and are free of inconsistencies.[52] But the Sinaiticus agrees with Jub. 32:15 (cf. 13:26 f.) in assigning to the priests the tithe of the cattle, and with Jub. 32:10-14 in allowing the layman to use the second tithe for his feasts at the Sanctuary. But Jub. 32:9 seems to agree with the standard text of Tobit in assigning the whole tithe to the priests, as specifically stated in Jth. 11:13 and as we know was done, in later times, at least in Galilee (Josephus, *Life*, ch. 12 [§63]). Philo and Josephus both contradict themselves in saying at times that the tithes belong to the Levites, and again to the priests.

In general, the Book of Tobit discloses true reverence for the Temple in Jerusalem and its worship. "The Temple of the habitation of God" (1:4, Sinait.) or "of the Highest" (Vat., Alex.) has been "sanctified and built for all generations of eternity" (1:4), in contrast with the shrines of Jeroboam at Dan and on all the mountains of Galilee dedicated to "the calf" ("Baal the heifer," Vat., Alex.) (1:5). The destruction of the Temple in 586 was a divine punishment, but the "tabernacle" will again be rebuilt with joy (13:9 f. [Gr. 13:10b-11]), but "not like the first" (14:5).

For the most part, however, Tobit describes the religious life of Jews in the Dispersion rather than at Jerusalem. Even this longing for the Temple and this vision of its superhuman significance and beauty (cf. also the picture of the New Jerusalem in 13:16-18 [Gr. 13:17 f.]) is characteristic of the Dispersion, beginning with Ezekiel.

> 'Tis distance lends enchantment to the view,
> And robes the mountain in its azure hue.
>
> Campbell
>
> Absence makes the heart grow fonder.
>
> T. H. Bailey

Indeed the Jews far from Jerusalem were "absent in body, but present in spirit" (I Cor. 5:3). This sense of nearness to the holy city[53] is symbolically expressed by turning one's face and hands in the direction of Jerusalem while praying in the lands of the Dispersion (3:11 f.; cf. I Kings 8:44, 48; Dan. 6:10 [Aram. 6:11]; Ps. 5:7 [H. 5:8]; 28:2; I [III] Esd. 4:58; Mishna *Berakoth* 4:5; Jerome, *ad* Ez. 8:16). This

---

[52] The problems involved are extremely complicated and cannot be dealt with in detail here. See in particular: G. F. Moore, in *Encyclopaedia Biblica*, Vol. 4, cols. 5102-5105; E. Schürer, *Geschichte*, Vol. 2, pp. 303-307; O. Eissfeldt, *Erstlinge und Zehnten im alten Testament*, pp. 118-121 (BWAT 22). Leipzig, 1917; R. Marcus, *Law in the Apocrypha*, pp. 109-112; S. Belkin, *Philo and the Oral Law*, pp. 67-78. Cambridge, Mass., 1940.

[53] "The Jews who lived in the lands outside of Palestine considered that country as their mother-land. Spiritually they were connected with the holy land. The home of Judaism, from its cradle up to the development of *nomocracy*, was in the land of Israel" (S. Zeitlin, in JQR 35 [1944] 218).

practice, perpetuated in the *kiblah* (*giblah*, what one faces) of the Moslem, is first attested among the Babylonians in the seventh century— if my interpretation of a letter from Erech to Ashurbanipal is correct (cf. JBL 47 [1928] 186 f.; R. H. Pfeiffer, *State Letters of Assyria*, p. 60).

This nationalistic trait of the Jews in the Dispersion (cf. 6:10-13 [Gr. 6:11-14]) expresses itself negatively by separation from the Gentiles among whom they live. This reaction against the danger of assimilation is particularly stressed in Tobit in the matter of food (1:10-12; cf. Dan. 1:8; Judg. 12:1-4) and marriage (1:9; 3:15; 4:12 f.; 6:11 [Gr. 6:12]; 7:12 f.). In Tobit, however, the proud realization of belonging to God's people, "the sons of the prophets" (4:12), who will eventually return to Jerusalem (14:5-7, Sinait.), does not express itself in that contempt for the heathen which is so conspicuous in books written *after* the persecution of the Jews by Antiochus Epiphanes in 168-165 (Daniel, Judith, and Esther).[54] Like the Second Isaiah, the author of Tobit expects the conversion of the Gentiles to the worship of Jehovah (13:11 [Gr. 13:13]; 14:6).

Judaism, however, in Tobit (as in Ecclesiasticus) is far more a personal than a national religion: its basic principle, addressed to the individual, is: "My son, be mindful of the Lord our God all thy days, and let not thy will be set to sin, or to transgress his commandments: do uprightly all thy life long, and follow not in the ways of unrighteousness" (4:5). We note here a parallel to the basic injunction of Jehovah to Abraham in Gen. 17:1 (Priestly Code); but the two rites of the patriarchal religion in the Priestly Code, characteristic of Judaism in the Dispersion, and mentioned by Roman writers[55] as typical of the Jews, i.e., the Sabbath and circumcision, are not mentioned in Tobit. The ritual prescriptions of the Law are taken for granted, but the Book of Tobit lays stress on "the weightier matters of the law" (Matt. 23:23): honesty (2:11-14), personal piety, integrity, and charity.

Personal religion finds its deepest expression in prayer. In times of distress petitions are addressed to God (3:1-6, 11-15) in a contrite spirit, with the assurance that they will ascend before the glory of God (3:16, Sinait.) or before Raphael (3:16, Vat., Alex. 12-12) and the six other archangels (12:15, Vat., Alex.). The pious Jew believed that God would protect him on dangerous journeys (5:16 [Gr. 5:17], Sinait.), through his angel (*ibid.*, Vat., Alex.); and that, in answer to prayer, God would save him from death (6:17 [Gr. 6:18], Vat., Alex.; cf. 7:18 [Gr. 7:17];

[54] Tacitus (*Histories* V, 5) expresses the point of view of Tobit, except for the hatred of the Gentiles which he polemically stresses: "Between themselves there is inflexible loyalty, ready mercy, but against all others hostile hatred; they separate themselves [from the Gentiles] with regard to food and marriage. . . ."

[55] The pertinent texts are conveniently collected in Th. Reinach, *Textes d'auteurs grecs et romains relatifs au Judaïsme*. Paris, 1895.

8:4-8). After the deliverance from danger and disease the pious Jew praised God (8:15-17; 11:14 f. [Gr. 11:13 f.]; 12:6 f., 22; 13) and invoked divine blessings upon his beloved (10:12 f. [Gr. 10:11 f.]). Earnest prayer should be accompanied by fasting and good works (12:8).

This assurance that prayer is effective rests on a firm faith in God's power and mercy, indeed in the certainty that he intervenes in human affairs (4:19; 12:18), sometimes even determining marriages long in advance (6:17 [Gr. 6:18]). The *power* of God is indicated by his appellations: the Most High (1:4, 13; 4:11), the King of Heaven (13:7, 11 [Gr. 13:9, 13]), the Great King (13:15 [Gr. 13:16]), the Everlasting King (13:6, 10 [Gr. 13:7, 11]), the Lord (*despótēs*; 8:17). God is the Holy One (12:12, 15), surrounded by glory (12:15). His perfect knowledge of the most secret matters is taken for granted (3:14). God dwells in heaven (5:16 [Gr. 5:17]; cf. 10:12 f. [Gr. 10:11 f.]; 13:7, 11 [Gr. 13:9, 13]), but also in the Temple at Jerusalem (1:4).

God's transcendent majesty and dominion are emphasized in Tobit not only by the avoidance of anthropomorphisms (except in standard poetic expressions, as in 13:6), but also by a doctrine about angels more elaborate than in any earlier or contemporary writing, comparable indeed to that of later books (Daniel, Ethiopic Enoch). Seven archangels[56] present the prayers of the pious Jews (cf. 12:12), or (according to another interpretation) of the angels,[57] to God (12:15, Vat., Alex.) and have immediate access to God's presence (*ibid.*). Angels praise God (8:15, Vat., Alex.) and are praised together with him (11:14). When Tobit expressed the wish that the angel of God should accompany Tobias and Azarias on their journey (5:16 [Gr. 5:17]) "with deliverance" (Sinait.), he did not realize that what he told his wife (5:21 [Gr. 5:22]), was literally true. For Azarias was the archangel Raphael in human form, but only as a "vision" (*horasis*) which only in appearance ate and drank (12:19). Raphael ("God heals"), as his name indicates, is the angel "who is set over all the diseases and all the wounds of the children of men" (Enoch 40:9): "he was sent to heal" (Tob. 3:16 f.) Tobit of his blindness and Sara of demonic persecution, and performed the cures by means of the inner organs of the fish that Tobias caught in the Tigris.

---

[56] It is possible (but not certain) that the notion of seven archangels in Judaism (12:15; Enoch 20:1-8; 81:5; 90:21; Rev. 8:2), called "angels of the presence" (Enoch 40:2, etc.), was derived from the seven *Amesha-Spentas* of Zoroastrianism. On the four or seven archangels in Judaism, see L. Ginzberg, *Legends of the Jews*, Vol. 5, pp. 23 f., n. 65; Vol. 6, pp. 81 f., n. 440.

[57] "Saints" may mean either strict Jews or angels. Angels elsewhere in Jewish writings never bring men's prayers to God but only God's messages to men. But in 8:15 (Vat., Alex.) God's "saints" (the Jews) and His "angels" are distinguished, and in 12:12 Raphael brought Tobit's and Sara's prayers before God (cf. 3:16 f. in Vat., Alex.).

But such therapeutic methods, as also the beliefs that sparrows' warm dung destroyed eyesight and that a demon (Asmodeus) killed Sara's seven husbands, belong to the realm of superstition and folklore, rather than to that of religion.

In Tobit, justice (3:2; "the Lord of righteousness" in 13:6 [Gr. 13:7]) is assumed to be a self-evident attribute of God: the discussion of the matter in Job had apparently failed to shake the reliance of the author, as of most of the pious Jews of his time, on the teaching of Amos and Isaiah. And yet, as in Job, pious and innocent persons such as Tobit and Sara suffer undeserved torments—caused by God himself in Tobit's case (11:15 [Gr. 11:14]) and by a demon in Sara's (3:8). Far from questioning, like Job, God's justice, or at least his equitable retribution of human conduct, the author reaffirms emphatically the standard doctrine of retribution: sin (4:13; 12:10) and virtue (4:6; 12:9) inevitably bring rewards or punishments; God himself judges men rightly (3:2), rewarding them for their good deeds (1:11-13; 4:14) and punishing them for their sins (3:3, 5), or even for their fathers' (3:4), in this life.

Like a father (13:4), God is not only just, but merciful: he scourges and has mercy (cf. 11:15 [Gr. 11:14]; 13:5, 9 [Gr. 13:10]); he leads down to the underworld and brings up again (13:2). His lovingkindness is manifest (8:16 f.; 11:17 [Gr. 11:16]), his ways are "mercy and truth" (3:2); he is compassionate (7:12, Vat., Alex.) and will have mercy on his people after they have been led into captivity (14:5).

Personal piety in Tobit is thus characterized by a strong feeling of trust and confidence in God, by love for God (14:7). This is the greatest of all treasures: the pious Jew who fears God, avoids sin, and does what is pleasing to God, even though poor in earthly goods, is the owner of good possessions (4:21); and through almsgiving he lays up for himself an earthly treasure against the day of necessity (4:9; Vat., Alex. [4:7-19a are lacking in Sinait.])—*not* the treasure in heaven of which Jesus spoke (Mark 10:21; Matt. 19-21; Luke 18:22; cf. Matt. 6:20; Luke 12:33). In addition to a firm faith in God, the personal religion in Tobit consists in observance of the Law of Moses and in philanthropic deeds.

The observance of the ritual prescriptions of the Law (such as the payment of tithes)[58] and the separation from the Gentiles, notably in the matter of food and marriage, has already been noted. The ethical prescriptions of the Law receive special emphasis in this book; they have a negative and a positive aspect.

The negative aspect of morality is summarized in the precept "What

[58] Note also the ritual purifications (2:5) and sleeping outside of the house when in a state of ceremonial pollution (2:9). The standard Greek text of 12:8 is more ritualistic than the Sinaiticus text.

you hate, do to no man" (4.15, Vat., Alex.); Jesus expressed the Golden Rule in a positive form (Matt. 7:12). Another general statement is in 4:5 (not to violate God's commandments). Tobit exhorts his son not to despise his mother (4:3), not to practice fornication (4:12; Vat., Alex.) nor to marry a Gentile wife (*ibid.*), not to retain the wages of an employee (4:14; Vat., Alex.), not to drink wine to excess (4:15b; Vat., Alex.), and not to give (alms) to the wicked (4:17; Vat., Alex.).

Raphael in his counsels (12:6-10) is more positive than Tobit: he stresses gratitude to God, doing good, prayer and almsgiving. But Tobit has likewise some positive advice for Tobias (4:3-19, of which 4:7-19a are omitted in Sinait.): Tobias should honor his mother and bury his parents properly, be mindful of God, live righteously, give alms in accordance with his substance, marry a Jewish wife, love the Jews, feed the hungry, clothe the naked, supply food for the graves of the righteous, seek advice from the wise, and turn to God with praise and prayer.

Aside from these precepts of Tobit and of Raphael, practical morality is inculcated elsewhere in the book by example and counsel; although often the point of view is narrowly Jewish and Gentiles are not taken into consideration, the moral ideal is by no means a low one. The family ties are particularly strong and affectionate (10:11-13 [Gr. 10:10-12]): money is as rubbish compared to a son's life, or (according to another interpretation of *perípsēma*) it is to be sacrificed for a son (5:18 [Gr. 5:19]). Special emphasis is placed on almsgiving (1:3, 16 f.; 14:2, 11) and on the burial of the Jewish dead whether members of the family (4:3 f.; 6:14 [Gr. 6:15]; 14:10) or utterly unknown (1:17 f.; 2:3-8; 12:12 f.).

In the person of Tobit the author has depicted a strict, law-abiding Jew, devoted to his God, his family, and his people; he is obviously presented as a model for the author's contemporaries, as an example of Jewish piety and right conduct. Even though Tobit is a character of fiction, he furnishes to modern historians a valuable likeness of those devout Jews in the early part of the second century B.C. who were the precursors of the Pharisees[59] and consequently of orthodox Jews through the centuries down to our own time.

---

[59] In contrast with the Pharisees (and Daniel in 164 B.C.), the Book of Tobit (3:6, cf. 3:10; 4:10), like Ecclesiasticus, knows nothing of a resurrection. But the beliefs in angels and demons, as also in the New Jerusalem, are characteristic of the Pharisees.

CHAPTER III

THE BOOK OF JUDITH

~~~~~~

This intensely patriotic and religious book is named, like the Book of Esther, after its heroine: Judith (Hebr. *Jehudith,* meaning "Jewess"; cf. Gen. 26:34). Both books relate fictitious stories about women who, through cunning and daring, brought about the death of their people's enemy and saved the Jews from impending massacre. Many centuries before, in ancient Israel, three women had wrought deliverance either by slaying the chief of the foes (Jael, Judg. 5:24-27; cf. 4:17-22; and a woman of Thebez, Judg. 9:53) or by shrewd counsel (II Sam. 20:14-22). These historical women, as also Deborah (Judg. 4-5), may have suggested to the authors of Judith and Esther the choice of a woman as a deliverer. The story of Judith may be summarized as follows:

PART I: THE ATTACK ON THE JEWS (1-7).

1. *Nebuchadnezzar's victory over Arphaxad* (1). In the twelfth year of Nebuchadnezzar, "who reigned over the Assyrians at Nineveh" (in reality Nebuchadnezzar king of Babylonia came to the throne in 605, seven years *after* the destruction of Nineveh!) and in the days of Arphaxad king of the Medes (otherwise unknown), who built mightily the fortifications of Ecbatana (cf. Herodotus I, 98, where the work is ascribed to Deioces), Nebuchadnezzar attacked Arphaxad king of Media in the plain of Ragau, presumably Rhagae (1:1-5; the long initial sentence [1:1-4] is left incomplete and merely gives the date; 1:5 looks like a gloss based on 1:15). Nebuchadnezzar summoned the forces of Persia, Cilicia, Damascus, the Libanus and Antilibanus, the Phoenician coast, Palestine, and Egypt to the war (1:7-10), but they refused to come (1:11). Angry and swearing that he would avenge himself on them (1:12), Nebuchadnezzar in his seventeenth year defeated the Medes (1:13), conquered Ecbatana (1:14), slew Arphaxad (1:15), and celebrated the victory in Nineveh during 120 days (1:16).

2. *Holofernes' subjection of the western nations, except the Jews* (2-3). In the first month of his eighteenth year, Nebuchadnezzar decided to destroy all western nations which had defied his orders (2:1-3) and ordered his commander in chief Holofernes to go forth with an army to

force their submission and slay the recalcitrants (2:4-13). Holofernes
assembled an Assyrian army of 120,000 foot soldiers and 12,000 mounted
archers (2:14-16), together with abundant supplies (2:17 f.), and
marched forth with these forces and innumerable contingents from other
nations (2:19 f.). In three days he reached Bectileth (unknown) (2:21),
then he devastated Put (Pontus?) and Lud (Lydia) (named together in
Ez. 27:10; cf. 30:5; Jer. 46:9), Rasses (Old Latin, *Thiras* and *Rasis*;
Syriac, *Tiras* and *Raamses*), and the Ishmaelites (2:22 f.); he crossed the
Euphrates, traversed Mesopotamia, and destroyed the cities on the
river Abrona or Arbonai (?) (2:24). He conquered Cilicia and came
to "the borders of Japheth" (?) near Arabia (2:25); he set fire to the
tents of the Midianites (2:26) and laid waste the plain of Damascus
(2:27). The cities on the coast—notably Sidon, Tyre, Sur (?), Ocina
(?), Jemnaan (i.e., Jamnia), Azotus, and Ashkelon—in their fear (2:28)
sent ambassadors to Holofernes offering unconditional surrender (3:1-6).
He was welcomed enthusiastically (3:7), although he destroyed the
sanctuaries and divine images in order that Nebuchadnezzar alone be
henceforth worshiped as god (3:8). Before invading Judea he stayed
a month near Scythopolis (ancient Beth-shean), reorganizing his army
(3:9).

3. *The resistance and seemingly hopeless plight of the Jews* (4-7). In
Judea, the Jews had recently returned from their Babylonian captivity
and had rebuilt the Temple in Jerusalem (the dating of these events in
the days of Nebuchadnezzar is incredibly absurd); they feared for their
Temple (4:1-3) and prepared for war (4:4 f.). Upon the orders of
Joakim, the high priest, and of the Sanhedrin, the people near the
plain of Esdraelon, particularly those living in Bethulia (otherwise
unknown), fortified the mountain passes to bar invasion from the north
(4:6-8). But, despairing of human means, the Jews cried mightily unto
their God and all of them, including their cattle (cf. Jonah 3:8), put on
sackcloth (4:9-13)—not excepting even the priests performing the
Temple rites (4:14 f.). Upon hearing of these military preparations,
Holofernes convoked the chiefs of the Moabites, Ammonites, and other
"sons of Canaan," asking for information about the Jews, who alone in
the western countries had dared defy him (5:1-4). In his reply, Achior,
the leader of the Ammonites, summarized the history of Israel from the
time of Abraham to the Jews' return from the Exile and the rebuilding of
the Temple (5:5-19), and concluded that the Jews could be overcome
only if their God failed to defend them on account of their sins (5:20 f.).
Indignant at these words, the listeners spoke of killing Achior and
proceeding with operations against the Jews (5:22-24). Holofernes
denied that the God of Israel could defend his people, because
Nebuchadnezzar, the sole god, would destroy the Jews (6:1-4); he

decided that Achior should be delivered bound to the Jews and suffer their fate (6:5-8): let him find comfort in his hope that they would be delivered (6:9)! Thus Achior was cast into fetters and thrown at the foot of the hill upon which Bethulia rose (6:10-13); he was, however, released by the men of the city. After reporting his speech to Ozias and the other leaders of the city, he was praised by the people and entertained at dinner by Ozias; meanwhile, the people continued to entreat God's help (6:14-21).

On the following day Holofernes moved his army of 170,000 foot soldiers and 12,000 horsemen against Bethulia (7:1-3; see 2:15), filling the inhabitants with terror (7:4 f.). One day later, at the head of the cavalry, he cut off some of the city's water supply (7:6 f.). Upon the advice of the Edomitic, Moabitic, and other leaders (7:8-15), Holofernes decided to lay siege to the city, forcing its capitulation through hunger and thirst, rather than to storm it at the cost of considerable losses (7:16-18). When the city had been under siege for thirty-four days and water had become so scarce that it was rationed scantily, the people lost heart (7:19-22); they angrily accused Ozias of having caused their plight and demanded that he surrender the city so that at least their lives might be saved (7:23-28). But Ozias persuaded them to endure five more days, pending God's help (7:29-32).

PART II: THE DELIVERANCE WROUGHT BY JUDITH (8-16).

4. *Judith's rebuke* (8). Judith, the daughter of Merari, whose genealogy was traced back to Jacob-Israel (8:1), was the widow of Manasses; her husband had died of sunstroke three years and four months before (8:2-4). Judith still wore mourning garments and fasted, except on Sabbaths, festivals, and on the eve of such days (8:5 f.). She was an extremely beautiful, wealthy, and pious woman (8:7 f.). Upon hearing of the murmuring of the people and of Ozias's reassurance, she summoned him with the other elders (8:9 f.) and upbraided them for promising to surrender the city in five days unless God delivered it before then (8:11): they had thus tempted God, whose purposes are unsearchable (8:12-14); God may save or destroy whenever he wishes, and cannot be forced by threats (8:15 f.). God may, however, hear their cry and rescue them (8:17), first of all because the idolatry of their fathers has now been suppressed (8:18-20), and secondly because the fall of Bethulia would involve the destruction of the Temple, as also the slaughter and captivity of the Jews (8:21-24). Let the people be grateful to God, who tests them through affliction, as he tested Abraham, Isaac, and Jacob, and who chastises them for their improvement (8:25-27). Ozias agreed entirely with Judith, but was bound to keep the promise

that the people forced him to make (8:28-30); let Judith pray for rain (8:31). Judith instead declared that she would go forth from the city with her maid that night and that God would deliver Bethulia within five days through her exploits (8:32-34). After invoking divine blessings on her, the elders returned to their stations (8:35 f.).

5. *Judith's prayer* (9). At the time of the evening sacrifice in the Temple (cf. Ex. 30:8), Judith, in sackcloth and ashes, prayed (9:1) to the God who through her ancestor Simeon had avenged Dinah's rape (9:2-4; cf. Gen. 34:25 f.), the God who determines the course of all events (9:5 f.), imploring his aid against the mighty Assyrians (9:7), who propose to defile the Temple (9:8); may he endow her with divine power that she might, through deceit, bring about the destruction of the foes (9:9-13): thus will Israel and the Gentiles know that God is the sole protection of Israel (9:14).

6. *Judith's preparations* (10-11). After her prayer, Judith, removing her mourning garments, bathed, anointed herself, and decked herself dashingly, to ensnare the eyes of all men who beheld her (10:1-4). With her maid, who carried victuals, wine, and vessels (10:5), she went to the city gate, where Ozias and the elders, entranced by her beauty, invoked divine blessings on her (10:6-8). At her request, they ordered the city gate opened for her, and she went down into the valley with her maid (10:9 f.). Stopped by an Assyrian outpost, she stated that she was a Jewess fleeing from her people to escape their imminent doom (10:11 f.), and that she would show Holofernes how to conquer the hill country without the loss of a man (10:13). The Assyrians reassured her and sent a hundred men to accompany her to the tent of Holofernes (10:14-17). Struck by her beauty as she stood awaiting admission, the Assyrians were saying that no Jew should be left alive lest, through the beauty of women like Judith, they entice the whole world (10:18 f.). Holofernes was resting on his bed, under a magnificent canopy; when he came forth to the vestibule of the tent, Judith remained prostrate before him until his servants raised her (10:20-23). Holofernes bade Judith to be of good cheer, for only those who refused to serve Nebuchadnezzar, like her mountain people, had reason to fear; she, on the contrary, would be treated well (11:1-4). Judith answered that she would speak the truth and show him how to attain his objective (11:5 f.); sent by Nebuchadnezzar to subjugate all men, he is renowned for his wisdom and valor (11:7 f.). Although what Achior has said (see 5:5-21) is perfectly true and should be taken to heart (11:9 f.), Holofernes will prevail over the Jews because they have incensed their God by their decision to lay hands on the sacrificial victims, the first fruits, and the tithes sanctified for the Temple, having already asked the approval of the Sanhedrin. Should permission be granted and the Law thus be

violated, the nation would be destroyed instantly (11:11-15). That is why she has forsaken her people and, being deeply religious, she has been commissioned by God to accomplish an astounding exploit with Holofernes (11:16). She will remain with the Assyrians and go forth by night into the valley to pray until God reveals to her that the Jews have sinned; then she will lead Holofernes to the conquest of Judea (11:17-19). Her words pleased Holofernes, who marveled at her beauty and wisdom, and he assured her that if she fulfilled her words he would worship her God and she would dwell highly honored in Nebuchadnezzar's palace (11:20-23).

7. *Judith's exploit* (12:1-13:10). Judith, conforming to the Jewish dietary laws, refused to partake of Holofernes' food; she had brought along her own victuals (12:1 f.). She assured Holofernes, who wondered what she would eat when her provisions were consumed, that before then the Lord's work through her would be accomplished (12:3 f.). She slept in her tent until the middle of the night, and at the morning watch, according to Holofernes' permission, she went into the valley to bathe and pray; thus she did for three days, returning to her tent in a state of purity and remaining there until the evening meal (12:5-9). On the fourth day Holofernes, who was fascinated by Judith's charms (cf. 12:16), gave a small banquet in her honor and sent the eunuch Bagoas, who was in charge of her, to invite her (12:10-13). Judith readily consented (12:14), decked herself in her finery, and reclined at the table on fleeces, partaking of her own food and drink (12:15-19). Her beauty so affected Holofernes that he drank more wine than ever before (12:20). After the guests had departed, Bagoas closed the tent and dismissed the servants, so that Judith was left alone with Holofernes, who was lying intoxicated on his couch (13:1 f.). Judith had ordered her maid to wait for her to go into the valley for prayer (13:3). Alone with the sleeping commander, Judith prayed silently (13:4 f.) and, seizing his sword, she took hold of his hair, and after another prayer smote his neck twice, severing the head. Then she calmly took along the canopy, gave the head to the maid, who put it in the bag of victuals. They passed through the camp as on previous nights and came undisturbed to the gate of Bethulia (13:6-10).

8. *Judith's triumph* (13:11-15:13). From a distance Judith asked the watchmen to open the gate, for "God is with us" (*Immanuel*). Joyfully they called the elders, opened the gate, and made a fire to dispel the darkness (13:11-13). Judith urged them to praise God and showed them the head of Holofernes and the canopy; ascribing her success to God, she assured them that she had enticed Holofernes without being defiled by him (13:14-16). The people blessed God (13:17), but Ozias blessed Judith together with God (13:18-20). Turning to practical matters,

Judith told the people to hang the head of Holofernes outside the city wall and to take up battle stations in the morning, pretending to attack the Assyrians, who would rouse their captains, seek Holophernes in vain, and flee in panic (14:1-4). Then she summoned Achior; he fainted at the sight of the head of Holofernes but, upon reviving, blessed her and heard from her a full account of her doings; then, believing in God, he was circumcised and became a Jew (14:5-10). In the morning, as Judith had anticipated, the Assyrians were dismayed when Bagoas reported that Holofernes had been treacherously slain by the Hebrew woman (14:11-19). As the Assyrian soldiers dispersed in mad terror, the Jews of all Palestine fell upon them, slaughtering them and pursuing them beyond Damascus (15:1-5). The Jews of Bethulia sacked Holofernes' camp, but the others on their return also took abundant spoil (15:6 f.). Joakim the high priest and the Sanhedrin came from Jerusalem to behold the work of the Lord for Israel and to bless Judith (15:8-10). After plundering the camp during thirty days, the people gave Judith the tent of Holofernes and its contents (15:11). Judith led the women in a round dance, after placing branches in their hands and olive garlands on their heads, while the warriors followed them singing (15:12 f.).

9. *Judith's psalm* (16:1-17). Judith then sang a hymn of praise (16:1). Sing unto the Lord, for he is victorious in battle (16:2 f.). The Assyrian hosts came down from the north to slaughter and to pillage (16:4 f.), but the Lord destroyed them by the hand of Judith, who ensnared their chief through her beauty and severed his neck (16:6-9). Persians and Medes were dismayed at her boldness (16:10). The weakest in Israel turned the Assyrians to flight and slew them (16:11 f.). "I shall sing unto my God a new song," for he is glorious and invincible (16:13), the creator, the animator of living beings through his spirit, the universal ruler (16:14); he is both almighty and merciful (16:15); sacrifices matter less to God than true piety (16:16). Any nation which attacks Israel will be condemned to perish in torment (16:17).

10. *Judith's later years and her death* (16:18-25). The people purified themselves and worshiped the Lord in Jerusalem, while Judith dedicated to the Lord the tent of Holofernes, which had been given her, and his canopy, which she had taken (16:18 f.). After feasting with the people in Jerusalem for three months, Judith returned to Bethulia (16:20 f.). She remained loyal to her deceased husband, refusing to marry any of her many suitors (16:22). She was greatly esteemed, freed her maid, and when she died at the age of 105 years she was mourned seven days; she bequeathed her property to her husband's kinsmen and her own (in accordance with Num. 27:11). After her exploit, and even long after her death, no enemy terrified again the children of Israel (16:23-25).

1. *Historicity and Date*

Before the Protestant Reformation in the sixteenth century, the story of Judith was accepted as a record of historical events.[1] Roman Catholic scholars have generally defended the historicity of the book, which the Council of Trent had declared canonical and therefore inspired.[2] In recent times, however, Roman Catholic scholars have frankly recognized the historical difficulties and the chronological absurdities inherent in the book, but by explaining them as the result of textual corruption and successive interpolations through the centuries, have defended to their own satisfaction the historicity and the inspiration of the lost original edition of the book.[3] Such an argument rests on dogmatic rather than on historical premises: since the book was originally divinely inspired, it must have been historically accurate; therefore the historical errors it now contains must be due to later hands. From a purely historical point of view it is much simpler to assume that the original author, like the authors of the Books of Daniel and Esther, had only the foggiest notions of the length of the period from Nebuchadnezzar to Alexander, when Jewish history is almost a blank, and regarded Nebuchadnezzar and Cyrus as almost contemporaries—unless he blundered deliberately to show that his story was fiction.

The first doubts about the historicity of Judith were expressed in the

[1] Judith was considered a historical character in the earliest reference to this book (Clement of Rome, I Corinthians 55: 4 f.; written in A.D. 90-100), and later by Tertullian, Clement of Alexandria, Origen, Jerome, and others. See: Schürer, *Geschichte*, Vol. 3, p. 235; A. Biolek, *Die Ansicht des christlichen Altertums über den literarischen Charakter des Buches Judith* (Weidenauer Studien 4), pp. 335-368. Wien, 1911. For echoes of Judith in English literature, see H. Pentin, *Judith*. London, 1908.

[2] Modern defenses of the historicity of the book on the part of Roman Catholic scholars are listed by Schürer, *Geschichte*, Vol. 3, p. 237; cf. P. A. Raboisson, *Judith: la véracité du livre de ce nom*. Rome, 1898. The following Roman Catholic scholars have, however, regarded the book as an allegory or a legend: A. Scholz (*Das Buch Judith eine Prophetie*. Würzburg, 1885). J. Jahn (*Einleitung in die göttl. Bücher des Alten Bundes*. Wien, 1802-1803), C. F. Movers (in *Zeitschr. f. Philos. u. kath. Theol.*, 13th issue [Köln, 1835], p. 47), F. Lenormant (*La divination chez les Chaldéens*, pp. 153 f. Paris, 1874).

[3] They generally assume that the personal names in the book (notably Nebuchadnezzar, Holophernes, and Bagoas) were not original, but were inserted by someone unfamiliar with the chronology of past historical events (cf. J. Goettsberger, *Einleitung in das A.T.*, p. 185. Freiburg i. B., 1928). The most elaborate and painstaking attempt to prove the historicity of the book through this hypothesis is that of F. Steinmetzer, *Neue Untersuchung über die Geschichtlichkeit der Juditherzählung*. Leipzig, 1907. In the original story, according to Steinmetzer, the events took place in the time of Ashurbanipal king of Assyria (668-625); in the second edition the king was Cyrus the Persian (550-530); in the third edition the events took place in the time of Ezra and Nehemiah (Artaxerxes I Longimanus? [465-424]); and the final edition transfers us to the Maccabean period (Antiochus IV Epiphanes, 176-164).

sixteenth century, and Protestant scholars have increasingly come to regard the book as fiction. Martin Luther considered the book as a religious allegory depicting the triumph of the Jews, through divine intervention, over their enemies: the author deliberately used a false chronology and erroneous names to warn the reader that it should be understood as a holy parable (see O. F. Fritzsche, Commentary, p. 126).[4] This view, according to which Judith is a sort of passion play, an epic, an apologue, an allegory, was defended by later writers until recent times. Only one Protestant critic, O. Wolff (*Das Buch Judith als geschichtliche Urkunde verteidigt und erklärt*. Leipzig, 1861), has defended the genuine historicity of the book. Others (including Jewish scholars) admit at most a historical kernel or at least allusions to actual events.[5] But the notion that Judith is fiction, pure and simple, was vigorously advocated by L. Cappellus (*Commentarii et notae criticae in Vet. Test.*, p. 575. Amsterdam, 1689), who denounced the book as "a most silly fable invented by a most inept, injudicious, impudent, and clownish Hellenist" to commend officious lies and pious frauds. Without such undeserved condemnation, the view that the book is fiction, defended by G. L. Bauer (*Theologie des Alten Testament*, p. 349. Leipzig, 1796) and L. Bertholdt (*Historisch-kritische Einleitung in die sämtlichen kanonischen und apokryphischen Schriften des alten und neuen Testaments*. Vol. 5, pp. 2492-97. Erlangen, 1815), has been steadily gaining ground among Protestants.[6]

Like Esther (and also Ruth), Judith purports to be history and, disregarding such exaggerations in the numbers (1:4, 16; 2:5, 15; 7:2, 17) as we find in genuine histories, it has verisimilitude—at least both books relate no supernatural events such as we read in Jonah, Daniel, Tobit, and other short stories. Nevertheless, the characteristics of fiction are no less pronounced in Judith than in Esther. Chronological, historical, geographical errors, and improbabilities of other kinds, are manifest.

The chronological data of the book span several centuries, although

[4] Jerome (*Explan. in Sophoniam; prologus*) was the first to discover an allegory in the book; Judith is the church decapitating the devil.

[5] H. Ewald, *Geschichte des Volkes Israel*, Vol. 3, Pt. 2, p. 541. Göttingen, 1852. H. Graetz, *Geschichte der Juden*, 2nd ed., Vol. 4, p. 132. Leipzig, 1866. Levi Herzfeld, *Geschichte des Volkes Israel*, Vol. 1, p. 319. Braunschweig, 1847. M. Galster (in PSBA, Vol. 16 [1893-94] 157). C. J. Ball (in Wace, *Apocrypha*, Vol. 1, pp. 245 f.). H. Willrich, *Judaica*, pp. 28-35. Göttingen, 1900. H. Winckler, *Altorientalische Forschungen*, Second Series, Vol. 2, pp. 266-276, Leipzig, 1900. S. Weissmann, *Das Buch Judith historisch-kritisch beleuchtet*. Wien, 1890. J. Lewy, "Enthalt Judith I-IV Trummer einer Chronik zur Geschichte Nebukadnezars und seiner Feldzuge von 597 in 591?" (ZDMG 81 [1927] lii-liv).

[6] O. F. Fritzsche, Commentary, p. 125 (1851). G. Volkmar, *Handbuch der Einleitung in die Apokryphen*, Vol. 1, p. 5. Tübingen, 1860. André, *Les Apocryphes*, p. 154. E. Schürer, *Geschichte*, Vol. 3, p. 232. A. E. Cowley, in Charles, *Apocrypha*, p. 243. O. Eissfeldt, *Einleitung*, p. 642.

the events narrated (aside from the epilogue, 16:23-25) take place within a few months. These data may be arranged as follows:

1. *Seventh century.* "Who reigned over the Assyrians in Nineveh" (1:1): Nineveh (cf. 2:21) was destroyed in 612; the kingdom of Assyria (whose last ruler was Ashuruballit) ceased to exist in 605, and the Assyrian nation disintegrated soon after. Throughout the book[7] the Assyrian Empire is still the dominating power in Western Asia, as it was until the death of Ashurbanipal in 625. "The great king" of Assyria is "the lord of all the earth" (2:5). In fact, F. Steinmetzer (*Die Geschichtlichkeit der Juditherzählung*, pp. 46-59), following Delattre, Vigoroux, Brunengo, and Winckler, has attempted to prove, not without some plausibility, that "the campaigns reported in chs. 1-3 are historically demonstrable during the reign of Ashurbanipal" (p. 46).[8]

2. *Sixth Century.* The only dates recorded in the book are the twelfth (1:1; thirteenth in the Syriac), the seventeenth (1:13; omitted in the Vulgate), and eighteenth (2:1; thirteenth in the Vulgate, where 1:13-16 is omitted) years of the reign of Nebuchadnezzar (605-561 B.C.), or 593, 588, and 587 B.C., respectively. Literally interpreted, the text manifestly dates the events in the reign of the famous Nebuchadnezzar king of Babylon:[9] the Babylonian Exile has already occurred (4:3; 5:18), the Medic Empire (550-525) is at the height of its power (1:1-4) but, with the capture of Ecbatana (by Cyrus in 550), comes to its end (1:13-15). This last event, however, brings us to the time of Cyrus the Great (550-530), as also the references to the return from the Babylonian captivity in 538 (4:3; 5:19), and to the cessation of the idolatry for which the Judeans were punished in 586 (8:18 f.).

3. *Fifth Century.* The situation of the Jews presupposed in the Book of Judith is that of the fifth century or later. The Second Temple, completed in 516, is standing, and the regular worship has apparently been performed in it for some time (4:2 f., 11, 13 f.; 5:19; 11:13; 16:18-20). It is true that the Jews are said to have returned "recently" from their captivity (4:3; 5:19), but the resumption of the Temple worship in accordance with the prescriptions of the Priestly Code, under the direction of a high priest (cf. 4:14; 11:13; 16:18-20), is inconceivable, historically, before 500 B.C. The hostility of the Moabites and Ammonites against the Jews (5:2; 7:8; 7:17 f.) has been adduced (e.g., by F.

[7] Jth. 2:1, 4, 14; 4:1; 5:1; 6:1, 7; 7:17, 20, 24; 12:13; 13:15; 14:2 f., 12, 19; 15:6; 16:4.

[8] Another reference to the seventh century is the fortification of Ecbatana (1:2). According to Herodotus (I, 98), Deioces (*ca.* 708-655) fortified Ecbatana about 700 B.C.

[9] Jth. 1:5, 7, 11 f.; 2:4, 19; 3:3, 9; 4:1; 6:2, 4; 11:1, 4, 7, 23; 12:13; 14:18. In reality Nebuchadnezzar did fight against the Judeans in the 18th year of his reign (cf. 2:1) and took Jerusalem in the 19th (II Kings 24:8).

Steinmetzer, *Geschichtlichkeit,* p. 80) as evidence for the time of Ezra and Nehemiah in the fifth century, but this enmity is not restricted to that time. A high priest Joakim (4:6, 8, 14; 15:8), apart from the unhistorical reference in Bar. 1:7, is, however, known only in the time of Nehemiah (Neh. 12:10, 26).[10]

4. *Fourth Century.* A number of critics (see Schürer, *Geschichte,* Vol. 3, pp. 332 f.; A. E. Cowley, in Charles, *Apocrypha,* p. 246) have discovered the historical background of the book in the campaign of Artaxerxes III Ochus (358-338) against Phoenicia and the Jews in 353 B.C.[11] As a matter of fact, one of his commanders was Holofernes, the brother of Ariarathes king of Cappadocia (Diodorus Siculus, 19:2 f.), who fought against the Egyptians; and Bagoas (in Jth. 12:11, 13, 15; 13:1, 3; 14:14 he is the eunuch of Holofernes), according to Diodorus (xvi, 47; xvii, 5:3), was one of the generals in the campaign of 353 and was a eunuch (Pliny, *Natural History* XIII, 41, even claims that eunuchs were called "Bagoas"). These two Persian names, Holofernes and Bagoas, are by no means uncommon, but their appearance together may indicate that the author had heard about them in connection with the campaign of Artaxerxes Ochus.

5. *Second Century.* The atmosphere of the book is decidedly that of the Maccabean period, when, as many (including this writer) believe, it was actually written. It is only in 168-165 that a king (Antiochus Epiphanes) forced the Jews to forsake their God and change their religion: no other historical event could have suggested such fantastic statements as we read in 3:8 and 6:2. There is unquestionably some resemblance between this imaginary picture of Nebuchadnezzar as the god of all nations and the character of Antiochus Epiphanes as depicted by another Jewish author of the same general period (II Macc. 9:4, 7 f., 10, 12). In Daniel, likewise, Nebuchadnezzar is the symbol of the hated Antiochus (Dan. 3:1-21; 4:22, 30, 36; cf. Darius in Dan. 6:7, 12). Moreover, Judith reflects the strong piety and strict observance of the Law characteristic of the Hasidim in the time of Antiochus and later of the Pharisees (4:9-14; 8:5 f.; 10:5; 11:10-15; 12:2, 5-9; 16:16 f.). In fact, the religious point of view is that of the Pharisees: the oral law is already observed in the avoidance of fasting on the eve of festivals (8:6).[12]

---

[10] The formula "to prepare earth and water" (2:7), meaning complete surrender, is Persian (cf. Herodotus VI, 48 f.; for later references in classical authors see Fritzsche, *Commentary,* p. 140).

[11] The sources of information on this campaign are given in Schürer, *Geschichte,* Vol. 3, p. 7, n. 11.

[12] Several critics recognize the Maccabean background of Judith, but they do not agree on the king represented by Nebuchadnezzar: C. J. Ball (in Wace, *Apocrypha,* Vol. 1, pp. 245 f.) recognizes the Pharisaic teaching of the book, which he dates in the time of Alexandra (76-67, not 79-70 B.C., as he says), but identifies Nebuchadnezzar with Antiochus Cyclops (governor of Phrygia and king of Asia Minor, 333-301); S. Weissmann (*Das Buch Judith* u.s.w. Wien, 1890) identifies Nebuch-

Moreover, the Jews are governed by a high priest (strictly speaking, not before Simon made the Jews independent in 142), whose orders are obeyed without question (4:6-8), and by the Sanhedrin, or *gerousía* (4:8, 11, 14; 15:8), mentioned by Josephus (*Antiquities* 12:3, 1) as existing in the time of Antiochus III the Great (233-187) and apparently known to the Chronicler (II Chron. 19:5-11) about 250 B.C. But even if this senate actually originated as early as 275 or 250 B.C., it did not play as important a role as it does in Judith before the Maccabean period. We may therefore regard the mention of the *gerousía* as another clue to the Maccabean background of the book. Since Galilee (1:8; cf. 15:5), the coastal cities (Jamnia and Ashdod, 2:28; cf. 2:6; 5:2, 22; 7:8), and the Idumeans (archaically called "the children of Esau" in 7:8, 18) are still apparently independent of the Jews, we may infer a time before the latter part of the reign of John Hyrcanus (135-104). Although the historical background is very confused and does not allow a final verdict on the date of the book, all in all it seems to belong after Daniel (164), about the middle of the second century (before Esther, which the present writer would date about 125).[13]

6. *The Second Century of Our Era.* The discovery in Judith of allusions to the victories of Trajan over the Parthians (G. Volkmar, *Handbuch der Einleitung in den Apokryphen,* Vol. 1, p. 5. Tübingen, 1860; G. Klein, "Über das Buch Judith" [*Notes du VIIIe Congrès international des Orientalistes,* Sect. Sem. B, p. 101. Leiden, 1891]) is mentioned here only for the sake of completeness. It rests obviously on hallucinations, for the book was known to Clement of Rome some years before.

Disregarding this last suggestion, we have found that one may plausibly discover in Judith a historical background in any of five centuries, from the seventh to the second B.C., and accordingly identify Nebuchadnezzar with a ruler living within that half of a millennium. Brunengo (*Il Nabucodonosor di Giuditta,* pp. 25 f. Rome, 1888. First published in *Civiltà Cattolica,* Ser. xiii, vols. 3-10, 1886-1888) has conveniently drawn up a table (reproduced by F. Steinmetzer, *Geschichtlichkeit,* pp. 41 f.) listing the kings with whom Nebuchadnezzar has been identified by critics. For convenience, we copy it here.

Adad-nirari III (Riessler); *Merodach-baladan* (Bellarmine); *Essarhaddon* (Montfaucon, Houbigant); *Ashurbanipal* (Robiou, Delattre, Vigoroux, Pal-

---

[13] adnezzar with Antiochus IV Epiphanes (176-164); cf. F. Steinmetzer, *Geschichtlichkeit,* pp. 99-105. H. Willrich (*Judaica,* pp. 28-35) sees in Nebuchadnezzar king Demetrius I Soter (162-150 B.C.).

[13] The date about 150 B.C. for the composition of the book is the one generally suggested. It has been adopted by Fritzsche (second century), Ewald, Reuss, Cornill, König, Strack, André, Löhr, Schürer, Nikel, Cowley, Eissfeldt, and others.

mieri, Cornely, Kaulen, Winckler); *Shamash-shum-ukin* (Lenglet-Dufresnoy); *Kandalanu* (Wolff, Gumpach); *Nebuchadnezzar* (Movers, Nickes, Danko, Neteler); *Cambyses* (Augustine, Suidas); *Darius I* (Gerardus); *Xerxes I* (Sanchez, Cornelius a Lapide); *Artaxerxes III Ochus* (Sulpicius Severus); *Seleucus I* (Raska); *Antigonus Cyclops* (Ball); *Antiochus IV Epiphanes* (Weissmann); *Demetrius I* (Willrich); *Trajan* (Volkmar); *Hadrian* (Klein).

These suggested rulers span almost a millennium (806 B.C. to A.D. 138), but only those from Ashurbanipal (668-625) to Antiochus Epiphanes (176-164) deserve serious consideration. Containing clear allusions to five centuries, the book teems with anachronisms: e.g, Nebuchadnezzar rules in Nineveh, destroyed before he became king, and is still king after the Jews have returned from captivity and have rebuilt the Temple (actually finished forty-five years after the death of Nebuchadnezzar).[14] The king of Media, bearing the fictitious name of Arphaxad (1:1, 5, 13, 15) taken from Gen. 10:22, has an even longer reign than this fabulous Nebuchadnezzar, for he joins in his person Deioces, who fortified Ecbatana about 700 B.C. (cf. 1:2-4), Cyaxares (625-593), the contemporary of Nebuchadnezzar, and Astyages (593-550), deposed by Cyrus after the conquest of Ecbatana (cf. 1:13-15): thus Arphaxad ruled 150 years!

In addition to anachronisms, the book contains a number of incredible stories. Without motorcars, Holofernes could never have moved a large army about 300 miles in three days, from Nineveh to Cilicia (2:21); the rest of his itinerary (2:23-27) is partly obscure, owing to mention of unknown localities, and partly insane or fantastic. We are not told how Holofernes could seize and garrison the spring at the foot of Bethulia's walls (7:3, 7; cf. 6:11) without dislodging the Jews occupying fortified positions on the hilltops round about (4:5; 5:1; 6:12), nor why the spring had to be conquered a second time by the Ammonites (7:12, 17), nor how Judith dared perform her ablutions at the spring (12:7) in the presence of the Assyrian garrison.

The geography of the book has defied interpretation. Most of the localities (1:6, 9; 2:21-27; 3:1; 4:4; etc.) are either given imaginary names or their correct names have been disfigured by copyists beyond recognition. Even the name of Judith's city, Bethulia (named nineteen times), remains a mystery, even though we are told that it was on a hill (10:10; etc.), near a spring (6:11; etc.), surrounded by mountains

---

[14] The ingenious attempt of Gottfried Brunner (*Der Nabuchodonosor des Buches Judith.* Berlin, Rudolph Pfau, 1940) to eliminate the difficulties connected with Nebuchadnezzar has not been successful. He identifies the Nebuchadnezzar of the Book of Judith with Nebuchadnezzar IV son of Nabonidus who became king of Babylon in 522-21 and was soon deposed by Darius I. Aside from the name, this weak and ephemeral ruler bears no resemblance to the mighty monarch in Judith.

(6:10-12; etc.), not far from Dothaim (4:6; 7:3, 18; 8:3), i.e., in Samaria.[15]

In view of this mass of anachronisms and incredible tales, the historicity of the book as a whole is out of the question. We must either, like most Roman Catholic scholars, regard the extant Greek text as highly corrupt and conflated, or conclude that the author wrote fiction rather than history. Following the first procedure, one could transform almost any short story into history by careful elimination and rewriting, thus leaving little of the original text intact; but who could then believe that the result was what the original author wrote, or how could it be shown that he intended to describe actual events and not merely tell an interesting story which uncritical readers might regard as history? Taking the book as we have it and assuming that it is a substantially accurate, though not always identical, copy of a faithful Greek rendering of a Hebrew scroll, our objective conclusion must be that the original author wrote historical fiction. His knowledge of past history and of the geography of Western Asia (outside of Palestine) was so limited that he committed numerous errors. Read as a good short story written by a Palestinian Jew about 150 B.C. to inflame the patriotism of his people, the book still retains a certain charm and is valuable as a mirror not only of the author's convictions but also of Palestinian Judaism at the time.

2. Literary Characteristics

The recognition that the Book of Judith is fiction rather than history does not exclude the possibility that Judith's slaying of Holofernes may be a more or less distorted account of a deed of valor like Jael's (Jud. 5:24-27), actually performed by a Jewish woman (cf. Eissfeldt, Einleitung, p. 643). More probably, Judith the daughter of Merari was (like Daniel) a well-known legendary character before the book was written. André (Les Apocryphes, p. 162) has suggested that the psalm extolling Judith's deed (16:2-17) may be older than the book and thus have furnished the plot. The style of this hymn is better than that of the rest of the book, and Fritzsche (Commentary, p. 209) classes it without hesitation among "the best poetic products of the Hebrew spirit."[16] If this poem furnished the plot of the book, it is also partly responsible for some of its chronological confusion, for it mentions Persians and

---

[15] The abundant literature on Bethulia is listed (to 1905) by E. Schürer, Geschichte, Vol. 3, p. 231, n. 20. See also F. Stummer, Geographie des Buches Judith. Stuttgart: Kathol. Bibelwerk, 1947. C. C. Torrey (JAOS 20 [1899] 160-172) is probably right in identifying Bethulia with Shechem (cf. Torrey, The Apocryphal Literature pp. 91-93).

[16] As in some of the Psalms, the speaker in the poem is the Jewish congregation, not Judith.

Medes (16:10) within the army of Assyria (16:4; for the Persians, cf. 1:7). If, however, the author of the book composed the poem for the climax, he made a slip in mentioning the Medes in 16:10; for in 1:12-15 the Medes are the defeated enemies of the Assyrian king.

Our Greek text is extant in three recensions: the standard edition (Codices Vaticanus, Alexandrinus, and Sinaiticus), the text of Codex Holmes and Parsons 58 (the prototype of the Old Latin and Syriac versions), and the text of Codices Holmes and Parsons 19 and 108 (perhaps Lucian's recension). Jerome tells us in his preface to Judith that he unwillingly and quickly made a free translation of Judith from a "Chaldean" (i.e., Aramaic) text; he also utilized extensively the Old Latin version.[17] This Aramaic text of Jerome can hardly be the lost Semitic original of the book (as J. Goettsberger, *Einleitung*, p. 183, still claims), for Origen (*Epistle to Africanus*, ch. 13) asserts emphatically that the Jews did not use Tobit and Judith, nor did they even have them among their apocryphal Hebrew writings. Jerome's Aramaic text was probably a free translation from the Greek.

The Greek text is manifestly a very close and faithful rendering from the Hebrew; in three Biblical quotations, however, the translator used the LXX (8:16, cf. Num. 23:19;[18] 9:2, cf. Gen. 34:7; 9:7, and 16:3 cf. Ex. 15:3; see also 3:7, cf. Judg. 11:34). According to C. J. Ball (in Wace, *Apocrypha*), 10:1-11:5 imitates Greek Esth. 5:1-15; the Titans and Giants of 16:7 are likewise Septuagintal. The Greek reproduces the syntax (e.g., the infinitive absolute: "completing you will complete," 2:13) and the idiomatic expressions of the Hebrew. "And" (*kai*), as in Hebrew, is used in a great variety of syntactical constructions (e.g., "in toil *and* brick" [5:11]). Some typical Hebrew idioms, reproduced literally in Greek, are: "a month of days" (3:10); "all flesh" (2:3; cf. "one flesh nor spirit of life" in 10:13); "to inherit" in the sense of "to take possession" (5:15); the figurative use of "eye" (2:11; 12:14; 16:9), "face" (2:7, 19, 25; 3:2, 9; 10:23; 11:5; 16:15; etc.), "mouth" (of the sword, 2:27), "hand" (2:12); the use of *en* (in) in the sense of "with, by means of," like the Hebrew *be* which has both meanings (although there are also traces of this usage of *en* in classical Greek) as, for instance, "to kill with (*en*) the sword" in 16:5 (Gr. 16:4) Codex Alexandrinus, cf. I Esd. 1:50; I Macc. 2:9; Rev. 6:8 (see Jth. 1:15; 2:19; 5:9, 11; 5; 6:4, 12; 7:14; 9:8; 11:11; 16:7 f.); "young man" (Hebr. *na'ar*) in the sense

[17] The Latin text of Judith in the Vulgate differs considerably from the Greek: it transposes (14:5-9 [Vulg. 13:27-31] appears after 13:20), it condenses, it omits 1:12b-16 and 4:3, it adds 4:11-14 (Vulg.) after 4:12, and it changes the diction considerably (cf. 4:14 f. with 4:15-17 in the Vulgate). See, for details, André, *Les Apocryphes*, pp. 165-168; and E. E. Voigt, *The Latin Versions of Judith* (Yale University Dissertation). Leipzig, 1925.

[18] See E. Nestle, *Marginalien*, p. 46, Tübingen, 1893.

of "servant" (10:10); the formula for oaths, "as a god liveth" (used for Nebuchadnezzar, who is called a god, 2:12 [cf. Num. 13:16; 14:21, 28]; 11:7; and also for Holofernes, 12:4). Some verses, like 3:8, could hardly be understood by a Greek unfamiliar with the Septuagint. Some puzzling texts become clear if we assume that they contain errors of translation, due generally to an incorrect reading of the Hebrew or to a defective or obscure Hebrew text.[19] In 2:2 instead of "he *finished* all the wickedness [or affliction] of the land out of his own mouth" Fritzsche would read, "he *revealed,* etc." (reading the Hebrew *galah* instead of *kalah*; likewise in 2:4). In 3:9 he suggests that the translator mistook *mîshōr* (plain) for *massōr* (saw), rendering "the great *saw* [instead of *plain*] of Judea." In 8:21 André suggests that "all Judea will *sit*" is an error for "will *be deported,*" due to a form of *shabah* being mistaken for a form of *yashab.* See also Fritzsche on 1:8; 3:1, 8 (Fritzsche 3:9), and Cowley on 9:2 (in Charles, *Apocrypha,* p. 258). According to Cowley (*op. cit.* p. 244), through the confusion in Hebrew writing between *r* and *d* the name *Achihud* (friend of the Jews) was read *Achior.*

The Hebrew style of the lost original work is fairly good, although at times more prolix (cf. 4:9-12) and bombastic than that of the Book of Esther. Like the author of the stories in Daniel, this writer is fascinated by the colossal (cf. 1:2-5; 2:14-20) and is fond of pompously grandiose speeches (cf. 2:5-13; 6:2-9; 8:11-27; 11:5-19), and of eloquent prayers of intercession (9:2-14; 13:4 f.) and praise (16:2-17).

The chief literary defect of the book is the lack of simplicity: the gorgeous Oriental *mise en scène*, the turgid style, the patent exaggerations, the stately pomp and ceremony throughout, unrelieved by a sense of humor, give to the book a baroque rather than a classic appearance. A comparison of the story of Judith's deed in prose (12:10-13:10) or in verse (16:6-9) with the similar assassination of a foe by Jael, as sung in Deborah's ode (Judg. 5:24-27) or told in simple prose (Judg. 4:17-22), is a contrast between the extravagantly ornate and the superbly natural, between sophistication and unadorned reality, between conscious and unconscious art.

Despite such literary blemishes, which are more or less characteristic of the period of Hebrew literature in which the book was written, the Book of Judith is a good example of an ancient short story. Even if the plot was previously known, the author displays considerable originality in working out the details, in injecting his patriotism and faith into the narrative, and in creating an imaginary, magnificent, historical background. His characters, in spite of their heroic stature, have psychological reality: Nebuchadnezzar, the imperial monarch whose ambition does not stop at world domination, but aspires to divine honors; Holofernes, the

[19] See Fritzsche, Commentary, p. 116; André, *Les Apocryphes,* pp. 158 f.

successful general to whom overconfidence and self-assurance bring sudden disaster; Judith, in whom noble devotion to God and nation is combined with feminine wiles, refined seductiveness, and unscrupulous resolve. With surprising candor, the author contrasts the assurance of the Ammonite Achior, who is certain that the Jews are unconquerable unless they have sinned against their God (5:5-21), with the abject terror of the Jews, who preferred surrender to defeat (7:19-28), and the weakness of their leaders, whose faint hope in divine help did not enable them to overcome the cowardly despair of the masses (7:30 f.; cf. 8:28-31) and thus provoked Judith's indignation (8:11-27).

The author was utterly sincere when he presented Judith as his ideal, and her deed as a heroic act approved by God—nay, God's own deed for the salvation of his people through her hand (13:11, 14, 18; 16:6; cf. 8:33; 9:10, 13). But at this point the verdict of readers is not always in agreement with the author's, and as in the case of the Book of Esther extreme praise and extreme abuse have been poured out upon the book.[20] Ultimately one's opinion is determined by one's attitude to the principle, "The end justifies the means." The author fully approves of deceit and imposture (9:10, 13; 11:5-19; 12:14, 18), of sensual entice-ment in cold blood (10:3 f.; 12:14-18; 16:7-9), and even of assassination (13:4-20; 14:7, 9; 15:9 f.; 16:2-17) in the interests of the nation and its religion: a noble end justifies ignoble means. But the opposite view has had its defenders, at least since the days of Hosea, who strongly de-nounced the political assassinations by Jehu (Hos. 1:4; cf. II Kings 10:11) which at the time had been ordered by Elisha in the name of Jehovah (II Kings 9:1-10; cf. I Kings 19:15-17). Like Fritzsche (Com-mentary, p. 128), one may take the middle of the road, between those who condemn Judith without allowing for extenuating circumstances and those who would justify her "theologically": he admits that morality cannot but protest against her conduct, but that in the desperate con-dition of her people attacked by a powerful army any ruse is generally regarded as permissible (cf. Cowley, in Charles, Apocrypha, p. 247).

Christian readers have also been shocked by the narrow, militant nationalism pervading the book. Thus André (Les Apocryphes, pp. 155 f.), for instance, lists among the defects of the book the author's bellicose mood, the "savage hatred" of the Israelites for the heathen (3:2-4, 8, 10; 13:5; 14:4; 15:5 ff.; 16:17), appearing also in the praises for Judith (13:17-20; 14:7; 15:9 ff.) and going so far as to extol (like

[20] Thomas Aquinas (Summa II, 2, quest. 110; a. 3), in contrast with Clement of Alexandria (Stromata 6) and Jerome (Adversus Rufinum I), who had excused Judith's lies, declares that Judith is praised not because she lied, but for her devotion to her people. Ambrose of Milan (De officiis ministrorum II, 13) regards Judith as religiously important because she saved the chosen people, and its holy customs and sacraments.

Jub. 30:16 f., cf. 31:13-17) the bloody deed of Simeon and Levi (9:2-4)
which the Old Testament had not condoned (Gen. 34:1-31; cf. 49:5-7
and IV Macc. 2:19), and the "religious character of war" (4:2; 5:12;
8:21-27; 9:8, 13 f.; 10:8; 13:4; 15:10), particularly of a war against a
king who wished to be worshiped as a god (3:8; 6:2). But before we
Christians cast a stone at Judith, let us remember that love for the
enemy instead of "an eye for an eye, a tooth for a tooth" has remained
in time of war a utopian private ideal, and that Judith was written in the
midst of the Maccabean struggles, when the Jews were fighting for
their very existence.

3. Religious Teaching

In contrast with the Book of Esther in Hebrew, Judith teaches not
only patriotism, but also religion, through example and precept.

In a book describing Israel's triumph over the heathen, God appears
primarily as the national God, the God of Israel (4:12; 6:21; 10:1; 12:8),
the Lord God of Israel (13:7), the God of Israel's inheritance (9:12),
Lord God of my father Simeon (9:2), the God of my father (Simeon)
(9:12), the God (or Lord) of our fathers (7:28; 9:12), the only protector
of Israel (9:14), who is his inheritance (13:5) and his children (9:13).
In the second place, as in Daniel, the vastness of his jurisdiction and the
immensity of his power (dýnamis, 9:8) and might (krátos, 9:11) are
stressed, since they make the divine protection of Israel effective against
all odds. Jehovah is Lord of heaven and earth, Creator of the waters,
King of all creation (9:12), the Creator of heaven and earth (13:18),
the God of Heaven (5:8; a favorite expression in the Persian period),
Lord God of all power (13:4), kýrios pantokrátōr (Lord Almighty; in
II Sam. 5:10, LXX, the translation of Yahweh Zebaoth: 4:13; 8:13;
15:10; 16:6, 18), the God of all power and might (9:14). "O Lord, thou
art great and glorious, marvellous in strength, unsurpassed" (16:13).
"And how shall ye search out God, who has made all these things, and
know his mind, and comprehend his purpose?" (8:14). Judith joins
intimately God's power and foreknowledge (prógnōsis): God not only
performs all things, past, present, and future, but they seem to exist in
his mind before becoming real and saying, "Here we are!" (9:5 f.).

The God of Israel, whose Name (i.e., his person) dwells in the Temple
of Jerusalem (9:8) and who in the day of judgment will destroy the
heathen enemies of Israel (16:17), is, however, also a god of justice,
who hates iniquity (5:17). It is true that he is compassionate (7:30),
for he is a God of the afflicted, a helper of the oppressed, an upholder
of the weak, a protector of the forlorn, a savior of them that are without
hope (9:11): he will not utterly forsake his people (7:30). But his cham-

pionship for Israel is morally conditioned: he tests (8:25 f.) and warns (8:27) Israel through minor misfortunes, and he allows enemies to triumph over the chosen nation on account of its sins (5:18, 20; 11:10-15) and the sins of the fathers (7:28), for he will defend Israel only when there is no lawlessness in it (5:21). Since Israel has now forsaken the idolatry of earlier times, Judith can firmly hope for God's help (8:17-20), inasmuch as God is with Israel when it sins not, granting prosperity (5:17) and victory (13:11; 16:3, 6), and destroying its foes (16:17).

Obedience to God's laws (11:12) is the supreme test of piety. Sin is violation of the Law of Moses, either unwitting (*agnóema*, oversight, 5:20) or conscious (*anomía*, lawlessness, 5:21): a departure from the divinely appointed conduct (5:18). Idolatry is the greatest national sin (8:18-20). Ritual prescriptions and their violations are emphasized throughout the book, although in 16:16 the attitude of mind (fear of the Lord) is regarded as superior to external performances (as in Ps. 51:16-19 [H. 51:18-21]), and in 8:11-17 an oath through which one attempts to force God is rightly denounced. Judith observed punctiliously the ritual laws, although she felt no compunction whatsoever in violating the basic moral laws in the interest of her people. She was careful in the observance of the dietary laws (10:5; 12:2, 12, 19), she fasted regularly except on festivals and on the eve of festivals (8:6), prayed at fixed times (12:6), performed her ablutions under difficulties (12:7), and avoided ritual pollution (12:9). Thus "she feared God exceedingly" (8:8). Judith believed that God was pleased with her deceits and the assassination she performed in the national interest, but that God was "provoked to anger" by the proposed feeding of the starving people of Bethulia, after obtaining permission from the Sanhedrin, by means of the firstlings, tithes, and first fruits set aside for the Temple (11:12-15)! To say with Cowley (in Charles, *Apocrypha*, p. 247) that she was "a perfect type of Pharisaic righteousness" seems to be too severe an indictment of the Pharisees!

The author of the book may well have been one of the early Pharisees, without however representing the views of the whole movement. The fact that the book did not attain canonicity in Judaism, in contrast with Esther (which attained that status through popular demand rather than through unanimous support of the rabbis), indicates that not all Pharisees agreed with its teaching. Nevertheless, Pharisaic doctrines and practice are by no means absent from the book. In addition to Judith's punctiliousness in observing the Law, there is also reference to national observance of the Temple rituals (including the *tāmîd*, or daily burnt offering, 4:14; cf. Joel 1:9, 13; 2:14; Dan. 8:11; 11:31; 12:11), to national repentance by sackcloth, ashes, fasting, and prayer (4:9-13; cf. Joel 2:12; Neh. 1:4; Esth. 4:3), to national purification and worship (16:18), and to the efficacy of prayer (*passim*). All this conforms to Pharisaic teaching, but is not characteristic of the movement. More significant is perhaps the reception of proselytes after they have been circumcised (14:10). Whether the author believed in the resurrection after death, a characteristic Pharisaic doctrine, must remain uncertain, for the interpretation of 16:17 is doubtful: some, like Cowley (in Charles, *Apocrypha*, p. 247) see in it an eternal punishment of the wicked after death (in a hell with material fire and worms, according to Roman Catholic interpreters); but others, like Fritzsche (Commentary, p. 208) and André (*Les Apocryphes*, pp. 157 f.) see merely a destruction of the flesh of Israel's enemies, or of their corpses, through fire and worms (cf. Is. 66:24)—a more probable interpretation, if we date the book as early as 150 B.C. Judith thus, like Daniel, is an invaluable source of information for the beginning of the Pharisaic movement. It already foreshadows some of the later tendencies, but it advocates a bellicose type of patriotism and piety which many Pharisees rejected later in favor of a pacifism founded on trust in almighty God—the universal Creator and at the same time the champion of Israel.

CHAPTER IV

THE REST OF THE CHAPTERS OF THE BOOK OF ESTHER

The Book of Esther soon after its appearance was, and later continued to be, one of the most popular and most widely circulated Biblical books. In addition to the standard Masoretic Hebrew text,[1] translated in the Authorized Version, the book is extant in a number of widely different recensions, all of which contain material lacking in the canonical book: the Greek ("LXX") translation in five variant forms;[2] two Aramaic versions or Targums, the first (*Targûm Rîshōn*) dating from about A.D. 700 and the second (*Targûm Shēnî*) published about a century later; and a number of homiletic and imaginative commentaries (*Midrāshîm*), listed in *Jewish Encyclopedia*, Vol. 5, p. 234. An Aramaic text of the "Dream of Mordecai" is printed in A. Merx, *Chrestomathia Targumica*, pp. 154-64. Berlin, 1888.[3]

The Greek text (and its Latin versions) is the only one of these enlarged editions of the canonical book which dates back to pre-Christian times, and therefore the only one with which we are here concerned. Disregarding the minor textual variants and additions of a few words here and there, the Greek text contains a number of longer narratives or other writings entirely lacking in the Hebrew canonical book, and occasionally contradicting the canonical story.[4] The Hebrew text includes 163 verses, the Greek 270, or 107 additional ones. These additions, conventionally indicated by the letters A-F, in the Greek are to be found in their proper

---

[1] The Peshitta (Syriac) version and Jerome's Vulgate reproduce the Masoretic text with great fidelity, although they exhibit some interesting variants which, at least in part, reflect a different Hebrew text. Jerome claims to have given a literal translation of the Hebrew, but added at the end the longer additions in the Greek version, which are lacking in the Peshitta.

[2] The standard LXX (codices *Aleph*, B, A, etc.), Origen's Hexaplar text, the recensions of Hesychius and of Lucian (the latter resembling the Old Latin version), and the text used by Josephus (*Antiquities* 11:6 [§§186-296]).

[3] A good summary of the characteristics of these expansions of the Book of Esther will be found in L. B. Paton, *The Book of Esther* (ICC). New York, 1908. In its expanded form, based on all extant texts, the story of Esther is told by L. Ginzberg, *Legends of the Jews*, Vol. 4, pp. 365-448 (for a learned discussion of the sources see Vol. 6, pp. 451-481).

[4] The chief contradictions are listed in André, *Apocryphes*, pp. 202 f.; in Charles, *Apocrypha*, pp. 66 f.; in L. B. Paton, *The Book of Esther* (ICC), pp. 43 f.

place in the narrative, as follows: A (before 1:1); B (after 3:13); C and D (after 4:17); E (after 8:12); F (after 10:3, the end of the book).

Jerome not only removed them from their context, placing them all in an appendix to the canonical book;[5] but leaving section F, as in Greek, immediately after the end of the book (10:3), he thus placed the final addition (F, provided with a final colophon) before all the others. Consequently, the interpretation of Mordecai's dream (F) precedes the dream itself (A). Accordingly, in the English editions of the Apocrypha the additions, following Jerome's order, are an incongruous sequence of six disconnected sections, beginning with the last. The contents of A-F, with the usual English chapter and verse citation corresponding to the Latin Vulgate, may be summarized as follows:

A. *The Dream of Mordecai* (11:2-12:6). In the second year of Artaxerxes (contrast 2:16, 21-23) Mordecai, a Jewish courtier in Susa, saw this dream (11:2-4). In the midst of tumult and earthquakes, two dragons went forth to fight (11:5 f.). At their cry, nations prepared for war and great danger threatened the righteous nation (the Jews) (11:7-9). When Israel cried to God, a little spring became a great river, the sun rose, and the humble [the Jews] prevailed over the mighty [i.e., Haman] (11:10 f.). Mordecai understood the dream to be prophetic and remained awake pondering its meaning (11:12; for the interpretation of the dream, see 10:4-11:1); and thus he heard two eunuchs (Gabatha and Tharra) plotting the assassination of the king; he informed the king (12:1 f.), who had them executed (12:3). The event was duly recorded (12:4; cf. 2:21-23; 6:2 f.). Mordecai was rewarded, but Haman sought his ruin on account of the eunuchs (12:5 f.).

B. *The Edict of Artaxerxes against the Jews* (13:1-7). The king wrote to the rulers of the 127 provinces as follows (13:1): Having at heart the welfare of his subjects (13:2) but having heard from Haman that an evil nation was ever threatening the peace of the realm (13:3 f.) through its opposition to all other men, the king decreed that they [the Jews] be rooted out to the last one on the 14th of Adar (13:5-7).[6]

C. *The Prayers of Mordecai* (13:8-18) *and of Esther* (14:1-19). The Lord, the universal King and Creator, whose power is irresistible

---

[5] Following 10:3 (and preceding "F"), Jerome inserted the following note in his Latin Bible: "The contents of the Hebrew text I have rendered most faithfully. The following passages, however, I found written in the 'Vulgate Edition' [the LXX]; they are couched in Greek language and letters. So for the time being this chapter has been placed after the end of [the Hebrew] book; and, according to our wont, we have marked it with the obelus, signifying truth."

[6] The "fourteenth" day is at variance with the Hebrew Esther, where the day is correctly the thirteenth (Esth. 3:13; 8:12; 9:1); likewise in the "E" addition (16:20).

(13:8-11), knew that Mordecai refused to bow before Haman not on account of pride (13:12 f.) but because he bowed only before God (13:14). But now the Lord should not allow his people to be destroyed (13:15-17). Then the Jews cried out, for they faced death (13:18).

Queen Esther, overcome with terror and in mourning attire (14:1 f.), prayed as follows: The Lord is her only helper in her danger (14:4). He chose Israel (14:5) and justly exiled his people for their sins (14:6). But now Israel's enemies have determined to destroy Judaism for the benefit of idolatry (14:7-10). Let not the Lord surrender his scepter to the idols (14:11), let him give courage and eloquence to Esther (14:12 f.), let him save his people (14:14). Esther detests being married to a heathen, abhors being a queen, and will not eat with Haman and the king (14:15-17); in fact her only joy at court has been the worship of the Lord (14:18): may he save Israel from the wicked and deliver Esther from her fear (14:19).

D. *Esther's admission before the king* (15:1-16; Vulg. 15:4-19). Three days later Esther, beautifully groomed and attired, but in dreadful fear (15:1-5), betook herself to the king (15:6). An angry royal look made her fall down in a faint (15:7). But God changed the king's mood (15:8) and his majesty encouraged the queen (15:9-12), who explained her fear and fainted again (15:13-15). The courtiers comforted her (15:16).

E. *The Decree of Artaxerxes in behalf of the Jews* (16:1-24). Many who have risen through favors, in their pride[7] seek to harm not only their inferiors but even their benefactors (16:1-4). Not seldom rulers, misled by the deceitful words of their ministers, have shed innocent blood and come to grief (16:5 f.). This may be seen not only in historical records but also in the present (16:7; the text is corrupt and the meaning uncertain). The ruler must maintain the peace of his realm, relying not on slander, but on just judgment (16:8 f.; slightly revised). Haman, a Macedonian (*sic!*), after becoming through royal favor the second in authority (16:10 f.), plotted to deprive the king of his throne; and Mordecai, the king's benefactor, and the queen, together with their whole nation, of their life (16:12 f.). Haman hoped thereby to transfer the Persian Empire to the Macedonians (16:14; anachronistic allusion to Alexander's conquests). The Jews, however, observe just laws and are sons of the living God (16:15 f.). The letters of Haman, who has been hanged, must be disregarded (16:17 f.). The present decree must be exhibited publicly everywhere; the Jews may observe their Law and should be aided on the 13th of Adar to avenge themselves of their enemies (16:19-21). The day shall become a joyful festival (16:22 f.).

[7] It is still a common observation that men are prouder of undeserved attainment than of achievement resulting from their own ability and effort.

Every city which violates this decree will be utterly destroyed (16:24).

F. *Interpretation of Mordecai's dream* (10:4-13; cf. A) and *Colophon* (11:1). Mordecai recognized that these events (the triumph of the Jews) were from God because they fulfilled his dream (10:4 f.). The spring which became a river is Esther (10:6); the two dragons are Mordecai and Haman (10:7). The nations are the enemies of the Jews (10:8) whom God saved from their hands (10:9). God made two lots ("lot" means both the die cast and the destinies thereby determined; cf. *Iliad* 8:69-74), one for the Jews and one for the Gentiles; and they were realized at the proper time (10:10 f.). So God remembered his people (10:12). The 14th and 15th of Adar were to be joyfully celebrated in all generations of Israel (10:13).

The "Epistle of Phrurai [i.e., Purim]," i.e., the Book of Esther in Greek, was brought to Egypt by Dositheus (a priest and Levite) and his son Ptolemy in the fourth year of Ptolemy and Cleopatra (probably 114-113 B.C.), after it had been translated by Lysimachus son of Ptolemy, a citizen of Jerusalem (11:1).

A comparison of the Greek and Hebrew texts of the Book of Esther shows that they represent radically different recensions of the story; in fact C. C. Torrey (JBL 61 [1942] 131) could even declare that the two principal Greek versions,[8] "in so far as they are translations from Semitic originals . . . render different texts"; and that neither renders the canonical Hebrew book, of which no Greek rendering exists. Students of the Greek text are accordingly faced with three problems. How much of the Greek text, if any, is a translation from a Semitic (Hebrew or Aramaic) original? Does the Greek represent a later edition than the Hebrew, or an earlier? What is the date of the "additions" and of the earliest edition of the book in Greek?

Protestant scholars generally seem inclined to believe that, with the exception of occasional brief glosses in the Greek,[9] the canonical parts of the Greek Esther were translated from the Hebrew, while, on the

---

[8] The standard Greek text (represented by codices *Aleph*, A, B, N, 55, 93b, 108a, 249, etc.) and the so-called Lucianic recension (codices 19, 93a, 108b, Athos 513) are edited separately in the following works: J. Ussher, *De graeca septuaginta interpretum versione syntagma* (London, 1655); O. F. Fritzsche, *Esther* (Zürich, 1848) and *Libri apocryphi Veteris Testamenti graece* (Leipzig, 1871); P. de Lagarde, *Librorum Veteris Testamenti canonicorum pars prior graece* (Göttingen, 1883); A. Scholz, *Commentar über das Buch Esther* (Würzburg 1892); A. E. Brooke, N. McLean, and H. St. John Thackeray, *The Old Testament in Greek*. Vol. III, Part I: Esther, Judith, Tobit (Cambridge University Press, 1940). The Old Latin version was made from a Greek text resembling Lucian's recension and has been published critically by B. R. Motzo (*La versione latina di Ester secondo i LXX*, in *Annali della Facoltà di Lettere della R. Università di Cagliari*, Vols. 1-2. Bologna, 1928).

[9] See the list in L. B. Paton, *The Book of Esther* (ICC), p. 33.

contrary the longer additions (A-F, above) were composed in Greek.[10] Conversely, Roman Catholic scholars, who regard the additions to Esther as canonical, or at least "deuterocanonical," and others[11] have maintained that the longer additions were translated from the Hebrew or Aramaic, and were an integral part of the first edition of the book. Three eminent Semitists have detected a difference in the "additions": in their opinion, four of them (A, C, D, F) were translated from Hebrew or Aramaic, while the two edicts of Artaxerxes (B and E) were written originally in Greek.[12] Finally, others[13] consider the evidence inconclusive and refuse to commit themselves to any of these theories. Such a verdict of *non liquet* may be defended, but the present writer is inclined to follow Nöldeke, Wellhausen, and Torrey, in regarding the edicts (B and E) as Greek compositions,[14] and the other additions as translations.[15]

Critical opinion is likewise divided as to the respective priority of the Hebrew and Greek texts of Esther. In general it is taken for granted that our Hebrew text gives the original form of the book, while the Greek is a translation and expansion thereof. However, those who regard the Greek version as canonical, and a few others, maintain, on the contrary, that the Hebrew book is a condensation and abbreviation of the Semitic text from which the Greek was translated.[16]

[10] See: O. F. Fritzsche, *Exeg. Handbuch zu den Apokryphen*, Vol. 1, p. 71 (Leipzig, 1851). J. M. Fuller in H. Wace, *Apocrypha*, Vol. 1, pp. 361-365. V. Ryssel, in E. Kautzsch, *Apokryphen und Pseudepigraphen*, Vol. 1, p. 196. L. E. T. André, *Apocryphes*, pp. 203 f. E. Schürer, *Geschichte*, Vol. 3, pp. 449 f. P. Haupt, in *Studies in Memory of W. R. Harper*, Vol. 2, p. 116. Chicago, 1908. L. B. Paton, *Esther*, pp. 44 f. J. A. F. D. Gregg, in Charles, *Apocrypha*, pp. 665 f. W. O. E. Oesterley, *An Introduction to the Books of the Apocrypha*, p. 191. New York, 1935.

[11] J. B. de Rossi, *Specimen variarum lectionum sacri textus et chaldaica Estheris additamenta*, Vol. 4, pp. 138-161. Rome, 1782 (2nd ed., pp. 122-149. Tübingen, 1783). G. Jahn, *Das Buch Esther nach der LXX hergestellt*. Leiden, 1901 (criticized in detail by J. Scheftelowitz, "Zur Kritik des griechischen und massoretischen Buches Esther," MGWJ 47 [N. F. 11] [1903] 24-37, 110-120). Cf. H. Willrich, *Judaica*, p. 15. Göttingen, 1900. See the Catholic authors mentioned by Paton, *Esther*, p. 42. The latest known to me is J. E. Steinmueller, *A Companion to Scripture Studies*, Vol. 2, pp. 141 f.

[12] Th. Nöldeke, *Die alttestamentliche Literatur*, pp. 88 f. Leipzig, 1867 (French translation, p. 129. Paris, 1873); and in Cheyne's *Encyclopaedia Biblica*, Vol. 2, col. 1406. J. Wellhausen, in *Göttingsche gelehrte Anzeige*, 1902, pp. 131 f. C. C. Torrey in JBL 61 [1942] 131 (cf. HTR 37 [1941] 2).

[13] C. Steuernagel, *Einleitung in das Alte Testament*, p. 789. Tübingen, 1912. O. Eissfeldt, *Einleitung in das Alte Testament*, p. 648. Tübingen, 1934.

[14] A literal, or at least a close, translation into Hebrew or Aramaic of such typical examples of Hellenistic Greek rhetoric as B, 2 (Lat. 13:2; Gr. 3:13b) or E, 2-9 (Lat. 16:2-9; Gr. 8:12c-i) would seem to be a *tour de force* beyond realization.

[15] Some striking evidence of translation from the Aramaic is presented by C. C. Torrey in HTR 37 (1944) 7-9.

[16] J. Langen, "Die beiden griechischen Texte des Buches Esther" (*Theolog. Quartalschrift*, 1860, pp. 263 ff.); *Die deuterokanonischen Stücke im Buche Esther*. Freiburg i. B., 1862. Henry Howorth, "Some unconventional views on the text of

The important monograph of C. C. Torrey (HTR 37 [1944] 1-40), in which the priority of the Greek over the Hebrew book has been maintained with new evidence and arguments, deserves more than passing notice. His main conclusions may be summarized as follows: 1. Both Greek texts are, in the main, independent translations from different Aramaic originals; but "Lucian" represents a separate Aramaic text only in 2:1-8:21 (2:1-8:17 constitutes the old short story, 8:18-21 is transitional); the rest is derived from the standard ("LXX") Greek text (pp. 6-9). 2. The "brief Hebrew version" of Esther, which became canonical for the Jews in the second century of our era, was abbreviated from the earlier Aramaic book (extant in Greek in two forms): when Purim became a "hilarious" celebration (long after 114 B.C.), all references to God and religion were removed from the book; the result was our Hebrew book which was edited later than Josephus (pp. 9-12). 3. The longer and shorter versions comprised the short story contained approximately in chs. 1-7 of the Hebrew text, and a supplement giving an account of the origin of Purim (chs. 8-9 in the Hebrew); the story dates probably from *ca.* 150 B.C. and is better preserved in the Aramaic texts underlying the Greek versions than in the Hebrew abridgment (pp. 12-25). 4. Lysimachus (according to the Greek colophon) translated the (Aramaic) "letter of Puraia" [*Phrourai*] in 114 B.C. for the Egyptian Jews while he was in Jerusalem, adding additions B and E. His Aramaic text contained two interpolations (additions A and F [without the colophon], i.e., the dream of Mordecai) dating from the period 130-114 B.C. (pp. 25-29). 5. Our abridged Hebrew Esther, called "the *second* letter of Purim" (9:29) to distinguish it from the longer Aramaic *first* "letter of Puraia" (9:29 in Greek), omitted "the false head and tail" (additions A and F, likewise recognized as spurious by Josephus), but not 10:1-3, "a worthless patch . . . not connected with Mordecai's dream." The Hebrew abridgment (made after Josephus) omits religious material and scenes or details belonging to the Persian décor of the story; otherwise the rendering of the Aramaic is quite literal; the name "Hadassah" was added in 2:7 (pp. 29-40).

Since this provocative but plausible theory of Torrey concerns the canonical book of Esther even more than the additions in the Apocrypha,

the Bible. VIII. The Prayer of Manasse and the Book of Esther" (PSBA 31, pp. 89-99, 156-168). A. Scholz, *Commentar über das Buch Esther mit seinen "Zusätzen" und über Susanna*, pp. xxi ff. Würzburg, 1892. F. Kaulen, *Einleitung in die Heilige Schrift des Alten und Neuen Testamentes*, 5th ed. by G. Hoberg, Vol. 1, pp. 2, n. 5; 108 ff. Freiburg i. B., 1911. J. Goettsberger, *Einleitung in das Alte Testament*, pp. 188-190. Freiburg i. B., 1928. J. E. Steinmueller, *A Companion to Scripture Studies*, Vol. 2, p. 142. C. C. Torrey, "The Older Book of Esther" (HTR 37 [1944] 1-40). The present writer is puzzled by Torrey's assertion that before him no one had doubted that "the Hebrew book is the original Esther" (*ibid.*, p. 12).

no full discussion of it is needed here.[17] As to the additions, Torrey's conclusions seem well established and extremely probable to the present writer: only additions C and D could possibly belong to the first edition of the book; additions A and F (without the colophon) were added to the Aramaic text; B and E were composed in Greek. It is thus probable that the Greek versions represent to some extent a stage earlier than the Hebrew text in the transmission of the book. A word remains to be said about the colophon in connection with the date of the additions.

The colophon that appears at the end of the Greek standard text and in 11:1 of the Vulgate (but not in "Lucian" and the Old Latin) has been translated as follows by E. Bickerman, at the end of his learned monograph on the subject (in JBL 63 [1944] 339-362). "In the fourth year of the reign of Ptolemy and Cleopatra [78-77 B.C.],[18] Dositheus—who said he was a priest,—and Levitas,[19] and Ptolemy his son deposited the preceding Letter of Purim, which they said really exists and had been translated by Lysimachus [son of] Ptolemy, [a member] of the Jerusalem community."

This subscription, as Bickerman has proved, was the attestation of the reported authenticity of the book and of its provenance, written by the librarian of the Jewish library in which the book was deposited, presumably in Alexandria. The Egyptian date, "in the fourth year of Ptolemy and Cleopatra," proves that the colophon was added to the manuscript in Egypt. This "fourth year" has been variously interpreted, but in recent years critics have followed B. Jacob (ZAW 10 [1890] 274-279) in identifying this Ptolemy with Ptolemy VIII (or IX) Soter II Lathyrus (117-81 or 116-80 B.C.) and thus date the colophon in 114-113. Bickerman, however, after discarding Ptolemy VIII—as also Ptolemy XIII (47-44, the husband of the famous Cleopatra [VII]) suggested by H. Ewald and H. Willrich—has presented strong arguments in favor of Ptolemy XII (or XI) Auletes and Cleopatra V and dates the colophon "between September 12, 78 and September 11, 77 B.C." (JBL 63 [1944] 346 f.). He infers, therefore, that the Hebrew Esther was written about 100 B.C. (*ibid.*, p. 355). While these conclusions are perfectly plausible, the present writer does not exclude the possibility that the Hebrew Esther was composed in *ca.* 125 and the translation was made about ten years later. Other dates seem unlikely.

[17] The present writer hesitates to accept Torrey's view that the first *written* edition of the book consisted only of the short story without any reference to Purim and its origin. There was possibly in circulation orally a folk tale about Esther, but the present writer is convinced that the original author wrote the Book of Esther in order to introduce the festival of Purim (possibly utilizing an existing folk tale).

[18] Bickerman was obviously unaware that this date had been previously suggested by J. Cohen, *Judaica et Egyptiaca*, pp. 28-30. Groningen, 1941.

[19] The usual translation, ". . . Dositheus—who claimed to be a priest and a Levite,—and Ptolemy . . ." is preferred by R. Marcus in JBL 64 (1945) 271.

According to the colophon, the translation was made by Lysimachus son of Ptolemy, "a member of the Jerusalem community." We may readily admit that the translation was made in Jerusalem, but was Lysimachus necessarily a native of Jerusalem and does his version of Esther present "a remarkable specimen of Palestinian Greek"? (Bickerman, *ibid.* pp. 355-357). In view of the manifest Egyptian coloring of the Greek diction, and the clear allusions to Egyptian conditions and institutions noted by B. Jacob (ZAW 10 [1890] 280-290), the present writer prefers to conclude with Th. Nöldeke (*Encyclopaedia Biblica,* Vol. 2, col. 1405) that, as suggested by his very name, the translator was "an Egyptian Jew" who, we may add, could very well have settled in Jerusalem and become a citizen thereof and thus have become familiar with Hebrew and Aramaic.[20]

The teaching of the book is not the same in the extant Hebrew and Greek redactions. The difference immediately obvious to all readers is that the Hebrew deliberately and consistently avoids all references to Jehovah and to Jewish religious rites and practices, while the Greek supplies prayers of Esther and Mordecai in which Judaism finds a noble expression. Another—less obvious—difference has been noted by Bickerman (JBL 63 [1944] 360-362): what was mere court intrigue and mutual personal dislike of Haman and Mordecai in the Hebrew, becomes in the Greek an eternal conflict between Jews and Gentiles. The note of "anti-Semitism," which hardly appears in the Hebrew (3:8), becomes dominant in the Greek. This mutual hostility between Gentiles and Jews is stressed in the king's accusation that the Jews are "an ill-disposed [*dysmenēs*] people," "standing continually alone in opposition to all men" (B, 4 f.; 13:4 f.). Likewise, according to the interpretation of Mordecai's dream, God made two lots, one for the Jews and the other for the Gentiles (F, 7; 10:10), implying that mankind is divided into these two opposed groups. The period about 100 B.C. is indeed characterized by violent hostility between Jews and Gentiles, both in Palestine and in Alexandria, and this feeling is reflected in other writings of the time. The injection of religion into a most unholy mutual hostility is characteristic of the Greek version, which was apparently prepared as an anti-Gentile tract.[21] Such a travesty of a noble religion, made for propaganda purposes, lowers the Greek book below the moral level of the Hebrew book, which is not particularly high. Thus, for instance, Mordecai's refusal to exhibit elementary common courtesy to Haman, ·

[20] E. J. Goodspeed (*The Story of the Apocrypha,* pp. 61-63. Chicago, 1939) says that "the Greek version, including the additions, was undoubtedly made in Egypt, and probably not far from 100 B.C."

[21] The anti-Hellenic spirit of the book appears, *inter alia,* in the transformation of the Agagite (i.e., Amalekite) Haman into a Macedonian plotter against the Persian king (E, 10 f., 14; 16:10 f., 14; cf. Josephus, *Antiquities* 11:6, 12).

according to the king's order (3:2), is unctuously—one would even say hypocritically—explained by Mordecai to God as dictated by reverence to the deity (C, 5-7; 13:12-14). In view of these facts it is not surprising that both in Hebrew and in Greek the Book of Esther has been the subject of controversy in religious circles. As late as the third century of our era an eminent rabbi could declare that Esther was not a sacred book (G. F. Moore, *Judaism*, Vol. 1, p. 244). Similarly some Church Fathers as late as Jerome rejected either the whole book or the additions in the Greek. And, beginning with Martin Luther, Esther has not been particularly popular in the Protestant Churches. But the Council of Trent in its decree "Sacrosancta" (April 8, 1546) ended all discussions on the Old Testament canon among Roman Catholics by canonizing officially the Latin Vulgate Bible, including Jerome's versions of the Hebrew Esther and of its additions in the Greek text.

CHAPTER V

THE WISDOM OF SOLOMON

~~~~~~~~~~~~~~~~~~~~~~~~~~~~~~~~

The English name of this book is a translation of the title occurring in the Greek Bible (LXX), *Sophia Salōmōnos* (or *Salomōntos, Solomōntos, Salōmōn*) and in the Old Latin, *Sapientia Salomonis*; but in the Latin Vulgate it is called *Liber Sapientiae* (Book of Wisdom). The book is an exhortation to seek wisdom, first, because it brings salvation to the pious Jews—damnation being the lot of ungodly Jews who disregard wisdom (1-5); secondly, because of its divine essence (6-9); and thirdly, because the history of Israel shows how wisdom brought blessings to the Israelites and calamities to the heathen (10-19). We may summarize the contents as follows:

I. *Wisdom's opposite attitude toward pious and wicked Jews determines their opposite destinies* (1-5).

1. The "judges [rulers] of the earth" should "love righteousness" in order to attain wisdom (1:1-5). God's universal spirit is aware of blasphemous thoughts and words (1:6-10) which, in spite of God's intentions in creating living beings for life eternal, result in death (1:11-15).

2. But the ungodly, by their deeds and words, have made a covenant with death (1:16-2:1a). Like Ecclesiastes, they argue that since human life is brief and miserable, beginning by chance and ending in extinction (2:1b-5), it should be devoted to the pleasures of banquets (2:6-9; cf. Is. 22:13), to oppression of the poor (2:10 f.), and to persecution of the righteous Jews (2:12; cf. Is. 3:10, LXX)—whose faith and life are a standing reproof to them (2:13-16)—in order to test the truth of Judaism and the patience of the pious under torture (2:17-20).

3. The faith of the righteous Jews (2:21-5:23). *a.* "Their hope is full of immortality" (2:21-3:9): the ungodly are in error (2:21 f.); God created man for immortality (2:23; cf. Gen. 1:26 f.), and it is only through the envy of the devil that death came into the world (2:24; cf. Gen. 3; Josephus, *Antiquities* I: 1, 4 [§41]). Accordingly, the souls of the departed righteous are at peace with God (3:1-3); after having been tested by affliction in this life (3:4-6), they will be glorified and will rule over nations (3:7-9). *b.* The lot of the righteous Jew in this life is preferable to that of the ungodly in two respects (3:10-4:19): the wicked man can

313

find no joy in his wife and children, but the righteous, even when
childless, will be remembered by God and man for his virtue (3:10-4:6);
and the premature death of the righteous is preferable to the wicked's
long life, for as in the case of Enoch (4:10 f.; cf. Gen. 5:22, 24, LXX),
God may snatch him from the world before his time to preserve him
from the contamination of sin (4:7-19). c. In the final judgment the
wicked will behold the salvation of the righteous (4:20-5:2) and in
their despair repent of their sins (5:3a [LXX 5:3]). These ungodly will
then recognize that the despised righteous have now become like angels
(5:3b-5 [LXX 5:4 f.]), while their own pride and riches profited nothing
(5:6-8), vanishing like a shadow (5:9-12). Devoid of virtue, they have
been ruined by their wickedness (5:13). Thus, while the hope of the
ungodly is like dust blown away by the wind (5:14), the righteous will
live forever, receiving from God a diadem of beauty (5:15 f.). d. On
the day in which God will put on his "panoply" (5:17a, 18-20a) and make
weapons of the whole creation (5:17b, 20b-23ab), he will triumph over
his adversaries: for iniquity devastates a land and evildoing overthrows
royal thrones (5:23cd).

II. *Solomon explains what wisdom is and how it may be attained*
(6-9).

1. The pagan kings, who have misused the power given them by God,
should learn wisdom in order to be acquitted in the impending divine
judgment (6:1-11).

2. Wisdom is accessible, for she seeks out those worthy of her
(6:12-16). Those who desire her may reach her and enjoy her blessings
by the following steps: the beginning of wisdom is desire of instruction,
which is love of her, which is observance of her laws, which is assurance
of incorruption, which is nearness to God (hence, dominion); therefore
the desire for wisdom raises us to a kingdom (6:17-20, a sorites or chain-
inference). Thus the kings on this earth, through wisdom, attain eternal
rule (6:21).

3. How Solomon attained wisdom (6:22-7:21). a. Solomon will instruct
the pagan kings in the mysteries of wisdom and will not treasure them
enviously (cf. 7:13), for he knows that a multitude of wise men is the
salvation of the world (6:22-25). b. Solomon attained wisdom not because
he was superior to mere human beings—on the contrary, being a descendant of Adam, he was born like other men (7:1-6)—but because he sought
it from God through prayer (7:7; cf. 8:21; 9; I Kings 3:9-12). c. He
preferred wisdom to thrones, riches, health, comeliness, and sunlight
(7:8-10), but through her he received all good things (7:11 f.). d. He
now imparts ungrudgingly the treasures of wisdom (7:13)—that wisdom
which not only implants in men friendship for God (7:14), but through
which God has taught him the several sciences (7:15 f.): philosophy

(7:17a), cosmology (7:17b), chronology and astronomy (7:18 f.), zoology (7:20a; cf. I Kings 4:33b [H. 5:13b]), demonology (7:20b; cf. Josephus, *Antiquities* 8:2, 5 [§45]), psychology (7:20b; cf. I Kings 3:16-27), botany (cf. I Kings 4:33a [H. 5:13a]) and pharmocology (7:20c). In brief, the knowledge of all things hidden or manifest (cf. also 8:8) was taught to him by wisdom, the artificer of all things (7:21-22a [Gr. 7:21]). *e.* The twenty-one (3×7) attributes of wisdom (7:22b-23 [Greek 7:22 f.]). More mobile than all motion, penetrating all things by virtue of her purity (7:24), wisdom is a breath of God's power, a pure efflux (or emanation) of his shining glory (7:25 f.); by entering holy souls she makes them friends of God and prophets (7:27 f.); she is superior to light, inasmuch as no night can obscure her brilliance (7:29 f.) and, reaching to the ends of the world, she rules admirably over the universe (8:1). *f.* Solomon has loved wisdom since his youth (8:2; cf. 7:8-10), first of all because she is God's friend and collaborator (8:3 f.), and secondly because she thus becomes the giver of all good things, both temporal, like wealth (8:5) and practical efficiency (8:6), and spiritual, like the four cardinal virtues of Plato and the Stoics (8:7; cf. IV Macc. 1:2-4, 18; 5:23 f.; Philo, *Legum allegoriae* I:19 [M I, 56]; *De posteritate Caini* 37 [M I, 250]), the knowledge of past and future, the understanding of complicated or obscure sayings, foreknowledge of signs and of the outcome of events (8:8). *g.* Solomon accordingly determined to take wisdom as his life companion—his counselor and comforter (8:9). Through her he would become a wise ruler, highly esteemed by his own subjects in life (8:10-12) and in death (8:13), as also by foreign peoples (8:14) and kings (8:15a), both in peace and in war (8:15b); through her his private life would be serene (8:16). *h.* Having thus reflected on the blessings resulting from communion with wisdom, he determined to take her unto himself (8:17 f.). Even though his soul was good and had entered into an undefiled body (8:19 f.), Solomon perceived that only God could bestow wisdom upon him, and he therefore uttered the following prayer (8:21). *i.* Solomon's prayer (9). God (the Lord of mercy, the creator by fiat, who in his wisdom formed man to rule over the creatures in holiness and righteousness [9:1-3]), should grant Solomon wisdom (9:4) because, though a weak human being (9:5 f.), he was chosen to reign (9:7) and to build the Temple (9:8); because he needs wisdom to fulfill these tasks (9:9-12); because human beings in general cannot understand the mind of God (9:13 f.)—since their corruptible body weighs down their soul (9:15; cf. Plato, *Phaedo* 81C) and they can hardly understand earthly things (9:16)—unless God grants them wisdom (9:17), through which he has guided and saved mankind (9:18).

III. *In past history wisdom has saved her friends (the Israelites) and punished her adversaries (the Egyptians and other heathen)* (10-19).

1. The heroes of wisdom (in contrast to the sinners) from Adam to Moses (10:1-11:1; cf. 4:10 f.). *a.* Adam (10:1 f.) contrasted with Cain (10:3). *b.* Noah contrasted with his contemporaries (10:4). *c.* Abraham contrasted with the builders of the Tower of Babel (10:5). *d.* Lot contrasted with the Sodomites and with his wife (10:6-9). *e.* Jacob contrasted with Esau (10:10-12). *f.* Joseph contrasted with his tormentors and with Potiphar's wife (10:13 f.). *g.* Israel contrasted with its Egyptian oppressors (10:15). *h.* Moses contrasted with Pharaoh (10:16). *i.* The exodus of the Israelites and their crossing of the Red Sea contrasted with the drowning of the Egyptians (10:17-11:1).[1]

2. Comparison (syncrisis) between the Egyptians and the Israelites (11:2-14,[2] continued in 16:1-19:22): "For by what things their enemies were punished, by the same they [the Israelites] in their need were benefited" (11:5). *a.* The Egyptians were punished with thirst—when the water of the Nile was turned into blood (Ex. 7:17-25)—for the drowning of the Israelite infants; on the contrary, when Israel thirsted in the desert, "water was given them out of the flinty rock" (11:2-14; cf. Ex. 17:3-6).

3. The first digression: God's punishment is just but mild (11:15-12:27); "wherewithal a man sinneth, by the same also shall he be punished" (11:16). *a.* Divine mildness in punishing the Egyptians (11:15-12:2). Although God in his almighty power could have sent the fiercest of beasts and monsters against the Egyptians or could have consumed them by a single breath, he made use of small creatures (11:15-20), not because God is limited in power, but because having created the world through his almighty power he loves his creation, and has "mercy upon all men" (11:21-12:2). *b.* Divine mildness in punishing the Canaanites (12:3-11). In spite of the detestable sins of the Canaanites (12:3-7), God sent against them hornets (Ex. 23:28; Deut. 7:20; Josh. 24:12) to destroy them little by little (12:8), not because God lacked power (12:9), but to offer them the opportunity for repenting—although they proved incorrigible (12:10 f.). *c.* Conclusion (12:12-27). The sole and almighty God (12:12-14) is just (12:15 f.) and merciful (12:17 f.), both to Israel's enemies and even more to his own people (12:19-22), who should follow his example (12:19b, 22b). Transition to the second digression: the pagans, who after being admonished by God through a mild punishment and being forced to recognize the "true God" remained obdurate, "shall experience a judgment worthy of God" (12:23-27).

[1] Wisdom is allegorically identified with the cloud and the pillar of fire in 10:17b (Philo, *Quis rerum divin. haeres* 42 [M I, 501], identifies the cloud with the divine *lógos* [word]).

[2] In some editions of the LXX, 11:5 is divided into two verses (11:5, 6) so that 11:6-26 become 11:7-27.

4. The second digression: the folly of heathenism (13-15). *a.* The adoration of natural elements and of the heavenly bodies instead of their Creator (13:1-9). *b.* The adoration of man-made idols (13:10-19; cf. Is. 44:10-20). An accursed wooden idol is contrasted with the blessed wood of Noah's Ark (14:1-11). *c.* The adoration of human beings, such as that of a deceased young son by his bereaved father (14:12-16) or of a remote living king by his subjects (14:17-21). (This theory that pagan gods were originally deified rulers had been popularized by Euhemerus, about 290 B.C.) *d.* The moral decay resulting from idolatry (14:22) is particularly evident in abominable ritual practices (14:23 f.), and in fifteen vices (14:25 f.) having their root in idolatry (14:27-29). God, not the idols, will punish the heathen for their false worship and false oaths (14:30 f.). *e.* In contrast with this corrupting influence of idolatry, the knowledge of the true and merciful God (15:1; cf. Ex. 34:6) prevents Israel's defection through sin (15:2a) and even its falling into sin (15:2b-3) under the lure of idolatry (15:4 f.). *f.* The author concludes the denunciation of man-made idols (13:10-14:11), after the general condemnation in 15:6, with a contemptuous picture of the potter, fashioning out of clay not only vessels for various uses (cf. Rom. 9:21), but also cheap clay copies of gold and silver idols (15:7-9): thus, for mere monetary gain, he offends his Maker (15:10-14). *g.* The Egyptians are the most foolish of all the heathen, for they worship not only foreign idols (15:15-17) but even the most miserable beasts (15:18 f.; cf. 11:15; 12:24).

5. Comparison (syncrisis) between the Egyptians and the Israelites (16:1-19:22), concluding 11:2-14 (No. 2, *a* above) and introduced by 11:15; 15:18 f. *b.* While the Egyptians were punished for their worship of beasts (11:15; 12:24; 15:18 f.) through a plague of small beasts (presumably the frogs, Ex. 8:1-6 [H. 7:26-8:2]) which prevented them from eating, Israel in the desert enjoyed a culinary delicacy, the quails of Ex. 16:13 and Num. 11:31 (16:1-4). *c.* While the Egyptians (16:9) were killed by locusts (cf. Ex. 10:12-15) and flies (cf. Ex. 8:16-24 [H. 8:12-20]), the Israelites, when bitten by the far more terrible snakes to remind them of the observance of the Law, were saved by God, who alone can rescue from death (16:5-14; cf. Num. 21:6-9). *d.* While the Egyptians were punished through wondrous downpours of rain and hail, while their crops were destroyed by thunderbolts passing unquenched through these showers and sparing the animals sent to plague the Egyptians (16:15-19, 22; cf. Ex. 9:22-26), God rained down manna—food of angels (Ps. 77:25), bread from heaven (Ps. 104:40 LXX [Engl. 105:40])—upon the Israelites in the desert. The manna miraculously assumed every conceivable flavor [cf. L. Ginzberg, *The Legends of the Jews* III, 44; VI, 17, note 99] and although similar to snow or hoarfrost (Ex. 16:14) it did

not melt in the fire (Ex. 16:23; Num. 11:8) but only under sunlight (Ex. 16:21)—a proof of nature's execution of God's rewards and punishments (16:15-29). *e.* While the Egyptians were haunted in the total darkness by frightening apparitions and were seized by a panic induced by their bad conscience (17:1-21;[3] cf. Ex. 10:21-23), the Israelites in Egypt enjoyed great light (18:1 f.; cf. Ex. 10:23) and in the desert were guided by the pillar of fire (18:3; cf. 10:17; Ex. 13:21 f.), being the future bearers of the light of the Law (18:4). *f.* While the Egyptians, having determined to slay Israel's infants (cf. 11:7; but Moses was saved, 18:5b; cf. 11:14), were punished through the loss of their first-born sons (18:5ac, 10-19; cf. Ex. 11:4-6; 12:29 f.) and through drowning in the Red Sea (18:5d; cf. 19:1-5), the Israelites celebrated the Passover and were spared (18:6-9; cf. Ex. 11:7; 12:21-28), and later, when stricken by a plague in the desert, they were saved through the intervention of Aaron (18:20-25; cf. Num. 16:41-50 [H. 17:6-15]). *g.* While the Egyptians, pursuing the Israelites after entreating them to leave, perished in the Red Sea, the Israelites crossed it on dry land (19:1-9; cf. Ex. 12:33; 14:5-9, 21-30; 15:1-21). *h.* Conclusion: how nature punishes the wicked and rewards the pious (5:17, 20; 16:17, 24; 19:6; cf. 18:8; 19:13, 22), being controlled by God who, without changing the essence of the elements nor disturbing the harmony of the world, changes the action of the elements as a harp player varies the duration and intensity of the musical notes (19:18; cf. Philo, *Vita Mosis* I, 17 [M II, 95-96]), is illustrated by the following examples: the Egyptian plagues of the flies and frogs, in contrast with the blessing of the quails (19:10-12; cf. 16:9, 1, 3, 2); the thunderbolts when the Egyptians drowned in the Red Sea (19:13;[4] cf. Ps. 77:17 f. [H. 77:18 f.]; Josephus, *Antiquities* II: 16, 3 [§343]); the punishment of the Sodomites, less inhospitable than the Egyptians (19:14-17; cf. Gen. 19); the change of land animals into marine animals and vice versa, at the crossing of the Red Sea (19:19, obscure); fire, unquenched in water, did not destroy the locusts (19:20-21a; cf. 16:17-19); icelike manna did not melt in the fire (19:21b; cf. 16:20-23). Thus did God in all things magnify his people (19:22).

The basic text of Wisdom is the Greek text included in the LXX (latest edition: A. Rahlfs, *Septuaginta*, Vol. 2. Stuttgart, 1935);[5] no

---

[3] In some editions of the LXX 17:9 corresponds to 17:9 f. of the Authorized Version, so that 17:11-21 in English correspond to 17:10-20 in Greek.

[4] In some editions of the LXX, 19:13 f. appears as 19:12 f., so that 19:15-22 become 19:14-21.

[5] For the text and versions of Wisdom (in addition to the commentaries) see: F. Feldmann, *Textkritische Materialen zum Buche der Weisheit.* Freiburg i. Br., 1902. For the Peshitta see: J. Holzmann, *Die Peschitta zum Buche der Weisheit.* Freiburg, 1903. Textual notes on the book have been published by B. Rissberg (ZAW 33 [1913] 206 ff.) and G. Kuhn (TSK 103 [1931] 445 ff.).

critical edition of the Greek text is available. The Latin is the most important of the versions. Prepared in North Africa about the middle of the second century of our era (D. de Bruyne, "Étude sur le texte latin de la Sagesse" [*Revue Bénédictine* 41 (1929) 101 ff.]), this version, incorrectly called *Itala*, was reproduced with scarcely a change by Jerome in his Vulgate. Two sentences, obviously genuine, are preserved in Latin but lost in Greek: "but unrighteousness is the acquisition of death" (at the end of 1:15); "let there be no meadow uncrossed by our revels" (at the end of 2:8). Other additions in the Latin text (see 2:17; 5:14; 6:1; 8:11; 9:19; 10:1; 11:5, 8, 13; 17:1) are glosses, paraphrases, or variant renderings. For the characteristics of the Latin Version, see P. Thielmann, *Über den Character der "Vetus Latina" des Buches der Weisheit* (*Archiv für lateinische Lexicographie und Grammatik* 8 [1893] 235-277). The other versions do not help materially to improve the text.

1. Critical Problems

In their investigation of the Wisdom of Solomon scholars have reached radically different conclusions on important points. Divergent views have been presented in solving the following problems: Was the book originally written in Greek or, at least in part, in Hebrew? Is it the work of a single author? When and where was it written? To what extent does the book as a whole or in its single parts disclose the influence of Greek philosophical thought? Before outlining the literary characteristics and the teaching of the book, it may be well to survey briefly the opinions of critics in regard to these four problems.

A. The Original Language

By attributing the book to Solomon, who certainly did not know Greek, the author naturally implied that it was originally written in Hebrew. Although Solomon is not actually named in the book, he is manifestly the speaker addressing the other kings in 6-9, for he is the king of Israel who built the Temple in Jerusalem (9:7 f.). Some Church Fathers (Clement of Alexandria, Tertullian, Cyprian, Hippolytus, and Lactantius), some medieval rabbis (see C. L. W. Grimm, *Das Buch der Weisheit*, p. 17, n. 3. Kurzgef. exeg. Handbuch zu den Apokr. des A.T., Vol. 6. Leipzig, 1860; cf. A. Marx, in JBL 40 [1921] 57-69), and, in recent times, S. Margoliouth (*Exp.* 6 [1900] 141-160, 186-193) have attributed the book, according to its title and the implications of chs. 6-9, to Solomon and have implicitly or expressly assumed that it was translated from classical Hebrew. But this critically absurd view was questioned early in the third century by the author of the Muratorian

Canon (lines 69-71), who says that Wisdom was written "by Solomon's friends in his honor," and by Origen (cf. E. Schürer, *Geschichte*, Vol. 3, p. 509). Later Augustine mentioned the attribution of the book to Sirach, the author of Ecclesiasticus (*De doctrina Christiana* 2, 8), but discarded it (*Retractationes* 2, 4). In any case he agreed with his most learned contemporaries in denying that Solomon wrote the book (*De civitate Dei* 17, 20): he presumably referred specifically to Jerome who, in his preface to the books of Solomon, not only regarded the book as pseudepigraphic but denied that it could have been translated from the Hebrew, since its style is that of Greek oratory.

But the general rejection of Solomonic authorship did not lead to the conclusion that no part of the book had been originally written in Hebrew. With the exception of S. Margoliouth, in the article cited and in a previous article ("Was the Book of Wisdom written in Hebrew?" JRAS 1890, 263-297; conclusively criticized by J. Freudenthal, in JQR 3 [1891] 722-753), no modern critic has regarded chs. 11:2-19:22 as a translation from the Hebrew. C. F. Houbigant (*Notae criticae in universos V. T. libros*, etc., I, ccxvi-ccxxiii. Frankfurt a. M., 1777; a reprint of the fuller Paris edition of 1753) regarded chs. 1-9 as written in Hebrew by Solomon and translated into Greek perhaps by the author of chs. 10-19. C. G. Bretschneider (*De libri Sapientiae parte priore Cap. I-XI e duobus libellis diversis conflata*, I, 25 ff. Wittenberg, 1804) limited the Hebrew original to 1:1-6:8; and W. F. Engelbreth (*Libri qui vulgo inscribitur Sapientia Salomonis latine conversi et explicati specimina*, II, 107 ff. Havniae [Copenhagen], 1816) to 1:1-5:23a; both adduced as evidence supposed misreadings or mistranslations of a Hebrew original. Similar evidence (in addition to "Hebraisms") is presented by F. Focke (*Die Entstehung der Weisheit Salomos*, pp. 66-74. FRLANT N.F. 5. Göttingen, 1913) to prove that chs. 1-5 were translated from the Hebrew (by the author of chs. 6-19). N. Peters (BZ 14 [1916] 1-14) has adopted these conclusions of Focke and has reconstructed a Hebrew psalm, having an alphabetic acrostic arrangement, out of ch. 9. Finally, E. A. Speiser (JQR N.S. 14 [1923-24] 455-482) and C. E. Purinton (JBL 47 [1928] 276-304) have attempted to prove, chiefly on the basis of presumable mistranslations, that 1:1-6:21; 8:1-9:18 or 1:1-11:1, respectively, have been translated from the Hebrew. C. C. Torrey (*The Apocryphal Literature*, pp. 98-103. New Haven, 1945) agrees with Purinton.

The evidence in support of the more generally accepted view that the Book of Wisdom was originally composed in Greek was presented, for the most part, in 1860 by C. L. W. Grimm, in his learned commentary (*op. cit.*, pp. 5-9); see also the commentaries of P. Heinisch (pp. xvi-xviii. EH. Münster i. W., 1912), F. Feldmann (pp. 3-5. HS. Bonn, 1926), and J. Fichtner (pp. 6 f. HAT. Tübingen, 1938; cf. his article in ZNW

36 [1937] 113-132). In brief, the literary diction and style (to be considered in a later section), the rhythm, combining Hebrew parallelism and Greek prosody (cf. for the latter H. St. J. Thackeray, in JTS VI [1904-05] 232-237), and the use of the Old Testament in Greek (LXX) rather than in Hebrew (cf. S. Holmes in Charles, *Apocrypha and Pseudepigrapha* I, 524 f.) militate in favor of a Greek rather than a Hebrew original. Particularly significant is the quotation of Is. 3:10, LXX (radically different from the Hebrew) in 2:12; and of Is. 44:20 (LXX) and Job 9:12, 19 (LXX) in the third part of the book (15:10 and 12:12, respectively): Margoliouth (*loc. cit.* in *Exp*, 1900) is forced to conclude that the Greek translators of Isaiah utilized the Greek text of Wisdom!

Moreover, as most critics agree, Wisdom contains not only echoes of Greek philosophies but even technical Greek terms which could hardly be expressed in Hebrew at the beginning of our era (see particularly 5:22; 7:17, 22-26; 8:1, 7, 19f; 9:15). One may become conscious, like Jerome, of the aroma of Greek eloquence in our book by comparing, for instance, the lyrical outbursts about the vanity of life in 2:1-9 and 5:8-13 with Ecclesiastes, who expressed similar thoughts in Hebrew. All in all, we must conclude that if any part of Wisdom (even the most Hebraic, like chs. 1 and 9) was translated from the Hebrew, the rendering was so free and so rhetorically Greek that it amounts to an original work with only the vaguest resemblances to its supposed prototype. It seems preferable to assume that the Alexandrian Jew who wrote chs. 1-9 (or the whole book) had little knowledge of Hebrew and composed his work in Greek.

B. Authorship

In regard to the subdivisions of the Book of Wisdom critics have not reached unanimous conclusions, although the subdivision into three main parts, as suggested at the beginning of this chapter (chs. 1-5; 6-9; 10-19), is the one most generally adopted. With a slight modification, the first two parts were joined together and the book was divided into two parts (chs. 1-9; 10-19) by C. F. Houbigant (*op. cit.*, 1753; 1777), followed by C. Gutberlet (*Das Buch der Weisheit*. Münster, 1874), F. W. Farrar (in H. Wace, *Apocrypha* I, 403-534. "Speaker's Commentary." London, 1888), C. H. Toy (in Cheyne's *Encyclopaedia Biblica*, Vol. 4, cols. 5336 f.), J. A. F. Gregg (in the *Cambridge Bible for Schools*. Cambridge, 1909), and E. H. Blakeney (*The Praises of Wisdom*. Oxford, 1937). The following subdivisions of the book have also been proposed, but seem less plausible:

a. 1:1-11:1; 11:2-19:22. J. G. Eichhorn, *Einleitung in die apokryphischen Schriften des A. T.* Leipzig, 1795. E. Gärtner, *Komposition und Wortwahl des Buches der Weisheit* (*Schriften der Lehranstalt für die Wissenschaft des Judentums* II, 2-4). Berlin, 1912. S. Holmes, in Charles, *Apocrypha and Pseudepigrapha* I, 321-324. Oxford, 1913. C. E. Purinton in JBL 47 (1928) 276-304. C. C. Torrey, *The Apocryphal Literature*, p. 98.

b. The two main parts (1-9; 10-19) contain the sayings of 79 sages, uttered in the course of two conventions of three sessions each: J. C. C. Nachtigal, *Die Versammlungen der Weisen, II: Das Buch der Weisheit.* Halle, 1799.

c. 1:1-6:8; 6:9-10:21; 12-19 (ch. 11 is editorial). C. G. Bretschneider (*op. cit.*, 1804).

d. 1-12; 13-19. L. Bertholdt, *Historisch-kritische Einleitung in die sämtliche kanonische und apokryphische Schriften des A. und N. T.*, Vol. 5, p. 2261. Erlangen, 1815.

e. 1:1-5:23a; 6:12-10:21; 11-19 (5:23b-6:11 is editorial). W. F. Engelbreth (*op. cit.*, 1816).

f 1:1-12:18 (written by a Samaritan); 12:19-19:22 (written by an Alexandrian Jew). L. Lincke, *Samaria und seine Propheten*, pp. 119-144. Tübingen, 1903.

g. 1:1-11; 1:12-6:12; 6:13-9:19; 10:1-11:4; 11:5-19:22 (five discourses). R. G. Moulton, *Ecclesiastes and the Wisdom of Solomon.* New York, 1903.

h. 1-5 (the eschatological book); 6:1-11:1 (the book of wisdom); 11:2-12:27 and 15:18-19:22 (the book of God's punitive method); 13:1-15:17 (the book of idolaters). W. Weber (in ZWT 47 [1904] 145-169). E. Gärtner (*Komposition und Wortwahl des Buches der Weisheit.* Berlin, 1912) agrees with Weber in the main. Weber regards the following as glosses: 1:4-6a; 3:11 f.; 11:15 f.; 14:2-7; Gärtner the following: 1:4-6a; 3:9; 3:11-4:19; 12:2-21; 19:10-12. Gärtner considers 11; 12; 16-19 as a midrash on the plagues of Egypt, which could have been derived from a Passover Haggadah (cf. Kohler, under *i.* below).

i. 1-6; 7:1-9:17 (on wisdom); 9:18-19:22 (an Alexandrian Passover Haggadah). K. Kohler (in *Jewish Encyclopedia*, Vol. 12, p. 539 New York, 1906).

j. 1:1-6:21; 6:22-19:22. R. Cornely, *Commentarius in Librum Sapientiae* (edited by Fr. Zorell). *Cursus Scripturae sacrae* II, 5. Paris, 1910.

k. 1:1-6:11; 6:12-19:22. J. K. Zenner (in ZKT 22 [1898] 417 ff.). J. K. Zenner and H. Wiesemann (*ibid.* 35 [1911] 21 ff.; 449 ff.; 665 ff.).

l. 1-5; 6-19. F. Focke (*op. cit.*, 1913); cf. A. Bertholet, *Biblische Theologie des Alten Testaments* (II) 475. Tübingen, 1911.

m. 1-6; 7-9; 10-19. A. T. S. Goodrick, *The Book of Wisdom* (Oxford Church Bible Commentary). London, 1913.

n. 1:1-6:21; 8:1-9:18 (first part); 6:22-7:30; 10–19 (second part). E. A. Speiser (in JQR N. S. 14 [1923-24] 455-482).

These critics (except Gutberlet, Farrar, Gregg, Moulton, Goodrick, Zenner, and Wiesemann) attribute the several parts into which they divide the Book of Wisdom to different authors. Some, as we have seen (A, above), regard the first part of the book as a translation from the Hebrew and inevitably attribute it to a different author; but this theory cannot be proved beyond cavil. The other arguments brought forth to prove multiple authorship are derived from differences in style and thought in the various parts of the book.

Obviously it is essential to determine at first the subdivisions of the book. The variety of opinions presented above shows that the subdivisions are not marked with sufficient clarity to exclude divergent views, although the general outline is far more logical than that of Proverbs or Ecclesiastes, where no plan is discernible. It would seem that the author of the book or, if it is composite, the final editor took special pains to disguise, by means of connective particles and transitional clauses, the lines of demarcation between the sections of his book. Whatever division is adopted, no part, in its present form, could be separated from what precedes and follows and be regarded as a separate work. And this mutual cohesion of the parts is the chief obstacle to the attribution of the book to more than one author.

One of the most clearly marked parts of the book is 6-9. Here Solomon is introduced addressing the kings of the earth in the first person (from 6:9 on, following the exordium in 6:1-8). And yet the opening of the address, "Hear *therefore* (*oûn*), O ye kings . . ." (6:1), which closely parallels the opening of the book (1:1), is unmistakably connected with what precedes: since thrones shall be overthrown by iniquity in the last judgment (5:23d), kings should receive Solomon's instruction and acquire wisdom. This part (6-9) is concluded with Solomon's prayer for wisdom (9), and 10:1 is therefore the opening of a new section. And yet, although ch. 10 opens the historical part of the book, it cannot be separated from 9:18 immediately preceding: "this one, she" (i.e., Wisdom) at the beginning of ch. 10 (cf. 7:29; 8:2, 7, 9; 10:5, 10, 13, 15) would be obscure without the immediately preceding mention of wisdom. Similarly 11:2, which begins the long comparison between Israelites and Egyptians, is intimately connected with the preceding section: no separate work could open with the words of 11:1, 11:2 or 11:5. As C. L. W. Grimm (*op. cit.*, p. 204) has rightly noted, 11:1 concludes ch. 10 ("here for the last time Wisdom is the subject"), but at the same time introduces the contrast between the Egyptians and the Israelites that follows immediately. Even the great digression on idolatry (13-15) is introduced by the preceding verse (12:27), with which it is connected: "*For* (*gar*) all men are vain by nature . . ." (13:1).

As F. Focke (*Die Entstehung der Weisheit Salomos*, pp. 6-20) has shown, chs. 6-19 deal with a variety of topics, but the various parts are so ably joined into a whole that, in their present form, they must have been written by a single author. Transitional clauses regularly mark the passage from one subject to another: thus 7:21 introduces 7:22-8:1; 8:21 introduces ch. 9; 10:1-11:1 are a general historical introduction to 11:2-19:22; 11:15 prepares for both digressions (11:16-12:22 and 13-15), the second of which is also ushered in by 12:23-27—a passage which is closely connected with 11:15 f.; similarly 15:18 f., while introducing chs. 16-19, is the logical sequel of 11:2-14. Characteristically, such transitional clauses (like 11:1) are connected with what precedes and with what follows, so that some critics regard them as conclusions and others as introductions—a false dilemma, for they were intended to serve in both capacities. This rhetorical device appears also in chs. 1-5: for instance, 4:16-19 concludes the preceding contrast between the pious and the wicked and prepares for the following description of the final judgment (similarly 1:15, as preserved in the Latin Bible). Throughout the book, another device for knitting its sections closely together is the repetition of the same thought at the beginning and at the end of a section or in successive sections: compare 1:13 f. with 2:23 f.; 2:1a with 2:21; 1:16 with 2:24; 2:17 f. with 3:1 f.; 3:13 with 4:1; 3:3 with 4:7; 5:3-13 is the counterpart of 2:1-16; compare 8:1 with 8:9 and 8:18; 11:15 with 12:24 and 15:18 f.; 10:17 with 18:3; 11:14 with 18:5 (Moses); 5:17, 20 with 16:17, 24 and 19:6; 16:17-19 with 19:21b; 16:17-23 with 19:20 f.; and the like.

Through these obvious stylistic devices a deliberate effort was made to give to the book the structural unity characteristic of Greek writings but entirely foreign to Hebrew wisdom books; in Prov. 1-9, the closest parallel to the Wisdom of Solomon in Hebrew, the use of such rhetorical devices is still rudimentary. The impression that the book was conceived as an organic whole is strengthened by a certain uniformity of diction and style (cf. Grimm, op. cit. pp. 5-8). Nevertheless, some of the critics named above have adduced evidence to prove that more than one author is responsible for our book.

The main arguments adduced to prove that Wisdom is composite are: the Hebrew origin of the first part (chs. 1-5, or 1:1-5:23a, or 1:1-6:8, or 1:1-6:8+8:1-9:18, or 1:1-11:1) and differences in thought and style between the two parts. In view of earlier discussions of these arguments (in particular by Grimm, op. cit., pp. 9-15; F. Feldmann, in BZ 7 [1909] 140-150, and in his commentary [HS, 1926], pp. 5-11) it seems unnecessary to refute them here in detail. It may be said in general, however, that where stylistic differences are not due to the variety of topics, they could conceivably result from the use of separate written sources, both Hebrew and Greek. Unfortunately, aside from the Old Testament (in

Hebrew and in Greek) no other sources used by the author of Wisdom can definitely be identified in extant Jewish and Greek literature, in spite of some rather striking parallels.[6] If the author seldom quoted his non-Biblical sources verbatim, but preferred to paraphrase them, the manifest differences of thought and style as well as the general uniformity of teaching and expression would be easily explained, without having recourse to hazardous guesses about multiple authorship.

Another consideration applies particularly to F. Focke, who has presented the most plausible arguments for the attribution of 1-5 and 6-19 to different authors (*Die Entstehung der Weisheit Salomos*, pp. 21-86). He notes that Greek philosophical terms do not occur in chs. 1-5; that Wisdom (aside from 1:3 f. and 3:11; he regards 1:6 as interpolated) plays no role in 1-5; that the deity is ethical in 1-5 and nationalistic in 6-19; that the resurrection from the dead is implicit in 1-5 but the insignificance of the body and the immortality of the soul are taught in 6-19; that 1-5 contrasts Pharisees and Sadducees, while 6-19 Israelites and heathen. He concludes that the first part is Palestinian and the second Alexandrian, explaining the uniformity of the Greek diction in the two parts (in spite of some differences) by supposing that the author of the second part translated the first from the Hebrew. In reality, these differences between the two parts, which Focke tends to exaggerate, do not prove diverse authorship. It is perfectly clear that chs. 1-5 are addressed to Jews and 6-19 to Gentiles. The first part strives to convert the wealthy, mundane, "wicked" Jews (so often denounced in the Psalms) to a true understanding of Jehovah and to an uncompromising fulfillment of his will. The second part is a defense of Judaism against the attacks of the heathen, a denunciation of paganism, and an effort to convert the Gentiles to Judaism. Obviously, in addressing Jews the author had no occasion to condemn idolatry nor to present the philosophical aspects of Judaism: he emphasized the *ethical* contents of Judaism as binding on individual Jews, for its *nationalistic* aspects were not in the least ignored by worldly Jews. On the contrary, in addressing Gentiles it was necessary to present the Jews as a whole as God's own people. The difference in the audience addressed in the two parts explains also the varying use of the divine names: "Lord" (*kýrios*), prevalent in the first part, stands for Jehovah, the god of Israel; "God" (*theós*), prevailing in the second part, serves to emphasize the identity of Israel's god with the only true God in existence.

In conclusion, no decisive arguments have been presented to prove

---

[6] The researches of P. Wendland and J. Geffcken (see F. Focke, *Die Entstehung der Weisheit Salomos*, pp. 8 f.) have shown that a written source was utilized for chs. 13-15. Of course, chs. 7-8 abound in thoughts generally emphasized in Stoic diatribes (cf. Focke, *op. cit.*, p. 104).

that Wisdom could not have been written by a single author. Like the Second Isaiah (Is. 40-55) the author addressed himself to the Jews, picturing for them a glorious future held in store for them by their God, and to the Gentiles, ridiculing their religion (nothing but idolatry!) and urging them to find salvation from the wrath to come by worshiping the one true God.

C. Date and Place of Composition

Like Proverbs and Ecclesiastes, Wisdom (at least in chs. 6-9) claims to be the work of Solomon. After this attribution, which is too absurd to need refutation, is dismissed as fiction (cf. above under A), the book lacks definite historical allusions for determining its date. We must rely exclusively on its general characteristics of thought and style. The same is true for the place of composition.

If, as everything indicates, Wisdom was written originally in Greek, its author could hardly have been a Palestinian Jew, living either before or after Alexander (d. 323 B.C.). He was obviously a Hellenistic Jew more familiar with Greek than with Hebrew, living in a Jewish center of the Dispersion—most probably Alexandria. His style and thought contrast strikingly with those of Palestinian sages of Hellenistic times, whether unfamiliar with Greek thought (like the author of Prov. 1-9 and Sirach) or acquainted with it in only the vaguest manner (Ecclesiastes). On the contrary, he is to be classed with Alexandrian-Jewish writers having some training in Greek rhetoric and some information about Greek philosophy, like the author of IV Maccabees, Aristobulus, and Philo. None of these three writers, nor any others known to us otherwise, could have written the Book of Wisdom, for in spite of some parallels (a few of which have been noted in the summary of Wisdom at the beginning of this chapter), this book has characteristics of its own. The attributions of Wisdom to one of the translators of the Pentateuch into Greek (LXX), to Aristobulus, or to Philo (Nicholas of Lyra, Martin Luther, and others) are now recognized to be erroneous (cf. Grimm, op. cit. pp. 21 f.; P. Heinisch, Das Buch der Weisheit [EH], p. xxix). Equally unsupported is the guess that the author was an Essene (E. Pfleiderer, Die Philosophie des Heraklit von Ephesus im Lichte der Mysterienidee, pp. 306 ff. Berlin, 1886. E. Zeller, Die Philosophie der Griechen III, 2, p. 296. 4th edit., Leipzig, 1903) or a Therapeute (J. G. Eichhorn, Einleit. in die apokr. Schriften, pp. 134 f., 150. A. F. Gfrörer, Philo und die Alexandrinische Theosophie II, 265 ff. Stuttgart, 1831. A. F. Dähne, Geschichtliche Darstellung der jüdisch-alexandrinischen Religionsphilosophie II, 170, note 96. Halle, 1834). Least of all can Wisdom be regarded as a Christian book (cf. the references in Grimm, op. cit. p. 25 f.), or a book written by

Apollos, before he became a Christian and eventually wrote (supposedly) the Epistle to the Hebrews (E. H. Plumptre, in *Exp.* I [1875] 329-348, 409-435). It is even highly improbable that, as H. Graetz (*Geschichte der Juden* III, 4, pp. 612 f.) believed, some verses are Christian interpolations (2:24; 3:13; 4:1; 14:7).

In general modern criticism has adopted the conclusions presented in 1860 by Grimm, in his great commentary: the author was "an Alexandrian Jew with a philosophical education" (p. 20), and lived in the period between 145 and 50 B.C. (p. 35) or, as E. Schürer said (*Geschichte des jüdischen Volkes* Vol. 3, p. 508), between Sirach and Philo. A date shortly after 100 B.C. or (C. Siegfried, in E. Kautzsch, *Apokryphen und Pseudepigraphen* I, 479) 100-50 B.C. cannot be far wrong. P. Heinisch in his commentary (pp. xx-xxiii) infers from the allusions to open persecution of pious Jews on the part of apostate Jews, with the tacit connivance of the Ptolemies (see 2:10-20; 5:3 f.), that the book was written in the period 88-30 B.C. (cf. R. Schütz, *Les idées eschatologiques du livre de la Sagesse*, p. 12. Paris, 1935). In reality, however, the author does not have in mind a general official persecution, but rather the ordinary anti-Semitic attitude of many Egyptians, which induced some of the wealthy Alexandrian Jews to forsake the religion of their fathers under the lure of social prestige and economic advantage. This would naturally lead them to assume the attitude of supercilious condescension or even bitter hostility toward the pious Jews, attributed to them in 2:12-16. This mutual contempt of pious and mundane Jews appears in the Psalms and has continued through the centuries. It is possible that, according to 2:17-20, occasionally a high-placed Jew brought about the death of a pious Jew through torture or through court proceedings; but the passage could be rhetorical exaggeration, like the references to shedding innocent blood in Ps. 10:8; 94:21; Prov. 1:11; 6:16 and often in Ezekiel, Jeremiah, and elsewhere. In any case, these allusions to the persecution of pious Jews offer no clue whatsoever to the date of the Book of Wisdom. It may be inferred, however, from the use of the Greek Bible (LXX) not only for the Pentateuch (translated about 250 B.C.), but also for Isaiah (2:12 quotes Is. 3:10, LXX; 15:10 quotes Is. 44:20), translated about 150 B.C., that our book was written after 150 B.C.

Like Heinisch, F. Focke (*op. cit.* pp. 74-86) believes that our book was written to encourage the victims of vicious persecutions: the Hebrew part of the book (chs. 1-5) was issued in Palestine when Alexander Jannaeus (103-76 B.C.) massacred the Pharisees opposed to him (88-86); an Alexandrian Jew translated this part into Greek (adding 5:23cd) and used it as the introduction for his own book (chs. 6-19), which he composed when Ptolemy VIII Lathyrus, upon his return from the war with Jannaeus in 88-87, persecuted the Jews of Alexandria (according to the legendary accounts in III Maccabees and Josephus, *Against Apion* II, 5 [§§51-56]). This attractive theory is based entirely on conjectures: the Hebrew origin of chs. 1-5 cannot be demonstrated; moreover, the alleged persecution by Ptolemy VIII rests on historical evidence of the most questionable sort (III Maccabees and Josephus do not name Ptolemy VIII, but Ptolemy IV and VII, respectively) ingeniously reconstructed by H. Willrich (*Hermes* 39 [1904] 244-258; cf. E. Schürer, *Geschichte* Vol. 3, p. 490, note 28).

It is extremely improbable that Wisdom was written later than 50 B.C., as isolated critics have suggested: S. Holmes (in Charles, *Apocrypha and Pseudepigrapha* I, 521) dates 1:1-11:1 in 50-30 B.C., and 11:2-19:22 in 30 B.C.-A.D. 10; A. T. S. Goodrick (in the *Oxford Church Bible Commentary*) in A.D. 37-41. A. Kuenen, F. W. Farrar, W. O. E. Oesterley (*An Introduction to the Apocrypha*, p. 209. New York, 1935) and E. J. Goodspeed (*The Story of the Apocrypha*, p. 90. Chicago, 1939) date the book about A.D. 40.

D. Greek Philosophy in the Book of Wisdom

None of the scholars who have studied our book has denied that its author used technical philosophical terms, chiefly Platonic and Stoic (particularly in 7:22, 24; 11:17; 14:3; 16:21; 17:2; 19:18), but paradoxically some have refused to admit that Greek philosophy influenced his thought. At one extreme E. Pfleiderer (*Die Philosophie des Heraklit*, pp. 289-348. 1886) and M. Friedländer (*Griechische Philosophie im Alten Testament*, pp. 182-208, particularly p. 189, note 4. Berlin, 1904) have discovered a pervasive influence of Greek philosophy in the book; at the other extreme P. Heinisch (*Die griechische Philosophie im Buche der Weisheit* [AA I, 4]. Münster i.W., 1908; cf. his commentary [EH, 1912] pp. xxxi, 149-158, 168 f.) regards the thought of Wisdom as substantially identical with that of the Old Testament, with scarcely an echo of Greek philosophy. Other scholars, taking a middle course, incline toward one or the other categorical view. Only a few scholars, however, deny that the author of Wisdom presents in 8:19 f. the Platonic doctrine of the preexistence of the soul.[7] Without going quite as far as Grimm in asserting that the author had a "higher and classical education" (Commentary,

[7] W. Weber (in ZWT 48 [1905] 409-444; 51 [1909] 314-332; 54 [1912] 205-239). M. J. Lagrange (in RB 4 [1907] 85-104). F. C. Porter (in AJT 12 [1908] 53-115; and in *Old Testament and Semitic Studies in Memory of W. R. Harper* I, 207-269. Chicago, 1908). P. Heinisch (*opera citata*, 1908 and 1912). F. Feldmann (*Das Buch der Weisheit* [HS] p. 19. Bonn, 1926). R. Schütz (*Les idées eschatologiques du Livre de la Sagesse*, pp. 26-30).

p. 19) and was "philosophically cultured" (*ibid.*, p. 20), the majority of scholars seem to agree with P. Wendland (*Archiv für Geschichte der Philosophie* 5 [1892] 112), when he writes: "On the whole, the author was not more deeply affected by genuine Greek philosophy than the cultured persons of his time; he has not appropriated much more than the notions which were beginning to penetrate into the general consciousness."[8]

2. Literary Characteristics

The Books of Proverbs and Ecclesiasticus are substantially transcripts of teachers' classroom lessons on the good and successful life (after the manner of Egyptian "Instructions"). For the most part the teaching, which is at times addressed to an individual, consists of miscellaneous aphorisms; occasionally, however, longer lectures on specific topics occur. The Book of Job, on the other hand, is a learned discussion of a theological problem among scholars holding divergent views; thus it faintly resembles the *Dialogues* of Plato. Like these books, the Book of Wisdom purports to be the transcript of spoken words, not, like Ecclesiastes, of the private reflections of a sage, published as an afterthought. In form the Wisdom of Solomon differs from these books in being not a teacher's instruction to pupils, nor a debate, nor a scholar's meditation, but, like IV Maccabees, a public address; not a sermon addressed to Jews, like IV Maccabees, but a diatribe or popular discourse delivered to a mixed audience of Jews (both pious and wicked) and Gentiles. In reality, however, neither IV Maccabees nor Wisdom was ever delivered orally in its present form: the oratorical manner is just as artificial as in the Deuteronomic Code (purporting to be the last sermon of Moses) and in Is. 40-55. More specifically, disregarding obvious differences, IV Maccabees and Wisdom are orations in the Hellenistic manner, consciously using the devices of Greek rhetoric: the first is intended for educated Jewish readers, the second is more popular, more "evangelistic," after the manner of the Cynic-Stoic diatribe, or literary imitation of a popular

---

[8] See in particular: E. Zeller, *Die Philosophie der Griechen* III, 2. 3rd ed., 1881, pp. 271-274; 4th ed., 1903, pp. 292-296. H. Bois, *Essai sur les origines de la philosophie judéo-alexandrine*. Toulouse, 1890. A. Bertholet, in K. Budde, *Geschichte der althebräischen Litteratur*, 2nd ed., pp. 412 f. Leipzig, 1909. E. Schürer, *Geschichte* Vol. 3, pp. 507 f. E. Gärtner, *Komposition und Wortwahl des Buches der Weisheit*, 1912. F. Focke, *Die Entstehung der Weisheit Salomos*, 1913. J. Heinemann, *Die Griechische Quelle der Weisheit Salomos* (Jahresbericht des jüdischen Seminar in Breslau, 1920; *Poseidonios' metaphysische Schriften* I. Breslau, 1921). Stella Lange, in *JBL* 55 (1936) 293-302. D. B. Macdonald, *The Hebrew Philosophical Genius; a Vindication*, pp. 96-127. Princeton, 1936. J. Fichtner, in *ZNW* 36 (1937) 113-132; and *Weisheit Salomos* (HAT), pp. 8f. Tübingen, 1938.

moral address, the best extant example of which is contained in Horace's *Satires* (III, 3).[9]

The author, however, does not adhere strictly to the pattern of a popular discourse. He does not expound logically a single theme according to a clear plan; he does not visualize a specific audience but addresses himself specifically to Jews in chs. 1-5, and to Gentiles in chs. 13-15; in the rest of the book he seems to have in mind both Jews and Gentiles. Moreover, here and there he drops the oratorical style and uses other literary forms: aphorisms (1:3; 3:11, 15; 4:9; 6:6, 24), prayers (ch. 9), psalms of praise (11:21-26; 12:12-25), verbatim reports of the words of the ungodly Jews (2:1-20; 5:3-13), praises of wisdom (6:12-16; 8:1-8), a description of the last judgment (4:20-5:16), pseudo-historical lists of ancient saints and sinners (10:1-11:1), accounts of God's miraculous interventions in behalf of his people in the past (11:2-14; 16:1-19:22) and in the future (5:17-23), a sorites or "mystic ladder" (E. R. Goodenough, *By Light, Light*, p. 274. New Haven, 1935) in 6:17-20 (cf. Plato, *Symposium* 210-212), a syncrisis (11:2-14; 16:1-19:22), a definition of fear (17:12 [LXX 17:11]), catalogues of the attributes of wisdom (7:22 f.), of the sciences (7:17-20), and of the vices (14:25 f.).

As frequently in eloquent orations, the tone tends to rise in a gradual crescendo from pianissimo to fortissimo. The book begins with a quiet, earnest exhortation in ch. 1; passes to the wicked Jews' lyrical outburst, abounding in metaphors, in ch. 2; subsides again in the objective contrast between the pious and the wicked in chs. 3-4, which culminates in the dramatic scene of the last judgment (far more tempestuous than Dan. 7) in ch. 5. Similarly the second part of the book begins again with a calm exhortation (ch. 6) and with Solomon's reminiscences (7:1-21), rising to a lyrical praise of Wisdom in general (7:22-8:1), and as Solomon's beloved comrade in particular (8:2-21), and culminating in an eloquent prayer (ch. 9). The third part, in spite of some brilliant though fantastic pieces (such as the nightmare of the Egyptian darkness in ch. 17), is decidedly inferior in literary quality to the other two: it combines argumentation with rhetorical outbursts, history and apocalypse, logic and fantasy, and does not rise to an oratorical climax like the other two (although there is a crescendo from 10:1-11:19 to 11:20-12:27, and to 13-15; 16-19). In fact, the conclusion (19:22) is so abrupt and pedestrian that some critics have surmised that the original end of the book is lost.

In style as well as in thought the author amalgamates Israel and Hellas. In the list of literary forms given above, the first ones are Hebrew,

---

[9] P. Wendland (*Die hellenistisch-römische Kultur*, pp. 39-50, in *Handbuch zum Neuen Testament* I:2. Tübingen, 1907; later editions) has penned the classical characterization of the diatribe. See also: J. H. Ropes, *The Epistle of James* (ICC), pp. 10-12; M. S. Enslin, *The Ethics of Paul*, pp. 41 ff. New York, 1930.

the last ones (sorites, syncrisis, definition, and catalogues) are Greek. Aiming to be an apology for Judaism as a way of salvation, the book is modeled both after Prov. 1-9 and after the diatribe. The poetry of the book (well sustained in chs. 1-5; 9; sporadic elsewhere, though more prevalent in 6-8; 10-12 than in 13-19, which are mostly prose) is a blend of Hebrew parallelism and Greek prosody, and at times is truly impressive.

The Hebrew elements of thought and expression are derived from the Greek Bible rather than from its Hebrew original. The poetic parallelism imitates that of the Psalms, Proverbs, and Job in their Greek version. A number of expressions are apparently borrowed from the LXX. The discovery of Greek papyri in Egypt has proved that the language of the LXX on the whole was the vernacular Greek of the time; we may, however, surmise that the following expressions (selected from a fuller list) are Biblical: "ye who judge the earth" (in the sense of rulers; 1:1; cf. 6:1); to seek God in simplicity of heart (1:1); *paideía* (Hebr. *mûsār*, education or discipline; 1:5); "reins . . . heart" (for feelings and thoughts; 1:6; cf. Jer. 11:20; 17:10; 20:12; Ps. 7:9 [H. 7:10]); "ear of jealousy" (meaning the jealous God; 1:10); "works of your hands" (with the omission of the article as in Hebrew; 1:12); law and discipline in parallelism (2:12; cf. 6:17 f.; Prov. 6:23); to be regarded as . . . (2:16; 3:17; 9:6; cf. Lev. 7:18; 17:4; Ps. 106:31); *diábolos* (devil; 2:24) is used in the LXX to translate "Satan"; "in the hand of . . ." is used in three meanings: under the protection of . . . (3:1; cf. Is. 51:16), in the power of . . . (7:16; cf. II Sam. 24:14), and through, by means of . . . (11:1; cf. Josh. 14:2; Acts 7:35; Gal. 3:19) ("in hands" [9:16; 19:3] means "at hand"); visitation or inquest (Gr. *episkópē*, Hebr. *peqûdāh*; 3:13; Ecclus. 16:16) is a Biblical word, meaning the divine revelation for blessing (2:20; 3:7; 4:15; cf. Luke 19:44) or for punishment (14:11; 19:15); "his [God's] saints" (Hebr. his *ḥasidim*, often in the Psalms; 4:15); "before the face of . . ." (5:1); "sons of God . . . saints" (5:5), either meaning angels (as in Job) or righteous human beings (cf. 2:13, 16, 18; 18:4); "to be found," in the sense of to be recognized as being . . . (7:29; 8:11); "with my whole heart" (8:21; cf. Deut. 6:5); "sons of men" (9:6); "well pleasing in thine eyes" (9:9; cf. 3:2); "abominations," meaning idols (12:23; cf. LXX in I Kings 11:5, 33; 21:22; Is. 2:8, 20); *aiōn* (like *'ōlām* in post-Biblical Hebrew) in the sense of world, not "eternity" (13:9; cf. IV Esd. 6:55, 59; in Wisd. 14:6; 18:4 it means the human world); to bless, blessing (14:7; 15:19); *skándalon* (stumbling block), meaning as in the LXX what induces men to sin (14:11); "they were stricken with blindness" (19:17; cf. Gen. 19:11). It is likely that *dýnamis* (power) in 1:3 (cf. 5:24) is a metonymy for God, translating *gebûrāh* (post-Biblical Hebrew); it would then be the first known occurrence of this usage, paralleled in Mark 14:62; Matt. 26:64, which paraphrase Ps. 110:1; for

the benefit of Gentile readers, Luke 22:69 writes "the power of God."
"Holy Spirit" (9:17; cf. 1:5; 7:22), however, does not occur for the first
time in our book, as F. Focke (*Die Entstehung der Weisheit Salomos*,
p. 62) states in accordance with Grimm (Commentary, p. 51), for we
find it in the LXX of Is. 63:10 f.; Ps. 51:13 (H. and Engl. 50:13).

Gentile Hellenistic expressions are much more conspicuous in Wisdom
than those derived from the Greek Bible.[10] In addition to vernacular
terms of common use, the author employs uncommon terms of various
types: philosophical terms (7:22, 24; 11:17; 14:3; 16:21; 19:18); poetical
expressions which are intensely lyrical (2:6-9; 5:9-13; 17:18-21) and not
unworthy of the great tragic authors of Greece (5:20; 10:3; 11:6);
unusual words which the author himself apparently coined (as *prōtó-
plastos*, first-formed [i.e., Adam], in 7:1; 10:1; the word is found elsewhere only in patristic literature [Clement of Alexandria, Tertullian,
Cyprian, Eusebius, etc.]) or obtained from recondite sources which are
now unknown (Grimm, in his Commentary, p. 6, lists seven compounds
which do not occur in other Greek writings). In general the author has
at his command a very copious vocabulary, abounding in synonyms and
antonyms (used in parallelism and antithesis), and in compound nouns
and adjectives. Although he makes repeated use of favorite expressions,
he displays considerable virtuosity in using a choice literary diction
without equal in the LXX and comparable to that of the best Hellenistic
writings. Nevertheless, he committed a curious blunder when he used
metalleúein (to dig for metals, cf. Deut. 8:9, LXX) twice (4:12; 16:25)
in the sense of *metallássein* or *metalloioûn* (to change). Likewise *philó-
psychos* (11:26) is wrongly used in the sense of "lover of souls" (it really
means "lover of his own life, coward").

The author's rhetorical skill appears also in the musical effects achieved
deliberately through the order and choice of words, through assonance,
rhyme, alliteration, paronomasia, and other devices (for examples, see
Grimm, *op. cit.* p. 7; Focke, *op. cit.* pp. 63-65). His sophisticated literary
elegance may be noticed by comparing, for instance, his vignette of the
idolmaker (13:11-19) with that of the Second Isaiah (44:13-20), which
served as his model. Here (13:11-15), and occasionally elsewhere
(12:3-7, 8-11, 27; 17:14 f., 17, 18 f. [LXX 17:13 f., 16, 17 f.]), the author
discloses his ability to construct in the Greek manner elaborate sentences
including subordinate clauses, although usually he adopts the simpler
Hebrew structure in which brief sentences are co-ordinated.

[10] On the vocabulary, syntax, and style of Wisdom see: Grimm, Commentary,
p. 6 f. F. W. Farrar, in H. Wace, *Apocrypha* I, 404-410. London, 1888. R. Meister,
Prolegomena zu einer Grammatik der LXX (*Wiener Studien* 29 [1907] 249 ff.).
P. Heinisch, *Das Buch der Weisheit* (EH) pp. xvi-xviii. 1912. E. Gärtner, *Komposition und Wortwahl des Buches der Weisheit*, 1912 (giving a full index of Greek
words in Wisdom). F. Focke, *Die Entstehung der Weisheit Salomos*, pp. 56-65.
1913. J. Fichtner, in ZNW 36 (1937) 113-132.

The order of words is varied deliberately for artistic effect and emphasis. In addition to the normal prosaic order of words, which is occasionally employed (1:2; 2:12; 7:1 f.; 9:1; 11:1-3; etc.), the author uses a chiastic arrangement such as this: "think of the Lord in uprightness, and in simplicity of heart seek Him" (1:1; see also 1:4, 8; 2:13; 2:4, 13; 3:12; 4:2; 5:5 f.; etc.); he places the accusative before its verb (3:11; 6:16; 11:10 [LXX 11:11]; 12:8, 17; etc.), the genitive before its noun (3:1, 14 f., 19; 4:2 f.; 5:6; 6:3 f., 7, 15, 17; 7:25 f.; 8:4; 9:4; 12:24; 14:5, 18; 15:7; 16:19, 22; 17:7; 18:5, 9, 13; 19:17; etc.), the verb between nouns and adjectives which belong together (1:7; 2:13, 22; 4:6; 5:10 f., 14; 6:4; 8, 14, 19; 7:3, 5, 12, 22 f., 25 f.; 8:2, 4, 6 f., 19; 10:8; etc.).

The style of Wisdom has certain general characteristics but at the same time is conspicuously varied in accordance with the topics. It has been observed that on the whole the diction is uniform throughout: typical words favored by the author occur repeatedly, as well as alliterations. Transitional and connective clauses serve to cement the several parts into a unit. Although the author refers to numerous Biblical heroes (4:10; 10; 10:1, 14; 12:3; 14:6; 15:14; 18:5, 21; 19:14, 17), none of them, not even Solomon, who is presented as the speaker in chs. 6-9, is ever named. The number seven has a special significance for the author: twenty-one attributes of wisdom (7:22 f.); seven wise men from Adam to Moses in ch. 10; seven sounds terrified the Egyptians in the darkness, 17:18 f. (Gr. 17:17 f.); seven contrasts between Israel and the Egyptians, chs. 11 and 16-19.

The style of the author runs the gamut from the sober exhortation in ch. 1 to the lyrical eloquence of ch. 8; from the realistic description of a carpenter (13:11-19) or a potter (15:7-9) at work making idols to the fantastic description of the horrors of darkness in ch. 17; from philosophical arguments (like the cosmological proof of God's existence in 13:1-5, or the explanation of the origin of death in 2:23 f.; cf. 1:13 f.) to impassioned denunciations of the heathen (14:22-28) and praises of wisdom (7:22-29; 8:4-8).

From the literary point of view, the best parts of the book are those written under the compulsion of a stirring emotion (as in the fine passage 3:1-9). The intensity of feeling expresses itself in eloquent, lyrical, imaginative language. The most brilliant use of metaphor and simile occurs in the elegies on the vanity of human life in general (2:2-5) or of the wicked's lot in particular (5:7-14); less musically lyrical is the image of God's panoply (5:17-22). Elsewhere metaphors appear only sporadically (3:6 f., 15; 4:3-5; 11:22; 15:10; 16:29; 18:4, 16; 19:9, 18) or not at all (in chs. 1, 6-10, 12-14 in particular). The author vividly personifies wisdom (chs. 6-9; cf. Prov. 8) and the divine *lógos* (18:15 f.), without, however, conceiving either one as an actual person distinct from God.

Of the numerous antitheses in the book the most apt and vivid shows
how futile it is to pray to idols (13:18 f.).

The allegorical interpretation of the Scriptures, used with such amazing virtuosity by Philo[11] not long after the time of our author, is conspicuously lacking in our book (cf. F. Focke, *op. cit.*, p. 100). The clearest
example is in 18:24, where Aaron's vestments are the symbol of the
world—a commonplace (Schürer, *Geschichte*, Vol. 2, pp. 319 f., n. 6)
familiar to Philo and Josephus (see Grimm, *ad loc.*) and present in the
Palestinian Midrash (C. Siegfried, *Philo . . . als Ausleger des Alten Testaments*, pp. 188 f. Jena, 1875). The other two examples cited by E. Bréhier
(*Les idées philosophiques et religieuses de Philon d'Alexandrie*, 2nd ed.
p. 47. Paris, 1925), the wife of Lot (10:7) and the brazen serpent (16:6),
are symbols rather than allegories. Conversely, the author (in 10-11;
16-19) is one of the first (together with Chronicles, Tobit, Jubilees, and
II Macc. 1:19-36; 2:1-8) to use the *haggadic* interpretation of the Scriptures, adding to their text fanciful legends (11:15; 16:1 f., 9, 18, 21 f.;
17:6, 9 f., 15-19; 18:12 f., 17-19; 19:11 f., 17, 21) in contrast with the
strict adherence to the Biblical accounts practiced by Sirach (Ecclus.
44-49).

In summing up, we may say that, despite some literary blemishes
(particularly evident to modern readers in chs. 10-19) and the rhetorical
prolixity that at times fails to conceal vagueness of thought, Wisdom is
"the most beautiful of all late Jewish [i.e., *ca.* 150 B.C.-A.D. 100] writings"
(R. Reitzenstein, *Zwei religionsgeschichtliche Fragen*, p. 109. Strassburg,
1901).

3. Religious Teaching

The author of the Book of Wisdom seems to have had three purposes
in writing his book: to strengthen and deepen the faith of the pious
Jews, to bring back to such a faith the worldly Jews, and to convince
the heathen of the foolishness of their idolatrous religion. In general
his polemic against the apostate Jews is found in chs. 1-5; his defense
of Judaism in chs. 6-12, 16-19; and his polemic against idolatry in chs.
13-15. The author, however, gave encouragement to afflicted pious Jews
also in chs. 1-5 and polemized against both apostates and infidels in 11-12,
16-19.

The danger to the faith of orthodox Jews arose from the disappointment of their hopes: misfortunes (such as disease, childlessness, poverty,
early death) and persecutions brought into question their assurance that
God would reward their piety. The author admits that *in this life* the
pious are frequently less prosperous and fortunate than the ungodly—

[11] See H. A. Wolfson, *Philo*, Vol. 1, pp. 115-138. Cambridge, Mass., 1947.

a bitter truth often evidenced in daily experience and lamented in the Scriptures since the days of Jeremiah (Jer. 12:1-3; Hab. 1:13 f.; Mal. 3:14 f.; Ps. 10; 37; 73; 92; 94; Job; Eccles.; etc.). The author of Wisdom deals with this problem first from the point of view of the individual— in the present (chs. 1-5) and in the past (ch. 10)—then with regard to Israel as a whole, in the past (chs. 11-12; 16-19).

"Righteousness is immortal, but the gain of unrighteousness is death" (1:15, Latin text) because God, the Creator of the world (1:14; 6:7; 9:1, 9; 11:17; 13:5; 16:24), whose rule over all that exists cannot be disputed (11:21 f.; 12:11b-14; cf. Is. 40:12-17; Dan. 4:34 f., 37 [Aram. 4:31 f., 34]), loves all things which he has made (11:23-26; cf. 1:13 f.; 12:16; 15:1) and, being almighty (7:25; 11:17, 21; 12:18; cf. 7:23; 18:15), rules justly and mercifully (11:23; 12:15-18; cf. Josephus, *Antiquities* IV: 8, 14). This idea of God, rooted in the Old Testament and paralleled in Palestinian Judaism, is not abstractly theological but intensely religious (G. F. Moore, *Judaism*, Vol. 1, pp. 368-380). God's ubiquity has a religious meaning—he is ever aware of secret sins (1:7-11; cf. Jer. 23:23 f.; Aristeas §132 f.) and is ever at hand to protect the righteous (2:18; 10:15; 19:22); God's almighty power "is the basis of justice," his universal rule makes him spare all (12:16). The conflict perceived by Job between the metaphysical (omnipotence) and the moral (justice and mercy) attributes of God is thus categorically denied, through an intense religious faith which also overcomes the skepticism and atheism of the ungodly (ch. 2).

On the basis of this faith, the author proceeds to explain the afflictions that beset the pious Jews—afflictions which Job had regarded as an insoluble mystery. Undeserved suffering is either a test (*peirasmós*) by which God tries the righteous "like gold in the furnace" (3:5cd-6; cf. Ecclus. 2:5), or a paternal chastisement, a disciplining (*paideía*) by which God improves their character (3:5a; 12:2; 16:6-13; cf. Deut. 8:5; Prov. 3:12; Lam. 3:27-33; Job 5:17; Ecclus. 18:13 f.).[12] The mildness of the divine chastisement of Israel's sins is contrasted with the merciless punishment of the Egyptians (11:9 f.; 12:20-22; cf. Ecclus. 35:18 f. [Gr. 32:22-25]). Even Enoch's untimely passing is explained as an act of divine kindness, "lest wickedness should alter his understanding" (4:10-15). Through the examples of the ancient heroes from Adam to Moses, the author shows how piety was rewarded in this life, while the wickedness of their contemporaries was punished (ch. 10).

In chs. 1-5, however, the author minimizes the temporal rewards for piety and wisdom (which are stressed in Proverbs). Two of the greatest

[12] R. Marcus, *Law in the Apocrypha*, pp. 29-31. New York, 1927. G. F. Moore, *Judaism* II, 248-256. W. Wichmann, in BWANT IV, 2 (1930), pp. 6 ff. A. Sommer, *Begriff der Versuchung* (Dissertation), p. 13. Breslau, 1935. H. J. Korn, in BWANT IV, 20 (1937), p. 13, note.

blessings in the eyes of the Jews, many children (Ex. 23:26; Deut. 7:14; Ps. 127:3) and a long life (Prov. 3:1 f.; 16:31), are said to be insignificant in comparison with virtue and wisdom (4:1-9); earthly rewards pale before the glorious brilliance of the heavenly ones. As Jesus said later, the righteous should lay up for themselves a treasure in heaven (Matt. 6:20; 19:21; and parallels). "For our light affliction, which is but for a moment, worketh for us a far more exceeding and eternal weight of glory" (II Cor. 4:17; cf. Rom. 8:18): this is a good general summary of Wisdom, chs. 3-4.

But when we attempt to gain a clear and detailed notion of the author's eschatology we are faced with serious difficulties. The vagueness and ambiguity of the language may be deliberate (cf. Stella Lange, in JBL 55 [1936] 300 f.): perhaps the author realized that living men cannot pierce the mystery of their destiny after death. But since our author attempted to combine mutually exclusive Hebrew and Greek ideas about life after death, his thought was inevitably indefinite, if not actually inconsistent. His interpreters have consequently reached opposite conclusions in their attempts to understand his teaching (see above, notes 7, 8).

In dealing with scientific and philosophical problems the author is a poet rather than a scientist, omitting essential details and using technical terms indiscriminately. In describing the conception, gestation, and birth of a human being (7:1-3) the author deals only with the body, ignoring completely the spiritual element in man, like the ungodly Jews who, in accordance with Epicurean notions, regarded *birth* as an accident, *thought* as a bodily process, and *death* as utter annihilation (2:2 f.). Elsewhere, however, the author mentions specifically the spiritual element in man, but refers to it indiscriminately by three terms connoting, in Greek philosophy, entirely different entities: *pneûma*, or spirit (5:3; 15:11, 16; 16:14); *psyché*, or soul (1:4, 11; 2:22; 3:1, 13; 4:11; 7:27; 8:19; 9:3, 15; 10:16; 14:11, 26; 15:8, 11, 14; 16:14; 17:1), which in some of these passages (cf. 10:7; 12:6; 17:8) may mean "person" (like its Hebrew prototype *nephesh*); and *noûs*, or mind (4:12; 9:15; cf. *diánoia*, 4:15). He actually uses *pneûma* and *psyché* (15:11; 16:14; cf. 15:8 with 15:16), and *psyché* and *noûs* (9:15), in parallelism, without the slightest difference; *psyché* (15:8; 16:14) or *pneûma* (16:14) leaves the body at death. According to Hebrew usage, "reins and heart" means man's innermost thoughts (1:6), "heart" (*kardía*) means mind (8:21; 15:10); through an extension of meaning, "heart" is identified with the ego, the self (8:17, 20).

While Greek philosophy distinguished in man three elements—the body, the animal soul, and the spirit or intellect (cf. I Thess. 5:23)— Jews generally believed, on the authority of Gen. 2:7 (cf. 3:9; Eccles. 3:19-21; 12:7), that two elements, the body and the spirit, constituted a "living soul" or person. Philo, of course, interpreted Gen. 2:7 philosophically (*De opificio mundi* 46 [M I, 32]) and even maintained, changing its meaning by joining it to Lev. 17:11, that man has, in addition to the body, both an animal and a rational soul (*Quod deterius potiori insidiari soleat* 22 [M I, 207]).[13] The author of Wisdom, on the contrary, seems to have accepted the literal meaning of this famous verse and conceived man as composed of a physical and a spiritual element (1:4; 2:3; 15:8), recognizing, however, with Plato that the soul is pre-existent (8:20) and pressed down by the body during man's earthly existence (9:15).

The other account of man's creation (Gen. 1:26 f.; cf. 5:1; 9:6) is likewise interpreted in accordance with Greek philosophy by both Philo and the author of Wisdom. Philo in fact gives two interpretations of man's creation in the divine image: this divine (non-physical) man is "the mind (*noûs*) which guides the soul" (*De opificio mundi* 23 [M I, 16]), or again "an idea, or genus, or seal, mentally perceptible, incorporeal, neither male nor female, incorruptible by nature" (*op. cit.* 46 [M I, 32]). The author of Wisdom inferred from Gen. 1:26 f. that "God created man to be immortal, and made him the image of his own *eternity* [*aidiotetos*; some important manuscripts read *idiotetos*, essence]" (2:23): the influence of Greek ideas (G. F. Moore, *Judaism* I, 448) is obvious (cf. Philo, *De opificio, loc. cit.*: "mortal as to his body, but immortal as to his intellect").[14] Death entered the world through the envy of the devil, the serpent in Eden (2:24; cf. Rev. 20:2).

These notions about the character of God and the nature of man are the philosophical presuppositions for the assurance given to the pious Jews that "their hope is full of immortality" (3:4), while that of the ungodly "is like the dust blown away by the wind" (5:14). The author of Wisdom, influenced by Hellenistic missionaries, is apparently the first Jew to regard a life of righteousness as the condition for eternal salvation. Like John the Baptist, Mohammed, and innumerable medieval and modern "evangelistic" preachers, he gave to the last judgment a central position in his exhortations. For the first time in extant Jewish writings the outlook is decidedly otherworldly, as in early Christianity. But in his fervor he joined confusedly (like St. Paul) traditional Jewish notions to echoes of Hellenistic thought and, like some eloquent preachers, he impresses us more by his poetic imagination than by the logic of his teaching.

From his reading in the Old Testament, the author knew of various

---

[13] On the conflict between rational and irrational soul, according to Philo and Plato, see H. A. Wolfson in HTR 35 (1942) 131-134.

[14] For four other inferences drawn from Gen. 1:26 f. in the Apocrypha and Pseudepigrapha, see L. Couard, *Die religiösen und sittlichen Anschauungen der alttestamentlichen Apokryphen und Pseudepigraphen*, pp. 105-107. Gütersloh, 1907.

notions, presented in the course of centuries, of the divine retribution for human deeds. Before Hellenistic times this collective (10:17-11:14; 16-19) and individual (10:1-16) retribution was conceived as preceding death, since in the underworld, or *Sheol*, the eternal home of all the dead, the same fate awaited both good and bad. The author of Wisdom ascribes this dismal survival after death in Sheol (which, following the LXX, he calls *Hades*) to the ungodly (2:1; cf. 2:5). But he himself believed that there is such a place (16:13; 17:14; in 1:14 Hades means death, as in Hos. 13:14). It is only for Israel as a whole that the early apocalypses inserted into the prophetic books, developing the ancient dream of "the day of the Lord" (Am. 5:18), predicted a glorious future in the Messianic age. The author's indebtedness to these writings appears not only in the apocalyptic traits of his description of Israel's triumphs over the Egyptians in the past (11; 16-19; note particularly 18:15 f.), but even more in his conception of Jehovah arming himself for the last onslaught against the heathen and destroying them by means of violent natural forces (5:17-23; cf. Is. 59:17; 66:15 f.; Ez. 38:18-23; Hab. 3; Ps. 7:12 f. [H. 7:13 f.]; 18:12-15 [H. 18:13-16]; etc.)

The Last Judgment is frequently related to this Armageddon, as, for instance, in Joel 3 (H. 4): this is probably why both are described in ch. 5, although here their juxtaposition is incongruous. The author uses a variety of expressions for the day of judgment (1:9; 3:7, 13, 17 f.; 4:6, 20; 14:11). All these expressions and their context bring out a basic difference between the judgment in Wisdom and in the Old Testament apocalypses. In Joel and elsewhere God judges between heathens and Jews, bringing about the triumph and dominion of the Jews (as in 5:17-23); but in Wisdom the judgment pertains not to nations and empires, but to individual Jews, separating the pious from the ungodly (4:20-5:16). The two groups face each other in the divine assize (4:20-5:2); the wicked confess the folly of their ways (5:3-13), repudiating their former opinions and actions (as stated in 2:1-21); although nothing is said of the judge (God) and his sentence, the opposite lots of righteous and ungodly Jews are succinctly described at the end (5:14-16). Logically this moral judgment, eliminating wickedness among the Jews, is much more connected with the religious judgment, eliminating paganism and its idols (14:10-14, inspired perhaps by Jer. 10:15 [note *episkopé* in the LXX, visitation, judgment], cf. Jer. 46:25; Is. 2:20; 30:22; 31:7), than with the destruction of pagan empires (5:17-23) that follows it.

The Jews attained their belief in a retribution after death in the Hellenistic period, when the Book of Daniel (Dan. 12:1 f.; cf. Is. 26:19, which perhaps refers to national resurrection) asserted that the most pious and the most wicked Jews would be raised from the dead to receive their rewards and punishments. Did our author derive his assurance of retribution after death from Daniel or from popular Greek philosophy? The latter alternative seems more probable, for nothing is said in Wisdom of a resurrection of the body; in fact it is clearly excluded in the case of the wicked (4:18). Some critics[15] have, however, maintained, more or less positively, that the doctrine of resurrection is implied in chs. 3-5 and alluded to, at least as a possibility, in 16:13 f. In reality the revivification of the body seems to be utterly alien to the author's thought. Believing with Plato and other Greeks that "the corruptible body presses down the soul" (9:15), he must have regarded a rebirth of the soul, a return into its "earthly tabernacle" (*ibid.*; cf. II Cor. 5:1, 4; II Pet. 1:13 f.; the figure of the tent for the body is common in Greek philosophy: cf. Grimm, Commentary, p. 188; E. Gärtner, *Komposition und Wortwahl des Buches der Weisheit*, p. 211, *s. v. skênos*), as the greatest conceivable calamity for the pious dead, "the *souls* of the righteous" who are in the hand of God (3:1). But could "the righteous that is dead condemn the living ungodly" (4:16), stand boldly after his death before his tormentors (5:1), or "judge nations and have dominion over peoples" (3:8), unless his body be restored to his soul? It is probable that all three verses are rhetorical outbursts intended to show how the tables will be turned and eventually the oppressed righteous will dominate over their oppressors. The author is fond of "poetic justice."[16] The third passage which, strictly speaking, implies for the pious dead a future life on this earth, may be a mere echo of Dan. 7:14, 27, penned without a realization of its far-reaching import; in the next verse the saved are spirits abiding with God in love (3:9). In general it should be remembered that the visible appearance of the ghosts of the dead is a necessary element in the *mise en scène*: it belongs to the dramatic poetry, rather than to the philosophy, of life after death. On this basis even Plato could be accused of believing in the resurrection of the body!

It is futile to seek in Wisdom (as some scholars have done) for a definite time-table of future life, such as was fixed later in Jewish apocalypses and even more in Christianity, beginning with the Revelation of St. John. The author speaks of a Last Judgment without telling us

[15] P. Heinisch, "Das jüngste Gericht im Buche der Weisheit" (*Theol. und Glaube* 2 [1910] 89-106). W. Weber, "Der Auferstehungsglaube des eschatologischen Buches der Weisheit" (ZWT 54 [1912] 205-239). F. Focke, *Die Entstehung der Weisheit Salomos*, pp. 33-35. Göttingen, 1913. R. Schütz, *Les idées eschatologiques du livre de la Sagesse*, pp. 187-195. But M. J. Lagrange (RB 4 [1907] 97) is less categorical than the preceding.

[16] "Wherewithal a man sins, by the same also shall he be punished" (11:16; cf. 12:23; 16:1; 17:3; 18:4 f.). In Judaism, generally, the old principle of *talio*, "an eye for an eye," was applied to divine retribution. See G. F. Moore, *Judaism* II, 251; R. Marcus, *Law in the Apocrypha*, pp. 26-28. H. L. Strack and P. Billerbeck, *Kommentar zum Neuen Testament aus Talmud und Midrasch* II, 192-197; 527-529. Munich, 1924.

whether it modified the state of the deceased, and if so, how. It would even seem that the Judgment (like Armageddon) is a Jewish tradition incongruously superimposed on the Greek notion that the souls go to their eternal rewards and punishments immediately after death. The author describes the opposite fates of the saved and the damned in general terms, without picturesque details. The pious are assured an eternal life (1:15; 3:4; 5:15; 6:18; 8:17; 15:3; cf. 2:23; in 4:1 and 8:13 "immortality" seems to mean only to be held in perpetual remembrance among the living) free from suffering (3:1), in peace (3:3), rest (4:7) and safety (4:17), under God's protection (5:16) and in communion with him (3:1, 9; 5:15; 6:19), among his angels (5:5 [?]). More concretely the author speaks of the shining brilliance of the saved (3:7; cf. Dan. 12:3; Enoch 39:7; 43; 104:2; Matt. 13:43); of their royal crown (5:16),[17] symbolizing their dominion over nations (3:8; 5:16; 6:20 f.). Since the fate of the deceased ungodly must be the exact opposite of that of the pious, the author contradicts himself: on the one hand, in contrast with immortality, the wicked must be utterly annihilated (1:11 f., 15b [Vulgate], 16; 2:24); on the other, in contrast with the heavenly bliss of the redeemed, they must be tormented eternally (4:19). Thus at death they become "a vile carcass" and at the same time an object of scorn among the ghosts in the underworld (4:18). The author may have believed that the ungodly destroyed through sin their immortal soul, although the common interpretation of 1:11 f. in the sense of "the second death" (Rev. 2:11) or Philo's "eternal death" (cf. Grimm, Commentary, pp. 59-61)—spiritual and moral death—is far from certain. In contrast with the hope of immortality of the pious, the ungodly have no hope (3:11, 18; 5:14; 15:6, 10), and while the first shine brilliantly, the latter are in utter darkness (17:21).

Such are the blissful hopes outlined to encourage the afflicted righteous Jew to remain steadfast, and at the same time to induce the prosperous wicked Jew to mend his ways before it is too late. It seems apparent that, in spite of the Biblical reminiscences noted above, the author's point of view in chs. 1-5 is Hellenistic rather than Palestinian—exactly the opposite of what F. Focke (*Die Entstehung der Weisheit Salomos*, pp. 28-41) attempted to prove. The contrast between the author's views and Palestinian Judaism is most marked in two points: he does not regard earthly blessings as God's reward for piety and he considers a blessed immortality the supreme goal of human life.

The Jewish mind was essentially realistic; in such diametrically opposite

[17] Instead of *diádēma* (originally the Persian royal crown), the New Testament uses *stéphanos*, the crown of victory in games (cf. Wisd. 4:2), of military valor, of festal gladness, for the glorification of the elect: I Cor. 9:25; 2 Tim. 4:8; Jam. 1:12; I Pet. 5:4; Rev. 2:10; 3:11; 4:4, 10.

books as Daniel and Ecclesiastes it strove after concreteness, whether in a dream-world or in the world of facts. It usually operated with the tangible, avoiding abstract problems and escape from the facts of life into the realms of metaphysics and mysticism no longer in contact with the phenomenal world—except under alien influences. A comparison between Sirach's Ecclesiasticus and the Wisdom of Solomon will show clearly the considerable influence of Hellenistic thinking on Wisdom. With realistic common sense Sirach clung to known facts, while the author of Wisdom peered into the invisible world. The attitude of Sirach toward life (Ecclus. 14:14-16) resembles that of the ungodly, which is anathema to the author of Wisdom (2:2-6; cf. Ecclesiastes): one should make the most of life on this earth, because "when a man dies, he inherits creeping things, beasts, and worms" (Ecclus. 10:11, LXX; similarly in Hebrew); "for the covenant from time immemorial is: 'Thou shalt die the death'" (14:17; Hebrew: "And the eternal decree is: 'Thou shalt surely die'"). The allusion is to Gen. 2:17. In Wisdom (2:23), on the contrary, "God created man to be immortal"—an inference from Gen. 1:26, which is totally alien to Sirach (Ecclus. 17:1-4) and flatly contradicts Gen. 3:22 f.

Consequently, Sirach and Palestinian Jews in general believed that God rewarded and punished human beings on this earth: "Prosperity and adversity, life and death, poverty and riches come from the Lord" (Ecclus. 11:14); even the resurrection from the dead as taught by Daniel, by the apocalypses, and by the Pharisees, provided a retribution *on earth*. Although the author of Wisdom did not entirely abandon this theory and believed that the wicked suffered for their sins before their death (as well as after), he knew of no earthly reward for the pious. In fact, he took issue with the current view and argued that the two supreme earthly rewards for piety in the eyes of Sirach—"He who honors his father will have joy of his children . . . (and) will have a long life" (Ecclus. 3:5 f.)—and of Jews in general, were insignificant and unreal. In the first place, the wicked can find no happiness in a large family and in a long life (Wisd. 3:12-19): their lot is less desirable than that of a barren woman and of a eunuch who are pious (3:13 f.), less enviable than that of Enoch, who was taken from this world before his time (4:10-15; cf. 4:7). In the second place, "better it is to have no children and to have virtue" (4:1) and "wisdom is the gray hair unto men, and an unspotted life is old age" (4:9; contrast Prov. 16:31). Thus for the author happiness has no relation to earthly goods, which are vain and transitory (5:8-12). For Palestinian Jews, on the contrary, "Beauty, strength, riches, honor, wisdom, [old age,] gray hair, children, are comely for the righteous and comely for the world" (*Sayings of the Fathers* [*Aboth*] 6:8; *Tosefta Sanhedrin* 11:8).

In transferring divine retribution to the invisible world, to the immortal life that follows death and is the *real* life, the author of Wisdom is closer to the Hellenistic mystery religions and to early Christianity than to the Palestinian Judaism of his time. Like these, his concern was to show how in this life men should strive for the supreme prize—the eternal salvation of their souls—and thus escape an eternity of torments. This preoccupation with the destiny of the soul after death; on the contrary, was totally alien to Palestinian Jews of the Maccabean period: they betrayed no anxiety about what awaits the soul beyond the grave, and their devotion to God (expressed in fulfilling his commandments) was an end in itself, not a "down payment" guaranteeing eternal bliss.

This brings us to the second purpose of the book. Having disclosed to the afflicted pious and to the affluent ungodly a dazzling vision of eternal glory and a terrifying picture of the eternal torments of the wicked, our author must now, in chs. 6-9, characterize, for their benefit and for the guidance of enlightened Greeks, the way of salvation. In giving an answer to the question, "What shall I do that I may inherit eternal life?" (Mark 10:17; Matt. 19:16; Luke 18:18), the author pens an apology for Judaism—as he conceives of it in Hellenistic garb. His answer to that question differs therefore radically from that of Jesus, which was not substantially different from that of the rabbis of Palestinian Judaism.

In principle the answer is stated in 15:3: "For to know thee [God] is perfect righteousness: yea, to know thy power is the root of immortality." In other words, immortality can be attained only by knowing God and doing his will. In these general terms the statement would have been accepted by a Pharisee; but our author's understanding of righteousness and knowledge of God was colored by Hellenistic notions.

The author's arguments to prove that immortality has its ultimate root in God are philosophical: God's ontological nature, his activity, and his moral character lead inevitably to this conclusion. Although the existence of God is regarded as axiomatic, the author, like Paul (Rom. 1:19-23), refutes polytheism and idolatry ("ignorance of God") by means of the cosmological argument: a consideration of the works of creation should demonstrate that there is a creator or "artificer" (13:1). In his essential nature, God is conceived both as "the existing one" (13:1; cf. Ex. 3:14, in the erroneous translation of the LXX), in harmony with Plato (*Timaeus* 27 D: "what exists forever, having no origin [or becoming]"), and the all-permeating universal intelligence (*lógos*) of the Stoics (7:23 f.; 8:1, with reference to wisdom; 1:7; 12:1 with reference to God's spirit; for Stoic parallels, see Grimm, Commentary, p. 159 f.).

God is of necessity incorruptible (12:1; cf. 6:19) and thus naturally the "root of immortality." In the second place, immortality is connected with God's activity in creating and upholding the world, which the author conceives in a general way after the manner of Plato in the *Timaeus* (27 D-57 C), but without disclosing any interest in the technical details. "He (the Creator) was good, and a good person could never feel envy for anyone [cf. Wisd. 2:23 f.]. Being free of this (feeling), he wished that all things should be as much as possible like himself. . . . God then, wishing that all things be good, and nothing evil, to the best of his power, having thus seized all that was visible [the "formless matter" in Wisd. 11:17] . . . brought it from a state of disorder to order, judging it preferable. . . . Having placed the intellect in the soul and the soul in the body, he built the universe so that the finished work should be by nature most beautiful and excellent. Thus . . . we must say that this cosmos became truly, through the providence of God [cf. Wisd. 14:3; 17:2], an animated being endowed with a soul and an intellect" (*Timaeus* 29 E-30 B).

That the author had some notion of this Platonic theory of creation seems certain, although he may never have read the *Timaeus*; I. Heinemann (*Poseidonios* I, 151) suggests that he derived his philosophical knowledge from the *Protreptikòs lógos* of Posidonius (*ca.* 130-50 B.C.). Like Plato, the author believes that God created the world (9:1) out of formless matter (11:17)—i.e., the four elements (first fire and earth, then water and air; *Timaeus* 31 B-32 C; cf. Philo, *Quis rerum div. haeres* 27 [M I, 492])—and placed a soul into it. In our book this *anima mundi*, or soul of the universe, is *Wisdom*; in Philo the immanent *Lógos*, "essentially the same as the Platonic universal soul" (H. A. Wolfson, HTR 35 [1942] 133). Accordingly, Wisdom, "the artificer of all things" (7:22; cf. 8:6; Prov. 8:30), like the Creator (13:1), oversees all things (8:23), renews all things (7:27), and ordains (*dioikeî*) all things well (8:1; so God in 15:1); cf. Plato, *Phaedrus* 246 C: "[the soul] ordains the whole world"; similarly *Laws* 896 E; for Josephus see *Antiquities* 4:3, 2 [§47]; on Philo see H. A. Wolfson, *loc. cit.* p. 131; E. Bréhier, *Les idées philosophiques . . . de Philon*, 2nd ed., p. 85. Like Plato, the author conceives the world as an animated being, a living creature endowed with intelligence: the world fights for the righteous against their enemies (5:20; 16:17-29; 19:6-8, 18-22; cf. 5:17).[18] But, like Philo, he differs from Plato in admitting the possibility of miracles, by which God reverses the course of natural laws (see, for Plato and Philo, H. A. Wolfson, *loc. cit.* pp. 139-146): the world is a psaltery, its strings are the elements that always give forth the same musical notes, no matter how God, the musician, varies the melodies (19:18).

[18] On "the participation of the physical world in the destinies of man" in the later Jewish Haggadah, see V. Aptowitzer in MGWJ 64 (1920) 227-231; 305-313; 65 (1921) 71-87; 164-187.

Thus God, being perfect, created a world which was as perfect as he could make it. Plato ended his *Timaeus* (92 C) with these words: ". . . this cosmos thus became a visible animated being containing the visible things; image of the intelligible, perceptible God; most great, good, beautiful, and perfect; this single heaven being sole of its kind." In Wisdom likewise the animated cosmos is morally good (fighting for righteousness, as we have seen), reflecting the character of its Maker (13:1) particularly in its superlative beauty (13:3, 5), in its power and activity (13:4), and in its greatness (13:5). Specifically, man (2:23), or rather his soul, and wisdom (7:26), the soul of the universe, are the "image" (*eikôn*, the word used by Plato) of God. Whence come, then, evil and death? Our author wavers between the Platonic notion that matter is corruptible (9:15) and the Jewish notion that death came into the world through the envy of the devil (2:24). In any case, since our author says that God "made not death" (1:13), but created all things that they might have being, without a poison of destruction in them (1:14; cf. 11:24-26), and man for immortality (2:23)—his incorruptible spirit is in all things (12:1),—he must have had a vague notion of a limitation to God's power (such as Plato postulates), in spite of his references to God's immortal power (7:25; 11:17, 21; 12:18; etc.).

Thus the author makes no original contribution to the discussion and solution of the problem of the existence of evil in a world created and controlled by an almighty and morally perfect deity; nor to the doctrine of theodicy, which attempts to maintain such a conception of the deity in the presence of the imperfection of the world, notably human wickedness and suffering. The author is not so great a thinker as the two philosophers who made the outstanding contributions to these problems in antiquity and are still unsurpassed in this field: the author of the Book of Job and Plato. Moreover, our author was more concerned with religious propaganda than with philosophical speculation.

His explanation of sin and of its consequence, death, in 2:23-24 (cf. 1:13) was destined, however, to play an important role in Jewish and Christian theology: "For God created man for immortality, and made him the image *of his own peculiar nature* [variant: *of his eternity*]; but by the envy of the devil death came into the world, and those who belong to his party make experience of it [i.e., of death]." *Diábolos* (the devil [without the article]) is the translation of the Hebrew *Satan*: not "the accuser, the slanderer," with the article, as in Zech. 3:1 f. and Job 1-2; but *Satan*, a proper name, as in I Chron. 21:1 (the LXX has *diabolos*, with or without the article, in all passages). With the exception of D. B. Macdonald,[19] no one seems to doubt that 2:24 refers to the temptation

---

[19] *The Hebrew Philosophical Genius*, pp. 104 f. Princeton University Press, 1936. Macdonald finds here an allusion to Cain's murder of Abel, "the cause of which was Cain's envy," and not to the "fall" of Adam and Eve.

of Eve and the fall of Adam (Gen. 3). Sirach, before Wisdom, had like-wise traced the origin of death to the sin of Eve: "Through a woman sin began, and on her account we all die" (Ecclus. 25:24, Hebrew text; cf. II Cor. 11:3; I Tim. 2:14).[20] New, however, or at least not attested in extant writings earlier than Wisdom, is the substitution of the devil for the serpent in Eden, as the tempter of Eve. It is not clear, however, whether the serpent of Eden is actually a form of appearance of the devil himself (as in III Bar. 9:7), an agent of the devil (Apoc. of Mos. 16), or the devil himself, either identified with the serpent (Rev. 12:9; cf. 20:2) or without mention of the serpent at all (as in Wisd. 2:24: see I Enoch 69:5 [Gadreel is the tempter]; II Enoch 31; Life of Adam and Eve 33; III Bar. 4:8).[21] These various alternatives presumably did not occur to the author of Wisdom: he was not a systematic theologian and was concerned, in ch. 2, with refuting the ungodly notion that death was a natural phenomenon ending all human activity. In contrast with the wicked Jews, the author asserted that death was not decreed by God as the inevitable end of man's life, but was merely the result of an acci-dent (the envy of the devil), nor was it the end of life for the righteous, whose souls are in the hand of God and whose death is but a passage to a more glorious life (ch. 3). Since God is immortal and incorruptible (12:1), death is contrary to his nature and could have no place in the divine plan of creation. Death is the gift of the devil to those who belong to his party (2:24b), but conversely, the knowledge of God is perfect righteousness and the root of immortality (15:3).

In the first two parts of his book the author has mainly preached salva-tion to the Jews, either strengthening the pious Jews in their devotion to God and his Law or persuading apostate Jews of the error of their ways. In so doing he has proved to his own satisfaction that Judaism is immeasurably superior to heathenism. Nevertheless, he devotes chs. 13-15 to proving the folly of the various types of paganism.

Attacks on rites, myths, and beliefs of the heathen religions as prac-ticed by the ignorant and superstitious masses were well known: in Judaism, the Second Isaiah (Is. 40:18-20; 41:6 f.; 44:9-20) had sarcasti-cally ridiculed the manufacture and worship of idols; and pagan philoso-phers had variously pointed out how irrational were some of the features

[20] In Rom. 5:12, however, Paul attributes the origin of sin and death to Adam instead of Eve. For the Jewish parallels, see G. F. Moore, *Judaism*, Vol. 1, pp. 474-478; H. L. Strack and P. Billerbeck, *Kommentar zum Neuen Testament*, Vol. 3, pp. 227 f.

[21] For additional details about Satan as the tempter in Eden, see L. Ginzberg, *The Legends of the Jews*, Vol. 5, pp. 94-124. H. L. Strack and P. Billerbeck, *Kommentar zum Neuen Testament*, Vol. 1, pp. 136-149.

of the popular cults.[22] Our author was manifestly familiar with earlier Jewish and pagan attacks on various phases of heathenism, and was indebted to both Jews and Greeks for his arguments. At times, when he used standard criticisms, it cannot be determined whether he borrowed from Jews or from Greeks.

The author begins his attack on heathenism (in chs. 13-15) with the worship of the phenomena of nature, and in particular of the heavenly bodies (13:1-9). This he presumably considered the noblest expression of paganism. Did not Socrates pray to the rising sun (Plato, *Symposium* 220d)? And did he not admit that sun and moon were gods (Plato, *Apologia* 26d)? And did not Plato himself assert that the worship of a certain number of heavenly deities should be ordained by law (Plato, *Laws* VII 821c; VIII, 828c)? And did he not place them first, as the greatest, among the four classes of gods: celestial, (the "gods of gods," *Timaeus* 41a), atmospheric, aquatic, and terrestrial (Timaeus 40a; cf. 41-43)? Plato's pupil Xenocrates, in a book on the nature of the gods, asserted more specifically than his great master that there are but eight gods: the five planets, one for all the fixed stars, the sun, and the moon (Cicero, *De natura deorum* I:13, 34). Through the influx of Babylonian astrology, the cult of the astral deities became popular among the masses in the Hellenistic period.

The author of Wisdom, while admitting that all men who are ignorant of the sole true God are foolish (13:1), considers the worship of the heavenly bodies the least reprehensible form of heathenism. Fascinated by the greatness and beauty of fire, wind, water, and the heavenly bodies, men have regarded them as the gods that rule the world and thus have failed to realize that their Maker was far superior to them (13:2-9). In the words of Paul, who may have read Wisdom, they "worshipped and served the creature more than the Creator" (Rom. 1:25). Philo likewise uses the same argument: "For some nations have made divinities of the four elements, earth and water, and air and fire. Others of the sun and the moon, and of the other planets and fixed stars. . . . And they have all invented different appellations, all of them false, for these false gods put out of sight that most supreme and most ancient of all, the Creator, the ruler of the great city [i.e., the world] . . . the pilot who always guides everything to its preservation" (*De decalogo* 12 [M II, 189]; cf. 13-14).

Far more severe is the author's verdict against the idolaters (13:10-14:11) who worship the inanimate "works of men's hands" (13:10; cf.

[22] See particularly, P. Decharme, *La critique des traditions religieuses chez les Grecs.* Paris, 1904. Bodo de Borries, *Quid veteres philosophi de idolatria senserint.* Dissertatio inauguralis. Göttingen, 1918. J. Geffcken, "Der Bilderstreit des heidnischen Altertums" (ARW 19 [1919] 286-315). A. B. Drachmann, *Atheism in Pagan Antiquity.* London and Copenhagen: Gyldendal, 1922.

Ps. 115:4; 135:15). Here again there was hardly anything new that the author could add to Jewish (Is. 44:10-20; etc.) and Greek[23] tirades against idols and their adoration. The Epistle of Jeremy describes in more detail the helplessness of idols.

Following the sarcastic description of an idolmaker in Is. 44, our author ridicules the manufacture of images (13:11-19). The closest parallel in classical literature is the following passage of Horace (*Satires* I:8, 1-3), which was written a few years before 35 B.C. and is therefore a little later than our book, although possibly inspired by an earlier Hellenistic work now lost.

> Olim truncus eram ficulnus, inutile lignum,
> cum faber, incertus scamnum faceretne Priapum,
> maluit esse deum. Deus inde ego. . . .[24]

This religious aberration known as idolatry the author of Wisdom traces back to a twofold origin (14:12-21): a father's affection for a deceased young son and the devotion of subjects for a distant king. This theory, tracing pagan worship back to reverence for human beings, was popularized in the first half of the third century B.C. by Euhemerus in a fictitious travel book in which he claims to have discovered an inscription recording the human exploits of Uranus, Cronus, Zeus, and other gods.[25] J. Geffcken (ARW 19 [1919] 292-294) rightly supposes that the author of Wisdom had read an unknown Euhemeristic author—not Euhemerus himself—before he penned his "singularly inept and yet very important" statements in 14:15-18. "This interpretation consists, as one sees at once,

[23] See the books cited above in note 22.

[24] "Once I was the trunk of a wild fig-tree—a useless log,—when the craftsman, in doubt whether he should make a stool or a Priapus [image] out of me, preferred that I should be a god. So from then on I became a god. . . ." The observations that the same craftsman makes idols and profane objects, and that the wood or other matter out of which an idol is made could have been used to make a piece of furniture or some other profane object (13:11-17) is frequently repeated by Christian apologists. Tertullian (d. *ca.* A.D. 230) says: "The man who carved a Mars [image] out of linden-tree wood, how much quicker could he not put together a chest?" (*De idolatria* 8); "As to the actual [divine] images, I can discover nothing but that their materials are sisters of ordinary small vessels and implements. . . ." (*Apologeticus* 12). See also: *Praedicatio Petri* 3; *Epistle to Diognetus* 2. The earliest text outside of the Bible is the story in Herodotus II 172: Amasis (Ahmose, 569-525 B.C.), when the Egyptian despised him at the beginning of his reign for his plebeian origin, ordered a golden vessel for washing the feet (*podaniptēr*) made into a divine image which soon received the ardent worship of the people; so Amasis called attention to the similarity of his own experience to that of the vessel (once a plebeian, now a king). Allusions to this story in early Christian literature are found in: *Epistula ad Diognetum* 2; Justin Martyr (d. *ca.* 165), *First Apology* 9; Theophilus of Antioch (second century), *ad Autolycum*, p. 344; Minucius Felix (third century), *Octavius* 23; Tertullian, *Apologeticus* 13; cf. Philo, *de vita contemplativa* 1 (M II, 472).

[25] Cf. T. S. Brown, "Euhemeros and the Historians" (HTR 39 [1946] 259-274).

of two entirely disparate explanations, one of which named the bereaved father, who made himself an image for the remembrance of the deceased son, while the other looked for the origin of the idols in the royal statues." It would seem that the same lost source utilized in Wisdom was used also by Minucius Felix (third century of our era) in his *Octavius* (20:5), where the two same roots of idolatry are specified.

> Our ancestors also went astray in the same manner with respect to the gods. Careless and credulous, they believed with an untutored simplicity. While they piously revered their kings, while they wished to see those dead (portrayed) in images, while they ardently longed to preserve their memories in statues, those practices which had been adopted for consolation became holy rites.

The same view is expressed by Lactantius early in the fourth century (*Divinarum institutionum* liber II:2, 3).

> For the custom of fashioning likenesses was discovered by men solely for one reason, namely that one might preserve the memory of those who were removed by death or separated by absence.

Echoes of this view are also found in the Letter of Aristeas (§134), where the idols are said to be images of great inventors. In the Sibylline Oracles (III, 108-113), Cronus, Titan, and Iapetus, the sons of Gaia and Uranus, were but human kings at first (as Euhemerus had claimed); but in a later section of these oracles (III, 552-555) these "haughty kings" are said to have misled mankind, which still clings to the idols of "deceased gods," or, in the words of III, 723, "idols and images of deceased men."

The author of the Wisdom of Solomon points out, not without good reason, that the popularity of idolatry is not only the result of strong affection (14:15) and royal command (14:16 f.), but also of the superb art of the sculptors who, improving on nature, made mortals appear as gods (14:18-20). The author is manifestly familiar with the official worship of living rulers (*ibid.*), although hardly with the much later insane claims to divinity on the part of Caligula in A.D. 40, as E. J. Goodspeed (*The Story of the Apocrypha*, p. 94. University of Chicago Press, 1939) believes.[26]

---

[26] On the worship of the rulers see, E. Kornemann, "Zur Geschichte der antiken Herrscherkulte" (*Klio* 1 [1901] 51 ff.); E. Fiddles, "The Beginning of Caesar-Worship" in *Owens College Historical Essays*, Vol. 1, pp. 1-16. London, 1932; J. Kaerst, *Geschichte des Hellenismus*, Vol. 2, pp. 376-404. Leipzig, 1926; Lily R. Taylor, *The Divinity of the Roman Emperor*. Middletown, 1931; W. Schubart, *Verfassung und Verwaltung des Prolemäerreiches*, pp. 35 f. (Der alte Orient 35, 4). Leipzig, 1937; U. Wilcken, *Zur Entstehung des hellenistischen Königskultes* (Preussische Akademie der Wissenschaften. Sitzungsberichte, Phil.-hist. Klasse, Berlin, 1938; pp. 298-321).

The author concludes his tirade against paganism with a sarcastic attack on the religion of the Egyptians whom, since he presumably lived in Alexandria, he does not name. They stand at the bottom of the scale and are the most contemptible of the heathen because they not only reverence foreign idols in addition to their own (15:15-17), but even "worshipped those beasts that are most hateful" (15:17-19; cf. 11:15; 12:24). Similarly we read in the Sibylline Oracles (III, 22-30): "Be ashamed of making gods of cats and beasts. . . . Ye witless folk, worshiping serpents, dogs, and cats, ye reverence winged creatures, and animals that creep on the earth, and images of stone and statues made with hands, and stones piled together by the roads." Philo of Alexandria expressed himself likewise, denouncing animal worship in unequivocal language (cf. Wolfson, Philo, Vol. 1, pp. 31 f.); cf. Josephus, Against Apion I, 25. Although some pagan authors attempted to justify the Egyptian worship of animals by asserting that the beasts were not regarded as deities but merely as representations of the various powers of God (Plutarch, De Iside et Osiride 74), others did not hesitate to ridicule this type of religion. Herodotus (II, 65-76) gives an objective and factual account of Egyptian animal worship, as likewise Strabo (XVII:1, 38-40 [p. 811 f.] and 47 [p. 817]). Cicero (Tusculanarum disputationum V:27, 78; De natura deorum I:29, 82; III:15, 39) does not conceal his low opinion for this type of worship, and Juvenal (XV, 1-13) lists some of the beasts worshiped by the "insane" Egyptians: some worship the crocodile, others the ibis; the golden statue of the cercopithecus monkey shines near the place where magical sounds proceeded from the truncated statue of Memnon,[27] and where Thebes of the hundred gates lies buried. Entire cities revere here cats, there a river fish, elsewhere a dog; no one cares about Diana. It is even a sacrilege to bite a scallion and an onion: O holy

[27] The two enormous statues of the sitting Amenophis III (1411-1375 B.C.), originally 64 feet (21 meters) high, west of the Nile at Thebes (not far from Medinet Habu and the Ramesseum, across the Nile from Luxor) in Roman times were regarded as the statues of Memnon, son of Eos and Tithonos, who was killed by Achilles in the Trojan War; he is mentioned in the Odyssey 11, 522; cf. 4, 188. The northern statue, which is less well preserved than the southern one, is the famous ágalma échoûn (Pausanias I:42, 3), or resounding, statue. At dawn a sound issued from the statue and it was said that Memnon greeted his mother Eos, the dawn. Strabo (XVII:1, 46 [p. 816]) is the first writer to report hearing this amazing sound "about the first hour" (at dawn), but he could not determine whether the sound was produced by the base, by the colossus, or deceitfully by one of those sitting around the base. Juvenal and Pausanias accepted the sound as a fact. Finally Septimius Severus (193-211) restored rather roughly the missing upper part of the statue and the sound ceased completely. The inscriptions in Greek and Latin, engraved by ancient tourists on the northern, vocal colossus, date from the time of Nero (54-68) to that of Caracalla (211-217); most of them (27) date from the reign of Hadrian (117-138), who spent several days there with his wife Sabina and a large retinue in 130.

people, whose gods grow in the vegetable garden! Beasts with wool are never served at a meal; it is a sacrilege to strangle a kid of the goats, but human meat is permitted.

It is characteristic of the Book of Wisdom that to these four types of false religion it does not simply oppose the Law of Moses as the guide to the true religion, but finds in wisdom (*sophía*)—which Moses mentions only twice in passing, at the very end of his life (Deut. 4:6; 34:9) as something pertinent to the true religion—not merely the ideal of human life, but also the power that enables men to attain it.

Wisdom, according to this book, comes from God himself (7:7; 8:21; 9:4; etc.), being in fact an emanation from God rather than a mere creation (7:25 f.), and lives in so close association with God (8:3 f.; 9:9 f.) that she seems to be a manifestation of the deity. Whatever a man may desire in this world (6:17-20; 7:11-14, 21, 27; 8:4-13, 18; 9:10) or in the next (8:13, 17; 9:18) may be attained only through wisdom. In order to obtain wisdom, man must desire her (6:13), think about her (6:15), seek her (6:2; 8:18), watch for her sleeplessly (6:15), pursue her early in the morning (6:14). He must learn wisdom (6:9 f.; 7:13). On her part Wisdom seeks those worthy of her (6:16). But without God's grace (8:21) Wisdom cannot be obtained by man, who therefore prays to God, "Give me . . . Wisdom" (9:2), as Cleanthes the Stoic prayed in his famous hymn: "Banish it [i.e., ignorance], Father, from their soul and grant them to obtain Wisdom whereon relying thou rulest all things with justice."

Wisdom existed before the creation of the world (9:9; cf. Prov. 8:24 ff.; Ecclus. 1:4), but God alone created the world through his word (9:1; cf. Gen. 1; but John 1:1-14 has no real connection with all this, even though the same word, *lógos*, is used there). Since the creation, however, wisdom has become *pántōn technítēs* (7:22 [Gr. 7:21]) or artificer of all things, the overseer of all (8:23), the renewer of all things (7:27), the performer of all things (8:5), and the excellent manager of all things (8:1). In other words, wisdom is responsible for the correct operation of the cosmos, rather than for its creation. This may of course merely mean that God governs the universe in a rational manner, *en lógō* (cf. 9:1).

What is wisdom? The author of our book attempts to define it in 7:22 f., where no less than twenty-one (7×3) qualities are ascribed to wisdom. Nevertheless, the nature of wisdom necessarily remain elusive and mysterious. We may safely assert that wisdom is not a "hypostasis," as A. Bertholet (*Biblische Theologie des Alten Testaments*, p. 394. Tübingen, 1911) and many others have claimed. The horrible word "hypostasis" should be avoided entirely in this connection, since it is only a bone of contention among ancient Christians, and the only problem raised by our book is whether the author thought of wisdom as a person (or thing) distinct from God. Wisdom is strongly personified: is that mere rhetoric or a real conviction of the author? Let better men decide. This author can only conclude that wisdom is like divine grace in Christianity, like the rays of the sun that flow out continually to bring life and joy wherever they go.

CHAPTER VI

ECCLESIASTICUS BY SIRACH

With the exception of the prophetic books and the Memoirs of Nehemiah, Ecclesiasticus is the only writing within the canonical and noncanonical Jewish Scriptures to which the author attached his name: all the others appeared anonymously or under a famous *nom de plume*. In the colophon (Ecclus. 50:27) the author gave his name as "Jeshua [i.e., Joshua; Greek: Jesus], the son of Eleazar, the son of Sira."[1] In English the author is usually called *Ben Sira* (in accordance with the Hebrew usage) or *Sirach* (according to the Greek); the mixture of the two (Ben Sirach) should be avoided.

The title of the book in Greek manuscripts is "Wisdom of Jesus the son of Sirach" (or, "Wisdom of Sirach"); in Syriac, "The Wisdom of Bar [son of] Sira"; in the Hebrew colophon, "The Words of [Simeon son of] Jeshua who is called Ben Sira" and "The Wisdom of [Simeon son of] Jeshua, son of Eleazar, son of Sira." Jerome (*Preface to the Books of Solomon*) reports that the Hebrew text of the book he found was not entitled Ecclesiasticus, "as among Latins," but *Parabolae* (Hebr. *meshālim*, Engl. Proverbs), cf. Ecclus. 1:25 and the "Proverbs of Salomon"; similarly Rabbi Joseph (see S. Schechter, in JQR 12 [1900] 460 f.) called it "The Proverbs of Ben Sira." In the Talmud it is called, "The Book [or, The Instruction] of Ben Sira." In the Authorized Version both the Greek and the Latin titles are used, "The Wisdom of Jesus the Son of Sirach, or Ecclesiasticus."

---

[1] The several texts differ slightly in giving the author's name. The Hebrew text (Cod. B) reads: "Simeon, the son of Jeshua, the son of Eleazar, the son of Sira" in 50:27; the colophon at the end of the book (after ch. 51) gives the name twice, the first time as "Simeon, the son of Jeshua, who is called *Ben Sîrâ* [the son of Sira]," the second time as in 50:27. This double mention in the colophon appears in the Syriac as follows: "Jeshua, the son of Simeon, who is called *Bar Asîrâ* [the son of the captive]," twice repeated (with minor variants). Saadia Gaon (d. 942) names the author "Jeshua, son of Simeon, son of Eleazar, son of Sira." The mention of Simeon is obviously a scribal error, due perhaps to the occurrence of this name earlier in the chapter (50:1 and [Hebr.] 24). The Greek manuscripts read "Jesus the son of Sirach [Seirach] of Jerusalem" or "Jesus, the son of Sirach, [the son] of Eleazar, of Jerusalem" [to be corrected by placing "Eleazar" before "Sirach"] in 50:27. The first Greek translator, in his prologue, names the author "my grandfather Jesus." The title of ch. 51 in Greek manuscripts reads, "Prayer of Jesus the son of Sirach." The final *ch* in Greek corresponds to an *aleph* in Aramaic (cf. *Akeldamach* in Acts 1:19); see G. Kuhn in ZAW N.F. 6 (1929) 289.

352

Sirach's book was not composed according to a definite plan, but is a collection of separate essays or collection of maxims, like Proverbs, the author's model. Presumably Sirach rewrote in verse for publication a number of his classroom lectures, but, except for 42:15-50:26, failed to mark clearly the individual parts. Consequently, scholars differ in their analysis of the book. O. F. Fritzsche in his commentary (*Exegetisches Handbuch zu den Apokryphen*, Vol. 5, p. xxxii. Leipzig, 1859) divided the book into seven parts: *a.* 1:1-16:21; *b.* 16:22-23:27; *c.* 24:1-33:16a (Gr. 24:1-30:24; 33:13-36:16a); 33:16b-18 (Gr. 30:25-27);[2] *d.* 33:19-36:17 (Gr. 30:28-33:33:13a; 36:16b-22); *e.* 36:18-26 [Gr. 36:23-31]; 37:1-39:11; *f.* 39:12-42:14; 42:15-50:26. R. Smend (*Die Weisheit des Jesus Sirach erklärt*, pp. xxx-xxxiv. Berlin, 1906) has noted that in chs. 1-41 a number of sections dealing with wisdom serve as introductions to individual parts of the book which follow them. These sections are the following: 1:1-20; 4:11-19; 6:18-37; 8:8 f.; 10:30-11:1; 14:20-15:8; 16:24 f.; 18:28 f.; 20:27-31; 24; 27:4-7; 30:1-13; 35:14-36:6; 31:1-20 (displaced); 36:23-37:15; 37:16-26; 38:24-39:11. These two examples may suffice to illustrate the differences of arrangement proposed by eminent scholars. What seems certain to this writer is that Sirach's book is divided into two distinct parts, chs. 1-23 and 24-50: this fact is not always sufficiently pointed out.

Ben Sira evidently not only arranged his book into two parts (1-23; 24-50) but published these as separate books, one after the other. It is no accident that both parts begin with the longest praises of wisdom written by him (1:1-20 [1:21 is a gloss]; and ch. 24). Exactly so, the Book of Proverbs opens with a sermon on wisdom (Prov. 1-9); incidentally, both Proverbs and Ecclesiasticus close with an alphabetic acrostic poem placed in an appendix (Prov. 31:10-31; Ecclus. 51:13-30). Moreover, at the beginning of his second volume (24:30-34) Ben Sira tells us in allegorical language that he had originally planned only the first volume, a small irrigation canal from the great stream of wisdom, intended to water his garden (24:30-31a); but since his material grew so that his book became a river and the river a sea (24:31b), he decided to make his instruction shine again like the dawn and pour out again

[2] In Greek manuscripts and in the versions derived from the Greek (with the exception of the Old Slavic) the section 30:25-33:16a (Gr. 33:13b-36:16a) has been displaced and now follows 33:16b-36:13a (Gr. 30:25-33:13a). The original order, adopted in the English versions following the Latin version, is preserved (apart from the Latin) in the Syriac, Armenian, and Hebrew texts. The error occurred through the accidental transposition of a quaternion, or a sheet folded twice (comprising eight pages), in the lost, relatively recent, archetype from which the extant Greek manuscripts were copied. In 31:1-36:13a (Gr. 34:1-36:16a) and in 34:1-36:13a (Gr. 31:1-33:13a) the verse numbers are identical. Here the correct reference (with the reference to the Greek wrong chapter number in brackets) will be given.

doctrine like prophecy (24:32 f.): thus he prepared his second volume for future generations.

Ben Sira, a scholar and teacher living in Jerusalem, published his book about 180 B.C. In 132 his grandson brought the work to Egypt and later translated it into Greek. In the preface to his translation (which is missing in the Syriac and Arabic texts, as naturally from the Hebrew from which they are directly [Syr.] or indirectly [Ar.] derived), the grandson first commends (in a long rhetorical sentence) his grandfather's book as the fruit of expert familiarity with the Scriptures and as a guide to a "life in harmony with the Law"; and then he apologizes for his imperfect translation, due to difficulties which his zeal and labors could not overcome; for even the Greek translation of the Scriptures (the LXX) is not always accurate.

The "Prologue made by an uncertain Author," which is printed before this preface in the Authorized Version, is found in Greek in the Complutensian Polyglot, in Codex 248 (see: J. H. Hart, *Ecclesiasticus. The Greek Text of Codex 248 Edited with a Textual Commentary and Prolegomena.* Cambridge, 1909), and in the "Synopsis of Holy Scripture" wrongly attributed to Athanasius and printed in his works. This prologue tells us that Jesus imitated Solomon and collected wise sayings in his book, which he left to his son Sirach in an unfinished condition. Finally Jesus, son of Sirach and grandson of the author, prepared the volume for publication, calling it "Wisdom." This mass of misinformation results from a misunderstanding of the names in 50:27 and of some statements in the grandson's preface. We may summarize Ecclesiasticus as follows:

I. The First Volume (1-23)

Introduction (1). *a.* "All wisdom comes from the Lord" (1:1-10). *b.* Religion ("fear of the Lord") and wisdom are essentially identical (1:11-21, omitting 1:21 with most Greek manuscripts). *c.* Self-control is a condition for wise speech (1:22-25). *d.* Only by keeping the commandments without hypocrisy and pride can wisdom be obtained from the Lord (1:26-30). The Syriac in 1:22-27 differs entirely from the received text.

1. On patience in tribulation, respect for one's parents, humility, and kindness to the poor (2:1-4:10). *a.* The man tested through affliction (2:1-5) should trust in God (2:6-11), for woe betide those who lose heart (2:12-14); the pious will always do God's will (2:15-18). *b.* Blessings come to him who honors his father and mother (3:1-11), particularly in their old age (3:12 f.); filial piety obliterates sins (3:14 f.), while its opposite incenses God (3:16). *c.* One should be humble in prosperity (3:17-20), and humble in recognizing the limitation of one's knowledge

(3:21-23), lest one be led astray by erroneous opinions (3:24 f.) and obstinacy (3:26 f.), and reap not the rewards of wisdom (3:29-31). *d.* The poor should neither be defrauded nor humiliated (4:1-6), but should be helped in a courteous manner (4:7-10).

2. "Wisdom instructs her sons" (4:11-19) in various matters pertaining to everyday life (4:20-6:17). *a.* Wisdom, addressing her pupils, promises that she will reward them after testing them (4:11-19). *b.* Practical counsels and warnings: beware of false shame and embarrassment (4:20-28), of boastfulness (4:29), harshness (4:30), cupidity (4:31), trust in wealth (5:1-3), a godless sense of security (5:4-7), unrighteous gain (5:8), and insincere, hasty, and violent talk (5:9-6:4); cultivate true friends but be on your guard against false ones (6:5-17).

3. The search after wisdom (6:18-37), and the avoidance of iniquity (7:1-3) rooted in pride (7:4-8:7). *a.* From youth on strive after wisdom (6:18 f.): wisdom is a burden to fools (6:20-22), but a joy to those who attain her (6:23-31) through hearkening to the instruction of the sages (6:32-36), through study of the Law, and through divine grace (6:37). *b.* "Do no evil" (7:1-3), in particular: beware of political ambition (7:4-7), of trust in religious rites (7:8 f.) devoid of piety and charity (7:10 f.), of harming others by word and deed (7:12 f.), of vacuous talk in the assembly and in prayer (7:14), of laziness (7:15), and of pride (7:16 f.). *c.* Deal justly and kindly with friends (7:18), wife (7:19), servants (7:20 f.), cattle (7:22), children (7:23-25), again wife (7:26), parents (7:27 f.), priests (7:29-31), indigent persons (7:32), departed friends (7:33), mourners (7:34). *d.* Be cautious in associating with men of power and wealth (8:1 f.) or with contentious (8:3) and foolish fellows (8:4); be considerate with repentant sinners (8:5) and old men (8:6); do not rejoice over a man's death (8:7).

4. Wise discrimination in social intercourse (8:8-9:16). *a.* One should learn from the wise and the aged (8:8 f.). *b.* It is well to avoid the company of the wicked (8:10 f.), loans and pledges (8:12 f.), lawsuits against judges (8:14), association with irascible men (8:15 f.), and intimate conversations with fools (8:17) and strangers (8:18 f.). *c.* Particular caution is advisable in the presence of women (9:1-9). *d.* "Forsake not an old friend" (9:10), "envy not a wicked man" (9:11 f.), avoid whoever has the power to kill (9:13), but consort with the wise (9:14-16).

5. Advice for the ruling classes and reflections on wealth (9:17-14:19). *a.* The welfare of a nation depends on the wisdom of its ruler (9:17-10:3). *b.* The government of the world is in God's hands (10:4 f.): pride is therefore unbecoming a ruler and brings ruin to his people (10:6-18). *c.* The pious and wise, whether princes or paupers, are most worthy of honor (10:19-25). *d.* Empty boasting may lead to a fall (10:26-29), but true wisdom may lift a humble man to positions of authority (10:30-11:1).

e. Avoid hasty opinions about men, based either on comeliness and dress (11:2-4), for a man's situation may change suddenly (11:5 f.), or on lack of information (11:7 f.); and meddle not in other people's quarrels (11:9). *f.* The true source of wealth is not frenzied business activity but is divine blessing (11:10-19; 11:15 f. are lacking in the earliest Greek manuscripts, although present in the Hebrew, and are probably spurious). *g.* Be therefore satisfied in your profession and place your trust in God rather than in riches, which may suddenly vanish (11:20-28). *h.* Avoid inviting to your house evil men who may cause your ruin (11:29-34). *i.* Similarly be discriminate in sharing your wealth with the needy (12:1-7; v. 7 repeats v. 4 and should be omitted; in vv. 4-7 the order of the clauses varies in the various texts), and in choosing your friends (12:8-13:1). *j.* If you are poor, avoid associating with the rich (13:2-8) and the powerful (13:9-13); choose rather associates from the lower classes (13:15-19; vv. 13c-14, appearing only in the Latin and late Greek manuscripts, are spurious); the ordinary attitude toward rich and poor is diametrically opposite (13:20-23). *k.* Only honest wealth is valuable (13:24), for without a good conscience (which manifests itself in a man's face, 13:25 f.) there is no happiness (14:1 f.); yet even honest wealth brings no joy to the miser (14:3-7) and to the envious (14:8-10). Therefore wealth should be used to make life pleasant for oneself and others, before death make all joy to cease (14:11-19).

6. The doctrine of God (14:20-18:14). *a.* "Blessed is the man who meditates on wisdom!" (14:20 f.) encamping by her house (14:22-25), and builds his nest in her branches (14:26 f.); being pious (15:1), he is welcomed by her (15:2) with the bread of understanding (15:3). He will find joy with her (15:4-6). But the wicked cannot reach her (15:7 f.) nor may they praise God (15:9 f.). *b.* God is not responsible for human sin (15:11-13), for he created man free to choose life or death (15:14-17); God is wise, mighty, all-knowing (15:18 f.), but not the author of sin (15:20). *c.* Godless children are no blessing (16:1 f.), nay, childlessness is preferable to them (16:3), for a wicked generation brings ruin to a city (16:4), as experience and history teach (16:5 f.), notably in four instances: the end of the semi-divine giants (16:7; cf. Gen. 6:1-4; Bar. 3:26-28; Wisd. of Sol. 14:6; Judg. 16:7; etc.), the destruction of Sodom (16:8; cf. Gen. 19), the dispossession of the "banned people," presumably the Canaanites (16:9), and the death of the murmuring Israelites in the desert (16:10; cf. 46:8; Ex. 12:37; Num. 14:22-24). *d.* In his mercy and wrath God still rewards and punishes in the present (16:11-16; vv. 15 f. are omitted by most Greek manuscripts), and only a fool could deny this, alleging the insignificance of man before the greatness and majesty of God (16:17-23). *e.* When God created the world he established an eternal cosmic order (16:24-28) and filled the earth with good things

and living creatures (16:29 f.). Then he formed man and gave him authority over animals (17:1-4); he endowed man with intelligence so that he might praise the Creator (17:5-10; v. 5 is a gloss lacking in the best authorities; the order in vv. 6-9 varies in the versions) and observe the divine covenant (17:11-14), in accordance with which God scrutinizes human conduct (17:15-20, omitting vv. 17 f.) in order to give each one his just reward or punishment (17:21-24). *f.* In a psalm (17:25-18:14), Ben Sira exhorts men to turn to God for forgiveness and salvation (17:25-28), for he is merciful (17:29-32) and just (18:1). Men, feeble and ephemeral as they are, cannot understand God's works (18:2-10): "therefore is the Lord patient with them" (18:11-14).

7. On kindness, foresight, and self-control (18:15-20:26). *a.* Add a kind word to alms given to the needy (18:15-18). *b.* As you should take the proper steps leading to a desired result (18:19 f.), so do not delay repenting of your sins and paying your vows (18:21-23), remembering that misfortune may be imminent (18:23-26). The wise man is on his guard (18:27) and ready to instruct others (18:28 f.). *c.* Control and restrain your lusts and appetites (18:30-33), for "wine and women" bring ruin (19:1-3); your urge to gossip (19:4-12); your tendency to believe accusations against friends without first remonstrating with them as the Law (Lev. 19:17) orders (19:13-17); (digression: there is no wisdom without piety [19:18-22, omitting vv. 18 f.] and folly is better than a "wisdom" used for abominable ends [19:23-30]). Such remonstrations should come at the right time, without violence (20:1-4, omitting v. 3), otherwise silence is preferable (20:5-8); appearances are misleading: adversity is sometimes salutary (20:9-12), whereas a fool's favors profit nothing (20:13-17). *d.* Control and restrain your tongue, for a slip of the tongue may be pernicious (20:18). Avoid speaking out of season (20:19 f.). Poverty may prevent false promises, often made to avoid embarrassment (20:21-23); in general, to lie is worse than to steal (20:24-26).

8. Sages and fools, saints and sinners (20:27-23:28). *a.* The wise man, promoted to a high position, must not allow bribes to induce him to conceal his opinions (20:27-31). *b.* "Flee from sin," for it leads to death (21:1-10). *c.* The character, conduct, and achievements of the wise and of the fool are diametrically opposite (21:11-28; rearrange vv. 22 f. as follows, according to the Hebrew: 22a, 23b, 23a, 22b); (digression on the public contempt for the slothful, 22:1 f.;) the contrast fits in particular uneducated and educated children (22:3-12, omitting vv. 9 f.). *d.* Consorting with a fool is a heavy burden (22:13-15), for one may rely on the counsel of a wise man, while that of a fool is no help in difficulties (22:16-18). *e.* A true friend should not be affronted (22:19-22), but should be helped in his adversity (22:23-26). *f.* A prayer for deliverance

from sins of speech and lust (22:27-23:6). g. "Discipline of the mouth" (23:7 f.): beware particularly of thoughtless oaths (23:9-11), as of blasphemy (?) and obscene language (23:12-15). h. Sexual offenses (23:16 f.), and adultery in particular (23:18-26), bring calamity in their wake and thus prove that "there is nothing sweeter than to observe the Lord's commandments" (23:27; 23:28 is a gloss).

II. The Second Volume (24-50)

Introduction on wisdom (24). a. Wisdom personified (24:1 f.) describes in a speech her divine origin (24:3), her sway over all creation and all nations (24:4-6), her permanent residence in Jerusalem (24:7-11), where she took root, flourished like a great tree (24:12-17; 24:18 is a gloss), and bore sweet fruit, of which all may partake (24:19-22). b. This wisdom, says Ben Sira, is "the Law which Moses commanded" (24:23; cf. 19:20; 21:11; Deut. 4:6; Ezra 7:25; IV Macc. 1:17), which pours out wisdom inexhaustibly like great streams overflowing their banks (24:25-28; v. 24 is a gloss) and whose deepest meaning has never been discovered (24:29). c. Ben Sira was but a watering ditch out of this great stream (24:30-31ab), but grew into a river and a sea (24:31cd); he has therefore prepared for all future generations a second volume filled with inspired doctrine (24:32-34).

9. On happy and unhappy marriages (25:1-26:27). Numerical proverbs occur in 25:1 f., 7-11; 26:5 f., 28. a. A happy married couple is one of the three loveliest things (25:1), while an adulterous aged fool is one of three contemptible types of men (25:2), for wisdom should be the crown of old age (25:3-6). Conversely, the husband of a wise wife is one of ten types of blessed men (25:7-9), of which the outstanding is the pious and wise man (25:10 f.; v. 12 is a gloss). b. Among four great misfortunes is the wickedness of a woman; "there is no wrath above the wrath of a woman" (25:13-15; in v. 15 the Greek and Latin read "enemy" instead of "woman," which is in the Syriac). c. A wicked woman causes her husband to sigh bitterly (25:16-18), particularly a malicious (25:19), garrulous (25:20), wealthy (25:21 f.), or evil (25:23) wife. A woman, Eve, brought sin and death into the world (25:24; cf. Gen. 3:6; II Cor. 11:3; I Tim. 2:14). A wicked woman should be divorced (25:26). d. Conversely, a good wife brings happiness to her husband (26:1-4). e. The worst of four scourges of the tongue is a wife jealous of another wife of her husband (26:5 f.). f. The following types of wicked women (26:7) are especially obnoxious: the drunken (26:8), lewd (26:9), shameless (26:10), unchaste (26:11 f.). g. "The grace of a [good] wife delights her husband" (26:13-18). h. Good and bad women are contrasted for the benefit of the young man, who should be true to his wife

(26:19-27; these verses occur only in two late Greek manuscripts, and in the Syriac and Arabic versions; although translated from the Hebrew, their authenticity is not unchallenged).

10. On caution and generosity in speech and in business transactions (26:28-29:28). *a.* It is sad to contemplate a rich man (so the Syriac; Greek: a warrior; the underlying Hebrew expression has both meanings) reduced to poverty, famous men (so the Syriac; Greek: men of understanding) deprived of honor, and righteous men turning to sin (26:28). *b.* Merchants, unless they be zealously pious, may easily become dishonest for the sake of gain (26:29-27:3). But sin, ultimately, expresses a man's nature and may be detected through careful tests (27:4-7). Man, however, can earn the rewards of righteousness (27:8-10). *c.* The tongue may sin in various ways. The conversation of fools (27:11-13) is filled with oaths and leads to strife (27:14 f.). Whoever discloses a friend's secrets destroys friendship (27:16-21). Still more detestable is the pretense of friendship for evil purposes (27:22-24); it often inflicts the proposed harm on the deceiver (27:25-29). One should therefore guard against anger and not take vengeance (27:30-28:1), for God pardons the sins of one who forgives an injury (28:2; cf. Matt. 6:12, 14 f.; 18:35), but not of a vindictive man (28:3-5): the pious is therefore merciful (28:6 f.). One should avoid strife, for it may lead to bloodshed (28:8-12), and slander, for it produces great ruin (28:13-16). In general, the tongue is worse than the whip and the sword (28:17 f.), but it has no power over the righteous (28:19-22)—only over the wicked (28:23-26). *d.* "Lend to your neighbor in time of his need" (29:1-3) in spite of the fact that many debtors are negligent in repayment (29:4-6); some refuse to lend for this reason (29:7), but one should be patient with the debtor (29:8) and help the poor (29:9 f.), thus laying up a spiritual treasure (29:11-13). *e.* Likewise, the good man becomes surety for his neighbor (29:14), although the latter is not always grateful (29:15-17) and suretyship has brought financial ruin to men of wealth (29:18-20). *f.* A simple life at home is preferable to traveling in foreign countries (29:21-28).

11. On bringing up children, caring for one's health, and behavior at dinners and banquets (30:1-32:13 [Gr. 30; 34:1-35:13]). *a.* A father should be strict and severe in bringing up his son (30:1-6), lest the child be spoiled by kindness (30:7-13). *b.* Sound health is preferable to riches (30:14-17), for without it one cannot enjoy the good things that wealth provides (30:18-20). Beware, therefore, of sorrow, anxiety, anger (30:21-24, 25 [Gr. 32:13bc]), and worry over wealth (31:1 f. [Gr. 34:1 f.]), for they make us prematurely old. Moreover, the *auri sacra fames* (accursed hunger for gold), as Vergil calls greed, is death for the soul (31:3-7): happy, therefore, the rich man who is not a worshiper of mammon (31:8-11 [Gr. 34:8-11])! (on mammon in the Hebrew of 31:8,

cf. Matt. 6:24; Luke 16:9, 11, 13). *c.* At dinners observe good manners: be not greedy (31:12 f. [Gr. 34:12 f]), but considerate of others in helping yourself (31:14 f. [Gr. 34:14 f.]) and in controlling your appetite (31:16-19 [Gr. 34:16-19]), thus avoiding indigestion (31:20 [Gr. 34:20], following the arrangement of the Hebrew, Latin, and Syriac: 20cdab), for which vomiting brings relief (31:21 [Gr. 34:21]). The polite guest is well spoken of, but the unmannered one has a bad reputation (31:22-24 [Gr. 34:22-24], according to the meaning of the Hebrew). *d.* Be likewise moderate in drinking wine (31:25 f. [Gr. 34:25 f.]), for while in moderation wine brings joy (31:27 f. [Gr. 34:27 f.]), in excess it ruins one's health and reputation (31:29 f. [Gr. 34:29 f.]). At banquets, avoid controversial topics (31:31 [Gr. 34:31]) and, if you are toastmaster, be modest and kind (32:1 f. [Gr. 35:1 f.]). Even elders should be silent during the singing (32:3-6 [Gr. 35:3-6]), and young men should speak only when requested, and then with becoming brevity and humility (32:7-10 [Gr. 35:7-10]). Leave fairly early, without lingering over the farewells (32:11-13 [Gr. 35:11-13]).

12. How to seek and teach wisdom when one has been chosen by God for this task (32:14-33:18 [Gr. 35:14-36:16a; 30:25-27]). *a.* Whoever seeks God and studies his Law will gain true understanding, but the hypocrite distorts the meaning of the Law to suit his convenience (32:14-18 [Gr. 35:14-18]). *b.* Never act rashly, without forethought, and you will not regret it later (32:19-24 [Gr. 35:19-24]); for the God-fearing man is divinely protected, while the godless has no help in trouble (33:1-3 [Gr. 36:1-3]). *c.* While a wise teacher gives well-prepared instruction, a fool is incapable of concentration of thought and steadfast affection (33:4-6 [Gr. 36:4-6]). *d.* Essentially all days are identical, but God has distinguished holidays from ordinary days; likewise, although by nature all men are made from clay, God exalted some (the Israelites) and abased others (the Canaanites), since men are under the power of God like clay in the hands of a potter (33:7-15 [Gr. 36:7-15]). *e.* Although Ben Sira is the last of a great line of teachers, he has gathered wisdom through divine blessing for the Jewish leaders (33:16-18 [Gr. 36:16a; 30:25-27]).

13. On the authority of the head of the family, false and true knowledge, false and true religion (33:19-36-17 [Gr. 30:28-33:13a; 36:16b-22]). *a.* The head of the family should not give his goods to his relatives before his death (33:19-23 [Gr. 30:28-32]), should be strict with an indolent servant (33:24-29 [Gr. 30:33-38]), but considerate with a servant if he is the only one (33:30 f. [Gr. 30:39 f.]). *b.* Place no trust in dreams, unless they be from God, nor in divinations, for they have deceived many (34:1-8 [Gr. 31:1-8]). *c.* Wisdom comes to those who, like Ben Sira, have had much practical experience and have traveled

extensively under God's protection (34:9-17 [Gr. 31:9-20]). *d.* True piety does not consist in ritual acts: the sacrifices of the ungodly are worthless, nay, abominable when the offerings are obtained through exploitation of the needy, for God will hear their appeals (34:18-25 [Gr. 31:21-30]); fasting is likewise useless without true repentance (34:26 [Gr. 31:31]). The acceptable sacrifice consists in keeping the Law, showing kindness, and abstaining from wickedness (35:1-3 [Gr. 32:1-5]). Nevertheless, in obedience to God's Law (and for no other rational reason) one must bring one's offering to the altar, for God will reward sevenfold the offering of the righteous (35:4-11 [Gr. 32:6-13]). Being just, God will not be bribed by offerings obtained dishonestly, but will intervene in favor of the oppressed and particularly of Israel (35:12-20 [Gr. 32:14-26]). *e.* In a psalm of petition the author begs the Lord to rescue Israel from its heathen oppressors, defeating their armies as in the past and gathering again the tribes of Israel, according to the prophetic promises, so that the whole earth may know that he is the true God (36:1-17 [Gr. 33:1-13a; 36:16b-22]).

14. On persons who help in difficulties: the wife, the friend, the counselor, the sage, the physician (36:18-38:23 [Gr. 36:23-38:23]). *a.* Just as the palate discriminates among foods, so the mind among persons (36:18-20 [Gr. 36:23-25]). *b.* The husband of a good wife is far more fortunate than a bachelor (36:21-26 [Gr. 36:26-31]. *c.* Not every friend is true: a faithless friend is a great sorrow, but a true friend is a comrade in battle (37:1-6). *d.* Likewise some counselors seek their own advantage and should be shunned (37:7-11); one should seek the counsel of a God-fearing man (37:12) and of one's own conscience (37:13 f.), praying for guidance (37:15): for deeds are rooted in words, and words in the thoughts of the mind (37:16-18). *e.* Some use their wisdom for their own benefit and enjoy pleasures and popularity; others serve the community disinterestedly (37:19-26). *f.* Eating to excess produces illness (37:27-31). *g.* Consult a physician, for God has given him knowledge and has provided remedies, as when Moses through a tree made sweet the waters at Marah (Ex. 15:23 f.); at the same time, however, "pray unto God, he can heal" (38:1-15). *h.* Mourn bitterly for your dead only a day or two instead of the customary seven days (see 22:12), then comfort yourself and forget him, for you cannot help him (38:16-23).

15. The noblest profession is that of the scribe; a psalm in praise of God (38:24-39:35). *a.* No one can become a scribe (or Biblical scholar) without leisure (38:24). The husbandman (38:25 f.), the seal engraver (Smend adds weavers of embroidered cloth) (38:27), the smith (38:28), and the potter (38:29 f.) perform indispensable work for the community, but are not prepared to be statesmen, leaders in the synagogue, judges, and teachers (38:31-34). The ideal scribe conversely devotes

himself to the study of the Scriptures (i.e., Law, wisdom, prophecies, speeches of famous men, parables and proverbs) (39:1-3). He will advise rulers, travel abroad, acquire experience, be devoutly religious, and receive from God understanding so that he can teach others (39:4-8): thus he acquires an imperishable reputation (39:9-11). *b.* Ben Sira will again (in this second volume) propound his doctrine (39:12), and he invites the pious to sing the following psalm in praise of the Creator (39:13-15). *c.* A psalm in praise of the Lord of creation (39:16-35). God's works are good and he supplies every need (39:16) through his omnipotence and omniscience (39:17-20). He provides good for the pious but evil for the ungodly (39:21-31). Therefore, "God's works are good and supply every need in its season" and his name should be praised (39:32-35; vv. 34 f. repeat 16-17a).

16. On suffering and death (40:1-41:13). *a.* Mental (40:1-7) and physical (40:8 f.) suffering is the lot of all men, notably of the wicked (40:10). What is earthly and false perishes, but what is from on high and true is eternal (40:11 f.). Dishonest wealth is swiftly swept away (40:13 f.), together with the generation of the ungodly (40:15 f.), but righteousness endures forever (40:17). *b.* The best of all good things is the fear of God (40:18-27), but a beggar's life is worse than death (40:28-30). *c.* Death is bitter to a happy and healthy man (41:1), but welcome to a man without strength and without hope (41:2); however, since death is the common lot of all men, it should be faced without fear (41:3 f.). Since the offspring of the ungodly is afflicted with want and disgrace, the death of the ungodly is for them the end of everything; the pious, on the contrary, leave behind an imperishable good name (41:5-13).

17. On legitimate and unwarranted shame, particularly the shame caused by wicked daughters (41:14-42:14). *a.* Hidden wisdom is unprofitable (41:14 f., identical with 20:30 f.). *b.* "Instruction concerning shame" (heading in the Hebrew). Of twenty situations or actions, which are enumerated, one should be ashamed (41:16-24 [Gr. 41:16-42:1d]), but not of the Law of God, of justice, of correct business practice, of disciplining sinners and lewd old men (42:1-8 [Gr. 42:1e-8]). *c.* Daughters cause much anxiety to fathers (42:9-14).

18. Praise of God for his works in nature (42:15-43:33); praise "of the fathers of old" who were loyal to him (44-49), and of the high priest Simon (50).

a. God created the world by fiat and controls its course (42:15); his glory shines from it like the sun (42:16) and not even the angels can describe his works (42:17), for God alone is all-knowing (42:18-21) and has organized the cosmos so that each part works harmoniously with the rest (42:22-25). Everything proclaims God's glory: firmament (43:1), sun (43:2-5), moon (43:6-8), stars (43:9 f.), rainbow (43:11 f.), lightning (43:13), clouds and hailstones (43:14 f), thunder, earthquake, and storms (43:17a, 16, 17b), snow (43:17cd-18), hoarfrost (43:19), ice (43:20 f.), dew (43:22), ocean (43:23-26). God is all; he is greater than his works and unfathomable; he should be praised although he is unknowable and his hidden works are greater than the visible; he has made everything and has given wisdom to the pious (43:27-33).

b. "Praise of the fathers of old" (heading in the Hebrew; in Greek: "Hymn of the fathers"). Introduction (44:1-15): "Let me praise the men loyal [to God]" (44:1, according to Hebrew), whom God honored (44:2): kings, heroes, counselors, seers, princes, conquerors, scholars, sages, psalmists, writers of proverbs, patriarchs, and rich men (44:3-6); all were famous when living, but only some after their death (44:7-9); nevertheless, the memory of their piety is imperishable in Israel (44:10-15). The following Biblical characters are praised: Enoch (44:16; cf. Gen. 5:24), Noah (44:17 f.; cf. Gen. 6:9; 7:1, 9:12-15), Abraham (44:19-21; cf. Gen. 17:4 f., 9-11, 24; 22:1-18), Isaac (44:22; cf. Gen. 26:3-5), Israel, or Jacob (44:22c-23e; cf. Ex. 4:22; Gen. 49), Moses (44:23f-45:5; cf. Ex. 4:16; 7-11; 33:18; etc.), Aaron (45:6-22; cf. Ex. 28; Lev. 6:19-23 [H. 6:12-16]; 8; Num. 16-18; etc.), Phinehas (45:23-26; cf. Num. 25:7-13), Joshua (46:1-8; cf. Num. 14; Josh. 8:18, 26; 10:11-14, 23; etc.), Caleb (46:9 f.; cf. Josh. 14:6-14; 15:16-19), the Judges (46:11 f.), Samuel (46:13-20; cf. I Sam. 1:11; 7:2 ff; 9:6 ff; 12:2 ff; 28:7 ff; etc.), Nathan (47:1; cf. II Sam. 7), David (47:2-11; cf. I Sam. 16:4-13; 17:34-36, 40-50; 18:6 f.; II Sam. 5:17-25; 8; 10; 12:13; I Chron. 16; 25; etc.), Solomon (47:12-22; cf. I Kings 3-11; Prov. 1:6; Cant. 1:1), Rehoboam (47:23a-d; cf. I Kings 12), Jeroboam I (47:23e-25; cf. I Kings 12; 14:15 f.), Elijah (48:1-11; cf. I Kings 17-19; II Kings 2:1, 11; Mal. 4:5 f. [H. 3:23 f]), Elisha (48:12-16; cf. II Kings 2:9, 11, 13; 3:13 f.; 6:15-17, 32 f.; 13:21), Hezekiah (48:17-21; cf. II Kings 18-19; 20:20; etc.), Isaiah (48:22-25; cf. Is. 6; 38:7 f.; 38:5-8; 40:1+61:3; 41:22 f.; 42:9; 44:7; etc.), Josiah (49:1-3; cf. II Kings 22-23), Jeremiah (49:4-6; cf. II Kings 25:9 f.; Jer. 1:5, 10; etc.), Ezekiel (49:8; cf. Ez. 1; 10), Job (49:9; cf. Ez. 14:14, 20; Job 1-2), the Twelve [Minor] Prophets (49:10), Zerubbabel (49:11; cf. Hag. 2:23), the high priest Joshua (Ezra 5:2; 6:14 f.), Nehemiah (49:13; cf. Neh. 3; 6:1; 7:1). *Conclusion* (49:14-16): Enoch was taken by God in his body (49:14; cf. 44:16; Gen. 5:24), and the body of Joseph was taken from Egypt to Palestine after his death (49:15; cf. Gen. 50:25; Ex. 13:19; Josh. 24:32); Shem, Seth, and Enoch (or Enosh?) were greatly honored; but Adam's glory is supreme (49:16).

c. Simon II the son of Jochanan (Gr. Onias, cf. Josephus, *Antiquities* XII:4, 10), the last devout and legitimate high priest (49:15b; 50:1-24). "Great among his brethren and the glory of his people" (49:15b; displaced in Greek, but the beginning of the poem in Hebrew) was **Simon**

(50:1a): the Temple was fortified and a large cistern was dug in his time (i.e., 198 B.C.; cf. Josephus, *Antiquities*, XII:3,3); and he strengthened Jerusalem (50:1b-4). During the celebration of solemn rites in the Temple (perhaps on the Day of Atonement, cf. Lev. 16), he officiated at the head of the priests, clothed in his "glorious vestments" (cf. Ex. 28:4-39) and blessed the people (50:5-21). "Now therefore bless ye the God of all" (50:22-24, conclusion to 44:1-50:21).

d. Ben Sira detests in particular the Edomites (Idumeans), the Philistines, and the Samaritans (50:25 f.).

e. Colophon: the author blesses the reader of his book and commends it to him (50:27-29).

III. Appendix (51)

a. A psalm of thanksgiving, praising God for his help in time of trouble (51:1-12). *b.* A liturgy (imitating Ps. 136). "Give thanks unto the Lord, for he is good; for his mercy endureth forever" (preserved only in the Hebrew, after 51:12, and cited as 51:12 a-p, i-xvi, or [1]-[16]). *c.* Alphabetic acrostic poem describing how Ben Sira acquired wisdom (51:13-22) and now offers it to the unlearned (51:23-30). *d.* Final doxology and colophon (in Hebrew and, with variations, in Syriac [following 51:30]).

1. *The Author, Jesus ben Sira*

Joshua (Gr., Jesus), the son of Eleazar, the son of Sira (Gr. Sirach)— as the author named himself in 50:27 (revised)—lived in Jerusalem before and after 200 B.C. and wrote his book about 180 B.C. The characteristics of thought and expression alone would have fixed the date between 250 and 168 B.C. (before the Maccabean rebellion), but the preface to the Greek translation and the mention of the high priest Simon (ch. 50) permit us to reach greater precision.

The translator in his preface calls the author "my grandfather Jesus" (there is no reason for translating, as do H. L. Strack and others, *páppos* as "ancestor" rather than "grandfather"). The grandson came to Egypt in the thirty-eighth year of King Euergetes and remained there some time. Since Ptolemy III Euergetes I (247-221 B.C.) ruled less than thirty-eight years, Ptolemy VII Euergetes II Physcon (170-117) is obviously meant, so that the translator came to Egypt in 132 B.C. and wrote his preface some years later (perhaps after the king's death in 117; cf. R. Smend, *Die Weisheit des Jesus Sirach*, pp. 3 f.). We may therefore infer that his grandfather, Ben Sira, was born between 250 and 210. The arguments of J. H. A. Hart (*Ecclesiasticus in Greek*, pp. 249-266. Cambridge, 1909) to prove that the book was written in the period 300-275 are utterly unconvincing.[3]

Sirach's glowing description (ch. 50) of the high priest Simon, son of Onias, officiating in the Temple at the celebration of a holyday (presumably the Day of Atonement), gives the impression of being the idealized remembrance of an actual sight. This Simon (or Simeon) seems to have died before Sirach composed his panegyric (cf. 50:1, particularly in the Greek, "who in his life . . ."), although 50:24b in Greek gives the impression that he is still alive. For Sirach concludes the poem with an exhortation to the sons of Simon (50:22-24; the Greek and Syriac omit v. 24bc; the Hebrew text is preferable): God should give them wisdom, and peace should prevail among them, so that "the covenant with Phinehas" (cf. 45:23; Num. 25:12 f.) might be established and Simon's seed endure forever. It seems obvious that after the death of Simon the dignity of the high priesthood was rapidly declining. When did Simon live? Josephus mentions two high priests named Simon son of Onias: Simon I (*Antiquities* XII: 2, 5 [§43]; cf. 4, 1 [§157]), of whom he knows only that he was called the Righteous on account of his piety and benevolence to his fellow citizens (about 300 B.C.); and Simon II (*Antiquities* XII:4, 10 [§224]; 5, 1 [§239]), the deposition of whose son Onias III (II Macc. 3-4) by Antiochus III Epiphanes (175-164) inaugurated the persecution of the Jews that precipitated the Maccabean rebellion (Simon II lived about 200 B.C.; cf. III Macc. 2:1). The Mishna (*Pirqê Abōth* or *Sayings of the Fathers* I, 2) knows a "Simeon the Righteous" whose motto was "The world rests on three pillars, on the Torah [revealed Law], on the cultus [in the Temple], and on works of charity." He is said to have been both one of the last survivors of the Great Synagogue in the time of Ezra (*ibid.*) and to have handed down the traditional law to Antigonus of Socho, who lived about 180 B.C. (*op. cit.* I, 3). We read, moreover, in the Talmud (*Bab. Menachoth* 109b; *Jer. Yoma* 6:3 [43cd]) that Onias the son of Simeon the Righteous built the temple in Egypt. Josephus in contradictory manner attributes the building of this temple at Leontopolis, where Jehovah was worshiped by Jews in Egypt from *ca.* 163 B.C. to A.D. 73, to Onias III son of Simon (*War* VII:10, 2-4 [§§420-436]; cf. I:1, 1 [§§31-33]) and to Onias IV son of Onias III (*Antiquities* XII:5, 1 [§237]; 9, 7 [§§386-388]; XIII:3, 1-3 [§§62-73]). From these scanty and partly unreliable sources, almost all scholars, beginning with Eusebius of Caesarea (*Demonstratio Evangelica* VIII:2, 71; cf. *Chronicon*, ed. Schöne, II:123 [Olympiad 137, 1]) and Jerome (commentary on Daniel, ch. 9 [*Opera*, ed. Vallarsi,

---

[3] Others have dated the book in 280-260 B.C. See J. K. Gasser, *Die Bedeutung der Sprüche Jesu Ben Sira für die Datierung des althebräischen Spruchbuches*, p. 20. Gütersloh, 1904.

V, 686]), have concluded that the Simon of Ecclus. 50 is identical with
Simon II of Josephus.[4] In reality the very existence of Simon I (mentioned
by Josephus) may be seriously questioned (cf. the works of Smend and
Moore cited in the footnote).[5] In *Abōth* Simeon the Righteous forms the
link, in the unbroken chain of witnesses who transmitted the tradition,
between the men of the Great Synagogue in the time of Ezra, and
Antigonus of Socho (about 180 B.C.), who was followed by the "Pairs"
down to Hillel and Shammai (about the beginning of our era). The
rabbis, who counted a single generation of thirty-four years between
the rebuilding of the Temple in 516 and the conquests of Alexander in
333, could thus span the gap between Ezra and Antigonus of Socho
with the single life of Simeon, and believe that this Simeon was the
high priest who welcomed Alexander the Great (*Yoma* 69a;[6] in Josephus,
Antiquities XI:8, 4 [§§325-328], this high priest is Jaddua, grandfather of
Simon I), and at the same time the father of the builder of the temple
at Leontopolis. While Simon II (the same as Simeon the Righteous of
rabbinical literature and Simon in Ecclus. 50) is unquestionably a genuine historical character, who lived about 200 B.C. (whether he was the
father or grandfather of Onias, the builder of the Egyptian temple is
immaterial), Simon I in Josephus (as presumably some other high priests
named by him as living between Jaddua and Simon II) is an artificial
substitute for a high priest whose name was not transmitted. To bridge
the dark period between Ezra and Antigonus of Socho, the rabbis (unaware of its real duration) extended the lifetime of Simeon the Righteous
fantastically, while Josephus manufactured an artificial list of high priests.
On the contrary, Ben Sira, being unable to discover in literature or
tradition any memory of a famous Jew living between Nehemiah (49:13)
in 444 and Simon (ch. 50) about 200, made no attempt to bridge the
gap. He did not feel compelled, like Josephus and *Abōth*, to provide an
unbroken history and chain of tradition.

The testimony of Sirach's grandson and the date of the high priest
Simon thus prove that Sirach wrote his book in an early decade of the

[4] The following publications are particularly important for their discussion of the
problem and for bibliographical references: R. Smend, *Die Weisheit des Jesus Ben
Sira*, pp. XV-XVII. E. Schürer, *Geschichte des Jüdischen Volkes*, Vol. 2, 4th ed., pp.
419 f. G. F. Moore, "Simeon the Righteous," in the Abrahams Memorial Volume,
pp. 348-364 (*Jewish Studies in Memory of Israel Abrahams*. New York, 1927) and
in *Judaism*, Vol. 1, pp. 34 f.; Vol. 3, pp. 8-10.

[5] H. Englander (*Hebrew Union College Jubilee Volume*, pp. 146-149), S. Zeitlin
(*Proceedings of the American Academy for Jewish Research* 3 [1932] 145 f.), and
others still assume the existence of both Simon I and Simon II despite G. F. Moore's
conclusion that "for the supposed Simon I there is no historical evidence" (Abrahams
Volume, p. 349).

[6] S. Zeitlin (*Nēr Ma'arābi* [Western Lamp] 1925, pp. 137-142 [in Hebrew])
believes that in the source of the story in *Yoma* 69a the high priest met Antiochus
III the Great, not Alexander.

second century, between the death of Simon (*ca.* 197-193) and 171, when Antiochus IV Epiphanes, having deposed the last legitimate high priest (descended from Zadok), Onias III son of Simon, in favor of his brother Jason (174), discarded the latter and made a Benjamite, Menelaus, high priest. Sirach did not yet know that the "covenant of Phinehas" (45:24; 50:24), reserving the high priesthood to the first-born descendants of Zadok, had been violated and discarded, although he seems to have been troubled by dire premonitions (45:26; 50:24). Nor did he witness the religious persecution and the Maccabean rebellion soon after the appointment of Menelaus. Although it is difficult to fix the date of the book exactly within the period from 190 (Smend, *op. cit.* p. 321, sees a possible allusion to the battle of Magnesia [190] in 33:12) to 171, the present writer would date it about 180. The date 174-171 proposed by N. Peters (*Das Buch Jesus Sirach* in EH, pp. xxxiv-xxxvii) is hardly correct (cf. Smend, *op cit.* p. xx, n. 1).

Writing with naïve candor, devoid of self-consciousness, Jesus the son of Sira has revealed more of his character than any other ancient Jewish author of a wisdom book. He not only expresses his views quite frankly on a variety of subjects, making no secret, for instance, of his intense dislike for the fair "weaker" sex (9:8; 23:22-27; 25:13-26; 26:6-12, 19-27; 42:6, 13 f.), but he also discloses something of his professional activity. Ben Sira was a teacher, and his book to a large extent consists of his classroom lectures edited in poetic form for publication. He invites the unlearned to attend his school, which he calls *bêth ha-midrāsh* (place [literally "house"] of learning), a term occurring in 51:23 (Hebrew text) for the first time in extant records, but common later as the name of advanced schools for Biblical studies. At the end of his book (51:29, Hebrew text) he expresses the wish that his soul may rejoice in his *yeshibāh* (audience, circle of students; later classroom, school). His pupils belonged to the upper classes of Jerusalem and received instruction aimed primarily at achieving happiness and success through diligence in work, honesty, caution, virtue, and piety. In inviting young aristocrats to attend his school (51:23-30), Sirach, besides more spiritual allurements, promises to charge no tuition (51:25; cf. Is. 55:1 f.)—if we may take his words literally—and, like earlier Egyptian and Hebrew teachers, stresses the pecuniary rewards of education (51:28; cf. *Pirqê Abôth* II:19 in contrast with I:3). With pardonable pride Sirach praises not only his oral teaching (51) but also his book (50:27-29).

Sirach was a teacher and a scholar. He acquired his knowledge through study, experience, and observation of life's varied scenes. This body of information and practical counsel (and at the same time the curriculum's chief subject) is called "wisdom," a term borrowed from the Book of Proverbs but in the new meaning of Judaism as revealed in the Scriptures (ch. 24). As R. Smend (*op. cit.*, p. xxiii) remarked, "subjectively wisdom is the fear of God, objectively the law-book of Moses." Sirach relates, in the first part of an alphabetic acrostic poem (51:13-22), how he acquired wisdom from God when he was still young, before he journeyed abroad (cf. 39:4); but unfortunately his poetic and allegorical language fails to convey a clear picture of his education. Elsewhere he speaks again of his foreign travels (34:11 f. [Gr. 31:12 f.]), during which he saw and experienced much, being often even in danger of death, and tells feelingly of humiliations in foreign countries (29:21-27). According to O. F. Fritzsche (Commentary, p. XI), the psalm of thanksgiving in 51:1-12 has reference to Sirach's deliverance from a deathly peril caused by slanderous accusations against him before a king. We may infer from Sirach's exhortation to his pupils in 6:32-37 that he attained "wisdom" (aside from practical experiences at home and abroad, cf. 34:9-12 [Gr. 31:9-13]) through listening to learned men (cf. 8:8 f.; 21:15), study of the Scriptures (cf. 32:15 [Gr. 35:15]), and even God's own instruction, for Sirach regarded his teaching as no less inspired than the ancient prophetic oracles (24:33; cf. 33:16-18 [Gr. 36:16a; 30:25-27]).

In an earlier period, when the several parts of the Book of Proverbs were written, the teachers of the young were called *ḥakāmim* (sages, wise)—a term used in a professional sense as early as the time of Jeremiah, if not of Isaiah. Sirach (38:24; cf. 44:4 in Hebrew) prefers a newer designation, originating after the Pentateuch was canonized about 400 B.C. and current after his time in the first century of our era—the term *sōfērim* (scribes, i.e., Biblical scholars), familiar to the readers of the Gospels (Gr. *grammateîs* or *nomikoí*). The earlier designation (sages, in the sense of learned) reappears in the second century of our era, but was eventually superseded by the title "rabbi." The scribes were a distinct professional group in the time of the Chronicler (*ca.* 250 B.C.), who traced back, with scant regard to historical facts, general instruction to the time of Jehoshaphat (II Chron. 17:7-9) and the scribes to Ezra (Ezra 7:11); but he correctly defined the professional activity of the scribes as study, practice, and teaching of the Law (Ezra 7:10). Ben Sira, however, combined in his own person and in his description of the ideal scribe (38:24-39:11) the functions of the scribes in the Chronicler's time with the earlier functions of the sages in Proverbs—a combination which is likewise apparent in *The Sayings of the Fathers* (*Pirqê Abōth*). The scribe derives his knowledge both from the Scriptures and from life, his "wisdom" is both Biblical and humanistic. In view of the fact that Ben Sira is (in extant sources) the first of those scribes who "became more and more the dominant factor in the conservation and development of Judaism through all the vicissitudes of the centuries" (G. F. Moore, *Judaism* I, p. 43), his historical importance cannot be overestimated.

Lacking datable sources of any kind from the Chronicler to Sirach (ca. 250-180), we cannot exclude his indebtedness to predecessors. But his enthusiasm, his zeal, his earnestness, his self-assurance, together with the immense popularity and influence of his book in later generations, which made it necessary to declare that it was not sacred Scripture (Moore, op. cit., pp. 44 f.), seem to indicate that he was the first to join deliberately in his teaching the lay and devout wisdom of Proverbs with the study of the Scriptures, particularly the Law (cf. 39:1-3): "Having given himself especially to the reading of the Law and the Prophets and the other books of his people, and having acquired much proficiency in them, he was moved himself to write something on subjects profitable for education and wisdom" (Preface of Sirach's grandson).

It is therefore probable that in portraying the exemplary scribe (38:24-39:11) Sirach idealized his own career rather than that of the average teacher of his day. This ideal scholar is for Sirach a man of culture, possessing sufficient means for devoting himself to study without the necessity of earning a living, a man who has had varied experiences in foreign travel, a gentleman received in the highest circles. Sirach (as perhaps Ecclesiastes) was apparently such a man, but the majority of later scribes (as also the Apostle Paul) supported themselves by working at a trade. Sirach instead (38:24 ff.), like the Egyptian author of the *Instructions of Duauf* (see A. Erman, *The Literature of the Ancient Egyptians*, p. 68. London, 1927) more than a millennium and a half before, denied that a craftsman or a husbandman, no matter how skilled, could acquire wisdom. He contrasts the scholar with the farmer, the gem engraver, the smith, and the potter: their work is indispensable to a city, but affords them not the leisure required to become learned and thus able to address the assembly, sit on a judge's bench, and teach. The scribe, on the contrary, devotes his time to study of the Scriptures (Law, wisdom books, prophecies, parables, and proverbs), to the service of rulers, and to travel; he tests the character of men, preaches the homily and leads in prayer in the synagogue (?), meditates, and lectures before a class.

Such was the ideal that Sirach placed before himself and the scholars of his day. He mapped out a field of research and teaching comprising both the practical wisdom of the sages and the study of the divine revelation embodied in the Scriptures, particularly the Law, to which the Scribes devoted themselves at least since the days of the Chronicler. Thus Sirach marks the transition from the Bible to the Talmud, from the authority of inspiration (which he still claims [24:33], although the rabbis denied it) to the authority of learning. The two phases of this study, wisdom and Law, remained basic in Judaism after Sirach and are called, respectively, *Haggadah*, aiming at "religious and moral instruction and edification" (G. F. Moore, *Judaism*, Vol. 1, p. 162), and *Halakah*, formulating juristically the rules of the traditional law and connecting them through ingenious exegesis with the revealed Law (cf. Moore, *ibid.* p. 161).

Wisdom, of course, looms much more prominently in Sirach's book than the Law with which he identified it. Essentially he carried on the instruction of the sages, and seems to have been impelled to stress the nationalistic, ritualistic (ch. 50), and legalistic aspects of Judaism—of which we can hardly discover a trace in the Book of Proverbs—to counteract the inclination of Jerusalem's upper classes to adopt the rapidly spreading Hellenistic civilization. To save Judaism from this corrosive influence, which is apparent in the skepticism of Ecclesiastes a few years later, he stressed the peculiarities of his religion, without, however, neglecting those universal principles of prudence and virtue which form the main topic of Proverbs.

During his travels abroad Sirach became familiar with some phases of Hellenistic culture and life. It is possible that he served a Hellenistic ruler (cf. 39:4) and learned some Greek. His book seems to contain allusions to Greek writings—mostly "familiar quotations" which he heard in his conversation with Hellenistic teachers and cultivated gentlemen. Some of the parallels between Sirach and Greek authors (notably Euripides and Theognis) which I. Lévi (*L'Ecclésiastique*, Pt. II, pp. lxiii-lxvi. Paris, 1901) has pointed out, represent commonplaces and generalities familiar in the teaching of ancient moralists, whatever be their nationality, as Lévi himself admits (p. lxv). Even if we conclude that through a mere coincidence Sirach and Euripides expressed the same hostility to women and the same indignation at false friendship (cf. Theognis), and warned against judging anyone happy before his death (11:26; cf. Euripides, *Andromache* 100-102; *Heracleidae* 865 f.; *Troades* 509 f.; etc.; similarly Aeschylus, *Agamemnon* 928 f.; Sophocles, *Oedipus Rex* 1528-30) —a truism in the time of Sophocles (*Trachiniae* 1-3) which had been stated by Solon to Croesus, according to Herodotus (I, 32)—we should not exclude in Sirach some slight acquaintance with Greek classics, as for instance Aesop's fable (No. 329) of the pot and the kettle (13:2) to warn against the association of the poor with the rich. When Sirach (3:17-25) asserted that human speculations concerning the ultimate mysteries of the universe are vain but that God reveals his secret to the humble, he apparently questioned the validity of Greek philosophy. Paradoxically he could have been inspired by Euripides, who wrote: "What man—who sees divine action [or fate] leaping hither and thither, and back again, in contrary unexpected turns—could say, after the most far-reaching investigation, that he has discovered what is God, or non-God, or the intermediary? . . . Nothing is positively known among men, but I have found that the word of the gods is true" (*Helena* 1137-49);

and "What we call wise is not wisdom, neither are our thoughts of what is not mortal. . . . Keep the wise understanding and the mind far from overly sophisticated men; whatever the humble crowd deems right and practices, that I would choose" (*Bacchae* 393 f.; 427-431). Although Sirach may occasionally have presented in Hebrew some Greek aphorisms from Theognis, Euripides, and other writers, his type of Judaism shows no influence of Hellenism.

The "height of Greek fashions and the influx of foreign customs" (II Macc. 4:13) in Jerusalem do not appear until 174-171, after Sirach wrote his book, and ended in 164. When Jason was high priest (174-171), young "modern" Jews scandalized their elders by wearing broad-brimmed Greek hats (similarly, until recent times Western hats have been anathema to pious Moslem); athletic priests hurried through their holy services to strip for sports in the gymnasium, built below the citadel on Zion; and some Jewish youths even had recourse to a surgical operation to escape the heathen's ridicule for the circumcised; finally, Jason sent a contribution to the sacrifices to Herakles (i.e., Melkart) of Tyre, on the occasion of quinquennial games (I Macc. 1:1-15; II Macc. 4:7-20). This tendency of the aristocrats to "make a covenant with the Gentiles" and to practice "the customs of the Gentiles" which were "forbidden by the Law [of Moses]" (I Macc. 1:11, 13; II Macc. 4:11) was noted by Sirach before it reached these impudent manifestations in the time of Jason. Back from his travels, he was shocked to see in Jerusalem Jews who were ashamed of their Law when in the company of Gentiles (42:2) and actually forsook it (41:8 f.), preferring to be in tune with Hellenism; he inveighed against the fearful of heart and faint of hand, against the "sinner that goeth two ways," who perhaps believed that he could be at the same time a Jew in religion and a Greek in culture (2:12 f.), and against those whose endurance had reached its end (2:14). He reminded these apostate or perplexed Jews that the humblest among the faithful is the true aristocrat, ranking high over Greek rulers (10:19-25), and that true piety implies uncompromising obedience to God's words and sincere submission before him (2:15-17).

It seems, from 1:22-24, that Sirach at first, under the spell of violent wrath, denounced the Hellenizers in Jerusalem with such fury that the authorities intervened and he found it advisable to "suppress his words" until a more suitable time. In any case he adopted a less impassioned tone in teaching and writing, and attacked Hellenism indirectly without ever referring to it clearly. He apparently refrained from becoming one of the Hasidim (pious), whose great spokesman was later the author of the Book of Daniel (164), but he detested the Hellenizers no less than they. He admired the Hasidim and seems to allude to their firmness in temptation, their courage in affliction, and their abiding trust in God (2:1-11; cf. 4:17; 33:1 [Gr. 36:1]; 44:20).

Sirach was convinced that Judaism was the only true religion, being the worship of the only God in existence, the almighty Creator of the world (42:15-43:33). No matter how depressing the situation of Judaism and the Jews might be in the present—and Sirach had no illusions about its seriousness (35:12-36:17 [Gr. 32:14-33:13a; 36:16b-22])—nothing can prevail against God, for the rule over the world is in his hands (10:4; cf. Dan. 2:21), and he will eventually glorify his people Israel (35:18-20 [Gr. 32:22b-26]; 44:21; 47:22; 48:10, 24 f.; 49:12; 50:24)—for "Israel is the Lord's portion" (17:17)—and vindicate the oppressed pious in its midst (2:7-11; 34:13-17 [Gr. 31:14-20]; 35:13-17 [Gr. 32:16-22a]).

That Judaism so conceived could be seriously threatened by Hellenism was unthinkable. Since the publication of the Pentateuch (ca. 400), when the Jewish congregation had been established as the earthly kingdom of the sole God, devout Palestinian Jews despised heathenism as falsehood and folly, and felt themselves to be impervious to its baleful influence. Even when Hellenism allured some aristocrats who became emancipated from the Law and the ancestral customs, even when Antiochus Epiphanes proscribed Judaism and made Hellenism compulsory, the strict Jews clung to their Law without the slightest inclination to engage in a theological controversy with pagan thinkers. The exclusive validity of Judaism was to them an axiom needing no demonstration, and its inevitable postulate was the falsehood of all other religions. There is no real polemic against Hellenism in Sirach and in Daniel, such as we find in Jewish writings in Greek intended also for Gentile readers (Aristeas, Wisdom of Solomon, Epistle of Jeremy, Sibylline Oracles; Josephus, Against Apion; etc.). It sufficed for Daniel to point out that heathen gods are nothing but idols (5:4, 23). Likewise Sirach's contempt for Hellenism finds expression merely in a passing allusion to idolatry (30:18 f.), and in two brief warnings: against trusting in divination and dreams (34:1-8 [Gr. 31:1-8]); and against vain speculations (Greek philosophy?) about the mysteries of the world (3:21-25). For the rest Sirach had no interest in polemics and apologetics: he conceived his task as that of an expounder of the inexhaustible riches of Judaism in its three aspects of fear of the Lord, observance of the Law, and wisdom (cf. 15:1), as will be seen in the following section of this chapter.

2. The Teaching of the Book[7]

Life's ideal, as presented by Sirach in his book, is a synthesis of religion (fear, or love, of the Lord), observance of the Law, and wisdom.

[7] See in particular: V. Merguet, *Glaubens- und Sittenlehre des Buches Jesus Sirach* (Vol. 1, 1874; Vol. II, 1901. Programm des königl. Friedrichs-Kollegium zu Königsberg); A. Büchler, "Ben Sira's Conception of Sin and Atonement" (JQR N.S.

A. Religion

Until the publication of the Deuteronomic Code in 621 B.C., the religion of Israel had been essentially national in character. But after the Exile, through the influence of Jeremiah and Ezekiel, Judaism became also a way of salvation for the individual: "the older ideas of national solidarity were supplemented and to some extent superseded by personal responsibility" (G. F. Moore, *Judaism*, Vol. 1, pp. 224 f.). Both aspects were stressed by Sirach and remained basic in later centuries.

The national feeling among the Jews after the loss of state and country is a unique historical phenomenon. It had its roots in Deuteronomy and the Priestly Code, and, kept alive by teachers like Sirach, it prevented the assimilation of the Jews. While the Persian Empire, whose liberal policy encouraged the development of national religions and cultures, had undoubtedly promoted the religious universality of the Second Isaiah (Is. 40-55)—one God and one faith for all men—the spread of Hellenism in Western Asia and its lure for some Jews inevitably produced the opposite reaction and led teachers like the Chronicler and Sirach to stress those nationalistic aspects of Judaism which had been repressed, following the Second Isaiah, in writings of the Persian period (Jonah; Ruth; Mal. 1:11; Gen. 10; some of Proverbs and Psalms; Is. 2:2-5 = Mich. 4:1-5). Sirach combines patriotism with the universality of God when he states: "For each nation he appointed a prince [i.e., angel], but the portion of the Lord is Israel" (17:17; cf. Deut. 32:8 f., reading with the LXX "angels of God" instead of "sons of Israel"; 4:19 f.). But when he forcefully expresses his abhorrence for three hostile neighboring nations, the Idumeans, the Philistines, and particularly the Samaritans (50:25 f.; cf. Jub. 24:28-33; 30; 35:14 f.; 37:13-38:14; Judith 9:2-4), when he prays God to crush the heathen oppressors of his people (36:1-10 [Gr. 33:1-12])—being assured that this judgment is imminent (35:18-20 [Gr. 32:22b-26])—and thus restore the tribes of Israel to their land, filling Zion with divine glory (36:11-17 [Gr. 33:13a; 36:16b-22]; cf. 48:10, which quotes Mal. 4:5 f. [H. 3:23 f.]), then Sirach's national feel-

---

13 [1922-1923] 303-335, 461-502; 14 [1923-1924] 53-83). Less in detail, the teaching of Sirach is described in the following general works: T. K. Cheyne, *Job and Solomon* (London, 1887); J. Köberle, *Sünde und Gnade im religiösen Leben des Volkes Israel bis auf Christum* (Munich, 1905); L. Couard, *Die religiösen und sittlichen Anschauungen der alttestamentlichen Apokryphen und Pseudepigraphen* (Gütersloh, 1907); H. M. Hughes, *The Ethics of Jewish Apocryphal Literature* (London, 1909); A. Bertholet, *Die jüdische Religion von der Zeit Ezras bis zum Zeitalter Christi* (Tübingen, 1911); H. J. Wicks, *The Doctrine of God in the Jewish Apocryphal and Apocalyptic Literature* (London, 1915); W. Bousset, *Die Religion des Judentums im späthellenistischen Zeitalter*, 3rd ed. by H. Gressmann (Tübingen, 1926); J. Fichtner, *Die altorientalische Weisheit in ihrer israelitisch-jüdischen Ausprägung* (Beih. ZAW 62. Giessen, 1933).

ing rings out loud and clear, without a trace of solicitude for the Gentiles. In a more religious mood this national pride is expressed in the assurance that Jerusalem, the holy city and the place of God's dwelling (36:13 [Gr. 36:18]), is beloved of God (24:11), and that Israel, God's portion (24:12) and first-born (36:12 [Gr. 36:17]), will endure forever (37:25; 47:22). In contrast with the glorious history of Israel, which Sirach summarizes as a succession of pious heroes blessed by God, from Enoch to Nehemiah and backwards from Enoch to Adam (44-49), God has overthrown throughout past centuries the proud kingdoms of the Gentiles (10:7-18). Israel will again triumph, through God's intervention, in the near future (35:19cd [Gr. 32:25]; 47:22; 48:10, 24 f.).

In its national aspect the religion of the Jews found expression in the public services, either in the Temple on Zion or in the synagogues. The Temple had a long history, but ceased to exist two and a half centuries after Sirach; the synagogues had perhaps originated less than two centuries before (although Philo and Josephus dated them back to the time of Moses) but were destined to endure. The silence of Sirach concerning the synagogues is puzzling; it should be noted, however, that synagogues are not mentioned before the Christian Era except in Greek inscriptions of Egyptian Jews (the earliest dated in the time of Ptolemy III [247-221]; cf. E. Schürer, *Geschichte des Jüdischen Volkes*, Vol. 2, pp. 499 f.) and perhaps in a Maccabean psalm (Ps. 74:8, "meeting places of God"; cf. Enoch 46:8). A possible allusion to the synagogue services may be found in 39:6: "The Scribe seems here to be thought of as holding discourse and leading the prayers in a religious assembly" (G. F. Moore, *Judaism*, Vol. 1, p. 41, n. 2). In 24:23 (cf. Deut. 33:4, LXX), the Greek mentions "the synagogues of Jacob."

Conversely, Sirach, although presumably not a priest, was intensely interested in the sacred rites of the Temple worship. Personified Wisdom ministered before God in the Tabernacle and was in it like the smoke of incense (24:10, 15); later she was established on Zion (24:10 f.). Jerusalem is God's holy city and dwelling; the Temple is filled with his glory (36:13 f. [Gr. 36:18 f.], according to the Hebrew; cf. 51:12 vii, xiii). There Sirach had beheld the high priest Simon celebrating the holy rites of the Day of Atonement—a solemn sight which made an unforgettable impression on him (50:1-21). Here and elsewhere Sirach discloses a profound reverence for the high priest: God has given him supreme spiritual authority among the Jews through the eternal "covenant with Phinehas" (45:24; 50:24; cf. Num. 25:11-13); the glory of Aaron, the first high priest, arouses his enthusiasm (45:6-22). Likewise reverence for the priests, "the sons of Zadok" (51:12 ix), manifested in contributions to their support, is inseparable from the fear of God (7:29-31), for God has allowed the priests to come near unto himself (33:12 [Gr. 36:12];

cf. Num. 16:5; Ez. 40:46; 45:4). Festivals (7:8-10; 33:7-9 [Gr. 36:7-9]; 43:7) and sacrifices (35:4-7 [Gr. 32:6-9]) are divinely ordained.

It would, however, be an error to assume from this that Sirach, like the Chronicler, regarded ritual ceremonies as the essential part of religion. On the contrary, right living and personal religion were far more significant for him. He mentioned ritual observances because, as part of Israel's heritage, they served to keep the holy nation (24:12; 36:12 [Gr. 36:17]) apart from the Gentiles, as God had ordained from the beginning (33:10-12 [Gr. 36:10-12]). Rites and ceremonies per se are really insignificant and ineffective. In a moment of candor, Sirach even admitted that the only reason for presenting offerings and sacrifices was that the Law commanded it (35:4 f. [Gr. 32:6 f.])! Sirach expresses here the basic principle and the logical attitude of all revealed religions: ritual observances are statutory and not a matter for discussion. The implications of this principle—the sacrificial cultus in itself consists of empty forms, religiously insignificant apart from the mental attitude of the worshiper—were accepted without qualms by the intelligent (including presumably the codifiers of the Levitical legislation), but the mass of the people through the centuries regarded the rites as the principal means of securing God's favor. Like Amos, Sirach unhesitatingly condemned the sacrifice of the unrighteous as a mockery, and regarded the offering of the despoiler of the poor as on a par with murder (34:18-26 [Gr. 31:21-31]), for God listens to the cry of the oppressed (35:12-20 [Gr. 32:14-26]). In itself, a sacrifice will not atone for sin (7:8 f.; cf. 35:12 [Gr. 32:14 f.]), exactly as fasting for one's sins is futile without true repentance (34:26 [Gr. 31:31]). Only the offerings of the righteous are acceptable to God (35:6 f. [Gr. 32:8 f.]), particularly when presented with joy and gratitude, without stint (35:8-11 [Gr. 32:10-13]). In his illness a man should pray, repent of his sins, and offer sacrifice (38:9-11); it is also advisable to call in a pious physician (38:12-15), although for the Chronicler (II Chron. 16:12) this indicates lack of faith. Finally, anticipating the general trend of Judaism (cf. Dan. 4:27 [H. 4:24]; Tob. 12:9), notably after the destruction of the Temple (A.D. 70), Sirach concludes from these premises that keeping the Law, practicing kindness and mercy, and avoiding wickedness are the equivalent of all sacrifices and oblations (35:1-3 [Gr. 32:1-5]). Thus, specifically, honoring one's parents (3:3, 14 f.) and giving alms (3:30; cf. 29:11-13), rather than sacrifices, atone for sin.

It is thus evident that moral conduct and personal piety in conformity with God's Law, rather than the national public worship, were for Sirach the essence of religion (17:11-27). His religion is nobler than that of the Book of Proverbs, although it does not quite attain the spirituality of some psalms. Nevertheless, the edition of the Psalms of David (cf. 47:8 f.) then current had a profound influence on him, as we see from the allusions to Psalms in his book and from the psalms which Sirach himself composed (17:29-18:14; 22:27-23:6; 36:1-17 [Gr. 33:1-13a; 36:16b-22]; 39:16-35 [introduced by 39:12-15]; 42:15-43:33; 44-49 [particularly 45:25 f., Hebrew text]; 50:1-24;[8] 51:1-12; 51:12 i-xvi [in Hebrew; cf. Ps. 136]; 51:13-30). Sirach's own personal piety and theology disclose his repeated reading of the Psalms.

Prayer was the innermost expression of Sirach's religious life. Of the psalms he included in his book, the following are prayers or songs of thanksgiving: 22:27-23:6, on the theme, "lead me not into temptation, but deliver me from evil"; 36:1-17 (Gr. 33:1-13a; 36:16b-22), a petition in Israel's behalf (God should annihilate its foes and restore the nation, as of old, on its land); 51:1-12, a song of thanksgiving to God, for deliverance from mortal danger; 52:12 i-xvi, an antiphonal liturgy of national thanksgiving; in 51:22 he praises God for fulfilling his prayer for wisdom (51:14). In all walks of life and in all circumstances, the pious pray unto God: the scribe (39:5), the diseased (38:9), the physician (38:14), the downtrodden (21:5; 35:13-17 [Gr. 32:14-22a]). Young men should pray for wisdom (51:14) and bless God for their good fortune (32:13 [Gr. 35:13]). In addition to these extemporaneous prayers, Sirach favors also regular formal prayers (7:10), although he warns against excessive repetition of the same words (7:14; cf. Matt. 6:7 f.).

Personal piety is called by Sirach, according to Old Testament usage, "fear of God" or "of the Lord" (the noun "fear" occurs 23 times; the verb "to fear" 31 times) or "love of God" (only in the form "those who love the Lord," occurring four times): since the publication of the Deuteronomic Code (621) the two expressions were used interchangeably and mean primarily obedience to God's Law (2:15 f.) including the ritual actions (7:29-31). The pious man seeks God (32:14 [Gr. 35:14]), believes in him trustfully (2:6, 8, 10, 13; 11:21; 32:24 [Gr. 35:24]), follows him (46:6e, 10), praises him (32:13 [Gr. 35:13]), clings to him (2:3). Faith and humility are well pleasing to God (1:27; cf. 3:17-20; 45:4; contrast 1:28-30; 40:12). The fear of God, more than anything else, brings joy and happiness to men (40:18-27; cf. 23:27; 25:11), and the God-fearing man is superior to a ruler (10:20-24).

Sirach's piety, consisting in fulfilling God's will as revealed in his Law,[9]

---

[8] Martin Rinckart's hymn, *Nun danket alle Gott* (changed in English to "Now thank we all our God"), was inspired by 50:22, "Now bless ye all God," in the standard LXX. The Hebrew reads "Bless ye Jehovah, the God of Israel"; many Greek manuscripts, the Latin, and other versions read "Bless ye the God of all" (cf. 36:1 [Gr. 33:1] and "He is all" [43:27]), which may be the original reading.

[9] See, e.g., 2:16; 10:19; 15:1; 19:20, 24; 21:11; 23:27; 33:1 f. [Gr. 36:1 f.]. Conversely, the Law of Moses does not seem to be mentioned as the norm of piety and ethics in the Book of Proverbs.

has a strong ethical element but lacks ascetic renunciation. Sirach not only has no objection to the pleasures of dinners and banquets, but on such occasions he emphatically refuses to let his enjoyment of music and song be ruined by an elderly bore, eager to discourse on serious topics (32:3-6 [Gr. 35:3-6]). He dislikes the practice of unnecessary oaths (23:9-11; cf. Matt. 5:33-37) and of thoughtless vows (18:22-24; cf. Deut. 23:21-23 [H. 23:22-24]; Prov. 20:25; Eccles. 5:4 f. [H. 5:3 f.]), and the reluctance, through religious scruples, to call in a physician (38:1-15). Although he does not conceal his mistrust of women, he advocates married life and pities the bachelor (36:22-26 [Gr. 36:27-31]).

Personal piety—fear of God expressed in obedience to his Law—will be rewarded in this life. This is one of the few dogmas of Judaism, and the discussion of it led to the beginning of a philosophy of religion. Sirach never doubted its validity: the controversy on the subject between Job and his friends made no more impression on him than on the authors of the Proverbs of Solomon and the Psalmists (with a few exceptions). For him, rewards and punishments for human conduct are confined to life on this earth: he discloses no knowledge of the Platonic doctrine of the immortality of the soul nor of the Pharisaic belief in the resurrection of the body. "When a man dies he inherits worm and maggot, lice and creeping things" (10:11, Hebr.; see also 7:17, Hebr.; 38:21-23, Hebr.; 40:1, 11; 41:1-4, Hebr.; cf. 17:32; 28:6). But in the first Greek translation of his book this dismal notion of death was occasionally softened (particularly in 7:17; 48:11), and some of the glosses appearing in the revised Greek translation actually teach a doctrine of eternal life for the pious (R. Smend, *Die Weisheit des Jesus Sirach*, pp. cxv f.; J. Fichtner, *Die Altorientalische Weisheit* [Beih. ZAW 62], p. 70. Giessen, 1933): "because an eternal gift with joy is his recompense" (2:9); "they who do the things pleasing unto him will enjoy the fruit of the tree of immortality" (19:19); "for he will lead out of darkness to the light of health [i.e., salvation]" (17:26a). The Latin version likewise refers to rewards and punishments after death in glosses to 17:23, 27; 21:10; 24:32; it is uncertain whether the one in 24:32 is of Jewish (so R. Smend) or Christian (so N. Peters) origin.

Sirach, on the contrary, conceived life after death, in accordance with the Biblical books existing at the time, as an endlessly gloomy existence in the darkness of the underworld, or Sheol (14:16; 17:27; 28:21; 41:4; 48:5; 51:5 f.). It is only here on earth that God rewards and punishes by awarding "good and evil, life and death, poverty and wealth" (11:14). Here the Lord has overthrown and annihilated wicked nations (16:6-13) and will vindicate Israel (35:12-20 [Gr. 32:14-26]). Here the pious man will receive rich rewards (1:11-13, 17-20; 2:8-11; 4:28; 16:14; 27:8 f.; 34:13-17 [Gr. 31:14-20]; 35:11 [Gr. 32:13]; 39:29; 40:10), but the wicked will suffer bitterly for his misdeeds (7:1-3; 10:12-17; 17:23; 27:3, 10;

28:1; 40:12-17; 41:5-10). Sirach's emphatic and repeated affirmation of the dogma of earthly rewards and punishments indicates not only that it was basic in his thought, but also that it was not unchallenged. He realized, in the first place, that, in actual life, men's destiny did not always correspond to their deserts; moreover, he heard some Jews, usually emancipated from orthodoxy under the influence of Hellenism (like Ecclesiastes later), reject this dogma *in toto*.

These doubters, called "ungodly, scoffers, liars, and wicked" (15:7-9) by Sirach in his holy wrath, considered themselves religious (15:9); they asserted (like the Epicureans) that God is too distant and the individual too insignificant for God to notice his conduct (16:17-23; 23:18 f.); that God created all men equal—so that Israel's election is an illusion (33:10-15 [Gr. 36:10-15])—and later determined their conduct, leaving them no freedom of choice (15:11-20); that God mixed evil and good in his creation without regard to men's deserts (39:16-35), allowing evil, however, to prevail in human life (40:1-17). Sirach indignantly rejects these objections to his theory (cf. the preceding passages and 1:9 f.; 40:18-27), and attempts to show that the facts do not refute it. The good fortune of the wicked should evoke no envy, for it may soon vanish (9:11 f. 18:24-26; 40:13-16): no man should therefore be pronounced happy before his death (11:23-28; cf. 21:10). The punishment may be delayed (5:4) but "the day of wrath" (5:8) is inescapable; often the nemesis is automatic and immediate (27:25-29).

On the contrary, "the fear of the Lord is honor and glory, and gladness and a crown of rejoicing" (1:11 cf. 10:19-24); it brings joy and long life (1:12), success to the day of death (1:13), good health (1:18), a good wife (26:3) who makes her husband happy (26:4), protection from harm (33:1 [Gr. 36:1]) and from need (40:26 f.).

Nevertheless, Sirach was aware, like some of the Psalmists, that the pious were not always blessed with these worldly goods. Like earlier Biblical writers, he solves this difficulty first by assuring the pious that their spiritual reward is more precious than temporal blessings (the fear of God is better than knowledge [19:24] and than wealth and strength [40:26]), and secondly by warning them to bear unflinchingly the misfortunes through which God may be testing their piety. The supreme rewards are spiritual: through the fear of the Lord the soul turns to God (21:6), obtains his favor and guidance (32:14, 16 [Gr. 35:14, 16]), and enjoys the blessing of communion with God (2:7-11; 34:13-17 [Gr. 31:14-20]).[10] Other intangible rewards are granted to the God-fearing

---

[10] How God grants wisdom is not clear: wisdom was with God (1:1) and he poured it out upon all his works (1:9), giving it both to all men and to them that love him (1:10); wisdom was created with the faithful in the womb (1:14); it was made to dwell in Zion, in the midst of Israel (24:7-12). But elsewhere wisdom is attained through one's efforts (6:18-37). Unless "wisdom" is used in a variety of meanings, Sirach contradicts himself.

man: the fear of the Lord, the best thing on this earth (23:27; 25:11), is his glory (10:22) and exalts him above potentates (10:23 f.); he overcomes temptations or trials (33:1 [Gr. 36:1]); he enjoys the friendship of kindred spirits (6:16 f.); after his death, his good fortune abides with his children and descendants (44:10 f.; 23:24 f.; contrast 41:5-9), who are like-minded (1:15; 4:16); and his good name survives forever (37:26; 39:9-11; 41:11-13). Going one step further, Sirach warns the pious man that he may fail to obtain a reward for his devotion to God: he should therefore prepare himself to endure patiently the calamities that may be in store for him, for God may test him in the furnace of affliction (2:1-6; 4:17 f.; cf. Prov. 3:11 f.; Job 5:17 f.; Wisd. of Sol. 3:5 f.) or chastise him for his improvement (18:13 f.; 21:6; 32; 14 f. [Gr. 35:14 f.]). In general, appearances may be deceiving, and misfortunes may be blessings in disguise (20:9-12).

As generally in Judaism, Sirach's doctrine of God is not based on metaphysical speculations (upon which he frowned, 3:21-24), but on piety. His theological views, like those of the Psalms, are closely connected with personal religion, particularly with the doctrine of divine rewards and punishments outlined above.

Monotheism, which is tacitly assumed in Proverbs and Psalms, is proclaimed by Sirach (and other writings opposing Hellenism) for polemical purposes, as long before by the Second Isaiah in his attack on heathenism: "Save us, O God of all, and send thy fear upon all the nations . . . that they may know, as we have known, that there is no other God but thee" (36:1-5 [Gr. 33:1-5]; cf. 36:17 [Gr. 36:22]). "From everlasting he is the same" (42:21, Hebr.); "he is all" (43:27).

"Mighty in power and all-seeing" (15:18b), his eyes look into the most recondite places (23:19; 39:19; 42:20): only a fool could believe that his secret sins will escape God's notice (16:17-23; 17:15, 19-24; cf. 23:18 f.). It was essential for personal religion that God should know human beings with a knowledge embracing their doings (23:19; 39:19 f.) and their hidden thoughts, past or future (42:18-20; cf. Wisd. of Sol. 1:6-11), and also that God should hear the prayers addressed to him (2:10; 35:13-17 [Gr. 32:16-21]; 36:17 [Gr. 36:22]; 48:20). At the same time God knows the secrets of the physical world in its entirety, from the beginning to the end of time: "For the Lord possesses all knowledge" (42:18) and nothing escapes him (42:20). Moreover, "all wisdom comes from the Lord and is with him forever" (1:1; cf. 1:8 f.; 15:18; 33:8, 11 [Gr. 36:8, 11]). Some dreams come from God (34:6 [Gr. 31:6]).

God's power is almighty: who can recount the might of his majesty (18:5)? Even his angels lack the power to describe his mighty works (42:17). He has created heaven and earth (16:26-17:9; cf. 18:1; 24:8;

42:15-43:33) by fiat (42:15; cf. 39:17; 43:10, 23), and has fixed the cosmic order regulating the relations between phenomena (16:26-30) so wisely that their harmony is eternal (42:22-25) in spite of their contrasting natures (33:7-9, 15 [Gr. 36:7-9, 15]): consequently, the works of God are all good (39:16 f. = 33 f.). He created man out of dust, in his own image (17:1-10; cf. 4:6; 7:30; 15:15; 32:13 [Gr. 35:13]; 33:10, 13 [Gr. 36:10, 13]). Because men are so insignificant in the cosmos, God is merciful to them (18:6-14; cf. 17:1-10) and controls the phenomena of nature for the benefit of the righteous and the punishment of the wicked (39:24-31; cf. Job 37:12; Wisd. of Sol. 16:24). The destiny of men is in his hand (33:10-14 [Gr. 36:10-14]; cf. 50:22); good and evil, life and death, come from him, and the success of human undertakings depends on him (11:14), not on human effort and ability (11:10-13; cf. 11:18 f.; 18:25 f.); but he does not control human conduct, for man's will is free (15:11-17). He exalts and abases both individuals (7:11b; 11:21) and nations (10:8, 13-17), for he is the supreme ruler of the human world (10:4 f.).

As the sovereign of mankind God is holy, merciful, and just. The Holy One (4:14) is incensed by wickedness (16:7-10; 5:6): he has sanctified himself by punishing Israel and will manifest his holiness in pouring his wrath on the Gentiles (36:1-10 [Gr. 33:1-12]). For he is just in his judgment of human conduct (35:12 [Gr. 32:14 f.]), requiting a man according to his deeds (11:26), in accordance with the doctrine of earthly retribution examined above. But he is also merciful (2:11; 48:20 [Gr.]; 50:19), and graciously forgives the sins of those who sincerely turn to him (17:25-29; cf. 18:20 f.), accept his chastening (18:13 f.; 32:14 [Gr. 35:14]), and show mercy to those who have done them an injury (28:2-5; cf. Matt. 6:12, 14 f.; 18:35). The inveterate sinner, however, who says, like Voltaire, "God will forgive me; it is his business," will find no mercy (5:4-6). God listens to the cry of the fatherless and the widow, to the appeal of the humble (35:14, 17 [Gr. 32:17, 21-22a]), and "saves in time of affliction" (2:11). For God is our Father (23:1, 4; 51:10, Hebr.).

Israel is a special object of God's mercy (35:19 f. [Gr. 32:24-26]; 36:12-17 [Gr. 36:17-22]). His blessings to his people are enumerated in the liturgy preserved in the Hebrew text after 51:12, and are described, in the course of Israel's history, in the "Praise of the Fathers of Old" (44-49). He separated Israel, his portion (17:17; 24:12), from other nations (33:10-13 [Gr. 36:10-13]) and gave them his covenant (17:11-14 [unless the passage refers to the covenant with Noah, 44:18]; 44:20 f.) and his Law (9:15; 19:17; 23:23; 24:23; 39:8; 41:8; 42:2; 45:5; 49:4, cf. 44:20). This brings us to our next topic.

B. The Law

The divine revelation of the Law, which Sirach repeatedly emphasizes in the passages just cited, is the basic principle of Judaism. Of course, the divine revelation embraced more than the Law, even if we understand Torah (Law) in its true and much wider meaning than legislation, i.e., religious and moral instruction. Sirach does not yet use Torah in the rabbinical sense of all "divine revelation, written and oral" (G. F. Moore, *Judaism*, Vol. I, p. 263), although the word means much more than the Pentateuch. When God "reveals his secret to the meek" (3:20b in the Hebrew, corresponding to 3:19b in the Syriac and the secondary Greek version; cf. 4:18; Am. 3:7; Ps. 25:15; Prov. 3:32), he makes known mysteries too deep for human investigation rather than his Torah, which is by no means hidden. Similarly, Sirach distinguishes between the Law, the wisdom of the ancients, and prophecies (presumably the Pentateuch, the prophetic books, and the wisdom books) in 39:1, where he describes the principal fields of a scribe's study. He does not seem to include in the Law the Messianic prophecies spoken in God's name (36:15 f. [Gr. 36:20 f.]; cf. 48:24 f.).

Sirach ordinarily understands by Torah the Pentateuch, "the Law which Moses commanded" (24:23; cf. 45:5). At the same time, however, he extends the import of the written Law considerably, and, like the rabbis later, makes it the revealed norm of human conduct, the standard of religion and morals. This expansion is accomplished in two ways: through the unwritten law—the "tradition of the elders" in the Gospels (Mark 7:3, 5, etc.; cf. Gal. 1:14)—and through the identification of Law with wisdom. Both of these notions may be older than Sirach, although they do not appear clearly in earlier writings, but he undoubtedly gave them a new significance and thus made his greatest contribution to the rise of Rabbinic Judaism.

The unwritten law is a sort of common law, more or less exactly formulated, which supplemented, interpreted, and applied the Pentateuchal statute law: it fixed the details of Temple rituals, it provided exact norms for procedure and decision in civil and criminal cases, and specified minutely the religious and moral duties and prohibitions regulating the conduct of the pious Jew. The scribes not only investigated the Pentateuch and the other Scriptures, but by ingenious exegesis derived the oral law from Biblical proof-texts and obtained norms and precedents for new situations. The immense labors of the scribes and their successors were eventually recorded in the Talmud, which is to a great extent a discussion of the oral law codified in the Mishna.

This great juristic development is still incipient in Sirach's book. A systematic study of our book from this point of view is still wanting, and should be undertaken by a scholar more familiar with the rabbinical literature than the present writer. Here Sirach's contributions will be illustrated by a few typical instances.

One of the earliest recorded articles of the unwritten law is that the sacred name "Yahweh" (English, Jehovah) is not to be pronounced by laymen; see, W. Bacher, in *Jewish Encyclopedia*, Vol. 11, pp. 262-264. A. Marmorstein, *The Old Rabbinic Doctrine of God*, pp. 17-40. Oxford University Press, 1927. G. F. Moore, *Judaism*, Vol. 1, pp. 424 f. The ineffable Name should be uttered only by the priest or the high priest in pronouncing the daily benediction in the Temple (Num. 6:23-27). On such an occasion, Sirach saw the high priest Simon descend from the altar[11] and lift his hands over the whole congregation of Israel: "and the blessing of Yahweh was upon his lips, and he glorified himself with [or, "took pride in"] the name of Yahweh" (50:20, Hebr.). The received Greek text ("to bless God") failed to recognize the reference to the "blessing of Aaron" (36:22, Gr.). Aaron was consecrated "to bless his people in his [Yahweh's] name" (45:15, Hebr.).[12] In contrast with this solemn utterance of the ineffable Name, Sirach strongly deprecates frequent oaths naming "the name of the Lord" (23:10, according to the correct reading of some Greek manuscripts, Chrysostom, and the Ethiopic version), casuistically distinguishing three kinds of wrong oaths (like Pseudo-Phocylides 16 f.): absent-minded false oath, deliberate perjury, and unnecessary oath (23:11; cf. R. Smend, *ad loc.*); or, in the Syriac, absent-minded oath, its breaking, and intentional perjury (rising to a climax). Another casuistic climax occurs in a numerical proverb denouncing the lustful, the onanist (so clearly the Syriac; Fritzsche and Smend understand the incestuous), and the adulterer (23:16 f.). Casuistic also is 23:23: an adulterous woman firstly violates the Law of God (the Seventh Commandment), secondly she injures her husband, and thirdly she commits adultery through fornication and bears children to a strange man.

Certain statutory laws in the Pentateuch ceased to be enforced rigidly and were suspended in the oral law. The death penalty for adultery (Deut. 22:22; Lev. 20:10), for instance, does not seem to have been enforced in the time of Ben Sira (23:24; cf. John 8:4-11). In general, however, Sirach recognizes the supreme authority of the written law: it must be fulfilled because it is God's commandment, even if for no other rational reason (35:5 [Gr. 32:7]). On the contrary, he does not

[11] On the contrary, according to Lev. 9:22 and *Mishna Yoma* 6, 2, the high priest blessed the people *before* (not after) descending from the altar.

[12] "Heaven" (cf. Dan. 4:26 [H. 4:23]; Is. 14:13, LXX; "the Kingdom of Heaven" in Matthew) was one of the substitutes for "Yahweh." Apparently the Greek translation in 26:16 erroneously translated "heaven," meaning here literally the sky, with "the LORD."

hesitate to disregard traditional practices lacking statutory enactment: it was customary for the Jews (and still is) to mourn seven days for a member of the family (22:12; cf. Gen. 50:10; Jth. 16:24), but Sirach recommends unhesitatingly to limit the mourning to a day or two, but not less "on account of gossip" (38:17).

Sirach was familiar with the Scriptures and especially with the Pentateuch. He discloses an expert knowledge (cf. 39:1) of the Mosaic legislation in all its aspects: ritual prescriptions (7:31; 45:6-26; 50; etc.), moral and religious precepts (3:1-16; 3:30-4:10; 7:26 f.; 18:22 f.; 19:13-17; 20:24 f.; 29:1, 9), and civil legislation (7:6 [cf. Lev. 19:15]; 41:19b, 20b, 21bc; etc.). Rules and regulations of the oral law which were eventually codified in the Mishna are already known to Sirach (cf. G. F. Moore, *Judaism*, Vol. 1, p. 40). He speaks of "dusting scale and balance, and wiping off the ephah and the stone [i.e. measures and weights]" (42:4a, Hebr.; the versions and modern interpreters miss the point), like the Mishna: "A shopkeeper must wipe his measures twice a week, and wipe off his weights once a week, and wipe his scales every time he uses them" (*M. Baba Bathra* 5:10).

While as a scribe Sirach was interested in such juristic definition of the statutes, as a teacher he laid the emphasis on right living and true piety, on the attitude of mind rather than on prescribed rituals. Like the rabbis of the Mishna and the Talmud, Sirach interpreted purely civil legislation not merely juristically, but in the spirit of moral and social principles: indeed, the authors of the Deuteronomic Code (under the influence of the prophets) had been guided in their codification and formulation of the Law by the ideals of love for God and man. In commercial transactions one should be not only honest (26:29-27:3), but generous to the point of self-sacrifice (29:1-20). In conversation one should never forget what harm may be occasioned by a careless, hypocritical, or malicious word (5:13; 26:5; 27:16-24; 28:8-26); when injured, one should not take vengeance, but forgive (27:30-28:7; cf. 19:17). Although the Pentateuchal legislation was largely concerned with ritual observances, Sirach's following summary stresses morals rather than ritual: "And he [God] said unto them, 'Beware of all unrighteousness;' and he gave them a commandment, to each one concerning his neighbor [Lev. 19:18]" (17:14). Perhaps the earliest of such summaries of the Law is in the Priestly Code: "Walk in my presence, and be blameless" (Gen. 17:1); Mic. 6:8 is well known, "to do justly, and to love mercy, and to walk humbly with thy God." Jesus summed up the Law in two verses, Deut. 6:5 and, like Sirach, Lev. 19:18 (Matt. 22:37-40); or in the Golden Rule (Matt. 7:12; cf. Luke 6:31), which states affirmatively Hillel's summary of the Law: "Do not do to your fellow what you hate to have done to you" (*Shabbat* 31a; cf. Tob. 4:15, "And what you hate, do to no man"). Leviticus 19:18 is likewise the summary of the Law for St. Paul (Gal. 5:14; cf. Rom. 13:8-10; Jam. 2:8) and for Rabbi Akiba (*Sifrā* on Lev. 19:18; etc.).[13]

Through this moral and religious interpretation of the Law, Sirach's second great contribution, the identification of the Law with wisdom was clearly foreshadowed. Already in Proverbs the ancient Oriental wisdom, which was primarily practical advice leading to a successful and happy life, had been more and more identified with the ethics (Prov. 8:13) and piety (Prov. 1:7, 29, LXX; 2:5; 9:10; 15:33) of Judaism, or with both (Prov. 2). Sirach not only adopted from Proverbs this Jewish notion of wisdom (1:10, 14, 16, 18, 20, 27; 2:3; 15:1a), but proceeded further to identify morals and piety with the keeping of God's commandments (2:15-17; 10:19; 23:27; 28:7; 29:1, 9; 41:8; 49:4 etc.). Thus the identity of Law and wisdom results from the syllogism: wisdom = piety and morals; piety and morals = Law; wisdom = Law (cf. 19:20; 21:11). Another factor contributing to this identification is the growth of the canon of Scriptures in which God had revealed himself: everything indicates that Sirach and his contemporaries regarded Psalms and Proverbs as inspired Scripture (cf. 39:1, mentioning Law, wisdom, and prophecies). As a result, the notion of divine revelation was enlarged beyond the earlier notion of Law and prophecy.

Before Sirach, the Mosaic Law had occasionally been called the wisdom of Israel or of Jehovah (Deut. 4:6 and Ezra 7:25 [compared with 7:14]), without a full realization of the implications involved. But Sirach is the first teacher known to us who regarded both the study of the Law and the search for wisdom as his task, believing that the two were not distinct undertakings. Repeatedly he stresses the identity of Law and wisdom (1:26; 6:37; 9:15; 15:1b, 15; 19:20; 21:11; 24:23; 34:8 [Gr. 31:8]). This notion reappears in later writings (Bar. 3:36-4:1; IV Macc. 1:16 f.; cf. 7:7, 21-23) and becomes basic in rabbinical Judaism (cf. G. F. Moore, *Judaism*, Vol. 1, pp. 263-265). The eternity of the Law (inferred by the rabbis from Prov. 8) is already stated by Sirach (24:9, cf. v. 23). It would be an error, however, to assume that wisdom for Sirach was merely the equivalent of the Law; and we must now determine more exactly Sirach's notion of wisdom.

[13] On these and other summaries of the law see G. F. Moore, *Judaism*, Vol. 2, pp. 83-88. W. H. P. Hatch, "A Syriac Parallel of the Golden Rule" (HTR 14 [1921] 193 f.). H. L. Strack and P. Billerbeck, *Kommentar zum Neuen Testament aus Talmud und Midrasch*, vol. I, pp. 353-364, 459 f., 905-908. Munich, 1922. G. B. King in *Journal of Religion* 8 (1928) 268-279; 15 (1935) 59-62. For the Golden Rule in ten different religions, see S. G. Champion, *The Eleven Religions and their Proverbial Lore*, p. xviii. New York, 1945.

C. Wisdom

Two parallel streams of thought, Law and wisdom, had at their source little connection with religion, being primarily the standards of right conduct for the benefit of the group or of the individual, respectively. Flowing through the centuries in Israel, both became increasingly saturated with morals and religion, until it was thought that both had their source in God and were revealed by him to his chosen people. It was therefore legitimate for Sirach to see the two separate streams come together into one great overflowing river, immense and inexhaustible (24:23-29), out of which his teaching flowed (24:30-34). Sirach's figure is correct, if we understand it to mean that his wisdom derived not only from this stream after it joined the Law, but also from its earlier separate course.

Sirach's teaching illustrates the whole growth of wisdom, from its mundane origins in Egypt to its identification with normative Judaism. His own task as a teacher, as he conceived it, was to prepare his pupils to meet successfully the innumerable problems of life by becoming upright men and pious Jews. Humanism and piety are still distinct in his teaching, as in Proverbs, in spite of his efforts to fuse them. In reality, practical wisdom in Sirach has three aspects: secular, ethical, and religious; they correspond to the three phases in its long development in Egypt, as well as in Israel.

At the same time he is also interested in theoretical wisdom, which searches for the solution of intellectual problems, although he warns his pupils against metaphysical speculations concerning the insoluble mysteries of the universe (3:21-25). Sirach's strong religious feeling colors his philosophical and scientific views no less than his practical advice. His theology, as has been noted, is determined by his religious aspirations, by his assurance that God rewards justly human conduct on this earth. As to man's nature and destiny, Sirach, like many thinkers before and after him, is unable to reconcile optimistic and pessimistic notions. Man was created out of dust (33:10 [Gr. 36:10]) and returns thereto (17:1; cf. 40:11a), being in life flesh and blood (17:31) and in death dust and ashes (10:9; 17:32). The days of his life are few (18:9 f.) and fixed (17:2a), ending inevitably (except for Enoch [44:16; 49:14] and Elijah [48:9]) in death (8:7; 10:9-11; 14:12, 17-19; 38:21-23; 41:3 f.), followed by the gloominess of the underworld (14:16; 17:27; 28:21; 41:4; 48:5; 51:5 f.). How bitter is death to a happy man (41:1), but how welcome, on the contrary, to the victim of an incurable disease (41:2; cf. 30:17; 38:18 f.; Job 3)! In addition to illness (see also 30:14-20; 38:7-14) many woes beset human life (40:1-9) or, through a sudden end of happy conditions (11:6; 26:28), may be imminently impending (18:24-26). For human situations are in continual flux (18:26), determined by God without human knowledge and collaboration (18:6; 42:21cd): destiny is in God's hands, and man's efforts cannot change it (11:2-28). Finally, all men are sinful (8:5; 17:31 f.), ever since Eve's fall (25:24).

There is, however, a reverse to this dismal picture. God created man in his own image (17:3), gave him authority over all earthly things including animals (17:2b, 4), and endowed him with free will (15:11-20), intelligence (17:6-8; 38:6), and wisdom (1:10a); at death the divine spirit returns "on high" to God (40:11b; cf. Eccles. 12:7). The world which God has created is essentially beautiful and good (39:16-22, 26 f., 32-35; 42:15-43:26). God established a cosmic order in the sky (16:26-28) and populated the earth (16:29 f.), so that every human need was supplied in its season (39:16 f., repeated in 39:33 f. and in part in 39:21); all things are different (even opposite, 33:7-15) and yet harmonious (42:23-25). Man's needs are very simple and easily satisfied (29:21; 39:26); happiness is essentially a state of mind free from sorrow and from pangs of conscience (13:25-14:2), for man's conduct and, to some extent, his destiny originate in his thought (37:16-18). Of course, good health is a condition of happiness (cf. 30:14-20). As for the misfortunes of life, they are a punishment of sin (3:26-28; 4:19; 5:7 f.; 6:2-4; 7:3, 16; 27:25-29; etc.), a result of stupidity (8:1-3, 12-19; 9:1-9; 11:29-13:1; 19:4-12; etc.) or gluttony (31:19-21 [Gr. 34:19-21]), an act of God (7:11; 11:14; etc.), a chastisement (18:13 f.; 21:6; 32:14 f. [Gr. 35:14 f.]), a test of piety (2:1-6; 4:17), or even a blessing in disguise (20:9-11). On the other hand, there is much in life that brings gladness (40:18-27) and should be enjoyed in the present, for the future is uncertain and death does not tarry (14:11-19). But one should avoid both self-denial on account of parsimoniousness (14:3-10; 30:18-20) and excess in eating and drinking (31:19-22 [Gr. 34:19-22]; 37:27-31).

We thus pass from Sirach's conception of human life to his practical counsel. As in the Book of Proverbs, his practical wisdom oscillates between good common sense and wishful thinking, between the teaching of daily experience and the teaching of faith.

The motives for right conduct range from self-interest to obedience to God's will for its own sake (cf. 23:23 f.). On the lowest plane, rewards and punishments, which make the strongest appeal to the average person, are presented by moralists of all periods as a powerful inducement for right living. Thus Sirach warns against riotous living, "wine and women," because it leads to poverty and illness (18:30-19:3; cf. 6:2-4; 9:2-9); against telling secrets, because one's reputation is ruined thereby (19:7-9); against protracted intense mourning, because lasting sadness may follow (38:18 f.), but also against omitting mourning entirely, on account of gossip (38:16 f.); against being jealous of one's wife, lest it produce the very realization of one's suspicions (9:1); against sorrow and anxiety, for they make us prematurely old (30:21-24); against receiving favors from fools, for they exact an excessive reward (20:14 f.); against contention with the mighty, for it is risky (8:1 f.; cf. 28:8-12); against going to law with a judge, associating with men of violence, and taking counsel with fools, for obvious reasons (8:14-19; cf. 8:4; 9:13; 11:29-34; 12:8-13:1); against disrespect for the aged (8:6) and joy over the death of a man (8:7; contrast 25:7); and the like. Likewise the following actions are enjoined for one's own advantage: fair treatment of slaves (33:30 f. [Gr. 20:39 f.]), help to a neighbor in need (22:23), almsgiving to the deserving pious (12:1-5; contrast the religious motivation in 4:1-10; 7:11; 12:6); and so forth. In general, evil actions should be avoided, because, like a boomerang, they return to smite their doer (7:1; 27:25-29) or at least, through remorse, destroy his peace of mind (14:2).

The motive of self-interest is dominant in Sirach's counsels concerning the family. Conceiving of the family in Oriental fashion as a patriarchal institution subject to the authority of the paterfamilias, Sirach fails to rate the welfare of the family above that of the father, its despotic chief. With an eye to his future happiness and success (36:22-26 [Gr. 36:27-31]), the young man should marry early in life (26:19-21; cf. 7:23, Hebr.) a worthy woman (36:22-26 [Gr. 36:27-31]) who will make him happy (22:4; 25:8; 26:1-4, 13-18, 26 cf. 7:19). It is a serious error to marry a woman either for her beauty or for her wealth (25:21 f.). Few misfortunes equal marriage to a bad wife (25:16-19, 23; 26:7), such as a garrulous woman (25:20; 26:27 contrast 26:14), one who is jealous of her husband's other wife or concubine (26:6; cf. 37:11; and perhaps 7:26; 25:14); or an intoxicated (26:8), bold (22:5), immoral (26:9-12), or adulterous (9:9; 23:22-26) woman. A wicked wife should be disciplined (25:25) and, if she remains obdurate, divorced (25:26). On the contrary, the husband of a good wife should not divorce her (7:19, 26) but remain true to her (23:18-21; 25:2; cf. 9:1-9; 19:2 f.; 41:17, 20-22).

Sirach is aware that the father's supreme authority (which should never be surrendered before death, 33:19-23 [Gr. 30:28-32]) entails a heavy responsibility, and he gives, in 7:18-28, a comprehensive summary of his duties with respect to wife, servants, cattle, sons, daughters, and parents. In bringing up his sons the father should be strict and not spare the rod (30:1-3, 7-13; cf. 7:23; 22:6; 42:5), so that in life and in death he may receive blessings through them (25:7; 30:4-6) instead of being disgraced (16:1-5; 22:3a). Daughters are a source of unending anxiety to the father: since women are born coquettes, daughters should be kept in strict seclusion until their marriage (7:24 f.; 22:3b-5; 26:10-12; 42:9-12); but whatever measures are taken, women, in Sirach's opinion, are so wicked that even their goodness is worse than a man's wickedness (42:13 f.). Servants should be treated fairly and kindly (7:20 f.; 33:29-31 [Gr. 30:38cd-40]; cf. 4:30; 10:25, Hebr.), hirelings should be paid their wages (34:22b [Gr. 31:27]), but strict discipline should be enforced (33:24-28 [Gr. 30:33-38b]; 42:5).

In conclusion, Sirach deals with family relations from the point of view of the husband and father, whose conduct is motivated primarily by selfish motives (16:1-6; 30:1-6), such as the fear of being publicly disgraced by wife or children—a horrible prospect (22:3a, 5; 42:11), since a good name lasts after death (41:12 f.)—and also eagerness to preserve the family patrimony and enjoy the prestige that it conferred (33:19-23 [Gr. 30:28-32]). Even the duty of honoring one's parents, which Sirach presents as a religious obligation and divine injunction in accordance with the Ten Commandments, is motivated not only by gratitude (7:27 f.) but also by selfish advantage (3:1-16), both temporal (3:5 f.) and spiritual (3:3 f., 14 f.; in 3:1b "that ye may be saved" [LXX] is rendered in the Syriac, "that ye may live the life which is eternal"). It should be noted in particular that a mother's curse may be grievous (3:9; cf. the Egyptian *Wisdom of Ani* [A. Erman, *The Literature of the Ancient Egyptians*, p. 239]) and that honor or respect for one's father atones for sins (3:3, 14 f.). Almsgiving likewise has atoning power (3:30; cf. 29:11-13)—an axiom of Jewish piety (Dan. 4:27 [Aram. 4:24]; Tob. 12:9; 14:11; according to R. Akiba [*Baba Bathra* 10a] benevolence saves from the torments of hell).

Self-advantage also is the keynote of Sirach's advice for social intercourse, although consideration for others is not lacking. Here again the parallel with the Egyptian wisdom literature is apparent. Experience teaches that one should be wisely discriminating in the selection of one's friends and companions (11:29-13:23): impulsive hospitality (11:29-34) and charity (12:1-7), offered to unworthy persons, may result in disappointment and serious harm, as also friendship with wicked or deceitful people (12:8-13:1; cf. 28:13-26) and association with those richer or mightier than oneself (13:2-23). One should cultivate the friendship of the pious (9:14-16), show sympathy to the unfortunate (7:32-36) and help them (4:1-10), behave with deference and self-restraint toward the upper classes (4:7; 8:1 f.; 9:13; 13:9-11), avoid the company of contentious and foolish fellows (8:4 f., 15-17; 22:13-16; 28:8-12), as also confidential conversations with strangers (8:18 f.). Positively Sirach urges respect for the aged (8:6) and the deceased (8:7), indulgence for repentant sinners (8:5), and self-restraint in the presence of scoffers (8:11).

Sirach devotes some attention to three special aspects of social intercourse: dinners, conversation, and friendship. The correct etiquette at dinners and banquets includes moderation in eating and drinking, consideration for others, and conversation which is both appropriate and restrained (31:12-32:6 [Gr. 34:12-35:6]; 37:27-31). The importance of talk in general, and its power for good and evil (37:16-18), is fully realized in our book, as later in the Epistle of James. Wisdom and folly are expressed in words (21:15-17, 25-27). "In talk there is glory and shame, and the tongue of man is his fall" (5:13). There are therefore times when silence is golden (5:12; 20:1-8; 32:4 [Gr. 35:4]), for "a slip on the pavement is better than a slip of the tongue" (20:18-20; cf. 22:27). The "discipline of the mouth" (23:7) implies thoughtful deliberation before talking (5:11), conciseness (32:8 [Gr. 35:8]) and decorum (7:14; 32:9 [Gr. 35:9]) in utterance, and steadfast sincerity of mind (5:10). One should therefore avoid the following sins of the lips: thoughtless and frequent oaths (23:9-12), impure speech (23:13 f.), lies (7:12 f.; 20:24-26; cf. 41:17), which will be detected (36:18-20 [Gr. 36:23-25]), slander (5:14-6:1; 21:28; 28:13-26), hypocrisy (1:28-30), disclosure of one's own (8:17-19) or a friend's (27:16-21) secrets, pretense of friendship (12:16-18; 27:22-24), gossip (19:6-12), hasty judgments based on hearsay (11:7; 19:13-17), provocative language (28:8-12; cf. 27:30-28:7), mockery (11:4-6; 27:28), and boasts (4:29). It is foolish to ask the advice of people who are hostile and prejudiced (37:10 f.).

Joseph Addison wrote a charming essay commending Sirach's precepts and observations on friendship (*The Spectator*, Vol. 1, No. 68; dated May 18, 1711). He observed that Ecclesiasticus "would be regarded by our modern wits as one of the most shining tracts of morality that is extant, if it appeared under the name of a Confucius, or of any celebrated Grecian philosopher." Sirach places a high value on friendship (6:14-17), particularly with an old friend whom he compares to old wine (9:10), although naturally a good wife (40:23) and a good son (30:3-6) are even more precious. A true friend should not be exchanged for money (7:18); on the contrary, one should gladly lose money for his sake (29:10) and, out of self-interest, remain loyal to him in his poverty (22:23, 25 f.; cf. 6:8-13; 10:23, 30; 13:21-23). Affability and cordiality (as also avoidance of loquacity, 20:8, 13) establish good relations with many acquaintances, but intimate friends are always few (6:5 f.): they should be chosen with care after a searching test (6:7-13) and never be condemned without affording them the opportunity to exculpate themselves (19:13-17), remembering that evil men delight in stirring up strife between friends (28:9). In general, one should choose one's friends within one's social class (13:15-23) and among persons of integrity and piety (9:11-16); one should not only refrain from doing them harm (7:12), but also help them generously in their hour of need (14:13; 37:5 f.; cf. 22:23, 25 f.). While good friends are thus "the medicine of life" (6:16; in the

Hebrew: "a bundle of life," cf. I Sam. 25:29), false friends are its poison. For false friends, impelled by self-interest, will not hesitate to give harmful counsel for their own benefit (37:7-11; contrast 37:12), to become enemies in days of affliction after pretending friendship in days of prosperity (6:8-13; 12:8 f.; 37:1-4), to make promises which they cannot keep (20:23), to betray secrets (19:4-10; 22:22; 27:16-21; 42:1). Hypocritical friends are really enemies in disguise (12:10-13:1; 27:22-24): heartless (41:21a) and treacherous (41:18c), they may cause unforgivable harm (22:19-22), although as often as not the evil they plot falls back upon their own heads (27:25-29).

The motive of self-interest, obvious in Sirach's counsels concerning family and social relationships, is prominent, in the third place, in his discussion of wealth, although ethical principles are not disregarded. Sirach regards the calling of the scribe or scholar as the noblest profession (38:24-34), because learning is a prerequisite for leadership in public assemblies (38:33), in courts of law (38:33; cf. 7:6), in schools (38:33), and in synagogues (39:5-8). Nevertheless, Sirach admits that other professions make essential contributions to the life of the community (38:32): without husbandmen (38:25 f.; cf. 7:15), seal engravers (38:27), smiths (38:28), potters (38:29 f.), and others (like merchants [42:4], physicians [38:1-7], and apothecaries [38:8]), no city can be inhabited. In the Egyptian wisdom books and still in Proverbs, education in the schools was chiefly vocational and prepared the young for careers as public servants. Sirach instead regards public office as only one of the secondary functions of the learned (39:4; cf. 11:1; 20:27); in fact, he distinctly exhorts his pupils to repress all ambition for high public office (7:4-7), in view of the pitfalls of politics with which he was familiar, possibly through a bitter personal experience but certainly through observation.

Sirach recognizes the advantages of wealth and tells his pupils how to acquire and preserve it. Hard work (7:15) is the basic requirement for accumulating a fortune honestly (20:28; 25:3; 31:3 [Gr. 34:3]); conversely, indolence (4:29), which is sometimes inspired by pride in one's education (10:26), leads to penury (10:27; 31:4 [Gr. 34:4]) and public contempt (22:1 f.). Preserving one's self-respect (10:28 f.), one should avoid becoming a vagabond (29:21-28) and a beggar (40:28-30). A man of substance is esteemed (10:30 f.; 13:23), attracts friends (13:21; cf. 6:8-13; 12:8 f.; 37:4) and supporters (13:22), retains the supreme authority in his family by keeping control of his patrimony until his death (33:19-23 [Gr. 30:28-32]), can (and should!) enjoy the pleasures of life (14:3-19), avoiding excesses (18:30-19:3), if he is in good health (30:14-20). He is able to help the needy, thus attaining favor with men and God (3:31; 4:1-6; 7:32; 18:15-18; 22:23; 29:1-20) while avoiding baneful curses (4:5 f.). In a word, "riches are good to him that is without sin" (13:24), although other blessings are even more precious (40:18-27), and occasionally wealth is a source of anxiety (31:1 f. [Gr. 34:1 f.]).

Sirach does not overestimate the value of wealth. He admits that poverty, in spite of disadvantages such as the loss of friends (13:21b), power (13:19 f.), and prestige (13:22 f.) usually resulting from it, is preferable to illness (30:14-17) and does not prevent a wise man from attaining honors and high positions (10:30-11:1); nay, it may even be useful in deterring from sin (20:21) and idleness (31:4 [Gr. 34:4]). Pride in the poor, like deceit in the rich, was particularly offensive to Sirach (25:2; cf. 13:24). Indeed wealth, when acquired and used improperly, is pernicious. Wealth may be amassed dishonestly through theft (cf. 20:25), misappropriation of funds (21:8), commercial fraud (26:29-27:2; particularly false weights, 42:4) and acceptance of bribes (20:29). But such apparent success is deceiving (20:9-11), for unrighteous gain is ephemeral (40:13-17) and the Lord may snatch away suddenly not only the wealth (cf. 16:13) but even the life of the man who feels secure in his riches (11:10-28; cf. Luke 12:16-21): "Trust not in deceiving treasures, for they avail nothing in the day of [God's] wrath" (5:8, Hebr.). In the presence of God, the power of wealth is but a snare and a delusion (5:1-3), notably when wealth is offered to God as a bribe (35:12 [Gr. 32:14 f.]). Love for gold and trust in it are grievous sins (31:5-11 [Gr. 34:5-11]), and excessive zeal in the pursuit of riches is both wrong and disappointing (11:10-13). Wealth gives to the wicked the power to oppress the needy (13:3-7, 19 f.), for their gold corrupts the judges (8:2) and blinds their eyes to the rights of the poor (20:29).

Wealth may be speedily lost through riotous living (9:6; 18:32-19:1), through distribution of one's estate to the family (33:19-23 [Gr. 30:28-32]), through indiscriminate lending (29:4-7) and becoming liable for the payment of another man's debt (29:18), and through an act of God, from whom come poverty and wealth (11:14), particularly in the case of dishonest riches (40:13-16; cf. 41:6). Sirach, however, enjoins the help of a neighbor in need, through charity, lending, and surety even in spite of the possible loss of money and ingratitude that may follow (29:1-20): "lose money for a brother and a friend" (29:10), but not for a man of higher social rank (8:12 f.); neither should alms be given to a sinner (12:4-7).

Common sense, with occasional ethical overtones, thus characterizes Sirach's discussion of economic conditions. Riches are presented as a good servant, able to accomplish much good, but as a bad master, crushing the noblest impulses of the human spirit. The man of substance should enjoy the pleasures and comforts he can afford (14:11-19), without forgetting that his wealth may vanish overnight (18:25 f.) and without squandering his property to satisfy his lusts (18:30-19:3). The man in modest circumstances should live within his means, remembering that life's necessities are merely food, clothing, and shelter (29:21), and that it is far better to live simply and independently than to enjoy luxuries in humiliating fashion at the expense of others (29:22-28).

D. Morals

Moral precepts and principles have been occasionally noticed above in dealing with religion, Law, and wisdom; it seems desirable neverthe-less to sketch separately the ethical system of Sirach.

His fundamental principle is derived from Amos and the other reform-ing prophets who followed him: the norm of ethical conduct is the will of God (2:15-17; 15:11-13; 25:1; 32:14 [Gr. 35:14]; 35:3 [Gr. 32:5]). But Sirach went one step further; in harmony with a tenet which became more and more basic in Judaism after the discovery of the Book of the Law in 621 B.C., he recognized that God had revealed his will in his Law (2:16, where God's good pleasure or approval is equivalent to the Law). As in Deuteronomy, to fear and love the Lord means to keep his com-mandments (10:19; 37:12; cf. 15:1). The Law was revealed to Moses (45:5) and Aaron (45:17), and is substantially identified with the Pentateuch, "the book of the covenant of God the Highest, the Law which Moses commanded" (24:23). But by identifying the Law with wisdom (ch. 24), which, according to Prov. 8:22-31, was born before God created the world (cf. Job 28), Sirach apparently concluded that the Law was as old as creation (a view held by later Jewish teachers, cf. G. F. Moore, *Judaism*, Vol. 1, p. 266). After speaking of the creation of mankind and of its divinely granted excellencies (17:1-10), Sirach proceeds at once to the revelation of the covenant and the Law (17:11-14), as if it had been made to Adam rather than to Moses; moreover, the divine covenant and commandments were known to Abraham (44:20).

Characteristically Sirach stresses the moral teaching of the Penta-teuchal law, which he summarizes (17:14) in the words "beware of all unrighteousness (*ádikon*)" (cf. Lev. 19:15, 35), and in the command-ment concerning one's neighbor (Lev. 19:18). He never enjoins the fulfillment of numerous ritual prescriptions in the Pentateuch, such as the observance of Sabbaths and festivals, dietary laws, purifications (cf. 34:25 [Gr. 31:30]); he does not even mention the ritual prohibitions in regard to idolatry, superstitions, and heathen customs (except divina-tion, 34:5 [Gr. 31:5]). Circumcision (44:20) and the Temple rituals are only mentioned in historical retrospects (reaching to the deceased high priest Simon), as if Sirach (like Amos) considered them secondary in the fulfillment of God's will. This attitude appears clearly in what Sirach has to say about sacrifice. On the one hand, he recommends the presentation of sacrifices and offerings (7:31; cf. 38:11; in 14:11b the LXX misunderstands the Hebrew), but only because such is God's command (35:1, 5 [Gr. 32:1 f., 7]) and with more emphasis on the right mental attitude of the worshiper (35:6-10 [Gr. 32:8-12]; contrast 34:18-20 [Gr. 31:21-24]) than on the monetary value of the sacrifice (7:8 f.); on the other hand, he regards right living as the offering most pleasing to the Lord (35:2 f. [Gr. 32:3-5]). In general, however, Sirach is chiefly concerned with virtues and faults in daily conduct, with right behavior in illness and in health, in prosperity and in poverty, in public and private affairs, in the circle of the family and in social relationships.

Nevertheless, Sirach seems to have given some thought to the speculative problem of the origin of moral evil. His starting point may have been Jeremiah's recognition that the obduracy of the human heart is the root of sin (Jer. 5:23 f.), which, as in this passage, is essentially, according to Sirach, a rebellion against God (10:12 f., contrast 10:19). It seems that the doctrine of the evil impulse (*yeṣer hā-ra'*, cf. G. F. Moore, *Judaism* I, 479-483; III, 146 f.), which appears in Old Testament passages later than Jeremiah (Gen. 6:5; 8:21; cf. Deut. 31:21; I Chron. 28:9; 29:18; Is. 26:3), was ultimately derived from this prophet; in his commentary on *Genesis* (3rd ed., Göttingen, 1910; p. 60), H. Gunkel on the contrary, claims that this notion of human sinfulness is preprophetic. Recognizing that this *yeṣer* (impulse) in man induces him to sin, Sirach was faced with three problems: Is man the slave of this impulse and thus incapable of choosing his conduct freely? Did God create the impulse? And if so, is God responsible for human sin?

Sirach emphatically asserts that man is free to choose between right and wrong (15:15-17; cf. Ps. of Sol. 9) and is thus responsible for his fate, although at times he may need divine help to overcome his evil inclinations (22:27-23:6, cf. Ps. of Sol. 16:6-15), for he is but "dust and ashes" (17:32) and "does not repress his *yeṣer* because he is but flesh and blood" (17:31 in the Syriac; the Greek, taking *yeṣer* as a verb, reads, "and an evil-doer [variants: evil; the man who] thinks of flesh and blood"). However, according to the Syriac in 21:11, "he that keeps the Law controls his *yeṣer* (Gr. *ennoēma*, thought; Lat. *sensus*); nevertheless, even the God-fearing must be vigilant, lest they fall (2:7). In fact, since all men have the evil impulse (17:31 f.), all men are sinners (8:5; 19:16; cf. I Kings 8:46; Job 4:17 ff.; 15:15-16; 25:5 f.; Prov. 20:9; Eccles. 7:20; etc.). Nevertheless, all may turn to God and forsake their iniquity (17:25 f.; cf. 5:4-7; 21:1; 34:25 f. [Gr. 31:30 f.]). It is clear that Sirach, like many after him, failed to reconcile logically the doctrine of free will, required by moral responsibility, with human sinfulness, the power of which seems at times irresistible.

The second problem is simple. On the premise that God is the creator of all that exists it follows that God placed in man the evil impulse. "God created man from the beginning and delivered him into the hand of his *yeṣer* (Gr., *diaboúlion*)" (15:14); the Hebrew adds, between the two lines, "and placed him in the hand of his spoiler." The gloss is a dogmatic correction, even though its meaning is ambiguous: man's spoiler is probably Satan, rather than human robbers as in 4:19, where the Hebrew uses another word variously misread or misunderstood in the versions (except in the Syriac, in which "spoilers" [as in the Hebrew text of 15:14] occurs). This identification of the evil impulse with the devil appears occasionally in rabbinical writings (cf. G. F. Moore, *Judaism*, Vol. 1, pp. 493 f.), and has been detected, by some interpreters, in 21:27 (Gr.), "When the ungodly [Syr., "fool"] curses Satan [*tòn satanân*; Latin, diabolum (the devil); Syr., "the one who has not sinned against him"], he curses his own soul." But "Satan" (as in the LXX of I Kings 11:14, cf. vv. 23 and 25 in some texts) may mean a human "adversary." The divine creation of the *yeṣer* seems to be mentioned likewise in 37:3, where the Hebrew text is usually emended to read: "O evil impulse! Why then were you created?" This emendation of the extant Hebrew text, which actually reads "Woe to the evil man who says, 'Why was I created?'" is supported by the Greek ("O wicked imagination, whence camest thou rolling in?") and the Syriac ("The enemy and the wicked, why were they created?"). The Greek text of 17:6 also refers to the creation of the *yeṣer*: "*Yeṣer* [*diaboúlion*, cf. 15:14] and tongue and eyes, ears and heart he gave them to understand"; but the Syriac may be correct in reading the consonants of *yeṣer* as a verb: "He *created* for them mouth and tongue, eyes and ears; and a heart to understand he assigned to them." Finally, Sirach's belief that the evil impulse was implanted by God in the first human beings he created may be inferred from their sin (cf. IV Esd. 3:21 f.): "From a woman [Eve] was the beginning of sin, and because of her we all die" (25:24, without important differences in the Hebrew and the versions). Incidentally, this is the earliest doctrinal interpretation of the story of the Garden of Eden (Gen. 3). The notion that man became mortal through the fall of Adam and Eve is unknown before Sirach and quite alien to Gen. 3, but prevailed later (Wisd. of Sol. 2:23 f.; IV Esd. 3:7, 21; 7:116-126; Syr. Bar. 17:3; 23:4; 48:42 f.; 54:15, 19; Rom. 5:12-21; for rabbinical parallels see, H. L. Strack and P. Billerbeck, *Kommentar zum Neuen Testament*, Vol. 3, pp. 227-229. Munich, 1926).

The third problem—whether God is responsible for human sin—is a phase of the problem of theodicy (in view of the presence of evil, is God both just and almighty?) and therefore ultimately insoluble. Sirach does not deal with it metaphysically, but from the point of view of faith, and fails to solve rationally the antinomies inherent in the problem.

The first contradiction is that God created a world which is good and beautiful (39:16-22, 32-35; cf. 42:15-43:33), and yet in which much is pernicious to human beings (39:27-31): according to Sirach, the pious understand that good things were created for both good and wicked persons (39:23-27), but good and evil things were created to punish the wicked (39:27-31).

A second contradiction is detected in man's nature. Human beings were created by God as miserable creatures beset by trouble during their brief span of life (40:1-10; cf. 10:9-11; 14:17-19; 17:1-2a; 18:8-10; 28:5 f.), but at the same time they were made according to God's image to have dominion over other creatures (17:2b-4), endowed with intelligence (17:6 f.; cf. 38:6 and the Stoic gloss in 17:15) and piety (17:8-14), and are the object of God's mercy (18:11-14). There is no logical solution for this contradiction, and Sirach refrains from explaining why man should be

> Half dust, half deity, alike unfit
> To sink or soar. . . .
>
> Byron, *Manfred*

The contradictory fate that besets men, some being fortunate and others unlucky, is generally explained by Sirach as a just divine retribution for their conduct. In one passage, however, he seems to recognize that God, who made all men out of clay, blessed and exalted some but cursed and abased others arbitrarily, as a potter fashions the clay (33:10-15 [Greek 36:10-15]). Whether Sirach means that God exalted Israel and debased the heathen (and the Canaanites in particular), or whether he means that human beings in general are born lucky or unlucky, he recognized that God does this "in his great wisdom" and no other explanation is possible.

The fourth dilemma follows from the third. If, as Sirach says in the preceding passage, man is in the power of his Creator like clay in the hands of a potter, is he a free and responsible agent? With little concern about logic Sirach emphatically asserts man's freedom of choice (15:14-19). Consequently, it is an error to attribute one's transgressions to God (15:11 f.)—this blasphemy is for Philo (*De profugis* 16 [M. I, 558]) an unpardonable sin. For God detests iniquity (15:13) and ordered no man to sin (15:20), even though he created the evil impulse in man. Sin originated with Eve, and because of her we all must die (25:24). God is at work to extirpate sinfulness: in his wrath he destroys the stiff-necked (16:6-11), but he chastises mercifully (16:12) and by reproof, chastisement, and teaching he brings men back to himself (18:13 f.). To those who love him he gives wisdom (43:33; cf. 1:26 f.; 14:20-27; 15:1; 19:20). Thus he has provided, through wisdom which is his Law, the means for overcoming the innate evil impulse (21:11). Sin, in conclusion, is a freely determined act of insolence against God (10:13), but such insolence is not the divinely given heritage of man (10:18).

Thus Sirach regards sin as a conscious and deliberate action or thought in defiance to God and his Law. He distinguishes between errors committed in ignorance and willful transgressions (23:2 f.): only the latter are stressed in his moral code, the best summary of which is furnished in ch. 23, beginning with 22:27 (23:1, repeated in 23:4a, should probably be omitted). Here Sirach prays for deliverance from two types of sin, wrong speech and sexual lust (22:27-23:6), which he proceeds to describe in detail (23:7-15 and 23:16-27, respectively). Elsewhere he condemns sins against God (the duties toward God form the subject of ch. 2, in particular; see also 5:4-7) and against fellow men, particularly in the family (3:1-16; 7:19-28; 30:1-13), in social intercourse (7:12 f., 18; 10:6; 27:16-28:36), in commercial transactions (5:8; 26:29-27:3; 42:1-7), and in political life (20:27-31). Sirach recommends patience in hardship (2:1-14) and humility in prosperity (3:17-25), and warns against pride (1:30; 7:16 f; 10:6-18), boastfulness (10:26-29), and envy (9:11 f.; 14:8-10). Nor does he forget man's duties to himself (13:24-14:27). In fact, his chief argument in urging the observance of the Law, the attainment of wisdom, piety, and the practice of right conduct is that they alone bring prosperity and happiness (cf. 3:17; 7:35; 12:1 f.); for wickedness results in misfortune. He summarizes this basic principle in 7:1-3 (slightly revised by comparison of the Hebrew with the versions): "Commit not evil, and evil will not overtake you; avoid iniquity, and it will turn away from you; sow not in the furrows of unrighteousness, lest you reap it sevenfold." Conversely, in a positive form, this principle is stated in 3:31a (Hebr.): "Whoever does good will meet it again on his ways."

This retribution of human conduct is not automatic but is definitely God's work. This doctrine, as has been noted, is basic in Sirach's thought and in contemporary Judaism. "He is a God of justice" (35:12 [Gr. 32:15], Hebr.), "the righteous judge" (35:16 [Gr. 32:21], Hebr.), who "gives retribution to man in accordance to his deeds and recompenses mankind according to its devices" (35:19 [Gr. 32:24], Hebr.; cf. 16:12; 17:23), sometimes only at death (11:26-28).

It is thus clear that Sirach's ethical system is essentially religious: it is God who in his Law, the Pentateuch, establishes the standards of right conduct, rewards virtue and punishes sin, and can wipe away sin and its ominous consequences. This third point remains now to be considered.

Although the righteous man strives to regulate his life by God's Law in piety and humility (2:15-18), prepared to endure afflictions patiently (2:1-6; 32:14 [Gr. 35:14]) in view of glorious rewards (1:11-20; 2:7-11) and of protection in time of trouble (32:24-33:1 [Gr. 35:24-36:1]), owing to the "inclination of flesh and blood" (17:31; cf. 23:4-6; 37:3) no man is sinless (8:5; cf. 4:26; 7:8. See G. F. Moore, *Judaism*. Vol. 1, pp. 467 f.), with the possible exception of Enoch (44:16), Noah (44:17), Abraham (44:19 f.), Moses (45:1-5), Aaron (45:6), Samuel (46:13), Jeremiah (49:7), and Job (49:9, Hebr.). It therefore becomes imperative for God to provide a remedy for universal human sinfulness, lest all men perish in their sins. God is both just and merciful: "mercy and wrath are with him, he forgives and pardons, but causes his wrath to rest on the wicked" (16:11). But the sinner should not count on God's great mercies and forgiveness for the remission of his sins (5:4-6) unless he turns to God contritely (5:7). It is only to those who sincerely repent that God "grants a return" (17:24), forgiving their sins: "Turn unto the Lord and forsake sins, supplicate in his presence and so lessen the offense" (17:25; cf. 17:26), for God's mercy and forgiveness are great unto those who turn to him (17:29), since he takes no pleasure in those that perish (17:27). The first condition for forgiveness is therefore true repentance, meaning forsaking evil deeds (21:2 f.) and intentions, and turning to God: "In the time of sins, show repentance" (18:21). Without repentance, neither fasting (34:25 f. [Gr. 31:30 f.]; 35:12 [Gr. 32:14 f.]) nor prayer (34:26 [Gr. 31:31]) nor sacrifices and offerings (7:9; 34:19 [Gr. 31:23]) are of any avail. But after a man has first "examined himself" (18:20), then "put away wrong doing, purified his hands, and cleansed his heart from all manner of sin" (38:10) in sincere repentance, he may atone for his sins through right living (35:3 [Gr. 32:5]), almsgiving (3:30 f.; 7:9), which is an acceptable sacrifice (35:2 [Gr. 32:3 f.]), and filial piety (3:3, 14 f.). The right attitude of mind following repentance is shown in the confession of sins (4:26), in supplication for forgiveness (2:10 f.; 7:10; 17:25; 21:1), in forgiving those who trespass against us (28:1-7; cf. Matt. 6:14 f.; 18:32 f.), and also in offering a sacrifice (38:11; cf. 35:6 f. [Gr. 32:8 f.]; 45:16). It is thus evident that Sirach, and contemporary Judaism in general, anticipated the Christian analysis of repentance into: *contritio cordis, confessio oris, satisfactio operis,* or grief of the heart (18:21), confession of the mouth (4:26), and atonement through deeds like almsgiving (3:30 f.).

In conclusion, Sirach has left us the earliest extant exposition of the tenets of normative Judaism. How much he learned from his teachers is unknown to us; for the rest, he derived his instruction equally from the Scriptures and from personal reflection on his observation of life in Jerusalem and abroad. Like other thinkers, he influenced later generations, although not all of his original teaching bore fruit in Rabbinic Judaism.[14]

3. The Style of Ecclesiasticus

As everyone knows, the style of an author can be characterized only by a study of his own words, *ipsissima verba*. Unfortunately we do not possess a fairly accurate transcript of Ben Sira's book, and cannot hope to reach conclusions valid in all details in a study of his literary art. It is true that we do not rely entirely on the two extant translations of his work, the Greek and the Syriac, for in 1896-1900 the bulk (about two-thirds) of the Hebrew text of the book[15] was recovered from four manuscripts dating from the eleventh and twelfth centuries, found in the Genizah ("hiding place," meaning the synagogue repository for worn-out manuscripts) at Fostat (*Fusṭâṭ*, Old Cairo), immediately south of Cairo. But it is clear that these manuscripts, written more than a millennium after Sirach's time, are seriously corrupt: the Jews did not regard the book as canonical Scripture and therefore did not take pains to preserve its text intact, as in the case of the Hebrew Bible. It will never be possible to recover the authentic Hebrew text of Sirach's book in all details; nevertheless, R. Smend, in his textual commentary (*Die Weisheit des Jesus Sirach*. Berlin, 1906) and in his edition of the Hebrew text with German translation (*Die Weisheit des Jesus Sirach hebräisch und deutsch*. Berlin, 1906; see also his *Griechisch-syrisch-hebräischer Index zur Weisheit des Jesus Sirach*. Berlin, 1907) has provided us with the standard textual apparatus. It was utilized in the critical English translation by W. O. E. Oesterley and G. H. Box (in R. H. Charles's *Apocrypha and Pseudepigrapha*, Vol. I. Oxford, 1913), which is based on a reconstructed text combining the readings of the Hebrew, Greek, and Syriac recensions. The best account of the textual history of Ecclesiasticus will be found in M. H. Segal's important monograph on "The Evolution of the Hebrew Text of Ben Sira" (JQR N.S. 25 [1934] 91-149). Although a few scholars in recent times (A. Büchler, in JQR N.S. 13 [1922-23] 320; C. H. Gordon, in JBL 56 [1937] 415; H. L. Ginzberg, in

---

[14] For quotations of Sirach in the Talmud, Saadia, and other rabbinical writings, see A. E. Cowley and Ad. Neubauer, *The Original Hebrew of a Portion of Ecclesiasticus*, pp. xix-xxx; cf. the Preface. Oxford, 1897. R. Smend, *Die Weisheit des Jesus Sirach*, pp. xlvi-lvi. Berlin, 1906.

[15] The following passages are *not* available in Hebrew: 1:1-3:5; 16:26-18:22; 18:24-30; 19:4-20:3; 20:8-12; 20:14-21:21; 21:24-25:1; 25:4-7, 9-12, 14-16, 25 f.; 26:4-27:4; 27:7-30:10; 33:4-35:8 [Gr. 36:4-16a; 30:25-32:10]; 38:28-39:14. The list has been compiled from R. Smend's edition of the Hebrew text (Berlin, 1906), in which Talmudic and rabbinical quotations are added to the text of the Genizah manuscripts. J. Marcus (JQR N.S. 23 [1930-31] 223-40) has since published 33:4-35:8, for the most part.

ZAW N.F. 14 [1937] 309; etc.) still consider the Hebrew fragments as a translation, Segal has proved, to the present writer's satisfaction, that they are an offshoot of Sirach's manuscript, although occasionally influenced by the three other early recensions (the first and second Greek, and the Syriac texts).

In view of the uncertainty of the text, any conclusion as to the type of Hebrew used by Ben Sira is apt to be precarious. It is obvious that the Hebrew fragments of his book contain words and expressions belonging to Rabbinic Hebrew. Although Aramaic was the vernacular of many Palestinian Jews in Sirach's day, Hebrew remained the language of scholars (*lešōn ha-ḥakhamîm*, tongue of the sages, as the Talmud calls it),[16] like Latin in the Middle Ages. As a literary language, Hebrew has remained alive until our time, when it has again become the vernacular of the Jews in Palestine. Inevitably in Sirach, as in the latest Old Testament books, a certain artificiality appeared in the vocabulary, imitation of ancient models produced archaisms, and the influence of the Aramaic vernacular proved irresistible.[17] On the basis of the characteristics of the Hebrew employed by Ben Sira opposite conclusions have been drawn. On the one hand, I. Lévi (*op. cit.*, Vol. 1, p. xxvii) and W. R. Taylor (*op. cit.*, p. 16) regard Sirach's book as unquestionably later than anything in the Old Testament; while, on the other hand Th. Nöldeke (*op. cit.* pp. 87-93) no less emphatically dates it before Daniel, Esther, and even Chronicles; and R. Smend (*op. cit.*, p. xliii) considers it rash to conclude from late Hebrew expressions in Sirach that certain Biblical books are earlier in date, stating that "Sirach masters the Hebrew language much better than the authors of Chronicles, Ecclesiastes, Daniel, Esther, and some Psalms" (cf. Cowley and Neubauer, *op. cit.*, pp. xliii f.). Since our information on the development of Hebrew between 300 B.C. and A.D. 100 is meager, and since some of the most modern expressions in the Sirach manuscripts may come from medieval scribes (cf. Nöldeke, p. 84), dogmatic conclusions are unwarranted. In any case, since the dates of Sirach (*ca.* 180) and of the Hebrew parts of Daniel (*ca.* 164) are known, it cannot be gainsaid that the Old Testament

---

[16] I cannot agree with Isr. Lévi, *L'Ecclésiastique*, Part I, p. xxii (Bibliothèque de l'École des Hautes Études, Sciences Religieuses II, I. Paris, 1898), when he claims that "Hebrew had not yet been supplanted by Aramaic, before the Christian Era, particularly in Judea."

[17] For examples of late Hebrew in Ben Sira see, in addition to the glossaries of R. Smend and others, the following publications. A. E. Cowley and Ad. Neubauer, *The Original Hebrew of a Portion of Ecclesiasticus*, pp. xxxi-xxxvi (by S. R. Driver). Th. Nöldeke, "Bemerkungen zum hebräischen Ben Sira" (ZAW 20 [1900] 81-94). Isr. Lévi, *L'Ecclésiastique*, Part II, xl-xlv. R. Smend, *Die Weisheit des Jesus Sirach*, pp. xliii-xlvi. W. R. Taylor, *The Originality of the Hebrew Text of Ben Sira in the Light of the Vocabulary and the Versions* (Doctoral Thesis, University of Toronto). Toronto, 1910. S. Lieberman, "Ben Sira à la lumière du Yerouchalmi" (REJ 97 [1934] 50-57).

contains writings later than Ecclesiasticus; thus Smend's view seems to be in harmony with the evidence accessible to us. In general, Sirach writes classical Hebrew, but he also reflects the language of his time. No better Hebrew was written in the second century B.C., as far as we know.

Sirach's book is generally classed as Palestinian wisdom literature and is often equated to the Proverbs of Solomon:[18] E. Schürer even calls it "the uncanonical duplicate [or "wraith," *Doppelgänger*] of the canonical Proverbs" (*Protest. Realenzycl.* of J. J. Herzog, 3rd ed. by A. Hauck, Vol. 1, p. 650). While superficially correct, such a comparison may become misleading. For although Sirach often echoes Proverbs and may possibly have used the book as his model (as A. Edersheim asserts in H. Wace, *Apocrypha*, Vol. 2, p. 20), his own book differs from the earlier one in general structure and teaching, as well as in numerous details. Wisdom, for instance, in Proverbs is either common sense or morality and religion, but in Sirach it is substantially identified with the Law of Moses; the "searching of the Scriptures" characteristic of Sirach and later Jews is totally foreign to the authors of Proverbs.[19]

Sirach, as noted above, was a Biblical scholar, a scribe. His grandson is correct in saying, in the preface to his Greek translation of the book, that Sirach "having devoted himself in a more than ordinary degree to the reading of the Law, and the Prophets, and the other books of the Fathers, and having acquired sufficient skill [or, "considerable familiarity"] therein, he was also himself induced to compose one [of the books] pertaining to education and wisdom . . ." Sirach indeed considers himself merely as the last one who kept the watch (at the gates of wisdom, Prov. 8:34; the Syriac reads, "I came last"), a mere gleaner after the grape gatherers, or canonical writers (33:16-18 [Gr. 36:16a] 30:25-27), a mere rivulet out of the (scriptural) river (24:30-32)—although, without false modesty, he believes that in his book he has poured out doctrine similar to prophecy (24:33).

A perusal of Sirach's book shows that he is familiar with the canonical books of the Old Testament in existence at the time. In addition to "The Law and the Prophets" (the Pentateuch; Joshua, Judges, Samuel, Kings, Isaiah, Jeremiah, Ezekiel, and the Twelve Minor Prophets), which were canonical in 200 B.C., Sirach refers to the three great poetical Hagiographa (Psalms, Proverbs, and Job) and Chronicles, Nehemiah (but not Ezra). He ignores Daniel (which was not yet written) and the "Five Scrolls"

[18] So already Saadia Gaon (d. 942) in his *Sefer ha-Galui*: "The Book of Ben Sira is a work on ethics, similar in form to Proverbs . . ."

[19] For a detailed comparison of Proverbs and Ecclesiasticus see J. C. Gasser *Die Bedeutung der Sprüche Jesu ben Sira für die Datierung des althebräischen Spruchbuches.* Gütersloh, 1904. See also W. Baumgartner, in ZAW 34 (1914) 195-197.

(Canticles, Ruth, Lamentations, Ecclesiastes,[20] and Esther), also ignored by Philo (although they were circulating in his time). A number of lists of scriptural allusions in Sirach have been compiled,[21] but, as Th. Nöldeke (ZAW 20 [1900] 87) and R. Smend (*op. cit.* p. xlii, n. 1) have observed, not all the parallels adduced are significant and valid. It is, however, clear that the language of Ben Sira is saturated with Biblical expressions and that he echoes the Scriptures, particularly in his Hymn to the Fathers (44-49) and in the prayers in chapters 36 (Gr. 33:1-13a; 36:16b-22) and 51. Owing to the similarity of the subject, Proverbs is naturally the book most frequently imitated by Ben Sira.

It would, however, be an exaggeration[22] to say, with Isr. Lévi, that "the diction employed is essentially imitative, being a mixture of Biblical centos and reminiscences" (*Jewish Encyclopedia* XI, 395), or that "the book is a 'digestive assimilation' of Scripture" (J. H. A. Hart, *Ecclesiasticus*, p. 235). A comparison with Proverbs and other wisdom books reveals the originality of thought and expression of Sirach, in spite of the biblical character of his language.

Divergent opinions on the structure and plan of Sirach's book as a whole have been noted at the beginning of this chapter, and the present writer's conclusions on the matter have been presented there in the summary of the book. Here we must examine only the structure of the individual sections within the book. While Proverbs (except in chs. 1-9 and the last chapters) consists chiefly of individual verses or distichs complete in themselves and unrelated to one another, such separate aphorisms are comparatively rare in Ecclesiasticus, which is a collection of longer essays in verse. In this respect the book resembles, in a general way, the Book of Job, without, however, approaching its unrivaled poetic brilliance.

The verse of Ben Sira is the standard Hebrew verse consisting of two hemistichs having four stress accents each (4:4 meter). In the Hebrew Codex B (containing most of 30:11-51:30), each verse is written on a separate line (18 to a page) and a space divides the two hemistichs (cf. the photograph of one page, containing 37:11-24, in the *Jewish Encyclopedia* XI, 394; a complete collotype facsimile of the Hebrew

---

[20] R. Smend (*Die Weisheit des Jesus Sirach*, p. 457) finds a possible allusion to Eccl. 2:20 in Ecclus. 47:23, and Th. Nöldeke (ZAW 20 [1900] 92) has been induced by S. Schechter to regard Sirach's acquaintance with Ecclesiastes as probable. In spite of the authority of these great scholars, the present writer believes that Ecclesiastes was written after Sirach's book.

[21] S. Schechter and C. Taylor, *The Wisdom of Ben Sira*, pp. 13-32. Cambridge, 1899. N. Peters, *Der jüngst wieder aufgefundene hebräische Text des Buches Ecclesiasticus*, pp. 81 f. Freiburg i. B., 1902. J. C. Gasser, *Die Bedeutung der Sprüche Jesu Ben Sira*, pp. 174-254 [the fullest list]. A. Eberharter, *Der Kanon des Alten Testamentes zur Zeit des Ben Sira*. Münster i. W., 1911.

[22] Cf. C. H. Toy in *Encyclopaedia Biblica* II, 1167 f.

fragments was published by the Cambridge and Oxford University Presses in 1901). The poetic units within the book range in size from the single distich, complete in itself, to the poem in praise of God (42:15-43:33), of the "Fathers of Old" (44-49), and of the high priest Simon (50) comprising exactly 300 distichs.[23] A strophic arrangement, such as we find in Job 3; 28; 31; 38-39, and elsewhere, appears in some of the poems: ch. 24 consists of six stanzas of six verses each; 43:6-26 of six stanzas of four verses each (for other examples see Smend, *op. cit.* pp. xxxix f.).

Among the Israelites the single distich, as a popular proverb (Is. 22:13; Ez. 18:2; etc.), was the earliest form of wisdom literature. Single verse epigrams composed by sophisticated literary sages constitute the bulk of Proverbs, and occur occasionally in Job and Ecclesiastes (where they are often later additions). In Sirach they are far less common than longer compositions, especially in his second volume (24-51). Usually the single-verse aphorisms in the book (e.g., 3:9, 21, 25, 30; 6:15; 13:1, 19; 21:8, 14; 25:16; 29:22; 31:1 [Gr. 34:1]) are not isolated, but joined to related verses as part of a larger unit; or they are used as texts for a fuller development of the thought. Sirach strings his pearls together, hardly ever mounting them individually.

The single-verse proverb (called *māšāl*, cf. 3:29; 44:5) varies considerably in form (cf. W. Baumgartner in ZAW 34 [1914] 165-169). We find exhortations (e.g., 4:7 f., occasionally attached to a conditional sentence, e.g., 21:1 f.), prohibitions (e.g., 4:1-4), and combinations of both (e.g., 4:25); statements of facts (e.g., 6:5, 14-16; 10:11), at times antithetical (e.g., 3:26); beatitudes (14:1 f., 20 ff.; 25:8 f.; 28:19; 31:8 [Gr. 34:8]; 48:11; 50:28) and their opposite woes (2:12-14; 41:8); and often similes such as are frequent in Proverbs (particularly Prov. 25-27). In form we may distinguish the similes as follows: ordinary similes (3:15; 20:4, 19 [Syriac]; 21:2 f., 8, 14, 16, 18 f., 21; 22:6, 17; 34:2 [Gr. 34:2]; 38:18), rarely joined to an exhortation (25:25; 28:24 f.); metaphorical identification of different things (22:7 f. [Gr. 22:9 f.]); comparisons expressing preference for the lesser of two evils (20:25; 22:15; 25:16; 30:14; 41:15) or for the more desirable of two goods (40:18-26); comparisons in negative (25:10, 15) or interrogative form (22:14); implied similes, in which the two terms of comparison are merely juxtaposed (3:25; 13:1, 15 f., 18; 22:19 f.; 27:5 f.; 30:8; 36:25 [Gr. 36:30]; cf. 41:14) or united by "so" (12:13 f.; 13:17, 19; 22:16, 18; 27:4).

---

[23] The round number "300" is hardly accidental, as R. Smend (*Die Weisheit des Jes. Sir.* p. xli) believed. Like ancient Hebrew poets and notably the author of the Book of Job, Sirach composed poems having a conventionally round number of verses: 36 (24; 50; 51:1-12), 30 (11:2-28; 37:27-38:23; 39:12-35); 20 (2; 40:1-17). It is true that other units have 39, 37, 35, 34, 31, or 17 verses (see Smend, *ibid.*), but in some cases the text may not have been preserved intact.

The riddle (called *ḥîdāh*; cf. 47:17; in 8:8 the word means wise sayings in general) is mentioned in Proverbs and in Ecclesiasticus, although none appears in these books. It is possible that certain questions (17:31; 22:14) are faint echoes of riddles, for they resemble the answer to Samson's riddle (Judg. 14:18), and that numerical proverbs developed from riddles and their answers. The earliest example of a numerical saying known to me occurs in one of the Ugaritic poems from Ras Shamra, and dates from the fourteenth century B.C. (Poem B, col. iii, lines 17-21. Text in J. A. Montgomery and Z. S. Harris, *The Ras Shamra Mythological Texts*, pp. 61 f. Philadelphia, 1935):

> Two sacrifices hates Baal,
> Three the rider of the clouds:[24]
> The sacrifice of shame and the sacrifice of *dnt*[25]
> And the sacrifice in which the maids wail.[26]

This stylistic device was used by Amos (1-2) in his oracles against foreign nations (also Job 5:19-22), before the sages standardized it in Prov. 6:6-19; 30:15-31. Sirach composed the following numerical proverbs: 23:16 f.; 25:7-11; 26:5 f., 28; 50:25 f. (cf. 25:1, 2 in which the second numeral, which should be one more than the first, is lacking).

Ben Sira's parallels to Proverbs are confined to the aphorisms mentioned above and to the praise of Wisdom personified in ch. 24 (cf. Prov. 8). For the rest, he displays his literary versatility in compositions of various other types, particularly lyrical poems both devout and worldly (cf. W. Baumgartner in ZAW 34 [1914] 169-195).

Sirach believed that the sages, when inspired by God, not only poured forth "wise sayings," but also praised God (possibly "gave thanks to God" or "confessed God") in prayer (39:6); for "in the mouth of the sage is the song of praise uttered" (15:10, Hebrew text; cf. Ps. 33:1; 147:1; the Greek has, "in wisdom is praise uttered"). In addition to such personal praise of God (as, in particular, after a banquet, 32:13 [Gr. 35:13]), Sirach admired the liturgical singing in the Temple (50:18 f., where congregation and choir sing antiphonally) and spoke enthusiastically of David's orchestral and vocal sacred compositions for the public worship, daily and on holydays (47:8-10).

So Sirach, after the manner of David, composed several psalms. The following are prayers: a petition for deliverance from sin (23:4-6; 23:1 repeats 23:4; 22:27-23:3 are introductory and express wishes rather than petitions); Israel's cry to God *de profundis*, called a prayer in 36:17 (Gr. 33:22), begging for vengeance against the heathen oppressors and

---

[24] "Rider of the clouds" should be read in Ps. 68:4 (Hebr. 68:5); cf. H. L. Ginsberg in JBL 62 (1932) 112 f.

[25] Meaning uncertain: baseness (?).

[26] Presumably for Adonis, the dead vegetation god (cf. Ez. 8:14).

for national restoration in accordance with the ancient prophecies (36:1-17 [Gr. 33:1-13a; 36:16b-22]). Some of his psalms are songs of praise and thanksgiving, hymns to the glory of God (*Te Deum*): "The works of God are all good" (39:16-20), with a double introduction (didactic [39:12-14a]; lyrical [39:14b-15]), a didactic epilogue (39:21-31, somewhat pedestrian), and a finale rising to a lyrical outburst (39:32-35); a praise of God's power and wisdom (42:15-25) revealed in the works of creation (43:1-26), concluded in a rhapsodic confession that God is greater than all his works and unfathomable, but nevertheless to be magnified enthusiastically (43:27-33). Related to the hymns of praise are the songs of thanksgiving, either public, as 51:12 i-xvi (preserved only in Hebrew), [27] which is a standardized liturgy to be sung antiphonally like Ps. 136:1-3 (cf. Ps. 118:1-4), or private, as 51:1-12, in which a pious man, slandered unjustly like Job, because he was ill unto death or in some other mortal danger, praises God for having "redeemed his soul from death." Indirectly, even the great "Hymn to the Fathers of Old" (44-49), concluded in the praise of the high priest Simon (50), although technically a panegyric, is akin to such hymns of praise and thanksgiving as Ps. 105; 135; 136 (lauding God for his ancient mighty deeds in Israel's behalf); for it is closely connected with the preceding hymn in praise of God (42:15-43:33) and contains passages in the style of the hymn (45:25 f.; 50:22-24). Psalmlike strains occur in the midst of didactic poems: 1:1-10 (inspired, like ch. 24, by Job 28 and Prov. 8); 10:14-18 (God's destruction of the wicked); within 16:24-18:14 (a long poem, or series of poems, describing God's work of creation culminating in man) the didactic tone occasionally becomes lyrical (cf. 17:29 f.; 18:1-14), and similarly 23:19 f. within 23:16-27. Elegiac laments occur in the prayers (22:27 and 23:2 f.; 36:1-17 [Gr. 33:1-13a; 36:16b-22]), songs of praise (51:1-12), and other poems (17:27 f. and 18:8-10) listed immediately above, as well as elsewhere (14:17-19; 38:16-23; 41:1-4).

The literary art of Ben Sira is thus primarily inspired by two books, Proverbs and Psalms, from which he derived his poetic forms and also some of his expressions and thoughts. Although he knew other types of literature in the rest of the Old Testament as it then existed (cf. 38:34-39:1), only occasionally did he use other literary genres occurring there. Like the Jews of his day, he failed to appreciate the "storm and stress" of the pre-exilic prophets and found in the prophetic books not so much fiery denunciations of national apostasy as chiefly predictions of Israel's future glory (36:15 f. [Gr. 36:20 f.]; 48:24 f.; 49:10). He naïvely believes that he is composing prophetic oracles in his book (24:33), and that his

---

[27] S. Schechter (cf. Th. Nöldeke in ZAW 20 [1900] 92) has suggested that this liturgy was omitted in the Greek version because the Sons of Zadok, praised therein, were no longer high priests in 132 B.C.

words are inspired (39:6). But it is only from the postexilic prophecy that he draws his picture of God's appearance in power to destroy Israel's enemies (35:17-19 [Gr. 32:22-25]) and to restore the dynasty of David (47:22).

Likewise in summarizing some portions of the historical books in his "Hymn to the Fathers" (44-49) Sirach has no interest in Israel's heroic feats, but rewrites history in the spirit of the Chronicler, who was chiefly interested in the Temple worship. As for the Pentateuch, it was for him divine Torah to be interpreted juristically, but to which nothing could be added: nothing in his book is written in the style of legal enactments. In harmony with a view appearing sporadically in the two or three preceding centuries (Deut. 4:6; Ezra 7:25), Sirach enthusiastically but unhistorically identifies wisdom with the Torah (24:23, 25-29; cf. 19:20; 21:11) and thus, as a writer of wise sayings but not of law, can regard himself as a rivulet flowing out of the Torah (24:30-34).

W. Baumgartner (ZAW 34 [1914] 189-191, 193) has observed that Sirach was familiar with other poetic genres but did not try his hand at them: the banquet song (32:3-6 [Gr. 35:3-6]; 40:21; 49:1), the funeral dirge (7:34; 22:11 f.; 38:16 f.), and the work song (38:25, Hebrew text); whether Baumgartner is right in regarding 14:20-27 and 51:13-21 (cf. Wisd. of Sol. 8:1-18) as "allegorical erotic reminiscences" (*allegorische Liebesgeschichte*) may be questioned.

Living in the late period of the silver age of ancient Hebrew literature, Sirach was probably one of the best poets in Jerusalem during the second century B.C., although Ecclesiastes occasionally surpasses him in originality of thought and brilliance of expression. He is by no means inferior to the latest authors of Psalms and Proverbs, but he cannot recapture the literary quality of the earliest parts of those books and is decidedly pedestrian in comparison with the superb poetry of Job. Being by temperament, training, and profession a teacher of youth, his didactic verse inculcating practical, moral, and religious wisdom is superior to his attempts at lyric poetry, for which he had no real talent. His lyrical outbursts are generally rhetorical, lack brilliance and swing, and instead of rising high usually fall flat. Notice, for instance, how one of his most pretentious psalms (39:12-35) begins in a pedagogical vein (39:12-14a), rises to a lyrical pitch (39:14b-15), which cannot be sustained in the following (39:16-31) rather uninspired lecture on the theme "The works of God are all good" (39:16-31), where the poet even descends to the level of listing man's daily necessities (39:26); then he winds up in a prosaic peroration (39:32-34), the dullness of which is unrelieved by another rhapsodic outburst at the end (39:35). A similar unsuccessful attempt at great poetry is found in 16:24-18:14. After a similar pedagogical introduction (16:24 f.), Sirach again tries to sing about God's

wisdom manifested in his works (16:26-30), notably in the creation of
man (17:1-14), but becoming involved in the divine retribution for human
deeds (17:15-24), he becomes increasingly rational and colorless, until,
after a passionate appeal for repentance (17:25 f.), he relapses into
devout speculations (17:27 f.), unrelieved by a brief lyrical outburst
(17:29 f.) which ends pessimistically (17:30 f.). In both cases Sirach
tried to say "The Heavens declare the glory of God" (Ps. 19:1 [H. 19:2]),
but was unable to emulate this magnificent hemistich.

In thus combining didactic and lyrical strains in some of his poems,
following the unattainable model of Job, Sirach attempted to relieve the
tedium of his moralizing lectures. In doing so he strained his moderate
poetic inspiration to the limit without even approaching literary brilliance. In contrast with Baumgartner (ZAW 34 [1914] 195), who is
inclined to see in such attempts the best expression of Sirach's poetic
talent, I greatly prefer, both for thought and for content, his epigrams.
It is in his observations of life and counsels to youth that Sirach sometimes achieves distinction. Here are a few examples, chosen more or less
at random, translated as far as possible from the Hebrew text:

> Without the apple of the eye light fails;
> Without knowledge wisdom fails (3:25).
>
> A flaming fire water quenches;
> Thus almsgiving atones for sin (3:30).
>
> Be not like a lion in thy household,
> Nor timid and frightened in thy work (4:30).[28]
>
> Let not thy hand be open to receive
> But closed at the time of giving (4:31).
>
> If capable, answer thy friend;
> But if not—thy hand upon thy mouth! (5:12).
>
> Those amicably disposed toward thee should be many,
> But the recipient of thy confidences one in a thousand (6:6).
>
> There is a friend who is a dinner companion
> But is not to be found in the day of trouble (6:10).
>
> Do not quarrel with a chatterer
> Nor add wood to the fire (8:3).
>
> New wine—new friend;
> When it has aged, then thou mayest drink it (9:10b).

[28] According to G. Kuhn (ZAW N.F. 6 [1929] 291) the second line exhorts Jews in
the service of a foreign ruler not to be afraid of him. For variants of this text see
Charles, *Apocrypha*, pp. 275 f.

Whoever touches pitch, it cleaves to his hand;
And whoever associates with a scoffer learns his way (13:1).

When a prince draws near, keep at a distance,
And so much the more will he bring you near (13:9).

How can the wolf associate with the lamb?
So the wicked with the righteous (13:18).

Like the leaves growing on a flourishing tree—
One fades and another sprouts—
So are the generations of flesh and blood:
One perishes and one ripens (14:18).

Like a drop of water in the sea or a grain of sand,
So are [man's] years in eternal time (18:10).

Presents and gifts blind the eyes of the wise
And, like a muzzle in the mouth, they remove reproofs (20:29).

The teacher of a fool is like one gluing together a potsherd:
He awakes a sleeper out of deep sleep (22:7 [Gr. 22:9]).

He who throws a stone at birds scares them away,
And he who upbraids a friend dissolves friendship (22:20).

No poison is worse than snake poison,
And no fury is worse than a woman's fury (25:15, revised).

Like a sandy ascent for the feet of the aged,
So is a chattering woman for a quiet man (25:20).

The stroke of a whip produces a weal,
But the stroke of the tongue breaks bones (28:17).

Better a beggar's life under one's own beams
Than choice fare among strangers (29:22).

Without a hedge the vineyard is ravaged,
Without a wife one is 'a fugitive and a vagabond.'
                              (36:25 [Gr. 36:30]; cf. Gen. 4:12)

All that comes from nothingness returns to nothingness,
So the wicked—from emptiness to emptiness (41:10).

While these aphorisms of Sirach are seldom as witty and as brilliant
as the best of those collected in the Book of Proverbs (notably in Prov.

25-27), they are superior to the majority of the Proverbs of Solomon. Here we have Sirach at his best: he is terse and pointed, vigorous and clear, imaginative and sensible. He discloses at times originality of thought, fine observation of life, and vividness of expression. Sirach was not a genius (his book excels neither in thought nor in style), but he was unquestionably a man of parts, an excellent teacher, a lover of learning, and a Jew utterly sincere in his piety, utterly devoted to his God and to his people.

THE BOOK OF BARUCH

~~~~~~

Several books were attributed to the pen of Baruch the son of Neriah, Jeremiah's secretary, but only one was included in the Septuagint, where it is called "Baruch," and in the Vulgate, where its title is "Prophecy of Baruch."[1] Although brief, this book is composite: the first part (1:1-3:8) is in prose, the second (subdivided into 3:9-4:4 and 4:5-5:9) in poetry. It is generally admitted that these two parts were written by distinct authors and that even the two subdivisions of the second part may be the work of different writers. The contents of the book may be summarized as follows:

PART I: A CONFESSION OF SINS FOLLOWING THE DESTRUCTION OF JERUSALEM
(1:1-3:8)

1. *Historical introduction* (1:1-14). According to the title, Baruch wrote this book in Babylon in the fifth year (presumably after 586, rather than after 597 B.C.) in the seventh day of the month (which month?)[2] when the Chaldeans had taken and burned Jerusalem (1:1 f.; cf. Jer. 29:1). Baruch read his book to the exiled king Jechonias (Jehoiachin) and to all the captives deported in 597, living in Babylonia by the (unknown) river Sud (1:3 f.). The audience wept, fasted, prayed, and sent a collection to the high priest Joakim at Jerusalem (1:5-7); Baruch sent at the same time (on the tenth of Sivan) the silver vessels which Zedekiah had ordered in place of the Temple vessels carried away by Nebuchadnezzar (1:8 f.; 1:9 quotes freely from Jer. 24:1). They requested that the priests in Jerusalem use the money for the Temple sacrifices, and that they pray for Nebuchadnezzar and his son Baltasar (Belshazzar, who was actually the son of Nabonidus [555-538]; the author erred under the influence of Dan. 5:2, 13, 18, 22), so that the Exiles may find favor in their sight (1:10-12). They should pray that God may for-

---

[1] In the Vulgate and in the Authorized Version the *Epistle of Jeremy* is joined to Baruch and forms its sixth chapter.
[2] Following J. J. Kneucker (*Das Buch Baruch*, pp. 9, 200. Leipzig, 1879) and others, W. O. E. Oesterley (*An Introduction to the Books of the Apocrypha*, pp. 256 f. New York, 1935) would revise the text to read "in the fifth *month*, on the seventh day of the month" (cf. II Kings 25:8) of 586, when the Chaldeans burned the Temple.

give the Exiles (1:13) and also read Baruch's book on feast days, as a confession of sins (1:14).

2. *The confession of sins* (1:15-3:8). *a.* Israel's transgressions (1:15-2:10).[3] The Lord is righteous, but the Jews have transgressed his Law (1:15-18, quoted, with slight variations from Dan. 9:7-10) ever since the Exodus from Egypt (1:19). Consequently, the curse of Deut. 28 has come upon them (1:20; cf. Dan. 9:11), but they have persisted in serving other gods in spite of the warnings of the prophets (1:21 f.). God has therefore fulfilled his threats (2:1 f.; cf. Dan. 9:12 f.), so that the Jews even ate their own children (2:3; cf. Deut. 28:53; Jer. 19:9) and were subjected and exiled by their enemies (2:4 f.; cf. Jer. 42:18). In spite of all calamities the Jews have refused to walk in the commandments of the Lord (2:6-10).

b. The Exiles' prayer for forgiveness (2:11-35). The Lord, who has performed mighty deeds in the past, should turn away his wrath from the remnant of Israel, now scattered among the heathen (2:11-13; cf. Dan. 9:15) and hear their petition for his own sake—that all nations may recognize his power and that some Jews may remain alive to worship him (2:14-18)—not for the righteousness of ancient Israel (2:19). God through his prophets had warned Judah to serve Nebuchadnezzar (2:20 f.; cf. Jer. 27:11 f.; 29:5 f.) lest the country be devastated (2:22 f.; cf. Jer. 7:34; 16:9; 33:11); but Judah rebelled and has suffered dire punishment (2:24-26). God has exiled the Jews in accordance with his revelation to Moses (2:27-29; cf. Deut. 28:62), knowing that they were a stiff-necked people; but they will repent in the land of their captivity (2:30-33) and will be brought back to their land by God (2:34), who will make an everlasting covenant with them (2:35; cf. Jer. 31:31; 32:40).

c. The Exiles' prayer for salvation (3:1-8). In anguish of soul the Exiles beg God to have mercy upon them because they have sinned (3:1-3); but now they have repented (3:4-7)—and yet they are still punished for the sins of their fathers (3:8).

PART II: PRAISE OF WISDOM (3:9-4:4) AND WORDS OF COMFORT (4:5-5:9)

3. *Israel should follow the rules of God's wisdom, embodied in his Law* (3:9-4:4). Hearken to the instruction of wisdom (3:9), for when Israel forsook the fountain of wisdom, it was led into exile (3:10-12): with wisdom are life and peace (3:13 f.). Neither the ancient heathen rulers, who accumulated wealth but vanished into the underworld (3:15-19), nor their youthful successors (3:20 f.), nor the renowned sages of Edom

[3] The first part (1:15-2:5) is a confession prepared for the Jewish community in Jerusalem; the second part (2:6-10), beginning like the first (cf. 1:15 with 2:6), seems to be a confession of the Babylonian Exiles, introducing their two prayers, which follow immediately.

(3:22 f.) ever found wisdom. The universe, God's house, is immense (3:24 f.); great giants lived in ancient times, but they perished for lack of wisdom (3:26-28). No one has ever found wisdom (3:29-31) except God, the all-knowing Creator of the world (3:32-36 [Gr. 3:32-37a]; cf. Job 28:12-27), and God gave wisdom to Israel (3:37 [Gr. 3:37b]), so that she dwelt among men (4:1a [Gr. 3:38]):[4] this divine wisdom is the book of the Law of Moses (4:1; cf. G. F. Moore, *Judaism*, Vol. 1, pp. 263-265), obedience to which brings life (4:2). Let Israel therefore walk in the light of the Law, happy in the assurance that God has revealed his will to his people (4:3 f.).

4. *"Comfort ye, comfort ye my people"* (4:5-5:9; inspired by Is. 40–55). *a.* Jerusalem laments her desolation (4:5-20) and comforts her exiled children (4:21-29). The everlasting God has exiled the Jews on account of their transgressions by which they grieved their mother, Jerusalem, but he will not destroy them (4:5-8). Addressing the women in Judea, Jerusalem bemoans her widowhood and the loss of her children carried away into captivity on account of their sins by a cruel nation (4:9-16). Turning to the Exiles, Jerusalem assures them that, though she cannot help them, she will mourn and pray for them always, certain that the Everlasting will deliver them (4:17-20). Before long the Everlasting will bring back to her her exiled children with joy and gladness, after destroying their persecutors (4:21-26). Let the Exiles therefore seek their God (4:27-29).

b. "Be of good cheer, O Jerusalem" (4:30-5:9). Babylon, the miserable enemy that has afflicted you, will soon be destroyed by God (4:30-35) and your exiled children will return unto you (4:36 f.). Put off the mourning garment and clothe yourself in divine righteousness and glory, for you will be called "the peace of righteousness and the glory of piety" (5:1-4). Stand on the mountain and behold your children gathered joyfully by God from the east to the west (5:5): they had been led away on foot, but God brings them back gloriously on a pathway made smooth and shady by him, who is their leader (5:6-9).

1. Unity of the Book

The Book of Baruch, according to the superscription (1:1), contains "the words of the book" or rather the "letter" (cf. Jer. 29:1, where *sepher* is rendered *biblion* in the LXX, as here, but means "letter") which Baruch, the son of Neriah, the son of Mahseiah (Jer. 32:12; cf. 51:59; Josephus *Antiquities* 10:9, 1), the secretary of Jeremiah, wrote in Babylon five years after the destruction of Jerusalem in 586 (1:2).

These statements are generally accepted as true by many Roman

[4] This verse is sometimes regarded as a Christian gloss.

Catholic scholars, beginning with R. F. R. Bellarmine (d. 1621): not long ago, for instance, E. Kalt (*Das Buch Baruch* [HS VII, 4], pp. 2-5. Bonn, 1932) strenuously maintained that Baruch wrote the whole book. Among Protestants, however, G. Whiston (*A Dissertation to prove the Apocryphal Book of Baruch Canonical*. London, 1727) is one of the few, and possibly the last, to defend this position.

In recent times even some Roman Catholic scholars have recognized that the book is not a unit. W. Stoderl (*Zur Echtheitsfrage von Baruch 1-3, 8*. Münster i. W., 1922) attributes to the pen of Baruch only 1:1-3:8. P. Heinisch (*Theologie und Glaube* 20 [1928] 696-710) accepts this conclusion and dates 3:9-4:4 soon after 516 B.C., and 4:5-5:9 shortly before 538 B.C. J. Goettsberger (*Einleitung in das Alte Testament*, pp. 307-310. Freiburg i. B., 1928) expresses himself more cautiously and vaguely, but admits that the poem on wisdom (3:9-4:4) is "presumably interpolated" in a book whose origin in the time of Baruch (sixth century) can be maintained with good arguments.

Every reader inevitably observes that the book consists of two parts (1:1-3:8; 3:9-5:9) which differ considerably in subject matter and style. Theodoret (d. *ca.* 457) seems to have noted the difference between the two parts when he said, "The admirable Baruch, having inserted this prayer of the people [1:1-3:8] into the book, put [there] also the divine answer [3:9-5:9]."[5] Accordingly, J. Jahn (1803) and W. M. L. De Wette (1817), in their introductions to the Old Testament, regard 1:1-3:8 as the introduction to the rest of the book; L. Bertholdt (*Einleitung*, 6 vols. Erlangen, 1812-1819), O. F. Fritzsche (Commentary, p. 173. Leipzig, 1851), and G. H. A. Ewald (*Geschichte des Volkes Israel* IV, 1864; *Die Propheten* u.s.w., III, 2nd ed., 1868) went a step further and recognized that the second part had been written by a different author. This conclusion has been generally adopted by Protestant scholars: see, e.g., E. Schürer, *Geschichte*, Vol. 3, p. 461; L. E. T. André, *Les Apocryphes*, pp. 259 f.

The integrity of each of the two parts has, however, been questioned. Schürer (in J. J. Herzog, *Realenzyklopädie für protestantische Theologie und Kirche*, 2nd ed. by G. L. Plitt and A. Hauck, Vol. 1, p. 500. Leipzig, 1877) and André (*Les Apocryphes*, p. 260) subdivide the second part and regard the poem on wisdom (3:9-4:4) as a separate work (cf. Heinisch and Goettsberger, above); according to André, the author of 4:5-5:9 added it to his poem, after interpolating 3:10-13. Similar conclusions

[5] Cf. J. J. Kneucker, *Das Buch Baruch*, p. 15, n. 22 (Leipzig, 1879). For patristic references to Baruch, see in particular F. H. Reusch, *Erklärung des Buches Baruch*, pp. 1-21, 268 ff. Freiburg i. B., 1853; and G. Hoberg, *Die älteste lateinische Übersetzung des Buches Baruch* u.s.w., pp. 7-19. 2nd ed. Freiburg, 1902.

were reached by O. C. Whitehouse (in Charles, *Apocrypha*, p. 570), who attributes 1:1-3:8; 3:9-4:4; and 4:5-5:9 to "different hands."

Others have found evidence of composition in the first part. J. J. Kneucker (*Baruch*, pp. 37-61, etc.) analyzes the book as follows: the original work or *Grundschrift* comprised the introduction in 1:1-2a (2b is a gloss) and 3 (expanded later with the addition of 1:4-14; v. 8 is a gloss to 1:1-2a) and the work itself in 3:9-5:9; the prayer in 1:15-3:8 is an addition. O. Eissfeldt (*Einleitung*, pp. 649-651) is inclined to follow Kneucker.

We may therefore hesitate to decide whether one, two (1:1-3:8; 3:9-5:5), three (1:1-3:8; 3:9-4:4; 4:5-5:9; or 1:1-3+3:9-5:9; 1:4-14; 1:15-3:8), or four (1:1-3+3:9-4:4; 1:4-14; 1:15-3:8; 4:5-5:9) authors are responsible for our book.[6] Since the two parts of the book (1:1-3:8 and 3:9-5:5) are sharply distinguished, even in form (the first being prose and the second poetry), it may be well to examine them separately.

2. *Authorship and date*
A. Baruch 1:1-3:8

The following facts militate against Baruch's authorship of the first part of the book. The chronological data in 1:2 are ambiguous in regard to both the month ("in the seventh day of the month" is meaningless, but attested in all versions) and the year. On the basis of II Kings 25:8, many critics read "the *fifth* month." But critics are divided in determining "the fifth year": they either follow J. J. Kneucker (*Das Buch Baruch*, pp. 10-16) in interpreting it as the fifth year after the captivity of Jehoiachin in 597, (cf. 1:9; Ez. 1:2) or O. F. Fritzsche (Commentary, p. 178) in understanding it as the fifth year after the captivity of Zedekiah and the burning of Jerusalem in 586. The latter view seems more probable, but is not without some difficulties, for 1:7, 10, 14; 2:16 seem to assume that the Temple is still standing (contrary to 1:2, 8; 2:26; cf. 2:3, which clearly refer to 586).

Whatever be the date meant in 1:2, there is no evidence that Baruch was ever in Babylonia. It appears from the Book of Jeremiah that Baruch remained with Jeremiah from 608 until after the destruction of Jerusalem in 586, when he went down to Egypt and settled there with his master (Jer. 43:5-7; cf. Josephus, *Antiquities* 10:9, 6). Thus Baruch could hardly have been in Babylonia before 586, and in all probability never went there later, for he presumably died in Egypt. Of course, Jewish

---

[6] The present writer is inclined to attribute the book to three authors, who wrote respectively 1:1-3:8 (including glosses); 3:9-4:4; and 4:5-5:9. J. T. Marshall (Hasting's *Bible Dictionary*, Vol. 1 [1898], p. 251) ascribes the book to four authors.

legends relate that when Nebuchadnezzar conquered Egypt[7] he brought
both Jeremiah and Baruch to Babylonia (*Seder 'Olam Rabba* 26; cf. the
attribution of Ps. 137, "By the rivers of Babylon," to Jeremiah in the
LXX), or, on the contrary, that Jeremiah went to Babylonia and Baruch
remained in Jerusalem (Paralipomena of Jeremiah), or that in Babylonia
Baruch was the teacher of Ezra, who refused to go to Judea before the
death of his old and feeble master (*Midrash Rabba ad Cant.* 5:5; *Megilla*
16b); or, on the contrary, that when Jeremiah went to Babylonia after
the destruction of Jerusalem, Baruch remained in the ruined city (Paralipomena of Jeremiah and Syriac Baruch). It is idle to seek in such
imaginary tales some confirmation for the hypothesis (which is supported
by no evidence and is highly improbable) according to which Baruch
was in Babylonia in 582 (Kalt, *Baruch*, p. 3). It is not to be excluded that
Baruch's alleged presence in Babylon at an uncertain date (1:1 f.) is the
result of some confusion between Baruch and his brother Seraiah, who
went to Babylon in 593 (Jer. 51:59).

Other historical difficulties, which critics have detected, contribute to
increase our skepticism with regard to Baruch's authorship of the book.
A "priest" (i.e., high priest; cf. I Macc. 15:1 f.; Acts 5:24) Joachim or
Joiakim (1:7) is unknown in Baruch's time[8] (see the list in I Chron.
6:13-15 [H. 5:39-41]; cf. Ezra 7:1-5), but turns up more than a century
later (Neh. 12:10, 12, 26). Similarly, the return of the sacred vessels of
the Temple (1:8) is reported much later, in the time of Ezra (Ezra
1:7-11); moreover, these "silver vessels" are said to have been made by
Zedekiah (597-586), after the first plundering of Jerusalem (cf. I Kings
24:13; II Chron. 36:10), but the vessels carried to Babylonia in the second
deportation (586) were not merely such silver vessels, but also brazen
and golden ones (II Kings 25:13-16; Jer. 52:17-19). Other objections are
less valid: the worship on Zion is said to continue after the destruction
of the Temple (1:10), but this is assumed in Jer. 41:5; Jechonias or
Jehoiachin was a prisoner, but he could conceivably have attended the
public reading of the book (1:3)—if it had taken place.

A serious historical error must be considered in connection with the
literary sources utilized in Bar. 1:1-3:8. The erroneous notion that Baltasar
(Belshazzar) was the son of Nebuchadnezzar (1:11 f.), who ruled from
605 to 561—whereas he was the son of Nabonidus (555-538)—is not an

---

[7] Nebuchadnezzar's conquest of Egypt is predicted by Jeremiah (43:10-13) and
Ezekiel (29:17-20; cf. 30:10-12), and reported as a fact by Josephus (*Antiquities*
10:9, 7) but, in spite of Nebuchadnezzar's victory over Amasis in 568, never
actually took place.

[8] A high priest Joachim at this time, i.e., during the reign of Nebuchadnezzar, is
mentioned elsewhere only in Jth. 4:6, 8, 14; 15:8. The coincidence is puzzling, but
neither Baruch nor Judith contain any valid historical information otherwise
unknown.

original blunder of our author, but is patently derived from the Book of Daniel (5:2, 11, 18), whose author confused Nebuchadnezzar and Nabonidus elsewhere (as in the story of Nebuchadnezzar's madness). The indebtedness of Baruch to Daniel is fairly certain: compare Bar. 1:15-20; 2:1 f., 7-14, 16-19 with Dan. 9:7-11, 12 f., 13-17, 18, respectively. Only those who cling to Baruch's authorship of Bar. 1:1-3:8, or at least to its relatively early date (586-300 B.C.), maintain that the author of Daniel excerpted and summarized Baruch.[9] It should be noted that, while in Daniel these verses are consecutive and connected, in Baruch they are separated by reminiscences of Jeremiah and of Deut. 28 (cf. the table in André Les Apocryphes, p. 252). In fact, most of Bar. 1:1-3:8 is a cento of Biblical expressions. Kalt (Baruch, p. 4) recognizes that out of 51 verses 33 are literal reproductions or paraphrases of scriptural passages (22 from Jeremiah, 5 from Deuteronomy, and 5 from I Kings 8), although he refuses to admit that exilic or postexilic books (Ezekiel and Daniel) are quoted. Ultimately, of course, Deuteronomy is the inspiration of the prayers in Dan. 9, Bar. 1:15-3:8, Neh. 1:5-11; 9:6-37, and Ezra 9:6-15; all of them are national confessions of sin, contrite recognitions that Israel has violated the Deuteronomic Law, and appeals de profundis for divine forgiveness and help. None of them is earlier than the fifth century; all of them are probably considerably later. The references to the prophets (Ezra 9:11; Neh. 9:30; Dan. 9:9; Bar. 2:20, 24) as God's servants who vainly attempted to induce Israel to obey the Law of Moses seem to indicate that not only was prophecy extinct, but that presumably the prophetic books were either canonized (ca. 200 B.C.) or at least in the process of attaining the status of sacred Scriptures.[10]

All attempts to fix the date of the first part of the book—nay, of the book as a whole—have failed because no definite clues are available. The relation of 1:15-3:8 to Dan. 9 is our main evidence, but even if we admit that Baruch is later (as seems probable), we cannot be certain that Dan. 9:4-19, which differs in style from the rest of Daniel and is sometimes regarded as interpolated, may not be earlier than 164. It does not necessarily follow that, because Bar. 1:11 f. is clearly dependent on Dan. 5 and is therefore later than 164, 1:15 ff. also is later, for the authorship of the two passages may be different. Baruch 1:15-3:8 may conceivably date from 250-150 B.C., but hardly earlier (Ewald would date it

[9] This is the view of Roman Catholics generally. Early Protestant scholars holding this opinion are listed by Kneucker (Baruch, pp. 31 f.). The latest detailed argument in favor of Daniel's dependence upon Baruch is that of W. Stoderl (Zur Echtheitsfrage von Baruch 1-3, 8. Münster i. W., 1922).

[10] In Zech. 1:4, 6; 7:7, 12 there is also a reference to the prophetic teaching, but two important differences should be noted: Zechariah speaks of "the former prophets" (not "the prophets" in general), and he carefully distinguishes the Law (i.e., Deuteronomy) and the words of the prophets (7:12); in fact, the words of the prophets are regarded as divine statutes (1:6).

ca. 350); later dates are possible but questionable. Fritzsche (Commentary, p. 173) and many others date the first part of the book in 150-100 B.C., but others believe that the references to the destruction of the Temple and the Exile (1:1; 2:23-26) must have been inspired by a contemporary event—Pompey's conquest of Jerusalem in 63 B.C. (H. Graetz) or, more literally, the destruction of Jerusalem by Titus in A.D. 70 (F. Hitzig, J. J. Kneucker, E. Schürer, O. C. Whitehouse, etc.). This assumption is false: the prayer was composed with reference to the destruction of Jerusalem in 586 B.C. and attributed to Baruch; it is futile to seek in this cento of Biblical passages the echo of a contemporary calamity. We may infer at most that the pervading pessimism and the wretched condition of the Jews depicted in this prayer reflect the plight of the Palestinian Jews between 586 and 142 B.C. In the first century of our era it would have been absurd for a Jew to say, "we are but few left among the heathen, where thou hast scattered us" (2:13) with reference to his times. In view of the widespread and numerous dispersion of the Jews in every city of the Mediterranean world (already about 85 B.C. Strabo [quoted by Josephus, *Antiquities* 14:7, 2] said it would be difficult to find a place in the world without Jews) such a statement would be inconceivable even as rhetorical exaggeration. In view of the similar prayers already mentioned (Ezra 9; Neh. 9; Dan. 9) and of Ps. 106 and 107 (praises of Jehovah's forgiving grace in spite of Israel's apostasies through the centuries), it would seem that this prayer of Baruch is merely a specimen of a favorite literary exercise, with little reference to actual calamities and wars at the time. All in all, the second century B.C. (perhaps the second half) seems to the present writer the most probable date for the first part of the book.

One cannot read the Greek text of 1:1-3:8 without being continuously impressed by its Hebraic character, which is more pronounced at times than in most of the Septuagint in general, and at times seems even to approach the literalness of Aquila. In fact, the Greek is often incomprehensible without a translation back into Hebrew. A few striking examples may suffice. In 1:10 the Greek reads literally, "buy with the money burnt offerings and *concerning sin* [i.e., trespass or sin offerings] . . . and make *manna* [i.e., prepare an oblation, Hebr. *minḥah*; cf. the LXX of Jer. 17:26; 41:5 (Gr. 48:5)]." A Hebrew idiom meaning "today" is rendered woodenly, "like this day" (1:15, 20; 2:6, 11), and the Hebrew construction in relative sentences is reproduced intact as "the house *which upon it*," i.e., upon which (2:4; cf. "which there" [where] in 2:13, 29; 3:8; similarly in Mark 1:7; 7:25). We may wonder how a reader unacquainted with Hebrew would understand the phrase "they will turn away from their hard back" (2:33; better in 2:30, "a stiff-necked people"). There are also cases of mistranslation from the Hebrew. "The prayer of the *dead* of Israel" (3:4; contrast 2:17) should have been "the prayer of the *men* (Hebr. *mēthê*, wrongly read as *methê* [dead]); the same error occurs in Aquila (Is. 41:14; Ps. 17:14) and in the LXX (Is. 5:13). In some instances Baruch reproduces errors occurring in the LXX of Jeremiah. "And he gave them as subjects to all the kingdoms . . . as a reproach and *an untrodden land*" (2:4; cf. Jer. 42:18 [Gr. 49:18]); the Hebrew word *shammah* has two meanings (desert and horror), and the translator mistakenly chose the first instead of the second. In Bar. 2:25 and Jer. 32:36 (Gr. 39:36) *apostolē* (a sending) is a mistranslation of the Hebrew word for pestilence.[11] The Hebrew origin of the first part is confirmed by the notes to 1:17 and 2:3 in the Syro-Hexaplar version: "not found in the Hebrew."[12]

Hardly any modern scholar doubts that the first part of Baruch was originally written in Hebrew, in spite of the fact that Jerome and Epiphanius (cf. Schürer, *Geschichte*, Vol. 3, p. 463) no longer could find the Hebrew text among the Jews. Th. Nöldeke (*Die alttestamentliche Literatur*, p. 214. Leipzig, 1867) and a few others regarded the Greek as the original text; and André (*Les Apocryphes*, p. 254) explains the Semitisms and the mistranslations as borrowings from the LXX on the part of an author writing in Greek. But if the Greek translator was familiar with the LXX, whether he was the same as the one (actually two)[13] to whom we owe the Greek version of Jeremiah (as Hitzig, Dillmann, Fritzsche, Ewald, and others believed; cf. Kneucker, *Baruch*, p. 83) or not, the contacts with the LXX noted above have a plausible explanation.[14] The Hebrew origin of the first part of Baruch seems certain beyond a doubt.

B. Baruch 3:9-4:4

The second part of the book consists of two poems (3:9-4:4 and 4:5-5:9) with no mutual connection and no relation to the first part except the (presumably fictitious) historical background, i.e., the Babylonian Exile. The final poem, even though different in form from the first part of the book, which is in prose, could be regarded as the hopeful answer

[11] For Hebraisms in Baruch see Kneucker, *Baruch*, pp. 25 f. (to be used critically), and André, *Les Apocryphes*, pp. 253 f.

[12] A. M. Ceriani, *Monumenta sacra et profana*, Vol. 1, Fasc. 1, pp. 2, 15. Milan, 1861.

[13] H. St. John Thackeray, in JTS 4 [1903] 245-266 (pp. 261-266 deal with Baruch), identifies the translator of the second part of Jeremiah with the translator of Bar. 1:1-3:8.

[14] In the quotations from Dan. 9, Baruch is closer to the Greek version of Theodotion than to the LXX. This is not to be regarded as evidence of lateness. Working in the second century, Theodotion obviously utilized an earlier version of Daniel, which is quoted in the New Testament and other writings of the first century.

to the despairing prayer in the first part. But the poem on wisdom (3:9-4:4), notwithstanding the introduction (3:9-13) which attaches it somehow to what precedes, is incongruous in this context: either it was inserted because 3:10-13 seemed appropriate for this context or these verses were added by the editor who placed the poem here. In any case, according to 3:10, the Exile of 586 is far in the past, whereas in 1:1-3:8 and 4:11-25 that calamity is very recent; consequently, there is no pretense of Baruch's authorship in the poem on wisdom, and no need to argue the point.

The date of the poem on wisdom (3:9-4:4) is uncertain, for the only historical allusion (the Exile of 586, in 3:10-13) may have been interpolated.[15] Our only clues are echoes of earlier writings in the poem. It is clear that the author is familiar with the wisdom literature existing at the time. When the poet, proud of Jewish wisdom, denies that the Edomites and their neighbors have found wisdom (3:22 f.), he may have been inspired by Jer. 49:7 and Obad. 8—the only other passages which (in Greek) deny Edom's claim to wisdom, supported by the Book of Job.

This poet attempted to combine three distinct notions of wisdom: the metaphysical plan of creation known only to God (Job. 28), the ethical wisdom that brings wealth and happiness (Prov. 8), and the peculiar wisdom of Israel that is the Law of Moses (Ecclus. 24). Obviously he could give us only an incongruous potpourri, for those three notions of wisdom are not easily reconciled. Our author was not a brilliant thinker and failed to unite metaphysics and ethics, as Prov. 8 did through the personification of wisdom; he is less original than Sirach (Ecclus. 24), who identified this personified wisdom with the Law of Moses; and he cannot attain the élan, the subtlety of thought, and the almost mystical soaring of Wisd. of Sol. 7:1-8:1—the closest approach to a synthesis—of which he was totally ignorant. He has, however, succeeded in summarizing the three stages of the development of wisdom in Israel: God's plan of creation, forever hidden from man (3:29-34 [Gr. 3:32-35], inspired by Job 28:1-27); the descent of wisdom among men (Prov. 8:31), particularly the Jews (3:35-37 [Gr. 3:36-38],[16] inspired by Ecclus. 24:8-12); the identification of wisdom with the Pentateuch (4:1, based on Ecclus.

[15] It consequently seems idle to discuss the views of those scholars who, finding historical allusions to the capture of Jerusalem by Ptolemy I (date unknown; cf. B. Niese, *Geschichte der Griechischen und Makedonischen Staaten*, vol. I, p. 230, n. 4. Gotha, 1893), Pompey (63 B.C.), or Titus (A.D. 70) in 4:5-5:9, date 3:9-4:4 accordingly, assuming a common authorship for the two poems (see Kneucker, *Baruch*, pp. 37-55).

[16] The last verse of Bar. 3 was often quoted in Patristic writings as a prediction of the incarnation of the Logos, and since H. Grotius it has been regarded as a Christian gloss by some critics (Kneucker, Schürer, Rothstein, etc.). In reality the verse is an echo of Prov. 8:1-4, 31.

24:23; see G. F. Moore, *Judaism*, Vol. 1, pp. 263-265). It thus seems clear that this poem was written after Ecclesiasticus, i.e., after 180 B.C., and in all probability about or before 100 B.C. It is possible that the author wished to correct the heresies of Ecclesiastes, as the Alexandrian Jew who wrote the Wisdom of Solomon did more directly and pointedly. In any case, the poem is interesting as the last product of Palestinian wisdom literature in the ancient tradition: later examples are concerned with wisdom as fulfillment of the Law of Moses or of ethical maxims, not with wisdom as God's plan or agent in the creation of the world. Our poet was one of the last Palestinian sages, living in a time when most of the teachers of youth were scribes, students of the Law. We may infer from 4:3 that he indirectly warned his pupils against the lure of Greek philosophy by assuring them that Israel, not Greece, possessed the true wisdom that comes from God and is most profitable.

If, as has been suggested, the author of the poem was a Palestinian sage writing in the period 150-100 B.C., it follows that he wrote in Hebrew or Aramaic, not in Greek. A number of critics[17] have, however, claimed that, judging from the character of the Greek style of 3:9-4:4, this poem was originally written in Greek: the references to *mythologoi* (3:23), literally the narrators and interpreters of myths, to the "house of God" (3:24), and to the sacrifices to demons (4:7; cf. Deut. 32:17, LXX) are adduced as evidence of Alexandrian provenance (Fritzsche, Commentary, pp. 168 f.). But the Greek Bible furnishes not a few examples of translations into excellent Greek (I Esdras, for instance), and the "mythologists," "house of God," and "demons" may well represent idiomatic renderings of Hebrew expressions (cf. Kneucker, *Baruch*, pp. 295 f. and 319 f., respectively).

The evidence for a Semitic original is less abundant and less obvious than in the first part of the book, but seems quite convincing to some critics,[18] including the present writer. The teaching of the poem on wisdom is strictly Palestinian, like Sirach's, in contrast with the Hellenistic

---

[17] Fritzsche (Commentary, pp. 172 f.), C. H. Cornill (*Einleitung in die kanonischen Bücher des Alt. Test.*, 3rd and 4th ed., p. 273), André (*Les Apocryphes*, p. 254), Schürer (*Geschichte*, Vol. 3, p. 461), etc.; cf. A. A. Bevan (*Encyclop. Bibl.* I, 493 f. London, 1899).

[18] The fullest argument for a Hebrew original of the whole book has been presented by Kneucker (*Baruch*, 1879), who has even attempted a reconstruction of the lost Hebrew original. His conclusion is adopted for the book as a whole by Roman Catholic scholars in general, by W. Rothstein (in E. Kautzsch, *Die Apokryphen u.s.w.*, p. 215. Tübingen, 1900), by R. R. Harwell (*The Principal Versions of Baruch*, Yale Dissertation. New Haven, 1915), and with less assurance by O. Eissfeldt (*Einleitung*, p. 650). The Hebrew origin of 3:9-4:4 is maintained by O. C. Whitehouse (in Charles, *Apocrypha*, p. 572), while J. T. Marshall (in Hastings's *Dictionary of the Bible*, Vol. 1, p. 253) argued, on the basis of a comparison of the versions of Baruch, for an Aramaic original without proving his case convincingly (cf. Charles, *Apocrypha*, pp. 571 f.).

atmosphere of Wisdom of Solomon: an Alexandrian Jew would have mentioned the Greeks rather than the Edomites and their neighbors as the searchers for wisdom (3:22 f.). A number of expressions have a pronounced Hebrew flavor: "thou art reckoned with them [that go down] into the underworld" (3:11; cf. 3:19; Ps. 28:1; 88:4 [H. 88:5]); "length of days" (3:14); "there is no end to their acquisition [or "possessions"]" (3:17); "there is no searching of their works" (3:18; cf. Job 5:9; 9:10; Is. 40:28);[19] "it was not heard . . . nor seen" (3:22); etc. It could be argued that some of these idioms were taken from the Greek Bible, but in some cases the text is clearly based on the Hebrew text of the Old Testament, as 3:26 (cf. Gen. 6:4). Moreover, some differences between the Greek and the Syriac can only be explained as independent renderings from the Hebrew;[20] the Hebrew manuscript used for the Syriac differed in minor points from the manuscript used for the Greek. Although not quite identical, the two manuscripts were obviously fairly accurate copies made from the same archetype, which seems to have contained the erroneous reading "Meran" (Gr. *Merrhan*) instead of the correct Midian or Medan[21] (3:23): *d* and *r* are easily confused in the Hebrew alphabet (and often are; cf. Friedr. Delitzsch, *Die Lese- und Schreibfehler*, u.s.w., pp. 105-107. Berlin, 1920) and in the LXX the *r*, which is hardly ever doubled in Hebrew, is frequently doubled in Hebrew proper names, as in *Gomorrah, Sarrah* (Sarah), etc. The following are some of the variants detected by scholars in the Hebrew prototypes of the Greek and Syriac versions: in 3:16 the Greek reads "peoples" (Hebr. *'mm*), the Syriac "world" (Hebr. *'lm*); in 3:18 the Greek seems to translate the Hebrew *ḥeqer* (searching) and the Syriac instead Hebrew *mispar* (number, but see below, note 19); in 3:21 the Syriac "her [wisdom's] way" (Hebr. *darkāh*) is preferable to the Greek's "their [i.e., their fathers'] way" (Hebr. *darkām*), but conversely in 3:34 the Greek "their watches" is preferable to the Syriac "their places"; etc. Nevertheless, it is clear that the Syriac translator utilized the Greek text in addition to the Hebrew original (cf. Kneucker, *Baruch*, pp. 163-173).

Errors and mistranslations in the Greek likewise indicate that it was translated from the Hebrew. The lack of vocalization and of "mothers of reading" (consonants representing long vowels) in the Hebrew ex-

---

[19] Curiously, the LXX translates "no number" in Job 5 and 9 (as the Syriac in Baruch 3:18) but "no searching" in Is. 40 (cf. the Greek of Bar. 3:18).

[20] For instance, in 3:18 O. C. Whitehouse (Charles, *Apocrypha*, p. 589) suggests that the Greek ("who fashion") and the Syriac ("who gain") are both translated from the Hebr. *qōnêy*; and that the Syriac "established" is a better translation of Hebr. *mēkhîn* than the Greek "prepared" (*ibid.*, p. 590).

[21] P. Heinisch (*Theologie und Glaube* 20 [1928] 708) reads Medan for Merran and Tema for Teman, thus finding a reference to Arabia instead of Edom.

plains the incorrect translations "he will bring her" instead of "he brought her" (3:30); "laws" (Hebr. *tôrôth*) instead of "Law" (*tôrath*) in 4:1. The ambiguity of the Hebrew explains the error in 3:17, where "there is no end" should have been "there was no end" (likewise in 3:18). It has been surmised (Kneucker, *Baruch*, pp. 280 f.) that in 3:11 the Hebrew *nidmētha* (thou art similar) was erroneously read *nitmētha* (thou art defiled); other examples of possible textual corruption in the Hebrew have been noted above. The most plausible explanation of these peculiarities of the Greek and Syriac texts is that they are both translations from the Hebrew.

C. Baruch 4:5-5:9

The final poem in Baruch differs so radically from the preceding poem on wisdom (3:9-4:4) that we may assume that it was written by another poet, who conceivably wished to pen a comforting reply to the national laments of the exiled Jews, which appear in the first part of the book (1:1-3:8). This poet drew his inspiration from the Second Isaiah (Is. 40-55), and not from Job, Proverbs, and Ecclesiasticus, as the author of 3:9-4:4.

Like many of the psalms, the poem deals with generalities and contains no specific contemporary historical allusions. The historical background is of course the Babylonian Exile, as in the first part of the book; but, after the destruction of Jerusalem (4:31, 33) and the Exile of 586 B.C. (4:14, 16, 24, 26, 32), the author, inspired by the Second Isaiah, looks forward to an imminent deliverance for the exiled Jews (4:22, 24 f.), to a sudden destruction of the (Babylonian) enemy (4:25, 33-35), and to a miraculous return of the Jews to Zion (5:5-9). This outlook and the obvious dependence on the Second Isaiah (cf. 5:7 with Is. 40:4) preclude a date earlier than 540 B.C. In fact, there are reminiscences of the Third Isaiah (Is. 56-66) in 5:2 (Is. 61:10), 5:5 (Is. 51:17 and 60:4), 5:6 (Is. 49:22; 60:4, 9; 66:20). How long after 500 B.C. was the poem written? The answer depends on whether it is merely a poetic exercise describing a situation in the past history of the Jews (like the psalm in Ex. 15:1-19 or Ps. 137) or whether the author felt compelled by a national calamity in his own time, resembling the Babylonian Exile, to comfort his people with words attributed to Baruch (Fritzsche, *Commentary*, pp. 172 f.). If, as the present writer believes, the poem is reminiscent and not a reflection of actual conditions, its date within the period 400-30 B.C. is uncertain, as in the case of many psalms; like the rest of the book it may well have been written about 100 B.C. (cf. Fritzsche, *op. cit.*, p. 178). On the other hand, if it is an actual picture of the misery of the Jews in captivity after the destruction of Jerusalem, then it is later than A.D. 70, when Titus stormed the city and burned the Temple: this date has been proposed by G. Volkmar (*Handbuch der Einleitung in die Apokryphen*, Vol. 1, p. 230; Vol. 2, p. 337. Tübingen, 1860), E. Schürer (in Herzog's *Realencyclopädie*, 2nd ed., Vol. 1, p. 501; *Geschichte*, Vol. 3, pp. 462 f.), F. Hitzig (*Geschichte des Volkes Israel*, Vol. 2, pp. 620-624. Leipzig, 1869), J. J. Kneucker (*Baruch*, pp. 46-54), J. T. Marshall (in Hastings' *Dictionary of the Bible*, Vol. 1, p. 253), André (*Les Apocryphes*, p. 259), C. Steuernagel (*Einleitung*, p. 790), O. C. Whitehouse (in Charles, *Apocrypha*, pp. 574-576), etc. The view that the book reflects the capture of Jerusalem by Pompey in 63 B.C. has found little favor (cf. Whitehouse, *op. cit.*, p. 574), for Jerusalem was not destroyed at the time.

Without denying that Bar. 4:5-5:9 *could* have been written in A.D. 70 or even a few years later, we should recognize that the evidence adduced for such a date is not convincing. The language of this poem, or of three poems beginning with "be of good cheer" (4:5, 21, 30), is too vague to disclose definite historical allusions. The ingenuity of critics has endeavored in vain to find allusions to historical events in the most general statements: the threat that the enemy capital (Babylon) will be destroyed by God through fire (4:35) has been interpreted as a reference to the eruption of Vesuvius in A.D. 79, and to the conflagrations in Rome during the reign of Nero and later (Kneucker, *Baruch*, pp. 51 f.), but that verse may be a mere echo of Jer. 51:58.[22] A Jew after A.D. 70 could have called the Romans "a nation from afar, a shameless nation speaking another language, without respect for the aged nor mercy for children" (4:15), but such an indefinite characterization could apply just as well to the Chaldeans, and is in fact applied to them in Deut. 28:49 f. Not a word definitely and unmistakably expresses the feelings of a Jew who survived the tragedy of A.D. 70.

It is not even certain, as frequently claimed, that Bar. 4:36-5:9 is a paraphrase of Ps. of Sol. 11:1-7 (cf. the parallels [in Greek] in Charles, *Apocrypha*, p. 572); see, for further details, H. E. Ryle and M. R. James, *Psalms of the Pharisees commonly called the Psalms of Solomon*, pp. lxxii ff. Cambridge, 1891. Both passages contain echoes of Is. 40-61; both, as Charles suggests (*op. cit.*, p. 574), could be variant recensions of the same Hebrew psalm.

As elsewhere in the book, the Palestinian provenance of this poem is obvious: no trace of Hellenistic Judaism has been detected in it, for the "demons" of 4:7 were suggested by Deut. 32:17. We may therefore assume that, like the rest of the book, the poem was originally written

---

[22] Even more farfetched is Kneucker's suggestion (*Baruch*, p. 73, 315 f.) that 4:1-4 may be a "warning against Christianity."

in Hebrew.[23] The Greek is fairly idiomatic (cf. Kneucker, *Baruch*, pp. 77-79), but reflects underlying Hebrew expressions (*ibid.*, p. 25). The presence of phrases like "seek him ten times more" (4:28), which are not easily reproduced in Hebrew, merely prove that the Greek translation is occasionally rather free. And the fact that once the Syriac is unquestionably based on a conflation of the Greek text (4:34: "I shall take away from her the idols [Gr. *agálmata*] and the exultation [Gr. *agallíama*]") merely confirms the view that the Syriac translator used the Greek text as well as the Hebrew.

3. Religious Teaching

The theme of the book as a whole is Israel's sin, punishment, and forgiveness, expounded somewhat differently long before in Judg. 2. Even the poem on wisdom (3:15-4:2), which dealt with individual rather than national conduct, is supplied with an introduction (3:9-14) and a conclusion (4:3 f.) addressed to the nation.

The author of the poem on wisdom attempted a synthesis between the teaching of the sages and the Jewish religion, following the previous, more original, identification of the Creator of the world with Jehovah made by the Second Isaiah (Bar. 4:35 [Gr. 4:36]: "our God," i.e., Jehovah, is the only god), and the identification of wisdom with the Law of Moses made by Sirach (Bar. 4:1). Having thus concluded that Israel's God is the sole god (the universe is his house, 4:24) and that Israel's Law is wisdom, he can, on the one hand, gloat over the failure of non-Israelites to discover wisdom (4:15-31), for God alone found it and gave it to Israel (4:32-37), and on the other, rejoice in Israel's possession of this treasure which is not to be given to another nation (4:4). Both the teaching and the absence of any missionary spirit, such as that of the Second Isaiah, place our author on the threshold of Rabbinic Judaism.

The poem on wisdom is incongruous within the book. It has no connection with the historical situation (except in the introduction, 3:9-13) and deals with entirely different matters. Even the notion of God is different. The deity is called *theós* (Hebr. *'elōhîm*), God (3:13, 24, 27; 4:1, 4; once "our God" [3:36]), in contrast with the divine names of LORD (Gr. *Kýrios*, Hebr. *YHWH*, pronounced *'adōnāy*) in 1:1-3:8[24] and "the

[23] Cf. A. Condamin, "Un poème du livre de Baruch"(*Études Religieuses*, Vol. 108, pp. 55-63). Conversely, Cornill (*Einleitung*, 3rd and 4th ed., p. 273), André (*Les Apocryphes*, p. 254), Schürer (*Geschichte*, Vol. 3, p. 461), Whitehouse (in Charles, *Apocrypha*, pp. 572 f.), and others are convinced that 4:5-5:9 was originally written in Greek.

[24] Usually *Kyrios* (1:5, 8, 12-14, etc.; 25 times in all), twice with the article (2:9, 17), sometimes with specifications: "Lord our God" (1:18 f. 22; 2:5; 3:8; in Hebrew: *YHWH 'elōhênû*), also with the article before *God* (1:13, 21; 2:12, 15, 19, 27; 3:6) or before *Lord* (1:13, 15; 2:6); "Lord the God of Israel" (2:11); "Lord their God" (2:31); "Lord almighty, the God of Israel" (3:1,4).

Everlasting" in 4:5-5:9.[25] In this poem God is the universal sole Creator, whose outstanding attribute is wisdom; he loved Israel and gave his Law to his servant Jacob (4:37; cf. 4:4). Nothing of this appears elsewhere: in the rest of the book God is just and merciful toward his sinful people. Anthropomorphisms occur elsewhere (2:11, 16 f., 29; 3:4) but not in the poem on wisdom; the same is true of human feelings and mental functions attributed to God (1:13; 2:13, 20; 3:5; 4:9, 25, 27; 5:5).

Turning now to the rest of the book (1:1-3:8; 4:5-5:9), we breathe a different air: the universal Creator becomes the God of Israel (3:1, 4, 6, etc.), solely concerned with the destinies of his chosen people, called by his name (2:15), with whom he makes a new "everlasting covenant" (2:35). The Almighty who is the God of Israel (3:1, 4) is a God of justice (1:15; 2:6, 9, 17) and mercy (2:27; 3:2). In his justice God punishes the sin of Israel; in his mercy he forgives it after Israel repents.

The sin of Israel is not specified exactly, as in the writings of the ancient prophets; we almost gain the impression that the sinfulness of the people was deduced from the destruction of Jerusalem in 586, but that the author had no accurate and detailed information about it. The people have disobeyed God and have not walked in his commandments (1:17-19; 2:5, 10, 12; 3:1-5; 4:12 f.); their fathers have committed iniquities and have departed from the Lord (3:5, 8); they have provoked God's wrath (4:6). But only one specific sin is mentioned: they sacrificed unto demons and not to the Lord (4:7), i.e., they worshiped heathen gods which are usually called idols, but called *daimonia* here, following the Septuagint (Deut. 32:17; Is. 13:21; 34:14; 65:11; Ps. 95:5 [H. 96:5]; 105:37 [H. 106:37]). The author seems to have believed in demons (cf. 4:35), but never mentions angels. This accusation of idolatry against the postexilic Jews is puzzling, being supported by hardly any evidence at all after 400 B.C. except during the proscription of Judaism by Antiochus Epiphanes in 168-165, when some Jews became apostates to save their lives. While such general accusations are common in epigonic writings and should be classed as rhetorical warnings with no historical basis, the identification of heathen gods with demons does not occur in the Septuagint except in Bar. 4:7 and the passages listed above; see also Jub. 1:11; 22:17; I Cor. 10:20 f.

It would thus seem that we have here a notion of sin which becomes more and more common after the Maccabean period: sin is rebellion against God. Consequently, sin provokes God's wrath (1:13; 4:6) and is

[25] "Everlasting" (Gr. *aiōnios*; cf. Is. 26:4; 40:28) occurs with the article as a divine name in 4:10, 14, 20, 22, 24, 35; 5:2; "God everlasting" once (4:8). Other appellations in this part of the book are: God (4:7, 12 f.; with the article: 4:6, 9, 21, 23-25, 27 f., 36 f.; 5:1-9), "the Holy One" (4:22, 37; 5:5); "The Everlasting, your Savior" (4:22).

punished by God. Every national calamity, notably that of 586 (2:24-26; 3:8; 4:6, 12), is therefore interpreted as a divine punishment for the people's sin; in fact it was inferred from a calamity that the people had sinned, though they had not been aware of it before. The nation is treated as a whole: nothing is said (as in 4:2) about the opposite fates of individuals who fulfill or disregard the prescriptions of the Law of Moses.

God had warned Israel through Moses (Deut. 28) that sin is inevitably punished (1:20) and repeated the warning through the prophets (2:1 f., 24). When Israel refused to obey, God fulfilled these threats (2:7), for he is just (2:9). The people recognize that they have deserved the punishment (1:15-2:12, 19-26; 3:2), and that even in chastising his people God is merciful (2:27) in not destroying Israel completely (4:6; cf. II Macc. 6:12-16). This merciful punishment has a salutary effect: in the land of exile Israel turns to its God (2:30, 32; 3:7) and the sorely afflicted soul praises the Lord (2:18). In humbly repenting of its sin after God has changed its heart (2:31; 3:7), in casting aside the iniquity of the fathers (3:7), Israel prays God for forgiveness and implores his mercy not on account of the merits of the fathers (2:19) but on account of God's covenant with Abraham, Isaac, and Jacob (2:34), on account of God's own honor (3:5; cf. 2:14). God's forgiveness requires an act of mercy (3:2) and an act of grace making possible true piety and avoidance of sin (3:7). When Israel returns to God wholeheartedly (4:28), he will bring the Exiles back to Jerusalem (2:34 f.; 4:23; 4:36-5:9). No other promise is made: there is no Messiah, no Jewish empire, no resurrection nor immortality (the deceased are in the underworld: 2:17; 3:3), no conversion of the Gentiles (only the destruction of Israel's enemies: 4:25, 31-35). The future hope is terrestrial, it is the restoration of the nation to its land as it was before the Exile; in this book (as in the Second Isaiah) apocalypse and eschatology do not disclose distant chimeric vistas and alluring mirages to a prostrate nation imploring salvation from its God, but merely another chance in the homeland.

CHAPTER VIII

THE EPISTLE OF JEREMY

The "copy of the epistle which Jeremiah sent to those who were to be led captive to Babylon by the king of the Babylonians, to make known unto them in accordance with what had been commanded to him by God" (v. 1 [Gr. 1a]; cf. Jeremiah's epistle in Jer. 29:1-23), as the title of this denunciation of Babylonian idolatry reads, is a separate book in the LXX, but is ch. 6 of Baruch in the Vulgate, in the A.V., and in Luther's Bible. Its contents, following this title, may be summarized as follows:

1. *Introduction* (1-7 [Gr. 1b-6]). The Jews whom Nebuchadnezzar will exile to Babylon on account of their sins shall remain there for seven generations (i.e., until 317 or 306 B.C., reckoning 280 years from 597 or 586, respectively), then God will deliver them (2 f. [Gr. 1b-2]). They must not worship the Babylonian idols there, but remain true to the Lord, whose angel will be with them (4-7 [Gr. 3-6]).

2. *The folly of idolatry* (8-73 [Gr. 7-72]; cf. Jer. 10:1-16; Is. 40:18-20; 41:6 f.; 44:9-20). *a.* Idols may be adorned with gold and silver, which priests sometimes steal for their harlots, but are unable to save themselves from rust, *moths* [so the Latin; Greek "food"], and dust (8-14 [Gr. 7-13]). They may carry a judge's scepter, but they cannot punish the guilty; they may have a warrior's sword, but cannot deliver themselves from soldiers, war, and robbers (15 f. [Gr. 14]).

b. Lacking all life, like a broken vessel, idols are unconscious of all indignities. Their eyes are filled with dust, they are locked in their temples for fear of robbers, they are illuminated through lamps which they cannot see, they are devoured by worms like beams, their faces are blacked by the smoke, and bats, birds, and cats (?) alight over them—but they feel nothing and are therefore not gods (17-23 [Gr. 15-22]).

c. Idols are incapable of any activity. They do not shine unless they are wiped, they felt nothing when they were molten, they are expensive but have no breath, they cannot walk nor move themselves. The offerings that are set before them, as if they were dead men, are sold by priests or preserved in salt by their wives, but not given to the needy; nay, even women in a state of impurity may touch these offerings (24-29 [Gr. 23-28]).

d. Idols can do nothing to others. Even priestesses [unknown in Juda-

426

ism] are allowed to minister in the temples; priests in mourning attire moan before them as in funeral ceremonies; priests may take an idol's garments for their families. But the idols, whether they obtain good or evil, can neither reward nor punish: they can neither crown nor depose a king, nor give riches, nor exact the payment of a vow made to them, nor save a man's life, nor protect the feeble, nor restore a blind man's sight, nor help those in need. They are like stones (30-40a [Gr. 29-39]).

e. Idols are treated contemptuously even by the Chaldeans. Dumb persons are brought before Bel (Marduk) as though he could restore their speech; and women sitting on the roadside are proud to be seduced by a passing man [an abominable practice in honor of Ishtar described by Herodotus I, 199] (40b-44 [Gr. 40-44]).

f. Idols are nothing but works of men's hands. They are only what the sculptors wish them to be and perish like their makers, who bequeath falsehood to posterity. In time of war or other emergencies they must be hidden by the priests, being but wood overlaid with gold and silver (45-52 [Gr. 45-51]).

g. The idols are helpless. They can neither set up kings nor give rain, neither judge nor redress a wrong, neither save themselves in a fire and in war (53-56 [Gr. 52-56a]).

h. The idols are useless. They cannot protect themselves and their property from robbers, being inferior to a valiant king. They lack the utility of a vessel, a door, a pillar of wood in a palace. Sun, moon, stars, lightning, wind, clouds, and consuming fire from heaven all fulfill divinely ordained functions, but idols cannot be compared with them in appearance and power (57-65 [Gr. 56b-64]); nor do they curse or bless kings, show signs in the heavens, and shine like sun and moon. Even beasts are better, because they can help themselves (66-69 [Gr. 65-68]).

i. In conclusion, the idols are like a scarecrow (literally, "amulet") in a garden of cucumbers, which protects nothing, or a white thorn in an orchard, on which every bird sits, or like a corpse cast into darkness. The idols and their garments will rot away, for they are not gods, and will bring reproach to the country. The righteous man who has no idols will therefore be free from reproach—a manifest *non sequitur* (70-73 [Gr. 69-72]).

The "Epistle of Jeremy" is neither an epistle nor was it written by Jeremiah. The author, living some centuries after that prophet, was inspired by Jeremiah's letter (or rather divine oracle) to the Exiles of 597 (Jer. 29:1-23) to prepare another letter of the prophet, dealing with weightier matters. Jeremiah had wisely exhorted the Exiles to mistrust the false prophets in their midst (who ostensibly announced their imminent return to Jerusalem) and to settle down permanently in Babylonia and live amicably with the native population. Shocked by the tenor of this message, which seemed to him either trivial or misleading, the author attributed to Jeremiah what he regarded as a more vital recommendation: let the Exiles beware lest they be frightened or attracted by the Babylonian gods, remembering that these deities are mere idols devoid of life; but let them worship the Lord alone (cf. Jer. 10:1-16, a late interpolation). Neither the genuine nor the forged letter of Jeremiah has the epistolary form—although both are called epistles in the superscriptions and are messages to the Exiles (using the second person plural).

The topic of this sermon attributed to Jeremiah, namely, the folly of idolatry, was not new when the tract was written—unless Jeremiah wrote it. The first known warning against Israel's worship of other gods is Elijah's in his attack against the introduction of Jezebel's Baal (Melkart of Tyre) in Samaria: Elijah failed, but Jehu's bloody *coup d'état* effectively eliminated this alien cult within Israel. Neither Elijah in denouncing the worship of Melkart nor Hosea in denouncing the worship of the Canaanite Baals (since Hos. 2:8b [H. 2:10b]; 11:2, and other references to idols in Hosea are glosses) felt the need of condemning idolatry, which they and the pre-exilic prophets in general obviously considered insignificant. The real polemic against image worship begins with the Deuteronomic Code found in 621 (cf. my articles in JBL 43 [1924] 229-233; 45 [1926] 220 f.). But even in the Ten Commandments, which were part of that code, the worship of alien gods (Deut. 5:7) and the worship of idols (Deut. 5:8-10) are sharply distinguished. It is only later that heathenism and idolatry were identified (so that eventually 'ābōdāh zārāh [foreign cult] came to mean idolatry) and all gods other than Jehovah were regarded as mere images carved out of inanimate matter,[1] as our author emphatically asserts, following Is. 40:18-20; 41:6 f.; 44:9-20, and perhaps even some later imitations of these sarcastic passages (Jer. 10:2-5, 9, 14 f.; Hab. 2:18 f.; Ps. 115:4-8 = 135:15-18; Dan. 5:4, 23). Our author, however, apparently had no knowledge of Wisd. of Sol. 13:10-15:17, which may have been written later than the Epistle of Jeremy. Needless to say, this Jewish denunciation of the religions of the ancient civilized nations, as a senseless adoration of inanimate images, is unfair and unfounded. None, except some of the most superstitious and stupid, identified a god with his image. When the Second Isaiah first equated the pagan gods to their idols, he was not describing actual reality, but drawing a theological inference: since Jehovah was for him the only God in existence, all the other gods could have no reality beyond their dead images, they could be nothing but wood and stone. Having reached this theoretical conclusion, he penned sarcastic caricatures of the idol-

---

[1] Cf. W. W. von Baudissin, *Studien zur semitischen Religionsgeschichte*, Vol. 1, pp. 80-96. Berlin, 1876.

makers to strengthen the Jews in their faith and to convert the heathen to the one true religion. Unfortunately these biting satires (notably Is. 44:9-20) and their later imitations merely gave to the Jews a proud sense of superiority over the Gentiles (cf. Wisd. of Sol. 15:1-6) and contributed to intensifying the animosity of the Gentiles against the Jews in the Graeco-Roman world. Second Isaiah's missionary zeal no longer inflamed his imitators in these tirades against idolatry,[2] but it reappears in a new form in the Apostle Paul (Rom. 1:16-2:16; idols are denounced in 1:22 f.).

This literary background of the Epistle of Jeremy is our only clue for dating the book. Even if it were originally written in Hebrew rather than in Greek, Jeremiah could hardly have been its author, as Roman Catholic scholars still claim,[3] in spite of the fact that Jerome (Preface to his Commentary on Jeremiah [Migne, P.L. 24,706]) did not hesitate to call it a *pseudepígraphon*, i.e., a book falsely attributed to an ancient writer. It is clear that it could not have been written before Is. 44:9-20 (written in 540 at the earliest), and everything indicates that this and similar imitations of that passage were written in the Greek period, after Alexander's death (323), for it was then that the Jews, not always insensitive to the lure of Hellenism, needed to be kept undefiled in the midst of Hellenistic heathenism: attacks against idolatry proved to be one of the most popular forms of antiheathen propaganda at that time. It would seem that the Epistle was written in the period 323-100 B.C., but it is not possible to fix the date more exactly. II Maccabees 2:2 (Jeremiah charged the Exiles "not to be led astray in their minds when they saw images of gold and silver and their ornaments") has been adduced as the earliest reference to our Epistle, but this view has been rightly rejected.[4] Equally unfounded is the suggestion of E. Nestle (*Marginalien und Materialen*, pp. 42 f. Tübingen, 1893) that the Targum to Jer. 10:11 (a verse in Aramaic) refers to our Epistle when it states that that verse is the copy of a letter of Jeremiah.

[2] In addition to the passages of the Old Testament listed above, the folly of idolatry is presented in the following passages from the Apocrypha and Pseudepigrapha (for Wisd. of Sol. see above): Bel 1-22; Jth. 8:18; Arist. 134 ff.; Jub. 11:3 ff., 16 ff.; 12:3 ff.; 20:8; 21:5; 22:17; Enoch 19:1; 46:7; Test. Napht. [Hebr.; M. Gaster, in PSBA 1893-4] 10; Sibyl. Prol. 60 ff.; 3:29 ff., 279, 605 f., 722 f.; 4:6 ff.; 5:356, 403 f. See also Philo, *De vita contemplativa* 1 (and elsewhere); Josephus, *Against Apion* II, 33-35. A faint trace of missionary spirit may be detected in the Alexandrian defenses of Judaism (Wisd. of Sol., Aristeas, Sibyllines, etc.), which at times seem to strive at the conversion of the heathen; but the main purpose of these apologies was the glorification of Judaism. In Palestinian literature a passage like Enoch 50:3 is exceptional.

[3] Cf., e.g., J. Goettsberger, *Einleitung in das Alte Testament*, p. 311. Freiburg i. B., 1928. E. Kalt, *Das Buch Baruch*, pp. 7 f. (HS VII, 4). Bonn, 1932.

[4] O. F. Fritzsche, Commentary to Epistle of Jeremy, p. 206; André, *Les Apocryphes*, p. 267; H. L. Strack, *Einleitung in das A. T.*, 6th ed., p. 173 (Munich, 1906); W. Naumann, *Untersuchungen über den apocryphen Jeremiasbrief* (Beih. ZAW 25), pp. 52 f. (Giessen, 1913); etc.

The book is usually dated either in the time of Alexander or in the Maccabean period. C. J. Ball (in Charles, *Apocrypha*, pp. 596 f.) discovers a clue in the "seven generations" (280 years) from the Exile of 597 or 586 (v. 3 [Gr. v. 2]): the date is accordingly 317 or 306 B.C. W. Naumann (*Untersuchungen*) believes that the account of Babylonian idolatry is an eyewitness report written in ·the time of Alexander, who restored the Babylonian worship. Neither of these arguments is in the least convincing. The present writer prefers to date the book considerably later, in 150-100 B.C., following De Wette, Fritzsche, André, Eissfeldt, and others.

While Roman Catholic scholars (as well as C. J. Ball and O. Eissfeldt) believe that the book was written in Hebrew, nearly all Protestants are convinced that it was originally published in Greek. The strongest argument for a Hebrew original has been presented by Ball (in Charles, *Apocrypha*, pp. 597 f.): he has discovered eight instances of mistranslations from the Hebrew. The most striking of them occurs in v. 72 (Gr. v. 71): "By the purple and marble [*mármaros*] which rots upon them. . . ." Obviously marble cannot rot. Ball ingeniously suggests that "marble" is a mistranslation of Hebrew *shēsh*, which means both "marble" (Cant. 5:15) and "fine linen" (Ex. 25:4, Greek *byssos*), and that the correct translation here should have been "purple and linen." While Ball's arguments are fairly plausible, other explanations may solve the exegetical difficulties of the text. While the evidence as to the original language ·is not conclusive, the present writer is inclined to regard this as an Aramaic book (following C. C. Torrey), although its Hellenistic Greek style is fairly good.

While the author was familiar with Old Testament attacks on idolatry, he discloses some originality in endeavoring to write his Epistle in the name of Jeremiah, in attacking specifically Babylonian idolatry, and in the rhetorical arrangement of his material. Even if Jeremiah were not specifically named as the author in the superscription (v. 1; cf. Jer. 29:1), the situation in vv. 2 f. (Gr. vv. 1b-2) would make an attribution to him nearly inevitable: the message is addressed to the Exiles of 597, and Jehovah promises them that he will bring them (or rather their descendants) back to Jerusalem (cf. Jer. 29:10-14). But our author fails to recapture the tenderness and compassion of Jeremiah (*ibid.*) when he stresses the past sins and the coming temptations of these unfortunate Exiles.

For they will see in Babylon "gods of silver and gold" (v. 4 [Gr. v. 3]) and multitudes worshiping them; but they must remain loyal to their God. After this introduction the author (vv. 8-73 [Gr. 7-72]) proceeds to prove the inanity and folly of Babylonian idolatry, forgetting that Jeremiah in 597 could hardly have known much about it. Even our author, long after, has only superficial and biased information about the

Babylonian religion. Of the numerous gods, he knows only Marduk, whom he calls Bel (i.e., Baal, lord) by his late name (cf. Is. 46:1; Jer. 50:2; 51:44; and Bel and the Dragon); before Bel the dumb are brought for healing (v. 41 [Gr. 40]). Only two religious practices more or less characteristic of Babylonia are mentioned: the mourning for dying gods, like Tammuz (vv. 31 f. [Gr. vv. 30 f.]); and the maidens' sacrifice of their virginity (v. 43 [Gr. vv. 42 f.]), described also by Herodotus (I, 199; cf. Strabo XVI: 1, 20), but with some differences in the details (that such a revolting custom was general is incredible). What our author says about the ritual care of the divine images is not peculiar to the Babylonians: the divine images, at times showing the tongue (v. 8 [Gr. v. 7]), are decked in luxurious garments (vv. 11 f. [Gr. vv. 10 f.]; cf. v. 72 [Gr. v. 71]) which are taken off at times (v. 33 [Gr. 32]); they are cleaned (v. 13 [Gr. v. 12]; cf. vv. 17, 21, 24 [Gr. vv. 16, 20, 23]), supplied with scepters (v. 14 [Gr. v. 13]), daggers, and battle axes (v. 15 [Gr. v. 14]), crowned (v. 9), presented with offerings (vv. 27-30 [Gr. vv. 26-29]) even by priestesses (v. 30 [Gr. 29]), provided with lighted lamps (v. 19 [Gr. v. 18]), and carried in procession (v. 26 [Gr. v. 25]). Despite all care, bats (cf. Strabo XVI, 7), swallows, birds, and cats perch on these images (v. 22 [Gr. 21]), and even though the gates of the temples are locked (v. 18 [Gr. v. 17]), priests (v. 10 [Gr. 9]; cf. v. 33 [Gr. v. 32]), robbers (vv. 15, 57 f. [Gr. 14, 56 f.]), and enemies (v. 56 [Gr. 55]; cf. vv. 48 f.) despoil these idols, or fire may destroy them (v. 55 [Gr. v. 54]). This is all the concrete detail given about the Babylonian religion. Curiously, although the author speaks of the heavenly bodies and meteorological phenomena, admiring (like Job 38:19-38) their submission to God and their beauty (vv. 60-63 [Gr. 59-62]; cf. v. 67 [Gr. v. 66]), he does not seem to realize that they played, in the Babylonian religion, as great a role, if not greater, than the divine images. It is clear that the Babylonian *mise en scène* is artificial and generic (as in Daniel) and fails to lend to Jeremiah's fictitious authorship even the appearance of reality. Like his predecessors in caricaturing heathenism, the author is trying to prove that all pagan religions, being (as he gratuitously claims) nothing but adoration of lifeless statues, are utterly absurd.

That such was his purpose appears from the tireless repetition that the idols are lifeless and helpless. After the introduction, the author divides his sermon into ten parts; in each the truism that wooden and metal images are inanimate is reiterated *ad nauseam*. Each part (except for the last, breaking off abruptly) ends with one of the following refrains, again stressing the obvious: "Thereby they are known not to be gods; therefore fear them not" (vv. 16, 23; cf. 29, 65, 69 [Gr. 14, 22; cf. 28, 64, 68]); "How then should it be thought and said that they are

gods?" (vv. 40 [Gr. 39], 44, 56); "By what [else] then shall it be known
that they are not gods?" (v. 52 [Gr. v. 51]). Once, in the middle of a
section, we read similarly, "How then is it possible not to perceive that
they are not gods?" (v. 49).

While superficially it may appear that the author wished to warn "his
compatriots against the dangers of idolatry" (André, *Les Apocryphes*,
p. 268), in reality this and similar Jewish-Hellenistic works of the time
were addressed to the Gentiles as much as to the Jews, if not more.
Ridiculed and persecuted in centers such as Alexandria, the Jews realized
that the best defense is the attack. Accused of despising the gods by
anti-Semitic writers from Apollonius Molon and Posidonius to Tacitus
(cf. Schürer, *Geschichte*, Vol. 3, p. 548), the Jews, like our author,
merely replied that those gods of the pagans were lifeless images made
by craftsmen. Therefore the Jews rejected them and said in their hearts,
"Thou [alone] art to be worshiped, O Lord [*déspota*]!" (v. 6 [Gr. v. 5]).

ADDITIONS TO THE BOOK OF DANIEL

~~~~~~~~~~~~~~~~~~~~~~~~~~~~~~~~~~~~~~~

The Greek and Latin Bibles in the Books of Daniel and Esther contain narratives and poems missing from the Hebrew Bible; in the modern editions of the English Bible these passages are taken out of their contexts and printed among the Apocrypha.

The additions to Daniel have come down to us in two quite different Greek recensions: the so-called *Septuagint* (LXX) text has survived in a single manuscript of the ninth century, the Codex Chisianus 2 (Holmes and Parsons 88, Field 87) in Rome (Chigi Library);[1] and *Theodotion's* revision of the LXX on the basis of the Hebrew Bible, which displaced the LXX of Daniel in the Greek Bibles used in the Christian Church and thus was the basis of the versions made for church use (Vulgate, Peshitta, Coptic, Ethiopic, Arabic, Armenian, Georgian, English Authorized and Revised versions, etc.).

These are the additions to Daniel found in the Greek texts: I. The Prayer of Azariah and the Song of the Three Children. II. The Story of Susanna. III. The Stories of Bel and of the Dragon. As shown in the following summary, these three groups actually comprise five or six separate compositions.

I. THE PRAYER OF AZARIAS AND THE SONG OF THE THREE HOLY CHILDREN

1. *The Prayer of Azarias* (vv. 1-22 [LXX and Vulgate: Dan. 3:24-45]). *a.* Introduction: Ananias, Misael, and Azarias (Hananiah, Mishael, and Azariah) praised God in the midst of the fiery furnace and Azarias prayed as follows (vv. 1 f.).

b. God is to be praised because he is always just (vv. 3 f.), even when he brought calamity on the Jews, through the destruction of Jerusalem and the Exile, on account of their sins (vv. 5-10). Yet God, for his name's sake, and on account of his Covenant and of his love for the Patriarchs, should not destroy them utterly (vv. 11-13). For the

---

[1] The Greek text is conveniently available in the editions of the Septuagint by Tischendorf (unsatisfactory), Swete, and Rahlfs; and in Fritzsche's edition of the Apocrypha. Besides the Codex Chisianus we have two other indirect witnesses to the LXX of Daniel: the Syriac version of Origen's edition of the LXX in his Hexapla, called the Syro-Hexaplar text and, in part at least, the Old Latin.

moment the Jews, being deprived of state and Temple, are inferior to all other nations (vv. 14 f.); but in a contrite heart they have turned to God (vv. 16-18), trusting that in his mercy and might he will deliver them and put to shame their oppressors (vv. 19-22).

2. *Narrative introduction to the Song of the Three Children* (vv. 23-28 [LXX and Vulgate: Dan. 3:46-51]). Fuel of various kinds was added to the furnace until the flames reached the height of 49 cubits and destroyed the Chaldeans in the vicinity (vv. 23-25). But an angel drove the flames out of the furnace and produced a pleasant wind in it, so that the three youths were not harmed (vv. 26 f.). They sang the following hymn (v. 28):

3. *The Song of the Three Children* (vv. 29-68 [LXX and Vulgate: Dan. 3:52-90]). *a.* God is blessed, praised, and exalted forever (vv. 29-34).

b. The *Benedicite* of the Prayer Book (vv. 35-65), a liturgy in which the second half-line of each verse is an identical refrain, as in Ps. 136; it resembles Ps. 148, 150. All the works of the Lord should bless the Lord (v. 35), in particular the heavens (v. 36) and what belongs to them (vv. 37-51), the earth (v. 52) together with inanimate things (vv. 53-56) and animals upon it (vv. 57-59), and mankind (v. 60), especially Israel (vv. 61-65).

c. Ananias, Azarias, and Misael should bless the Lord (v. 66), as also all the pious (vv. 67 f.; v. 67 reproduces the LXX of Ps. 135:1 [Hebr. and Engl. 136:1]).

II. SUSANNA

1. *According to the Greek text of Theodotion* (and the Latin and English Bibles). Joakim, a wealthy Jew in Babylon, married Susanna, who was very pious and beautiful (vv. 1-3). Prominent Jews came to the house of Joakim, which was surrounded by a park (v. 4); among them two aged judges to whom the Scriptures refer saying that wickedness came out of Babylon from aged judges (v. 5; presumably an allusion to the false prophets Ahab and Zedekiah in Jer. 29:21-23): these two were frequent visitors (v. 6).

In the afternoon, after the visitors had left, Susanna used to walk in the park (v. 7), and the two elders saw her often and became so inflamed with love for her that they gave no thought to God and his judgments (vv. 8 f.). They were ashamed to confess their passion to each other (vv. 10-12). But one day, after leaving Joakim's house at dinnertime, each one of the elders returned secretly and upon meeting again were forced to acknowledge their lust; they agreed to seek the opportunity of finding Susanna alone (vv. 13-14).

One day, while the elders were hidden in the park, Susanna sent her two maids to fetch oil and cosmetics, asking them to close the doors; she wished to bathe in the garden pool, for the day was hot (vv. 15-17). The two elders, no sooner had the maids departed, ran to Susanna and threatened to accuse her of committing adultery with a young man unless she yielded to their passion (vv. 18-21). Faced with death whatever she did, Susanna chose to be falsely accused rather than to sin in the sight of God (vv. 22 f.). She shouted for help, but the elders cried out and one of them ran to open the door, while the maids returned and were shocked in hearing the accusation against their mistress (vv. 24-27).

On the morrow the two elders asked that Susanna be brought before Joakim and the people gathered in his house (vv. 28 f.). When she came with her family, the elders, to enjoy her beauty, commanded her to unveil; her friends wept and laid their hands on her head (vv. 30-34). She wept, and they testified that they had surprised her in the park with a young man, who escaped (vv. 30-40). The assembly believed them and condemned her to death (v. 41), but Susanna's prayer was heard by God (vv. 42-44).

While Susanna was being led to execution, God inspired Daniel; he berated the people for condemning a woman without thorough examination and accused the elders of having borne false witness (vv. 45-49). When the case was reopened, Daniel cross-examined the two elders separately (vv. 50 f.): the first one testified that Susanna committed adultery under a mastic tree (vv. 52-55), the second under a holm oak (vv. 56-59). In accordance with the law of Deut. 19:18 f., as interpreted in 105-79 B.C. by the Pharisees (who, in opposition to the Sadducees, condemned to death a false witness in a criminal case even if the defendant had not been executed), the two elders were put to death (vv. 60-62). Susanna's family praised God for her innocence (v. 63), and Daniel henceforth enjoyed public esteem (v. 64).

2. *According to the Greek text of the Septuagint.* (The omitted verses were lacking in the original LXX.) Two elders, denounced in Jer. 29:21-23, were appointed as judges and decided cases from other cities (vv. 5 f.). They saw Susanna walking in the park of her husband Joakim at eventide and were so inflamed by love for her that they ceased to give thought to God and right decisions (vv. 7-9). They concealed their passion from each other and Susanna was unaware of it (v. 10). At dawn each elder came secretly to look at her and, finding each other, they made a mutual confession of their passion (vv. 12-14). Together they came to Susanna and tried to force her to yield to their lust (v. 19), but in her dilemma she chose to arouse their enmity rather than to commit sin (vv. 22 f.). Planning vengeance, the two elders came to the synagogue (v. 28) and asked the assembly to summon Susanna (v. 29). She came

accompanied by her parents, five hundred servants of both sexes, and her children (vv. 30 f.). The lawless pair had her unveil to enjoy her beauty (v. 32), but her attendants and friends wept (v. 33). The elders and judges laid their hands on her head (v. 34; cf. Lev. 24:14). Susanna prayed silently, and God listened to her entreaty (vv. 35). The two elders testified that, coming to the stadium in her husband's park, they spied a woman consorting with a man (vv. 36-38); coming closer, they recognized Susanna, but the young man was masked and escaped (v. 39). She refused to tell who he was (vv. 40-41a). The whole synagogue believed them (v. 41b).

As she was being led to execution, an angel bestowed discernment on Daniel (vv. 44 f.). He berated the crowd for condemning her without thorough examination and asked leave to cross-examine them (vv. 48, 51). The first elder, in answer to Daniel's question, stated that Susanna had been surprised under a mastic tree (vv. 52-55); the other under a holm oak (vv. 56-59). The synagogue condemned them to suffer the penalty of their intended victim, in accordance with Deut. 19:18 f. (vv. 60 f.). They gagged them and hurled them into a chasm where an angel hurled fire in their midst: so was innocent blood kept safe (v. 62). This is why young men were beloved of Jacob for their sincerity (v. 63); therefore young men should be guarded, so that they may become valiant, pious, and understanding (v. 64).

III. BEL AND THE DRAGON
a. The Story of Bel (vv. 1-22)

A. *According to the Greek text of Theodotion.* Astyages died, and Cyrus reigned in his stead (contrast Herodotus I, 130) (v. 1; Vulgate: Dan. 13:65; vv. 2-42 in the Greek are vv. 1-41 in Latin). At the Babylonian court Daniel was greatly honored (v. 2). The Babylonians provided for their idol, Bel (or Marduk), fine flour, sheep, and wine daily in good measure (v. 3). Daniel told Cyrus that he would not worship Bel—an idol made with hands—instead of the Creator of heaven and earth (v. 4 f.). To the king's objection that Bel ate quantities of food daily (v. 6), Daniel replied that, being made of clay covered with brass, Bel never ate anything (v. 7). In anger the king summoned the priests (seventy in number) and declared that unless they told him who consumed Bel's food they would die, but if they proved that Bel consumed it, Daniel would die; then the king and Daniel went into the temple (vv. 8-10). The priests agreed to let the king set forth Bel's food and seal the temple door overnight (vv. 11 f.), having little fear of dying, for they could enter the temple by a trap door under the god's table to consume the food (v. 13). So the king placed the food before Bel, but Daniel, without the knowledge of the priests, had servants strew ashes over the floor (v. 14). In the night the priests and their families came as usual to eat the food (v. 15). In the morning the king and Daniel came to the temple and Daniel certified that the seals were intact (vv. 16 f.). Seeing the food gone, the king praised Bel (v. 18), but Daniel laughingly called the king's attention to the footprints on the floor (v. 19). Recognizing footsteps of men, women, and children, the king forced the priests to show him the secret trap door and slew them with their families (vv. 20 f.). Daniel destroyed the image of Bel and its temple (v. 22).

B. *According to the Greek text of the Septuagint.* "From the prophecy of Habakkuk the son of Jesus of the tribe of Levi" (v. 1). Daniel, a priest, was a companion of the king of Babylon (v. 2). The Babylonians worshiped the idol of Bel (or Marduk), and provided for him wheat flour, sheep, and oil daily in good measure (v. 3). The king worshiped Bel daily and asked Daniel why he did not; Daniel replied that he worshiped only the Lord who created heaven and earth (vv. 4 f.), and added that the king should not be deceived by the food that was apparently consumed by Bel, for, being nothing but clay and bronze, it never ate anything (vv. 6 f.). The king summoned the overseers of the temple, threatening them with death if other than Bel consumed the food but condemning Daniel to death if Bel really consumed it (vv. 8 f.). Bel's seventy priests conducted the king into the temple (v. 10) and the food was laid before Bel (v. 11). Then Daniel requested that the king seal the door (vv. 12 f.); after Daniel's attendants had put the people out of the temple and sprinkled the floor with wood ashes, he had the door sealed with the signets of the king and of priests of high rank (v. 14). When they returned on the morrow, the priests, entering through secret doors, had consumed the food and drunk the wine (v. 15). Daniel asked the priests and the king to verify the seal impressions (vv. 16 f.). On entering they saw that the table was empty and the king praised Bel (v. 18). But Daniel, laughing heartily, invited the king to see the deception of the priests and asked him whose footprints were on the floor (v. 19). The king recognized the footprints of men, women, and children and, going to the priests' house, found Bel's food and wine; Daniel showed the king the secret doors (v. 21). The king delivered the priests to Daniel and gave him the remnants of Bel's food; but Bel was destroyed (v. 22).

b. The Story of the Dragon (vv. 23-42)

A. *According to the Greek text of Theodotion.* The Babylonians also worshiped a great dragon (v. 23). The king asked Daniel to worship the dragon, for he was alive, ate, and drank; but Daniel would worship only the Lord (vv. 24 f.). Daniel obtained leave to slay the dragon without sword or staff (v. 26): he boiled together pitch, fat, and hair; the dragon ate the lumps thus obtained and burst asunder (v. 27). But the Babylonians conspired against the king, accusing him of having become a Jew (v. 28), and asked him to deliver Daniel unto them (v. 29). So Daniel was cast into the lions' den, remaining there six days with seven lions who had not been fed (vv. 30-32). In Judea the prophet Habakkuk was on the point of bringing pottage and bread to the reapers (v. 33) when the angel of the Lord ordered him to bring the food to Daniel in the lions' den (v. 34). Habakkuk objected, but the angel carried him by the hair of his head to the lions' den (vv. 35 f.). Habakkuk delivered the dinner, and Daniel praised the Lord (vv. 37 f.). Daniel ate, and the angel instantly brought Habakkuk back (v. 39). On the seventh day the king came to bewail Daniel but found him sitting in the den (v. 40). The king then praised God, drew Daniel out, and cast his enemies into the den, where they were devoured instantly (v. 41 f.).

   B. *According to the Greek text of the Septuagint.* The Babylonians worshiped also a dragon (v. 23). The king asked Daniel to do homage to the dragon, for he was alive, ate, and drank (v. 24).[2] Daniel asked and received permission to slay the dragon without sword and staff (vv. 25 ff.). Daniel took thirty minas of pitch, fat, and hair; and boiling them together, he made a cake, which he threw into the dragon's mouth: the monster burst asunder; then Daniel asked the king whether the fragments would be worshiped (v. 27). The Babylonians arose against the king, saying that he had become a Jew (v. 28). Seeing the mob, the king delivered Daniel to them (v. 30), and they cast him into the den where seven lions were fed daily with two corpses of traitors: thus he would have no burial; and he was there six days (vv. 31 f.). On the sixth day Habakkuk was taking a bowl of crumbled bread loaves and a jar of mixed wine to the reapers (v. 33), when the angel of the Lord ordered him to take them to Daniel (v. 34). Habakkuk objected, but the angel brought him over the lions' den by the hair of his head (vv. 35 f.). Habakkuk gave the dinner to Daniel, who said that God does not forsake those who love him (vv. 37 f.). While Daniel ate, the angel set Habakkuk back where he had been; God remembered Daniel (v. 39). Going to the den to bewail Daniel, the king peered in and saw him sitting there (v. 40). The king then praised God, led Daniel out, and cast his enemies into the den, where they were devoured (vv. 41 f.).

1. The Greek Texts

The Christian Church, to which we owe the preservation of the Greek Old Testament (commonly called the Septuagint [LXX]), at an

---

[2] Verses 25 and 29 of Theodotion are omitted in the Septuagint, but following A. Rahlfs's *Septuaginta*, both texts have here the same number for parallel verses.

early date discarded the old Alexandrian Greek version of the books of Chronicles-Ezra-Nehemiah and of Daniel, substituting the revision thereof made by Theodotion early in the second century of our era. The old Alexandrian version (LXX) has survived only in part for Chronicles-Ezra-Nehemiah in the "apocryphal" I Esdras (the Greek Ezra), but for Daniel we have the complete text in the Codex Chisianus and in a Syriac version.

Jerome (d. 420) was at a loss to explain this preference of Theodotion to the Septuagint, on the part of the Church. In his preface to Daniel (Migne, PL 28, 1291) he writes: "The churches of the Lord Savior do not read the prophet Daniel according to the Seventy Interpreters [LXX], using [instead] the edition of Theodotion; and why this happened I do not know. . . . This only I am able to assert, that [the LXX] disagreed greatly from the truth [i.e., the Hebrew-Aramaic text], and was rightly rejected." Since Jerome, others have made guesses as to the reason for the unpopularity of the Septuagint: the liberty taken with the text by the translator, particularly in chs. 4-6, the erroneous rendering of the "weeks" (9:24-27) with "seventy" (a confusion easily made in reading an unpointed Hebrew text), and the like.[3]

A. Bludau (op. cit., p. 24) believes that the decisive reason for the rejection of the LXX on the part of the Christians was that the above-mentioned misinterpretation of Dan. 9:24-27 ended the availability of the passage as a prophecy of the coming of the Messiah in the person of Jesus.

Like Jerome, we can only make inferences and guesses about the reasons for the rejection of the LXX of Daniel in favor of Theodotion on the part of the Christian Church. Modern scholars, with few exceptions, have re-echoed and variously specified the harsh judgment of Jerome: F. Field, in his famous edition of Origen's Hexapla, even wrote that the LXX of Daniel was translated so absurdly that no healing hand could adapt it for Church use.[4] With greater fairness, A. Bludau (op. cit. p. 87) considers the LXX, in view of the difficulties facing the translator, a surprising achievement; and J. A. Montgomery (Daniel, in the ICC, pp. 36 f. New York, 1927), admitting the peculiarities of the original text translated in Dan. 4-6 and recognizing that this original was glossed throughout, praises the translator as "a writer of skill in Greek and of ingenious spirit."

It is possible that the LXX of Daniel dates back to the period 160-132,

---

[3] The most detailed study of the differences between the Hebrew-Aramaic text of Daniel and the Greek "Septuagint" text is that of August Bludau, Die alexandrinische Übersetzung des Buches Daniels. (Bibl. Stud. II, 2-3. Freiburg i. B., 1897).

[4] "Tam putide et praepostere jacet, ut nulla manu medica ad Ecclesiae usum accommodari posset" (F. Field, Origenis Hexapla, Vol. 1, p. xxxix. Oxford, 1875).

if the grandson of Ben Sira (preface to Ecclesiasticus) included it in "the other books of our fathers" and "the rest of the books" which had been translated into Greek by 132, in addition to the Law and the Prophets. This cannot be positively established, although it has been maintained that the same translator prepared the LXX versions of Daniel and I Esdras (cf. Montgomery, *Daniel*, p. 38) and that the latter was known to Eupolemus in 150 B.C. (C. C. Torrey, *Ezra Studies*, p. 82. Chicago, 1910). But it may be safely assumed that the LXX of Daniel is not later than about 100 B.C., for it was used by the Greek translator of I Maccabees soon after that date (Bludau, *op. cit.*, pp. 8 f., n. 6; Montgomery, *loc. cit.*). No one doubts that the LXX of Daniel was prepared in Egypt, presumably at Alexandria.

It is now necessary to say a word about the text of the LXX accessible to us. Ancient works, Hellenistic, Jewish, and classical, which did not enjoy much popularity among the Christians either perished or survived accidentally. The LXX of Daniel, no longer in official use after Theodotion had taken its place in the Church Bible, has survived through unexplained circumstances in a ninth-century cursive manuscript (Codex Chisianus in Rome)[5] which contains also the version of Theodotion: in Holmes and Parsons' great edition of the LXX both versions in this manuscript are indicated by the same symbol: "88" (Field uses "87" to indicate the LXX part). Pope Alexander VII (d. 1667), a member of the Chigi family to whom the manuscript belonged, allowed the Vatican librarian, Leo Allatius, to edit it. But it was only a century later that an incomplete edition was prepared by Vincent de Regibus and Joseph Bianchini; this was finally completed and issued anonymously by Simon de Magistris (des Maîtres) in 1772 at Rome (*Daniel secundum Septuaginta ex Tetraplis Origenis*). This edition was reprinted, with improvements, by J. D. Michaelis (Göttingen, 1773; with Latin translation and notes, Göttingen, 1774), by C. Segaar (Utrecht, 1775), H. A. Hahn (Leipzig, 1845), and others. The edition of the Septuagint prepared by R. Holmes and J. Parsons (Oxford, 1798-1927) unfortunately reproduced merely the copy of the Chisianus made by Leo Allatius. In his edition of the Greek Bible, C. Tischendorf reproduced the text of 1772, correcting it partially according to the unsatisfactory text of Holmes and Parsons. The best editions of the LXX of Daniel are those of O. F. Fritzsche (*Libri Apocryphi Vet. Test.* Leipzig, 1871), J. Cozza (*Sacrorum Bibliorum vetustissima fragmenta graeca et latina*, Pt. 3. Rome, 1877), H. B. Swete (*The Old Testament in Greek*, Vol. 3. Cambridge, 1894; and later editions), and A. Rahlfs (*Septuaginta*. Stuttgart, 1935). While Cozza gave a very exact reproduction of the codex, E. Nestle (in the

---

[5] C. Tischendorf, C. Vercellone, J. Wellhausen, and M. Löhr date the Codex Chisianus in the eleventh century (cf. A. Bludau, *Alexandr. Übersetz.* p. 25, n. 2).

6th and 7th editions of Tischendorf's Septuagint, 1880 and 1887), Swete, and Rahlfs utilized for the critical apparatus the only other extant witness to the LXX of Daniel: the Ambrosian manuscript of the Syriac version of Origen's edition of the LXX (the "Syro-Hexaplar" version prepared in 617 by Bishop Paul of Tella), edited for Daniel by C. Bugati (Milan, 1788) and reproduced sumptuously in photo-lithography by A. M. Ceriani (*Monumenta sacra et profana*, Vol. 7. Milan, 1874). The colophon both of the Chisianus and the Ambrosian Syro-Hexaplar states positively that the text is that of the LXX. The Greek colophon reads: "Daniel according to the LXX; it was written from a copy having this note, 'It was written from the Tetrapla from which it was supplied [with critical notes].' "[6] Origen's critical marks occur in both the Chisianus and the Ambrosianus, and his asterisks indicate that in the Hexapla (as well as in the Tetrapla copied from it) the text of the LXX was supplemented from Theodotion and other versions, as for instance in Susanna vv. 1-5. On the whole the Chisianus and the Syro-Hexaplar correspond very closely, even in minute details: thus, for instance, in Dan. 11:42 the same error (Greek *gais* instead of *tais*) occurs in both; for a good comparison of the two, see M. Löhr, "Textkritische Vorarbeiten zu einer Erklärung des Buches Daniel" (ZAW 15 [1895] 75-103; 193-225; 16 [1896] 17-39). German translations of both the LXX and Theodotion are printed in parallel columns in E. Kautzsch, *Die Apokryphen und die Pseudepigraphen*, Vol. 1; and English translations similarly in R. H. Charles, *Apocrypha and Pseudepigrapha*, Vol. 1. All other English versions of the Apocrypha, from John Wycliff's (1382) to E. J. Goodspeed's (1938), as also the versions prepared for Church use in other languages, are based on Theodotion.

The origin of Theodotion's version is not clear. While it is certain that Theodotion prepared his edition of the Greek Bible in the period A.D. 100-130, readings characteristic of Theodotion occur in earlier writings, notably in the New Testament (especially in Revelation and Hebrews). It has been plausibly inferred from these facts that Theodotion merely revised slightly a Greek version which was circulating in the first century of our era by the side of the LXX version of Daniel.[7]

For our present purposes it is important to know whether the LXX of Daniel, in its first edition about 100 B.C., contained the additions lacking

[6] In the Syro-Hexaplar the colophon reads: "It was written from copies having this subscription: 'It was written from the Tetrapla, with which it has been compared.' "

[7] Bludau, *Die Alexandr. Übersetz.*, pp. 12-25. H. B. Swete, *Introd. to the Old Test. in Greek*, pp. 46-49. E. Schürer (*Geschichte*, Vol. 3, p. 441). J. A. Montgomery, *Daniel*, pp. 46-50. Montgomery (p. 50) is certain that this "Ur-Theodotion" existed before our era, but may not have been committed to writing, being merely "a Hellenistic oral Targum."

in the Masoretic text: if this can be demonstrated, we are supplied with a valid clue for dating these "apocryphal" additions. Since L. Bertholdt (*Daniel*. Erste Hälfte, pp. 151-154. Erlangen, 1806), no other scholar has doubted that the additions were an integral part of the LXX of Daniel. In fact, it seems to be the accepted view that the LXX contained them from the beginning, since, as O. F. Fritzsche (Commentary, p. 114) and others later have noticed, the style of the additions agrees with that of the rest in the most minute particulars:[8] the contrast between the diction and style of the LXX and of Theodotion is most illuminating in this respect. Needless to say, Theodotion (and therefore "Ur-Theodotion") contained the additions from the first. The references to "Ananias, Azarias, Misael" in this order—as given in the Song of the Three Children (v. 65; Gr. Dan. 3:88; cf. LXX 3:24) but never found in the canonical Daniel (cf. Dan. 1:6 f., 11, 19; 2:17)—in I Macc. 2:59; IV Macc. 16:21; 18:12 seem to indicate that the Greek Daniel with its additions (or at least with this addition; cf. also III Macc. 6:6 [quoting Gr. Dan. 3:46, 50]; IV Macc. 16:3) enjoyed canonical standing among the Jews in Alexandria.[9] This fact confirms, indirectly, the conclusion that the Greek version or versions of Daniel circulating before our era contained the additions. Everything indicates, however, that Aquila undoubtedly (as may be inferred from Origen, *ad Africanum* §2), and Symmachus presumably, omitted them.

The canonicity of the additions to Daniel was questioned even before Jerome expressed some misgivings in his *Preface to Daniel*. Julius Africanus wrote about 240 from Palestine to his friend Origen, expressing his surprise that Origen did not notice that the story of Susanna was a spurious portion, recent and fictitious, of the Book of Daniel; the same was true of the two additions at the end, i.e., Bel and the Dragon (Migne, PG XI, 44; *Origenis Opera*, ed. Lommatzsch, Vol. 17, pp. 17 ff.). Africanus adds that these passages are lacking in the Hebrew Scriptures, which are normative for the Greek Old Testament; the Greek puns in Susanna (*schînos, schízein* [mastic tree, to cut in two], vv. 54 f.; *prínos, príein* [holm oak, to saw in two], vv. 58 f.) prove that the story was written

[8] Cf. C. J. Ball (in H. Wace, *The Apocrypha*, Vol. 2, pp. 308 f.). A. Bludau (*Alex. Übers.*, p. 161). W. Rothstein (in E. Kautzsch, *Apokryphen*, p. 176). C. Julius (*Die Griechischen Danielzusätze und ihre kanonische Geltung*, pp. 16 f. Bibl. Stud. VI, 3-4. Freiburg, i. B., 1901). L. E. T. André (*Les Apocryphes*, p. 210). Among modern scholars only Wm. Robertson Smith (*The Old Testament in the Jewish Church*, p. 154) says "these are perhaps later additions to the Greek version."

[9] Likewise the following early Christian writers name "Ananias, Azarias, Misael" in this order, according to the Greek Bible: Clement of Rome [d. *ca.* 100] (*Corinthians* 45:7); Justin Martyr [d. *ca.* 165] (*First Apology* 46:3). Conversely, the order in Josephus, *Antiquities* X:10, 1 (§§188 f.), is that of the Masoretic text: Ananias, Misael, Azarias.

originally in Greek and not in Hebrew.[10] Origen replied in a long letter: he admitted that the Jews could not tell him how the puns would have sounded in Hebrew, but for the rest stoutly maintained the canonicity of the Greek Bible and not seldom quoted the additions to Daniel as Scripture;[11] he even accused the Jews of deliberately removing the additions from their own Scriptures.

Reserving for a later discussion the problem of the original language in which each addition was written, we must inquire into the date of the substitution of Theodotion for the LXX in the Christian Church, and into the date of the latter's disappearance from circulation.

At least as early as the first century of our era we find Daniel quoted according to Theodotion's Greek text, as we have noticed above. The Greek text of Baruch, chs. 1-2 (cf. André, *Apocryphes*, pp. 251 f.; but see Montgomery, *Daniel*, p. 50), the Epistle to the Hebrews (11:33; cf. Dan. 6:22), the Revelation of St. John (cf. Bludau, *Alex. Übers.*, pp. 14 f.; Montgomery, *op. cit.*, p. 49), the Gospel of Matthew (cf. Montgomery, *ibid.*), and Clement of Rome (*To the Corinthians* 34:6; cf. Dan. 7:10) occasionally quote Daniel according to Theodotion's Greek text. It is thus clear that Theodotion was beginning to be used at least in the first century of our era. In the second century, however, the LXX was still occasionally used side by side with Theodotion, as may be seen in the quotations from Daniel by Justin Martyr (cf. Montgomery, *Daniel*, p. 48). But at the end of the second century, as shown by the consistent use of Theodotion in the writings of Irenaeus (d. *ca.* 202), this version had definitely prevailed over the LXX; Hippolytus (d. *ca.* 235), a disciple of Irenaeus, and Origen (d. *ca.* 254) definitely used Theodotion's text as the basis of their commentaries on Daniel. In the Latin Church, however, the Old Latin version of Daniel based on the LXX was exclusively used by Tertullian (d. *ca.* 230) and Victorinus of Pettau (d. 303). However, the Latin Bible of Cyprian (d. 258) already discloses readings from Theodotion as well as from the LXX, and already in the third century (in the tract *De Pascha computus*, dated in 243, and in Commodian, who flourished about 250) a new version of Daniel definitely based on Theodotion was in use and prevailed exclusively in the fourth

---

[10] Porphyry (quoted by Jerome in the preface to his commentary on Daniel) makes the same observation as Africanus. In his preface to Daniel, Jerome quotes Africanus approvingly and illustrates the force of the puns for his readers through some similar examples in Latin; in English the best I can suggest as a parallel is: pine tree, pine away; ash tree, turn to ashes. J. T. Marshall (Hastings, *Dictionary of the Bible*, Vol. 4, p. 632a) suggests puns in English and Aramaic similar to the Greek. See also C. J. Ball in Wace, *Apocrypha*, Vol. 2, p. 324.

[11] References to the additions to Daniel in ancient Christian literature are given, among others, in: C. Julius, *Die Griechischen Danielzusätze Bibl. Stud.* VI, 3-4. 1901; W. H. Daubney, *The Three Additions to Daniel*, Cambridge, 1906; E. Schürer, *Geschichte*, Vol. 3, pp. 454-456.

and later centuries.[12] We may thus conclude that Theodotion in Daniel triumphed over the LXX in 150-200 in the Greek Church and in 230-250 in the Latin Church.

Daniel in the Greek text of the LXX disappeared gradually. Origen was still familiar with it; although he preferred Theodotion, he included the LXX in his Hexapla and Tetrapla. Jerome knew Origen's Hexaplar edition of the LXX, but he regarded it as corrupt (*multum a veritate discordat*) and made Theodotion the basis of his version of the additions to Daniel. Manuscripts of the Hexaplar LXX were still available in Alexandria in 615-617, when the Syro-Hexaplar version was prepared by Paul of Tella and his collaborators.[13] But after that time the LXX of Daniel became more and more inaccessible: after the ninth or eleventh century, when the sole extant copy of the LXX of Daniel (Codex Chisianus) was prepared, the LXX text disappeared entirely from view until the publication of this manuscript in 1772. The Church had by then read the additions to Daniel for many centuries in Theodotion's text or in translations therefrom, and from all indications, whatever be the scholarly opinion, the Church will continue to ignore the LXX text of these additions.

2. The Song of the Three Holy Children

Under this title the English Bible includes: 1. Narrative sections supplementing the story in Dan. 3 (vv. 1 f., 23-28; Gr. and Lat.: Dan. 3:24 f., 46-51); 2. The confession and prayer of Azarias (vv. 3-22; Gr. and Lat.: Dan. 3:26-45); 3. The song of praise of the three youths (vv. 29-68; Gr. and Lat.: Dan. 3:52-90).

Jerome prefixed to this addition (following Dan. 3:23) a note stating: "What follows I have not found in Hebrew scrolls."[14] Nevertheless, Roman Catholic scholars, in harmony with the practice of their Church, generally regard 3:24-90 as an original, integral part of the Book of Daniel,[15]

---

[12] See F. C. Burkitt, *The Old Latin and the Itala*, pp. 6 f., 18-31. (Texts and Studies IV, 3). Cambridge, 1896.

[13] The earliest edition of the Old Latin and the Syro-Hexaplar are the only ancient versions based on the LXX. The following are based on Theodotion's Greek text, at least for the additions lacking in the Masoretic text: the second edition of the Old Latin, the Vulgate, the Syriac Peshitta, the Coptic (Bohairic and Sahidic), the Ethiopic, the Arabic, the Armenian, the Georgian, as well as the later versions in European languages.

[14] At the end, Jerome adds after 3:90 the following note, "Thus far it is lacking in the Hebrew; and what we have set down was translated from Theodotion's edition."

[15] J. Goettsberger, however, regards all the additions to Daniel as secondary (*Einleitung in das Alte Testament*, p. 323. Freiburg i. B., 1928. *Das Buch Daniel* [HS VIII, 2], pp. 28, 94. Bonn, 1928).

a view which has been defended occasionally by Protestant scholars, like Howorth.[16]

Three different theories have been advanced by scholars: all of Gr. Dan. 3:24-90 was part of the original Hebrew-Aramaic Daniel, or was added in a later edition; it was composed in Greek or translated from stray Semitic material by the Greek translator responsible for the LXX; only the bulk of the narrative sections (vv. 1, 23-27; Gr. 3:24, 46-50) belonged to the first edition of Daniel; the poems, however, were circulating separately.

To reach some conclusion in the matter we should determine, if we can, the original language of the poems and narratives. The evidence furnished by the two versions of the Greek (LXX and Theodotion), which differ but slightly, and the Syriac (rendered from the Greek) is not decisive, and competent scholars have reached opposite conclusions. Thus, for instance, Fritzsche, Schürer, Strack, König, and other Protestant scholars regard Greek as the original language; but all Roman Catholic scholars, down to J. E. Steinmueller (1942), not a few Protestants (Rothstein, Ball, Howorth, Marshall, Daubney, Bennett, Goodspeed, Eissfeldt, Torrey) and Jews (J. Fürst, *Der Kanon des Alt. Test*, pp. 102 f. Leipzig, 1868; M. Waxman, *A History of Jewish Literature*, vol. I. p. 17. New York, 1938) believe that the Greek text was translated from a Semitic original. This latter view seems more plausible. The Greek abounds in Semitic idioms and expressions[17] which are either a sign of "translation Greek" woodenly reproducing the Semitic idioms or a deliberate imitation of the language found in some parts of the Septuagint. The latter explanation is unlikely, for the remnants of Hellenistic-Jewish literature usually do not exhibit such an abundance of Semitic expressions in Greek. Linguistic clues for determining whether the poems and the narratives were written in Hebrew or Aramaic are lacking; nevertheless, we may surmise that the two psalms were composed in Hebrew, which was the sacred language of prayer and praise, while the narratives could well have been written in Aramaic, like the rest of Dan. 3, for which they were manifestly composed.

There is no reason for attributing the poems and the narrative to the same author. The poems, as in the case of some poems inserted in the Old Testament narratives from poetic anthologies (I Sam. 2:1-10; Is. 38:9-20; Jonah 2:1-9 [H. 2:2-10]), are not entirely appropriate to the story and were not composed *ad hoc*. An editor found copies of the poems and, considering them appropriate for the occasion, inserted them

---

[16] Henry Howorth, "Some Unconventional Views on the Text of the Bible," Part VII (PSBA 29 [1907] 31-38, 61-69).

[17] Cf. A. Bludau, *Die Alex. Übers.*, p. 160; J. T. Marshall (in J. Hastings, *Dictionary of the Bible*, Vol. 4, p. 755); W. H. Daubney, *The Three Additions to Daniel*, pp. 49-53; W. H. Bennett (in Charles, *Apocrypha*, p. 628).

into the Semitic manuscript of Daniel from which the LXX was trans-lated. This editor merely added an introductory verse for each poem (v. 2; Gr. and Lat. 3:25; and v. 28; Gr. and Lat. 3:51) and at least one verse to the second poem (v. 66; Gr. and Lat. 3:88), or possibly its end (vv. 66-68; Gr. and Lat. 3:88-90), in order to name Ananias, Azarias, and Misael specifically among the creatures praising God.

The remaining narrative portions (v. 1; Gr. and Lat. 3:24; and vv. 23-27; Gr. and Lat. 3:46-50) may or may not be the work of the same redactor. Exactly as C. C. Torrey believes that he has discovered in Greek Ezra some genuine verses which were omitted from the standard Masoretic text of Ezra (*Ezra Studies*, pp. 28-30), so some critics regard either the whole addition[18] (vv. 1-68; Gr. and Lat. 3:24-90) or at least the narrative verses[19] as an integral part of the first edition of the Book of Daniel in Hebrew-Aramaic. J. A. Montgomery (*Daniel*, p. 9) at first accepted the latter view (as presented by Rothstein), but later con-cluded that the story in the canonical text "is far more striking in leaving the discovery of the marvel to the heathen king's eyes, rather than with the *banal* explanation made to precede it. Which is all a matter of taste!" We shall never know for certain whether the narrative verses in Greek Ezra and Daniel preserved in the LXX but not in the Hebrew were really an original part of the Hebrew-Aramaic canonical books. What is certain is that they were in early copies of these books accessible to the first Greek translators. Thus both Biblical books written partly in Hebrew and partly in Aramaic (Ezra and Daniel) were current for a while in two editions of the original, a longer and a shorter one. Whether the longer edition was the original one or not, the oldest Greek version, commonly called the LXX, was made from the longer one; but while Theodotion in Ezra is based on the shorter version, in Daniel it runs parallel to the LXX. Eventually, the shorter version of both books in the original was canonized by the rabbis, while Alexandrian Jews preferred the longer version.

The religious teaching of the poems is that of the immediate precursors of the Pharisees, and does not lack parallels in the Psalter. The prayer of Azarias (vv. 3-22; Gr. and Lat. 3:26-45), being a liturgical confession

---

[18] It has been said that without the whole addition there would be a lacuna in the text and Nebuchadnezzar's words following it would be inexplicable: see the references in A. Bludau, *Alex. Übers.* p. 165, n. 1.

[19] W. Rothstein (in E. Kautzsch, *Apokryphen*, pp. 175 f.) regards vv. 1-2a, 23 (in Theodotion), 24-27 (Gr. and Lat. 3:24-25a, 46 [Theod.], 47-50) as original; he is followed by L. E. T. André (*Apocryphes*, p. 215), who considers vv. 1, 23-27 (Gr. and Lat. 3:24, 46-50) as a genuine part of the canonical text. G. Jahn (*Das Buch Daniel nach der Septuaginta hergestellt*. Leipzig, 1904) limits the original section to vv. 26-28 (Gr. and Lat. 3:49-51). W. H. Bennett (in Charles, *Apocrypha*, p. 629) is inclined to regard vv. 1 f., 23-27 (Gr. and Lat. 3:24 f., 46-50) or some-thing like it as original (standing between Dan. 3:23 and 24).

of national sin closely resembling Daniel's prayer in Dan. 9:4-19 (cf. Jer. 26; 32; 44; Ezra 9; Neh. 1; 9; Bar. 1:15-3:18), is unsuited to the plight of a pious martyr in the midst of the fiery furnace. It may confidently be asserted that the prayer was copied from an anthology and was not composed for Azarias. Aside from the fact that the Jerusalem Temple has been destroyed by Nebuchadnezzar, only the absence of "prince, or prophet, or leader, or burnt offering, or sacrifice, or oblation, or incense, or place for divine offerings" (v. 15; Gr. and Lat. 3:38) can serve as a clue for dating the prayer. But the poet, presumably writing in Jerusalem a considerable period later, described imaginatively the condition of the Exiles in Babylonia during the reign of Nebuchadnezzar, although he erred both in fact and in doctrine when he denied that there were prophets in their midst; he may have been misled by texts referring to a later period, such as Ps. 74:9. The prayer was probably written in the second century B.C.

As in Ps. 51:17 (cf. Is. 57:15), "a contrite heart and a humble spirit" are a substitute for sacrifice (v. 16; Gr. and Lat. 3:39) in atoning for sin. The people's transgression is described in the most general terms as sinning in all things and committing iniquity by departing from God and violating the commandments of his Law (vv. 6 f.; Gr. and Lat. 3:29 f.; Theod. has "thy commandments" instead of "the command of thy Law" in the LXX). The God of the Fathers (v. 3; Gr. and Lat. 3:26) is just and right (v. 3; 3:27) and has in his true judgment delivered his people into the hands of lawless enemies and the most wicked of all kings (v. 9; 3:32). For his name's sake (v. 11; 3:34), for the sake of the promises to Abraham (vv. 12 f.; 3:35 f.), and in view of the repentance (vv. 16 f.; 3:39 f.) and conversion of the Jews (v. 18; 3:41), God should save them (vv. 19 f.; 3:42 f.) and humiliate their foes (vv. 21 f.; 3:44 f.).[20]

The second poem (vv. 29-68; 3:52-90) is a liturgical hymn of praise, adapted to the situation of the three youths in the fiery furnace through the addition of v. 66 (3:88),[21] in which the three singers of this hymn, Ananias, Azarias, and Misael, exhort themselves to sing God's praises (second person plural) because he has delivered *us* in the fire. The

[20] Needless to say, the last verse (22; 3:45) is not "a petition for the conversion of the Gentiles," as W. H. Daubney (*Three Additions to Daniel*, p. 63) asserts: the Gentiles should merely recognize that Jehovah is the only God, glorified in the whole earth—a very different thing from conversion to Judaism.

[21] In all probability, as assumed by L. E. T. André (*Apocryphes*, pp. 220 f.), W. H. Bennett (in R. H. Charles, *Apocrypha*, p. 637), and others, vv. 66-68 (3:88-90) are a spurious conclusion of this psalm, intended to connect it with its present context. In the *Odes* or *Cantica* placed at the end of the Psalter in some manuscripts of the Greek Bible (cf. the editions of the Septuagint of Swete and Rahlfs), this psalm ends with v. 66a (3:88a): "Bless, O Ananias, Azarias, Misael, the Lord, sing his praises and extol him exceedingly forever." The rest is lacking. Most of vv. 67 f. (3:89 f.) was quoted verbatim, anyhow, from the LXX of Ps. 135:1 f. (Hebrew and English 136:1 f.).

change of person per se indicates interpolation. In all probability the poem was quoted from a Hebrew psalmbook because it seemed appropriate to such a miraculous deliverance.

This liturgical psalm may have been sung antiphonally, in its original form. The second half of the verses (except for the first and last ones) looks like the response of the congregation: "praise and exalt him above all for ever." One poem in the Psalter (Ps. 136, Gr. 135) presents a similar antiphonal structure: the second half of all verses is "for his mercy endureth forever." But as for the contents, Ps. 148 is very close to our poem, and it is difficult to escape the conclusion that one composition influenced the other, although it is not possible to determine with assurance which of the two is the earlier. In both all creatures are invited to praise the Lord. The order in Ps. 148 is as follows: (heavens, heights) angels, hosts, sun and moon, stars, heavens of heavens, upper waters, (earth) sea monsters and deeps, fire and hail, snow and vapour, stormy wind, mountains and hills, trees, beasts, cattle, creeping things, birds, men. The order in the psalm of the Three Children is: heavens, angels, upper waters, hosts, sun and moon, stars, rain and dew, winds, fire and heat, nights and days, light and darkness, cold and heat, frost and cold, frost and snow, lightning and clouds, earth, mountains and hills, vegetation, fountains, seas and rivers, whales, birds, beasts and cattle, men, etc. It is possible that both poems were inspired by Ecclus. 43 and were influenced by considerably earlier compositions describing God's creative activity or poems on the theme "The heavens declare the glory of God" (Ps. 19): Job 38, Ps. 104, Gen. 1, etc. The hymn of praise of the Three Children is thus far from original and vital; it is rather a standardized composition molded on well-known patterns. Nevertheless, this *Benedicite opera omnia* has achieved a place in Christian hymnology and has been used in the liturgy, both in the East and in the West, since early times. In his *Holy Year* (1864) Bishop Wordsworth alludes to it in his Michaelmas Hymn (No. 102):

> Angelic voices we shall hear
> Joined in our jubilee,
>   In this thy Church, and echoing
> Our Benedicite.

3. The History of Susanna

The story of Susanna is of course pure fiction. It is of interest as one of the first examples of a favorite modern literary form: the detective story (as also the story of Bel, but not the story of the Dragon), and it has been included at the beginning of some recent collections of typical detective stories. The earliest example of a story containing at least the germ of criminal detection is, I believe, the story of the judgment of Solomon in I Kings 3:16-27—a tale of Indian origin which had originally nothing to do with Solomon. Just as such a tale would be attached to Solomon, famous for his wisdom, so other tales like Susanna would be told of Daniel, nearly as celebrated as Solomon for his wisdom (Ez. 28:3; cf. a poem from Ras Shamra-Ugarit) and also regarded as a paragon of piety (Ez. 14:14, 20). Such stories would inevitably gravitate toward the Book of Daniel and become part of it in some of its editions.

Like the stories of Ahikar, of the Three Youths at the Court of Darius (in I Esdras), Tobit, and others, Susanna is a good example of a tale of pagan origin, told in Aramaic in the Persian period or later, and adopted with slight retouches by the Jews. It is of course impossible to tell exactly where Susanna originated or when; we have it in a Greek version made at Alexandria about 100 B.C. It seems most unlikely to the present writer that, as many scholars assert, it was written originally in Greek— in spite of the strong argument made by Julius Africanus in the time of Origen on the basis of the Greek puns previously mentioned, as well as of the characteristics of the Greek style. While all Roman Catholic scholars have maintained that Susanna and the other additions to Daniel were translated from the Hebrew or Aramaic, most Protestant scholars have followed Africanus in asserting that Susanna "could only have been written in Greek" (André, *Apocryphes*, p. 228). Following J. G. Eichhorn, Franz Delitzsch, Paul de Lagarde, C. J. Ball, however, some recent Protestant scholars have defended the Hebrew or Aramaic origin of Susanna.[22] Although a final solution of this problem may never be possible, and one should perhaps give "a verdict of 'non liquet'" (W. H. Daubney, *Three Additions to Daniel*, p. 34; cf. O. Eissfeldt, *Einleitung*, p. 646), the present writer believes that the evidence favors a Semitic original.

On the date and place of origin of Susanna's story no information is available. Internal clues are vague. Since the story is contained in the "LXX" Greek version of Daniel, which can be dated with some assurance about 100 B.C., we may conclude that the story is not later than that date, and probably not more than half a century earlier. The most natural place of origin, if the original story was written in Hebrew or Aramaic, would be Judea. As shown by the Book of Esther (which the present writer would date about the same time as Susanna), stories were written in Jerusalem in the late second century B.C. about Jewish

[22] W. Rothstein (Kautzsch, *Apokryphen*, p. 178); J. T. Marshall (Hastings, *Dictionary of the Bible*, vol. 4, p. 632); D. M. Kay (Charles, *Apocrypha*, pp. 641 f.), R. H. Charles (*Encyclopaedia Britannica*, 14th edition, Vol. 7, p. 30a: Theodotion was translated from the Hebrew, the LXX probably from the Aramaic); E. J. Goodspeed (*The Story of the Apocrypha*, p. 68. Chicago, 1939); C. C. Torrey, *The Apocryphal Literature*, p. 56; and others.

heroines living in the lands of the dispersion; the story of Sara in the Book of Tobit (which is somewhat earlier) offers another example of a wrongly suspected innocent Jewess, whose virtue was finally vindicated through divine help. Those who believe that the story of Susanna was written originally in Greek would naturally regard Egypt, or more exactly Alexandria, as its place of origin.

The interpretations of the meaning of the story and the guesses about the author's purpose may be classed into two groups: the story was written to teach a lesson; the story is no more didactic than the tales of the *Arabian Nights.* We may dismiss without discussion a third interpretation: the story is the record of actual historical events. The historicity of the book can only be asserted to support its canonicity, and is therefore based on dogmatic postulates; here, in a purely objective inquiry, we may accept the findings of some early critics, like J. D. Michaelis (*Mosaisches Recht,* Vol. 6, pp. 129 ff., 300. Biehl, 1877) and J. C. Eichhorn (*Einleitung in die Apokryphischen Schriften des Alten Testaments,* pp. 449 ff. Leipzig, 1795), and regard the story as fiction.[23] The two didactic and the three fictional interpretations that are worthy of notice are the following:

1. A didactic book with moral and religious purpose. Respected old men do not always deserve unqualified confidence, for a pious youth is preferable to aged rascals (J. G. Eichhorn [1795], Johannes Jahn [1802]). Divine providence does not abandon an innocent person falsely accused (E. Reuss, *La Bible,* Old Test., Vol. 6, p. 611. Paris, 1878; L. E. T. André, *Apocryphes,* pp. 227 f.). According to A. Bertholet (in K. Budde's *Geschichte der althebräischen Litteratur,* pp. 384 f. 2nd ed. Leipzig, 1909) the story was inspired by Daniel's name (meaning, "God is my judge") and presents the model of the upright young man and of the virtuous young wife.

2. A didactic book with a juristic purpose. Moritz Duschak (*Mosaisch-talmudische Strafrecht,* pp. 94 f. Vienna, 1869) considers the story of Susanna as a legend which dates back into exilic times the painstaking care of a certain Ben Zakkai (identified by the Talmud with Johanan ben Zakkai [d. *ca.* A.D. 80]) in cross-examining witnesses in criminal cases. When the witnesses declared that a murder had taken place under a fig tree, he wished to know whether the tree's stems were thick or thin,

---

[23] For the sake of completeness we may add two other interpretations, which we need not discuss here. Hippolytus (d. *ca.* 235) in his commentary on Daniel interprets the story of Susanna allegorically: Joakim represents the Christ, Susanna the Church, the bath is the baptism, the two elders are the Jewish and pagan persecutors of the Church. A Scholz (*Esther und Susanna,* p. 139. Würzburg, 1892) solved the difficulties inherent in the theory that Susanna is genuine history by regarding the book as the report of a vision.

its figs dark or pale.[24] The obvious objection to this view is the necessity of dating Susanna in the late first century of our era if not later, disregarding our evidence for a considerably earlier date.

A more elaborate juristic theory has been presented by N. Brüll[25] and has found considerable favor among some British scholars.[26] In brief, Susanna is, according to Brüll, a polemical pamphlet of the Pharisees attacking the Sadducees for their laxity in court procedure during the reign of Alexander Janneus (103-76 B.C.). The leader of the Pharisees at that time, Simeon ben Shetach, advocated greater strictness in cross-examining witnesses and the death penalty for false witness. His motto was "Examine the witnesses thoroughly, and [in doing so] be cautious with your words lest they learn [from them] to utter falsehood" (Sayings of the Fathers [Pirqē Abōth] 1:9). It is related that after he had sentenced to death eighty women from Ashkelon for sorcery, their relatives brought capital charges, through false witnesses, against Simeon's son. The latter protested his innocence so eloquently on the way to execution that the witnesses confessed their false testimony. When the judges would have freed the young man, he protested that a witness withdrawing his former statement must not be believed, and he said to Simeon, "Father, if you wish that help come through you, use me as a threshold" (Jerus. Sanhedrin VI, 23b). During the reign of Alexandra, the widow of Janneus (76-67 B.C.), Simeon reformed the court procedure and, according to Brüll, Susanna was written in Pharisaic circles to attack the Sadducees (represented by the wicked elders) and extol the Pharisees (represented by Daniel).

The most serious objection to such a theory is that the average reader, even when the story first appeared, would hardly consider the story of Susanna as an appeal for a stricter administration of justice—unless a scholar explained it to him in that sense. In any case the redactor of the LXX text (v. 63) draws from the story the lesson that God-fearing young men have in them knowledge and discernment, while Theodotion (v. 64) merely regards the incident as the beginning of Daniel's growing reputation among the Babylonian Jews.

[24] Bab. Sanhedrin 41a; cf. Mishna Sanhedrin V, 2. These rabbinical parallels to Susanna had been pointed out previously by: Zecharias Frankel (Der gerichtliche Beweis nach mosaisch-talmudischen Recht, u. s. w., p. 199. Berlin, 1846) and Abr. Geiger (Urschrift und Übersetzungen der Bibel, pp. 195 f. Breslau, 1857).

[25] "Das apokryphische Susanna Buch" (JJGL 3 [1877] 1-69).

[26] The following accept and summarize Brüll's theory: C. J. Ball (in Wace, Apocrypha, Vol. 2, pp. 325-331. London, 1888); J. T. Marshall (in Hastings's Dictionary of the Bible, Vol. 4, pp. 631 f.); D. M. Kay (in Charles, Apocrypha, pp. 638, 643 f.); W. O. E. Oesterley, The Books of the Apocrypha, p. 393 (London, 1914); and An Introduction to the Books of the Apocrypha, pp. 283-285 (New York, 1935). Cf. also M. Waxman, A History of Jewish Literature, Vol. 1, p. 15 (2nd ed. New York, 1938).

The present writer agrees with W. Baumgartner when he says (ARW 24 [1926-27] 264), "All such attempts to interpret [Susanna] in accordance with the history of law take the story far too seriously. It is wasted effort to seek to find here any kind of juristic instruction or reform, or even an exact picture of prevailing juristic conditions. Daniel is not the better jurist, the cleverer judge, but the man sent by God and endowed with the needed wisdom to deliver a condemned innocent woman."

3. A legendary tale. This view is presented very briefly by O. F. Fritzsche in his Commentary (p. 118. Leipzig, 1851), and more fully by others. According to a Jewish legend,[27] a variant of which Origen[28] and Jerome[29] heard from their Jewish teachers, the two false and adulterous prophets denounced by Jeremiah (Jer. 29:21-23) vainly attempted to seduce the daughter or wife of Nebuchadnezzar and were executed in the fiery furnace. A number of scholars[30] have recognized in this haggadic interpretation of Jer. 29:21-23 the source of the first part of the story of Susanna. The obvious parallels between the two narratives should, however, not overshadow the important differences between them. At most we may say that both stories are variants of a well-known folkloristic motif, that of the virtuous woman who rejects improper advances; but the theme of the innocent woman wrongly accused is lacking in the Jewish Haggadah.

4. The echo of a myth. H. Ewald (*Geschichte des Volkes Israel*, Vol. 4, p. 636; 3rd ed., 1864), followed by A. Kamphausen (Cheyne's *Encyclopaedia Biblica*, Vol. 1, col. 1014 [1899]), discovered in the story of Susanna the echo of a Babylonian myth (to which Mohammed alluded in the Koran, 2:96): two elders were seduced by the goddess of love. The parallels are too vague to prove anything.

Others have searched Greek mythology for the source of the Susanna story.[31] K. Fries ("Schuschanna" in OLZ 13 [1910] 337-350; reprinted in his *Kleine Beiträge* u.s.w., 1911) believed that Susanna, like the hetaera Phryne, was originally a virgin goddess, and that the two elders were the slaves who helped her bathe, and were then put to death. W. Schultz (*Memnon* 4 [1910] 137 f.) saw in Susanna the virgin swan, spied amo-

[27] See, for the version of the story in English, L. Ginzberg, *Legends of the Jews*, Vol. 4, pp. 336 f. (Philadelphia, 1913); for references to the original texts, see *op. cit.* Vol. 6, p. 426, n. 106 (cf. p. 415, n. 79). See also W. Baumgartner, ARW 24 (1926-27) 264-266; C. J. Ball, in Wace, *Apocrypha*, Vol. 2, pp. 325-328.

[28] *Letter to Africanus*, 52 ff. (Migne, PG, Vol. 11, pp. 61 ff.) and *Stromata* X (Migne, *op. cit.* p. 101).

[29] Commentary on Jer. 29:20-23 (Migne, PL, Vol. 4, pp. 862 f.).

[30] L. Bertholdt (*Historisch-kritische Einleitung in sämtlichen Schriften des Alten und Neuen Testaments*, Vol. 4, p. 157, n. 5 [1812 ff.]); Z. Frankel (MGWJ 17 [1868] 447 f.); N. Brüll (JJGL 3 [1877] 5 ff.); C. J. Ball (Wace, *Apocrypha*, Vol. 2, pp. 325 ff.); J. T. Marshall (Hastings, *Dict. of the Bible*, Vol. 4, p. 631.

[31] Cf. W. Baumgartner in ARW 24 (1926-27) 266-268.

rously in her bath, as well as the eponym goddess of Susa, the capital of Elam. According to E. Siecke (*Memnon* 5 [1911] 123 ff.), Susanna was the sun-goddess spied by the moon-god, shortly before conjunction, in her bath. It is a sign of real progress in Biblical research that such fantastic mythological interpretations of Jewish tales are no longer fashionable.

5. A folk tale. That the story of Susanna is fiction without an ulterior purpose, "a pure invention suggested by facts of not infrequent occurrence . . . a folk-tale in laudation of the famous prophet Daniel" (C. H. Toy, in *Jewish Encyclopedia*, Vol. 11, p. 603 [1905]), is the most probable opinion, and seems destined to prevail.[32] This appears to have been the view of Sextus Julius Africanus (*ca.* A.D. 200) in his polemic with Origen; and it is not without significance that the story of Susanna appears, substantially intact, in the *Arabian Nights*—without seeming to be out of place.

It is clear that at least two folkloristic motifs have been utilized in the story of Susanna: the innocent woman falsely accused and the clever young judge.

The tale of the chaste wife repudiated or condemned to death on the word of a rejected suitor is usually called the "Genoveva-type" of story (cf. the article "Geneviève" in the *Encyclopaedia Britannica*. 11th or 14th ed.). The earliest known occurrence of this motif, in a variant form, is the story of Tamar in Gen. 38; its opposite is the story of Potiphar's wife (Gen. 39:7-20), based on the Egyptian *Tale of the Two Brothers* (A. Erman, *The Literature of the Ancient Egyptians*, pp. 151-153. London, 1927. G. A. Barton, *Archaeology and the Bible*, pp. 300 f. Philadelphia, 1916, and later editions). Numerous parallels occur in Eastern and Western folk tales up to modern times.[33]

The other principal motif is that of a clever judge or helper (often a young boy) who delivers a person out of an apparently desperate situation or cleverly reaches a just decision in a previously falsely settled court action.[34]

---

[32] The best presentations of the folkloristic elements in Susanna are: G. Huet, "Daniel et Susanne. Note de littérature comparée" (RHR 65 [1912] 277-284; cf. 66 [1917] 129 f.); W. Baumgartner, "Susanna: die Geschichte einer Legende" (ARW 24 [1926-27] 268-280; cf. 27 [1929] 187 f.).

[33] See H. Gunkel, *Das Märchen im Alten Testament*, p. 126 (Religionsgeschichtliche Volksbücher II, 23/26). Tübingen 1921; the articles of Huet and Baumgartner cited in the preceding footnote; and particularly Stith Thompson, *Motif-Index of Folk-Literatures*, Vol. 4, pp. 480-482. Bloomington, Ind., 1934.

[34] Numerous variants of this motif are cited by Huet and Baumgartner, cf. the preceding notes. See also, for the literature on the subject, Stith Thompson, *Motif-Index of Folk-Literatures*, Vol. 4, p. 81; cf. pp. 76-80. Huet notes correctly that the youth of the judge or helper (Daniel was twelve years old when he saved Susanna, according to early exegetical tradition) was at times a trait added subsequently to stories told originally of older men.

Aside from these two main motifs, some details of the story of Susanna may have been derived from Oriental folklore: thus, for instance, the trees are witnesses in lawsuits in a number of tales (cf. Baumgartner, *op. cit.*, p. 269, and n. 2); we should add the Syriac *Kalilah we-Dimnah* (F. Schultess, *Kalila und Dimna syrisch und deutsch*, Vol. 2, pp. 45 f. Berlin, 1911).

Leaving to folklorists further investigation of this interesting topic, we may conclude that the story of Susanna was pagan in origin and had no didactic purpose at first. When the Jews adopted it and inserted it into the Book of Daniel in one of its editions, they identified the clever youth with Daniel and changed all the other characters into Jews living in Babylonia during the Exile. The religious elements, which are strictly Jewish, were likewise part of the same process, for which we have parallels in the adaptation, for a Jewish public, of alien folklore in Ahikar, Tobit, and the Three Youths at the Court of Darius.[35] The action takes place, as in all ancient Jewish stories, in a pious Jewish milieu (v. 3), in Babylonia, where criminal justice among the Jews was administered in strict adherence to the Law of Moses (vv. 60-62; cf. Deut. 19:16-21). The scriptural reference in v. 5 (Theodotion) is not to be found in the Old Testament, and seems to be a confused reminiscence of Jer. 29:23. The Jewish editor patriotically regards the Judean women as more moral than those of the Ten Tribes of Israel (v. 57); and naturally, for in his day the detested Samaritans regarded themselves as the heirs of North Israel.

The religious teaching of the book is in harmony with that of Tobit and Judith, the latter of which is more or less contemporary with Susanna. The sorely troubled turned in their distress to God on high in fervent prayer (v. 35; Susanna's prayer is given in v. 35b in the LXX and in 42 f. in Theodotion); and the Lord, who knows all secrets including the future (v. 35b, LXX; v. 42, Theod.), rescues his servants from death. Through his angels (vv. 44 f., LXX) or directly (v. 45, Theod.), God inspired Daniel and thus saved Susanna. Angels are said to execute the divine sentence (v. 55; cf. v. 62, LXX). Thus God is represented as close to the individual; the sense of God's nearness is so strong that when determined to commit a sin the two elders perverted their mind first and avoided to look toward heaven (either literally or meaning "toward God," cf. Dan. 4:23) in order to forget God and his Law (v. 9). Thus by these additions[36] and slight retouches, what had been a tale of clever detection of criminals became an edifying account of God's vindication of the innocence of the pious and of his infallible punishment of the wicked.

[35] Numerous instances of a similar later use of alien folklore in Jewish tales and legends will be noticed in the collection of L. Ginzberg (*The Legends of the Jews*).

[36] W. Baumgartner (*op. cit.*, p. 280) lists the following additions in the LXX: vv. 5, 9, 35, 35a, 44 f., 52 f., 57.

4. Bel and the Dragon

These two stories have the primary purpose of ridiculing heathenism, particularly as practiced in Babylon, and the secondary purpose of exhibiting Daniel's brilliant wisdom in police detection and in chemical concoctions. As to the historicity of these two tales and of Susanna, one is tempted to repeat with Horace, *credat . . . Apella, non ego* (Horace *Sermones* I, 5:100 f.). Jerome called them rightly "fables" (Preface to Daniel): *"Belis draconisque fabulas."*

It is a commonplace in the Old Testament that idols cannot eat (Deut. 4:28) and, being merely wood and stone, the work of men's hands, are incapable of all functions characteristic of living beings (a list of passages has been compiled by the writer in JBL 43 [1924] 239). Such is the theme of the Epistle of Jeremy; polemic against idolatry in the Bel story assumes the form of a detective tale.[37] Bel (Is. 46:1; Jer. 50:2; 51:44) is philologically the same word as the Hebrew Baal, and became eventually a name for Marduk, the god of Babylon, whose temple built by Nebuchadnezzar was one of the seven wonders of the ancient world. This temple of Marduk was plundered by Xerxes I (485-465 B.C.), who carried away even the golden statue of the seated god and killed a priest who attempted to stop him (according to Herodotus I:183). Strabo (XVI:1, 5) tells us that the "sepulcher of Bel" (i.e., the Marduk temple) in Babylon was found in ruins by Alexander (332 B.C.) and that he planned to rebuild it. But actual information about the destruction of the temple, sometime between Xerxes and Alexander, is lacking—aside from our unhistorical book in Theodotion's version, which erroneously dates the destruction in the time of Cyrus the successor of Astyages. In any case, it may be safely assumed that the author of the story knew that the Marduk (Bel) temple in Babylon was in ruins at the time he was writing his tale.[38]

While the worship of Bel (Marduk) at Babylon is known through innumerable Neo-Babylonian inscriptions (625-538 B.C.), not to mention

[37] In the text of Theodotion, but not in the LXX, special emphasis is placed on the contrast between the sole living God and the idols of the heathen (Bel, v. 5); Daniel laughed at the Idol (v. 7) and will die for blasphemy against God if the facts do not prove him right (v. 9). In Theodotion the priests of Bel are put to death by the king (Cyrus in Theod.) and Daniel overthrew Bel and his temple; in the LXX the king delivered to Daniel the priests and the balance of what had been expended on Bel, but the king destroyed the statue of Bel (v. 22).

[38] A student inclined to check the amount of food placed before Bel according to the story (v. 3) with a Babylonian account of the same may read the text of Nebuchadnezzar published in cuneiform in H. C. Rawlinson, *The Cuneiform Inscriptions of Western Asia*, Vol. 1, p. 65, col. I, lines 13-28 (London, 1861); translated in S. Langdon, *Die Neubabilonischen Königsinschriften*, p. 91 (Vorderasiatische Bibliothek. Leipzig, 1912). The differences are more conspicuous than the similarities.

later sources, there is of course not the slightest historical evidence (outside of our book) for the worship of a living dragon alleged in the second tale, although some have equated the mythical dragon with a living snake supposed to be adored in Babylon.[39] In any case the two stories are slightly connected by their opposite conclusions about food for pagan gods: divine images do not partake of it, but divine animals may be killed by eating indigestible food.

The slaying of the dragon in the second tale is a distant echo of a well-known myth, circulating through the whole Mediterranean world from very ancient times and continuing in Christian times in the stories of St. Michael or St. George slaying the dragon. The earliest known version of this myth is Sumerian, and dates from the third millennium B.C. or before.[40] It has been suggested that the story of Daniel's destruction of the dragon was inspired by the well-known Babylonian story of Marduk's slaying of Tiamat:[41] the most emphatic defender of this view is H. Gunkel (*Schöpfung und Chaos in Urzeit und Endzeit*, pp. 320-323. Göttingen, 1895).[42] While his argument is based in part on farfetched resemblances, it is probable that the author of our tale knew of the Babylonian myth and it is even possible that he may have deliberately written a caricature of it. This sarcastic note is apparent in the absurd notion that the eating of a cake made of pitch, fat, and hair (LXX), or lumps made thereof (Theodotion), could possibly cause a dragon to burst asunder. The author could hardly have expected to be taken seriously, and we may dismiss these tales as samples of popular Jewish fiction of little literary and no religious significance, dating from about 100 B.C.[43]

[39] W. H. Daubney, *The Three Additions to Daniel*, p. 212; cf. J. T. Marshall, in Hastings, *Dictionary of the Bible*, Vol. 1, p. 268a. The evidence for Babylonian worship of serpents, particularly of live ones, is scanty and questionable (cf. J. Hastings's *Encyclopaedia of Religion and Ethics*, Vol. 11, p. 403; S. Landersdorfer, "Der Drache zu Babylon" in BZ 11 [1913], 1-4).

[40] See S. N. Kramer, *Sumerian Mythology*, pp. 76-83. Memoirs of the American Philosophical Society, Vol. 21. Philadelphia, 1944.

[41] A transcription and translation may be found in R. W. Rogers, *Cuneiform Parallels to the Old Testament*, pp. 3-44 (New York, 1912) and elsewhere; for a recent translation see A. Heidel, *The Babylonian Genesis*, Chicago, 1942.

[42] The theory of Gunkel was adumbrated before him by C. J. Ball in Wace, *Apocrypha*, Vol. II, p. 347. After Gunkel, this theory was defended by J. T. Marshall (Hastings, *Dictionary of the Bible*, Vol. 1, p. 267) and C. H. Toy (*Jewish Encyclopedia*, Vol. II, p. 650). On the other hand the theory is rejected by W. Davies (in R. H. Charles, *Apocrypha*, pp. 653 f.), following P. Jensen and W. W. Baudissin.

[43] For the stories of Bel and the Dragon in later Jewish literature, see L. Ginzberg, *Legends of the Jews*, Vol. 5, p. 291, n. 136; Vol. 6, p. 427, n. 112; p. 432, n. 6; p. 434, n. 8; p. 435, n. 13; 436, n. 18. An apparent survival of the story of the Dragon in a Christian environment is reported by Ruy Gonzalez de Clavijo (d. 1412), who was sent by Henry III of Castile on a diplomatic mission to Tamerlane in 1403. On this journey, he was told in Antioch in that year that the thumb of the relic of St. John was fed to the dragon and made it burst asunder (Clavijo, *Embassy to Tamerlane, 1403-1406*. Translated by Guy Le Strange, pp. 65 f. New York, 1928).

CHAPTER X

THE PRAYER OF MANASSES

~~~~~~

This penitential psalm is entitled in the printed editions of the Vulgate "The Prayer of Manasses, King of Judah, when he was held captive in Babylon," and "The Prayer of Manasses" in Greek and Latin manuscripts. It was composed with reference to II Chron. 33:11-13, according to which Manasses repented and prayed when a captive in Babylonia; and 33:18 f., according to which the prayer was "contained both in the acts of the kings of Israel" and in "the history of *Hozai* [or, *the seers*]." This poem was included in the *Didascalia* (a Christian writing of the third century, later incorporated into the *Apostolic Constitutions*) and in some manuscripts of the Septuagint (for instance, the Codex Alexandrinus); it was included among the Odes or Canticles appended to the Psalter (so in A. Rahlfs, *Septuaginta* II, 180 f.). In the Vulgate it is printed after the New Testament (in late manuscripts after II Chronicles). Its contents may be summarized as follows:

O Lord almighty, God of Israel (v. 1), maker of heaven and earth (v. 2), through whose command the sea and the abyss were restrained (v. 3 f.; cf. Job 38:8-11; Ps. 104:9), before whom all things tremble and the sinner cannot endure (v. 5) but whose mercy is infinite (vv. 6 f.), thou hast appointed repentance not for the righteous but for me, a sinner (v. 8). I have committed innumerable transgressions and now I am in fetters, weighed down by my sins through which I provoked thy wrath (vv. 9 f.). And now I bend the knee of my heart (v. 11), confessing my sins (v. 12) and beseeching thy forgiveness (v. 13). Thou wilt save me, unworthy as I am, in thy mercy; and I shall praise thee during my whole life (v. 14). For the hosts of heaven praise thee, and thine is the glory forever (v. 15).

No information on this prayer is available before the third century of our era, when it is found in Syriac in the *Didascalia*.[1] The earliest Greek

---

[1] The Syriac text has been published in a critical edition by P. de Lagarde (*Didascalia apostolorum syriace*. Leipzig, 1854; reprinted in 1911). For the English translation see: R. H. Connolly, *Didascalia Apostolorum*, Oxford, 1929. A German translation has been published by H. Achelis and J. Flemming (*Die syrische Didaskalia*. Leipzig, 1904. The prayer is on pp. 36 f.). See also E. Hennecke, *Neutestamentliche Apokryphen*, 2nd ed., pp. 583-587. Tübingen, 1924. A Syriac edition of the prayer has been published also by F. Nau (*Revue de l'Orient chrétien* [1908] 134-141). For additional bibliography, see O. Bardenhewer, *Geschichte der altkirchlichen Literatur*, 2nd ed., Vol. 2, pp. 310-312. Freiburg i. B., 1914.

text is that of Codex Alexandrinus (British Museum), written in Egypt in the fifth century, where it is the eighth of the Odes or *cantica* (appropriately following Is. 38:9-20) copied after the Psalter; it is the ninth poem in the *Psalterium Turicense* (Zürich).[2] E. Nestle (*Septuaginta-studien* III, pp. 4-22; IV, pp. 5-9. Stuttgart, 1899, 1903) and F. Nau may be right in assuming that the Greek text in the manuscripts of the Septuagint was derived from the *Didascalia*, but nothing indicates that the Christian author of that work composed the obviously Jewish Prayer of Manasses, as Nau (*op. cit.*, p. 137) regarded probable (following J. A. Fabricius, *Liber Tobiae, Judith, Oratio Manasse, Sapientia et Ecclesiasticus*, p. 208. 1691). Since Origen and Jerome manifestly did not find the prayer in the manuscripts of the Greek Bible accessible to them, the suggestion of Sir Henry Howorth (PSBA 31 [1909] 89-99), according to which the Prayer of Manasses and the related narrative in the *Didascalia* are a remnant of the original LXX version of Chronicles-Ezra-Nehemiah (discarded in favor of Theodotion), must remain an attractive conjecture unsupported by clear evidence.

Neither of these views on how the Prayer of Manasses found its way into the Greek Bible (either from the *Didascalia* or from the original LXX) helps us to solve a second problem: Was it originally written in Hebrew (or Aramaic) or in Greek? For the Greek Bible contains some additions to the Hebrew canonical books translated from the Hebrew-Aramaic and others composed in Greek. Here again, owing in part to the brevity of the text, the evidence is ambiguous and critical opinion is divided.[3] An examination of the Greek text leads to no certain conclusion. We find a number of Semitic idioms reproduced literally, such as: "from the face of thy power" (v. 4); "evil in the sight of . . ." (Hebr. "in the eyes of . . .") (v. 10); "angry for an eternity" (v. 13; cf. Ps. 103:9, LXX [H. 102:9]; Jer. 3:12, LXX); etc. There are also evidences of the use of the LXX, as in vv. 1 (Gen. 1:1; 2:1), 7 (Joel 2:13), 13 (Gen. 19:15 and Ps. 138:15 [H. 139:15]), 15 (Ps. 32:6 [H. 33:6]); see also C. C. Torrey, *The Apocryphal Literature*, pp. 68 f. In some instances, expressions unknown or extremely rare in the LXX occur: *eúsplanchnos*, tender-hearted (v. 7; cf. Eph. 4:32; I Pet. 3:8), "God of the righteous"

---

[2] The best critical edition of the Greek text is in A. Rahlfs, *Psalmi cum Odis*, Göttingen, 1931; also in his *Septuaginta*, 2 vols. Stuttgart, 1935.

[3] Howorth (see above) as well as a few others (L. Couard, *Die religiösen und sittlichen Anschauungen der alttestamentlichen Apokryphen und Pseudepigraphen*, p. 5. Gütersloh, 1907; R. H. Charles, *Apocrypha*, p. 614, n. 1; C. C. Torrey, *The Apocryphal Literature*, pp. 68 f.) regard the prayer as a translation from Hebrew-Aramaic. Most critics, however, regard Greek as the original language: Fritzsche (*Commentary*, p. 157), André (*Les Apocryphes*, p. 241), Schürer (*Geschichte*, Vol. 3, p. 144), H. E. Ryle (in Charles, *Apocrypha*, pp. 614 f.), O. Eissfeldt (*Einleitung*, p. 644), etc.

(v. 8) or "of those who repent" (v. 13), *psámmos*, sand (v. 9; in the LXX the later form *ámmos* is used, except Wisd. of Sol. 7:9), *atenízō*, to look intently (v. 9; twice in the LXX, frequent in Acts), *anáxios*, unworthy (v. 14; three times in the LXX). Thus in some cases the diction is closer to that of the New Testament than to that of the LXX (cf. also v. 15 with Luke 2:13; Matt. 6:13).

These instances illustrating the characteristics of the Greek of this prayer may be adduced to prove either that a Hebrew or Aramaic text was translated idiomatically by a Hellenistic Jew familiar with the LXX, or that such a Jew wrote it originally in Greek. For identical, typically Jewish expressions occur in the LXX and in the New Testament both in translations and in original writings: thus, for instance, *bdélugma* (abomination) and *prosóchthisma* (detestable thing) in v. 10 occur in the LXX both in translated passages and in passages originally written in Greek, in the sense of heathen deities or idols.

Although the linguistic evidence is ambiguous, the present writer is inclined to regard the prayer as a translation from the Hebrew, chiefly on the basis of the content, which presents no trace of the characteristic ideas of Hellenistic Judaism but is entirely in harmony with Palestinian Judaism: thus, for instance, there is no immortality, for the dead go to Sheol (cf. v. 13). Allowing for the difference in the imaginary historical background, the Prayer of Manasses (placed in the pre-exilic period) resembles the Prayer of Azariah in the Greek Daniel (referring to the Exile). But unfortunately the linguistic evidence is equally undecisive for that prayer.

The notion of God in the Prayer of Manasses combines incongruously, after the manner of the Second Isaiah, the universal Creator of the world (vv. 2-4) and the God of the Jews only. Specifically he is the God of the sinless Patriarchs and of the righteous Jews, the strict observers of the Law, belonging to their seed (v. 8; cf. v. 1; cf. Ecclus. 10:19-24): "For not all those belonging to Israel are [the true] Israel; neither, because they are of Abraham's seed, are they all children" (Rom. 9:6 f.).

The Almighty (v. 1), the Most High (v. 7) is a God of power, majesty, and glory (vv. 5, 15), praised by the heavenly hosts (v. 15), dreaded by all things (v. 5), whose wrath is kindled against sinners (vv. 5, 10), particularly idolaters (v. 10), but whose mercy saves the repentant transgressors (vv. 7, 14). Sinners are punished (vv. 9 f.), but if they confess their misdeeds (vv. 8-10, 12) and, bending the knee of their heart (v. 11), contritely beg for God's forgiveness (vv. 11, 13), they may hope for salvation (v. 14): for Jehovah is "the God of them that repent" (v. 13).

This prayer, typical of Judaism after 400 B.C., was presumably composed in Palestine between 250 B.C. (the probable date of Chronicles, which suggested it) and the beginning of our era, presumably in the first century B.C. Its style is comparatively simple and clear, concise and expressive, but the thought does not attain the spiritual level of the prayer of another repentant sinner, Ps. 51. For Manasses is chiefly eager for deliverance from his captivity, and does not, like the Psalmist, crave for a clean heart and the bliss of God's presence.

CHAPTER XI

I MACCABEES

～～～～～～～～～～～～～～～～～～～～～～～～

The English, Latin (*Machabaeorum I*), and Syriac titles of this book reproduce its title in Greek (*Makkabaíōn A*).[1] "Maccabee" was originally a surname first applied to Judas, "called Maccabeus" (I Macc. 2:4; 3:1; Josephus, *Antiquities* 12:6, 1 [§266]; cf. I Macc. 2:66; 5:24; 8:20; II Macc. 2:20; 5:27; 8:1; 14:6). The surname became so famous that "the Maccabee" alone sufficed to identify Judas in twenty passages of II Maccabees (8:5, 16; 10:16, 19, 21; etc.) and is even used without the article in I Macc. 5:34 and II Macc. 10:1, as if it were a proper noun. Eventually the term, in the plural, came to refer to the brothers and followers of Judas and was used in the title of four books (I-IV Maccabees); the earliest instances of this usage are to be found, however, in patristic writings (cf. C. L. W. Grimm's *Commentary* on I Maccabees, p. x).

Curiously, the term "Maccabee" does not occur in Hebrew and Aramaic writings until a few centuries after the close of the Talmud about A.D. 500. In Talmud and Midrash, Judas and his family are called the Hasmoneans (cf. Josephus, *Antiquities* 14:16, 4 [§490]; 20:8, 11 [§190]; etc.), from the name of Hashmon,[2] an ancestor of Judas's father, Mattathias (*ibid.* 12:6, 1 [§265])[3]—a term which never occurs in the Apocrypha and Pseudepigrapha.

Philological imagination often is allowed free play in suggesting the etymology of obscure words. "Maccabeus" is a case in point: what was its Hebrew or Aramaic original? The Greek spelling (*Makkabaios*) seems to presuppose a Semitic spelling *mqb* (given by the Syriac), but the Latin (*Machabaeus*) the form *mkb*: both occur in medieval Hebrew.

---

[1] Origen (on Ps. 1; see Eusebius, *Hist. Eccl.* 6:25, 2) writes "*Tà Makkabaïká.*"

[2] The ethymology of the name Hashmon is unknown. Its connection with the obscure (possibly corrupt) *ḥašmannîm* in Ps. 68:32 (Engl. 68:31), suggested (among others) by L. E. T. André (*Les Apocryphes de l'Ancien Testament*, p. 65), seems to have been generally discarded. C. C. Torrey (JBL 62 [1943] 5) has abandoned his previous view (*Encycl. Bibl.* 3, 2852) and has reached a conclusion like that of J. Wellhausen (*Die Pharisäer und die Sadducäer*, 1874, p. 94, n.; *Nachrichten der Gesell. der Wiss. zu Göttingen*, 1905, p. 133), when he suggests tentatively that Simeon in I Macc. 2:1 is an error for *Hashmon* (Josephus, *Antiquities* 12:6, 1). According to Wellhausen, *Hashmon* is a variant of *Simeon*.

[3] In *War* 1:1, 3, however, Josephus calls Hashmon the father of Mattathias.

Accepting the first spelling, with a *q*, many regard the word as a honorific title given to Judas after his victories: *Maqqabi*, meaning "The Hammerer" (cf. "Charles Martel" [Charles the Hammer], the grandfather of Charlemagne), from *maqqebeth*, small hammer (Judg. 4:21; I Kings 6:7; Is. 44:12; Jer. 10:4). The chief objection, often raised, is that *maqqebeth* does not mean, as one would expect in this connection, a sledge hammer or a battle mace (cf. Jer. 50:23), but a mallet or workman's hammer unsuitable for war. Even the honorific use of *Maccabeus* has been questioned: C. C. Torrey (*Encycl. Bibl.* 3, 2851) regards it as the given name, while *Judas* would be his honorific title; conversely, F. Perles (JQR N.S. 17 [1926-27], 403-406) regards *mqbi* as a nickname meaning "one with extraordinary nostrils." Here are some other curious explanations of *maqqabi* as a title of Judas: *a.* "He who tracks or traces out" or "he who pierces through" (C. J. Ball, in H. Wace, *Apocrypha*, Vol. 1, p. 248, n.). *b.* "The one who has been made chief" (L. E. T. André, *Les Apocryphes*, p. 64). *c.* "General" (Conrad Iken, *Symbolae litterariae*, Vol. 1, p. 184. Bremen, 1744), from the Arabic *manqab. d.* The banner of Gad, in whose territory Modein (Judas's city) was located, allegedly bore the letters *m-q-b*, which are the final consonants of "Abraham, Isaac, and Jacob" in Hebrew.[4]

The second spelling (*mkb*) likewise offers considerable scope for etymological fancies, like the following: *a. Mkby* has been regarded as an acrostic giving the initials of the Hebrew words (in Ex. 15:11) meaning "Who is like thee among the gods, O Jehovah?" (H. Grotius, and others). *b.* It is the acrostic for "Mattathias priest (*kōhēn*), son of (*ben*) Johanan" (Franz Delitzsch, *Geschichte der jüdischen Poesie*, p. 28. Leipzig, 1836). *c.* It is a contraction of *māh khā ʾābî* meaning, "what is like my father?" (Fr. Delitzsch, quoted by H. Bévenot, *Die Beiden Makkabäerbücher* [HS], p. 3. Bonn, 1931). *d.* S. J. Curtiss (*The Name Machabee.* Leipzig, 1876) interprets the word as "The Extinguisher" (from the root *kby*; cf. Is. 43:17).

At least four books are named after the Maccabees. I Maccabees relates the history of the Jews from the accession of Antiochus IV Epiphanes (175) to the death of Simon (135). II Maccabees begins one year earlier (176), gives a fuller account of the intrigues of the Hellenizing high priests before the Maccabean rebellion, but comes to an end with the death of Nicanor in 161. Thus I. Macc. 1:10-7:50 is more or less parallel to II Macc. 4:7-15:36. III Maccabees, despite its title, has nothing to do with the Maccabees, but is a legendary account of earlier events, during the reign of Ptolemy IV Philopator (221-203): frustrated in his attempt to enter the Holy of Holies in Jerusalem, he vainly attempted

---

[4] A. A. Bevans (JTS 1929, pp. 191 ff.) believes that the original spelling of "Maccabeus" was "Maqqabyahu."

to destroy the Jews in Alexandria. IV Maccabees is a diatribe or sermon on the Stoic theme "pious reason controls affections and feelings," illustrated with the stories of Jewish martyrs in II Maccabees (Eleazar, the seven brothers, and their mother). In addition to these four books preserved in Greek, there is an Arabic chronicle (sometimes called V Maccabees) dealing with Jewish history from Heliodorus' attempt to plunder the Temple (II Macc. 3) in 176 to the reign of Herod the Great (d. 4 B.C.). The Arabic text with the Latin translation of Gabriel Sionita are printed in the Paris Polyglot (Vol. 9) and in the London Polyglot (Vol. 4). It is closely parallel to parts of the Hebrew *Josippon* of Joseph ben Gorion (or Gorionides)—a chronicle from Adam to Titus's destruction of the Temple (A.D. 70) written probably in the tenth century (see E. Schürer, *Geschichte*, Vol. 1, pp. 159-161). In the Ambrosian manuscript of the Peshitta published by Ceriani, the Syriac version of the sixth book of Josephus, *War of the Jews*, is entitled "V Maccabees." The Ethiopic Book of Maccabees is fiction pure and simple (cf. J. Horowitz in *Zeitschr. für Assyriologie* 19 [1905-06] 144-233).

The contents of I Maccabees may be summarized as follows:

Introduction. A summary of the conquests of Alexander the Great (336-323 B.C.) and of his rule (1:1-4). His division of the empire and the evil rule of his successors (1:5-9).

PART I: CAUSE AND INCEPTION OF THE MACCABEAN REVOLT (1:10-2:70)

1. *The hostility of Antiochus against the Jews* (1:10-64). *a.* When Antiochus IV Epiphanes (d. 164), the son of Antiochus III the Great (223-187), came to the throne in 175 (1:10), the Jews favorable to Hellenism built a gymnasium in Jerusalem and strove to appear uncircumcised (1:11-15). Antiochus invaded Egypt in 170 and defeated the forces of Ptolemy VI Philometor (181-146) (1:16-19). On his return from Egypt, Antiochus plundered the Temple in Jerusalem (1:20-24; cf. II Macc. 5:21) and caused bitter mourning and lamentation among the Jews (1:25-28, in verse).

b. Two years later (168) Antiochus sent a tax collector (Apollonius, according to II Macc. 5:24) who, after a show of friendship, fell upon the Jews (on a Sabbath, according to II Macc. 5:25), plundered and destroyed part of Jerusalem (1:29-32), and placed a garrison in a fortress (the Acra) on Zion (1:33-36). Jerusalem and the Temple were subjected to horrible indignities (1:37-40, a second lamentation in verse; cf. 1:25-28).

c. To amalgamate the various nations in his kingdom, Antiochus prescribed the Greek cults and culture for all his subjects. The practices of

Judaism were forbidden under penalty of death, and heathen altars were erected throughout Judea. Some Jews promptly fulfilled these ordinances, but some of the faithful went into hiding (1:41-53).

d. On the 25th (1:54 reads erroneously the 15th, but see the Syriac text in the *Codex Ambrosianus* published by A. M. Ceriani, and 1:59) of Chislev (approximately December) of 168 they placed on the altar in the Temple the "abomination of desolation" (a small altar dedicated to the Olympian Zeus; cf. 4:43; 6:7; II Macc. 6:2; Dan. 9:27; 11:31; 12:11; Josephus, *Antiquities* 12:5, 4) and offered sacrifices upon it. Scrolls of the Law were burnt, circumcision was forbidden, and the faithful Jews (Hasidim) who refused to become apostates were put to death (1:54-64).

2. *Mattathias' rebellion against Antiochus* (2:1-70). *a.* The genealogy and the five sons of Mattathias (2:1-5).

b. Mattathias mourned the desecration of the Temple (2:6-14; a third lamentation in verse [see 1:25-28, 37-40] is found in 2:8-13).

c. When a Syrian officer came to Modein to enforce the decree of Antiochus and invited Mattathias to offer a heathen sacrifice, the latter not only refused, but slew both a Jew who came forward to sacrifice and the royal officer; then he fled to the mountains with his sons (2:15-28).

d. Some pious Jews (Hasidim) hiding in the wilderness refused to fight when attacked on the Sabbath, and were slain with their families— about a thousand souls (2:29-38).

e. Mattathias and the Hasidim with him decided to fight on the Sabbath when attacked (2:39-41); they collected an army, slew apostate Jews, pulled down the heathen altars, circumcised the children, and enforced the Law (2:42-48).

f. On his deathbed, Mattathias exhorted his sons to be zealous for the Law, remembering the example of Abraham (Gen. 22:1; 15:6), Joseph (Gen. 39:9), Phinehas (Num. 25:7-13), Joshua, Caleb (Num. 13:30; 14:24; Josh. 14:14), David (II Sam. 7:16), Elijah (I Kings 18:40; 19:10; II Kings 2:11), Hananiah, Azariah, and Mishael (Dan. 1:6-20; 3:17 f.), Daniel (Dan. 6:22 [Aram. 6:23]). Thus would they attain glory(2:49-64). Among them Simon would be as a father and Judas Maccabeus their captain (2:65). After urging them to take vengeance among the heathen (2:67 f.) and blessing them, Mattathias died at the age of 146 years and was buried at Modein (2:69 f.).

PART II: JUDAS MACCABEUS (3:1-9:22)

Introduction. A panegyric in verse extolling the deeds of Judas Maccabeus (3:1-9).

1. *Judas's fight for religious liberty* (3:10-4:61). *a.* His victory over

Apollonius and Seron (3:10-26). Judas Maccabeus defeated and slew Apollonius (cf. 1:29) and henceforth carried his sword (3:10-12). Seron marched against Judas with a strong force, but Judas, trusting in God's help, attacked him suddenly at the pass of Beth-horon and forced his retreat (3:13-26).

b. Lysias was placed in command of the operations against the Jews (3:27-37). When Antiochus, to replenish his treasury, undertook a campaign against Persia (166-165), he placed Lysias in charge of the lands west of the Euphrates and appointed him guardian of his son Antiochus. He left with him half of the army, including the military elephants, to crush the Maccabean rebellion (3:27-37).

c. Judas's victory over Gorgias (3:38-4:25). Lysias sent out an army of 40,000 infantry and 7,000 cavalry under the command of Ptolemy, Nicanor, and Gorgias; they encamped near Emmaus (3:38-41). Judas gathered his men at Mizpeh (3:42-46; v. 45 is a fourth poetic lament; cf. above, under 2:8-13). They fasted, mourned, and performed religious ceremonies (3:47-54). Judas organized the army for battle, granting the military exemptions ordered in Deut. 20:5-8 (cf. Judg. 7:3), and after encamping south of Emmaus urged the men to be valiant (3:55-60). Informed that Gorgias would march against his camp that very night with 6,000 soldiers, Judas boldly attacked the enemy position and routed the Syrians (4:1-15). The army of Gorgias fled in panic (4:16-25).

d. The victory over Lysias (4:26-35). In 164 Lysias, with an army of 60,000 infantry and 5,000 cavalry, encamped at Beth-zur (4:26 f.). After blessing the Lord, through whose help David and Jonathan triumphed against superior foes, Judas defeated Lysias (4:28-35).

e. The Rededication of the Temple (4:36-61). The Maccabees, having expelled the Syrian forces from Judea except for the garrison in the Acra (cf. 4:41), went up to Jerusalem. At the sight of the desolate and desecrated Temple they lamented and mourned (4:36-40). Judas appointed soldiers to keep the garrison in check (4:41) and proceeded with the cleansing of the Temple. The defiled altar's stones were placed aside, awaiting instructions from a prophet (4:42-46), and a new altar was erected (4:47). The buildings were restored (4:48), new vessels were provided (4:49), and sacrifice was offered (4:50-53). The dedication of the Temple was celebrated on the 25th of Chislev, exactly three years after its profanation (4:54-58; cf. 1:54, 59), and the day became an annual festival (*Hanukkah*) lasting eight days (4:59; cf. the superscription of Ps. 30 and John 10:22). Then Judas fortified Jerusalem and Beth-zur (4:60 f.).

2. *Wars against the enemies of the Jews* (5). *a.* The success of the Maccabees spurred the Gentiles to persecute the Jews in their midst (5:1 f.). *b.* Victory of Judas over the Idumeans (5:3). *c.* Victory over

the "Children of Baian" (Baean) (5:4 f.). *d.* Victory over the Ammonites (5:6-8).

e. Victories in Galilee and in Gilead (5:9-54). Appeals for help against the heathen came to Judas from oppressed Jews in Gilead (5:9-13) and in Galilee (5:14 f.). Judas sent his brother Simon to Galilee, and decided to go to Gilead with Jonathan (5:16 f.), leaving Joseph and Azarias in charge of Judea, with orders not to wage war (5:18 f.). Simon took 3,000 men, and Judas 8,000 (5:20). Simon was victorious in Galilee (at Ptolemais) and brought the Jews residing there to Judea (5:21-23). Judas, after reassuring the Nabateans (5:24-27), captured Bosora (5:28), delivered the Jews besieged by Timotheus in Dathema (5:29-34), and took Mizpeh and other cities (5:35 f.). With a new army Timotheus met Judas near Raphon, but was driven into the temple at Carnaim; there he perished when the temple was burnt (5:37-44). When Judas was returning together with the Gileadite Jews, the city of Ephron refused passage (5:45-48) but was quickly destroyed (5:49-51). Then they returned to Jerusalem by way of Beth-shean (5:52-54).

f. An ill-fated attack on Jamnia (5:55-64). Meanwhile Joseph and Azarias, who had been left in charge of Judea (cf. 5:18 f.), eager to gain military glory, undertook a campaign against Jamnia, but were routed by Gorgias: they were not of the seed of the Maccabees through whom Israel was to be delivered (5:55-64).

g. Successful expeditions of Judas against Hebron in Idumea (5:65), and, after a failure at Marisa (5:66 f.), against Azotus in Philistia (5:68).

3. *Death of Antiochus Epiphanes and Lysias' war against the Jews* (6). *a.* The end of Antiochus (6:1-17). Antiochus failed in his attempt to plunder the riches of Elymais [?] in Persia (6:1-4). Upon hearing of the successes of Judas Maccabeus (6:5-7), Antiochus, ill from grief, realized that he was about to die because he had plundered the Jerusalem Temple (6:8-13) and appointed Philip regent during the minority of Antiochus V Eupator (6:14 f.). But at the death of Epiphanes, Lysias made himself regent (6:16 f.).

b. The war between Lysias and Judas (6:18-63). The *casus belli* was furnished by Judas, when he began to besiege the Syrian garrison in the Acra on Zion (6:18-27). At the head of an army of 100,000 infantry, 20,000 cavalry, and 32 military elephants, Lysias and Antiochus Eupator crossed Idumea and besieged Beth-zur (6:28-31). To relieve this citadel, Judas encamped at Bethzacharias (6:32). The Syrians formed phalanxes of one thousand infantry and five hundred cavalry around each elephant, which carried a tower of wood with thirty-two (?) men and the Indian mahout (6:33-38). Six hundred Syrians fell in the battle (6:39-42). A brother of Judas, Eleazar (cf. 2:5), slew the largest of the elephants, thinking that the king was on it, and was crushed to death when it fell

(6:43-47). Beth-zur surrendered owing to lack of food, because it was a sabbatical year (6:48-50). For this reason the Jews besieged in the Temple were unable to resist (6:51-54). Lysias, however, upon hearing that Philip (cf. 6:14) had come to Antioch, persuaded the young king to sign a peace treaty with the Jews, allowing them to practice their religion (6:55-61). After dismantling the fortifications of Jerusalem (except the Acra), Lysias attacked Philip and took Antioch by force (6:62 f.).

4. *Judas's conflict with Demetrius I, ending with Judas's death* (7:1-9:22). *a.* Ascendancy of the Hellenizing Jews supported by Demetrius I (7:1-20). In 162-161, Demetrius I Soter, son of Seleucus IV Philopator, returned from Rome, where he had been held as hostage, and after slaying Lysias and Antiochus V became king (7:1-4). At the instance of Alkimus, the leader of the Hellenists in Jerusalem (7:5-7), Demetrius sent Bacchides against Judas (7:8 f.). Alkimus with his friendly overtures deceived some of the scribes and of the pious (Hasidim), but not Judas (7:10-15). After slaying sixty men, in accordance with the words of Ps. 79:2 f., Alkimus, supported by a contingent of troops left by Bacchides, became master of Jerusalem (7:16-20).

b. Judas's victory over Nicanor (7:21-50). Alkimus, the high priest of the Jews, again appealed to Demetrius for help against Judas, who was reorganizing his forces (7:21-25). Nicanor was sent to Jerusalem and at first tried to seize Judas by deceit (7:26-30); then, after the battle of Capharsalama (7:31 f.), he withdrew into Jerusalem, where he insulted the priests in the Temple (7:33-38). In the battle of Adasa (near Beth-horon) Nicanor was defeated and slain by Judas (7:39-49): this victory was celebrated annually on the 13th of Adar (7:50).

c. The signing of a treaty between Judas and Rome (8). Judas heard of the Roman conquests in Galatia (through Manlius Vulso in 189), in Spain (the Carthaginian portion of which was conquered in 206), and elsewhere (8:1-4); and also of their victories over Philip (197) and Perseus (168), kings of Macedonia, and over Antiochus III the Great (defeated at Magnesia in 190 by Scipio Africanus), whose territories in India (?), Media (?), and Lydia were given to Eumenes II, king of Pergamum (8:5-8). He also heard of the Roman conquest of Greece—which actually occurred in 147-146, fifteen years after Judas's death (8:9 f.)—and of the islands in the Mediterranean (8:11) and kingdoms near and far (8:12). He heard that the Romans crowned and deposed kings, but were themselves governed by a senate of 320 (actually less than 300) members sitting daily (?) and by one consul (actually two) appointed yearly (8:13-16).

Judas sent Eupolemus and Jason to Rome to make an alliance (8:17-22); the text of the Roman treaty, written on tablets of brass, is given in 8:23-32.

d. The death of Judas Maccabeus in 161 (9:1-22). When Demetrius I Soter heard of the defeat and death of Nicanor (see 7:39-50), he sent again Bacchides and Alkimus (9:1). Their forces were 20,000 infantry and 2,000 cavalry, while of Judas's 3,000 men all but 800 fled at the sight of the enemy (9:2-6). Against the advice of his men, who recognized that victory was impossible (9:7-9), Judas ordered the attack at Elasa and fell valiantly in the battle (9:10-18). He was buried at Modein in the family grave (9:19) and was sorely lamented with the words of David in II Sam. 1:19, 25, 27 (9:20 f.). The rest of his deeds were not recorded (9:22).

PART III: JONATHAN (9:23-12:53)

1. *The conflict between Jonathan and Bacchides* (9:23-73). *a.* Sorely pressed by Bacchides and the Hellenists among the Jews, the followers of the Maccabees chose Jonathan as their leader (9:23-31).

b. Jonathan and the Arabs (9:32-42). Jonathan and his followers sought refuge in the wilderness of Tekoah, but fled over the Jordan to escape from Bacchides (9:32-34). Jonathan sent his brother John to deposit the baggage with the friendly Nabateans, but near Medaba John was robbed and killed by a band of Sons of Ambri (an otherwise unknown Arabic tribe) (9:35 f.). In retaliation, Jonathan plundered a wedding procession of the Sons of Ambri (9:37-42).

c. Jonathan and Bacchides (9:43-73). In the marshes where the Jordan empties into the Dead Sea, Jonathan was met by Bacchides and, even though a thousand Syrians fell in the battle, the Maccabees could save themselves only by swimming across the Jordan (9:43-49). Bacchides fortified the strongholds of Judea and took Jewish hostages (9:50-53). Alkimus died in 159, while demolishing a wall in the Temple (9:54-56); Bacchides returned to Antioch, and Judea had peace for two years (9:57). Upon the appeal of the Hellenizing Jews, Bacchides returned, besieged Jonathan in Bethbasi without success (9:58-69), and finally signed a peace treaty with him (9:70-72). Jonathan took up his residence in Michmash, ruling over the countryside, while the Hellenizing Sanhedrin ruled in Jerusalem (9:73).

2. *Jonathan and Alexander Balas* (10:1-11:19). *a.* When Alexander Balas, with the support of the king of Pergamum, laid claim to the throne of Syria, pretending to be a son of Antiochus IV Epiphanes, Demetrius I made considerable concessions to Jonathan in an attempt to gain his support (10:1-14). But Alexander Balas appointed Jonathan as high priest and made him a "king's friend" (10:15-21). Although Demetrius granted the Jews immunity from taxation, virtual independence, and increased territory (10:22-45), Jonathan mistrusted him and remained

faithful to Balas (10:46 f.). Demetrius fell in battle against Balas (10:48-50), who made a treaty with Ptolemy VI Philometor, king of Egypt, and married the latter's daughter Cleopatra at Ptolemais (10:51-58). Jonathan was invited to the wedding, gave gifts to the two kings, and was greatly honored by them, receiving from Balas the titles of military and civil commander (10:59-66).

b. Victories of Jonathan over Apollonius (10:67-89). Demetrius II Nicator came from Crete to claim the kingdom of his father Demetrius I (10:67 f.) and sent Apollonius against Jonathan (10:69-73). With 10,000 men Jonathan conquered Joppa (10:74-76) and, with the help of his brother Simon, defeated Apollonius at Azotus (Ashdod) and burned the city together with its famous temple of Dagon (10:77-85); then he received the homage of Ashkelon (10:86). Balas rewarded Jonathan with a golden buckle reserved to the "king's kinsmen" (10:87-89).

c. The death of Alexander Balas (11:1-19). The cities of Philistia and Jonathan welcomed Ptolemy VI, the father-in-law of Balas (11:1-7), but he made an alliance with Demetrius II, gave him Cleopatra, Balas's wife, in marriage, and crowned himself king of Syria at Antioch (11:8-13). Balas returned from Cilicia and was defeated; in Arabia he was beheaded by Zabdiel (11:14-17). Ptolemy, however, died three days later, and thus Demetrius II ruled unopposed in 145 (11:17-19).

3. *Jonathan and Demetrius II* (11:20-12:53). *a.* After becoming the sole ruler of Syria, Demetrius II granted Jonathan increased powers and increased territory (11:20-37). Demetrius II demobilized most of his troops, thus causing considerable resentment among them on account of their loss of pay (11:38). Taking advantage of this disaffection, Tryphon, a former partisan of Balas, decided to place on the throne Antiochus VI, the young son of Balas who was being reared by an Arab named Imalkue (11:39 f.). Jonathan requested Demetrius II to remove the garrisons in the Acra and in other strongholds (11:41). Upon receiving a favorable answer, Jonathan sent 3,000 Jewish soldiers to Antioch to put down a revolt against Demetrius: they slew 100,000 of 120,000 rioters (!) and returned laden with spoil (11:42-51); but Demetrius broke his deceitful promises to Jonathan (11:52 f.).

b. Jonathan and Antiochus VI (11:54-74). Tryphon placed Antiochus VI on the throne and took possession of Antioch (11:54-56). The new king confirmed the authority of Jonathan and placed Simon in command of the Philistian coast (11:57-59). Jonathan received the homage of Ashkelon, forced the surrender of Gaza, and reached Damascus (11:60-62). While Simon forced the capitulation of Beth-zur, Jonathan defeated the forces of Demetrius II at Kadesh in Galilee (11:63-74).

c. Alliance of Jonathan with the Romans and the Spartans (12:1-23). Jonathan's ambassadors were well received in Rome (12:1-4) and brought to the Spartans a letter of his (12:5; the text is given in 12:6-18). Formerly Areios, king of the Spartans, had written to the high priest Onias that, like the Jews, the Spartans were descended from Abraham (!) (12:19-23).

d. Jonathan met the forces of Demetrius II near Hamath, but they withdrew across the Eleutherus (*Nahr el-Kebir*) river (12:24-30). After defeating the Gabadean (error for Zabadean) Arabs, Jonathan came to Damascus (12:31 f.). Simon occupied Ashkelon and Joppa (12:33 f.), Jonathan fortified Jerusalem, and Simon strengthened Adida (12:35-38).

e. The capture of Jonathan (12:39-53). Tryphon, planning to displace Antiochus VI on the throne and wishing to rid himself of Jonathan's opposition, marched to Beth-shean, where Jonathan met him with 40,000 men (12:39-41). Through flatteries and promises, he induced Jonathan to come to Ptolemais with a bodyguard of a thousand men: there Jonathan was captured and his bodyguard was slain (12:42-48). Tryphon sent troops into Galilee and Esdraelon, but they returned without attacking Jonathan's troops (12:49-51). The Jews mourned for Jonathan, while the Gentiles plotted against them (12:52 f.).

PART IV: SIMON (13-16)

1. *Simon's relations with Tryphon and Demetrius II* (13:1-14:3). *a.* Simon, seeing that the people were troubled by Tryphon's hostile preparations, offered to lead them as Judas and Jonathan had heretofore, and was elected (13:1-9). He completed the fortifications of Jerusalem (cf. 12:36 f.) and sent Jonathan son of Absalom to occupy Joppa (13:10 f.).

b. Tryphon's unsuccessful campaign (13:12-24). Marching from Ptolemais with Jonathan his prisoner, Tryphon found Simon well entrenched in Adida (13:12 f.); he promised to free Jonathan against payment of a hundred talents of silver and delivery of two of Jonathan's sons as hostages (13:14-16). Simon complied, although he suspected treachery, but Jonathan was not set at liberty (13:17-19). Tryphon failed to invade Judah (13:20) and (owing to a snowstorm) to send supplies to the garrison in the Acra (13:21 f.); on his way back, he executed Jonathan at Bascama (13:23 f.). Jonathan was buried in the family grave at Modein, where Simon erected elaborate mausoleums (13:25-30).

c. Immunities granted to the Jews by Demetrius II (13:31-42). In 162 Tryphon arranged the assassination of Antiochus VI and assumed the royal power (13:31 f.). Simon fortified Judea and requested tax immunity from Demetrius II (13:33 f.). In a letter (the text of which is in 13:36-40) Demetrius confirmed his former immunities (see 10:28-35) and extended them (13:35-40). Thus in 141 the Jews became independent and began to date their contracts by the first year of Simon (13:41 f.).

d. Simon's victories (13:43-53). Simon forced the capitulation of Gazara (Gezer), exiled the inhabitants, and settled Jews therein (13:43-48). Facing starvation, the Syrian garrison in the Acra surrendered on the 23rd of Iyyar, 141, an event celebrated annually (13:49-52). Simon's son John was placed in charge of Gazara (13:53).

e. Demetrius II was captured by Arsaces (i.e., Mithridates I), king of the Parthians (14:1-3).

2. *Simon's rule* (14:4-49). *a.* Simon's achievements are described in prose (14:4 f.) and in poetry (14:6-15).

b. The Romans (cf. 8:1 ff.; 12:1-4; 15:15-21) and the Spartans (cf. 12:5-23; 15:23) renewed with Simon their former treaties of friendship (14:16-24; see the sequel in 15:15-24).

c. In recognition of the services of the Maccabees, and particularly of Simon, to the nation, it was decreed on the 18th of Elul, 140, that Simon and his line should fill the offices of high priest, military commander, and civil ruler of the Jews in perpetuity—at least until a divine revelation through a reliable prophet should order otherwise (14:25-49). The text of the decree (contained in 14:27-47) was engraved on tablets of brass set up conspicuously in the Temple, while a copy was deposited in the archives (14:48 f.; cf. 14:26).

3. *Simon and Antiochus VII Sidetes* (15-16). *a.* Antiochus VII (138-129), the son of Demetrius I and brother of Demetrius II (then prisoner of the Parthians), wishing to become king of Syria, wrote a letter to Simon (the text is given in 15:2b-9) confirming his authority, allowing him to coin money, and promising to glorify him and the Jews when he would attain his purpose (15:1-9).

b. In 138 Antiochus VII came to Syria, collected a large army, and besieged Tryphon by land and sea in Dor (15:10-14).

c. The Jewish ambassadors returned from Rome bearing a letter (the text of which is given in 15:16-21) of Lucius, the Roman consul, to Ptolemy VII Euergetes II (170-117) and to other kings and nations, confirming the Roman friendship for the Jews (15:15-24; cf. 14:16-24).

d. Ultimatum of Antiochus VII to Simon (15:25-41). Simon sent two thousand men to help Antiochus at the siege of Dor (cf. 15:10-14), but Antiochus, feeling sufficiently strong, revoked his concessions (cf. 15:2-9) and demanded that Simon give back the Acra in Jerusalem and the conquered cities, or pay an indemnity of 1,000 talents of silver (15:25-31). Simon offered 100 talents for Joppa and Gazara (15:32-36). Tryphon escaped by ship from Dor to Orthosia (15:37). Cendebeus was ordered to attack Judea while Antiochus pursued Tryphon (15:38-41).

e. The defeat of Cendebeus (16:1-10). Simon's son John came from Gazara (cf. 13:53) to report to Simon on the hostile operations of Cendebeus (16:1). Simon, being old, placed his two sons Judas and John in command of the army (16:2 f.). In the vicinity of Modein they routed Cendebeus (16:4-10).

f. Simon's death (16:11-24). Simon's son-in-law Ptolemy, governor of the plain of Jericho, assassinated Simon and his two sons Mattathias and Judas at a banquet in 135 (16:11-17). Ptolemy offered to Antiochus VII to bring Judea under his authority (16:18) and sent assassins to Gazara to do away with John Hyrcanus (cf. 16:1), but John was notified in time and slew the assassins (16:19-22). The rest of the deeds of John Hyrcanus are recorded in the chronicles of his high priesthood—a lost work (16:23 f.).

1. A Comparison between I and II Maccabees

The differences and parallels between the first two books of Maccabees furnish valuable clues for determining not only their possible literary relationship but also their respective point of view, purpose, and date. Beginning with a comparison of their contents, we may present the facts briefly as follows:

A. *Parts of I Maccabees lacking in II Maccabees.* 1. The empire of Alexander the Great (1:1-4) was divided among his successors (1:5-9). 2. Mattathias and his sons begin the Maccabean rebellion against Antiochus IV Epiphanes (2:1-48); the last words of Mattathias and his death (2:49-70). 3. A poem in praise of Judas Maccabeus (3:1-9). 4. Victory of Judas over Apollonius and Seron (3:10-26). 5. Antiochus Epiphanes led an expedition against Persia and left Lysias in command in Syria (3:27-37). 6. Judas defeated Gorgias (3:38-4:25). 7. Judas defeated the "Children of Baian" and the Ammonites (5:4-8). 8. At Jamnia, Gorgias routed the Jews led by Joseph and Azarias (5:55-64). 9. Judas raided Idumea (5:65) and Philistia (5:66-68). 10. Judas besieged the Acra in Jerusalem (6:18-27). 11. Demetrius I Soter sent Bacchides to support the high priest Alkimus against Judas (7:8-20); but Alkimus was forced to appeal for help against Judas (7:21-25). 12. Judas signed a treaty with Rome (8). 13. Judas died in battle (9:1-22). 14. Jonathan continued the fight for Jewish independence (9:23-12:53). 15. Simon became an independent ruler (13-16).

B. *Parts of II Maccabees lacking in I Maccabees.* 1. Letters from Palestine to the Jews in Egypt (1:1-2:18). 2. Preface, stating that the book is a summary of a history written by Jason of Cyrene (2:19-32). 3. Divinely frustrated attempt of Heliodorus to plunder the Temple (3). 4. Onias III appealed to Seleucus IV (4:1-6); but, under Antiochus IV Epiphanes, Jason became high priest in place of Onias (4:7-10) and sent a contribution to Tyre for the festival of Heracles (4:18-20). He gave a public reception to Antiochus Epiphanes (4:21 f.). 5. Menelaus was appointed high priest in place of Jason and plotted the assassination of Onias (4:23-50). 6. Visionary portents in Jerusalem (5:2-4); Jason's brief occupation of Jerusalem and his death (5:5-10). 7. Judas Maccabeus in the wilderness (5:27; cf. I. Macc. 2:28). 8. The author's explanation of the persecution of the Jews (6:12-17). 9. Outstanding Jewish martyrs (6:18-7:42). 10. Victories of Judas over Nicanor (8:1-29), and over Timotheus and Bacchides (8:30-33); Nicanor's return to Antioch (8:34-36). 11. Suicide of Ptolemy Macron (10:12 f.). 12. Lysias' first treaty of peace with Judas (11:13-15). 13. Letters of Lysias to the Jews (11:16-21), of Antiochus V to Lysias (11:22-26) and to the Jews (11:27-33), and of the Romans to the Jews (11:34-38). 14. Judas at Joppa (12:1-9). 15. Execution of Menelaus (13:3-8). 16. Razis chose a self-inflicted death rather than capture (14:37-46). 17. Nicanor failed to attack Judas in Samaria on a Sabbath (15:1-5). 18. Judas encouraged by a dream (15:6-16). 19. Epilogue (15:37-39).

C. *Parallel stories in I and II Maccabees.* 1. Accession of Antiochus Epiphanes (I 1:10; II 4:7). 2. Hellenization of Jerusalem (I 1:11-15; II 4:11-17); Eupolemus' embassy to Rome (I 8:17; II 4:11). 3. Expedition of Antiochus Epiphanes against Egypt (I 1:16-19; II 5:1). 4. Antiochus plundered the Temple and massacred the Jews (I 1:20-28; II 5:11-23). 5. Military occupation of Jerusalem (I 1:29-40; II 5:24-26). 6. Proscription of Judaism and persecution of the Jews (I 1:41-64; II 6:1-11). 7. First campaign of Lysias against Judas (I 4:26-35; II 11:1-12). 8. Rededication of the Temple (I 4:36-61; II 10:1-9).[5] 9. Campaigns of Judas in Idumea (I 5:1-3; II 10:14-23) and in Transjordania (I 5:24-54; II 10:24-38; 12:10-31). 10. Death of Antiochus Epiphanes (I 6:1-16; II 9). 11. Accession of Antiochus Eupator under the tutelage of Lysias (I 6:17; cf. 3:32; II 10:10 f.). 12. Second campaign of Lysias against Judas, dated in 150 (I 6:20) or 149 (II 13:1) of the Seleucid Era (I 6:28-63; II 13:1 f., 9-26). In I Maccabees (6:57-62) Lysias granted the Jews religious freedom after the second campaign, in II Maccabees (11:13-15) after the first. 13. Demetrius Soter became king (I 7:1-4; II 14:1 f.) and made Alkimus high priest (I 7:5-7; II 14:3-11). 14. Judas's victory over Nicanor (I 7:26-50; II 14:12-36; 15:17-36).

It may be convenient to present these data in tabular form, repeating the numbers given above to each passage under the three divisions, A, B, and C. An asterisk (*) marks passages in II Maccabees which appear here out of their original context (beginning with ch. 9).

Although superficially the similarities and differences between I and II Maccabees remind us, in a general way, of those between Kings and Chronicles, it is most improbable that II Maccabees utilized I Macca-

[5] In I Maccabees (6:1-16) Antiochus Epiphanes died *after* the rededication; in II Maccabees (9), *before.*

Subject	I Macc.	II Macc.
A1. Alexander and the Diadochi	1:1-9	
B1. Letters to Egypt		1:1-2:18
B2. Preface		2:19-32
B3. Heliodorus (Seleucus IV)		3
B4. (1) Onias		4:1-6
C1. Accession of Antiochus Epiphanes	1:10	4:7a
B4. (2) Jason		4:7b-10, 18-22
C2. Hellenism in Jerusalem (cf. B4).	1:11-15	4:11-17
B5. Menelaus		4:23-50
C3. Antiochus IV in Egypt	1:16-19	5:1
B6. Portents; death of Jason		5:2-10
C4. Plunder and massacre	1:20-28	5:11-23
C5. Military occupation	1:29-40	5:24-26
B7. (Flight to the wilderness)	(2:28)	5:27
C6. Religious persecution	1:41-64	6:1-11
B8. Persecution as chastisement		6:12-17
B9. Famous Jewish martyrs		6:18-7:42
A2. Mattathias	2	
A3. Judas Maccabeus (poem)	3:1-9	
A4. Apollonius and Seron	3:10-26	
A5. Antiochus in Persia; Lysias	3:27-37	
A6. Defeat of Gorgias (and Nicanor?)	3:38-4:25	
B10. Defeat of Nicanor (and Gorgias)		8:1-29
Defeat of Timotheus and Bacchides		8:30-33
Nicanor's return		8:34-36
B11. Suicide of Macron		10:12 f.
C7. First campaign of Lysias	4:26-35	*11:1-12
B12. First treaty of peace (Lysias)		*11:13-15
B13. Official letters		*11:16-38
C8. Rededication of the Temple	4:36-61	10:1-9
C9. Judas in Idumea and Gilead	5:1-3, 9-54	*10:14-38;
		*12:10-31
A7. Judas and the Ammonites	5:4-8	
A8. Defeat of the Jews at Jamnia	5:55-64	
B14. Judas at Joppa		12:1-9
A9. Judas in Idumea and Philistia	5:65-68	
C10. Death of Epiphanes	6:1-16	ch. 9
C11. Accession of Eupator	6:17; (3:32)	10:10 f.
A10. Judas besieged the Acra	6:18-27	
C12. Second campaign of Lysias	6:28-63	13:1 f., 9-26
B15. Execution of Menelaus		13:3-8
C13. Demetrius I and Alkimus	7:1-7	14:1-11
A11. Bacchides and Alkimus	7:8-25	
C14. Victory over Nicanor	7:26:50	14:12-36
		15:17-36
B16. Suicide of Razis		14:37-46
B17. Nicanor's failure at Samaria		15:1-5
B18. Judas's dream		15:6-16
B19. Epilogue of II Maccabees		15:37-39
A12. Judas's treaty with Rome	8	
A13. Judas's death	9:1-22	
A14. Jonathan	9:23-12:53	
A15. Simon	13-16	

bees as a source[6] (the reverse is hardly credible),[7] as Chronicles excerpted and rewrote Kings. Similarities in parallel accounts are to be expected in reports of identical events, but the differences in language, style, and concrete detail seem to preclude direct literary borrowing.

Let us consider the far-reaching differences in contents, order of events, incidents, historicity, and point of view. The style need not be contrasted here, for it will be characterized later in the literary appreciation of each book.

As the preceding tabulation has shown, the two books are partly parallel (I Macc. 1:10-7:50; II Macc. 4:7-15:36) and partly distinct (the rest): I Maccabees deals with the history of forty years (175-135 B.C.), II Maccabees instead begins and ends earlier and describes the events of fifteen years (176-161 B.C.). Thus the two books have in common only a period of fourteen years, from the accession of Antiochus Epiphanes (175) to the death of Nicanor (161). Although the main events of this time are related by both authors, their choice of incidents does not always coincide, so that at times they supplement each other. Aside from numerous legends and tales which are purely imaginative and aside from valuable information in ch. 4, II Maccabees adds some historical details to the more reliable account of I Maccabees (cf. B. Niese, *Kritik der Beiden Makkabäerbücher*, pp. 27-32, and *passim*), such as three incidents also found (independently) in Josephus: the Samaritan temple on Gerizim was dedicated to Zeus Xenios or protector of guests (6:2; Josephus, *Antiquities* XII: 5,5, says Zeus Hellenios); Menelaus was executed at Berea (13:3-8; Josephus, *Antiquities* XII: 9,7); Demetrius I landed at Tripolis (14:1; Josephus, *Antiquities* XII: 10,1).[8] The preceding table indicates in a general way how the books supplement each other.[9] For instance, I Maccabees never mentions Jason and Menelaus, and II Maccabees ignores Mattathias.[10] Historians may use II Maccabees critically for genuine information, but they will generally agree with J. Wellhausen (*Israel. und Jüd. Geschichte*, 4th ed., p. 246, n. 1. Berlin,

[6] Cf. B. Niese, *Kritik der beiden Makkabäerbücher* (a reprint from *Hermes* 35 (1900) 268-307; 453-527), pp. 25 f. Berlin, 1900; D. M. Sluys, *De Maccabaeorum libris I et II quaestiones* (Dissertation), pp. 2-33. Amsterdam, 1904.

[7] A. Schlatter (*Jason von Kyrene*. Munich, 1891) regards I Maccabees (as well as II Maccabees) as a summary of the history of Jason of Cyrene (II Macc. 2:19-23).

[8] Valid information is also furnished by II Macc. 4:11-12, 21, 29 f.; 5:7 f., 22-24; 8:32-33; 12:2, 19, 35; 13:24; 14:17-19; etc.

[9] See, for details, W. Kolbe, *Beiträge zur syrischen und jüdischen Geschichte* (BWAT N. F. 10), pp. 124-150. Stuttgart, 1926.

[10] B. Niese (*Kritik d. beid. Makk.*, pp. 43-47) explains this inconsistency as due to the tendencious *parti pris* of I Maccabees. E. Bickermann (*Der Gott der Makkabäer*, p. 149. Berlin, 1937) explains the omission of Mattathias in II Macc. through the author's literary art: he wished to achieve a dramatic unity by confining himself to the heroic figure of Judas.

1901): "We must not indeed look at everything through the spectacles of the first book. Nevertheless we have no alternative but to make it our basis."

The difference in order of events related by both books raises more difficult problems. In the preceding table, which follows the sequence of I Maccabees, it will be noted that two chapters of II Maccabees (9 and 11) appear outside of their original context, as also 10:14-38 and 12:10-31. Other differences in chs. 9-13 are less significant.[11]

The most obvious anachronism in II Maccabees is the dating of the death of Antiochus IV Epiphanes (ch. 9; cf. 10:9) *before* the campaigns of Judas (10:14-38; 12:10-31), before the first expedition of Lysias (ch. 11) and the rededication of the Temple (10:1-8). In I Maccabees the correct sequence is: first campaign of Lysias (4:26-35), rededication of the Temple (4:36-61), campaigns of Judas (5),[12] death of Epiphanes (6:1-16). Even B. Niese, who has attempted to prove that II Maccabees is older and more accurate than I Maccabees, admits that "the rededication of the Temple took place during the reign of Epiphanes, although his death was described before. II Macc. 10:1, 9" (*Kritik der beiden Makkabäerbücher*, p. 75, n. 2).[13] Why, then, does the account of Epiphanes' death precede that of the rededication? A number of explanations have been given by critics. In general they admit that ch. 9 (the death of Antiochus) was deliberately placed before 10:1-9 (rededication). But there is no unanimity about the reasons that dictated the displacement.

Some scholars believe that it is merely a literary device: the author of II Maccabees described the rededication after the death of Antiochus "in order to end the first part of his book with the inauguration of the Feast of Dedication" (Grimm, Commentary to II Maccabees, p. 12); in order to produce a psychologically powerful climax (F. X. Kugler, *Von Moses bis Paulus*, pp. 359-370, especially pp. 366 f. Münster i. W., 1922).

---

[11] E. Bickermann (*Der Gott der Makkabäer*, pp. 150, 162-168) has discussed a less obvious discrepancy. According to I Macc. 1:16-23, Antiochus Epiphanes plundered the Temple after his *first* Egyptian expedition (fall of 169), but according to II Macc. 5:1, 11-15, he did it after the *second* expedition (summer of 168). Bickermann rightly follows I Maccabees and dates the plundering in 169 and the military occupation through Apollonius, following riots, in 168. He traces the error of II Maccabees back to a Seleucid account which justifies the plundering of the Temple by alleging a Jewish rebellion.

[12] As will be noted later, not all of the campaigns of I Macc. 5 occurred before Epiphanes' death.

[13] C. L. W. Grimm (in his Commentary to II Maccabees, pp. 8, 12, 158) likewise infers from II Macc. 10:9 f. that the author of II Maccabees "knew perfectly well that the cleansing of the Temple was performed before the death of Antiochus IV, or anyhow before this event had become known in Syria and Palestine" (p. 12). But Niese is not consistent: on p. 62 he admits the possibility that "the death of Epiphanes offered to Judas the needed opportunity for cleansing the Sanctuary and restoring the worship" (in n. 1, however, he regards this possibility as improbable).

H. Ewald (*Geschichte des Volkes Israel*, Vol. 4, 3rd ed., pp. 606 ff. 1864) and C. F. Keil (*Kommentar über die Bücher der Makkabäer*, p. 264 f. Leipzig, 1875) agree with Grimm.

Other critics have found in the letters of ch. 11 the reason for the anachronism. Two of these (11:23, 33) imply that Epiphanes died before April, 164 (Xanthicus of 148, Seleucid Era), while in reality he died a year later. B. Niese (*Kritik d. b. Makk.*, pp. 66-84) has vigorously defended not only the authenticity of these letters, but also the correctness of the date of Epiphanes' death. R. Laqueur (*Kritische Untersuchungen zum zweiten Makkabäerbuch*, pp. 37 ff. Strassburg, 1904), on the other hand, regarded the letters as genuine but, since the date of Epiphanes' death was wrong, concluded that the dates and the allusions to Eupator were interpolated (the letters in 11:22-33 were written by Epiphanes). Such outstanding scholars as J. Wellhausen (*Nachr. d. Götting. Ges. d. Wissensch.* 1905, 142; *Isr. u. Jüd. Gesch.*, 6th ed., p. 256), who, however, regards the fourth letter (11:34-38) as spurious, and E. Meyer (*Ursprung und Anfänge des Christentums*, Vol. 2, p. 212) adopted the view of Laqueur; but H. Willrich (*Urkundenfälschung in der hellenistisch-jüdischen Literatur* [FRLANT N.F. 21], p. 35. Göttingen, 1924) without hesitation asserts that "the letters of Lysias and Eupator are an embellishment, prepared by Jason [of Cyrene] for the report, also utilized in I Macc. 6:55 ff., in an older, well informed source."

Whatever conclusion we may reach in regard to the genuineness of these official letters,[14] it is natural to assume that whoever inserted them into the book felt obliged to place the death of Epiphanes before the rededication of the Temple—if he accepted the date in 11:33 as exact. E. Bickermann (*Der Gott der Makkabäer*, pp. 149 f.) attributes the anachronism to the original author himself, Jason of Cyrene, whose work was summarized in II Maccabees: after erroneously assuming that the letter in 11:22-26 was written in March, 164 (according to 11:33), he concluded that Epiphanes had died before then and corrected those of his sources which contradicted this inference. "Precisely this arbitrary procedure shows that he [Jason] felt himself to be a real historian, possessing in his own eyes the authority to correct traditional accounts on the basis of documents" (*ibid.*, p. 150). On the contrary, W. Kolbe, after adducing evidence to prove that the letters in II Macc. 11:16-38 are spurious (*Beiträge zur syrischen und jüdischen Geschichte*, pp. 74-95), attributes them to the forger who concocted the letters in 1:8-2:18: the epitomizer was responsible neither for this material nor for its addition to his summary of Jason's work (*op. cit.*, pp. 121 f., 127). The redactor who inserted it was forced to change the order of events,

[14] A bibliography on the opposite views is given by W. Kolbe, *Beiträge zur syrischen und jüdischen Geschichte*, pp. 74 f.

originally given in Jason's work as follows: early victories of Judas and occupation of Jerusalem (8), rededication of the Temple (10:1-8), death of Epiphanes (9:1-29, followed by 10:9), accession of Antiochus Eupator (10:11 f.), suicide of Ptolemy Macron (10:12 f.), campaigns of Judas (10:14-38), first expedition of Lysias and first peace treaty (11:1-15), renewed campaigns of Judas (12), and so on to the end of the book (*op. cit.* pp. 124 f.). In other words, after adding the letters in chs. 1 and 11, the redactor merely moved 10:1-8 from before to after ch. 9. Similarly, F. X. Kugler (*Von Moses bis Paulus*, pp. 364 f.) had previously adopted the following order as chronologically correct: 8:1-29, 34-36, 30-33; 10:1-8; 9:1-29; 10:9 f. But, while Kolbe attributes the present confused order to a redactor, Kugler (*ibid.*) ascribes it to the Epitomist himself. R. Laqueur (*Kritische Untersuchungen* u.s.w., pp. 30 f.) would transfer 10:1-8 and ch. 11 before 8:30.

The second difference in the chronology of the two books appears in the different positions of the campaigns of Judas against neighboring nations. In I Maccabees they are related together in ch. 5 as if they had taken place in the few months elapsing from the rededication of the Temple to the death of Epiphanes. In II Maccabees, however, they are all dated after the death of Epiphanes and occur at three different times: before the rededication (8:30-33), after it (10:14-38), and between the two campaigns of Lysias (12). E. Meyer (*Ursprung und Anfänge des Christentums*, Vol. 2, p. 228, n. 1), while admitting that the sequence in I Maccabees may not be exact in every detail, believes that on the whole it is correct and that in II Maccabees the right connection between events, presumably given by Jason, has been disarranged. Nevertheless, as B. Niese (*Kritik der beiden Makkabäerbücher*, p. 58) and W. Kolbe (*Beiträge* u.s.w., p. 134) have noted, it is hardly credible that these campaigns of Judas could all have occurred within the space of a few months, as appears from I Maccabees. It seems more probable that the author of I Maccabees, after correctly reporting the beginning of Judas's guerrilla warfare shortly before the death of Epiphanes (163), for purely literary reasons decided to narrate together the campaigns of Judas in the east, west, and south, which continued until Lysias' second campaign in 162. Similarly Matthew combined in the Sermon on the Mount sayings of Jesus uttered at various times and on different occasions.

A third discrepancy appears in the campaigns of Lysias, two of which are reported in each book. In I Maccabees the first campaign occurs before the rededication of the Temple in the days of Epiphanes (4:26-35); in II Maccabees (11:1-12) after the rededication, in the time of Eupator (cf. 11:21). The second campaign (I Macc. 6:28-63; II Macc. 13:1-26) is dated in 150, Seleucid Era, in I Macc. 6:20, but in 149 in II Macc. 13:1. In I Maccabees a treaty of peace followed only the second campaign, but in II Maccabees both campaigns were concluded by treaties.

Various solutions have been proposed to solve these difficulties. Seventeenth- and eighteenth-century scholars (particularly Roman Catholic) regarded the two accounts of the first campaign as reports of two different military actions (cf. Grimm, Commentary on I Maccabees, pp. 70 f.), a view defended by J. Knabenbauer (*Commentarius in duos libros Machabaeorum* [Cursus Scripturae Sacrae]. Paris, 1907) and F. X. Kugler (*Von Moses bis Paulus*, pp. 358-405): thus Lysias would have led three expeditions, not two. According to Kugler, the first expedition is that of I 4:26-35, the second that of 11:1-38; and the third that of I 6:28-63 and II 13:1-26 (*op. cit.* pp. 375, 405).

Others, conversely, believe that Lysias led only one expedition against Judas. E. Meyer (*Ursprung und Anfänge des Christentums*, p. 233, n. 3, and p. 459) regarded the two stories in II Maccabees (chs. 11 and 13) as variant accounts of the same campaign—a view held long before by H. Ewald (*Geschichte des Volkes Israels*, Vol. 3, Pt. ii, p. 365) and first suggested by H. Grotius (*Annotationes in Vet. Test.*, *ad* II Macc. 13:1. Paris, 1644). Both accounts would refer to the second campaign in I Macc. 6:28-63, while II Maccabees omits the first campaign (I Macc. 4:26-35). Going a step further, O. Procksch ("Der Friede des Lysias vom Frühling 164 v. Chr." in *Theologisches Literaturblatt* 24 [1903] 457-464, 481-484; see especially p. 458) and W. Kolbe (*Beiträge u.s.w.*, pp. 81, 126) concluded that the first campaign (I Macc. 4; II Macc. 11) was unhistorical: the narratives about it are a distorted echo of the events of the second campaign and were concocted for the glory of the Jews.

The majority of critics still admit the historicity of both campaigns and regard the stories in I Maccabees as more accurate (except for the omission of the peace treaty after the first campaign).[15] Even B. Niese (*Kritik der beid. Makkab.*, p. 77) is forced to recognize that I Maccabees is preferable for the history of the second campaign.

In the third place, in addition to their variations in the contents and in the sequence, the two books differ considerably in matters of details pertaining to identical events. At times the dates in the two books cannot be reconciled: we have noted the contrast between I 6:20 (150 Seleucid Era) and II 13:1 (149 Sel.); according to I 4:52 the Temple was rededicated exactly three years after it was polluted (I 1:54, 59), but according to II 10:3 only two years had elapsed. The other dates

---

[15] H. Bévenot (*Die Beiden Makkabäerbücher* [HS IV, 4], pp. 10 f., 32, 221 f.), following S. Zeitlin (JQR 1919-20, p. 56) and F. M. Abel ("Topographie des campagnes machabéennes" in RB 1923-26), solves the difficulties involved in the stories of Lysias' campaigns by simply transferring II Macc. 11 before II Macc. 8:30 (cf. R. Laqueur, *Krit. Unters.*, pp. 30 f.).

correspond exactly, as for instance 151 Seleucid Era for the landing of Demetrius I (I 7:1; II 14:1, 4), and apparently the death of Nicanor in the same year (I 7:1, 43; II 15:28, 36 [compared with II 14:4]). This raises the vexing question of the beginning of the Seleucid Era according to I and II Maccabees.[16] This era celebrates the founding of the Seleucid Empire through the victory of Seleucus I, in alliance with Ptolemy I, against Demetrius (son of Antigonus) at Gaza, and his conquest of Babylonia in 312-311 B.C. But the exact beginning of the era was not fixed uniformly; there are four possibilities: spring (March 21) or fall (September 21) of 312, or of 311. The court at Antioch, using the Macedonian calendar, reckoned from the fall of 312; the Babylonians, however, reckoned from the spring (when their year began) of 311, six months later.

The following dates have been suggested for the beginning of the Seleucid Era in I Maccabees:

1. March-April, 312 B.C.: C. L. Ideler, *Handb. der . . . Chronol.*, Vol. 1, pp. 532 ff. (1825). Grimm, on I Macc. 1:10, p. 10; but cf. on II Macc. 13:1, pp. 186 f. (1853, 1857). E. Schürer, *Geschichte des Volkes Israel*, Vol. 1, pp. 32 ff. (1901). F. K. Ginzel, *Handb. der . . . Chronologie*, Vol. 2, pp. 60 f. 1911. E. Mahler, *Handb. der jüdischen Chronologie*, pp. 140 ff. Leipzig, 1916. F. X. Kugler, *Von Moses bis Paulus*, p. 344 (1922). H. Volkmann, in *Klio* 19 [1925] 395.

2. September-October, 312 B.C.: G. Wernsdorf, *Commentatio historico-critica de fide historica librorum Maccabaicorum*, pp. 18-31. Vratislavia [Breslau], 1747. J. von Gumpach, *Über den altjüdischen Kalender*, pp. 217 ff. (1848); *Zwei chronol. Abhandlungen u.s.w.*, pp. 100 ff. Heidelberg, 1854. H. F. Clinton, *Fasti Hellenici*, Vol. 3, 2nd ed., p. 379 (Oxford, 1851). H. Ewald, *Geschichte des Volkes Israel*, Vol. 4, 3rd ed., 1864. B. Niese, *Kritik d. b. Makk.*, p. 94 (1900). J. Wellhausen, *Israel. und jüd. Geschichte*, p. 260, footnote. 5th ed., 1904 (omitted in the 7th ed., 1914). O. Procksch, in *Theol. Literaturbl.* 24 [1903] 457 ff., 481 ff. K. J. Beloch, *Griechische Geschichte*, Vol. 3, Pt. II, p. 138. Berlin, 1904. R. Laqueur, *Kritische Unters. z. zweit. Makk.*, p. 9 (1904). E. Meyer, *Ursprung und Anfänge d. Christ.* II, 248 f., n. 1; 208, n. 2; 255, n. 3 (1921).

3. March-April, 311 B.C. M. Gibert, "Mémoire sur la chronologie de l'histoire des Maccabées" (*Mém. de l'Acad. des Inscr. et Belles-Lettres* 26 [1759] 112-156). L. Hertzfeld, *Geschichte des Volkes Israel* II, 1, p.

[16] For the abundant literature on the subject, see in particular: Grimm, on II Macc. 13:1 (pp. 186 f.). E. Schürer, *Geschichte des Jüdischen Volkes*, Vol. 1, pp. 32 ff. 4th ed. Leipzig, 1901. W. Kolbe, *Beiträge u. s. w.*, p. 19; and *Hermes* 62 [1927] 225-242. E. Bickermann, in Pauly-Wissowa, *Realenzyklopädie* XIV, 783 ff. (1928); and *Der Gott der Makkabäer*, pp. 155-168 (1937). H. Bévenot, *Die beide Makkabäerbücher*, pp. 1 f., 24-28 (1931).

448 (Nordhausen, 1855). G. F. Unger, "Die Seleukidenära der Makkabäerbücher" (*Sitzungsber. der München. Akad. der Wiss.*, phil. hist. Kl., 1895, pp. 244 ff.). D. M. Sluys, *De Maccabaeorum libris I et II quaestiones*, pp. 89, 95. Amsterdam, 1904. W. Kolbe, *Beiträge z. syr. u. jüd. Geschichte* (BWAT N.F. 10), p. 33. Stuttgart, 1926; *Hermes* 62 (1927) 225-242. H. Bévenot, *Die Beiden Makkabäerbücher*, p. 27. Bonn, 1931.

4. September-October, 312 b.c. for Seleucid history, March-April, 311, for Jewish history. E. Bickermann, in Pauly-Wissowa, *Realenzykl.* XIV, 783 ff.; *Der Gott des Makkabäer*, pp. 154-157 (1937); *Berytus* 8 (1944) 73-83.

For II Maccabees the following beginnings of the Seleucid Era have been suggested:

1. March-April, 312. Schürer, *Geschichte*, Vol. 1, p. 39.
2. September-October, 312. Scaliger, Gibert, Clinton, Niese, Kugler (p. 352), Bickermann (Pauly-Wissowa, *Realenz.* XIV, 1, p. 784; *Gott der Makk.*, p. 157).
3. March-April, 311. Grimm, Hertzfeld (p. 448), Unger (pp. 246 ff.), Kolbe (p. 44).
4. September-October, 311. Wernsdorf, Ideler (p. 533), Mahler (p. 140 f.), Bévenot (p. 27).
5. March-April, 311, for II Macc. 1:7, 10; fall of 312 for 11:21, 33, 38; 13:1; 14:1, 4. Sluys (pp. 116 f.).

This wide divergence of opinion among experts indicates per se that our data (particularly for II Maccabees) are too meager and too ambiguous for a final solution of the problem. The present writer has no new contribution to make on this question, but he believes that as a Palestinian Jew the author of I Maccabees, since in his calendar the year began in March-April, followed the Babylonian usage (I Macc., No. 3, above: March-April, 311), while Jason of Cyrene probably followed the usage at Antioch (II Macc. No. 2, above: September-October, 312). But this assumption does not eliminate all the difficulties.

The two books differ also in the numbers of soldiers engaged in certain battles. In the first campaign, Nicanor had 40,000 footmen and 7,000 horsemen facing 3,000 Jewish foot soldiers who slew an equal number of Syrians, according to I Macc. 3:39; 4:6, 15; but according to II Macc. 8:1, 9, 16, 24, 20,000 Syrians, of which 9,000 were killed, faced 6,000 Jews. In his first campaign, Lysias had 60,000 footmen and 5,000 horsemen to fight against 10,000 Jewish footmen, and lost 5,000 of his soldiers (I Macc. 4:28 f., 34); the figures are increased in II Maccabees (11:2, 4, 11) to 80,000 footmen, thousands of horsemen, and 80 elephants, of which 11,000 footmen and 1,600 horsemen fell. In his second expedition Lysias commanded 100,000 footmen (50,000 in Josephus, *War* I, 1),

20,000 horsemen, and 32 elephants, according to I Macc. 6:30; Lysias forces are 110,000 footmen, 5,300 horsemen, 22 elephants, and 300 chariots armed with scythes according to II Macc. 13:2. Needless to say, these figures are greatly exaggerated (though not so fantastically as in Chronicles); but the differences between the two books are significant.

Aside from dates and figures, the two books do not always agree in regard to concrete details in their stories of identical events. Thus, for instance, we have in the two books three accounts of the death of Epiphanes (I 6:1-16; II 1:12-16 and ch. 9) which cannot be mutually reconciled.[17] The numerous contrasts between the two books are emphasized by B. Niese (*Kritik d. b. Makk.*) in order to prove the superiority of II Maccabees over I Maccabees, but they are minimized by W. Kolbe (*Beiträge z. syr. u. jüd. Geschichte*) in order to prove that both books utilized the same source—Jason of Cyrene. In reality the comparison between parallel stories in the two books shows that the two authors worked independently, seldom using the same source material, and not only had no knowledge on each other's work, but pursued different aims and were animated by different ideals. And in spite of Niese's valuable *Kritik* as to their relative historicity, the verdict must still be in favor of I Maccabees (cf. Grimm, Commentary on II Maccabees, pp. 8 f.), in view of the numerous unhistorical and even supernatural events related in II Maccabees.

Looking at the two books *in toto*, we note a far-reaching difference in the two authors' points of view. Although both are zealous and ardent in their devotion to Judaism, the author of I Maccabees extols the patriotism and national power of the Jews, while the second stresses their religious superiority over the Gentiles and the Almighty's special care for them. In the first book the reward is purely terrestrial; in the second a celestial reward is expected by the pious martyrs. In I Maccabees the Jews suffer persecution because of the wickedness of the heathen; in II Maccabees, because of their own sins: God, in his loving-kindness, chastises the Jews before they have reached the ultimate measure of wickedness, lest he be required to "destroy" them "from off the face of the earth," as the prophet Amos had threatened. The achievements of Judas and the later Hasmoneans form the chief topic of the first book; God's care for his Temple and his people are the subject of the second. While in I Maccabees nothing is said of God's direct intervention in favor of the Jews, supernatural manifestations abound in II Maccabees.

[17] See H. Willrich, *Judaica*, pp. 140-144. Göttingen, 1900. B. Niese, *Kritik d. b. Makk.*, pp. 19, 29, 84 f. J. Döller, "Der Tod des Königs Antioch IV Epiphanes" (*Theologisch-praktische Quartalschrift* 68 [1915] 929-931). F. X. Kugler, *Von Moses bis Paulus*, pp. 350 f.

The comparison of the two books thus indicates that they did not influence each other; seldom, if at all, did they use the same sources. I Maccabees was written in Hebrew by an author whose knowledge of Greek was probably limited, while Jason of Cyrene, whose five books were summarized in II Maccabees, like most of the Jews in the Diaspora, wrote in Greek and apparently knew hardly any Hebrew and Aramaic: it would be strange indeed, under the circumstances, if we could discover a very close similarity between the two books.

2. Literary Features of I Maccabees
A. *The Hebrew Text*

The Greek text of I Maccabees, which has come down to us in the Septuagint (LXX) Old Testament of the Christian Church, is manifestly a translation from a Hebrew original. The original did not survive for long after the beginning of the Christian Era, if until then, for the book seems to be unknown to the rabbis of the Mishna and Talmud: they never use the term "Maccabeus," but refer to Judas and his family as the "Hasmoneans" (a term unknown in the Apocrypha).

The references to a Hebrew text on the part of Origen and Jerome do not prove that the original survived until their time, for it is not to be excluded that this "Hebrew" book was a version from the Greek.[18] In commenting on Ps. 1, Origen (see Eusebius, *Eccles. Hist.* VI, 25:2) wrote: "Outside of these [the canonical books of the Old Testament] there is *tà Makkabaiká* which is entitled *Sarbēth Sabanaiel* [or *Basanaiel, Sarbane el*]." We may assume that the general term *Makkabaiká* (Maccabean matters) indicates I Maccabees, although it could apply to all the books about the Maccabees, but even so we have no proof that this was the original and not an Aramaic history based on I Maccabees. The same applies to Jerome's words: "Machabaeorum primum librum hebraicum repperi, secundus graecus est, quod ex ipsa quoque phrasi probari potest" (*Prologus Galeatus*). Even if the current interpretation is adopted ("I found I Maccabees in Hebrew; II Maccabees is Greek, a fact which can be proved by the very style"), we are still in the dark as to the origin of this Hebrew book.[19] The original Hebrew text of I Maccabees may have disappeared from circulation some time before A.D. 100, for Josephus demonstrably utilized I Macc. 1-13 in the Greek text which is extant, reproducing some obvious corruptions in it, but patently knew nothing

[18] Cf. C. C. Torrey in *Encycl. Bibl.* III, 2858. H. W. Ettelson, *The Integrity of I Maccabees* (Transact. of the Connecticut Acad. of Arts and Sciences, Vol. 27 [August 1925] 249-384), pp. 331-335. New Haven, 1925.

[19] Ettelson's other interpretation (*op. cit.*, p. 333) is most improbable: "I found the first Book of Maccabees to be Hebrew, the second Greek, which fact can be proved by the style itself."

of the Hebrew original (cf. H. W. Ettelson, *The Integrity of I Macc.*, pp. 335-341).

The nature of the Maccabean book known to Origen is no less mysterious than its Semitic title, *Sarbeth Sabanaiel*. In general the words are regarded as Hebrew, but none of the numerous suggested interpretations is convincing.[20] G. Dalman,[21] on the other hand, with some slight revisions sees in the words a transcription of the Aramaic *Sefar beth Hasmonaie* (Book of the Hasmonean Dynasty): this was in his opinion the title of a Hasmonean history in Aramaic, quite distinct from I Maccabees.

The First Book of Maccabees (in contrast with the second) is unquestionably a translation from a Semitic original. "The Greek of I Macc. is, like the LXX, translation Greek and intensely Hebraistic" (A. T. Robertson, *Grammar of the Greek New Testament in the Light of Historical Research*, p. 87. 3rd ed. New York, 1919). Although an occasional scholar has suggested in the past that I Maccabees was written in the current vernacular of the Jews, Palestinian Aramaic,[22] critical opinion is now unanimous in maintaining that the original was in Hebrew.[23]

The Greek version is so faithful that we are frequently able to recognize the Hebrew text from which it was translated, particularly when the author, as was his habit, used Biblical expressions. A few examples from ch. 1 may suffice.[24] "Many evils have found us" (1:11, cf. Deut. 31:21; see also I Macc. 6:13; Tob. 12:7). "They sold themselves to do evil" (1:15, cf. I Kings 21:20). "And the kingdom was established . . ." (1:16, cf. I Kings 2:12, and elsewhere). "With a heavy crowd," meaning "a great army" (1:17, cf. Num. 20:20). "And there fell many wounded" (1:18; 3:11; 8:10; 9:17, 40; 16:2; literally from Judg. 9:40; cf. Dan. 11:26; I Chron. 5:22). "And after two years of

[20] See on the meaning of *Sarbeth Sabanaiel*: Grimm, Commentary on I Maccabees, p. xvii. S. J. Curtiss, *The Name Machabee*, p. 30. H. E. Ryle, *The Canon of the Old Testament*, p. 185. London, 1892. S. Sachs, in REJ 26 (1893) 161-166. L. E. T. André, *Les Apocryphes*, pp. 60-62. Böhmer (no initials given), in TSK 76 (1903) 332-338. A. Schulte, in BZ 7 (1909) 254. Cf. also E. Schürer, *Geschichte*, Vol. 3, p. 195.

[21] *Grammatik des jüdisch-palästinischen Aramäisch*, p. 6. Leipzig, 1896. 2nd ed., p. 7; 1905. C. C. Torrey (*Encycl. Bibl.* III, 2857) agrees with Dalman's interpretation.

[22] E. Reuss, *Das Alte Testament*, Vol. 7, p. 25. Braunschweig, 1895. L. E. T. André, *Les Apocryphes*, p. 69.

[23] The evidence is scanty but clear. See C. C. Torrey, in *Encycl. Bibl.* III, 2859. W. O. E. Oesterley, in R. H. Charles, *Apocrypha and Pseudepigrapha*, Vol. 1, p. 61. P. Joüon, in *Biblica* 3 (1922) 204-206. H. W. Ettelson, *The Integrity of I Macc.*, p. 309.

[24] H. W. Ettelson (*The Integrity of I Maccabees*, pp. 303, 308-314, 317-330) presents numerous other illustrations of the Hebrew words and idioms underlying the Greek text (see also the bibliography in Ettelson, *op. cit.*, p. 308, n. 7).

days," a Hebrew idiom meaning "two full years" (1:29, cf. Gen. 41:1).

The author obviously was well versed in the Hebrew Scriptures and generally wrote in good classical Hebrew learned from the ancient models. Of course, like other Hebrew writers of the third and second century B.C., he is not free from Aramaic expressions such as occur in the latest books of the Old Testament (cf. Grimm, Commentary on I Maccabees, p. xvii). Nevertheless, I Maccabees in Hebrew was a notable historical work, not inferior in style and historicity to the Books of Kings, although below the high level of literary excellence attained by the most ancient parts of Judges and especially Samuel.

As Sirach had taken Proverbs for his model, so our author studied the historical books of the Old Testament and strove to equal them. It was the misfortune of Ecclesiasticus and I Maccabees that the Jewish dogma, according to which divine inspiration ceased after Ezra and Nehemiah, excluded them from the Hebrew canon of Scriptures, for they deserved such a distinction no less than a considerable portion of the Old Testament. In Luther's opinion (cf. Grimm's Commentary, p. xxii, n. 3), I Maccabees was "not unworthy" of canonicity.

Twice (9:22; 16:23) the author uses the well-known standard formula from Kings (negatively in 9:22): "Now the rest of the acts of Solomon, and his wisdom, are they not written . . ." (I Kings 11:41). The author would presumably have loved to insert prophetic oracles and stories about prophets into his book, after the manner of Kings, but no prophet had appeared in Judah for a long time (9:27), and he could only admit honestly that no prophet was available when divine guidance was needed (4:44-46; 14:41). But the author did not hesitate to follow Chronicles (rather than Kings) when he inserted into his history pious addresses and poems, and when he incorporated into the narrative, after the manner of the Book of Ezra, official dossiers of public documents. We may detect another sign of the Chronicler's influence in the author's interest in a priestly genealogy (2:1; 14:29) through which Mattathias is assigned to the course of Joarib (Jehoiarib in Chronicles), the very first in the list of I Chron. 24:7-18 (but not in Neh. 12:1-7, 12-21). Finally, in the use of exact dates, in the quotation of state papers, in the combination of biography and national history, and in the avoidance of miraculous interventions of the deity in human affairs, our book resembles Ezra-Nehemiah and, beginning as it does with Alexander's conquests, it may have been planned by the author as a sequel to the Chronicler's work. The century between Nehemiah's second visit and Alexander's conquests was naturally skipped, for it is a blank in all Jewish histories and practically disregarded in the Jewish chronology: Daniel (11:2 f.) seems to confuse Xerxes and Darius III of Persia; the *Seder Olam Rabbah* (second century of our era) reckoned only thirty-four years from the rebuilding of the Temple in 516 to Alexander in 331.

If our surmise is correct and the author really wished to bring the Biblical history almost down to his own time by writing a sequel to the Chronicler's work, his use of Hebrew language and of Biblical style was inevitable. And this would also explain his predilection for archaic terminology, which B. Niese (*Kritik*, pp. 48 f.) has noted. Scythopolis (II Macc. 12:29) is still called Beth-shean (I Macc. 5:52; 12:40 f.), although Akko is regularly called Ptolemais. Special prominence is given to sites famous in Israel's ancient history, such as Mizpeh (3:46; 5:35), Michmash (9:73), and the Plain of Hazor (11:67). Jerusalem and the Temple Hill are called "Zion" (4:37, 60; 5:54; 6:48, 62; 7:33; 10-11; 14:27)—a name which survived only in poetry; the Acra (4:2; 6:18) is sometimes called "the City of David" (1:33; 7:32; 14:36). In speaking of the Jews, the author delights to use the ancient term "Israel" (40 times)—a term never used, however, in those diplomatic negotiations and documents which the author has not rewritten in his own style (cf. H. W. Ettelson, *Integrity of I Macc.*, p. 301); once he calls the Jews "the race [variant: seed] of Jacob" (5:2). He still speaks of the Philistines (*allóphyloi* [foreigners] in the Greek; cf. the LXX), who had long since disappeared and had bequeathed their name (in Greek writings) to "Palestine" (3:41; 4:22, 30; 5:66, 68). He even speaks of "Sons of Esau," meaning Idumeans (5:3), and of "Canaanites" (9:37). The author was obviously aware that he was using obsolete names, and occasionally he took pains to explain them: so in the case of "City of David" (1:33; 14:36), "Sons of Esau" (5:3), and "land of Chittim" (1:1; contrast 8:5)—properly Cyprus, here Macedonia or Greece (cf. 6:2).

B. *Speeches, Prayers, and Documents*

The speeches and the prayers are of course adapted to the situation in which they were pronounced but manifestly were composed by the author of I Maccabees either freely or on the basis of some slight recorded reminiscences. Such was the practice of Greek and Roman historians, which Thucydides (I, 22) frankly admitted in his own case. Good evidence, for instance, that Mattathias could not have uttered verbatim the deathbed speech attributed to him (2:49-68) is furnished by the allusions to chapters 3 and 6 of Daniel in 2:59-60 (cf. III Macc. 6:6 f.), for, when Mattathias died, the Book of Daniel (or even its first part) could hardly have been written. This address of Mattathias, the most notable in the book, is a panegyric in praise of Old Testament heroes of faith (like Hebr. 11), possibly suggested by Ecclus. 44-49. This recollection of the deeds of the "fathers" from Abraham to Daniel serves not only as an inspiring example to the Maccabees, but also as a connecting link between the Scriptures and I Maccabees, a book written as a supplement to sacred history. The unbroken continuity in Israel's devotion to God and his Law, and in God's deliverance of his people, appears in the prayers of Judas (4:30-33; 7:40-42) and of the priests (7:37 f.); it is also stressed in several addresses (2:19-22, 27, 34, 37; 3:18-22; 4:8-11). If at times the speeches seem to attribute the victory to human valor rather than to divine help (3:58-60; 5:18; 13:3-6; 16:2 f.; cf. 14:25 f.), this is because God has chosen the Maccabees to deliver his people (5:62): the Hasmoneans are thus like the Judges of old (except that they are never said to be filled with God's spirit): "And Jonathan began to *judge* the people" (9:73). When God's wrath raged violently against Israel (1:64; cf. 2:49; Dan. 8:19; 9:16; 11:36), Judas through his campaigns "turned away the wrath from Israel" (3:8)—neither repentance (as in Daniel) nor the blood of the martyrs (as in II Maccabees) brought about this result. This incongruous combination of pride in human achievement and trust in God is totally foreign to Daniel, where Judas's military achievements are dismissed merely as "a little help" (Dan. 11:34).

The poetry in the book stresses the human rather than the divine factor in the deliverance of Israel. It is not to be excluded that some poems were quoted from anthologies,[25] but it seems more probable that the author of the book, when carried away by his enthusiasm, lapsed into verse. The poems are well connected with the narrative but lack brilliance and originality, being usually replete with scriptural reminiscences. They fall into two groups: laments over the sad plight of Jerusalem and Israel (1:25-28, 36-40; 2:7-13; 3:45); and panegyrics in honor of Judas (3:1-9;[26] in 9:21 he is called "savior of Israel") and of Simon (14:6-15).[27] In addition, after relating a particularly dramatic event, the author sums up the tragedy in a single line of poetry (9:41; 16:17). In 7:17 the author summarizes Ps. 79:2 f.; and in 4:24 f., Ps. 118:1-4 and 136. Occasionally a metrical line seems to occur in the midst of prose: 2:44; 3:51; 4:38.

In the third place, besides speeches and poems, the author introduces into his history various dossiers of diplomatic and other official docu-

[25] But it is unlikely that all metric passages are quotations, as E. Kautzsch (*Die Apokryphen und Pseudepigraphen*, p. 26. Tübingen, 1900; cf. T. K. Cheyne, *Origin of the Psalter*, p. 23. London, 1891; E. Bickermann, *Der Gott der Makkabäer*, p. 146) asserts.

[26] Cf. C. F. Burney, "An Acrostic Poem in Praise of Judas Maccabaeus (I Macc. iii, 1-9)" (JTS 21 [1920] 319-325).

[27] Ps. 110, having the acrostic šm'wn (Simon) in vv. 1-4, is another extant poem in honor of Simon, earlier in date. It was composed to celebrate Simon's installation as high priest in 142 B.C.

ments—a practice for which there is no evidence before the Book of Ezra. We may classify these state papers as follows:[28]

A. Communications between Jews. 1. Summary of a letter from the Jews in Gilead, besieged in Dathema (probably an error for Ramoth, cf. Ettelson, *Integrity*, p. 335), appealing to Judas for help (5:10-13). 2. National decree (incised on tablets of brass) conferring on Simon the authority of leader and high priest in perpetuity, issued in 140 B.C. (it is not clear whether the text of the decree is limited to 14:27-45 or, less probably, includes either 14:27-47 or 14:27-49).

B. Negotiations between Jews and Romans. 3. Treaty of alliance made by the Roman Senate with Judas (8:23-32), inscribed on tablets of brass (161 B.C.). 4. Letter of the Roman consul Lucius Caecilius Metellus to Ptolemy VII Euergetes II Physcon (15:16-21) in 142; a copy was sent to Simon.

C. Letters of Seleucid kings to the Jews and others. 5. Letter of Alexander Balas to Jonathan (10:18-20) in 152. 6. Letter of Demetrius I Soter to the Jewish nation (10:25-45) in 152. 7. Message of Alexander Balas to Ptolemy VI Philometor (10:52-54) in 151. 8. Reply of Ptolemy to Balas (10:55 f.) in 151. 9. Letter of Demetrius II Nicator to Jonathan (11:30-37), containing a copy of his letter to Lasthenes, in 145. 10. Letter of Demetrius II to Simon (13:36-40) in 142. 11. Letter of Antiochus VII Sidetes to Simon (15:2-9) in 138.

D. Jews and Spartans. 12. Letter of Areios, or Areus (*sic*, instead of *Dareios*), king of Sparta (309-265 B.C.) to Onias (12:21-23). 13. Letter of Jonathan (160-142) to the Spartans (12:6-18). 14. Letter of the Spartans to Simon (14:20-24) in 142.

In appraising the origin and historical value of these fourteen documents scholars have reached the most divergent opinions. We are faced by two problems with reference to each document: Is it authentic? Was it an integral part of the first Hebrew edition of I Maccabees?

The two documents which do not involve foreign nations (A, Nos. 1-2), like the speeches considered above, seem to be from the pen of our author. The appeal of the Jews in Dathema (Ramoth) to Judas (No. 1) is historical, but is not preserved verbatim. It is possible that a national decree (No. 2) was promulgated in favor of Simon, but the extant text cannot be its accurate translation. As Grimm (Commentary, pp. 219 f.) has noted, the order of the events in the first years of Simon differs considerably in the preceding narrative and in the decree. Moreover, if the purpose of the decree was to show tangibly the nation's appreciation to Simon and his sons (14:25) for making Judah independent, it should have added something to his present authority and dignity (which the decree does not increase) by making them hereditary.

---

[28] Other documents of this period, quoted by II Maccabees and Josephus, are listed by E. Bickermann (*Der Gott der Makkabäer*, pp. 174 f.).

But this the decree fails to specify in clear legal language, and it is probable that the author of I Maccabees rewrote the crucial passage in 14:41 ". . . that Simon should be their leader and high priest *forever*"; but he added immediately "until a faithful prophet should arise" (cf. 4:44-46), thus depriving Simon's *perpetual* tenure of complete legal certainty (contrary to what such a decree would have ordained).[29]

The documents involving other nations have been defended as genuine (except perhaps for some slight verbal revisions) by Roman Catholic and early Protestant scholars, while on the contrary H. Willrich rejects them as spurious. The various shades of opinion may be classified as follows:

1. All the documents are authentic and formed an original part of I Maccabees. In addition to Roman Catholic scholars, who regard I Maccabees as inspired Scripture, this view has been maintained by E. Meyer (*Ursprung und Anfänge des Christentums*, Vol. 2, p. 246, n. 4; p. 255, n. 1; cf. 211) and even more vigorously by E. Bickermann (Pauly-Wissowa, *Realenzykl.* XIV, 1 [1928], pp. 779-800), who lists as authentic (*Gott der Makkab.*, p. 174 f.) the documents listed above, except Nos. 1 and 7-8 (presumably omitted as irrelevant).

2. All the documents are an integral part of I Maccabees, although hardly all authentic, at least in their present form. The critics who have reached this general conclusion differ in their verdict on the authenticity of the documents.

   a. E. Renan (*Histoire du peuple d'Israël*, Vol. 4, pp. 384, n. 3; 398, 400, 402; 405, n. 2. Paris, 1893) declares all the documents to be "false and apocryphal," but contemporary with the book.

   b. C. C. Torrey (*Ezra Studies*, pp. 145 ff.) states that the documents were not technically forgeries, but were freely composed by the author as embellishments for his book, like the speeches interspersed in it.

   c. Grimm (Commentary, pp. 130, 189 f.), H. Drüner, (*Wocheschrift für Klassische Philologie* 1901, No. 25), Schürer (*Geschichte*, Vol. 1, pp. 220, n. 32; 250, n. 19), Niese (*Kritik*, p. 88; *Geschichte der Griechischen und Makedonischen Staaten*, Vol. 3, pp. 261 f. Gotha, 1903), and Ettelson (*Integrity*, p. 346) recognize that the diction of these documents is frequently that of the author, but that their substance is derived from genuine state papers.

3. Most of the documents, whatever their degree of authenticity, were inserted by the author into I Maccabees; but a few are later interpolations. With differences in detail, the following critics have adopted this conclusion: F. Rosenthal (*Das erste Makkabäerbuch*, pp. 14 ff.),

---

[29] "Whatever one may think about the authenticity of the contents, the form and structure are unquestionably the contribution of the author [of I Maccabees] himself" (Niese, *Kritik*, p. 51).

Kautzsch (*Apokryphen*, pp. 27 ff.), André (*Les Apocryphes*, pp. 78 f.), C. Steuernagel (*Lehrb. d. Einleitung in das Alte Test.*, p. 776. Tübingen, 1912), Oesterley (in Charles, *Apocrypha*, pp. 61-65), and O. Eissfeldt (*Einleitung in das Alte Test.*, p. 635. Tübingen, 1934).

4. All the documents are interpolated forgeries. H. Willrich (*Judaica*, pp. 40-47), on rather flimsy evidence, tries to prove that Philo and his comrades made for Caligula (in A.D. 40) a summary of the official dossier allegedly collected by Judas Maccabeus and sent to Alexandria (II Macc. 2:14 f.). Later Philo's epitome was expanded into the "Collection of Agrippa I." All documents in these various collections were forged by the Jews for apologetic purposes. A detailed argument for the falsity of each document is given by Willrich in his monograph *Urkundenfälschung* (FRLANT N.F. 21. Göttingen, 1924).

As is often the case when historical evidence is not sufficiently definite for a final solution of the problems, scholars have in this instance suggested almost all conceivable theories, buttressing them with more or less convincing arguments. The present writer regards the second of these four theories as the most probable, and endorses the words of Niese (*Kritik*, p. 100): "In reality the documents, whatever one may think of their authenticity, constitute an essential part of the narrative and cannot be dispensed with. If one imagined them absent, not much would be left." The evidence from context, diction, and style adduced by Ettelson (*Integrity*, pp. 365-375) is significant, to say the least: the author of I Maccabees must have placed them in his book and must have retouched them—unless he drafted them entirely. So much seems fairly certain, but we may hesitate in deciding whether the author merely revised existing documents (Ettelson) or composed them *in toto*, inventing them "to the best of his ability and in perfect good faith" (Torrey, *Ezra Studies*, p. 149, n. 17).

I Maccabees as a whole is so uniform in diction and thought that it is idle to search for interpolations of any length. In particular the theory of J. von Destinon (*Die Quellen des Fl. Josephus in der Jüd. Archäologie, XII-XVII und Jüd. Krieg, I.* Kiel, 1882), regarding I Macc. 14:16-16:24 as "from the hand of another author" (*op. cit.*, p. 89) because Josephus ignored it, after a period of vogue[30] seems to have been abandoned.[31]

[30] It was accepted by Wellhausen, Kautzsch, Roth, G. Schmidt, G. Hölscher, Benwitch, Steuernagel, Büchler, and others (see Ettelson, *Integrity*, pp. 257 f.). In a general way this theory had been previously advanced by F. Rosenthal (*D. erste Makkab.*, 1867).

[31] Destinon's theory has been refuted in detail by H. Drüner (*Untersuchungen über Josephus* [Dissertation]. Marburg, 1896) and especially by Ettelson (*Integrity*, pp. 255-341). It was rejected by Willrich, Oesterley, Fairweather, André, Streane, Barton, Niese, Torrey, and others (cf. Ettelson, *op. cit.*, p. 262); and more recently by Eissfeldt (*Einleitung*, p. 635).

Even if some or all of the official documents were freely composed by the author, like the speeches and poems interspersed in the book, I Maccabees remains a historical source of basic importance, as critics (not excluding Niese, who regards I Maccabees as inferior to II Maccabees; cf. his *Kritik*, pp. 52 f.) generally recognize.[32] Not only do we find here information not available elsewhere and a considerable number of exact dates,[33] but supernatural events are conspicuously lacking, in contrast to II Maccabees. While the historicity of the book as a whole is not questioned, in a number of cases the author fails to adhere to the facts, either through bias or through ignorance. Speeches, prayers, and official letters freely composed or revised; the omission of the disgraceful intrigues of Jason and Menelaus; fantastic numbers of soldiers in battle (3:39; 4:15, 28, 34; 6:30; 11:45, 47; 12:41) or riding on an elephant (6:37); and the like (5:54; 7:46) reveal the author's pride in the achievements of his people—a pride apparent in the selection of incidents and in their presentation. On the other hand, the author betrays a naïve ignorance concerning foreign nations and commits a number of errors about them (1:1-9; 6:1 [Elymais is not a city]; 8:1-16; 10:1 [Balas was *not* the son of Epiphanes]; Antiochus VI was actually killed *after* [Josephus, *Antiquities* 13:7, 1; §218] Demetrius II was captured by the Parthians [13:31; 14:1-3]). But such inaccuracies, errors, and exaggerations are fairly common in historians of the time and do not seriously impair the credibility of this valuable history, which is based on accurate written sources, unusually exact in the topography and chronology.

C. *The Author*

What information about the nameless author of I Maccabees can we glean from his book? If the last two verses of the book are genuine, as seems certain, the author wrote late in the rule of John Hyrcanus I (134-104)[34] or more probably after his death (when "the chronicles of his priesthood" would have been completed), presumably about 100 B.C. or soon after: certainly before Pompey conquered Jerusalem in 63, for the Romans are consistently presented as friends of the Jews (8:1-32; 15:15-21).

The author was a Palestinian Jew and presumably lived in Jerusalem.

---

[32] Cf. Ettelson, *Integrity*, p. 376.

[33] Dates according to the Seleucid era are given in the following passages: 1:10, 20, 54; 2:70; 3:37; 4:52; 6:16, 20; 7:1; 9:3, 54; 10:1, 21, 57, 67; 11:19; 13:41, 51; 14:1; 15:10; 16:14. Less exact chronological data are found in: 1:59; 4:28; 7:43=49; 9:57; 10:50; 13:22.

[34] C. C. Torrey (*Encycl. Bibl.* Vol. 3, cols. 2859 f. London, 1902) and W. O. E. Oesterley (in Charles, *Apocrypha* I, 60) date the book in 140-125 and 125-100, respectively; E. Bickermann (*Der Gott der Makkabäer*, p. 146) dates it in 123-113.

He spoke Aramaic and wrote Hebrew well. His knowledge of Greek must remain a matter of conjecture. Niese (*Kritik*, pp. 50:53) has of course presented some arguments to prove that he knew Greek well, since some of his sources (notably in the second half of the book) must have been Greek in origin and the decree in behalf of Simon is patterned after honorary decrees of Greek cities. But it is not impossible that a history of the Ptolemies and Seleucids was available in Aramaic or Hebrew (cf., for the earlier period, Dan. 11:5-20), and Niese himself shows that in 3:32 the Greek title "kinsman" or "cousin" (*syngenés*) of the king (II Macc. 11:1) was misunderstood and taken as indicating actual blood relationship: such an error does not indicate a thorough familiarity with Greek.

Like earlier Hebrew historians, the author is passionately patriotic, uniting (as only the Jews did in antiquity) nationalism and religion in a single ardent devotion. In this respect he stands between the Book of Daniel, in which religion overshadows nationalism, and the Hebrew Esther, in which religion is subordinated to nationalism. His main, and perhaps only, bias is his pride in national achievement under the guidance of God. In contrast with Daniel, expressing the hopes of the Hasidim, according to whom God would perform the deliverance of Israel and the annihilation of the heathen powers "without [human] hands" (Dan. 2:34, 45; cf. 8:25), our author stresses (as has been noted above) the achievements of Judas and his successors, which Daniel dismissed as "a little help" (Dan. 11:34). The author reports that some pacifist Hasidim before the rededication of the Temple made common cause with the belligerent Maccabees (2:42-44, cf. 7:12 f.); he was not a member of this group, and much less a Pharisee, as some have asserted. In contrast with II Maccabees, he did not regard Judas as the leader of the Hasidim (II Macc. 14:6); he approved defensive warfare on the Sabbath (2:41, cf. 9:43-47), in contrast with the practice of the strict Hasidim (2:32-38; II Macc. 6:11) and with II Macc. 15:1-5. The faith in God and zeal for the Law, so conspicuous in I Maccabees, are not found in the Hebrew Book of Esther.

Since the author is not a Pharisee (*inter alia*, he ignores life after death and the Messianic hope), it has been argued that he must have been a Sadducee (André, *Les Apocryphes*, p. 82; Oesterley, in Charles, *Apocrypha* I, p. 59)—as if all Palestinian Jews about 100 B.C. belonged of necessity to one or to the other group.[35] More plausibly it has been asserted that the author wrote I Maccabees in the interests of the Hasmonean dynasty (cf. Schürer, *Geschichte*, Vol. 3, p. 193), as an

---

[35] On the academic discussion as to whether the author was a Pharisee or Sadducee, see A. Momigliano, *Prime linee di storia della tradizione maccabaica*, pp. 12 ff. Rome, 1930.

"unofficial" (*offiziös*; E. Bickermann, *Gott der Makkabäer*, p. 145) or even as an official history of the Maccabean rebellion, being the "state historian of the Hasmonean dynasty" (A. Geiger, *Urschrift und Über-setzungen der Bibel*, p. 206. Breslau, 1857). The strongest evidence for this view is of course 5:62, according to which the Hasmoneans are "the seed of those men through whose hands deliverance was given to Israel." But while the enthusiasm of the author for the heroic deeds of the Maccabees is unmistakable, it is by no means certain that their dynastic interests were uppermost in his mind. As a matter of fact, opposite conclusions have been reached on the subject. While B. Niese (*Kritik*, pp. 44-46) decided that the author distorted the facts (in ch. 2) in order to "prove the hereditary right of Simon and his sons," F. Rosenthal (*Das erste Makkab.*, pp. 18 f., 31-33), on the contrary, by removing 2:65; 14:4-48; 15:15-24, discovered that the author's attitude was intensely unfavorable toward Simon. This disagreement is significant, for Simon was the real founder of the Hasmonean line.

No, the writer was not an amanuensis of the Maccabees. Like the author of Judges, he admired the leaders who defeated the enemy, but regarded them as mere tools in God's hand for the deliverance of Israel (5:62). Moreover, the most important decisions were not taken by the leader alone but by the assembly of the people, called *synagōgē megalē* (14:28; cf. 3:44). This "great synagogue" is neither the questionable institution of the same name in the time of Ezra (Mishna and Talmud) nor the later Sanhedrin, but a popular assembly, Israel as a whole (cf. 5:16). Not Mattathias, as Josephus asserts, but his followers decided to fight defensively on the Sabbath after a free deliberation and discussion (2:40 f.). That Israel, not the Hasmoneans, was supreme, according to our author, appears also from a number of decisions made by the people (3:43 f.; 4:59; 5:16; 7:48 f.; cf. 14:19), and especially by the national decree (14:27-47) by which the assembly (14:26-28) confirmed the authority that Simon already enjoyed. There is no trace of such "democracy" in II Maccabees. Clearly our author is more concerned with the fate of Israel than with that of the ruling dynasty.

By this ancient and hallowed name "Israel" the author means at the same time the chosen nation, the Jewish state, and especially the holy congregation headed by the high priest. Like the Chronicler (who followed the Priestly Code), he envisaged the Jewish commonwealth as a church rather than as a political state or a nation. Citizenship in this commonwealth required obedience to the Law of Moses rather than purity of race or residence in Judah. In the heroic figure of Mattathias the author has presented the ideal Israelite; the requirements of citizenship in Israel are stated by Mattathias in ringing words: "I and my sons and my brothers will walk in the covenant of our fathers. Heaven forbid that we should forsake the Law and the ordinances" (2:20 f.; cf. 2:27); "Now therefore, my sons, be ye zealous for the Law and give your lives for the covenant of your fathers" (2:50).

All those who do not "observe the Law" (2:67; cf. 2:68), be they Jews or Gentiles, are outside of the holy congregation. Israel is a zone of light surrounded by utter darkness, a marvelous island in the midst of a stormy sea. Israel is being attacked by the enemies of God, as clearly stated in Ps. 2, composed for the marriage and coronation of Alexander Janneus in 103 (the Hebrew acrostic reads, "For A. Janneus and his wife") and therefore more or less contemporary with I Maccabees: the heathen and their kings are raging and plotting "against Jehovah and against his anointed." Our author traces the beginning of this hostility back to the conquests of Alexander, who "became exalted" and whose "heart was lifted up" (1:3). Like the author of Daniel, he is acutely aware of the menace of Hellenism: Greek culture and observance of the Law were for him irreconcilable; the battle between them, within the religious sphere, was a fight to the finish.

The outcome of the fight was never in doubt, for Israel under the protection of its God, whose wrath Judas had turned away (1:64; 2:49; 3:8), is invincible. Israel is indeed the center of world history. The glory of Antiochus Epiphanes, that "sinful shoot" (1:10), is but "dung and worms" (2:62), but the heroes of Israel have "great glory and an ever-lasting name" (2:51), though not (as in II Maccabees) eternal life. The policy of the Gentile kingdoms is determined by Israel. Epiphanes did not lead a campaign into Persia on account of Parthian aggression, but to replenish his treasury for the war against the Jews (3:27-31). Foreign powers, not only the kings of Egypt and Syria (10:4-47; 11:3-7, 44-52) but even the distant Romans and Spartans (14:16-23), were eager to gain the friendship of Israel: was not the glorious name of Simon "proclaimed to the ends of the world"? (14:10).

The enemies of Israel are the enemies of God, and are therefore doomed like the mighty army of Sennacherib, destroyed in one night by the angel of the Lord (7:41 f.). "And thus consider ye throughout all ages, that none that put his trust in him shall be overcome" (2:61). Conversely, the enemies of the Jews came to a sudden and tragic end; the dramatic death of Judas (9:1-21) and of Simon (16:11-17) are entirely different, being the result of ill-considered heroism or base treachery, respectively.

In all events of the history which he relates the author discovers the hidden hand of God. His "wrath" allows the persecution by Antiochus Epiphanes (1:64; 2:49), but his power brings about the triumph to the Jews.[36] Out of reverence, the author avoids naming God, and regularly

---

[36] God intervenes to give victory not through miracles but through natural means: 2:20-28; 3:18-24; 3:60-4:25; 7:33-50; 11:71 f.; 16:2-10; etc.

employs the substitute "Heaven"[37] or vague pronouns.[38] He deliberately omits references to God where they are expected (1:64; 2:20 f., 53, 55; 3:8; 7:37, 41 f.; 16:3) and even when they appear in Biblical texts which he is paraphrasing (2:58 [cf. I Kings 19:10]; 4:24 f. [cf. Ps. 118:1-4; 136]). When we recall the later discussions of the rabbis about the sacredness of a book containing God's name (Bab. *Shabbat* 116a) and the author's realization that divine inspiration had ceased in his day, since prophecy was extinct (4:46; 9:27; 14:41), we shall conclude that the writer, even though he deliberately penned a sequel to the Chronicler's history, fully realized that his book could not become one of the *biblia hágia* (holy books) which brought comfort to the Jews in times of trouble (12:9; cf. 1:56 f.; 3:48). The author realized that an epoch had come to its end with Ezra and Nehemiah: God no longer manifested himself directly to men through miracles and revelations, but he still was the omnipotent champion of Israel.[39]

Like the Chronicler, the author writes to glorify Israel, God's holy congregation: he combines an apology of the Jews with a substantially accurate historical account, while the Chronicler had felt impelled to disguise the facts he could not suppress and to invent incidents freely in order to exaggerate the piety and the power of ancient Judah. Our author differs from the Chronicler in another respect: in his attitude toward those outside the congregation. This is the result of changed historical circumstances: in the time of the Chronicler Hellenism was not yet a menace for Judaism, but the controversies with the Samaritans had not yet ceased; but in the time of Hyrcanus and Janneus the Samaritans could be ignored, and the advocates of Hellenism within and without the Jewish nation were the most dangerous foes. While the Chronicler could still hope for the conversion of non-Jews to the true religion, our author, after Epiphanes' attempt to suppress Judaism and the wars that followed, advocated the motto "Recompense the Gentiles to the full, and take heed to the commandments of the Law" (2:68). Judaism was beginning to entrench itself and to build a fence around the Law, isolating itself from the outside world—a process completed in the Talmud.

[37] "Heaven" is used for God in: 3:18 f., 50, 60; 4:10, 24, 40, 55; 9:46; 12:15; 16:3. It is not exact to say, as most books do, that divine names never occur in our book, for we find *kýrios* (Lord) in 4:24; 7:37, 41, and *theós* (God) in 3:18; but these divine names are rightly considered interpolations by textual critics. The substitute "Heaven" occurs before our author in Dan. 4:23 and later in the familiar "Kingdom of Heaven" of Matthew (the equivalent of "Kingdom of God" in Luke).
[38] I Macc. 2:57, 61; 7:37, 41.
[39] The author's faith in God's help for Israel is expressed in no uncertain terms in the speeches and prayers that he placed into the mouth of Mattathias and his sons: 2:19-22, 27, 34, 37; 3:18-22; 4:8-11, 30-33; 7:37 f., 40-42; 16:3. In contrast with II Maccabees, our author hardly ever (cf. 3:44; 4:24) speaks of the divine attributes.

The opposition between Israel and the outside world dominates the thought of our historian (cf. E. Bickermann, *Der Gott der Makkabäer*, p. 28). As an ardent apologist of Israel he must prove that all armed conflicts were provoked by Gentiles or apostate Jews: this is his strongest bias, his most serious lapse from objective historicity. Israel is immaculate: whatever would cast discredit on the congregation is omitted, as for instance what is told in II Macc. 3:1-4; 4:1-50; 5:1-10; 10:20-22; 12:38-40; 13:21. On the contrary, the enemies of the Jews, animated by their hatred for the true religion, plan to "destroy the seed of Jacob" (5:1 f.). It is characteristic of our author that he attributes this attack of the Gentiles to religious (cf. 7:33-35) rather than political anti-Semitism: they were displeased because the Temple has been rededicated, exactly as had been the heathen in Ps. 83 (which refers to the same event)—an attitude regarded by the Jews as a conspiracy against God. The Chronicler, similarly, speaks of the opposition of the enemies of the Jews to the rebuilding of the Temple (Ezra 4:4-6). Conversely Judas is depicted by our author as a crusader, zealous in fulfilling the Law (3:47-56) and in destroying heathen temples (5:44, 68; cf. 10:83 f.).

The heathen, in their "fullness of insolence and lawlessness" (3:20; cf. 1:21; 2:47; 7:47), with blasphemies (7:38; cf. 2:6) and with treacherous deceit (1:30; 7:10, 18, 27; 11:53; 13:17, 31; 16:13, 15) are always the aggressors of Israel (6:18; 7:7; 9:23 f., 57 f.): "they come to destroy us . . . but we fight for our lives and our laws" (3:20 f.). But even greater is the mischief done against Israel by apostate Jews (7:23). They "joined themselves to the heathen and sold themselves to do evil" (1:10-15), fighting in the ranks of the enemies of Israel (3:15), accusing the Jews before kings (6:21-27; 7:5 f., 25; 10:61; 11:21, 25), urging rulers and generals to make war against Israel (7:7-9; 9:58), assassinating the Hasidim (7:16), desecrating the Temple (9:54), thus bringing great tribulation on Israel (9:23-27). But the Maccabees gave them no quarter and "smote sinners in their anger and lawless men in their wrath" (2:44; cf. 3:6, 8; 9:61, 73).[40]

We may conclude from these clues that the author, inspired by his devotion to Israel's God and Law, and proud of the achievements of the family through whom deliverance came to Israel at a most critical time, wrote down for future generations the account of Israel's triumphs over its foes—the Jews and Gentiles who vainly attempted to force Israel to adopt the Hellenistic culture in place of the Law and Covenant of Jehovah.

[40] E. Bickermann (*Der Gott der Makkabäer*, p. 29) believes that these lawless and sinful Jews were the enemies of the Hasmonean dynasty, which had the support of a strong party but not of the whole nation. Such does not seem to me to be the opinion of the author: these enemies of Israel (cf. 11:21) are regularly called godless and lawless, and are accordingly the Jews who, allured by Hellenism, forsook the strict observance of the Law.

D. *The Greek Text*

The loss of the Hebrew text at an early date, as in the case of the other Palestinian Apocrypha (except Ecclesiasticus), makes the Greek text preserved in the Christian manuscripts of the Septuagint (LXX) our basic text.[41] All ancient versions were made from it, and it is obviously in Greek that Josephus read I Maccabees (cf. Ettelson, *Integrity*, pp. 331-341). The translation was undoubtedly made between 100 B.C. and A.D. 90 (Josephus), but its date cannot be fixed more precisely: the translator's use of the Greek versions of late Psalms and of Daniel is of no help.

If the translation was made in Alexandria by a Jew native to that city, as we may surmise, the translator knew Greek better than Hebrew. This may be inferred from the text itself. It has been noted that occasionally the translator misunderstands the Hebrew text. In 1:28 he renders "the land shook *against* [or "*over*"] its inhabitants," instead of "*for* [out of compassion for] its inhabitants." In 2:34 the Hebrew text probably meant "we shall not do the king's commandment *nor shall we* profane the Sabbath" rather than ". . . commandment to profane. . . ." In 4:24 he mistranslates a quotation from Ps. 118 and 136, rendering "for beautiful, for unto eternity is his mercy," failing to notice the correct translation of the LXX, "for he [God] is good, for his mercy [endures] forever." In 6:1 he apparently misunderstood *'ēlām ha-medīnāh* (the *province* of Elam, so correctly in the LXX of Dan. 8:2), inventing a nonexistent *city* called Elymais: *Medinah* has both meanings. Other instances of mistranslation are given by Ettelson, *Integrity*, pp. 313 f.

Although, as we have seen, in 4:24 and 6:1 the translator ignored the correct rendering of the Septuagint, in general he shows great familiarity with the Greek version of the canonical books. The condensed quotation of Ps. 79:2 f. in 7:17 discloses a fairly accurate reminiscence of the LXX version of the passage, as also the allusions to Ps. 92:7 in 9:23, and to Zech. 8:4 in 14:9. Direct influence of the LXX can also be detected in

[41] The most important manuscript of the LXX (*Vaticanus Gr.* 1209, Codex B) never contained the books of the Maccabees (E. Nestle, TLZ 1895, pp. 72 ff.), because the *Vaticanus,* and consequently the Ethiopic version, conformed to the canon of Athanasius (cf. A. Rahlfs in ZAW 1908, pp. 63 f.). The Greek text is found in three uncial LXX manuscripts (the *Sinaiticus* or *Aleph,* the *Alexandrinus* or Cod. A, and the *Venetus* or No. 23 in Holmes and Parsons) and in many minuscules. The manuscripts have been classified into "families" by W. Kappler, *De memoria alterius libri Maccabaeorum* (doctoral dissertation), Göttingen, 1929. The most important versions are the Syriac (cf. G. Schmidt in ZAW 17 [1897] 1-47, 233-262) and the Old Latin (revised in the current Vulgate). D. de Bruyne (in RB 31 [1922] 31-54; 39 [1930] 503-519) has discovered that the Greek text from which the Old Latin was translated was better than that of the Greek manuscripts and is a criterion for determining the best readings of the Lucianic recension. The best recent editions of the text are: W. Kappler, *Maccabaeorum liber I* (Septuaginta: Vet. Test. Graec. etc., IX, 1). Göttingen, 1936. A. Rahlfs, *Septuaginta.*

1:54 (the "abomination of desolation" of Dan. 12:11, cf. 9:27) and 7:9 (cf. Ps. 149:7, "take vengeance"; contrast I Macc. 2:68); and in certain standard phrases like "and there fell many wounded" (1:18; 3:11, 8:10; 9:17, 40; 16:8), reproduced verbatim from the Greek text of Judg. 9:40 (cf. Dan. 11:26; I Chron. 5:22); see also Ettelson, *Integrity*, p. 303. The language of I Maccabees resembles that of considerable parts of the LXX in being typical "translation Greek," replete with Semitic expressions, idioms, and constructions literally rendered into Greek (cf. Ettelson, *op. cit.*, pp. 309-311).

Nevertheless, in spite of the translator's familiarity with the Greek Bible ("the holy books," 12:4), his vocabulary and style are not entirely dependent on the LXX. He uses a number of words not found elsewhere in the LXX (Ettelson, *op. cit.*, pp. 322-325), and occasionally his style and diction are more classical than those of the LXX as a whole: e.g., *epistolaí* (in the plural) in the sense of "a letter" (10:3, 7, 17, and eight other occurrences; cf. II Macc. 11:16) does not occur in the LXX nor in the New Testament; *allotrioûn* in the passive with the dative (to become estranged: 11:53; 15:27) occurs elsewhere in the LXX with *apó* and the genitive; words like *xenologeîn* (to hire mercenary troops: 4:35; 11:38; 15:3), *koinológeisthai* (to converse, to confer: 14:16; 15:28), and *déltos* (writing tablet: 8:22; 14:18, 27, 48) are unknown elsewhere in the LXX.

Within the limitations of a very close rendering of a Hebrew original, and in spite of the innumerable Semitisms that this procedure involved (contrast the freer rendering into idiomatic Greek in I Esdras), the translator writes simply and clearly, without the rhetorical embellishments so conspicuous in II-IV Maccabees. Inspired perhaps by the Greek Pentateuch, he strove to reproduce a Hebrew book in Greek and succeeded so well that we are able to reconstruct the lost Hebrew original, with fair accuracy, from his version.

CHAPTER XII

II MACCABEES

The contents of II Maccabees may be summarized as follows:

INTRODUCTION (1-2)

1. *The first letter to the Jews in Egypt* (1:1-10a), written in 123 B.C. (1:10a). After the greeting (1:1) and a series of good wishes (1:2-6) the Palestinian Jews recall a letter written to their Egyptian brethren in 142 concerning their extreme tribulation (cf. I Macc. 11:53) which began when Jason (cf. II Macc. 4:7-22) persecuted the pious Jews (1:7). But the Temple worship has been restored and the Egyptian Jews should observe the festival of the rededication of the Temple (1:8 f.; on this festival see 1:18; 10:5-8; I Macc. 4:59).

2. *The second letter to the Jews in Egypt* (1:10b-2:18), written by the Sanhedrin and Judas Maccabeus in 164, just before the rededication of the Temple, to Aristobulus (presumably the Jewish philosopher; cf. E. Schürer, *Geschichte*, Vol. 3, pp. 512-522), the teacher [?] of Ptolemy VI Philometor, and to the Egyptian Jews (1:10b). *a.* Antiochus IV Epiphanes, the persecutor of the Jews, was killed in Persia by the priests of Nanea (perhaps the Babylonian goddess Nanâ or Ishtar), whose treasure he intended to plunder (1:11-17; cf. ch. 9; I Macc. 6:1-16; Polybius 31, 2; Josephus, *Antiquities* 12:9, 1). The Jews are now about to celebrate the rededication of the Temple on the 25th of Chislev, and urge their Egyptian brethren to observe the festival (1:18a).

b. When Nehemiah restored the Temple service (which in reality had been reorganized long before), he searched for the sacred fire, which some pious priests had hidden carefully in a dry cistern when the Jews were taken captive to Persia (really to Babylonia) (1:18b-20a). A black liquid was found, instead of fire, and when it was sprinkled on the sacrifices and on the wood, it was ignited by the sun's rays (1:20b-22). While the sacrifices were being consumed by the flames, the priests prayed that God might accept the offering and bring back the exiled Jews, punishing their oppressors (1:23-29), and they sang hymns (1:30). The rest of the liquid was poured on some stones and remained ignited until extinguished by the rays of the flame on the altar (1:31 f.). The king of Persia ordered the place where the liquid was found to be enclosed and sanctified (1:33 f.), and exchanged gifts (1:35). Nehemiah called the liquid *Nephtar*, meaning cleansing (?), but the people usually called it *Nephtai* (i.e., naphtha) (1:36).

c. The same record telling how Jeremiah gave instructions for hiding the sacred fire (cf. 1:19) also reports that he gave the Law to the Exiles, urging them to keep it (2:1-3); and that he hid the Tabernacle, the Ark, and the altar of incense in a cave of Mount Nebo (2:4 f.), warning his followers that the spot would remain unknown until the scattered Jews be brought together and the divine glory appear (2:6-8).

d. The record also told that when Solomon consecrated the Temple, heavenly fire consumed the offerings (cf. II Chron. 7:1), exactly as when Moses prayed (cf. Lev. 9:23 f.); as in the time of Judas, so Solomon's dedication (I Kings 8:66) lasted eight days (2:9-12).

e. These events are also recorded in Nehemiah's archives, which report that he founded a library containing "the books about the kings and the prophets, the books of David, and letters of kings about sacred gifts" (2:13). Judas has collected the scattered writings, and the Egyptian Jews may obtain copies thereof (2:14 f.).

f. The Egyptian Jews may participate in the coming Festival of Dedication (2:16). God, who has delivered the Jews, may speedily gather them together (2:17 f.).

3. *Preface* (2:19-32). The history of the wars of the Maccabees against Antiochus IV Epiphanes and Antiochus V Eupator, compiled by Jason of Cyrene in five books, has been condensed by the author of II Maccabees into one book (2:19-23), in order to supply the information to the general reader (2:24 f.). Although the work of condensation has been difficult, like the preparation of a banquet, the author has undertaken it gladly in view of the gratitude of many for this service (2:26 f.). Depending on the original work for scholarly researches on matters of detail, the Epitomist has aimed merely at conciseness and simplicity (2:28-31). Now he will proceed with the story, for a long preface is out of place before a mere epitome (2:32).

PART I: THE CAUSES OF THE MACCABEAN REBELLION (3-7)

1. *Intrigues for the high priesthood* (3-4). a. Simon's charges against Onias III (3:1-4:6; ch. 3 has been utilized in IV Macc. 3:19-4:14). The peace of Jerusalem under the high priest Onias III (deposed in 175) was disturbed by Simon, a high Temple official who could not prevail against Onias in a dispute over the management of the market (3:1-4). To avenge himself, he reported to Apollonius, the governor of Coele-Syria and Phoenicia, that immense sums, rightfully belonging to the king, were

lying idle in the Temple (3:5 f.). Informed of this by Apollonius, Seleucus IV Philopator sent Heliodorus (who, according to Appian, *Roman History* XI:8, 45, had the king assassinated in 175) to confiscate the treasure (3:7 f.). Deaf to the entreaties of Onias, who assured him that the Temple funds were only deposits of widows and orphans, and money belonging to Hyrcanus son of Tobias, Heliodorus was determined to obey the king's orders (3:9-13). On the appointed day priests and citizens lamented and prayed, while Onias' distress was apparent on his countenance (3:14-21). When Heliodorus reached the treasury, a miracle occurred: a horseman in golden armor rushed upon Heliodorus and two youths scourged him unmercifully until he fainted and was carried out (3:22-30). Upon the request of friends of Heliodorus, Onias offered a sacrifice in his behalf (3:31 f.). The two youths informed Heliodorus that he owed his life to Onias, and he gave testimony to God's power both in Jerusalem and to his king (3:33-40).

Simon then accused Onias of having plotted against Heliodorus and even permitted his followers to commit murders; so Onias went to Seleucus IV to request him to restore law and order (4:1-6).

b. How Jason, through bribes, supplanted his brother Onias as high priest (4:7-22). When Antiochus IV Epiphanes succeeded his brother Seleucus IV on the throne, Jason ingratiated himself with him and, by payments of money and promises to Hellenize the Jews, was appointed high priest by the king (4:7-10). Jason built a gymnasium and induced young noblemen to wear the Greek broad-brimmed felt hat; athletic games became so popular that young priests hurried through the services in order to participate in them (4:11-17). Jason even sent a contribution to the quadrennial games celebrated at Tyre in honor of Melkart-Heracles, but his messengers contrived to have the money used for the fleet (4:18-20). When Antiochus Epiphanes came to Jerusalem on a tour of inspection occasioned by the hostility of the new king of Egypt, Ptolemy VI Philometor, Jason tendered him a magnificent reception (4:21 f.).

c. How Menelaus, the brother of Simon, supplanted Jason as high priest and maintained himself in power through criminal plots (4:23-50). After three years Jason sent Menelaus on an embassy to Antiochus, but Menelaus secured the high priesthood by outbidding Jason (4:23 f.). Jason fled into the country of the Ammonites (4:25 f.). Failing to pay the money, Menelaus was summoned before Antiochus and left his brother Lysimachus as his deputy (4:27-29). But Antiochus had gone to Tarsus to put down a rebellion, and Menelaus gained the favor of Andronicus, who had been left in authority, through gifts of vessels stolen from the Temple (4:30-32). From the sanctuary of Daphne, where he had sought asylum, Onias denounced this sacrilege but was assassinated by Andronicus on the request of Menelaus (4:33 f.). This crime aroused general indignation; even Antiochus was grieved and put Andronicus to death (4:35-38; according to H. Willrich and J. Wellhausen, Andronicus actually killed Seleucus, a young prince). The Temple robberies of Lysimachus, with the connivance of Menelaus, stirred the Jews to revolt; Lysimachus was killed in the riots (4:39-42). Three ambassadors appeared before Antiochus to bring charges against Menelaus, who bribed Ptolemy and thus was acquitted; the ambassadors were executed but the Tyrians, shocked by this iniquity, gave them splendid obsequies (4:43-50).

2. *Persecution of the Jews by Antiochus Epiphanes* (5-7). *a.* The profanation of the Temple (5). While Antiochus made his second campaign into Egypt (cf. I Macc. 1:16-19; Dan. 11:25-28) and visions of battling horsemen were seen in Jerusalem (5:1-4), it was falsely rumored that Antiochus had died (5:5a). Jason, through a sudden attack, conquered Jerusalem and forced Menelaus to seek refuge in the citadel; but through his reckless slayings Jason aroused such hostility that he fled again to the Ammonites and after wandering through various countries died at Sparta (5:5b-10). Antiochus, believing Judea to be in revolt against him, massacred 80,000 people in Jerusalem and, accompanied by Menelaus, entered the Holy of Holies, polluting the Temple (5:11-16; cf. I Macc. 1:20-28). Antiochus did not fare like Heliodorus (cf. 3:22-30), because God was incensed with his people on account of their sins, yet cared less for the Temple than for the people (5:17-20). Antiochus, departing in triumph with the plunder from the Temple, left governors behind to oppress the people (5:21-23) and sent Apollonius with an army to massacre the Jews (5:24-26; cf. I Macc. 1:29-32). But Judas Maccabeus hid in the mountains with nine others (5:27).

b. The proscription of Judaism (6). Antiochus forbade the observance of the Law, dedicated the Temple in Jerusalem to the Olympian Zeus and the Samaritan temple to Zeus Xenios (patron of guests), and allowed obscenities in the Temple; festivals in honor of Dionysus were to be celebrated monthly (6:1-9; cf. I Macc. 1:44-64). Two women were executed for circumcising their infants (1:10; cf. I Macc. 1:60 f.); pious Jews were burnt to death in a cave, where they were observing the Sabbath (1:11; cf. I Macc. 2:29-38).

These calamities were a chastisement of God for his people's sins: for while God allows other nations to fill their measure of iniquity and then destroys them, he chastises the Jews in his mercy before the ultimate limit of wickedness has been reached (6:12-17).

The aged scribe Eleazar preferred to die in tortures a martyr's death rather than partake of swine's meat (6:18-31; cf. IV Macc. 5:3-7:23). Seven brothers and their mother likewise died painfully for their faith (7:1-42; cf. IV Macc. 8-17).

PART II: THE MACCABEAN REBELLION (8:1-10:9)

1. *Early victories of Judas Maccabeus* (8). *a.* Judas Maccabeus mustered a force of 6,000 pious Jews and, since God's anger was now turned to mercy (cf. 6:12-17), harassed the heathen incessantly (8:1-7).

b. Ptolemy, the governor of Coele-Syria and Phoenicia, at the request of Philip (cf. 5:22), sent an army of 20,000 under Nicanor and Gorgias against Judas; Nicanor, certain of the victory, offered Jewish slaves for sale in advance (8:8-11). Judas exhorted his 6,000 men to trust in God (8:12-18), remembering the destruction of Sennacherib's army of 185,000 men (8:19; cf. 15:22; II Kings 19:35; III Macc. 6:5) and the slaying of 120,000 Galatians in Babylonia by 8,000 Jews (8:20; nothing is known of this battle). Judas divided the army into four contingents of 1,500 men at the orders of himself and his three brothers and routed the army of Nicanor—interrupting the pursuit only because it was the eve of the Sabbath—and divided abundant spoil (8:21-28; cf. I Macc. 3:38-4:25). Then they prayed God for his complete reconciliation (8:29).

Judas defeated Timotheus and Bacchides, killing over 20,000 men and obtaining enormous booty (8:30-32; this story is unhistorical). At the celebration in Jerusalem they executed Callisthenes and others (8:33). Nicanor fled alone to Antioch (8:34-36).

2. *The death of Antiochus Epiphanes* (9). Antiochus was routed when he attempted to rob a temple in Persepolis (9:1 f.; contrast I Macc. 6 and II Macc. 1:12-16). In Ecbatana, upon hearing of the defeats of Nicanor and Timotheus, he determined to avenge himself, but was suddenly stricken by the Lord (9:3-6) and was run over by his chariot (9:7 f.); worms and decay destroyed his body while he was still alive (9:9 f.). Broken in spirit, he made a vow to glorify the Jews and even to become a Jew (9:11-17). On his deathbed he wrote a friendly letter to the Jews, informing them of his disease and urging them to be loyal to his successor Antiochus V Eupator (9:18-27). Philip took his body to Antioch but, fearing Antiochus V, went to Ptolemy VI Philometor in Egypt (9:28 f.).

3. *The cleansing of the Temple and the Feast of Dedication* (10:1-9; cf. I Macc. 4:36-61). Heathen altars were demolished, a new altar was erected in the Temple, and unpolluted fire for the sacrifice was obtained by striking flints: thus the rituals that had lapsed for *two* (an error for *three*) years were inaugurated anew (10:1-3), and prayers were offered (10:4), on the very day (the 25th of Chislev) in which the Temple had

been defiled three years before (10:5). The Feast of Dedication was celebrated during eight days, after the manner of the Feast of Tabernacles, and its annual observance by all Jews was decreed (10:6-9).

PART III: THE CAMPAIGNS OF JUDAS MACCABEUS (10:10-15:36)

1. *First victory over Lysias* (10:10-11:38). *a.* Antiochus V Eupator chose "a certain Lysias" as his chancellor and governor of Coele-Syria and Phoenicia (10:10 f.; contrast I Macc. 3:32; 6:17) in place of Ptolemy Macron (cf. 5:22; 8:8), who had been a friend of the Jews and had poisoned himself when accused of treason (10:12 f.).

b. When Gorgias (10:14; cf. 8:9) and the Idumeans harassed the Jews, Judas stormed the Idumean strongholds and executed some of his brother Simon's captains who had allowed a number of Idumeans to escape on payment of 70,000 drachmae (10:15-23; cf. I Macc. 5:3, 65).

c. Timotheus (cf. 8:30, 32; 12:2-24) invaded Judea with huge forces, but Judas met him, after earnest prayers, near Jerusalem and routed him with the help of five angelic horsemen (10:24-30). Timotheus fled to Gazara, which Judas stormed after a siege of twenty-four days (10:31-38). This story (10:24-38) is a distorted and legendary echo of I Macc. 5:6-8.

d. The first victory over Lysias, followed by a treaty of peace (11). Lysias, invading Judea from the southeast with a force of 80,000 infantry, much cavalry, and 80 elephants, invested Bethsuron, i.e., Beth-zur (11:1-5). But Judas, led by a heavenly horseman, routed the Syrians (11:6-12), forcing Lysias to offer favorable peace terms (11:13-15), specified in a letter of Lysias (11:16-21), and in letters of Antiochus V to Lysias (11:22-26) and to the Jews (11:27-33). These terms were approved by the Romans through a letter of their ambassadors Quintus Memmius and Titus Manlius (11:34-38). The story in 11:1-15 is perhaps based on I Macc. 4:26-35, but adds to it details from the second campaign of Lysias (I Macc. 6; II Macc. 13).

2. *Other campaigns of Judas* (12). *a.* In spite of the peace treaty some Syrian governors vexed the Jews (12:1). At Joppa some people invited the Jews to embark and drowned two hundred of them (12:2-4). Judas burned the boats in the harbor and killed the murderers (12:5); while planning further revenge, he heard that the same plot was being planned in Jamnia, so he burned the fleet there (12:6-9).

b. Judas defeated a force of Arabs near Jamnia and made an alliance with them (12:10-12; a distorted reminiscence of I Macc. 5:37-39).

c. Judas captured the fortified city of Kaspis (12:13-16).

d. Judas went to Charax to help the Jews in Tubiene. After capturing the city, he pursued Timotheus and his army of 120,000 infantry and 2,500 cavalry. Timotheus was captured at Carnaim, but freed upon his promise to release the Jewish prisoners in his power (12:17-25; possibly a parallel to I Macc. 5:37-43).

e. The fortresses of Carnaim (in which was a temple of Atargatis) and Ephron were taken (12:26-38). Scythopolis (Beth-shean) was spared at the request of the Jews; then Judas returned to Jerusalem to celebrate the Feast of Pentecost (12:29-31).

f. Gorgias, governor of *Jamnia* (not *Idumea*; cf. 12:40), was almost captured in battle by Dositheus; his troops were routed (12:32-37).

g. After keeping the Sabbath at Adullam, Judas and his men, preparing to bury the fallen Jews, discovered on their corpses images of the idols of Jamnia: they had died for this violation of the Law (12:38-40). After praying for their forgiveness and exhorting his army to avoid sin, Judas raised a collection of 2,000 drachmae for a sin offering in behalf of the dead; this proves that he was a firm believer in the resurrection (12:41-45).

3. *Second victory over Lysias* (13). *a.* Judas heard that Antiochus V and Lysias were marching against Judea, each commanding 110,000 infantry, 3,000 cavalry, 22 elephants, and 300 chariots armed with scythes (13:1 f.; cf. I Macc. 6:28-30). Menelaus attached himself to them, but Antiochus, on the advice of Lysias, had him executed in Beroea by being dropped into hot ashes (13:3-8).

b. After three days of fervent prayers (13:9-12), Judas encamped at Modein (13:13 f.) and through a night attack in which the largest elephant was stabbed (cf. I Macc. 6:43-46) threw the enemy camp into confusion (13:15-17).

c. Antiochus attacked Beth-zur without success—in spite of information furnished by a Jewish traitor, Rhodocus—and signed a peace treaty (13:18-22). Defeated by Judas, Antiochus accepted the peace terms dictated by the Jews (13:23 f.). The men of Ptolemais were indignant at his treaty until Lysias in a public address won their approval for it (13:25 f.). The stories in 13:9-26 give a distorted and biased account of the events told in I Macc. 6:28-63.

4. *Victory over Nicanor* (14:1-15:36). *a.* Upon the advice of Alkimus, a Hellenizing high priest (see I Macc. 7:5-25; 9:1, 54-56), Demetrius I, who had killed Antiochus V and Lysias, sent Nicanor to Judea as governor, and appointed Alkimus as high priest (14:1-13; cf. I Macc. 7:1-21).

b. The heathen joined Nicanor, but the Jews mourned and prayed (14:14 f.). After Simon had been forced back by Nicanor, the armies met at *Dessau* (variant: *Lessau*; both unknown), but Nicanor made peace and became a friend of Judas (14:16-25; cf. I Macc. 7:26-29).

c. Greatly vexed, Alkimus accused Nicanor of conspiracy, and Demetrius ordered Nicanor to send Judas to Antioch under guard (14:26 f.). Reluctantly Nicanor planned to seize Judas by a stratagem, but Judas

went into hiding (14:28-30). Nicanor asked the priests who were sac-
rificing to deliver Judas, and threatened to erect a sanctuary to Dionysus
on the site of the Temple if they failed to do it (14:31-33). The priests
prayed God to preserve his Temple (14:34-36). These stories are not
in I Macc. 7.

d. Razis, a highly esteemed elder in Jerusalem, committed suicide in
a horrible manner in order not to fall into the hands of Nicanor
(14:37-46).

e. Nicanor, in defiance of the divine ordinances, proposed to attack
Judas in Samaria on a Sabbath, but he failed to accomplish his shocking
purpose (15:1-5).

f. Judas encouraged his men by relating a dream in which he saw the
deceased high priest Onias invoking blessings on the Jews, and the
prophet Jeremiah presenting a golden sword to Judas (15:6-16).

g. Thus encouraged, the Jews, more anxious about the Temple than
about their kinsmen, decided to attack the army of Nicanor, which
included elephants and cavalry (15:17-21). Judas prayed unto the Lord,
who had destroyed the army of Sennacherib (15:22-25).

h. In the battle the Jews slew 35,000 Syrians and, discovering the
corpse of Nicanor, took his head and (right) arm to Jerusalem, where
his tongue was cast piecemeal to the birds and his arm and head were
hung from the citadel (14:26-35; cf. I Macc. 7:47). The victory was
celebrated annually on the 13th of Adar, on the day preceding the Feast
of Purim or "the day of Mordecai," instituted in the Book of Esther
(14:36; cf. I Macc. 7:49).

EPILOGUE (15:37-39)

Here ends the story, for Jerusalem remained safely in Jewish hands
after Nicanor's death in 161 (this is contrary to the facts) (15:37). The
Epitomist has striven to blend together historical fact and colorful style,
as water and wine are delicious when mixed, to please his readers
(15:38 f.).

1. Jason of Cyrene

The Second Book of Maccabees, according to 2:23, is the summary
(*epitomé*, 2:26, 28) of a history in five volumes written by Jason of
Cyrene. This history, now lost, we are told (2:19-22), dealt with "Judas
Maccabeus and his brothers" (Jonathan and Simon; the other brothers
are listed in I Macc. 2:2-5), with "the purification of the great Temple,"
with the wars against Antiochus IV Epiphanes and his son Antiochus V
Eupator, and with divine manifestations (*epipháneiai*) in behalf of the
loyal Jews (cf. 3:24; 5:2-4; 11:8; 15:27). This is all that is known about

Jason of Cyrene and his work in five books (if we accept the statement in 2:19-23 as trustworthy), except for what may be preserved of it in II Maccabees.

Few have questioned the substantial truth of 2:19-21. The view of W. H. Kosters (TT 12 [1878] 491-558) and of A. Kamphausen (in E. Kautzsch, *Apokryphen und Pseudepigraphen*, I, pp. 81, 84), according to which that passage is pure fiction, has been generally rejected.[1] But in regard to the contents, date, and nature of Jason's history there is still a wide difference of opinion.

In regard to the contents, the problem has two sides. Was everything in II Maccabees contained in Jason's history? Did Jason's history continue after the death of Nicanor, with which II Maccabees closes?

Some parts of II Maccabees were not taken from Jason, but inserted from other sources by the Epitomist or by a later redactor. The letters to the Jews in Egypt (1:1-2:18) have been the subject of more discussion than any other part of the book. Critics even disagree in regard to the number of the letters. The view now prevalent (adopted in the preceding summary) recognizes that there are two letters (1:1-10a; 1:10b-2:18), but others have identified either a single letter or three separate ones (1:1-7a; 1:7b-10a; 1:10b-2:18).[2] As for the authenticity and the presence of these letters in the work of Jason and the first edition of II Maccabees, nearly every possibility has been suggested by critics.

1. The letters were composed by Jason and included in his history (H. Willrich, *Urkundenfälschung*, p. 26).[3]

2. The letters were composed by the Epitomist as part of his preface (B. Niese, *Kritik*, p. 24); similarly G. Wernsdorf, *Commentatio hist.-crit. de fide hist. libr. Maccab.*, pp. 65 ff., 181 ff. Breslau, 1747.

3. The Epitomist probably composed 1:18b-2:15, found the rest in a source other than Jason, and "prefixed 1:1-2:18 to his abridgment" (J. Moffatt, in Charles, *Apocrypha*, p. 130).

4. The Epitomist translated the letters from the Aramaic and added them to his book (C. C. Torrey, *The Apocryphal Literature*, pp. 78 f.).

---

[1] Kosters, following A. Geiger (*Urschrift und Übersetzungen*, pp. 219-230), believed that II Maccabees was written to discredit I Maccabees because the Pharisee who wrote II Maccabees was hostile to the Hasmoneans. Kosters adds that the author of II Maccabees invented Jason of Cyrene to give prestige to his work, lest it be dismissed merely as a polemical writing (p. 557).

[2] Cf. the bibliography in W. Kolbe, *Beiträge z. Syr. u. Jüd. Gesch.*, pp. 108-110. The following selected lists illustrate the division of opinion: *One Letter* (Herzfeld, H. Graetz, B. Niese, W. Kolbe); *Two Letters* (G. Wernsdorf, C. L. W. Grimm, C. C. Torrey, L. E. T. André, E. Schürer, J. Moffatt, H. Herkenne, A. Kamphausen, F. X. Kugler, E. Bickermann in ZNT 32 [1933] 233); *Three Letters* (C. Bruston, H. Willrich, R. Laqueur, J. Wellhausen, E. Meyer, H. Bévenot).

[3] But in *Juden und Griechen* pp. 67 and 76 f., Willrich regards 1:1-10a, 13-16 as interpolated.

5. The letters are a late interpolation in II Maccabees (C. L. W. Grimm, Commentary to II Maccabees, pp. 22-25; L. E. T. André, *Les Apocryphes*, p. 94; E. Schürer, *Geschichte*, Vol. 3, p. 486; W. Kolbe, *Beiträge*, pp. 119-121; J. Goettsberger, *Einleitung in das Alte Testament*, p. 206. Freiburg i. B., 1928; H. Bévenot, *Die beide Makkabäerbücher*, p. 170. Bonn, 1931; O. Eissfeldt, *Einleitung in das A. T.*, p. 637).

It seems fairly certain that the letters in 1:1-2:18 were not included in Jason's history; presumably they were even lacking in the first edition of II Maccabees. In spite of the arguments adduced by E. Bickermann (ZNT 32 [1933] 233-254; cf. *Der Gott der Makkabäer*, pp. 34, 175), these documents can hardly be genuine *"Festbriefe,"* letters of the community in Jerusalem to the Egyptian Jews, urging them to observe the new Feast of Dedication (Hanukkah). It is even uncertain that they were translated from the Hebrew or Aramaic, as C. C. Torrey (ZAW 20 [1900] 225-242) claims. It is possible that they are "specimens of the Alexandrian epistolary literature which was fond of producing such documents for purpose of edification" (J. Moffatt, in Charles, *Apocrypha*, p. 129); specifically they seem to have been composed to discredit Onias' temple at Leontopolis and to prove that the Temple in Jerusalem, whose rededication the Egyptian Jews should celebrate annually (1:9, 18; 2:16), is still the only legitimate earthly abode of the Lord.[4]

Besides the letters in 1:1-2:18, other passages in the book cannot be attributed to the pen of Jason. This is obvious for the preface (2:19-32) and epilogue (15:37-39), which the Epitomist himself wrote in the first person. It is more difficult to determine whether personal reflections on the events narrated are to be attributed to Jason or to the Epitomist.[5] While a final solution of this problem may not be possible, the present writer would suggest that the reflections of Jason may be separated from those of the Epitomist. Brief moralizing remarks, closely connected with the narrative (which often leads up to them), and pointing out extreme perfidy (4:2), errors of judgment (5:6), and in particular the infallible divine retribution of human deeds (3:39; 4:16, 38; 5:9 f.; 8:34, 36; 9:6, 8, 13, 18, 28; 10:38; 13:4, 7 f.; 15:32-35) may be attributed to Jason. But *obiter dicta*, loosely connected with the stories and expounding general doctrines, seem to be the contributions of the Epitomist (4:17; 5:17-20; 6:12-17; 12:43b-45): in one instance (6:12-17) he addresses the reader, speaking in the first person, as he does in the preface.

[4] G. Rawlinson (in Wace, *Apocrypha*, Vol. 2, p. 544) and H. Willrich (*Juden und Griechen*, pp. 66-68) believe that such was the purpose of Jason; Willrich regards II Maccabees as a "Hanukkah letter."
[5] Berthe, De Wette, Ewald (cf. Grimm's Commentary, p. 17), André (*Les Apocryphes*, p. 110), Niese (*Kritik*, pp. 37 f.), Sluys (*De Maccab. libris*, p. 77), and others attribute these reflections to the Epitomist; conversely, Eichhorn and Grimm (cf. Grimm, *op. cit.*, p. 18) to Jason.

It has been argued that the official documents of ch. 11, whether genuine (noting that 11:22-26 is a letter of Epiphanes, not of Eupator), as maintained by R. Laqueur (*Kritische Untersuchungen zum zweitem Makkabäerbuch*, pp. 38 ff., 75), or apocryphal, as claimed by W. Kolbe (*Beiträge*, pp. 75-107), were not included in Jason's history (nor in the first edition of II Maccabees). Conversely, H. Willrich (*Urkundenfälschung*, pp. 35 f.) and E. Meyer (*Ursprung und Anfänge des Christentums*, Vol. 2, p. 460) assert that they belonged to Jason's work; but while Willrich regards them as Jason's concoctions, Meyer (following B. Niese, *Kritik*, pp. 65-78; similarly E. Bickermann, in Pauly-Wissowa XIV, 1, p. 789) considers them authentic. As shown by this radical divergence of critical opinion, the evidence is not clear and no conclusion is final. To the present writer the authenticity of the documents does not seem to be above suspicion; they either stood in Jason's work (as seems probable to this writer) or they were added by a later redactor, rather than by the Epitomist.

It has been suggested, without sufficient reasons, to omit from Jason's work the following passages of II Maccabees: chs. 3-7 (A. Büchler, *Die Tobiaden und Oniaden im II Makkabäerbuche*, p. 356, etc. Vienna, 1899); ch. 7 (B. Niese, *Kritik*, p. 38); the stories of the martyrs (H. Willrich, *Judaica*, p. 132. Göttingen, 1900; D. M. Sluys, *De Maccabaeorum libris*, pp. 77 f.); chs. 12-15 (cf. Grimm, Commentary, pp. 14 f.). We lack all objective criteria for such excisions, which are made only on the basis of subjective notions of what Jason's plan and purpose was, or on the assumption that his work was entirely free of contradictions.

The second problem in connection with the contents of Jason's work is about its possible extension beyond the end of II Maccabees, which closes with the death of Nicanor in 161. The information furnished by the Epitomist on this point is contradictory. On the one hand, he says that Jason dealt with "Judas Maccabeus and his brothers" (2:19), which can only mean, literally, that the rule of Jonathan (160-143) and of Simon (143-134) was also described; but, on the other hand, only "the wars against Antiochus Epiphanes and Eupator his son" (2:20) are mentioned, and they cover less than the extent of II Maccabees since they lasted from 168 to 162. Some critics, like B. Niese (*Kritik*, p. 38), conclude that the history of Jason did not extend beyond the end of II Maccabees; and H. Bévenot (*Die beide Makkab.*, p. 10; cf. Grimm, Commentary, p. 77; J. Moffatt, in Charles, *Apocrypha*, p. 125) believes that 3:40; 7:42; 10:9; 13:26; 15:37 may mark the end of each of Jason's five books. On the contrary, others believe that Jason's history continued beyond the end of II Maccabees (André, *Les Apocryphes*, p. 109), to Simon's ordination as high priest in 142 (E. Meyer, *Ursprung und*

Anfänge des Christentums, Vol. 2, pp. 456 f.), or even to Simon's death (134) or the time of Hyrcanus I (D. A. Schlatter, *Jason von Kyrene*, p. 50. Munich, 1891; cf. H. Willrich, *Judaica*, p. 134). Schlatter reached the conclusion (adopted likewise by W. Kolbe, *Beiträge*, p. 148) that Jason's history was excerpted not only in II Maccabees but also in I Maccabees, and therefore reached at least as far as I Maccabees, which ends with the death of Simon.

If I Maccabees is left out of the discussion, as having been neither the source (H. Willrich, *Juden und Griechen*, pp. 68, 76; later, in *Judaica*, p. 134, Willrich denied that Jason knew I Maccabees) nor the summary (Schlatter) of Jason's work, we lack clear evidence to determine whether Jason's five books ended with the celebration of "Nicanor's Day" (like II Maccabees) or continued with the story of later events. In any case, since the remnants of Jason's work are preserved only in II Maccabees, which is said to be a summary of Jason's complete work in five books (2:23), we can only estimate Jason's work for the period covered by II Maccabees: no inferences can be drawn from alleged narratives dealing with a later period which (if they existed) were lost without leaving a trace. Moreover, it is doubtful that Jason's history would have been entirely lost if it had contained important stories glorifying the Jews which had no parallels in I and II Maccabees.

If Jason's five books corresponded in scope to II Maccabees, they may (as suggested by Moffatt and Bévenot) have been arranged as follows: I. Heliodorus (ch. 3). II. Idolatrous "sacrificial feasts and extreme tortures" (7:42) (chs. 4-7). III. The Maccabean rebellion, the death of Epiphanes, and the cleansing of the Temple (8:1-10:9). IV. Campaigns against Antiochus V Eupator and Lysias (10:10-13:26). V. Victory over Nicanor (14:1-15:36). A better arrangement of the first two "books" is the following: I. Intrigues for the high priesthood (chs. 3-5). II. Persecution of the Jews (chs. 6-7). On the other hand, if, as seems less probable, Jason's history reached the death of Simon, the five books might have been divided as follows: I. The events that precipitated the Maccabean rebellion (chs. 3-7). II. The rebellion and the cleansing of the Temple (8:1-10:9). III. The victories of Judas (10:10-15:36). IV. Jonathan. V. Simon.

Omitting the times of Jonathan and Simon, which may never have been described by Jason, we note that the Temple in Jerusalem—not Israel, as in I Maccabees—is the pivot around which the action revolves. The drama is in two acts: in the first the Temple is threatened by Heliodorus, desecrated by Antiochus, and finally cleansed by Judas; in the second the Temple is endangered by Lysias and Nicanor, but finally God preserved "his own place undefiled" (15:34). Each act culminates in the institution of a new annual festival: Hanukkah (rededication)[6] and the Day of Nicanor (later absorbed by Purim), respectively.

The paramount significance of the Temple is repeatedly emphasized by Jason. The theme of his book is well expressed by Heliodorus: "He whose abode is in heaven above has his eye on that place and defends it; those who approach it with evil intent he slays with a blow" (3:39). It has pleased the Lord of all things, who has need of nothing, to have among the Jews a Temple to dwell in (14:35): he chose it for the sake of the nation (5:19). This sanctuary is accordingly the "greatest" (14:13, 31), the "holy" (14:31), the "sanctified" (15:18), the "most holy temple on earth" (5:15); even Jerusalem is "the holy city" (3:1). Incidentally, it may be noted that such enthusiasm for the Temple is typical of Jews living in the lands of the Dispersion rather than of Palestinian Jews; in I Maccabees, for instance, except for an Old Testament expression in a prayer (I Macc. 7:37; cf. I Kings 8:43), we find only "the sanctuary" (I Macc. 4:36, 38, 41, 43) with reference to the Temple. In glorifying the Temple, Jason reports that even heathen kings honored and enriched it with their gifts (3:2 f.; 5:16; cf. 13:23), or at least planned to do so (9:16); and that God had repeatedly prevented or punished the profanation of his sanctuary (3:24-40; 13:6-8; 15:32 [cf. 14:33]; see also 8:33). It is true that once God allowed his Temple to be sacrilegiously profaned (5:15 f.; 6:2-4). This bitter fact could not be ignored but was minimized as much as possible: no explicit mention is made of the "abomination of desolation" (I Macc. 1:54)—the Temple "was to be called after Zeus Olympius" (II Macc. 6:2)—nor of sacrifices of swine (I Macc. 1:47; Josephus, War I, 1:2 [§34]), to which Jason alludes delicately as "abominable [sacrifices] which the Law prohibited" (6:5). On the other hand, the author feels compelled to explain this "sore and dreadful visitation of evil" (6:3). For Gentile readers he has a rational explanation: Antiochus Epiphanes plundered the Temple because he believed Judea was in revolt (5:11), and later he compelled the Jews to "conform to Greek manners" (6:9). But for Jewish readers he had a theological explanation, which the Epitomist takes pains to expound clearly (5:17-20; 6:12-17): "We suffer these things on our own account, for having sinned against our God" (7:18); "We suffer on account of our sins, but although our living Lord is angry for a brief while in order to rebuke and chasten us, he will be again reconciled to his servants" (7:32 f.; see also 12:42). This is why Jason of Cyrene described so fully the intrigues

---

[6] Although Antiochus Epiphanes died *after* the rededication (cf. 9:9 f., and the celebration of victory [8:33] before Antiochus's death), Jason (or the Epitomist?) transposed the order of events in order to make Hanukkah the final climax of the first part of the work, just as Nicanor's day marks the end of the history. Among the deeds of Judas, Jason, according to the Epitomist, stressed particularly "the purification of the great temple and the dedication of the altar" (2:19).

and plots in Jerusalem that preceded the persecution of the Jews (ch. 4).

Many features through which II Maccabees is sharply distinguished from I Maccabees are readily understood when we keep in mind Jason's purpose—the glorification of the Temple. Jason is much more interested in theology than is the author of I Maccabees, for the Temple is God's abode in the midst of Israel (14:35). The existence of God (15:3 f.) and monotheism (7:37) are taken for granted. The Lord is the master of all authority (3:24), dwelling in heaven (3:39; 15:4), and ruling over the heavens (15:23) and the angels ("lord of the spirits," 3:24, according to some Greek Mss., Syriac, Vulgate; the standard LXX has "lord of the fathers"). God sees and oversees all things (12:22; 15:2); he manifests himself on earth in behalf of his people (12:22; 15:34), usually through angels (3:25 f., 33 f.; 5:2 f.; 10:29 f.; 11:8) or in dreams (15:12-16). He is at the same time the God of Israel (9:5; cf. 1:17; 2:17), and the highest (3:31) and greatest (3:36) God, the king of kings (13:4), the creator (7:23, 28 [creation *ex nihilo!*]; cf. 1:24) and lord of the world (7:9; 12:15), the animator of every human being (7:11, 23, 28). Among the divine attributes Jason stresses particularly omnipotence (3:22, 28, 30; 5:20; 6:26; 7:35, 38; 8:11, 18, 24; 9:8; 11:13; 15:8, 32, etc.), omniscience (7:6, 35; 9:5; 12:22, 41; 15:2; etc.), self-sufficiency (14:35), holiness (8:4; 14:36), justice (8:13; 12:6, 41; cf. 1:25) manifested in the punishment of evildoers (7:19, 31, 35 f.; 8:4; 9:6, 18; etc.), and loving-kindness (6:13; 7:37; 8:29; 10:26; 11:9; 13:2).

God punishes the sinners according to the ancient *jus talionis*, "an eye for an eye, a tooth for a tooth," and makes the penalty conform as much as possible to the offense. Thus did outstanding sinners suffer their penalty, according to poetic justice, at their death: Andronicus (4:38), Lysimachus (4:42), Jason (5:9 f.), Callisthenes (8:33), Antiochus Epiphanes (9:8-10, 28), Menelaus (13:5-8), and Nicanor (15:31-35). Conversely, God's wrath at the sins of Israel (5:20; 7:38; 8:5) lasts but a moment (7:33, 37 f.; 8:5), for God has established his people, forever and ever upholds his own portion (Israel) through miraculous manifestations (14:15), defending his Temple (3:25 f., 33 f., 38 f.) and his human hosts (10:29 f.; 11:8; cf. 5:2-4) through heavenly beings. By "the help of God's protection" (13:17) Judas is said to have slain more than 229,700 of his enemies in battle, not counting the wounded and 120,000 Galatians (8:20) slain in an earlier day (8:24, 30; 10:17, 23, 31; 11:11; 12:19, 23, 26, 28; 13:15; 15:27): in his enthusiasm Jason has increased the actual figures ten- or twentyfold! On the contrary, the Jews are invincible: they sustained only one temporary slight reverse, promptly rectified (14:17), and their only casualties were a few soldiers wearing heathen amulets (12:39 f.)! God's activity is thus miraculous, and God is therefore called *teratopoiós* (worker of wonders; 15:21; cf. III Macc. 6:32). As when the

Lord destroyed the mighty army of Sennacherib in one night (8:19; 15:22; cf. I Macc. 7:41), so in the present the victory is not decided by weapons but given by the Lord to those he judges worthy (15:21).

To Israel God has given his holy Law (6:23; cf. 3:15; 6:1) contained in "the holy book" (8:23; cf. I Macc. 12:9; II Macc. 2:1, 4), which before the New Testament is called "the Law and the Prophets" only in 15:9 and in the preface to the Greek translation of Ecclesiasticus. To "obey the commandment of the Law given by Moses" to the fathers (7:30; cf. 3:1) is Israel's supreme task, and by following the divine laws Israel becomes invulnerable (8:36): God has made a covenant with Israel (cf. 7:36; 8:15), and a Jew should rather die than transgress the Law (7:2; cf. 6:30 f.; 7:37; 13:14). The Jews are sharply divided into the ungodly (8:2) and the Pious, or Hasidim (14:6). The ungodly not only violate the prescriptions of the Law, as when they wear heathen amulets (12:40) and swear falsely (4:34; cf. 15:10), but skeptically doubt God's judgment (8:13). On the contrary, the Pious trust absolutely in the Lord, even when put to death for their faith (7:40), and punctiliously fulfill the Law in every detail: Sabbath observance, even stricter than in I Macc. 2:41 (II Macc. 6:11; 15:5), circumcision (6:10), purifications (12:38), dietary prescriptions (6:18-31; 7:1 ff.), execution of traitors (10:22), burial of the dead (12:39; contrast 5:10), protecting the moneys deposited by widows and orphans (3:10, 12, 15; cf. Ex. 22:7-13 [H. 22:6-12]), and prayer of intercession for unfortunate Jews (8:14; cf. 1:6; 15:12)—even for deceased sinners, according to the Epitomist (12:43-45).

Of all violations of the Law, the profanation of the Temple and the attempted Hellenization of the Jews ("new customs forbidden by law," 4:11) particularly horrified Jason of Cyrene (4:7-20; 5:15-26; 6:1-9). Although in 5:9, as in I Macc. 12:6, 21, the Spartans are regarded as kinsmen of the Jews, II and III Maccabees, like the Pharisees, stress the separation of the Jews from the heathen and all their customs, anathematizing Hellenistic culture (4:12-20; 14:38; cf. 11:24 f., 31). Almost as virulent as in Judith, this hostility against the "blasphemous and barbarous" (10:4) heathen finds expression in the invectives against the enemies of the pious Jews—a veritable *thesaurus* of Greek vituperation. Jason calls them apostates and hangmen (5:8), blasphemers (9:28; 10:36), murderers (9:28), impious wretches (7:34), godless (10:10), ungodly (3:11; 8:14; 9:9; 15:33), accursed (12:35), the greatest of villains (4:19; 7:34; 9:13; 15:32; cf. 5:16), scoundrels (12:23; 13:4; 14:42), wild beasts (4:25), thrice-scoundrels (8:34; 15:3), utterly wicked (14:27). The basic sin of the heathen is arrogant pride, insolent conceit (5:17, 21; 9:4, 7). Like Sennacherib, Epiphanes did not realize that he was merely "the rod of God's anger" (Is. 10:5-8, 13 f.): "Shall the ax boast against him that hews therewith?" (Is. 10:15) For comparing their power with God's (15:5 f.), the heathen rulers not only failed in their wicked purposes (15:5) but received through God's judgment the just penalty of their arrogance (7:36).

In contrast with God's inexorable judgment against the heathen is his mercy toward Israel: his anger for Israel's sins lasts but a brief while. We must note here a difference, in the notion of divine retribution, between the Wisdom books (Proverbs and Ecclesiasticus in particular) and II Maccabees: in those books each individual received *on this earth* the rewards and punishments which his conduct deserved. But in II Maccabees, as in the ancient prophetic books, the nation is judged as a whole, and consequently the good Jews (notably the martyrs) suffer with the wicked; through their steadfastness and suffering they leave behind at their death "a noble example" (6:28; cf. 6:31) and bring to an end God's wrath (7:38; cf. 8:5). Nevertheless, God rewards the outstanding piety of the martyrs who suffered torments and death rather than violate the Law: after descending into the underworld (6:23), the martyrs will be raised to eternal life (7:9, 11, 14, 23, 29, 36; 12:43-45) and be reunited with their deceased kinsmen (7:29). Whether Jason of Cyrene believed in the sole resurrection of the pious Jews (as in Is. 26:19) or in the double resurrection of the most pious and most wicked Jews (as in Dan. 12:2 f.) is uncertain; but apparently he did not believe in a general resurrection of all the dead (John 5:29: "resurrection of life and . . . resurrection of judgment"). II Maccabees, in any case, is the only book in the Apocrypha that teaches the doctrine of the resurrection *of the flesh* (7:11; 14:46), in sharp contrast with the immortality of the spirit adopted from Plato by Wisdom of Solomon, IV Maccabees, and Philo. The fate after death of the most arrogant and wicked of the heathen, Antiochus Epiphanes, is not described clearly: of course he will not partake of the "resurrection unto life" which is the reward of the Jewish martyrs (7:14) and he cannot escape from the judgment of God (7:31, 36); but nothing indicates that he will be raised to "everlasting contempt" (Dan. 12:2). In all probability his punishment, as in the case of other villains, consists of the manner of his death (cf. 9:4, 18) and of an eternity in the underworld (cf. 7:14). Conversely, according to the Epitomist, even sinful Jews may hope to be delivered from the underworld and raised unto life (12:43-45). Manifestly God's judgment occurs during the earthly life of each person (7:36; 9:4, 18), and not (as in later writings) at the end of time.

Jason of Cyrene, if this summary (II Maccabees) reflects *his* thought and not the Epitomist's, obviously did not intend to write an objective history of the Maccabean Rebellion, but rather a book of religious instruction, illustrated by historical events which he retold, when it served his purposes, in legendary form. Jason wished to strengthen the faith of the Jews by showing that their God would defend his Temple and his nation against any attack. He was unquestionably a Jew of the Dispersion, born in Cyrene and presumably writing in Alexandria about 100 B.C. He wrote in Greek, which was his vernacular, primarily for the Jews of Egypt, although he also kept in mind possible Gentile readers. D. M. Sluys (*De Maccabaeorum libris*, pp. 74 f.) is convinced that Jason was a Gentile—a patently absurd view, unless Sluys means a Gentile convert to Judaism (which is extremely improbable). The horror of Jason for Hellenism and the heathen and his accurate information about the tenets of Judaism seem to indicate that he was a Jew by birth. His theology is distinctly Palestinian rather than Jewish-Hellenistic, as appears in particular in his belief in the resurrection of the flesh; but this is not sufficient, even if his zeal for the strict observance of the Sabbath in war (6:11; 15:5) is taken into account, for regarding him as a Pharisee. In contrast with Ben Sira he discloses little, if any, knowledge of the oral law; and he is not interested in Messianic hopes. There is no trace of Greek philosophy in his thought, and even God's wisdom, which was the connecting link between Hellenism and Judaism at that time, is entirely disregarded. But, while his theology is commonplace, his history to a great extent fanciful or legendary, his ethical teaching negligible, and his juristic learning superficial, Jason's contribution to religion has left its mark, particularly in Roman Catholicism. The stories about the Jewish martyrs (6:18-7:42; cf. 14:37-46) inspired the eloquent peroration of the famous eulogy of the heroes of faith in the Epistle to the Hebrews (Hebr. 11:35 alludes to II Macc. 6:19, 28; Hebr. 11:35-38 refers in general to the Maccabean martyrs) and furnished Christian martyrs with examples to be followed. Origen (*Exhortatio ad martyrium* IV, 10 [ed. Lommatzsch XX, 261-268; cf. VI, 305]) presents the death of Eleazar and of the seven brothers as a glorious example for the Christians (cf. Cyprian, *Ad Fortunatum*, ch. 11). Later Church Fathers alluded to these stories (see André, *Les Apocryphes*, p. 114; Bickermann, *Gott der Makkabäer*, p. 36), which became the pattern for the *Passiones* of early Christianity and the later *Acta Martyrum*; nay, Eleazar and the seven brothers became Christian saints (Schürer, *Geschichte*, Vol. 3, p. 487)! In Judaism, likewise, the stories of the martyrs were retold with embellishments, for edifying purposes, in IV Maccabees and in the Haggadah (see Lévi, in REJ 54 [1907] 138-141). It would seem that Jason of Cyrene is the first author of *Acta Martyrum*, for the stories of pagan martyrs in Hellenistic literature[7] are not earlier than the first century A.D.

As early as Origen, likewise, II Maccabees furnished proof texts for

---

[7] See W. Schubart, *Einführung in die Papyruskunde*, pp. 152-154. Berlin, 1918. H. Lietzmann, *Griechische Papyri*, No. 21 (Kleine Texte 14, second edit.). Berlin, 1910.

important doctrines:[8] the creation *ex nihilo,* out of nothing, in 7:28 (*Comment. in Johan.* I, 18 [Lommatzsch I, 37]; *de principiis* II: 1, 5 [Lommatzsch XXI, 142]); and the intercession of the saints in 15:14 (*Comment. in Johan.* XIII, 57 [Lommatzsch II, 120], and elsewhere). For the following Roman Catholic doctrines confirmation is also found in II Maccabees:[9] the "eternal death" of the wicked (7:9, 14); the resurrection of the flesh (7:11; 14:46); the intercession of the living in behalf of the dead (12:43); the possibility for the living to make expiation for the dead and thus deliver them from Purgatory (12:43-45);[10] the doctrine of angels (3:24-28; 10:29 f.; 11:8; cf. 5:2-4). Conversely, the Protestants, beginning with Luther, accused the Catholics of misinterpreting these passages, and not only contested the canonicity of II Maccabees but judged it more adversely than any other book in the Apocrypha (cf. Grimm, Commentary, pp. 27-29, 185 f., etc.).

Before leaving Jason of Cyrene, we must consider his lost work from the literary point of view. The book can hardly have been written as early as 161-152 B.C., as suggested by Niese (*Kritik,* p. 37) and Schürer (*Geschichte,* Vol. 3, 484), unless all evidence of a later date be attributed to the Epitomist to whom we owe II Maccabees: the reference to the Feast of Purim (the Day of Mordecai, 15:36), for instance, can hardly be earlier than the Greek version of Esther (113 B.C.?). Moreover, Jason hardly drew his information "from the lips of contemporaries" of Judas Maccabeus (Schürer, *loc. cit.*), but utilized sources written in Greek (cf. Bickermann, *Gott der Makkabäer,* pp. 18, 34).

Jason did not know I Maccabees, neither in Hebrew nor in Greek, but excerpted at least one pagan source, a Seleucid history in Greek, which was known also to Josephus (who apparently ignored Jason and II Maccabees). As was observed in the preceding chapter, II Maccabees and Josephus report, presumably from this source, three historical details (see II Macc. 6:2; 13:3-8; 14:1), as also the story of the intrigues for the high priesthood that preceded the Maccabean Rebellion (ch. 4). That *Jewish* sources for the life of Judas Maccabeus were scarce or nonexistent in 100 B.C. may be inferred from I Macc. 9:22, and from the fact that Josephus knew only one—I Maccabees. Traces of a *pagan* source in Jason's work may be detected in the references to the cult of Dionysus (6:7; 14:33); in erroneous notions about the topography of Palestine (11:5; 12:17; the distances given in 12:9, 29 are, however, correct); in the apparent assumption that Jerusalem, "the city" (4:39; 5:2; 8:3; 10:1;

---

[8] Cf. Schürer, *Geschichte,* Vol. 3, p. 486; André, *Les Apocryphes,* p. 114.

[9] Cf. H. Bévenot, *Die Beiden Makkabäerbücher,* pp. 38-41.

[10] Dom D. de Bruyne (cf. Bévenot, *op. cit.,* p. 40) has plausibly detected, particularly from the Old Latin version, two contradictory glosses in 12:43-45. The first is Jewish and skeptical: "it is superfluous and silly to pray for the dead!" (v. 44); the second is Christian (or written by a pious Jew): "a holy and pious thought!" (v. 45).

13:13), was the only city in Judea (contrast I Macc. 1:29, 44, 51, 54: "the cities of Judah"), other localities being "villages" (8:1; see, however, 8:6); in the correct use of Hellenistic titles (11:1, contrast I Macc. 3:32 [see Niese, *Kritik*, p. 51]; 3:5, 7; 4:29; 5:24; 8:9; 9:29; 14:12; etc. [*ibid.*, pp. 28 f.]); in the acquaintance with details of Seleucid history (4:21, 27; 5:22 f.; 8:8; 9:29; 10:13 f.; 13:25 [*ibid.*, pp. 27 f.]); and in other minor matters.

It is clear that sometimes Jason superimposed on the Seleucid point of view of his sources his diametrically opposite Jewish explanation of the facts. The campaigns of Judas after the rededication of the Temple are explained in I Macc. 5:1 f. as a crusade for the suppression of the pogroms which the heathen had initiated out of hatred for Judaism; Jason's source, conversely, showed that the Idumeans were welcoming refugees escaping from Judas's "purge" against Hellenizing Jews in Jerusalem (II Macc. 10:15); finally, Jason regarded the unprovoked attacks of Gorgias and the Idumeans (cf. I Macc. 5:3) against Judas as the *casus belli* (10:14 f.). The religious anti-Semitism, after the death of Antiochus, which is stressed in I Macc. 5:1 f., 9, 13-15, 27 and even more in Ps. 83 (an echo of the same events), is totally lacking in II Maccabees, as also the Maccabean zeal against pagan cults manifested in the destruction of pagan temples (I Macc. 5:44;[11] 10:83 f.; 11:4). Another example of Jason's revision of the Seleucid source is offered by the events of 168 (cf. Bickermann, *Gott der Makkabäer*, p. 167): while the Seleucid source reported that Jerusalem rebelled, Jason states that Antiochus Epiphanes "*thought* that Judea was in revolt" (5:11), whereas the trouble was merely a contest between two Jewish supporters of the king, Menelaus and Jason, for the office of high priest (5:5-7).

Traces of Jason's Seleucid source have been detected in a comparatively pure form in Josephus, *War* I:1, 1 to 2, 3 [§§31-56]; and, in conjunction with I Maccabees, in *Antiquities* XII: 5, 3-4; 6, 1-2. If, as G. Hölscher (*Die Quellen des Josephus*, pp. 4 ff. Leipzig, 1904; Pauly-Wissowa, *Realenzyklopädie*, Vol. 9, p. 1944) maintains, Josephus used here the history of Nicholas of Damascus, the secretary of Herod the Great, then Jason's source was known to Josephus only through the intermediary of Nicholas. Echoes of this source survive in Diodorus Siculus XXXIV (incorporating parts of the history of Posidonius of Apamea), Tacitus (*Historiae* V, 8), Porphyry (preserved in Jerome's commentary on Daniel), and John Malalas (sixth century).[12] Conceivably the story that

---

[11] On the contrary in II Macc. 12:26 the temple of Carnaim, correctly named *Atargateion*, or temple of Atargatis (Derketo), in Jason's pagan source, is not said to have been destroyed by Judas.

[12] The latest discussion of Jason's source is that of Bickermann (*Gott der Makkabäer*, pp. 150, 162-168). Some valuable data may be also found in H. Willrich, *Judaica*, pp. 131-163, although the conclusions reached there are questionable.

Epiphanes died by falling from his chariot (9:4-9) is a distorted version of the story, possibly derived from this Seleucid source, told by Granius Licinianus (p. 9, Bonn ed.): "When his [Antiochus'] corpse was being brought to Antioch, through the sudden fright of the horses it was carried away by the river and was never seen again."[13]

Out of the materials derived from the Seleucid and possibly also other sources, Jason has produced a highly romantic history, in which fact and fancy, drama and faith are thoroughly mixed. The result is a typical example of rhetorical Hellenistic historiography. Rhetorical art furnished Jason with both style and method. Jason's style, to judge from what is left of his work, was ornate and flowery, often poetic in diction, abounding in rare, farfetched, elegant expressions (cf. Grimm, Commentary, p. 7; Niese, Kritik, p. 33); see, for instance, 3:30; 4:13, 15, 26, 47; 5:6, 9; 8:18; 13:22-26; 14:24 f. In a number of cases we find parallels with the diction of Polybius (Grimm, ibid.).

Although Jason was a strict Jew and wrote his five books to glorify the institutions of Judaism, and particularly the Temple, the manner of his historical writing is typically Hellenistic: few historians in the centuries around the beginning of our era, like Polybius, avoided the passionate tone, the dominating parti pris, the concoction of miraculous tales, the search for dramatic effect, the subordination of facts to moral lessons, and in general the conformity to the prevailing rhetorical fashions, characteristic of Jason (cf. Niese, Kritik, pp. 34-36). Stories about heavenly riders (3:25) and other wonders (cf. Niese, ibid.), reports of ominous dreams (15:12-16; cf. ibid.), descriptions of the "ghastly spasm of racking torture" (Milton) at the death of tyrants (9:5-10; cf. Niese, ibid.; Willrich, Urkundenfälschung, p. 31), and other standard motifs in Jason can be paralleled in Greek and Hellenistic historians. In fact, as Bickermann (Gott der Makkabäer, p. 147; cf. R. Reitzenstein, Hellenistische Wundererzählung. Leipzig, 1906) has observed, II Maccabees is the sole complete specimen of the "pathetic historiography" of Hellenism. Such a narrative stirred the feelings of the reader; kindled in him terror, horror, and enthusiasm; stressed the author's own point of view; depicted feelingly the emotions of the characters; and dramatized intensely the events narrated. To us such romanticized history and rhetorical style may be less attractive than the objectivity and simplicity of I Maccabees; nevertheless, Jason of Cyrene, with all his faults, deserves to be investigated as a typical Hellenistic historian and as a writer not lacking in ability.

[13] Cf. Willrich, Judaica, p. 142 f.; Sluys, De Maccab. libris, p. 77. According to the Arabic Maccabean History, ch. 8 (published in the Paris [Vol. 9] and London [Vol. 4] Polyglots), and the medieval elaboration of Josephus (called Yosippon) by Josephus Gorionides (III: 12, 13), the horses were frightened by the trumpeting of elephants (cf. Grimm, Commentary, p. 148).

2. *The Epitomist*

The unknown Alexandrian Jew who condensed the five books of Jason of Cyrene into II Maccabees (2:23) has briefly explained his purpose and his method (2:19-32; 15:37-39). The reason for preparing this *epitomé* (2:26, 28) was to supply the general reader with an elementary manual (2:24 f.). Jason's work was difficult to read, owing to "a flood" of statistics (dates, distances, numbers of troops, etc.)[14] and a mass of details intended for scholars; conversely, the epitome is intended for the entertainment of those who are fond of reading, for the ease of those who like to memorize passages, and for the aid of readers in general.

The task of abridging was taken seriously by our Epitomist: it was not easy, he says, but rather to be accomplished through sweat and night work (2:26). In general, labors for the benefit of others, like that of a toastmaster at a banquet (cf. Ecclus. 32:1 f. [Gr. 35:1 f.]; John 2:8 f.) or of one furthering other people's interests, are wearisome. But the Epitomist has gladly undertaken this chore to gain the gratitude of many (2:27).

His method, substantially, was to follow the accepted rules for the preparation of an epitome, leaving all research about particulars to the historian, Jason (2:28). In other words, Jason is the architect and builder, who erects the structure of the edifice, while the Epitomist is the decorator, who through encaustic and fresco painting adorns the interior (2:29). The Epitomist takes credit for the form alone; the substance of the book is the result of the detailed researches and elaborate discussions of Jason (2:30-31). His own endeavor has been to tell the story agreeably and in order, mixing Jason's wine (historical matter) with his water (good style) for the delight of the reader (15:38 f.).

This is all the Epitomist tells us. There is no reason to doubt that on the whole he is speaking the truth: his book (II Maccabees) is really an epitome of Jason's five books. Since this could be verified easily, as long as Jason's work was still circulating, it is incredible that the Epitomist should have falsified the facts. Nor is it probable that he should have invented a mythical Jason and a nonexisting history of his— a fiction likewise easily disproved in the lifetime of the Epitomist; for forgers are wont to attribute their work to celebrities, not to otherwise unknown authors. But, though substantially correct, the Epitomist's statement presents serious difficulties.

The problem of the contents of Jason's history has been considered

[14] The statistics about troops in II Maccabees have been mentioned in the preceding section, as also distances. Dates occur in II Macc. 1:10; 11:21, 33, 38; 13:1; 14:4. The first was not in Jason's work, and the dated documents in ch. 11 are regarded by some as an interpolation.

earlier in this chapter: in spite of some ambiguity in 2:19-23, it seems probable that the original history embraced the same period as II Maccabees, and that the Epitomist did not utilize other sources nor make any important additions to it. A second problem is raised by the comparison of Jason to an architect and builder, and of the Epitomist to a decorator (2:29). As Grimm (Commentary, p. 64) observes, the comparison (as also that of wine and water, 15:38 f.) does not fit an ordinary epitome, but rather a rhetorical rewriting of a factual and statistical manual; nor does a mere condensation require quite so much labor as the Epitomist (2:26 f.) claims to have devoted to this work. We are thus faced by a dilemma: either the Epitomist greatly exaggerates his contribution, when he claims that the facts are Jason's but the form is substantially his; or he is actually responsible for the rhetorical style, the pedagogical purpose, and the dramatic theology of the book. We lack the evidence needed for a final solution of the dilemma: while Niese (Kritik, pp. 37 f.) and particularly Willrich (Judaica, pp. 131-134) and Sluys (De Maccabaeorum libris, pp. 76-78) choose the second horn, the present writer follows Grimm (Commentary, pp. 16-19) in preferring the first. As Grimm says, we know neither the moral caliber of the Epitomist, in order to ascertain his credibility, nor his literary ability, in order to ascertain whether he limited himself to stylistic rewriting or whether in dramatic scenes (3:15-22; 6:18-7:42; 14:41-46) he actually contributed to the contents. Did he really sweat and sit up late making the abridgment (2:26), or is he deceitfully boasting or joking when he says so? To judge from what the Epitomist has written (2:19-32; 15:37-39; and presumably 4:17; 5:17-20; 6:12-17; 12:43b-45), he appears to be a *beschränkter Kopf* (Grimm), a man of limited intelligence, rather than a creative writer of considerable ability and originality. His comparisons in 2:27 and 15:39 are commonplace and not fully appropriate; his moralizing in 6:12-17 is a platitude (taken from 7:32-35) which rhetoric fails to make eloquent in tone and original in thought (cf. Wisd. of Sol. 11:9 f.; 12:22). All in all, he is a well-intentioned, somewhat pompous, devout Jew who, after graduation from an Alexandrian school, sought fame as a writer (2:25, 27) in summarizing and popularizing the work of a scholar (2:23 f., 30 f.) after discovering that he lacked the talent for original research and independent literary production.

In reducing Jason's five books to the size of one, the Epitomist followed several methods. Some passages of Jason, which he liked particularly for their edifying and inspiring lessons, he reproduced virtually intact: so, for instance, the stories of Heliodorus (ch. 3), of the martyrs (6:18-7:42; 14:37-46), and of Nicanor's death (15:1-36). Other passages he seems to have abridged slightly (4:1-6:17) or more considerably (ch. 8; 10:1-8). In the story of the death of Antiochus Epiphanes (ch. 9) he seems to have rewritten some parts. Elsewhere he condensed detailed stories into a very brief outline (13:18-26; 14:18-25). Finally, he entirely omitted some sections of Jason's work and tried to bridge over the gaps as inconspicuously as possible (cf. Grimm, Commentary, p. 18 f.). But traces of the omissions can still be detected in the sudden appearance on the scene of persons who had apparently been mentioned earlier by Jason: Timotheus and Bacchides (8:30), Zacchaeus (10:19), Allophanes (10:37), Esdris (Authorized Version: Gorgias) (12:36), Hegemonides (13:24). Similarly, certain contradictions may be best explained as the result of drastic curtailment: in 11:11 f. the Jews have completely routed Lysias, but in 11:29 f. they are besieged and are allowed to go to their homes within fifteen days (Grimm, *ibid.*); Timotheus, after being killed (10:37), reappears in 12:2 ff. (cf. Niese, *Kritik*, p. 6, n. 3). It is possible that the erroneous dating of Antiochus Epiphanes' death *before* the cleansing of the Temple (9:1-10:9) is to be attributed to the Epitomist, as also the assumption that the seven brothers were killed in the presence of Antiochus Epiphanes, while in reality (5:21; cf. 6:1) the king was in Antioch.[15]

If such was the Epitomist's procedure in summarizing Jason's work, it cannot be said with Grimm (*op. cit.*, p. 19) that he produced a selection rather than a summary; for the parts omitted without even a passing reference can hardly be extensive and numerous. As Grimm himself believes (*ibid.*), they were confined to incidents in battles (like 12:35) and anecdotes (like 13:21; 14:37-46).

Our final verdict on the Epitomist cannot be very favorable. He did not deal with Jason in a manner quite so arbitrary as that of the Chronicler in excerpting Samuel and Kings, but he proceeded with great freedom and confessedly with greater concern for public recognition of his own literary ability than for an objective, concise presentation of Jason's work. He manifestly took considerable liberties, rearranging the order of events wrongly, stressing the religious teaching, exaggerating horrors and miracles, and generally showing less respect for historical reality (cf. 15:37) than Jason, who himself cannot be accused of excessive accuracy. Thus he aggravated the defects of Jason, without making any important contributions.[16] However, we owe the Epitomist a debt for preserving, even though in curtailed and fragmentary form, something

[15] Other contradictions in II Maccabees (disregarding the letters at the beginning) are: Philip fled to Egypt immediately after the death of Epiphanes (9:29; but see 13:23); Antiochus V was in full authority at his accession (10:11; 11:15, 18 f., 22-33; but see 13:2).

[16] The letters in chs. 1-2 were written originally in Hebrew and seem to have been added (in a Greek translation) to the Epitomist's book.

of Jason's history; and we should judge him leniently, because he intended to write a popular book—not a scholarly history—for the entertainment and instruction of the general reader among the Alexandrian Jews. If his intentions were better than his achievement, he should be excused, for from all appearances he is right in saying (15:38) that this is the best he could achieve.

ABBREVIATIONS

ABBREVIATIONS

A. OLD TESTAMENT

Am.	Amos	Judg.	Judges
Cant.	Canticles (Song of Sol.)	Lam.	Lamentations
Chron.	Chronicles	Lev.	Leviticus
Dan.	Daniel	Mal.	Malachi
Deut.	Deuteronomy	Mic.	Micah
Eccl.	Ecclesiastes	Nah.	Nahum
Esth.	Esther	Neh.	Nehemiah
Ex.	Exodus	Num.	Numbers
Ez.	Ezekiel	Obad.	Obadiah
Gen.	Genesis	Pr.	Proverbs
Hab.	Habakkuk	Ps.	Psalms
Hag.	Haggai	Sam.	Samuel
Hos.	Hosea	Song	Song of Solomon (Cant.)
Is.	Isaiah	Zech.	Zechariah
Jer.	Jeremiah	Zeph.	Zephaniah
Josh.	Joshua		

B. NEW TESTAMENT

Acts	Acts of the Apostles	Pet.	Peter
Col.	Colossians	Phil.	Philippians
Cor.	Corinthians	Philem.	Philemon
Eph.	Ephesians	Rev.	Revelation
Gal.	Galatians	Rom.	Romans
Hebr.	Hebrews	Thess.	Thessalonians
Jam.	James	Tim.	Timothy
Matt.	Matthew	Tit.	Titus

C. APOCRYPHA

Bar.	Baruch	Macc.	Maccabees
Bel	Bel and the Dragon	Sus.	Susanna
Ecclus.	Ecclesiasticus	Tob.	Tobit
Esd.	Esdras	Wisd.	Wisdom of Solomon
Jth.	Judith	of Sol.	

525

Arist.	Letter of Aristeas	Mart. Is.	Martyrdom of Isaiah
Ass. Mos.	Assumption of Moses	Ps. of Sol.	Psalms of Solomon
Enoch	Ethiopic Enoch	Sibyl.	Sibylline Oracles
Epist.	Epistle	Slav. En.	Slavic Enoch
of Jer.	of Jeremy	Syr. Bar.	Syriac Baruch
Gr. Bar.	Greek Baruch	Test. XII	Testaments of the XII
Jub.	Jubilees		Patriarchs
Macc.	Maccabees		

ad loc.	on the passage	Gr.	Greek
apoc.	apocalypse	H.	Hebrew Bible
Beih.	Beiheft	*ibid.*	same place
Beitr.	Beitrag, Beiträge	*op. cit.*	work quoted
ca.	about	LXX	the Septuagint
cf.	compare	Ms., Mss.	manuscript, manuscripts
ch.	chapter	n.	footnote
cod.	codex	N.F., N.S.	Neue Folge, New Series
d.	date of death	R.V.	Revised Version
ed.	edition, editor	u.s.w.	etc.
f.	following verse or page	v.	verse
ff.	following verses or pages	Zeitschr.	Zeitschrift

AA	Alttestamentliche Abhandlungen (edited by J. Nikel). Münster i. W.	Bibl.	Biblica
		Bibl. Stud.	Biblische Studien
		BS	Bibliotheca Sacra
AASOR	Annual of the American Schools of Oriental Research	BWANT	Beiträge zur Wissenschaft vom Alten und Neuen Testament
AJSL	American Journal of Semitic Languages and Literatures	BWAT	Beiträge zur Wissenschaft vom Alten Testament
		BZ	Biblische Zeitschrift
AJT	American Journal of Theology	EB	Études Bibliques
AO	Der Alte Orient	EH	Exegetisches Handbuch zum Alten Testament. Münster i. W.
ARW	Archiv für Religionswissenschaft		
ATR	Anglican Theological Review	ET	Expository Times
		Exp.	The Expositor
Bab.	Babylonian Talmud	FRLANT	Forschungen zur Religion und Literatur des Alten und Neuen Testament. Göttingen
BASOR	Bulletin of the American Schools of Oriental Research		

HAT	Handbuch zum Alten Testament. Tübingen	NTT	Nieuw Theologisch Tijdschrift
HKAT	Handkommentar zum Alten Testament. Göttingen	OLZ	Orientalistische Literaturzeitung
HS	Die Heilige Schrift des Alten Testaments. Bonn	PSBA	Proceedings of the Society of Biblical Archaeology
HTR	Harvard Theological Review	RB	Revue Biblique
HUCA	Hebrew Union College Annual, Cincinnati	REJ	Revue des Études Juives
		RHPR	Revue d'Histoire et de Philosophie Religieuses
ICC	International Critical Commentary, Edinburgh and New York	RHR	Revue de l'Histoire des Religions
JAOS	Journal of the American Oriental Society	RR	Ricerche Religiose
		TLZ	Theologische Literaturzeitung
JBL	Journal of Biblical Literature	TQ	Theologische Quartalschrift
JBR	Journal of Bible and Religion	TSBA	Transactions of the Society of Biblical Archaeology
Jer.	Jerusalem Talmud	TSK	Theologische Studien und Kritiken
JJGL	Jahrbuch für Jüdische Geschichte und Literatur	TT	Theologisch Tijdschrift
JQR	Jewish Quarterly Review	ZA	Zeitschrift für Assyriologie
JRAS	Journal of the Royal Asiatic Society	ZAW	Zeitschrift für die Alttestamentliche Wissenschaft
JTS	Journal of Theological Studies	ZDMG	Zeitschrift der Deutschen Morgendländischen Gesellschaft
KAT	Kommentar zum Alten Testament. Leipzig	ZKT	Zeitschrift für Katolische Theologie
M	Th. Mangei, *Philonis Judaei Opera Omnia*, 2 vols. Paris, 1742.	ZNW	Zeitschrift für die Neutestamentliche Wissenschaft
MGWJ	Monatschrift für Geschichte und Wissenschaft des Judentums	ZWT	Zeitschrift für Wissenschaftliche Theologie

ABBREVIATIONS

SELECTED BIBLIOGRAPHY

SELECTED BIBLIOGRAPHY

~~~~~~~~~~~~~~~~~~~~~~

NOTE. The bibliography on Hellenism and on the Jewish Diaspora has been given in Part I, Chapters IV, V, and VI, and need not be repeated here. Attention should be called to the excellent "Selected Bibliography (1920–1945) of the Jews in the Hellenistic-Roman Period" published by Professor Ralph Marcus in the *Proceedings of the American Academy for Jewish Research* (16 [1946–47] 97–181), which is far more complete;[1] see also his chapter on "The Future of Intertestamental Studies" in H. R. Willoughby, *The Study of the Bible Today and Tomorrow* (University of Chicago Press, 1947)—a book which contains also a valuable chapter by J. Coert Rylaarsdam on "Intertestamental Studies since Charles' Apocrypha and Pseudepigrapha." An earlier survey of "Intertestamental Studies" was published by the late Prof. A. T. Olmstead (JAOS 56 [1936] 242–257). The best bibliography of nineteenth century books on all topics treated in this volume will be found in E. Schürer, *Geschichte des jüdischen Volkes im Zeitalter Jesu Christi* (4 vols., 3rd and 4th ed. Leipzig, 1901–11). A comprehensive edition of the Apocrypha and Pseudepigrapha, giving in separate volumes the text and the English translation of each book (with introductions and notes), has been projected by the Dropsie College in Philadelphia, under the general editorship of Professor Solomon Zeitlin.

PART I: GENERAL WORKS

1. Political History

B. Stade, *Geschichte des Volkes Israel*, Vol. 2, pp. 271–674 (by O. Holzmann). E. Renan, *Histoire du peuple d'Israël*, vols. 4 and 5. Paris, 1893 and 1894 (English translation). J. Wellhausen, *Israelitische und jüdische Geschichte*. Berlin, 1894; 7th ed., 1914 (English translation: "Israel" in the 9th ed. of the *Encyclopaedia Britannica* [1875–89] and in Wellhausen, *Prolegomena to the History of Israel*. Edinburgh, 1885). H. Guthe, *Geschichte des Volkes Israel*. Tübingen, 1899; 3rd ed. 1914. C. F. Kent, *History of the Jewish People*, vol. 2 (by J. S. Riggs). New York, 1900. E. Schürer, *Geschichte des jüdischen Volkes im Zeitalter Jesu Christi*, 4 vols. 3rd and 4th. ed. Leipzig, 1901–1911 (English translation: *A History of the Jewish People in the Time of Jesus Christ*. 5 vols. Edinburgh, 1886–90). J. Juster, *Les Juifs dand les l'empire romain*, 2 vols. Paris, 1914. W. O. E. Oesterley and Th. H. Robinson, *History of Israel*, vol. 2 (by Oesterley). Oxford University Press, 1932. E. R. Bevan, in *Cambridge Ancient History*, vol. 9, pp. 397–434. Cambridge University Press, 1932.

---

[1] The valuable bibliographies on special topics (dealt with in this book) prepared by Professor Marcus in the appendixes of vols. VI and VII of his translation of Josephus in the *Loeb Classical Library* were discovered by me after this volume was in gallery proofs, and could not be utilized. As my excuse, I may say that for Josephus I used the *editio minor* of his works by B. Niese (which I own), having been unable to purchase the volumes in the Loeb Classical Library, of which only vol. VII has now been sent to me by the publishers.

G. Ricciotti, *Storia d'Israele*, vol. 2. Turin, 1934. A. Momigliano, in *Cambridge Ancient History*, vol. 10, pp. 316–39; 849–65. Cambridge, 1934. E. Bickermann, *Die Makkabäer*. Berlin, 1935 (English translation: E. Bickerman [*sic*], *The Maccabees*. New York, 1947); *Der Gott der Makkabäer*. Berlin, 1937. A. H. M. Jones, *The Herods of Judea*. Oxford University Press, 1938.

2. Religious History

P. Volz, *Jüdische Eschatologie von Daniel bis Akiba*. Tübingen, 1903. O. Holzmann, *Neutestamentliche Zeitgeschichte*. 2nd edit. Tübingen, 1906. L. Couard, *Die religiösen und sittlichen Anschauungen der alttestamentlichen. Apokryphen und Pseudepigraphen*. Gütersloh, 1907. H. M. Hughes, *The Ethics of Jewish Apocryphal Literature*. London, 1909. A. Bertholet, *Die Jüdische Religion von der Zeit Esras bis zum Zeitalter Christi* (Vol. II of B. Stade's *Biblische Theologie des Alten Testaments*). Tübingen, 1911. R. H. Charles, *Religious Development between the Old and New Testaments* (Home University Library). London and New York, 1914. F. C. Burkitt, *Jewish and Christian Apocalypses*. London, 1914. H. J. Wicks, *The Doctrine of God in the Jewish Apocryphal and Apocalyptic Literature*. London, 1915. L. Ginzberg, "Some Observations on the Attitude of the Synagogue towards the Apocalyptic-Eschatological Writings" (JBL 41 [1922] 115–136). W. Bousset, *Die Religion des Judentums im späthellenistischen Zeitalter*. 3rd ed. by H. Gressmann. Tübingen, 1926. G. Kittel, *Urchristentum, Spätjudentum, Hellenismus*. Stuttgart, 1926; *Die Probleme des palästinischen Spätjudentums und das Urchristentum*. (BWANT 3, 1) Stuttgart, 1926. A. Büchler, *Studies in Sin and Atonement in the Rabbinic Literature of the First Century*. London, 1928. A. Marmorstein, *The Old Rabbinic Doctrine of God*. 2 vols. London, 1927 and 1937. G. F. Moore, *Judaism in the First Centuries of the Christian Era: The Age of the Tannaim*. 3 vols. Harvard University Press, 1927 and 1930. R. T. Herford, *Judaism in the New Testament Period*. London, 1928. M. J. Lagrange, *Le Judaïsme avant Jésus Christ* (EB). Paris, 1931. G. H. Box, *Judaism in the Greek Period*. Oxford, 1932. S. Zeitlin, *The History of the Second Jewish Commonwealth: Prolegomena*. Philadelphia, 1933; *Who Crucified Jesus?* New York, 1942; 2nd edit., 1947. P. Volz, *Die Eschatologie der jüdischen Gemeinde im neutestamentlichen Zeitalter*. Tübingen, 1934. J. Bonsirven, *Le Judaïsme palestinien au temps de Jésus-Christ*. 2 vols. Paris, 1935. C. Guignebert, *Le monde juif vers le temps de Jésus*. Paris, 1935; English translation: *The Jewish World in the Time of Jesus*. London, 1939. E. Sjöberg, *Gott und die Sünder im palästinischen Judentum* (BWANT). Stuttgart, 1938. W. O. E. Oesterley, *Judaism and Christianity*. 3 vols. London, 1937–38; *The Jews and Judaism During the Greek Period*. New York, 1941. N. Johansson, *Parakletoi: Vorstellungen von Fürsprechern . . . in der alttestamentlichen Religion, im Spätjudentum und Urchristentum*. Lund, 1940. H. H. Rowley, *The Relevance of Apocalyptic:* A Study of Jewish and Christian Apocalypses from Daniel to the Revelation. London, 1944. Norman B. Johnson, *Prayer in the Apocrypha and the Pseudepigrapha:* A Study of the Jewish Concept of God (JBL, Monograph Series, vol. 2. Philadelphia, 1948).

3. Literary History

A. EDITIONS OF THE ANCIENT VERSIONS

P. de Lagarde, *Libri Veteris Testamenti apocryphi syriace*. Leipzig, 1861. O. F. Fritsche, *Libri apocryphi Veteris Testamenti graece*. Leipzig, 1871; *Libri*

Veteris Testamenti pseudepigraphi selecti. Leipzig, 1871 (Psalms of Solomon, IV and V Esdras. Apocalypse of Baruch, Assumption of Moses). Editions of the LXX (for the Apocrypha).

B. Modern Translations

E. Kautzsch (Editor), *Die Apokryphen und Pseudepigraphen des Alten Testaments,* 2 vols. Freiburg i. B. and Leipzig, 1900. R. H. Charles (Editor), *The Apocrypha and Pseudepigrapha in English,* with Introductions and Critical and Explanatory Notes to the Several Books. 2 vols. Oxford, 1913. W. O. E. Oesterley and G. H. Box, *Translations of Early Documents.* London, 1916 ff. A series of translations of individual books. *Les Livres apocryphes de l'Ancien Testament.* Societé Biblique de Paris, 1909. P. Riessler, *Altjüdisches Schrifttum ausserhalb der Bibel übersetzt und erläutert.* 1928. G. Luzzi, *La Bibbia,* tradotta dai testi originali e annotata. Vol. X: *Apocrifi dell'Antico Testamento,* Florence, 1930. E. J. Goodspeed, *The Apocrypha.* An American Translation. Chicago, 1938.

C. Commentaries

O. F. Fritzsche and C. L. W. Grimm, *Kurzgefasstes exegetisches Handbuch zu den Apokryphen des Alten Testamentes.* 6 vols. Leipzig, 1851–1860 (still unsurpassed). H. Wace (Editor), *The Holy Bible* . . . ("Speaker's Commentary"): *Apocrypha.* London, 1888. O. Zöckler, *Die Apokryphen nebst einem Anhang über die Pseudepigraphenlitteratur* (in Strack and Zöckler's *Kurzgefasster Kommentar*). Munich, 1891. H. A. Fischel, *The First Book of Maccabees.* New York, 1948. Roman Catholic commentaries, as well as some Protestant ones, deal with the Apocrypha.

D. Critical Introductions

E. Schürer, *Geschichte des Jüdischen Volkes im Zeitalter Jesu Christi.* Vol. III, 4th ed., Leipzig, 1909 (with full bibliography). The English translation (*A History of the Jewish People in the Time of Jesus Christ*) is antiquated, but the latest edition in German is still indispensable. C. C. Torrey, *The Apocryphal Literature.* Yale University Press, 1945.

On the Apocrypha Alone

L. E. T. André, *Les apocryphes de l'Ancien Testament.* Florence, 1903. W. Christ, *Geschichte der griechischen Literatur bis auf die Zeit Justinians.* 6th ed. edited by O. Stählin and W. Schmidt. Pt. II, vol. 1, pp. 535–658 (by Stählin). *Handbuch der Altertumswissenschaft* (edited by W. Otto), Abt. VII. Munich, 1921. W. O. E. Oesterley, *The Books of the Apocrypha: Their Origin, Teaching and Contents.* London, 1914; *An Introduction to the Books of the Apocrypha.* New York, 1935. B. Motzo, *Saggi di storia e letteratura giudeo-ellenistica* (Contributi alla scienza dell'antichità 5). Florence, 1924. R. Marcus, *Law in the Apocrypha* (Columbia University Oriental Studies 26). New York, 1927. J.-B. Frey, "Apocryphes de l'Ancien Testament" (in Pirot's *Supplément au Dictionnaire de la Bible* [of F. Vigoroux], vol. 1, columns 354–459. Paris, 1928). E. J. Goodspeed, *The Story of the Apocrypha.* University of Chicago Press, 1939. The following authors deal with the Apocrypha and Pseudepigrapha in their Introductions to the Old Testament: König, Strack, Cornill (only 3rd and 4th ed.), Sellin, Steuernagel, Eissfeldt; also A. Bertholet in K. Budde's *Geschichte der althebräische Literatur.* Roman Catholic Introductions deal with the Apocrypha. See also the articles in Bible Dictionaries and

Encyclopaedias, particularly E. Schürer (in Herzog-Hauck, *Realenzyklopädie*, vol. 1, pp. 622 ff.; on the Apocrypha) and G. Beer (*ibid.*, vol. 16, pp. 229 ff.; on the Pseudepigrapha).

PART II: THE BOOKS OF THE APOCRYPHA

1. I [III] Esdras

C. C. Torrey, *Ezra Studies*. Chicago, 1910. P. Bayer, *Das dritte Buch Ezra und sein Verhältnis zu den Büchern Ezra-Nehemia* (Biblische Studien XVI, 1). Freiburg, 1911. B. Walde, *Die Esdrasbücher der Septuaginta* (Bibl. Stud. 18, 4). Freiburg i. B., 1913. S. S. Tedesche, *A Critical Edition of I Esdras*. (Yale University Dissertation, 1928). Printed in Leipzig, no date.

2. II [IV] Esdras

Texts, versions, commentaries: G. H. Box, *The Apocalypse of Ezra* (II Esdras 3–14). London, 1912. B. Violet, *Die Ezra-Apokalypse*. Vol. I: *Die Überlieferung*. Leipzig, 1910; Vol. II: *Die Apokalypsen des Ezra und des Baruch in Deutscher Gestalt* (with textual notes by H. Gressmann). Leipzig, 1924. R. P. Blake, "The Georgian Version of Fourth Esdras" (HTR 19 [1926] 299–375; 22 [1929] 57–105). W. O. E. Oesterley, commentary in the Westminster Commentaries (London, 1933).

Investigations: C. Sigwalt, "Die Chronologie des 4. Buches Esdras (BZ 9 [1911] 146–148). D. Völter, "Die Gesichte vom Adler und vom Menschen im 4. Ezra, nebst Bemerkungen über die Menschensohnstelle in den Bilderreden Henochs" (NTT 1919, 241–273). J. Keulers, *Die eschatologische Lehre des vierten Ezrabuches* (Biblische Studien XX, 2–3). Freiburg, 1922. W. Mundle, "Das religiöse Problem des IV. Ezrabuches" (ZAW N.F. 6 [1929] 222–249). A. Kaminka, "Beiträge zur Erklärung der Ezra Apocalypse und zur Rekonstruktion ihres hebräischen Urtextes" (MGWJ 76–77, 1932–1933); reprinted in *Schriften der Gesellschaft zur Förderung der Wissenschaft des Judentums*, Vol. 38, 1934. L. Gry, *Les dires prophétiques d'Esdras*. 2 vols. Paris, 1938.

3. Tobit

Margarete Plath, "Zum Buch Tobit" (TSK 74 [1901] 377–414). J. Müller, *Beiträge zur Kritik des Buches Tobit* (Beih. ZAW 13). Giessen, 1908. A. Schulte, *Beiträge zur Erklärung und Textkritik des Buches Tobias* (Bibl. Stud. XIX, 2). Freiburg, 1914. G. Huet, "Le conte du 'mort renaissant' et le livre de Tobie" (RHR 71 [1915] 1–29). P. Haupt, "Asmodeus" (JBL 40 [1921] 174–178). C. C. Torrey, "'Nineveh' in the Book of Tobit" (JBL 41 [1922] 237–245). P. Jüon, "Quelques hébraïsmes du Codex Sinaiticus de Tobie" (*Bibl.* 4 [1923] 168–174). G. Priero, *Il libro di Tobia: testi e introduzioni*. Como, 1924. H. G. Bévenot, "The Primitive Book of Tobit" (BS 83 [1926] 55–84). E. Sereni, "Il libro di Tobit" (RR 4 [1928] 43–55, 97–117, 402–439; 5 [1929] 35–49). M. Schumpp, commentary in EH, 1933.

4. Judith

A. Scholz, *Kommentar über das Buch Judith und über Bel und Drache*. 2nd ed., 1896.

C. Meyer, "Zur Entstehungsgeschichte des Buches Judith" (*Bibl.* 3 [1922] 193–203). F. Zimmermann, "Aids for the Recovery of the Hebrew Original of Judith" (JBL 57 [1938] 67–74).

5. Additions to Esther

Roman Catholic commentaries to Esther (A. Scholz, 1892; M. Seisenberger, 1891), and L. B. Paton's in ICC, 1908.

D. B. Jacob, "Esther bei den LXX" (ZAW 10 [1890] 241–298).

E. Bickerman, "The Colophon of the Greek Book of Esther" (JBL 63 [1944] 339–62); cf. R. Marcus in JBL 64 (1945) 269–71. C. C. Torrey, "The Older Book of Esther" (HTR 37 [1944] 1–40).

6. Wisdom of Solomon

Commentaries: W. J. Deane, *The Book of Wisdom.* Oxford, 1881. A. T. S. Goodrich in "Oxford Church Bible Comm.," London, 1917. J. A. F. Gregg, *The Wisdom of Solomon* (Cambridge Bible for Schools). Cambridge, 1909. P. Heinisch in EH, 1912; and F. Feldmann in HS, 1926 (cf. his *Textkritische Materialen zum Buch der Weisheit.* Freiburg, 1902; and BZ 1909, 140 ff.). J. Fichtner, *Die Weisheit Salomos.* HAT, Tübingen, 1938.

Original Language: D. S. Margoliouth, "Was the Book of Wisdom written in Hebrew?" (JRAS 1890, 263 ff.); J. Freudenthal, "What is the Original Language of the Wisdom of Solomon?" (JQR 1891, 722 ff.); E. A. Speiser, "The Hebrew Origin of the First Part of the Book of Wisdom" (JQR N.S. 14 [1923–1924] 455–482); C. E. Purinton, *Translation Greek in the Wisdom of Solomon* (Yale University Dissertation). New Haven, 1928 (also JBL 47 [1928] 276–304). Cf. A. Marx, "An Aramaic Fragment of the Wisdom of Solomon" (JBL 40 [1921] 57–69).

Greek Philosophy in Wisdom: E. Pfleiderer, *Die Philosophie des Heraklitus von Ephesus im Lichte der Mysterienidee,* pp. 289–352. Berlin, 1886. F. C. Porter, "The Pre-existence of the Soul in the Book of Wisdom and in the Rabbinical Writings" (*Old Testament and Semitic Studies in Memory of W. R. Harper,* vol. I, pp. 207–269. Chicago, 1908). P. Heinisch, *Griechische Philosophie und Altes Testament,* vol. II (Bibl. Zeitfragen VII, 3). Münster, 1914. F. Focke, *Die Entstehung der Weisheit Salomos.* (FRLANT 22). Göttingen, 1913 (cf. H. J. Elhorst in NTT 3 [1914] 1–21). S. Lange, "The Wisdom of Solomon and Plato" (JBL 55 [1936] 293–302).

Miscellaneous: N. Peters, "Ein Alphabetischer Psalm in der Weisheit-Salomos" (BZ 14 [1916] 1–14). L. Heinemann, "Die Griechische Quelle der 'Weisheit Salomos'" (Jahresber. des jüd.-theol. Seminar Fränkelscher Stiftung 1920, 135–153). A. Causse, "La propagande juive et l'hellénisme" (RHPR 3 [1923] 397–414. B. Motzo, "L'età e l'autore della Sapienza" (RR 2 [1926] 39–44). D. de Bruyne, "Etude sur le texte latin de la Sagesse" (*Revue Benedictine* 41 [1929] 101–133). G. Kuhn, "Beiträge zur Erklärung der Weisheit" (ZNW 28 [1929] 334–341); "Exegetische und textkritische Anmerkungen zum Buche der Weisheit" (TSK 103 [1931] 445–452). A. Dupont-Sommer, "Les 'impies' du Livre de la Sagesse sont-ils les Épicuriens?" (RHR 111 [1935] 90–110). R. Schütz, *Les idées eschatologiques du Livre de la Sagesse.* Paris, 1935. J. Fichtner, "Die Stellung der Sapientia Salomonis in der Literatur- und Geistesgeschichte ihrer Zeit" (ZNW 36 [1937] 113–32). H. Bückers, *Die Unsterblichkeitslehre des Weisheitsbuches* (AA 13, 11). Münster i. W., 1938. P. W. Skehan, *The Literary Relationship between the Book of Wisdom and the Protocanonical Wisdom Books of the Old Testament.* Washington, D.C., 1938. A. Dupont-Sommer, "Adam père du monde dans la Sagesse de Salomon" (RHR 119 [1939] 182–203).

7. Sirach's Ecclesiasticus

Editions of the Hebrew fragments with translation and commentary: I. Lévi, *L'Ecclésiastique ou la Sagesse de Jésus fils de Sira:* texte original hébreu (Bibliothèque de l'École des Hautes Etudes). 2 vols. Paris, 1898 and 1901. R. Smend, *Die Weisheit des Jesus Sirach.* 2 vols. Berlin, 1906; *Griechisch-syrisch-hebräischer Index zur Weisheit des Jesus Sirach.* Berlin, 1906 (Smend's is the outstanding work on the subject).

Manual editions of the text: N. Peters (1905), with translation and notes (1902); H. L. Strack (1903); I. Lévi (Leiden, 1904). J. Marcus, *The newly Discovered Original Hebrew of Ben Sira.* Philadelphia, 1931; "A Fifth Manuscript of Ben Sira" (JQR 21 [1930–1931] 223–240).

Commentaries: N. Peters (EH, 1913), P. Volz (*Schriften des Alten Testaments in Auswahl,* 2nd ed., 1921), A. Eberharter (HS, 1925), and Roman Catholic commentaries.

Translation: W. O. E. Oesterley in *Translations of Early Documents.* London, 1916.

Miscellaneous: W. Baumgartner, "Die literarischen Gattungen in der Weisheit des Jesus Sirach" (ZAW 34 [1914] 161–198). A. Büchler, "Ben Sira's Conception of Sin and Atonement" (JQR N.S. 13 [1922–1923] 303–335, 461–502; 14 [1923–1924] 53–83). D. de Bruyne, "Le prologue, le titre et la finale de l'Ecclésiastique" (ZAW N.F. 6 [1929] 257–263). G. Kuhn, "Beiträge zur Erklärung des Buches Jesus Sirach" (ZAW N.F. 6 [1929] 289–296; 7 [1930] 100–121). M. H. Segal, "The Evolution of the Hebrew Text of Ben Sira" (JQR N.S. 25 [1934] 91–149). S. Liebermann, "Ben Sira à la lumière de Yeroushalmi" (REJ 191–192 [1934] 50–70).

8. Baruch

Commentaries: F. H. Reusch (Freiburg, 1853); J. J. Kneucker (Leipzig, 1879); J. Knabenbauer (in *Cursus Scripturae Sacrae.* Paris, 1891); L. A. Schneedorfer (in *Kurzgefasster wissenschaftlicher Kommentar.* Vienna, 1903); E. Kalt (in HS, 1932).

Miscellaneous: R. R. Harwell, *The Principal Versions of Baruch* (Yale University Dissertation, 1915). W. Stöderl, *Zur Echtheitsfrage von Baruch 1–3, 8.* Münster, 1922. H. St. John Thackeray, *The Septuagint and Jewish Worship* (Schweich Lectures for 1920), lect. III. London, 1921; 2nd ed., 1923.

9. The Epistle of Jeremy

Commentary: E. Kalt (in HS, 1932).

W. Naumann, *Untersuchungen über den apokryphen Jeremiasbrief* (Beih. ZAW 25). Giessen, 1913. H. St. John Thackeray, *Some Aspects of the Greek Old Testament,* pp. 53–64. London, 1927. E. S. Artrom, *L'origine, la data e gli scopi dell'Epistola di Geremia* (Annuario di Studi Ebraici I [1935] 49–74).

On the Apocryphon of Jeremiah see: A. Mingana, "A New Jeremiah Apocryphon" (*Bulletin of the John Rylands Library* 11 [1927] 329–498). A. Marmorstein, "Die Quellen des neuen Jeremia Apokryphon" (ZNW 27 [1928] 327–88). A. M. Vitti, "Apocryphum Jeremiae nuper detectum" (*Verbum Domini* 8 [1928] 316–20).

10. Additions to Daniel

Commentaries: A. Scholz, *Esther und Susanna,* 1892; *Judith und Bel und der Drache,* 1887; 2nd ed., 1896. Roman Catholic commentaries on Daniel.

N. Brüll in JJGL 3 (1877) 1–69 [on Susanna]; 8 (1887) 22–27 [on Song of the Three Children]; 28–29 [on Bel and the Dragon]. C. Julius, *Die griechischen Danielzusätze* (Biblische Studien VI, 3–4). Freiburg, 1901. G. Jahn, *Das Buch Daniel nach der LXX hergestellt*. Leipzig, 1904. G. Huet, "Daniel et Susanne" (RHR 76 [1917] 129 f.). W. Baumgartner, "Susanna: Die Geschichte einer Legende" (ARW 24 [1926] 259–280; 27 [1929] 187 f.). C. Kuhl, *Die drei Männer im Feuer* (Dan. Kap. 3 und seine Zusätze), u.s.w. (Beih. ZAW 55). Giessen, 1930. I. L[évi?], "L'histoire de Susanne et les vieillards" (REJ 190 [1933] 157–171).

11. Prayer of Manasseh

F. Nau, "Un extrait de la Didascalie: La Prière de Manassé" (*Revue de l'Orient Chrétien* 13 [1908] 134–141); with a critical edition of the Syriac text.

12. I Maccabees

Commentaries: C. F. Keil (Leipzig, 1875); W. Fairweather and J. C. Black (in *Cambridge Bible for Schools*, Cambridge, 1897); J. Knabenbauer (in *Cursus Scripturae Sacrae, Paris*, 1907); C. Gutberlet (AA VIII, 3–4). Münster, 1920; H. Bévenot (in HS, 1931).

Miscellaneous: B. Niese, *Kritik der beiden Makkabäerbücher*. Berlin, 1900, (also *Hermes* 35, 1900). J. Wellhausen, "Über den geschichtlichen Wert des zweiten Makkabäerbuchs im Verhältnis zum ersten" (*Nachrichten der Götting. Gesellsch. der Wissensch.*, phil.-hist. Kl. 1905, 117–163). C. F. Burney, "An Acrostic Poem in praise of Judas Maccabaeus (I. Macc. iii, 1–9)" (JTS 21 [1920] 319–325). B. Risberg, "Textkritische und exegetische Anmerkungen zu den Makkabäerbüchern" (*Beiträge zur Religionswissenschaft*, Stockholm, 2 [1914–1915] 6–32). D. de Bruyne, "Le texte grec des deux premiers livres des Maccabées" (RB 31 [1922] 31–54). H. Bévenot, "Prolegomena to the Maccabees" (BS 81 [1924] 480–492). H. Willrich, *Urkundenfälschung in der hellenistisch-jüdischen Literatur* (FRLANT N. F. 21). Göttingen, 1924. H. W. Ettelson, *The Integrity of I Maccabees*. (Transactions of the Connecticut Academy of Arts and Sciences, vol. 27, pp. 249–384). New Haven, 1925. A. Momigliano, *Prime lines di storia della tradizione maccabaica*. Rome, 1930. L. Salamina, *I Maccabei*. Turin, 1933. H. Bévenot, "The Armenian Text of Maccabees" (JPOS 14 [1934] 268–282). C. C. Torrey, "Three Troublesome Proper Names in First Maccabees" (JBL 53 [1934] 31–33).

13. II Maccabees

Commentaries: see for I Maccabees.

Miscellaneous: H. Willrich, *Juden und Griechen vor der makkabäischen Erheburg*, pp. 64 ff. Göttingen, 1895; *Judaica*, pp. 131–176. Göttingen, 1900. R. Laqueur, *Kritische Untersuchung zum zweiten Makkabäerbuche*. Strassburg, 1906. V. Kappler, *De memoria alterius libri Maccabaeorum* (Dissertation). Göttingen, 1929. D. Bruyne, "Le texte grec du deuxième livre des Maccabées" (RB 39 [1930] 503–519). C. Mugler, "Remarques sur le second livre des Maccabées" (RHPR 11 [1931] 419–424). E. Bickermann, "Ein Jüdisches Festbrief vom Jahre 124 v. Chr. (II Macc. 1:1–9)" (ZNW 32 [1933] 233–254). C. C. Torrey, "The Letters Prefixed to Second Maccabees" (JAOS 60 [1940] 119–50). E. Bikermann (*sic*), "Héliodore au temple de Jérusalem" (Annuaire de l'Institut de Philologie et d'Histoire orientales et slaves 7 [1939–44] 5–40).

14. III Maccabees

I. Abrahams, "The Third Book of Maccabees" (JQR 9 [1897] 39–58). H. Willrich, "Der historische Kern des III. Makkabäerbuches" (*Hermes* 39 [1904] 244–258). S. Tracy, "Aristeas and III Maccabees" (Yale Classical Studies 1 [1928] 239–52). J. Cohen, *Judaica et Aegyptiaca: de Maccabaeorum libro III quaestiones historicae*. Groningen, 1941.

PART III: THE BOOKS OF THE PSEUDEPIGRAPHA

1. Jubilees

Commentary: R. H. Charles, *The Book of Jubilees*. London, 1902.

Miscellaneous: J. A. Montgomery, "An Assyrian Illustration to the Book of Jubilees" (JBL 33 [1914] 157 f.). E. Tisserand, "Fragments syriaques du livre des Jubilées" (RB 30 [1921] 55–86, 206–232). L. Finkelstein, "The Book of Jubilees and the Rabbinic Halaka" (HTR 16 [1923] 39–61; cf. MGWJ 76 [1932] 525–534). A. Büchler, "Studies in the Book of Jubilees" (REJ 82 [1926] 253–274); "Traces des idées et des coutumes hellénistiques dans le Livre des Jubilées" (REJ 89 [1930] 321–48). H. Albeck, *Das Buch der Jubiläen und die Halakah*. Berlin, 1932. R. Uhden, "Die Erdkreisgliederung der Hebräer nach dem Buche der Jubiläen" (ZS 9 [1934] 210–233). S. Klein, "Palästinisches im Jubiläenbuch" (ZDPV 57 [1934] 7–27). S. Zeitlin, "The Book of Jubilees: its Character and Significance" (JQR 30 [1939–40] 1–32). L. Finkelstein, "The Date of the Book of Jubilees" (HTR 36 [1934] 19–24). H. H. Rowley and S. Zeitlin, "Criteria for the Dating of Jubilees" (JQR 36 [1945–46] 183–190).

2. The Letter of Aristeas

H. St. John Thackeray, *The Letter of Aristeas*, translated, etc. London, 1917; cf. his edition of the Greek text in H. B. Swete's *Introduction to the Old Testament in Greek*. Cambridge University Press, 1900; 2nd ed., 1902. R. Tramontano, *Il più antico saggio d'esegesi biblica allegoristica* (Aristea, §§128–171), *Scuola Cattolica* di Milano, Quaderno di Settembre 1919; *La lettera di Aristea a Filocrate*. Naples, 1931. J. Herrmann and F. Baumgärtel, *Beiträge zur Entstehungsgeschichte der Septuaginta* (BWAT 30), pp. 39–80. Stuttgart, 1923. E. J. Fébrier, *La date, la composition et les sources de la Lettre d'Aristée*. Paris, 1925. O. Michel, "Was spricht der Aristeasbrief über Gott?" (TSK 102 [1930] 302–6). E. Bickermann, "Zur Datierung des Pseudo-Aristeas" (ZNW 29 [1930] 280–298). G. Stählin, "Josephus und der Aristeasbrief" (TSK 102 [1930] 324–331). A. Momigliano "Per la data e la caratteristica della lettera di Aristea" (Aegyptus 12 [1932] 161–172). H. G. Meecham, *The Letter of Aristeas: A Linguistic Study with Special Reference to the Greek Bible*. Manchester, 1935.

3. The Books of Adam and Eve

M. R. James, *The Lost Apocrypha of the Old Testament*, pp. 1–8. London, 1920. J. H. Mozley, "The *Vita Adae*" (JTS 30 [1929] 121–149).

4. The Martyrdom of Isaiah

R. H. Charles, *The Ascension of Isaiah*. London, 1900. I. Flemming and H. Duensing, in E. Hennecke, *Neutestamentliche Apokryphen*, 2nd ed., pp. 303–314. Tübingen, 1924. V. Burch, "The Literary Unity of the *Ascensio Isaiae*"

(JTS 20 [1919] 17–23); "Material for the Interpretation of the *Ascensio Isaiae*" (JTS 21 [1920] 249–265). K. Galling, "Jesaja-Adonis" (OLZ 33 [1930] 98–102).

5. The Book of Enoch (Ethiopic Enoch)

R. H. Charles, *The Ethiopic Version of the Book of Enoch*, etc. Oxford, 1906. F. C. Burkitt, *Jewish and Christian Apocalypses*. London, 1914. G. Kuhn, "Beiträge zur Erklärung des Buches Henoch" (ZAW 39 [1921] 240–275). N. Messel, *Der Menschensohn in den Bilderreden des Henoch* (Beih. ZAW 35). Giessen, 1922. A. C. Welch, "A Zealot Prophet" (*Exp.* 25 [1923] 273–287). G. H. Dix, "The Enochic Pentateuch" (JTS 27 [1925] 29–42). N. Schmidt, "The Apocalypse of Noah and the Parables of Enoch" (*Oriental Studies for Paul Haupt*, pp. 111–123. Baltimore, 1926). C. Kaplan, "Angels in the Book of Enoch" (ATR 12 [1930] 423–437); "The Pharisaic Character and the Date of the Book of Enoch" (*ibid.*, pp. 531–537); "The Flood in the Book of Enoch and Rabbinics" (JSOR 15 [1931] 22–24); "Versions and Readings in the Book of Enoch" (AJSL 50 [1934] 171–177). A. Vitti, "Ultime critiche su Enoc etiopico" (Bibl. 12 [1931] 316–25). F. Stier, "Zur Komposition and Literaturkritik der Bilderreden des äthiopischen Henoch" (in R. Paret [ed.], *Orientalische Studien . . . Enno Littmann überreicht*, pp. 76–88. Leiden, 1935). C. Bonner, *The Last Chapters of Enoch in Greek* (Studies and Documents, 8). London, 1937. H. L. Jensen, *Die Henochgestalt: eine vergleichende religionsgeschichtliche Untersuchung*. Oslo, 1939. F. Zimmermann, "The Bilingual Character of I Enoch" (JBL 60 [1941] 159–72). C. C. Torrey, "Notes on the Greek Text of Enoch" (JAOS 62 [1942] 52–60). G. Zuntz, "Notes on the Greek Enoch" (JBL 61 [1942] 193–204); "The Greek Text of Enoch 102:1–3" (JBL 63 [1944] 53 f.).

6. The Book of the Secrets of Enoch (Slavonic Enoch)

G. N. Bonwetsch, *Die Bücher der Geheimnisse Henochs*. Das sogenannte slavische Henochbuch (Texte und Untersuchungen 44, 2). Leipzig, 1922. J. K. Frotheringham, "The Date and Place of Writing of the Slavonic Enoch" (JTS 20 [1919] 252); "The Easter Calendar and the Slavonic Enoch" (JTS 23 [1921] 49–56). K. Lake, "The Date of the Slavonic Enoch" (HTR 16 [1923] 397 f.).

7. The Testaments of the XII Patriarchs

W. Bousset, "Die Testamente der 12 Patriarchen" (ZNW 1 [1900] 141–175). J. W. Hunkin, "The Testaments of the Twelve Patriarchs" (JTS 16 [1915] 80–97). M. R. James, "The Venice Extracts from the Testaments of the Twelve Patriarchs" (JTS 28 [1926–27] 337–348). R. Eppel, *Le piétisme dans les Testaments des Douze Patriarches*. Paris, 1930. P. A. Munich, "The Spirits in the Testaments of the Twelve Patriarchs" (*Acta Orientalia* 13 [1935] 257–263).

8. The Sibylline Oracles

I. Geffcken, *Komposition und Entstehungszeit der Oracula Sibyllina* (Texte und Untersuchungen 23, 1). Leipzig, 1902; also in E. Hennecke, *Neutestamentliche Apokryphen*, 2nd ed., pp. 399–422. H. N. Bate, *The Sibylline Oracles, Books iii–v* (Translations of Early Documents). London, 1918. A. Pincherle, *Gli oracoli sibillini giudaici*. Rome, 1922. H. H. Rowley, "The Interpretation and Date of Sibylline Oracles III, 388–400" (ZNW N.F. 3 [1922] 324–27). F. X. Kugler, *Sibyllinischer Sternkampf und Phaeton u.s.w.*, Münster, 1927.

G. Crönert, "Oraculorum sibyllinorum fragmentum" (Symbolae Osloenses 5 [1927] 38–40; 6 [1928] 57–9). A. Kurfess, "Horaz und Vergil und die jüdische Sibylle" (Pastor Bonus 45 [1934] 414–23); "Das Mahngedicht des sogenannten Phokylides im 2ten Buch der Oracula Sibyllina" (ZNW 38 [1939] 171–81); "Oracula Sibyllina" (ZNW 40 [1941] 151–165). H. Youtie, "Sambathis" (HTR 37 [1944] 209–18).

9. The Assumption of Moses

Text: C. Clemen, Die Himmelfahrt des Mose (Kleine Texte, 10). Leipzig, 1904.

G. Hölscher, "Über die Entstehungszeit der Himmelfahrt Moses" (ZNW 17 [1916] 108–27; 149–58). G. Kuhn, "Zur Assumptio Mosis" (ZAW 43 [1925] 124–29). C. C. Torrey, " 'Taxo' in the Assumption of Moses" (JBL 62 [1943] 1–8). H. H. Rowley, "The Figure of 'Taxo' in the Assumption of Moses" (JBL 64 [1945] 141–43); cf. C. C. Torrey, ibid., pp. 395–97.

10. The Syriac Apocalypse of Baruch

B. Violet, Die Apocalypsen des Ezra und des Baruch in deutscher Gestalt. Leipzig, 1924. X. Vallisolato, "Christologia in Apocalipsi Baruch syriaca" (Verbum Domini 11 [1931] 212–21). L. Gry, "La date de la fin des temps selon les révélations du Pseudo-Philon et de Baruch" (RB 48 [1939] 337–56).

11. The Greek Apocalypse of Baruch

Greek text, with English translation of the Slavic text: M. R. James, Apocrypha anecdota (Texts and Studies V, 1). Cambridge, 1897. W. Lüdtke, "Beiträge zu slavischen apokryphen" (ZAW 31 [1911] 219–222).

12. The Psalms of Solomon

Greek text: H. B. Swete, The Old Testament in Greek, 2nd ed., vol. III, pp. 765–787. Cambridge, 1899; O. von Gebhart, Psalmoi Solomontos (Texte und Untersuchungen 13, 2). Leipzig, 1895. Syriac text: Rendel Harris and A. Mingana, The Odes and Psalms of Solomon. 2 vols. Manchester, 1916 and 1920.

J. Wellhausen, Die Pharisäer und die Sadduzäer. Eine Untersuchung zur inneren jüdischen Geschichte, 1871; 2nd ed., Hanover, 1924. H. E. Ryle and M. R. James, The Psalms of the Pharisees. Cambridge, 1891. W. Frankenberg, Die Datierung der Psalmen Salomos (Beih. ZAW 1). Giessen, 1896. F. Dölger, "Zum 2ten Salomonischen Psalm" (Antike und Christentum 1 [1929] 291–94). K. Kuhn, "Die älteste Textgestalt der Psalmen Salomos" (BWANT). Stuttgart, 1937. J. Begrich, "Der Text der Psalmen Salomos" (ZNW 38 [1939] 131–64).

13. IV Maccabees

C. C. Torrey, in Encyclopaedia Biblica, vol. III, cols. 2882–2886. London, 1902. H. Winckler, in Altorientalische Forschungen III, 1, pp. 79–89. Leipzig, 1902. E. Norden, Die Antike Kunstprosa. 3rd ed., Leipzig, 1915. Rendel Harris, "Some Notes on IV Maccabees" (ET 32 [1920–1921] 183–185). H. Dörrie, Passio SS. Machabaeorum: die antike lateinische Übersetzung des IV Makkabäerbuches (Abhandlungen der Gesellschaft der Wissenschaften zu Göttingen, 22). Göttingen, 1938. A. Dupont-Sommer, Le quatrième livre des Maccabés. Paris, 1939.

14. The Story of Ahikar

Text and Translation: R. H. Charles, *Pseudepigrapha*, pp. 715–784. F. C. Conybeare, Rendel Harris, and Agnes S. Lewis, *The Story of Ahikar*. 2nd ed., Cambridge, 1913. A. Cowley, *Aramaic Papyri of the Fifth Century B.C.*, pp. 204–248. Oxford, 1923.

Investigations: F. Nau, *Histoire et sagesse d'Ahikar l'Assyrien*. Paris, 1909. B. Meissner, *Das Märchen vom weisen Achiqar*. Leipzig, 1917.

15. Documents of Jewish Sectaries at Damascus

S. Schechter, *Documents of Jewish Sectaries*, Vol. I: *Fragments of a Zadokite Work*, Edited from Hebrew Manuscripts in the Cairo Genizah Collection now in the Possession of the University Library, Cambridge, and Provided with an English Translation, Introduction, and Notes. Cambridge University Press, 1910. J. Juster, *Les Juifs dans l'empire romain*, vol. 1, pp. 26–31 (with full bibliography). Paris, 1914. R. H. Charles, *Pseudepigrapha*, pp. 785–834. W. Staerk, *Die jüdische Gemeinde des Neuen Bundes in Damaskus* (Beiträge zur Förderung Christlicher Theologie 27, 3). Gütersloh, 1922. L. Ginzberg, *Eine unbekannte jüdische Sekte*. New York, 1922. H. Preisker, "Zum Streit um die Geniza-Texte der jüdischen Gemeinde des Neuen Bundes in Damaskus" (TSK 98–99 [1926] 295–318). G. F. Moore, *Judaism*, pp. 200–204. Harvard University Press, 1927. G. Hölscher, "Zur Frage nach Alter und Herkunft der sogenannten Damaskusschrift" (ZNW 28 [1929] 21–46). F. Hvidberg, "Die 390 Jahre der sogenannten Damaskusschrift" (ZAW N.F. 10 [1933] 309–311). L. Rost, *Die Damaskusschrift* (H. Lietzmann, Kleine Texte, 167). Berlin, 1933. R. Eisler, "The Sadoqite Book of the New Covenant: its Date and Origin" (B. Schindler and A. Marmorstein, Editors, *Orient and Occident, in Honor of Dr. M. Gaster's 80th Birthday*, pp. 110–43. London, 1936). Bo Reicke, *The Jewish "Damascus Documents" and the New Testament* (Symbolae Biblicae Upsalienses, 6). Supplement to *Svensk Exegetisk Årsbok* 11. Uppsala, 1946.

INDEX OF AUTHORS

Abel, F. M., 11, 479
Abydenus, 106
Achelis, H., 457
Adams, J., 140
Addison, Joseph, 389
Adeus of Mytilene, 114
Aenesidemus of Knossos, 121
Aeschylus, 102, 129, 370
Aesop, 108
Africanus, Julius, 107, 203, 442, 449, 453
Agatharchides of Cnidos, 209
Albright, W. F., 18 f.
Alcaeus, 115
Alexander of Aphrodisias, 118, 134
Alexander of Pleuron, 116
Allatius, Leo, 440
Ambrose of Milan, 143, 300
Ammonius Saccas, 146
Amometus, 110
Anaxarchus, 121
André, L. E. T., 255, 259, 274 f., 292,
  297 ff., 308, 412, 415, 417, 419, 422 f.,
  429, 432, 442 f., 446 f., 450, 461 f.,
  484, 490, 492, 507 ff., 515 f.
Andrews, H. T., 224
Andronicus of Rhodes, 118
Antagoras of Rhodes, 102
Antigonus of Carystus, 107, 114 f.
Antimachus of Colophon, 115
Antiochus of Ashkelon, 118
Antipatros (or Antipater) of Sidon, 103
Antipatros (or Antipater) of Tarsus, 122
Antiphanes of Berge, 110
Antisthenes of Athens, 120
Antonius Diogenes, 110
Apion Pleistonikes of Alexandria, 176,
  198 f.
Apollodorus of Athens, 104, 107
Apollonius Molon, 432
Apollonius of Perga, 112 f.
Apollonius of Rhodes, 102
Apollonius of Tyana, 145
Apollos, 327
Appian, 501
Aptowitzer, V., 343
Apuleius, 154, 157 f., 160
Aquilas, 442
Aquinas, Thomas, 300
Aratus of Soli, 104, 115, 215

Aratus of Sykyon, 107
Arcesilaus of Pitane, 117
Archemachus the Euboean, 154
Archilochus of Paros, 133
Archimedes of Syracuse, 112 f.
Aristarchus of Samos, 112
Aristarchus of Samothrace, 115
Aristeas of Alexandria, 70, 202
Aristides, P. Aelius, 155
Aristippus of Cyrene, 119
Aristobulus of Cassandreia, 105, 212
Aristocles, 121
Ariston of Ceos, 118
Ariston of Chios, 122
Aristophanes, 100, 115, 129, 131 ff.
Aristophanes of Byzantium, 115
Aristotle, 95, 98 f., 102, 113 ff., 117 ff.,
  123, 130, 139 f., 142, 192
Aristoxenos of Tarentum, 115, 118
Arnim, H. von, 117, 122, 140
Arnold, W. R., 115, 171
Arrian, Flavius, of Nicomedia, 105, 122,
  144
Artemidorus of Ephesus, 111
Asclepiades of Bithynia, 103, 114
Asclepiades of Samos, 103
Athanasius, 354
Athenaeus, 10, 252
Athenodorus of Tarsus, 153
Augustine of Hippo, Saint, 135, 143, 146,
  155, 227, 296, 320
Ausfeld, A., 108

Bacher, N., 382
Bailey, T. H., 280
Ball, C. J., 292, 294, 296, 298, 430, 442 f.,
  449, 451 f., 462
Bardenweher, O., 457
Barlow, C. L., 143
Barnabas, 130
Barnes, W. E., 57
Barton, G. A., 490
Bate, H. N., 226
Baudissin, W. W. von, 159, 428, 456
Bauer, B., 144
Bauer, G. L., 292
Bauer, W., 139, 145
Baumgarten, F., 93

Baumgartner, W., 400, 402 f., 405 f., 452 ff.
Bayer, E., 239, 241, 243, 251, 255
Becker, C. H., 108
Belkin, S., 180
Bell, H. I., 93, 167, 173 ff.
Bellarmine, R. F. R., 295, 412
Beloch, K. J., 93, 96, 100, 129, 173, 480
Benfrey, Th., 269 f.
Bennett, N. H., 445 ff.
Benveniste, E., 162
Benwitch, 490
Berendts, A., 210
Berger, H., 110
Berossus, 106, 199
Bertheau, E., 250
Bertheau, Karl, 508 (where *Berthe* should be read "Bertheau")
Bertholdt, L., 292, 322, 412, 442, 452
Bertholet, A., 57, 128, 188, 244, 322, 329, 350, 373, 450
Bevan, A. A., 419, 462 (where *Bevans* should be read "Bevan")
Bevan, E. R., 93
Bévenot, H. G., 272, 462, 479 ff., 507 ff., 516
Bianchini, J., 440
Bickermann, E. (also spelled Bikerman, Bickerman), 9 ff., 13, 310 f., 475 ff., 480 f., 487 ff., 491, 493, 496, 507 f., 515 f., 518
Billerbeck, P., 125, 168, 194, 339, 345, 384
Biolek, A., 291
Bion of Borysthenes, 143
Bissell, E. C., 237
Bixler, J. S., 137
Blakeney, E. H., 321
Bloch, H., 209
Bludau, A., 167, 439 f., 442, 446
Boccaccio, Giovanni, 108
Boeckh, A. 155
Böhmer, 484
Boethius, 146
Bois, H. 329
Boissier, G., 128, 148
Boll, F., 134
Bonaiuti, E., 137
Bonhöffer, A., 117, 122, 144
Bonner, C., 77
Borries, Bodo de, 346
Botti, G., 155
Bouché-Leclercq, A., 93, 134
Bouriant, M., 77
Bousset, W., 66, 187 f., 253, 273
Box, G. H., 86, 398

Breasted, J. H., 151, 153
Breccia, E., 155
Bréhier, E., 126, 145, 206, 212, 214, 334
Bretschneider, C. G., 320, 322
Brooke, A. E., 258, 307
Brown, T. S., 109, 347
Brüll, N., 451 f.
Brunengo, 293, 295
Brunner, G., 296
Bruston, C., 507
Bruyne, D. de, 319, 497, 516
Büchler, A., 372, 398, 490, 509
Budge, E. A. W., 108
Bugati, C., 441
Burkitt, F. C., 444
Burney, C. F., 487
Burrows, M., 59
Bury, J. B., 93
Buttenwieser, M., 45

Caesar, Julius, 107
Callimachus of Cyrene, 102 ff., 116
Callippus, 112
Callisthenes, 105
Callixenus of Rhodes, 114
Calvin, J., 125
Campbell, Th., 280
Cappellus, L., 292
Carcopino, J., 148
Carneades of Cyrene, 118, 135
Cary, M., 93
Case, S. J., 148
Cassius, Dio, 45, 178
Castor of Rhodes, 107
Catullus, 150
Celsus, A. C., 113, 226
Ceriani, A. M., 72, 79, 417, 463
Chaeremon, 198 f.
Chamaeleon of Heraclea Pontica, 115, 118
Champion, S. G., 384
Chares of Mytilene, 105
Charles, R. H., 49, 57 f., 66, 73, 76 f., 79, 86 f., 89 f., 109, 132, 218, 268, 304, 406, 441, 449
Cheyne, T. K., 373, 487
Christ, W. von, 101
Christensen, A., 252
Chrysippus of Soli, 116, 122, 124 f.
Ciasca, A., 259
Cicero, M. T., 99, 104 f., 115 f., 122, 126, 134 ff., 139, 142 f., 191, 193, 217, 269, 346, 349
Clavijo, Ruy Gonzales de, 456
Clay, A. T., 69
Cleanthes of Assos, 112, 121, 124, 140
Clearchus of Soli, 107, 118, 190, 192, 350

Clemen, C., 148, 153
Clement of Alexandria, 135, 198, 200, 211, 213, 226, 256, 275, 291, 300, 319
Clement of Rome, 291, 442 f.
Cleodemus (or Malchus), 202
Cleon of Syracuse, 111
Clinton, H. F., 480 f.
Clitarchus, 105
Clitomachus, 118
Cohn, L., 221
Colson, F. H., 221
Commodianus, 135, 443
Condamin, A., 58, 423
Confucius, 129
Connolly, R. H., 457
Conon of Samos, 112 f.
Conybeare, F. C., 268
Cook, A. B., 128
Cook, S. A., 251
Copernicus, N., 112
Cornelius a Lapide, 296
Cornely, R., 296, 322
Cornill, C. H., 419, 423
Cosquin, E., 270
Couard, L., 132, 337, 373
Cowley, A. E., 170, 172, 252, 268, 292, 294, 299 ff., 398 f.
Cozza-Luzi, J., 259, 440
Crantor, 117
Crates of Athens, 117
Crates of Thebes, 117, 120 f.
Creed, M. N., 210
Critolaus of Phaselis, 118
Ctesibius of Alexandria, 113
Cumont, F., 133 ff., 148, 161, 193
Curtiss, S. J., 462, 484
Cyprian, Th. C., of Carthage, 256, 319, 443, 515

Dähne, A. F., 326
Dalman, G., 484
Damascius, 146
Danko, 296
Dante Alighieri, 110, 114, 125, 133
Darembourg, 135
Daubney, W. H., 443, 445, 447, 449, 456
Davies, W., 456
Decharme, P., 212, 346
Deissmann, A., 147, 167
Deissner, K., 148
Delattre, 293, 295
Delitzsch, Franz, 449, 462
Delitzsch, Friedrich, 420
Demetrius, Jewish historian, 200
Democritus of Abdera, 119, 121
Derwacter, F. M., 188

Destinon, J. von, 209, 490
De Wette, W. M. L., 412, 508
Dibelius, M., 210
Dicaearchus, 115, 118
Dietrich, A., 110, 128, 131, 133, 161
Diller, A., 111
Dillmann, A., 73, 259, 417
Diodorus Cronus, 121
Diodorus Siculus, 10, 105 f., 138, 152 f., 192, 294, 517
Diogenes Laërtius, 100, 107, 115 f., 122
Diogenes of Seleucia, 122, 134
Diogenes of Sinope, 117, 120, 142
Diogenes the Bematist, 95
Dionysius of Halicarnassus, 107
Dionysius of Heracleia, 122
Dionysius Thrax, 116
Dios (or Dius), 106, 199
Dodd, C. H., 182 f.
Dölger, F. J., 147
Döller, J., 482
Dorotheus of Tyre, 66
Dositheus of Pelusium, 112
Dow, S., 153
Drachmann, A. B., 346
Driver, S. R., 399
Droysen, J. G., 93
Drummond, J., 206, 212, 214
Drüner, H., 489 f.
Dübner, 211
Duris of Samos, 114, 118
Duschak, M., 450
Dyroff, A., 122

Edersheim, A., 400
Eichhorn, J. G., 238, 321, 326, 449 f., 508
Eisler, R., 210
Eissfeldt, O., 76, 130, 160, 243, 270, 274, 280, 292, 297, 308, 413, 419, 430, 445, 449, 490, 508
Eliezer (or Eleazar), Rabbi, 190
Elter, 214
Empedocles, 139
Engelbreth, W. F., 320, 322
Englander, H., 366
Ennius, 138
Enslin, M. S., 35, 167, 330
Ephippus, 105
Epictetus of Hierapolis, 99, 118, 122, 126 f., 140 f., 144
Epicurus of Samos, 117, 119, 136, 140
Epiphanius, 42, 66
Erasistratus of Iulis, 114
Eratosthenes of Cyrene, 99, 107, 111, 116

Erbt, W., 268, 270, 276
Erman, A., 151, 369, 388
Ettelson, H. W., 483 f., 486, 488 ff., 498
Euclid, 112
Euclides of Megara, 120
Eudemus, 114, 118
Eudoxus of Cnidus, 112
Euhemerus, 109, 120, 130, 138, 347 f.
Euphorion, 103
Eupolemos, 440
Euripides, 102, 129, 370 f.
Eusebius of Caesarea, 42, 56 f., 70, 107, 121, 198, 200 f., 203, 206 f., 210 f., 215, 223, 365, 483
Ewald, G. H. A. (or H.) 15, 238, 250, 292, 310, 412, 417, 452, 477, 479 f., 508

Fabricius, J. A., 458
Fagius, P., 259
Fairweather, 490
Farnell, L. R., 128
Farrar, F. W., 321, 328, 332
Feldmann, F., 318, 320, 324, 328
Ferguson, W. S., 93
Fichtner, J., 64, 320, 329, 332, 373, 377
Fiddles, E., 348
Fiebig, P., 270
Field, F., 439
Figulla, H. H., 161
Filson, F. V., 13
Finkelstein, L., 69
Firmicius Maternus, 135
Flemming, J., 457
Focke, F., 320, 322 f., 325, 327, 329, 332, 334, 339 f.
Frankel, Z., 451 f.
Frazer, J. G., 148, 159
French, J. M., 101
Freudenthal, J., 198, 212
Friedländer, L., 148
Friedländer, M., 183, 328
Fries, K., 271
Fritzsche, O. F., 272, 292, 297, 299, 300, 302, 307 f., 353, 368, 412 f., 417, 419 f., 429, 433, 440, 442, 452
Fürst, J., 445
Fuchs, C., 72
Fuchs, L., 167
Fuller, J. M., 272, 308

Gertringen, F. H. von, 155
Gall, A. von, 253
Gardiner, A. H., 151
Gärtner, E., 321 f., 329, 332, 339
Gasser, J. K., 365, 400 f.

Gaster, M., 259, 292 (where Galster should be read "Gaster")
Gavin, F., 188
Geffcken, J., 128, 147, 212, 226, 325, 346 f.
Geiger, A., 451, 493, 507
Gelzer, H., 107
Geminus, 112
Gerardus, 296
Gercke, A., 128
Gerould, G. H., 269 ff.
Gfrörer, A. F., 326
Gibert, M., 480 f.
Gieseler, 73
Gilbert, G. H., 144
Ginsberg, H. L., 59, 68, 90, 403 f.
Ginzberg, L., 57 f., 267, 269, 271, 282, 304, 317, 345, 398, 452, 454, 456
Ginzel, F. K., 480
Glover, T. R., 148
Goettsberger, J., 274, 291, 298, 309, 412, 429, 444, 508
Gonzenbach, Laura, 270
Goodenough, E. R., 145, 148, 167, 206, 222, 330
Goodart, H. L., 206
Goodrick, A. T. S., 322, 328
Goodspeed, E. J., 272, 275, 311, 328, 348, 441, 445, 449
Gordon, C. H., 131, 159
Gorgias, 120
Gorionides, see Joseph son of Gorion in the Index of Subjects
Graetz, H., 272, 274, 292, 327, 416, 507
Graillot, H., 148
Granius Licinianus, 518
Greene, W. C., 134
Greenough, C. N., 101
Gregg, J. A. F. D., 308, 321
Grenfell, B. P., 73, 155
Gressmann, H., 112, 134, 253, 373
Grimm, C. L. W., 122, 209, 218, 319 f., 323 f., 326 f., 328, 332, 334, 339 f., 461, 476, 479 f., 482, 484 f., 488 f., 507 ff., 516, 518, 520
Groome, F. H., 270
Grotius, H., 418, 462, 479
Grünebaum, G. E. von, 108 (where Grünebaum should be read)
Gruppe, O., 128, 155, 157
Guignebert, Ch., 167
Gumpach, J. von, 296, 480
Gunkel, H., 269, 453, 456
Gutberlet, C., 274, 321
Guthe, H., 167
Gwynn, J., 249

Haarhoff, T. J., 93
Hahn, H. A., 440
Hall, I. H., 66
Harnack, A., 128, 188
Harris, J. Rendel, 258, 268
Harris, Z. S., 403
Harrison, Jane E., 132
Hart, J. H. A., 354, 364
Harvey, W., 114
Harwell, R. R., 419
Hastings, J., 53, 135
Hatch, W. H. P., 384
Hauck, A., 400, 412
Haupt, P., 271, 308
Haxthausen, A. von, 270
Heath, T., 112
Hecataeus of Abdera, 106, 110, 138 f., 192
Hedylus of Athens, 103
Hegesios, 119
Hegesis, 105
Heidel, A., 456
Heinemann, I., 143, 145, 174, 191, 329, 343
Heinisch, P., 320, 326 ff., 332, 339, 412, 420
Hennecke, E., 73, 133, 457
Hepding, H., 149
Heracleides Ponticus, 154
Heracleides of Tarentum, 114 f.
Heraclitus of Ephesus, 124, 129, 226
Herillus of Chalcedon, 122
Herkenne, H., 507
Hermesianax, 103
Herodas, 104
Herodotus, 130, 153 f., 163, 169, 172, 199, 252, 275, 285, 293 f., 347, 349, 370, 431, 455
Hierophilus of Chalcedon, 114
Hertz, W., 269
Hertzfeld, L., 292, 480 f., 507
Hesiod, 128, 215
Hesychius, 304
Heuten, G., 153
Hieronimus of Rhodes, 115, 118
Highet, G., 128
Hillel, 383
Hipparchus of Nicea, 112 f.
Hippe, M., 269, 271
Hippocrates, 113
Hippolytus, 319, 443, 450
Hitzig, F., 274, 416 f., 422
Hoberg, G., 309, 412
Hoffmann, G., 269
Holmes, S., 321 f., 328
Hölscher, G., 207, 209, 244, 490, 517

Holzmann, J., 318
Homer, 102, 115, 128, 138, 215, 228, 271
Hopfner, Th., 153
Horace (Q. Horatius Flaccus), 120, 143, 184, 217, 330, 455
Horowitz, J., 463
Houbigant, C. F., 295, 320 f.
Howorth, Sir Henry, 243, 248 ff., 445, 458
Huet, G., 270 f., 453
Hughes, H. M., 373
Hultsch, 111
Hunt, A. S., 73, 155, 260
Hyde, W. W., 15, 147 f.

Iamblichus of Chalkis, 146
Ideler, C. L., 480
Ignatius of Antioch, 220
Iken, C., 462
Ilgen, K. P., 276
Irenaeus of Lyons, 443
Isocrates, 95

Jackson, F. J. F., 55, 59, 93, 167
Jacob, B., 310 f.
Jacobs, I. R., 159
Jacobs, V. R., 159
Jacoby, F., 105, 202
Jaeger, W., 128
Jahn, G., 243, 308, 446
Jahn, J., 291, 412, 450
Jakoby, A., 148
James, M. R., 70 ff., 133, 422
Jensen, P., 163, 456
Jerome, Saint, 9, 143, 164, 249, 259, 271 f., 280, 291 f., 298, 300, 304 ff., 319 ff., 365, 439, 442, 444, 455, 483
Johnson, Sh. E., 86
Jones, H. S., 167
Josephus, Flavius, 8, 10, 13, 19-24, 26-30, 33-44, 53-56, 59, 62, 69, 98, 107, 157, 167, 169, 173, 175-178, 180 f., 183, 185 f., 190, 194 f., 198, 200 ff., 212 f., 226, 241 f., 244, 249, 256, 280, 295, 304, 309, 311, 313, 317, 328, 334, 349, 365 f., 372, 411, 413 f., 416, 429, 442, 461, 475, 480 f., 483, 491, 511, 516 f.
Jouget, P., 93
Joüon, P., 258, 484
Julius Africanus, see Africanus
Julius, C., 442 f.
Juster, J., 45, 57, 167, 175 f., 178 f., 188 f., 191 f., 194 ff., 198, 210, 212
Justin Martyr, 163-165, 189, 213, 226, 347, 442 f.
Justinus, Junianus, 106

Juvenal, 44, 144, 156, 158, 184, 191, 195, 349

Kabisch, R., 86
Kaerst, J., 93, 348
Kalt, E., 412, 414 f., 429
Kamphausen, A., 452, 507
Kant, Immanuel, 256
Kappler, W., 497
Kaulen, F., 274, 296, 309
Kautzsch, E., 66, 72, 88, 244, 441, 487, 490
Kay, D. M., 449, 451
Keil, C. F., 237, 477
Kennard, J. S., Jr., 35, 210
Kennedy, H. A. A., 148
Kephalas, Constantine, 103
Kepler, J., 112
Kerényi, K., 108
Kern, O., 130, 132
Kidenas, see Kidinnu
Kidinnu of Sippar, 113
King, G. B., 384
Kittel, G., 148
Kittel, R., 15
Klauser, Th., 147
Klausner, J., 148, 167, 181, 183, 187 f., 189, 194, 196, 212
Klein, G., 295 f.
Klostermann, E., 35
Knabenbauer, J., 479
Kneucker, J. J., 409, 412 f., 415 ff.
Köberle, J., 373
Kohler, K., 70, 322
Köhler, R., 269 f.
Kohut, A., 275
Kolbe, W., 475, 477 ff., 480 f., 507 ff.
König, E., 237, 271
Korn, H. J., 335
Kornemann, E., 348
Kosters, N. H., 6, 507
Kramer, S. N., 159, 456
Krappe, A. H., 210
Krauss, S., 183, 226 (where Krauss should be read)
Kroll, W., 108, 174
Krüger, P., 198
Kuenen, A., 6, 328
Kugler, F. X., 476, 478, 480 ff., 507
Kuhn, G., 318, 352, 406
Kuiper, K., 144

Lactantius, 142, 226 f., 348
Lagarde, P. de, 259, 307, 449, 457
Lagrange, M. J., 58, 328, 339
Lake, K., 55, 59, 93, 167

Lakydes of Cyrene, 118
Lancaster, H. C. O., 226
Landersdorfer, S., 456
Langdon, S., 455
Lange, Stella, 329, 336
Langen, J., 308
Lao-tse, 129
La Piana, G., 148, 167, 180
Laqueur, R., 93, 202, 477, 479 f., 507, 509
Lattey, C., 79
Laurence, R., 73
Lehman, E., 128
Leipoldt, 148
Leisegang, H., 221
Lemm, O. von, 108
Lenglet-Dufresnoy, 296
Lenormant, F., 291
Leonidas of Tarentum, 103
Le Strange, Guy, 456
Lévi, I., 399, 515
Lévy, I., 188, 261, 268, 272
Lewis, Agnes S., 268
Lewy, J., 292
Leyen, F. von der, 269
Lieberman, S., 183, 399
Lietzmann, H., 57, 147, 167, 515
Liljeblad, S., 269 f.
Lincke, L., 322
Linford, I. M., 132
Linschmann, Th., 270
Livy, T., 97
Lobeck, C. A., 130
Löhr, M., 260, 269, 272, 275, 440 f.
Loisy, A. F., 137
Longinus, D. C., 146
Lovagnini, B., 109
Lucian of Samosata, 110, 132, 159 f., 266
Luckenbill, D. D., 161, 166
Lucretius, Carus, 119, 137, 140, 149
Luther, H., 210
Luther, Martin, 292, 312, 326, 516
Lycon of Troas, 113, 118
Lycophron of Rhegium, 103, 116
Lycos of Rhegium, 111
Lysimachus, 198 f.

Macalister, R. A. S., 18
Macchioro, V., 130
Macdonald, D. B., 329, 344
Macrobius, 32, 154
Magistris, S. de (des Maîstres), 440
Magoun, F. P., Jr., 108
Mahler, E., 480 f.
Mai, Angelo, 70
Malalas, John, 517

Manetho, 106, 154, 158, 198 f.
Manzoni, A., 32
Marcus Aurelius Antoninus, 117, 122,
  126 f., 140 f.
Marcus, R., 48, 57, 183, 191, 206, 279 f.,
  310, 335, 339, 398, 531
Margoliouth, S., 319 ff.
Marmorstein, A., 58, 382
Marquart, J., 243, 250
Marshall, J. T., 267, 274, 413, 419, 422,
  443, 445, 559, 451 f., 456
Marx, A., 319
Massebieau, L., 207
Maury, L. F. A., 128
Maynard, J. A., 253
McCormack, T. J., 161
McCown, C. C., 189
McLean, N., 307
Megasthenes, 106, 138
Meissner, B., 6, 172, 252, 268
Meister, R., 332
Meleager, 103
Menander, 100, 104, 106
Menippus of Gadara, 120
Meno, 114
Merguet, V., 372
Merx, A., 304
Meyer, E., 47, 57, 93, 160, 477 ff., 480,
  489, 507, 509
Meyer, P., 108
Michaelis, J. D., 440, 450
Migne, 271, 439
Mills, L. H., 253
Milne, H. J., M., 103
Milton, John, 518
Minucius Felix, 347 f.
Mittelhaus, K., 174
Mnaseas, 198
Modona, A. N., 167
Moffatt, J., 507 ff.
Molière, 100
Molon, Apollonius, 198
Momigliano, A., 492
Montfaucon, 295
Montgomery, J. A., 69, 249, 403, 439 ff.,
  441, 443, 446
Moore, G. F., 11, 55, 60, 64, 148, 186,
  188 f., 194 ff., 212, 254, 280, 312, 335,
  339, 344, 368 ff., 373, 381 f., 384,
  393 f., 396, 411, 419
Moret, A., 153
Motzo, B. R., 167, 307
Moulton, J. H., 271, 275
Moulton, R. G., 322
Moulton, W. J., 239, 248
Movers, C. F., 291, 296

Mowinckel, S., 233
Müller, C., 70, 105, 138 f., 153, 192, 198,
  201 f., 209, 211
Müller, I. von, 101
Müller, J., 260, 262, 268, 270, 272 f.,
  275 f.
Müller, T., 105
Münster, S., 259
Murray, G., 128, 132
Musonius, 144

Nachtigal, J. C. C., 322
Nau, F., 268, 270, 457 f.
Naumann, W., 429 f.
Nestle, E., 237, 258, 298, 429, 440, 458
Neteler, 296
Neubauer, A., 258, 398
Nicander, 104
Nicholas of Damascus, 22, 27, 30, 54,
  101, 106 f., 181, 209, 517
Nicholas of Lyra, 326
Nickes, 296
Niese, B., 93, 209, 418, 475 ff., 481 f.,
  486, 489 ff., 507 ff., 516 ff., 520 f.
Nilsson, M. P., 128
Nock, A. D., 148
Nöldeke, Th., 108, 259, 272, 275, 308,
  311, 399, 401, 404, 417
Norden, E., 109, 128, 140, 147
Nymphodorus, 111

Obermann, J., 131
Oesterley, W. O. E., 86, 270, 274, 308,
  328, 398, 409, 451, 484, 490 f.
Oldfather, C. H., 103
Olivieri, A., 132
Onesicritus, 105
Orelli, J. C., 137
Origen, 79, 116, 210, 213, 256, 271 f.,
  291, 298, 304, 441 ff., 452, 461, 483
Otto, W., 93
Ovid, 104, 109, 143, 158, 266

Page, D. L., 103
Palmieri, 295 f.
Panaetius of Rhodes, 122, 126, 143
Panini, 116
Parmenides of Elea, 120
Paspati, A. G., 270
Paton, L. B., 304, 307 f.
Paton, W. R., 103
Paul of Tarsus, 104, 107, 127, 130, 140,
  143, 145, 147, 156, 183, 186, 188 f.,
  191, 194, 213, 220, 342, 345 f., 384
Paul of Tella, 249, 259, 441, 444
Pausanias, 156, 349

Pentin, H., 291
Perles, F., 77, 462
Persius, 143 f., 184
Petazzoni, R., 148
Peters, N., 320, 367, 401
Pfeiffer, E., 134
Pfleiderer, E., 326, 328
Pfleiderer, O., 147
Pheidias of Syracuse, 112
Philetas of Cos, 103, 115
Philinus of Cos, 114
Philo Byblius, 106, 198
Philodemus, 103
Philo of Alexandria, 30, 36 f., 56, 69, 116,
    122, 126, 134, 139, 145, 166, 173-177,
    179, 192 ff., 196, 206, 212 f., 215, 254,
    315 ff., 326, 334, 337, 340, 343, 346,
    349, 395, 429
Philo of Byzantium, 113
Philo of Larissa, 118
Philostratus, 106
Phocylides of Miletus, 225
Photius, 106, 110, 192, 210
Pindar, 129, 131
Pinson, K. S., 191
Planudes, M., 109
Plath, Margarete, 269 ff.
Plato, 102, 118, 123, 126, 129, 131 f.,
    139 f., 142, 145, 215, 220, 315, 330,
    337, 339, 342 ff.
Pliny the Elder, 56, 133, 140, 159, 294
Plitt, G. L., 412
Plotinus, 146
Plumptre, E. H., 327
Plutarch of Chaeronea, 96, 99, 101,
    106 f., 116, 122, 132, 141, 145, 151,
    153 f., 162 f., 202, 226, 252, 349
Pohlmann, A. A., 249
Poland, F., 93
Polemon of Athens, 117, 121
Polybius, 10, 12, 105 f., 203, 209, 518
Polycarp, 275
Polyhistor, Alexander, 198 ff., 210, 226 f.
Pope, H., 249
Porphyry (Porphyrius), 9, 146, 157, 164,
    443, 517
Porter, F. C., 328
Poseidippus of Alexandria, 103
Posidonius of Apamea, 102, 105, 112 f.,
    122, 134, 143, 145, 192, 198, 343, 432,
    517
Pottier, 135
Pratt, Ida A., 93, 170, 253
Praxagoras of Cos, 114
Praxiphanes of Mytilene, 115
Preisendanz, K., 103

Preiss, H., 270, 274
Preuschen, E., 139
Procksch, O., 479 f.
Proclus, 146
Prodicus of Ceos, 125, 139
Protagoras of Abdera, 129
Prudentius, 151
Pseudo-Callisthenes (Aesop), 108
Pseudo-Clement, 275
Pseudo-Dionsus the Areopagite, 146
Ptolemaeus, Claudius, 112
Purinton, C. E., 320, 322
Pyrrho of Elis, 107, 117 ff., 121
Pythagoras, 115, 139, 145, 215
Pytheas of Messalia, 111

Quintilian, 33, 103 f.

Raboisson, P. A., 291
Radin, M., 167
Rahlfs, A., 258 f., 318, 433, 440 f., 457 f.,
    497
Raska, 296
Raspe, R. E., 110
Rawlinson, G., 508
Rawlinson, H. C., 455
Redpath, H. A., 182
Regibus, V. de, 440
Reinach, Th., 49, 106, 167, 184, 190-193,
    198, 207, 268, 281
Reitzenstein, R., 130, 134, 334, 518
Renan, E., 30, 161, 269, 271, 489
Reusch, F. H., 258, 412
Reuss, E., 450, 484
Rhianus, 102
Ricciotti, G., 207
Riessler, P., 243, 249 f., 295
Rigg, H. A., Jr., 107, 202
Rinckart, Martin, 376
Rissberg, B., 318
Roberts, C. H., 103
Robertson, A. T., 484
Robinson, C. A., 93
Robiou, 295
Rogers, R. W., 456
Rohde, E., 109 f., 130 f.
Ropes, J. H., 330
Roscher, W. W., 135
Rose, V., 134
Rosemann, M., 266
Rosenthal, F., 274, 489, 493
Rossi, J. B. de, 308
Rost, L., 57
Rostovtzeff, M. I., 93, 101, 161
Roth, 490
Rothstein, 418 f., 442, 446, 449

Rowley, H. H., 57, 70, 76, 79 f., 89, 188, 196
Rufus, C. Musonius, 122
Ryle, H. E., 422, 484
Ryssell, V., 308

Saadia Gaon, 352, 400
Sabatier, P., 258
Sachau, E., 170, 268
Sachs, S., 484
Saglio, 135
Sanchez, 296
Sanchuniathon, 106
Sarton, G., 110
Satyrus of Alexandria, 107
Saussaye, Ch. de la, 128
Scaliger, 481
Scaurus, 107
Schaefer, H., 153
Schechter, S., 352, 401, 404
Scheffer, T. von, 148
Scheftelowitz, J., 253, 308
Schemann, F., 209
Shermann, Th., 66
Schiller-Szinessy, 168
Schischmanoff, Lydia, 270
Schlatter, D. A., 475, 510
Schmekel, A., 122
Schmid, W., 101
Schmidt, G., 490, 497
Schnapp, F., 66
Schneider, H., 271
Schollmeyer, A., 252
Scholz, A., 291, 307, 309, 450
Schubart, W., 93, 148, 348, 515
Schütz, R., 327 f., 339
Schürer, E., 13, 35, 40, 49, 69, 71, 90, 124, 132, 167 ff., 172, 174 ff., 180 f., 183 ff., 188, 190-193, 195 f., 198, 200, 203, 207, 209 ff., 214, 226, 237, 249, 258, 260, 268, 270, 272, 274, 279, 280, 291, 294, 297, 308, 320, 327 ff., 334, 366, 374, 400, 412, 416 ff., 422, 432, 441, 443, 463, 480 f., 484, 489, 492, 507, 515 f.
Schulte, A., 258 f., 268, 272, 484
Schultess, F., 454
Schultz, W., 452
Schultze, V., 128
Schumpp, M., 258
Scotus Erigena, 146
Second Isaiah, 129
Seeligmann, I. L., 182
Seethe, K., 153
Segaar, C., 440
Segal, M. H., 398
Segré, A., 174

Seleucus of Babylon, 112
Sellers, O. R., 18 f.
Seneca, L. A., 111, 118, 122, 126 f., 140-145, 193
Serapion of Alexandria, 114
Sextus Empiricus, 121, 134, 136
Shepherd, M. H., 86
Shoverman, G., 134, 149
Siecke, E., 453
Sieger, J., 270
Siegfried, C., 126, 212, 327
Silberschlag, E., 183
Simeon ben Shetach, 451
Simpson, D. C., 258, 263, 267 f., 270, 272, 274
Simrock, K., 269
Sionita, Gabriel, 463
Sluys, D. M., 475, 481, 515, 518, 520
Smend, R., 238, 266, 276, 353, 364, 366 ff., 377, 382, 398 ff.
Smith, G. A., 35
Smith, W. R., 275, 442
Söder, Miss R., 108
Solon, 370
Sommer, A., 335
Sophocles, 102, 129, 131, 370
Sosibius Lakon, 107
Spartianus, Aelius, 45
Speiser, E. A., 320, 322
Speusippus, 117
Stadmüller, H., 103
Staehle, K., 145
Stähelin, F., 167
Stählin, O., 101
Statius, 136
Stearns, W. N., 106, 200, 214
Stein, L., 122
Steinmetzer, F., 291, 293 ff.
Steinmueller, J. E., 271, 274, 308 f., 445
Stephens, G., 269
Steuernagel, C., 308, 422, 490
Stilpon of Megara, 120 f.
Stinespring, W. F., 148, 165
Stoderl, W., 412, 415
Strabo, 99, 111, 152, 159, 167, 173 f., 186, 190, 192, 209, 252, 349, 431, 455
Strack, H. L., 125, 168, 194, 339, 344, 364, 384, 429
Strato of Lampsacus, 113, 118 f.
Streane, 490
Stummer, F., 252, 297
Suetonius, 39, 134
Suidas, 296
Sulla, 107
Sulpicius Severus, 296
Susemihl, F., 101

Swete, H. B., 224, 249, 258, 259, 433, 440 f.
Swift, Jonathan, 110
Symmachus, 442
Syncellus, 77

Tacitus, 10, 134, 154, 157, 184, 191 f., 198, 281, 432, 517
Tarn, W. W., 93, 101, 108, 167, 180, 183
Tate, J., 130
Taylor, C., 401
Taylor, Lily R., 348
Taylor, W. R., 399
Tcherikover, V., 179
Tennyson, A., 99
Tertullian, 114, 164 f., 195, 291, 319, 347, 443
Thackeray, H. St. John, 27, 106, 182, 207, 224, 238, 246, 249, 307, 321, 417
Thallus, 107
Theagenes of Rhegium, 130, 213
Theis, J., 243, 250
Theocritus, 103 f., 159
Theodoret, 412
Theodorus, 119
Theodothion, 249, 417, 433, 439, 442
Theognis, 370 f.
Theophilus of Antioch, 226 f., 347
Theophrastus, 100, 113 ff., 189
Theopompus, 107
Thielmann, P., 319
Thompson, Stith, 269, 453
Thucidides, 105
Tibullus, 157
Timaeus, 111
Timagenes, 107
Timon of Phlius, 121
Timosthenes of Rhodes, 111
Timotheus of Eleusis, 154
Timotheus the Eumolpid, 158
Tischendorf, C. von, 72, 433, 440 f.
Tisserant, E., 73
Tod, M. M., 179
Tolman, H. C., 252
Torrey, C. C., 58, 66, 70, 73, 76 f., 79 f., 86, 233, 238 ff., 272 ff., 297, 307 ff., 320, 322, 440, 445 f., 449, 458, 461 f., 483 f., 489 ff., 507 f.
Toutain, J., 128, 148
Townshend, R. B., 218, 220
Toy, C. H., 276 f., 321, 401, 453, 456
Trever, J. C., 59
Trogus, Pompeius, 106
Tscherikover, A., 167
Turchi, N., 148
Tyrannion, 118
Tyrrell, G., 137

Überweg, F., 117
Unger, G. F., 481
Ungnad, A., 170
Usener, H., 136
Ussher, J., 307

Valerius, J., 108
Valerius, M., 193
Vallarsi, 365
Varro, M. T., 143, 190, 192
Vercellone, C., 259, 440
Vergil, 102, 104, 143, 226
Verne, Jules, 110
Vetter, P., 269, 272, 275
Victorinus of Pettau, 443
Vigoroux, F., 293, 295
Vincent, A., 170
Violet, B., 88
Voghano, A., 137
Voigt, E. E., 298
Volkmann, H., 480
Volkmar, G., 292, 295 f., 422
Volz, P., 253

Wachsmuth, C., 105
Wagner, F. G., 211
Wagner, R., 93
Walde, B., 238 ff.
Wallach, L., 186 f.
Walton, B., 259
Waszink, J. H., 147
Waxman, M., 445, 451
Weber, W., 322, 328, 339
Weidner, E. F., 161
Weissbach, F. H., 252
Weissmann, S., 292, 294, 296
Wellhausen, J., 15, 21, 308, 440, 461, 475, 477, 490, 507
Wells, L. S. A., 72
Wendland, P., 93, 101, 135 f., 143 f., 147, 187, 221, 224, 325, 329 f.
Wenger, L., 147
Wernsdorf, G., 480 f., 507
Wesley, John, 100
Whiston, G., 412
Whiston, W., 207, 412
Whitaker, G. H., 221
Whitehouse, O. C., 413, 419, 422
Wichmann, W., 335
Wicks, H. J., 373
Wide, S., 128
Wielkie, W., 99
Wieneke, J., 211
Wiesemann, H., 322
Wilamowitz-Moellendorff, U. von, 93, 100, 101
Wilcken, U., 167, 348

Willoughby, H. W., 148
Willrich, H., 19, 292, 295 f., 308, 477, 482, 488, 490, 507 ff., 517 f., 520
Winckler, H., 161, 292 f., 296
Windelband, W., 117
Wissowa, G., 128
Wolff, O., 292, 296
Wolfson, H. A., 37, 126, 134, 139, 146, 167, 173, 194, 196 f., 206, 212, 215, 221, 334, 337, 343, 349
Wordsworth, Bishop, 448
Wright, G. E., 13
Wünsch, R., 161
Wycliff, John, 441

Xenocrates of Athens, 114, 139, 346
Xenocrates of Chalcedon, 117

Xenophanes of Colophon, 129
Xenophon, 106, 125

Yonge, C. D., 221
York, H. C., 249

Zahn, Th., 144
Zeitlin, S., 59, 80, 210, 336, 479
Zeller, E., 117, 326, 329
Zenner, J. K., 322
Zeno of Citium, 100, 117, 120 f., 124, 141
Zeno of Tarsus, 122
Zenodotus of Ephesus, 115 f.
Ziegler, J., 182
Zimmermann, F., 77
Zöckler, O., 237, 272
Zorell, F., 322

INDEX OF SUBJECTS

Abimelech, 74
Abydos, 153
Acra, 13, 15 ff., 19
Adam, 81 ff., 85, 88
A-D-A-M, 277
Adasa, 16
Adiaphora, 121, 125
Adida, 22
Adonis, 131, 147, 150, 159
Aelia Capitolina, 45
Aeneas, 228 f.
Aerarium, 36
Aesculapius, 154
Agathocles, 110
Age to come, 82, 87
Agrippa I, 31, 34 ff., 209
Agrippa II, 31, 38 ff., 44, 209
Agrippa, the son-in-law of Augustus, 111
Agrippeion, 30
Ahikar, 109, 252 f., 268
Ahura-Mazda, 162, 252, 254
Akatalepsia, 121
Akiba, Rabbi, 54, 72
Albinus, 38, 40
Alcimus, 16 f.
Alexander, son of Aristobulus II, 22 ff.
Alexander, son of Herod, 31 f.
Alexander the Great, 8, 76, 95 f., 108, 110, 173
Alexander romances, 108
Alexandra, mother of Mariamne, 27, 29
Alexandra, see Salome Alexandra
Alexandreion, 30
Alexandria in Egypt, 37, 41, 43, 96
Alexandrium, 24
Alexas, 31
Allegorical interpretation, 142, 212 ff., 334
Amathus, 21, 24
Amenophis III, 349

'Am ha-areş, 55
Amixia, 191
Ammonites, 16
Amon, 147
Amos, 67
Amyntas, 95
Ananel, 27
Ananaias, 40
Anankē, 133
Ananus, 40
Andronicus, 12
Androsthenes of Thasos, 95, 110
Angels, 58, 70, 75, 282
Angra-Mainyu, 162
Anileus, 169
Annas, 40
Anthedon, 21, 29
Anthropomorphisms, 215
Antigonus of Phrygia, 8
Antigonus, son of Aristobulus II, 24 ff.
Antigonus, son of Hyrcanus I, 21
Antioch, 96
Antiochus I, of Commagene, 163
Antiochus I Soter, 96, 129
Antiochus III the Great, 9, 203
Antiochus IV Epiphanes, 10 ff., 14 ff., 76, 79, 129 f., 216 ff.
Antiochus V Eupator, 16
Antiochus VI Theos, 18
Antiochus VII Sidetes, 19 f.
Antiochus VIII Grypus, 20
Antiochus IX Cyzicenus, 20
Antiochus XII Dionysos, 22
Antipas, son of Herod, 33 ff.
Antipater, ruler of Macedonia, 8

Antipater, father of Herod, 23 ff.
Antipater, son of Herod, 31
Antipatris, 30
Antipsychon, 220
Anti-Semitism, 311, 496
Antoninus Pius, 45
Antony, Mark, 24 f., 27 ff., 175
Apama, 255
Aphorisms, 330
Aphrodite, 142, 147
Apocalypse, 74 ff.
Apocalypse of Moses, 72
Apocalypse of Peter, 133
Apollo, 149
Apollonius, 12, 14, 17
Apologies, Jewish, 198 f.
Arabia, 29
Aramaic literature, 251 f.
Archelaus, son of Herod, 31 ff., 35
Archelaus, King of Cappadocia, 32
Archangels, 75 f., 282
Ares, 142
Aretas, 22 f., 34
Argolai, 87
Ariarathes V, 17
Aristeas, Letter of, 224 ff., 256
Aristobulus, 95
Aristobulus I, 21
Aristobulus II, 22 ff.
Aristobulus III, 27
Aristobulus of Alexandria, 214
Aristobulus, son of Herod, 31 f.
Ark of the Covenant, 67
Arsinoë, 203
Artapanus, 201
Artaxerxes III Ochus, 294
Aryans, 161
Asar-Hapi, 154
Ascension of Isaiah, 73
Asclepios, 114

555

Asha, 253
Ashdod, 16 f.
Ashkelon, 18, 41
Ashurbanipal, 163
Asidaîoi, 11, 13
Asineus, 169
Askesis, 120
Asmodeus, 271
Assumption of Moses, 79
Astarte, 147
Astrology, 134 f.
Asvins, 162
Ataraxia, 119, 121, 136
Atargatis, 159 f.
Atellanae, 104
Athena, 138, 142
Athens, 98
Atonement, 220
Attalus I, King of Pergamum, 149
Attalus II, 17
Attis, 131, 149 f.
Augustus, see Octavian
Auranitis, 29, 34
Aurelian, 160
Autarkeia, 126
Avesta, 252 f.
Azarias, 16
Azizus, 31, 39

Baal of Heaven, 13
Baal of Doliche, 160
Baalbek, 160
Babas, 29
Bacchides, 16 f.
Baeton, 95
Bagoas, 294
Balas, Alexander, 17
Balkira, 73
Bantu, 95
Baptism, 55, 193
Bar Cocheba, 45, 178
Barbarians, 95
Baron Munchausen, 110
Baruch, 74
I Baruch, 409 ff.
II Baruch, 86 ff.
Barzaphranes, 26
Bassus, C., 25
Bassus, L., 43
Batanea, 29, 34
Bechira, 73
Behistun Inscription, 252 f.
Belial, 58
Beliar, 69, 73 f.
Belos, 138

Belsamim, 160
Bematists, 95, 110
Benedicite, 434, 448
Benjamin, 11
Berenice I, 31 f.
Berenice II, 31, 44
Bêth dîn, 44
Bether, 45
Bethhoron, 14
Bethramphtha, 34
Bethsaida, 35
Bethulia, 296 f.
Beth-Zacharias, 16
Beth-zur, 15 ff.
Bilgah, 11
Bismarck, Otto von, 97
Boethus, 40
Bouriant, M., 77
Bride of the monster, 270 f.
Brutus, M., 25
Buddha, 129
Buto, 152

Caesar, Julius, 25
Caesarea on the Sea, 29 f., 36, 39, 41
Caesarea Philippi, 9, 35
Calendar, 68, 76
Caligula, Gaius, 34 ff., 157, 175 f., 207
Callisthenes, 95
Cantherus, 40
Caracalla, 149
Cardinal virtues, 126, 215 f., 222, 315
Carrhae, 24
Cassander, 8, 94
Cassius, C., 25
Catalogues, 330
Cendebeus, 19
Cerealis, Vettulenus, 43
Chaeronea, 94
"Chaldean," 134
Chosroes I, 146
Chosroes II, 5
Christians in Jerusalem, 42
Christianity, 161, 164
Christmas, 15, 164
Chrysippus, 99
Circumcision, 49, 70
Claudius, 35, 37 ff., 150, 173 f., 177
Cleodemus, 202
Cleopatra III, 21
Cleopatra VII, 26 ff., 175

Cleopatra, wife of Herod, 31
Collegia, 147
Conscience, 65, 145
Cosmos, 140 (see Rosmos)
Constantine, 161
Covenanters of Damascus, 57
Crassus, M. L., 24, 26
Criobolium, 151
Cronus, 227 f.
Cross examination of witnesses, 451
Crusaders, 5
Cumanus, V., 38 f.
Cybele, 147, 149 f.
Cynics, 117, 120, 136
Cyrenaic School, 119
Cyrene, 43, 117
"Cyrenius" (P. Sulpicius Quirinius), 35
Cyril of Alexandria, 178
Cyrus the Great, 7, 79

Daimon, 133
Dalios, 110
Damascus, 18, 23, 41
Danaus, 138
Dangerous bride, 269 ff.
Daniel, 67
Daniel, Book of, 63
Darius I, 6, 252
Demeter, 129, 131, 138, 147, 149
Demetrius, Jewish historian, 200
Demetrius of Phalerum, 224
Demetrius I Poliorcetes, 129
Demetrius I Soter, 8, 16 f.
Demetrius II Nicator, 17 ff.
Demetrius III Eucerus, 22
Demodamus of Miletus, 110
Derketo, 159
Devil, the, 79
Diaspora, 166
Diatribe, 143, 329 f.
Dicaearchus, 95, 111
Dictionaries, 116
Dietary prescriptions, 58, 302
Diogenes, 95

Dinah, 71
Dionysus, 129, 131, 139, 147, 149, 204
Dioscuri, 162
Dispersion, Jewish, 166 ff., 280
Divine justice, 81
Divinized mortals, 139 f.
Dogs, 266
Dor, 19
Doris, 31
Dositheans, 53
Drusilla, 31, 39
Dualism, 118
Dumuzi, 159
Dura Europos, 161

Ebionites, 53
Ecbatana, 293
Eccelsiastes, 136
Ecclesiasticus, 268, 352 ff.
Eden, 65
Edfu, 183
Egypt, 64, 138, 151 ff.
Ekron, 17
Elagabalus, 160
Elasa, 16
Eleazar, 39
Eleazar the martyr, 216 f.
Eleazar, son of Ananias Nedebai, 41 f.
Eleazar, son of Simon, 43
Elements, the four, 139
Elephantine, 169 ff., 268
Eliezer, Rabbi, 168
Elihu, 71
Elisha, 67
Emmaus, 14 f.
End of the world, 230
Enoch, Book of, 75 ff.
Ephesus, 180
Epicureans, 136
Epoché, 121
Era, Seleucid, 8, 480 f.
Eranoi, 147
Esbon, 30
I Esdras, 233 ff.
II (IV) Esdras, 81 ff.
Essenes, 53, 56, 223
Esther, 64, 304 ff.
Eternal bliss, 217 f., 220
Eternal life, 58
Eternal torments, 217
Eucharist, 164
Eupolemus, 201
Eutychides, 133

Evil impulse, 65, 81, 85, 393 f.
Expiatory martyrdom, 221
Ezekiel, the prophet, 67
Ezekiel, the dramatist, 211

Fadus, 38
Fall of the angels, 75 ff.
Family, 387 f.
Fatalism, 134
Fate, 124
Fearers of God, 194
Felix, A., 31, 38 f.
Festus, P., 38 ff.
Fiscus, 36
Flaccus, A. A., 37, 175 f., 207
Flood, 75 f.
Florus, G., 38, 40 f.
Fools, in Stoicism, 125
Freedom of choice, 395
Free will, 63
Future age, 52

Gaba, 30
Gabinius, 24, 29
Gadara, 21, 24, 29
Galba, 43
Galileans, 189
Galilee, 16, 21, 33, 42
Galli, 150
Gallus, C., 41 f.
Gamala, 22
Gamaliel, 38
Gaugamela, 94
Gaulanitis, 34
Gaza, 21, 29, 94
Gazara, 19, 24
Gehenna, 52, 80, 82, 86, 90
Genius, 133
"Genoveva-type," 453
Gerasa, 22
Germanicus, 175
Gerousia, 174
Gezer, 18
Gerizim, 20, 36
Gilead, 16
Gilgamesh, 109
Glaphyra, 31, 33
God, conception of in Plato and Aristotle, 123; in Stoicism, 140 f.; in Neoplatonism, 146; in Judaism, 47; in Hellenistic Judaism, 186 ff.;

in Wisdom of Solomon, 335, 342 ff.; in II Maccabees, 512 f.; in Ecclesiasticus, 379; in Tobit, 282 ff.; in Judith, 301 ff.; in I Maccabees, 494 f.; in the Prayer of Manasses, 459
Golden Rule, 65, 383 f.
Gorgias, 14 ff.
Gortheni, 53
Grammars, 116
Granicus, 94
Grateful dead, 269 f.
Great Synagogue, 46, 53
Graeco-Roman works on the Jews, 198
Greek Anthology, 103
Greek city, the, 96
Greek customs, 96
Greek philosophy, 116 ff.; in the Book of Wisdom, 328 ff.

Habakkuk, 67
Hadad, 160
Hadrian, 45, 178
Haggadah, 69
Halakah, 69
Haman, 311
Hamath, 18
Hanukkah (Feast of Re-dedication), 15
Harpocrates, 151
Hasîdîm, 11, 13 f., 16, 36, 48, 53, 72, 294
Hattushash, 161
Hattushil III, 107
Hazor, 18
Heaven, 75
Heavenly bodies, 139
Hebrew Bible, 84
Hebron, 16
Heimarmenē, 123, 133, 140
Heliodorus, 9
Hell, 132
Hellenism, 93 ff.
Helenistic Judaism, 181 ff.
Hellenists, 96
Hellenizers, 11
Hemerobaptists, 53
Hephaestus, 138
Hera, 142, 227
Heracles, 11, 139
Herod of Chalcis, 31, 38

Herod the Great, 25 ff.,
    31, 33, 59, 80, 181
Herodians, 53
Herodias, 31, 34
Herodium, 42 f.
Hezekiah, "bandit chief,"
    25
Hierapolis, 185
Hillel, 28
Hipparchia, 120
Hippus, 24, 29
Hispalus, C. C., 193
Holophernes, 294
Horus, 151 ff.
Hybrys, 230
Hypomnemata, 102
Hyrcania, 24, 30
Hyrcanus I, 29, 190
Hyrcanus II, 22 ff., 28 f.

Iapetus, 227
Identity of Law and Wisdom, 384
Idolatry, 49, 186, 426 ff.,
    453
Idumea, 33, 42
Idumeans, 16, 20, 190
Immortality, 54, 220, 230;
    in the Wisdom of Solomon, 337 ff.
Inanna, 159
Indar, 161 f.
Individualism, 51 f.
Ineffable Name, 382
Iphigenia, 137
Ipsus, 8
Isaiah, 67
Iseum, 156
Ishmael, son of Phabi, 40
Isiac associations, 156
Isidore, 177
Isis, 138, 147, 151 ff.
Israel's affliction, 82
Issus, 94
Iturea, 34 f.
Itureans, 21

James, 40, 210
James and Simon, sons of
    Judas the Galilean, 38
Jamnia, 37
Janneus, Alexander, 21 f.,
    190
Jason, high priest, 10 ff.,
    216
Jason of Cyrene, 506 ff.

Jeconiah (Jehoiachin), 87
Jeremiah, 67, 74
Jericho, 24, 28 f., 33, 41
Jerusalem, 43
Jesus Christ, 33, 36, 66 f.,
    74, 98, 140, 210, 230,
    284, 383
Jesus, son of Ananus, 40
Jesus, son of Damneus, 40
Jesus, son of Gamaliel,
    40
Jesus, son of Sapphias,
    42
Jesus, son of Sira, 53,
    364 ff.
Jewish-Hellenistic literature, 61, 197 ff.
Jews, history of, 5 ff.; in
    classical literature, 190
Job, 70 f., 267 f.
Jobab, 71
John Hyrcanus I, 19, 22
John of Giscala, 42 f., 59
John, son of Simon, 19
John the Baptist, 34, 210,
    337
Jonah, 67
Jonathan Maccabeus, 16 f.
Jonathan ben Zakkai, 44
Jonathan, high priest, 39
Joppa, 17 ff., 25 f., 29
Joseph, brother of Antipater, 31
Joseph, brother of Herod,
    26, 28, 31
Joseph, Jewish commander, 16
Joseph, son of Gorion,
    42, 463, 518
Josephus, Flavius, 42,
    199, 207 f.
Juba, king of Lybia, 31
Jubilees, Book of, 68 ff.
Judah ha-Nasi, 50
Judaism. 47 ff.
Judas Maccabeus, 14 ff.
Judas, son of Hezekiah,
    59
Judas, son of Simon, 19
Judas the Galilean, 35,
    59
Jude, 79
Judgement, final, 51, 75
    ff., 82 ff., 86 f., 90, 229
Judith, 63, 285 ff.
Julian the Apostate, 161
Julias, 34 f.

Jupiter Capitolinus, 45,
    178
Jupiter Dolichenus, 160
Justinian, 117, 146, 156
Justus of Tiberias, 210

Katharsis, 146
Kiblah, 281
Kingdom of God, 80
Koinē, 98 f.
Kore, 149
Kosmos, 213 (see cosmos)
Kostobar, 29, 31
Kypros, stronghold near
    Jericho, 30
Kypros I, 29, 31
Kypros II, 31, 37
Kypros III, 31
Kyrios pantokratōr, 301

Laenas, Popilius, 12
Lampon, 177
Laomedon, 8
Last Judgement, 65, 330,
    338
Law (Torah), 49, 55, 65,
    184 f., 381 ff., 513
Leontopolis, 43, 178 f.
Life after death, 377 f.
Linus, 215
Lives of Adam and Eve,
    72
Lives of the prophets,
    66 f.
Livias, 34
Logic, 22
Logoi spermatikoi, 123
Logos, 122 f., 140, 253 f.,
    316, 333, 343
Longinus, C. C., 24
Lost Ten Tribes, 168
Lucius, 155
Lucullus, 23
Lupus, M. R., 178
Lyceum, 117 f.
Lyons, 34
Lysias, 14 f.
Lysimachus, 8, 94

Mâ, 149
Maccabean Rebellion, 9 ff.
I Maccabees, 461 ff.
II Maccabees, 472 ff.,
    499 ff.
III Maccabees, 203 ff.
IV Maccabees, 215 ff.

"Maccabeus," meaning of, 483
Machaerus, 24, 30, 41 ff.
Maenads, 131
Magna Mater, 147
Magnesia, 97
Malchus, 202
Malichus, 25, 28
Malthace, 31
Man's nature, in Ecclesiasticus, 385 f.
Marcellus, 36
Mariamne I, 27 ff., 31 f.
Mariamne II, 32
Marriage, 58
Martyrdom of Isaiah, 73
Masada, 26, 30, 41 ff.
Mastema, 69
Mattathias, 14, 80
Mattathias, son of Simon, 19
Mattiwaza, Hittite king, 161
Medaba, 20
Megara, 117
Megarian School, 120
Megasthenes, 111
Memnon, 349
Menahem, son of Judas the Galilean, 41
Menelaus, Jewish high priest, 11 ff., 16
Mesopotamia, 168
Messiah, 50, 52, 58, 65, 77 f., 82, 84, 86, 88 ff., 228, 230
Messiah, the Son of Man, 75, 78
Messianic Age, 50, 76
Messianic Hope, 63
Michael, 51, 79 f.
Michmash, 17
Millennium, 52
Miracles, 206, 330
Mishna, 50
Missionary work, 188 ff.
Mithra, 161 ff.
Mithraeum, 163
Mithridates I, 19
Mithridates, King of Pontus, 23, 163
Modin, 14
Mohammed, 337, 452
Moira, 133
Monotheism, 186, 379; in Graeco-Roman paganism, 154

Morality, 65, 283
Motives for right conduct, 386
Muratorian canon, 319 ff.
Museum in Alexandria, 224
Mystai, 131
Mystery cults, 147 ff.
Mysticism, 145 f.

Nabateans, 21, 28
Nasatya, 161 f.
National feeling, 373
Nationalism, 47
Nature of man, 336 (see Man's nature)
Nazarenes, 53
Neapolitanus, 41
Nearchus, 95, 105, 110
Nebuchadnezzar, 293
Nedebai, Ananias, 41
Nehardea, 169
Nehemiah, 6; his Memoirs, 107
Neoplatonism, 146
Neo-Pythagoreanism, 145
Nephthys, 152
Nero, 39, 41; *Nero redivivus,* 229
New Jerusalem, 65, 77, 81, 83
New Testament, 55
Nicanor, 14, 16
Nineveh, 273 f., 275, 293
Noah, 76
Numerical proverbs, 403

Oaths, 58
Obadas, 21
Oceanus, 138
Octavian Augustus, 26, 28 f., 32 f., 36, 174 f.
Odyssey, 109, 131 f., 266, 349
Offerings for the dead, 266
Oikoumenē, 99, 111
Olympian gods, 128
"One World," 99
Oniads, 12
Onias III, 10, 12
Onias IV, 179
Oral Law, 55, 58, 381 ff.
Origin of sin, 393
Orion, 153
Orodes, 26
Orpheus, 131, 215

Orphism, 131, 133
Osiris, 131, 138, 151 ff.
Osseans, 53
Otho, 43

Pacorus, 26
Palestine, History of, 5 ff.
Palestinian Literature in Aramaic, 61 f., 67 ff.
Palestinian Literature in Hebrew, 60-67
Palingenesia, 124
Palmyra, 160
Pampras, 18
Panias, 34 f.
Panium, 9
Pannychis, 57
Paradise, 52, 82, 86, 90, 132
Paralipomena of Jeremiah, 74
Parmenio, 94
Parthian Empire, 97
Parthians, 20, 24, 26
Parysatis, 94
Passions, 216
Paul of Tarsus, the Apostle, 39, 44, 214, 337
Patrocles, 110
Pella, 22, 24
Pentateuch, 46, 265 f.
Perdiccas, 96
Perea, 33 f., 42
Pergamum, 96
Persephone, 131
Persian Literature, 252 f.
Pericles, 98
Persian Period, 6 ff.
Personal Piety, 281 ff., 376 ff.
Personifications, 253 ff.
Petra, 23
Petronius, P., 37
Pharisees, 11, 22, 28, 36, 48, 53 ff., 65, 284, 294, 302 f.
Pharos, 157
Pharsalus, 25
Phasael, son of Antipater, 25, 31
Phasael, son of Phasael, 31
Phasaelis, 30
Pheroras, 31 f.
Phidias, 98
Philae, 156
Philip II of Macedon, 94

Philip, son of Herod, 29, 31 ff., 37
Philo, naval officer, 110
Philo of Alexandria, 37, 206 f., 221 ff.
Philo the Elder, 211
Phlyakes, 104
Phoenix, 153
Pilate, 207
Pitholaus, 24
Placidus, 42
Planets, 134
Plato, 98, 117
Pleiads, 103
Pleistarchus, 94
Pluto, 154, 227
Pneuma, 123, 138
"Poison maiden," 269 ff.
Polemon of Cilicia, 31
Polis, 98 ff.
Politeuma, 173 f.
Pollio (Abtalion), 28
Pollio, C. V., 37, 176
Polygnotus, 131 f.
Pompey, 23 ff., 63, 163, 229
Pontius Pilate, 36 (cf. Pilate)
Poseidon, 227
Praise of God, 403
Prayer, 281 f., 376; prayers, 278
Pre-existence of the soul, 328
Problem of evil, 344
Problem of Theodicy, 81, 394 ff.
Procurators of Judea, 38
Pronoia, 123, 140
Prophets, 267
Proselytes, 188 ff.
Proverbs, 267 f.
Providence, 124
Psalm 2: 21, 48; Psalm 110: 19, 48; Psalms: 60, 267 f., 330, 376
Psalms in Ecclesiasticus, 408
Psalms of Solomon, 63
Psalter, 52, 62 f.
Pseudo-Hecateus, 201
Pseudo-Phocylides, 225 f.
Physics, 123
Ptolemais, 18, 21 f., 42
Ptolemy, general of Alexander, 95

Ptolemy, governor of Jericho, 19 f.
Ptolemy I Lagos, Soter, 8, 94, 105, 153 f., 173, 209
Ptolemy II Philadelphus, 224
Ptolemy III Euergetes, 154, 179, 203
Ptolemy IV Philopator, 221-203 B.C.
Ptolemy V Epiphanes, 203-181 B.C.
Ptolemy VI Philometor, 181-145 B.C., 17
Ptolemy VII, Physcon, 145-116 B.C., 20, 107
Ptolemy VIII Lathyrus, 116-108 and 88-80 B.C., 21
Ptolemy, Syrian general, 14
Pulcinella, 104
Purim, 16

Quadratus, 39
Quirinius, see "Cyrenius"

Ragaba, 22
Ramiel, 89
Ransom, 217, 220
"Ransomed Woman," The, 269 ff.
Raphia, 21
Ras Shamra (Ugarit), 131, 159, 403, 448
Re, 152
Reason, 216, 219
Reconciliation, 66
Repentance, 65
Resurrection, 51, 54, 63, 65, 75, 78 f., 82, 86, 88 ff., 220, 514
Retribution, 338, 377 ff.
Revelation of St. John, 80 f.
Rhea, 147, 227
Ritual prescriptions, 302
Rome, 16, 18, 98, 149 ff.
Romulus and Remus, 229
Roxana, 94
Rufinus, 157
Rufus, M. R., 178

Sabazios, 147
Sabbath, 14, 49, 53, 56, 58, 70

Sabinus, 33
Sabouaei, 53
Sacrifice, 393
Sadducees, 41, 53, 56
Sadduk, 35
Saints, 282
Salampsio, 31
Salome Alexandra, 21, 23
Salome I, sister of Herod, 28 f., 31, 33
Salome II, 31, 35
Samaga, 20
Samaria, 18, 20, 24, 29, 32
Samaritans, 36
Sameas, 28
Sampseans, 53
Sanhedrin, 22, 25, 36, 44, 295
Sarbēth Sabanaiel, 483
Sardis, 180
Sargon II, 168
Satan, 58, 69, 71, 80
Scaurus, 23
Scipio Africanus the younger, 122
Scipio, L. C., 9
Schools, Jewish, 49, 367
Scribes, 16, 53, 368 ff., 390
Scythopolis, 18, 20, 24, 41
Sebaste, 29
Second Isaiah, 51
Sefer ha-Hāgō, 58
Sejanus, 175, 207
Seleucia, 22, 96 f.
Seleucid Era, see Era
Seleucus I, Nicator, 8, 94, 96, 129
Seleucus II, Callinicus, 247-226 B.C.
Seleucus III Soter, 226-223 B.C.
Seleucus IV Philopator, 9 f., 216
Sennacherib, 169
Sepphoris, 24, 34
Separation of the Jews from the Gentiles, 281
Septuagint (LXX), 179, 182 f., 189, 212, 224 f.
Septimius Severus, 349
Serapeum, 156
Serapis, 114, 151 ff.
Sermon on the Mount, 188

Seron, 14
Sesostris I, 153
Seth, 152
Seven brothers, 217
Sextus Caesar, 25
Shalmaneser V, 168
Shammai, 28
Shealtiel, 81
Shechem, 20, 211
Shubbiluliu, Hittite King, 161
Sibyls, 226
Sibylline Oracles, 226 ff.
Sicarii, 39 f., 59, 178
Signs of the end, 82 f., 87
Silo, 26
Siloah, 67
Silva, Flavius, 43
Simon bar Giora, 42
Simon ben Shetach, 22
Simon, high Temple official, 11
Simon Maccabeus, 16, 18 f.
Simon, son of Onias, 365 ff.
Sin, 65, 396, 424
Sirach, 364 ff.
Sirius, 153
Sisyphus, 131
Sitidos, 71
Skeptical School, 120 f.
Skepticism, 135
Smyrna, 181, 185
Social intercourse, 388 ff.
Socrates, 99, 117, 120, 127, 129, 215
Son of Man, 52, 84
Sophia, 122, 214
Sophists, 121, 129
Sophocles, 98
Sorites, 330
Sosius, 27
Sotēr, 101
Sparta, 18
Statira, 94
Stoicheîa, 139
Stoicism, 99, 121, 138, 140 ff.; Stoicism and Christianity, 143 f.
Stoics, 135, 215, 219, 315, 342
Story of the Three Youths, 249 ff.
Strato's Tower, see Caesarea on the Sea

Summaries of the Law, 266, 383 f.
Sunday, 164
Susanna, 434 ff.
Swine's meat, 49
Synagogue, 49 f., 179 f., 374
Syncretism, 148
Syncrisis, 330
Syrian deities, 159

Talmud, 50, 69, 190
Tantalus, 131
Tarquinius Superbus, 149
Taurobolium, 151
Taxo, 80
Tekoa, 16
Temple of Jerusalem, 13, 15, 30, 44, 48 f., 88, 278 ff., 510 ff.
Temple worship, 374
Ten Tribes, 90
Teshub, 160
Testament of Job, 70
Testaments of the XII Patriarchs, 64 ff.
Thallus, 202
Theodicy, 85
Theodosius I, 156, 161
Theodotus, 179, 211
Theophilus of Alexandria, 156
Theophrastus, 95
Therapeutae, 57, 206, 223
Theudas, 38
Thiasoi, 147
Thoth, 152
Tiberias, 34, 37
Tiberius, 34, 36, 134, 157, 175
Tiberius Alexander, 38, 177, 181
Tiglath-pileser III, 166, 168
Tigranes, 23
Titans, 227 f.
Tithes, 279
Titus, 42 f.
Tityus, 131
Tobiads, 10 ff.
Tobit, 258 ff.
Tower Antonia, 29, 37
Trachonitis, 29, 34
Tradition of the ancients (oral Law), 55, 266, 381
Trajan, 44, 178

Tree of life, 78
Triumvirate, 227
Trust in God, 65
Tryphon, 19
Tyche, 133
Tyre, 11, 94

Underworld, 75
Undeserved suffering, 335
Universalism, 51 f.
Uranus, 227
Uriel, 81, 83

Varuna, 161 f.
Varus, 59, 80
Venice, 30
Ventidius, 26
Vespasian, 42 f., 178
Vienna in Gaul, 33
Virtue, 120; in Stoicism, 125; see also "Cardinal virtues"
Vision of Isaiah, 73 f.
Vita Adae et Evae, 72
Vitellius, 34, 36, 43
Vows, 58

Waidrang, 172
Way of salvation, 342
Wealth, 390 ff.
Wisdom, 216, 219, 343, 350, 385 ff., 418, 423
Wisdom Literature, 64
Wisdom of Solomon, The, 313 ff.
Wise, in Stoicism, 125
World state, 120, 127

Yasht, 162
Yeṣer, 59, 65

Zabinas, 20
Zadok, 56
"Zadokite" Document, 57
Zagreus, 131
Zarathustra, 162
Zealots, 35 f., 39, 41 f., 59
Zedekiah, 87
Zenodorus, 29
Zerubbabel, 6
Zeus, 138, 141 f., 147, 154, 227; Olympian Zeus, 13, 15; Zeus Xenios, 13
Zodiac, 134
Zoroaster, 129
Zoroastrianism, 148, 282